THE ROUTLEDGE COMPANION TO LATINA/O POPULAR CULTURE

D0074537

Latina/o popular culture has experienced major growth and change with the expanding demographic of Latina/os in mainstream media. In *The Routledge Companion to Latina/o Popular Culture*, contributors pay serious critical attention to all facets of Latina/o popular culture including TV, films, performance art, food, lowrider culture, theater, photography, dance, pulp fiction, music, comic books, video games, news, web and digital media, healing rituals, quinceñeras, and much more.

Features include:

- consideration of differences between pop culture made by and about Latina/os;
- comprehensive and critical analyses of various pop cultural forms;
- concrete and detailed treatments of major primary works from children's television to representations of *dia de los muertos*;
- new perspectives on the political, social, and historical dynamic of Latina/o pop culture.

Chapters select, summarize, explain, contextualize and assess key critical interpretations, perspectives, developments, and debates in Latina/o popular cultural studies. A vitally engaging and informative volume, this compilation of wide-ranging case studies in Latina/o pop culture phenomena encourages scholars and students to view Latina/o pop culture within the broader study of global popular culture.

Contributors: Stacey Alex, Cecilia Aragón, Mary Beltrán, William A. Calvo-Quirós, Melissa Castillo-Garsow, Nicholas Centino, Ben Chappell, Fabio Chee, Osvaldo Cleger, David A. Colón, Marivel T. Danielson, Laura Fernández, Camilla Fojas, Kathryn M. Frank, Enrique García, Christopher González, Rachel González-Martin, Matthew David Goodwin, Ellie D. Hernandez, Jorge Iber, Guisela Latorre, Stephanie Lewthwaite, Richard Alexander Lou, Stacy I. Macías, Desirée Martin, Paloma Martínez-Cruz, Pancho McFarland, Cruz Medina, Isabel Millán, Amelia María de la Luz Montes, William Anthony Nericcio, William Orchard, Rocío Isabel Prado, Ryan Rashotte, Cristina Rivera, Gabriella Sanchez, Ilan Stavans.

Frederick Luis Aldama is Arts and Humanities Distinguished Professor of English and University Distinguished Scholar at the Ohio State University where he is also founder and director of LASER and the Humanities & Cognitive Sciences High School Summer Institute. He is author, co-author, and editor of over 24 books, including *The Routledge Concise History of Latino/a Literature* and *Latino/a Literature in the Classroom*.

THE ROUTLEDGE COMPANION TO LATINA/O POPULAR CULTURE

Edited by Frederick Luis Aldama

Routledge
Taylor & Francis Group

LONDON AND NEW YORK

First published 2016 by Routledge

2 Park Square, Milton Park, Abingdon, Oxfordshire OX14 4RN
52 Vanderbilt Avenue, New York, NY 10017

Routledge is an imprint of the Taylor & Francis Group, an informa business

First issued in paperback 2019

Library of Congress Cataloging in Publication Data
Aldama, Frederick Luis, 1969- editor. The Routledge companion to
Latina/o popular culture / edited by Frederick Luis Aldama. New York,
NY ; London : Routledge, 2016.
    Includes bibliographical references and index. Hispanic Americans
    in popular culture--History. | Popular culture--United States--
    History. E184.S75 R75 2016
    LCC E184.S75 (ebook)   973/.0468--dc23

ISBN: 978-1-138-63894-5 (hbk)
ISBN: 978-0-367-87692-0 (pbk)

Typeset in Goudy
by HWA Text and Data Management, London

CONTENTS

List of Figures ix

List of Contributors xi

Introduction: Putting the Pop in Latina/o Culture 1
FREDERICK LUIS ALDAMA

PART I
Televisual, Reel, Animated, Comic, Digital, and Speculative Pop Spaces 21

1 Latina/os On TV!: A Proud (and Ongoing) Struggle Over Representation
  and Authorship 23
  MARY BELTRÁN

2 Latino Film in the End Times 34
  CAMILLA FOJAS

3 "¡Vámonos! Let's Go!": Latina/o Children's Television 44
  ISABEL MILLÁN

4 Branding "Latinohood," Juan Bobo, and the Commodification of Dora
  the Explorer 59
  CRISTINA RIVERA

5 Canta y no Llores: Life and Latinidad in Children's Animation 68
  LAURA FERNÁNDEZ

6 Beyond the "Digital Divide" and Latina/o Pop 76
  KATHRYN M. FRANK

7 Why Videogames: Ludology Meets Latino Studies 87
  OSVALDO CLEGER

8 The Industry and Aesthetics of Latina/o Comic Books 101
  ENRIQUE GARCÍA

9   Science Fiction and Latino Studies Today ... and in the Future   110
    FABIO CHEE

10 The Technology of Labor, Migration, and Protest   120
    MATTHEW DAVID GOODWIN

PART II
Pop Poetics of Tongues Untied   129

11 Performing *Mestizaje*: Making Indigenous Acts Visible in Latina/o
    Popular Culture   131
    CECILIA JOSEPHINE ARAGÓN

12 Brown Bodies on the Great White Way: Latina/o Theater, Pop Culture,
    and Broadway   142
    WILLIAM ORCHARD

13 Siempre Pa'l Arte: The Passions of Latina/o Spoken Word   151
    DAVID A. COLÓN

14 Postindustrial Pinto Poetics and New Millennial Maiz Narratives:
    Race and Place in Chicano Hip Hop   162
    PANCHO MCFARLAND

15 Punk Spanglish   173
    ILAN STAVANS

16 Latino Radio and Counter Epistemologies   179
    STACEY ALEX

PART III
Pop Artivist Reclamations   189

17 Hermandad, Arte and Rebeldía: Mexican Popular Art in New York City 191
    MELISSA CASTILLO-GARSOW

18 Inexact Revolutions: Understanding Latino Pop Art   205
    ROCIO ISABEL PRADO

19 Installation Art, Transnationalism and the Chinese-Chicano Experience 214
    RICHARD ALEXANDER LOU AND GUISELA LATORRE

20 Revising the Archive: Documentary Portraiture in the Photography
    of Delilah Montoya   226
    STEPHANIE LEWTHWAITE

CONTENTS

PART IV
Quotidian Pop   237

21   Farmworker-to-Table Mexican: Decolonizing Haute Cuisine   239
      PALOMA MARTÍNEZ-CRUZ

22   The Rituals of Health   256
      AMELIA MARÍA DE LA LUZ MONTES

23   Lowrider Publics: Aesthetics and Contested Communities   267
      BEN CHAPPELL

24   Barrio Ritual and Pop Rite: Quinceañeras in the Folklore–Popular
      Culture Borderlands   279
      RACHEL GONZÁLEZ-MARTIN

25   Cultura Joteria: The Ins and Outs of Latina/o Popular Culture   291
      ELLIE D. HERNANDEZ

26   Raza Rockabilly and Greaser Cultura   301
      NICHOLAS CENTINO

27   Bodies in Motion: Latina/o Popular Culture as Rasquache Resistance   310
      MARIVEL T. DANIELSON

28   Claiming Style, Consuming Culture: The Politics of Latina Self-Styling
      and Fashion Lines   323
      STACY I. MACÍAS

29   Latina/os and the American Sports Landscape   334
      CHRISTOPHER GONZÁLEZ

30   Latina/os in the American High School, Collegiate, and Community
      Sporting Landscape   345
      JORGE IBER

PART V
Pop Rituals of Life in Death   355

31   Saints and the Secular: La Santísma Muerte   357
      DESIRÉE MARTÍN

32   Day of the Dead: Decolonial Expressions in Pop de los Muertos   370
      CRUZ MEDINA

CONTENTS

33 Liberanos de Todo Mal/But Deliver Us from Evil: Latina/o Monsters
    Theory and the Outlining of our Phantasmagoric Landscapes   381
    WILLIAM A. CALVO-QUIRÓS

34 Narco Cultura   394
    RYAN RASHOTTE

35 Smuggling as a Spectacle: Irregular Migration and Coyotes in
    Contemporary U.S. Latino Popular Culture   413
    GABRIELLA SANCHEZ

Afterword: A Latino Pop Quartet for the Ontologically Complex
Smartphone Age   424
WILLIAM ANTHONY NERICCIO

Index   434

FIGURES

1.1	NBC's *The High Chaparral*	26
1.2	NBC's *Chico and the Man*	27
2.1	Michael Piña as César Chávez in Diego Luna's *César Chávez* (2014)	36
2.2	Latinas in Vicky Funari's and Sergio De La Torre's *Maquilapolis* (2006)	38
2.3	Danny Trejo as Machete in Robert Rodriguez's *Machete* (2010)	40
3.1	*Carrascolendas* cast members on set	48
3.2	*Maya & Miguel* online game	52
4.1	Hi! I'm Dora	60
4.2	Jennifer Lopez (JLo) standing in as a backup dancer	62
4.3	King Bobo and Dora	63
4.4	*Juan Bobo Busca Trabajo*	64
4.5	Ambiguous Dora	66
7.1	How the video game industry beat some of its rivals in the entertainment world	88
7.2	Who plays video games?	89
7.3	Who makes video games?	89
7.4	Major video game releases featuring Latin American locations and/or portraying Latino characters and themes	90
7.5	Havana Cathedral	95
7.6	Detail of the Havana Cathedral, as seen in *Assassins Creed: Black Flag*	95
9.1	Memo (Luis Fernando Peña) connects his body to the infomaquila network	114
9.2	Captain William Adama (Edward James Olmos) contemplating aboard the Battlestar Galactica	116
11.1	*Huitzilopochtli* traditional Aztec dancers	135
17.1	Sarck Har's "Mexica Style" tattoo work	195
19.1	Richard Lou, *Stories on My Back*	215
20.1	*Contemporary Casta Portraiture: Nuestra "Calidad"*	228
20.2	*Terri 'Lil Loca' Lynn Cruz*	232
20.3	*San Sebastiana: Lengua Negra*	234
27.1	Leigh-Anna Hidalgo Newton	316
31.1	Santa Muerte (Saint Death)	358
33.1	Deadly Vulnerability	390
34.1	Jesús Malverde	396
34.2	El Gallo	400
34.3	Santa Muerte	406

FIGURES

36.1   Lalo Alcaraz's "Liberty's On the Run"   425
36.2   Trump Statue of Liberty   430
36.3   Hollywood sign near Griffith's Park in LA   431

CONTRIBUTORS

Frederick Luis Aldama is University Distinguished Scholar and Arts and Humanities Distinguished Professor of English, Spanish, and Portuguese at The Ohio State University. He specializes in Latina/o and Latin American literature, comic books, film, and pop culture generally. He is the author, co-author, and editor of over twenty-four books. He is editor and co-editor of five book series, including *Latino Pop Culture, Latino and Latin American Profiles*, and *Global Latino/a Americas*.

Stacey Alex is a PhD student at The Ohio State University where she creates theoretical bridges between Latin American and Latina/o cultural phenomena. She investigates literary and other cultural representations of Latina/o identity as shaped by education, immigration, and living in the Midwest. She is especially interested in Chicana/o literature for young adults.

Cecilia Josephine Aragón is an associate professor of Multicultural Theater at the University of Wyoming. She publishes and teaches in the areas of world drama, multicultural theater, performance theory, and theater for social change. In addition to publishing numerous articles, she is co-editor of *Rudolfo Anaya: Billy the Kid and Other Plays* (2011). Her directing credits include, but are not limited to: *Where the Wild Things Are, Lilly's Purple Plastic Purse, Alicia in Wonder Tierra, Bocón, Beauty and the Beast*, and *Naked Words Hip-Hop Revolution*.

Mary Beltrán is an associate professor of Radio/Television/Film, Mexican American and Latina/o Studies, and Women's and Gender Studies at the University of Texas at Austin. Her research focuses on the construction of race, class, and gender in U.S. television, film, and celebrity culture, particularly in relation to Latina/o and mixed race representation. She is the author of *Latina/o Stars in U.S. Eyes* (2009) and co-editor (with Camilla Fojas) of *Mixed Race Hollywood* (2008).

William A. Calvo-Quirós is an assistant professor of American Culture at the University of Michigan. His current research investigates the relationship between state violence, imagination, and the phantasmagoric along the U.S./Mexico border region, exploring how this sociopolitical space of conflict and struggle is a "haunted" land inhabited by many imaginary creatures and fantastic tales. His other areas of interest include Chicana/o aesthetics, Chicana feminist and queer decolonial methodologies, and the power of empathy and forgiveness in order to formulate new racial, gender, and sensual discourses.

Melissa Castillo-Garsow is a PhD student in American Studies and African American Studies at Yale University. Her short stories, articles, and poetry have been published in numerous journals. She is the co-editor with Jason Nichols of *La Verdad: The Reader of Hip Hop Latinidades*, forthcoming with The Ohio State University Press's Global Latino/a Americas book series, as well as the editor of a forthcoming anthology of Afro-Latino poetry with Arte Publico Press. She is author of the novel *Pure Bronx* (2013) and a forthcoming volume of poetry, *Coatlicue Eats the Apple*.

Nicholas Centino is a scholar of Chicana/o Studies who works to provide a critical look at intersections of race, culture, and the economy in his research. He currently conducts research with the University of California Irvine Community and Labor Project and the UCLA Labor Center.

Ben Chappell is an associate professor of American Studies at the University of Kansas. He has authored numerous articles and the book, *Lowrider Space: Aesthetics and Politics of Mexican American Custom Cars* (2012). He is currently writing about Mexican American fastpitch softball tournaments in the Midwest and Texas.

Fabio Chee is a poet, writer, and adjunct professor in Mexican and Chicana/o Studies in the Department of Modern Language Studies at California State University, San Marcos. He received a PhD in Spanish from the University of California, Irvine, and an MA in Hispanic Literatures from the University of Texas, Austin.

Osvaldo Cleger is an assistant professor in the School of Modern Languages at the Georgia Institute of Technology. His research focuses on the impact that recent technological developments have on the cultural and literary field. His articles on video games, visual culture, blogging, and hypertext fiction have appeared in numerous journals and edited volumes. His book *Narrar en la Era de las Blogoficciones: Literatura, Cultura y Sociedad de las Redes en el siglo XXI* (2010) offers a systematic approach to blog-narratives written by Hispanic authors. He is also co-editor of the volume *Redes hipertextuales en el aula* (2015).

David A. Colón is an associate professor of English and the Director of the Latina/o Studies Program at Texas Christian University. His essays have appeared in numerous journals. He edited an anthology, *Between Day and Night: New and Selected Poems 1946–2010*, by Miguel González-Gerth (2013), named an "outstanding title" by the Association of American University Presses. His novel, *The Lost Men* (2012), was nominated for the Arthur C. Clarke Award. He is currently researching dynamics between masculinity and matriarchy in Mexican-American novels.

Marivel T. Danielson is an associate professor in the School of Transborder Studies at Arizona State University. She is the author of *Homecoming Queers: Desire and Difference in Chicana Latina Cultural Production* (2009). She has published numerous articles and chapters in edited volumes. Her research and teaching focuses on Chicana Latina literary and cultural studies, performance, and gender/sexuality studies. She is a founding member of the Phoenix-based production collective Entre NosOtr@s and a board member of the national organization Association for Jotería Arts, Activism, and Scholarship (AJAAS).

CONTRIBUTORS

Laura Fernández is a PhD student in the Department of Spanish and Portuguese at The Ohio State University. Her areas of interest include Latina/o gangs (culture and literature), Latina/o pop culture, and Latina/o cultural studies.

Camilla Fojas is Vincent de Paul Professor of Latin American at DePaul University. She is co-editor and author of several books, including *Cosmopolitanism in the Americas* (2005), *Border Bandits: Hollywood on the Southern Frontier* (2008), and *Islands of Empire: Pop Culture and U.S. Power* (2014).

Kathryn M. Frank received her PhD in Communication from the University of Michigan in 2015. She is broadly interested in the intersections of race/ethnicity, gender, and sexuality, and representations of these topics in visual and popular media. She is the author of several articles and is currently examining the history of live-action comic book adaptations as a genre deeply intertwined with representations of race.

Enrique García is associate professor of Hispanic Visual Culture in the Department of Spanish and Portuguese at Middlebury College. His research is focused on transnational Hispanic cinema and comic books written in Spanish. He has published essays on Mexican comics and on U.S. Latino director Robert Rodríguez. He has published *Cuban Cinema* (2014) and has in production a book on Gilbert and Jaime Hernandez, forthcoming with the University of Pittsburgh Press's Latino and Latin American Profiles series.

Christopher González is assistant professor of English at Texas A&M University–Commerce. His research and teaching focuses on twentieth- and twenty-first century literature, film, and comics of the U.S. Latino popular culture, and narrative design. González is co-author of *Latinos in the End Zone: Conversations on the Brown Color Line in the NFL* (2013), author of *Reading Junot Díaz* (2015), and co-editor of *Graphic Borders: Latino Comics Past, Present, and Future* (2016).

Rachel González-Martin is an assistant professor of Mexican American and Latina/o Studies at the University of Texas at Austin. Her work investigates the lived experiences of Latina/o identifying communities across the United States, focusing on material practices and notions of consumer belonging.

Matthew David Goodwin is an assistant professor in the Department of English at the University of Puerto Rico at Cayey. His research is centered on the experience of migration in Latino/a literature. He is currently at work on a full-length study of Latino/a science fiction. His edited anthology of Latino/a science fiction and fantasy is forthcoming with Wings Press.

Ellie D. Hernandez is an associate professor in the Department of Chicana/o Studies at the University of California at Santa Barbara where she teaches and writes extensively on Jotería popular culture, citizenship, transnational Chicana/o and Latina/o cultural production, as well as issues of gender and sexuality. She is author of *Postnationalism in Chicana/o Literature and Culture* (2009), as well as co-editor of *The UnMaking of Latina/o Citizenship: Culture, Politics and Aesthetics* (2014).

Jorge Iber, PhD, is Associate Dean in the College of Arts and Sciences and professor of History at Texas Tech University in Lubbock. He is the author, co-author, editor, and co-editor of seven books, including *Latinos in US Sport: A History of Isolation, Cultural Identity, and Acceptance* (2011), *More than Just Peloteros: Sport and US Latino Communities* (2015), and *Mike Torrez: A Baseball Biography* (2016). He is also the author of dozens of scholarly and encyclopedia articles, and serves as series editor for the Sport in the American West series for Texas Tech University Press.

Guisela Latorre is associate professor at The Ohio State University where she specializes in modern and contemporary U.S. Latina/o and Latin American art with a special emphasis on gender and women artists. She is the author of *Walls of Empowerment: Chicana/o Indigenist Murals from California* (2008) which explores the recurrence of indigenist motifs in Chicana/o community murals from the 1970s to the turn of the millennium. She has published numerous articles and is co-editor of the feminist journal *Frontiers: A Journal of Women Studies*. She is currently at work on a second book project on the graffiti and mural movement in Chile during the post-dictatorship era.

Stephanie Lewthwaite is a lecturer in the Department of American and Canadian Studies at the University of Nottingham, United Kingdom. She is the author of *Race, Place, and Reform in Mexican Los Angeles: A Transnational Perspective, 1890–1940* (2009) and *A Contested Art: Modernism and Mestizaje in New Mexico* (2015). Her interests lie in the field of contemporary Latino/a visual culture, especially in photography, and its connection with historical memory.

Richard Alexander Lou is a professor and Chair of the Department of Art at the University of Memphis. He has curated over 30 exhibitions, and continues to produce and exhibit art. His art work has been published and cited in dozens of newspapers, magazines, catalogs, electronic media, and over 30 books.

Stacy I. Macías is an independent scholar who earned her PhD from UCLA in Women's Studies. She was a Carlos E. Castañeda Postdoctoral Fellow at the Center for Mexican American Studies, University of Texas, Austin, and has since taught courses at UC Santa Barbara and the University of Nevada, Las Vegas. Her research and activism are in the areas of Chicana/Latina studies, feminist transnational praxis, and queer of color studies with a focus on aesthetics, femininity, and queer cultural production.

Desirée Martín is an associate professor at the University of California, Davis, where she teaches, researches, and writes in the areas of U.S.-Mexico border studies and theory, Chicana/o and Latina/o studies, transnational American studies, and nineteenth and twentieth century Mexican cultural production. She is the author of *Borderlands Saints: Secular Sanctity in Chicano/a and Mexican Culture* (2013), and is currently working on a book-length project on cultural translation and the mistranslation and refusal of identity, tentatively titled *Untranslatable*.

Paloma Martínez-Cruz is an assistant professor of Latino/a Cultural and Literary Studies at The Ohio State University working in the areas of contemporary hemispheric literature and culture, women of color feminism, performance, and alternative epistemologies. She is the author of *Women and Knowledge in Mesoamerica: From East*

L.A. to Anahuac (2011). She is the translator of *Ponciá Vicencio*, the debut novel by Afro-Brazilian author Conceição Evaristo, as well as the editor of *Rebeldes: A Proyecto Latina Anthology* (2013), a collection of stories and art from 26 Latina women from the Midwest and beyond. Currently Martínez-Cruz is at work on a book publication centered on sonic Latinidad.

Pancho McFarland is associate professor of sociology at Chicago State University. He conducts research on hip hop in Mexican American communities and food justice in Chicago. His writings on Chicana/o culture have appeared in numerous journals, edited volumes, and encyclopedias. He is author of *Chicano Rap: Gender and Violence in the Postindustrial Barrio* (2008) and *The Chican@ Hip Hop Nation: Politics of New Millennial Mestizaje* (2013). He is currently writing *Food Justice in the City: Essays on CommUnity, Autonomy and Struggle in Chicago*, and co-editing *Decolonial Food for Thought: Mexican-Origin Foods, Foodways and Social Movements* (University of Arkansas Press).

Cruz Medina is an assistant professor of Rhetoric and Composition at Santa Clara University, where he teaches courses in rhetoric, social justice, digital writing, and multicultural literature. Medina is the author of *Reclaiming Poch@ Pop: Examining the Rhetoric of Cultural Deficiency* (2015) in the Latino Pop Culture Series edited by Frederick Luis Aldama. His writing appears in *Latino/a Literature in the Classroom: 21ˢᵗ Century Approaches to Teaching* (2015), *Alter/nativas: Latin American Cultural Studies Journal*, *College Composition and Communication*, and other publications.

Isabel Millán is an assistant professor in the Department of American Ethnic Studies at Kansas State University. Her recent publications include "Contested Children's Literature: Que(e)ries into Chicana and Central American Autofantasías" (*Signs: Journal of Women in Culture and Society*), "Engineering Afro-Latina and Mexican Immigrant Heroines: Bio/Border Politics in Dystopian Speculative Fiction and Film" (*Aztlán: A Journal of Chicano Studies*), and a chapter on Latina comics in *Graphic Borders: Latino Comics Past, Present, and Future* (2016).

Amelia María de la Luz Montes is an associate professor of English and Ethnic Studies at The University of Nebraska, Lincoln. Her scholarly publications and teaching include Chicana/U.S. Latina literatures and theory, late nineteenth-century and contemporary American literatures. Her Penguin Classics edition of Ruiz de Burton's novel *Who Would Have Thought It?* was listed on the Latino Books Month List from the Association of American Publishers. She is currently finishing a critical text on Chicana and Latina Midwest writers, and a creative non-fiction book entitled *The Diabetes Chronicles*. Dr. Montes is one of 11 writers for the largest national/international Chicana/Chicano and Latina/Latino blogsite, *La Bloga*.

William Anthony Nericcio is a professor and Director of the MALAS Cultural Studies Graduate Program at San Diego State University. He also serves as Lead Faculty for the Digital Humanities Initiative, as well as affiliated faculty for the Center for Latin American Studies and Chicana/o Studies. The author of *Tex[t]-Mex: Seductive Hallucinations of the "Mexican" in America*, he is presently working on his follow up study of American visual culture, *Eyegiene: Permutations of Subjectivity in the Televisual Age of Sex and Race*.

William Orchard is an assistant professor at Queens College of the City University of New York. With Yolanda Padilla, he has co-edited *The Selected Plays of Josephina Niggli* and the forthcoming volume *New Chicana/o Narratives: History, Form, and Nation in the 21st-Century.*

Rocío Isabel Prado is a PhD student at The Ohio State University. Her research interests include Latino graphic novels, queer and postcolonial theory, and postmodernism and contemporary stand-up comedy. Her creative work can be found on the Black Girl Dangerous Project and the upcoming Jota anthology through Kórima Press.

Ryan Rashotte is an independent scholar and author of *Narco Cinema: Sex, Drugs, and Banda Music in Mexico's B-Filmography* (2015). He has a PhD in English from the University of Guelph, Canada.

Cristina Rivera is a graduate student at San Diego State University. She is editor of the *Pacific Review: A West Coast Arts Review Annual* and works as an editorial assistant for *The Lion and the Unicorn.* Her current research is on terror in folktales.

Gabriella Sanchez is assistant professor in Human Security Studies at the University of Texas at El Paso. A sociocultural anthropologist whose work explores the social dynamics of criminal/ized markets along border regions, her primary research areas involve human smuggling and trafficking and the drug trade. She is the author of *Border Crossings and Human Smuggling* (2014) that documents the day-to-day interactions among *coyotes* in the U.S. Southwest. As a Fulbright fellow, Sanchez also conducted ethnographic fieldwork in North Africa, the Middle East, and Australia.

Ilan Stavans is Lewis-Sebring Professor in Latin American and Latino Culture at Amherst College. His most recent books include the anthology *The FSG Book of Twentieth Century Latin American Poetry* (2012), the graphic novel *El Iluminado* (2012, with Steve Sheinkin), the children's book *Golemito* (2013, with Teresa Villegas), *Thirteen Ways of Looking at Latino Art* (2014, with Jorge J.E. Gracia), *A Most Imperfect Union: A Contrarian History of the United States* (2014, with Lalo Alcaraz), *Quixote: The Novel and the World* (2015), and a new translation of *Lazarillo de Tormes* (2016).

INTRODUCTION
Putting the Pop in Latina/o Culture

Frederick Luis Aldama

As the scholarship in this volume attests, Latina/os are actively educating the way people in the U.S. hear, taste, see, smell, touch, think, and feel. To varying degrees of complexity, as creative agents or subjects of created cultural phenomena, Latina/os appear in all variety of today's pop culture: TV (web and otherwise), film, animation, comic books, video games, art, slam poetry, music, food, sartorial wear, and so much more. In this whirlwind of pop culture making and consuming, one way or another, the scholarship that makes up this volume asks: how are the different pop cultural formats being created representing—or more accurately, distilling then reconstructing—the many complex ways we exist and identify as Latina/os in the U.S.?

First, what is meant by Latina/o pop culture—as opposed to, say, Latina/o culture? For some this might be the artificial division between mass or lowbrow culture and highbrow culture. For these scholars (and media pundits) this is the difference between a beach-read like Alisa Valdez's *Dirty Girls Social Club* (2003) and Salvador Plascencia's *People of Paper* (2005); or, the difference between mural, or graffiti street art and that which appears in a museum. In this scenario, pop culture is created to appeal to the masses—masses not considered, say, sophisticated in their taste. Scholars such as those identified by the European Frankfurt School go a step further, identifying mass created and consumed pop culture as a kind of opiate that clouds truths of global capitalist exploitation and oppression. For other scholars like those of the Birmingham School, consumption of pop culture is an active re-interpretive process, especially by those at the socioeconomic, racial, and political margins. No part of pop culture is swallowed whole; all of it is metastasized and made one's own in new and meaningful ways. And, in one of the chapters in this volume, William Orchard links popular culture with community and resistance and pop to those cultural objects created with profit margins in mind that constrain aesthetic aspirations.

Certainly, I'm a scholar who considers humans generally and Latina/os specifically as active transformers of culture—pop or otherwise. Common sense (and the recent advances in the cognitive and neurosciences) more than suggests that there is *not* a one-to-one correspondence between what children see and play with and how they self-identify. The imagination—and especially the child's imagination—isn't a tabula rasa to be etched upon indelibly. Indeed, it is the opposite. The child's exercising of his or her causal, counterfactual, and probabilistic mechanisms allows them not only to map their present social and natural worlds, but also to imagine new and possible ways of existing in the world in the future. Children and adults, we Latina/os are such active transformers.

As it is, whether or not we deem a pop cultural phenomenon by and about Latina/os well done—and this meaning-making and evaluating is an important part of cultural production—it will not change this fact: children (and we adults) are extraordinarily creative and *re-creative* in what they do with products that enter the world with more or less set or delimited functionalities. Such products could be a TV show, comic book, or video game. While the latter rely less on determining a physical functionality, they do establish storylines and characters that direct (more or less) our gap-filling capacities; but where we go in our gap filling—our imagination—is not predetermined. Rather, it is ultimately limitless. So we can and do evaluate and interpret mediated Latina/o cultural products, keeping in mind that in spite of the delimitations built into these objects, when we couple them with our limitless capacity to imagine, they become unlimited in their function.

Indeed, the study of the making and consuming of pop culture by and about Latina/os can tell us much about Latina/os in time (history) and place (region) as well as about prejudices and worldviews. It can teach us much about human creation and consumption, and how in this process objects are made to establish patterned, new relationships between subjects and objects. It can and does say something about our human nature generally. For thousands of years we have transformed our environment, and by transforming nature, we have transformed ourselves constantly and in this dialectical manner. While this transformative capacity applies to all organisms and is not just a feature of humans, we are, as far as we know today, the only organisms capable of transforming nature not only as a means of survival but more and more over the millennia the only species capable of transforming nature in a *purposeful* way! That is, according to a plan and no longer only as a means of immediate survival in reaction to our environment.

For Latina/os and humans the planet over, planning is a central activity for us. Aristotle's observation holds true today: we transform nature aand in turn are transformed by this changed nature – and we are the only part *of nature that can do this according to plan*. This is important for our evolution and also in the education of each individual starting from when we are born. In this sense, just as there is no rigid distinction between pop culture and culture, there is no rigid distinction between nature and culture. With advances in socio-neurobiology we know this to be the absolute case.

Another way to look at this is to hold at bay any impulse to reify what I'm identifying as pop culture by and about Latina/os. Latinoness, or Latinidad, varies from each subgroup that makes up the Latina/o whole. Latino Cuban culture in the US is not identical to Cuban island culture, nor is it identical to the culture of other U.S. Latinos of different ethnic origins. Latinidad is variable, movable, and changeable.

And yet, in spite of all its ancestral variability and constant transformation, Latinoness is something we can touch, smell, taste, and hear. It is something that is distilled, reconstructed, and consumed anew in all variety of cultural phenomena. Here, rather than think of binaries, perhaps we should be considering degrees of willfulness involved in the distillation, reconstruction, and consumption of cultural phenomena that feature Latina/os. In the willful metastasizing of this slice of reality we're calling Latina/o, there are those who put a lot of work and skill into their reconstructions and those who slip into lazy, comfortable habits; there are those who pull us more deeply into the cultural objects that feature Latina/os and those who lazily reproduce more of the stereotypical same. There's a DC comic book that features a superhero Latino who is called Vibe and who speaks with heavily accented and truncated English; and there's El Muerto, given life through Javier Hernandez's deft drawing ability, who creates a new superhero mythos built on Mesoamerican history and today's *día de los muertos* ceremonies. There's the complexly rendered graphic novel, *In My Darkest Hour* (2004), whereby Wilfred Santiago distills then reconstructs the experience of a Latino suffering from manic depression during the 9/11 events; his psychological suffering leads to increased isolation and the obliteration of a sense of self. And, there's the less graphically layered and more playful serape-wearing donkey superhero as created by Carlos Saldaña's *Burrito* (1990).

Pop culture by and about Latina/os has gone through historical ebbs and flows. With a seemingly sudden gush of music, film, and art generally during the 1980s, *Time* magazine announced this period to be "The Hispanic Decade." I do recall the excitement around Gloria Estefan and the Miami Sound Machine as well as those films of Luis Valdez such as *Zoot Suit* (1981), *La Bamba* (1987) and Gregory Nava's *El Norte* (1984), and Cheech Marin's *Born in East LA* (1987). The 1990s continued to experience a seeming explosion in pop culture by and about Latina/os with the ever evolving Santana, Jon Secada, Selena, Marc Anthony, JLo, and Ricky Martin booming across the radio airwaves; and, I recall those films that complexly reconstructed the Latina/o experience such as Edward James Olmos's *American Me* (1992), Robert Rodríguez's *El Mariachi* (1992), Allison Anders's *Mi Vida Loca* (1993), Darnell Martin's *I Like it Like That* (1994), Gregory Nava's *Mi Familia* (1995), and Paul Espinosa's *... and the earth did not swallow him* (1995).

Increasingly, too, pop culture by and about Latina/os has begun to, say, naturalize its presence; by this I mean that today one might have a Latina cheerleader or an aspiring singer on a television show without much ado about the character's ethnic background. The character simply *is* Latina just as another simply *is* Anglo. This is not always the case, of course. Indeed, we still have the kinds of exaggerations and caricatures that marked the presence of Latina/os during earlier decades such as the 1970s, with Freddy Rodriguez's over-the-top Chico Rodriguez in *Chico and the Man* (1974–1978). And, we see the bumbling buffoonery today as we did with the heavily Spanish-accented Ricky Ricardo in *I Love Lucy* (1951–1957). And, while it seems like those Anglo actors who regularly appeared in Brownface in Hollywood are a part of our shameful silver screen history—Marlon Brando as Zapata in *Viva Zapata!* (1952) and Natalie Wood as María in *West Side Story* (1961)—this still happens today when Anglos and Euro-Spaniards continue to be cast as Latina/os or to play their voices, such as Robin Williams as Ramone in the animated feature *Happy Feet*.

That Latina/os are an active part of the making of U.S. pop culture writ large is not surprising. Some might consider this a by-product of what has been identified by scholars and media pundits as the "Browning of America." There has been a massive growth in the demographic presence of Latina/os in the U.S. in the first decade of the twenty-first century. Today, Latina/os are the largest minority in the U.S., numbering upward of 51 million on the 2010 U.S. census, plus 12 million undocumented. In contrast, in 1980, Latina/os numbered 14.6 million. And this increased population is a U.S.-Latina/o-born demographic: playgrounds across the country have more and more Latina/o children.

This massive demographic presence has led to a greater existence of Latina/os (and Latina/o culture writ large) in the mainstream—a mainstream itself that has changed by the very presence of Latina/os and Latina/o pop culture. Dora teaches children the alphabet and counting, and not Sally. In *Glee* (2009–2015), Santana Lopez (Naya Rivera) is on the Cheerio cheerleading squad along with Brittany, and all other shades of brown and white on the squad.

The building blocks of reality in the U.S. look, smell, sound, and feel different as a result of the Latina/o presence. Creators of shows, comics, films, blogs, and any other media format pull the building blocks from this reality in the making of their stories. The shows themselves reflect a Latina/o-transformed reality just as they contribute constantly to this transformation. Otherwise stated, today we see much more visibly a two-way flow of influence between the Latina/o and mainstream culture. The more the presence of Latina/os grows, and the visibility of its culture with it, the more it impacts the mainstream cultural setting materially, intellectually, and sensorially.

Just as the tastes of the average U.S. American have changed, so too have those of Latina/os—and not just when it comes to cuisine. Our massive demographic presence brings with it a wide array of Latina/o consumer tastes. We are as likely to hunger for the clear-cut worlds presented in *telenovelas* such as *Eva Luna* (2010–2011) as those presented on shows such as *Lost* (2004–2010) or *Mad Men* (2007–). We are just as likely to be interested in American Girl Dolls such as the Latina Marisol as the Anglo McKenna. We are just as likely to crave the complexity of a Junot Díaz fictional narrative as we are to want to read an instructional *chica lit* novel by an Alisa Valdes. We are just as likely to pick up a Marvel high-gloss superhero comic book such as Ultimate Spider-Man with the Afro-Latino Miles Morales as Spidey as we are a Fantagraphic produced, innovative, and daring stand-alone noir graphic novel by Gilbert Hernandez. We are just as likely to play a shooter game such as *Gears of War* (2006–) as we are the magical-realist puzzle-game, *Papo y Yo* (2012).

One way or another (with greater or lesser degrees of willfulness), as creators (authors, directors, bloggers, software developers, for instance) and participants (actors, athletes, musicians, for instance) Latina/os exist as a vital presence in all layers of today's U.S. pop cultural tissue.

Content and Form

I'm all about opening doors and making widely available any and all kinds of pop cultural phenomena to satisfy the huge range of tastes out there. However, not all pop cultural phenomena by and about Latina/os are made alike. As mentioned earlier, some products evince a greater degree of *willfulness* in their distillation and reconstruction of Latina/os than others. Put simply, some are driven by corporate profits and others by the desire to innovate, and make *new* our perception, thought, and feeling about Latina/os in the U.S.

For corporate America, the Latina/o demographic represents a one-trillion-dollar buying potential. Viewed with somewhat cynical and skeptical eyes, the increased representation of Latina/os in the entertainment industry is a result of this push to capture the Latina/o consumer market. The U.S. Latina/o market ranks as the twelfth largest economy in the world. Was Marvel's introduction of the Afro-Latino Spidey to *make new* the superhero universe, or to take advantage of the purchase power of the two largest minority populations in the United States: blacks and Latina/os? Was the Latina/o-focused content in a special bilingual issue of *Rolling Stone* (November 22, 2012) that included pieces on Latino musicians Pitbull and Calle 13 as well as fiction by Junot Díaz, a *new* way to engage its readership or a marketing ploy for Latina/os to purchase?

The massive demographic growth of Latina/os has had cable and the networks jumping on the Latina/o bandwagon too. The joint Fox and Colombian RCN Television production of MundoFox aims to capture a portion of this 51-plus million demographic by introducing American-style programming to Spanish speaking audiences. Its tagline: "Americano Como Tú" (or, American Like You); MundoFox wants to move into an area missed entirely by

American broadcast networks. This adds to the telenovela, sports, and reality programming already offered by networks located across the U.S.–Mexico border such as Univisión and Telemundo. In 2014, Robert Rodríguez launched his Austin-based El Rey Network (Comcast) which targets second- and third-generation Latina/os with original programming like the series *From Dusk Till Dawn* and *Lucha Underground* in English aimed at third-generation Latina/os.

This phenomenon of Spanish-language and Latina/o-oriented television programming should come as no surprise. At any given time, there are 48 million Latina/os in the United States watching television, according to the Nielson ratings. And while demographics have done much to push the envelope on representation—and also media watchdog entities such as the National Council of La Raza, American Entertainment Marketing, and the National Hispanic Media Coalition—we still remain largely invisible in pop cultural phenomena. We are few in front of cameras and even fewer behind the scenes in mainstream media creation and production.

As already mentioned, not all pop cultural products are the same. Some have a greater degree of willfulness in the shaping of forms to convey interesting Latina/o content. I identify this elsewhere as the degrees of presence of the "will to style": the responsibility of the creator (or creators) to understand well the building blocks of the reality they are reconstructing as well as the degree of presence of a willful use of skills and technical devices to give shape to the making of new pop cultural phenomena by and about Latina/os. The presence of this will to style can be strong or weak in any given pop cultural object. Here are a few examples that come readily to mind.

Disney's Marvel Studios seeks profits, but even here this is not enough to put Latina/os into the filmic comic book universe. While the Marvel universe has plenty of important Latino superheroes and super villains, they have yet to appear on the big screen. When Latinoness does appear, it's either to convey a sense of danger or as the bumbling side-kick comic relief. Take Peyton Reed's *Ant-Man* (2015). As the trademark Marvel Comic book pages flip to introduce the film, we hear salsa music—a sound bridge used as the camera moves into the interior of a jail to introduce the Anglo protagonist, Paul Rudd as Scott Lang (Ant-Man); he's picked up by his former cellmate (arrested for stealing a smoothie machine) and friend Luis (Michael Peña), who, while driving a beat up van, tells him in quick fire succession of his girlfriend leaving him, his "ma" dying, and his dad getting deported. While the writers of the film's script try to complicate the caricature of the Latino—Luis mentions how he prefers neo-cubism to abstract art and rosé wine to red—he's largely figured as the brainless buffoon, to an infantilizing degree.

Ant-Man is one of many examples of the way Latinoness shadows the mainstream film imaginary. The latest Bond franchise, *Spectre* (2015), opens with the words "the dead are alive" across the screen then follows with a long shot of Mexico City celebrating *día de los muertos*; the camera then zooms in to track the masked and dangerous looking (in a calavera costume) Anglo protagonist James Bond (Daniel Craig) navigating through the masses. *Día de los muertos* establishes the scene of danger and death, something the Anglo cosmopolitan aristocrat Bond can wear then discard. In *Elysium* (2013) director Neill Blomkamp chooses to depict earth as a massive shanty/favela filled with brown people. The film's Earth-bound scenes were shot in a dump in the poor Iztapalapa district on the outskirts of Mexico City while the scenes for Elysium were shot in Vancouver and the wealthy Huixquilucan Interlomas suburbs of Mexico City. Yes, we are absolutely present, but in ways whereby the film narrative locates issues of overpopulation and pollution in the brown subject—and replays ad nauseum the white savior myth with the Latino-raised Anglo Max (Matt Damon) as the figure who saves the planet.

And, when Latina/os are not used as cultural signifiers of danger, our Latinidad is made visible in other simplistic ways. In Sean McNamara's *Bratz: the Movie* (2007) the high school Latina character (Mexican and Jewish), Yasmin, is played by the light-skinned Spanish and Australian actress, Manuela Nathalia Ramos. While her phenotype and action largely "whitewash" her Latinidad, the film's beginning does establish her as a Latina—and in an extremely lazy way. In the morning when Yasmin first enters the kitchen to greet her abuelita there's an entire mariachi band sitting around eating pan dulce—we know not why. And, in Disney's *Camp Rock* (2008) it is the light-skinned Latina actress Demi Lovato who plays the lead, Mitchie Torres. The details of her Latinidad are slim to none: her family name, "Torres", and the mother Connie's Spanish-accented English (she's played by the Cuban American María Canals Barrera); she's also a cook—a possible marker in the mainstream imagination of Latinidad. And in Disney Channel's TV show and spin-off film, the *Wizards of Waverly Place* (2009), we see some hints at a Latinidad, but in ways that are not integrated into the story in a central way. It makes clear that the family of wizards at the center of the story is Italian-Mexican. Yet again, the writers decide that the show's Latinoness can be conveyed by having the mother Theresa Russo (played again by María Canals Barrera) as a cook and light-skinned Latina actress Selena Gomez cast as the daughter, Alex.

As one can imagine, not only do the distillations and reconstructions lack much will to style, but they trigger much anxiety around the issue of what it means to be Latina/o in pop cultural phenomena generally. Are these shows representing an assimilated Latina, or a Latina who *is Latina* in a United States where Latinidad (smells, sights, touch, sounds) is so interwoven into a mainstream culture that it now passes us by in these stories as indistinguishable?

We have TV shows like *Desperate Housewives* (2004–2012), *Modern Family* (2009–), *Devious Maids* (2013–), *Jane the Virgin* (2014–), *Cristela* (2014–2015), *East Los High* (2013–), *Ugly Betty* (2006–2010), and many others. Taken on their own terms and as a whole, the shows code differently a Latina/o identity and experience. For instance, in *Desperate Housewives* we see the upper-middle-class Solis family deal with issues typical of those living on Wisteria Lane, such as deceit and infidelity. But the show also distinguishes them from the other families as hot tempered, oversexed, and, finally, downwardly mobile. They are the family that slips into a non-country club-going group when Carlos (Ricardo Antonio Chavira) goes blind, loses his job, and takes up massage therapy. Rather than pass through the front doors of the country club, they find themselves welcome only by way of the servant's entrance—an indication generally of their lower status in the community once they are not members of the professional, bourgeois class. In *Ugly Betty*, the show focuses on the upward mobility of Betty (America Ferrera) whose smarts (street and book) and much coincidence lead to her arrival in the upper-middle professional class—and London, romancing the Anglo boss. While there's much importance placed on food (Mexican), dance, and code-switching (especially during heightened emotional moments and by the older generation, represented by the father who peppers his English with "Dios mío!" and "mija," and so on) as expressions of their Latinidad, the show subordinates this to its fairytale vision of the Latina/o family: that hard work and the pursuit of one's passion will lead to a Cinderella-like, socioeconomic transformation. With their blessing, Betty leaves behind her unemployed (single mother) sister Hilda (Ana Ortiz), her gay nephew Justin Suarez (played by the Italian/Puerto Rican actor, Mark Indelicato), and the father, Ignacio (played by Cuban American actor, Tony Plana). Certainly, one could read the show and even further exaggeration of the *telecomedia* mode, with its flamboyant mood and over-the-top slapstick-like characterizations, as a self-reflexive move to foreground its up-from-the-bootstrap ideological worldview. Perhaps, however, it simply is a fairytale centered on a Latina/o family.

Other prime time shows play their comedy in a more straightforward manner; by this I mean not cloaked in the garish reds, blues, and greens that make up the sartorial landscape of *Ugly Betty*, nor in the extreme, Fellini-esque caricatures it portrays. While not the representation of a family unit, we do have the whisper of a Latinidad in *Scrubs* (2001–2010). This is given shape in the interaction between the nurse Carla Espinosa (played by Judy Reyes) and her significant other, the African American character Christopher Turk (played by Donald Faison). It's not so much the show's depiction of her as hot tempered, gossipy, and sassy that is innovative, but rather in the way the show uses Reyes's mixed, Afro-Latina features to disrupt stereotypes. While the television viewers learn over the eight seasons that she's of Dominican origin, migrating to Chicago as a child, others, including Turk, constantly try to pigeonhole her as something else: Mexican, Puerto Rican, you name it, but not Afro-Latina—or Blatina. In so doing, the show also calls into question the very construction of Latina/o as a category: who is included and who is not.

In ABC's *Modern Family*, there is the focus on the family unit as such, but one that looks nothing like the Suarez or Solis family in the other shows mentioned earlier. The Latina/o family unit is made up of the Columbian émigré character Gloria (played by Sofía Vergara) and her son Manny (played by Rico Rodriguez); Gloria reconstitutes the traditional family structure with her marriage to Jay (Ed O'Neill), effectively tying herself and Manny to a larger, upper-middle-class Anglo-American family unit. The show plays Gloria as a hyperbolic embodiment of all stereotypes of Latinas. She speaks English with a very heavy Spanish accent (unlike any other Latina character on prime time today) and she relishes in her body and sexuality. As with other mainstream TV shows, cultural signifiers (language and body) are used largely to garner laughs. We can read this, as some have, as offensive, or as self-reflexive parody. I leave this for others to decide. However, what is clear is that the show seeks to counterbalance Gloria's histrionics with the staid, careful, smart, and wise presence of her son, Manny.

There's the Latina/o family unit that appears in *The George Lopez Show* (2001–2007). The show focuses on the everyday ins and outs of a working-class Mexican/Cuban family living in Los Angeles. Most of the comedy revolves around different cultural and generational tensions between these two Latina/o groups: George (George Lopez) as the Mexican and his wife Angie (Constance Marie) and especially her father, Vic, as the Cuban. Here, too, while Vic speaks English with a pronounced Spanish accent (not quite that of Gloria in *Modern Family*, but close), Spanish itself is not spoken. This is a generation of Latina/os who self-identify as Mexican American or Cuban American, constantly using their own cultural traditions and histories as punch lines to jokes, but who communicate via the common language of English.

And then there are all sorts of interesting ways Latinidad is represented in animation aimed at children. There's the clearly sloppy way that Disney's multiple directors decide to tell the story *Road to El Dorado* (2000), which not only conflates all historical periods of Mesoamerican epochs, but also presents the tired white savior myth once again. While Rosie Perez is cast as the character Chel, there's nothing indigenous about her. In fact she's all body, slinking around with lots of skin showing and willing to betray her people and romance a Spaniard to get to Europe. This is not to mention the brownface that happens in animation. So, someone like Robin Williams ventriloquizes (channels) the passionate, romantic persona of the Latino Ramon in the *Happy Feet* (2006) franchise behind his mic. And, the same happens with Penelope Cruz as Agent Juarez in *G-Force* (2009). As a Euro-

Spaniard she's in Latina/o brownface, and in the choice of the way the animators move her guinea pig body, she's hypersexualized. She causes one of her male compadres to get so sexually excited that he "drops a pellet."

Like *Dora the Explorer* (2000–), *Handy Manny* (2006–) uses Spanish in a didactic way; moreover, Manny is associated with tools and fixing things; not that there is anything wrong with this, but stereotypes already abound about the Latino as only good with his hands. To make matters worse, without a hint of irony, his Anglo neighbor Mr. Lopart constantly ignores and disregards Manny's handy advice. The Australian-made flash animation, *Mucha Lucha!* (2002–2005), uses lots of Spanglish and references to pre-Columbian and present day culture and is innovative in form. De Casanova writes how the characters's features are "stylized rather than being naturalistic" (40) and how there's a diversity of Spanish: Buena Girl and Rikochet's Chicano-inflected Spanglish; Flea's Spanish-as-second-language inflections. And while it incorporates *cumbia* into its theme song and *rock en español* generally, in the end she considers how the "campy, hybrid sensibility" of the show leads to the creating of "floating cultural signifiers" (41). As Stacy Hoult-Saros writes, "Moving beyond tortillas and well-known musical forms to incorporate more nuanced cultural references would be a positive step, as would a more sustained use of Spanish (in its many regional variations) in meaningful communication" (157).

Maya and Miguel gets its cultural references right, for the most part, and anchors them in context, as well as code-switches English/Spanish more naturally, but it abides by conventions of realist animation; more Disney than, say, Tex-Avery. Here we might consider, then, not only getting the content right, but also how the use of shaping devices *make new* this content. We see this with Gutierrez's *El Tigre*—where *El Tigre* pushes the envelope of realism and *Miguel and Maya* abides by conventions of realism. In *El Tigre* the use of Spanish is non-didactic and used as unique expression of Latinidad. *El Tigre* includes cultural signifiers like churros, but done in a way that speaks to a Latino audience already in the know and playfully so. Its techniques are constantly exposing the device of its own storyworld construction. Some have identified this as a "postmodern Latinidad". (See Philip Serrato's "Postmodern Guacamole", for instance.) But perhaps it's simply *making new* our perception of Latinoness within the conventions of animation storytelling. *Maya and Miguel* naturalizes Latino-ness and *El Tigre* denaturalizes the way the mainstream represents referents of Latinoness as floating signifiers.

And, you don't have to be Latina/o to get it right. There's Karyn Kusama's *Girlfight* (2000) which offers one of the most powerful portrayals of a Latina yet in a feature film. In *Girlfight* we meet the character Diana Guzman (played by Michelle Rodriguez in her breakout role) who literally boxes her way out of a troubled family life (an aggressive and violent father). She decides to grow her skill in an otherwise highly gendered (male) sport as a form of empowerment and way out of an otherwise suffocating Latina/o domestic space. We see, too, how Larry Clark does his homework when making his films that center on Latina/os: the LA-set *Wassup Rockers* (2005) and U.S./Mexico borderlands set, *Marfa Girl* (2012). The former chooses to focus on second-generation Central American ancestral U.S. Latina/os. And, importantly, he shows audiences that Latina/o teens today don't necessarily conform to a hip hop and gang culture branding. His ragtag group of Latina/os wear skin-tight pants, listen to punk rock, play video games, and ride skateboards—all while still anchored in Latina/o familial rituals and traditions. In *Marfa Girl* (2012) Clark not only conveys the beauty of Latina/o youth as portrayed in their total (sexual) exploratory innocence, but constructs whiteness as the repository of perverse violence and sexual dysfunction.

In addition to interesting explorations of gender roles, films and TV shows have also reconstructed Latina/o sexuality in interesting ways. Justin Suarez from *Ugly Betty* was one of prime time TV's youngest out gay Latino characters. And, the Latina Naya Rivera as Santana in *Glee* (2009–) was out as a lesbian—and in a matter of fact way. The character Dr. Callie Torres (Sara Ramirez) was a lesbian orthopedic surgeon in *Grey's Anatomy*. There was the Latino accountant, Óscar Martínez, on NBC's *The Office* (2005–2012), who is outed by his boss, Michael; the show pokes fun at Latina/o stereotypes by having coworkers tease him in exaggerated ways for being a gangbanger, a baseball player or boxer, the voice of the Taco Bell Chihuahua, and everybody buys him presents like *Will & Grace* memorabilia that he tries to get rid of at a garage sale. And, there was Jesus Velasquez (Kevin Alejandro) as gay shamanic bad boy in HBO's *True Blood* (2008–2014).

Complex reconstructions of Latina/o sexuality appear in films such as the Latina/o-created *La Mission* (2009) directed by Benjamin Bratt's brother, Peter, and that follows the tense and violent father–son relationship after the son Jes comes out as gay. After a violent separation there's a reconciliation that takes place after the father, Che, experiences a kind of rebirth in and around a *danza Azteca* ritual. (See Cecilia Aragón's chapter in this volume.) In the like-spirited *Gun Hill Road* (2011), director Rashaad Ernesto Green focuses on the intergenerational struggle between Puerto Rican father and son; this time, however, the son Michael (played by Harmony Santana) is rejected because she identifies as Vanessa.

In these cases and others, we see Latina/os stepping in as the creators of film and pop cultural phenomena generally—a counter optic to all those films that follow lazy formulas such as seen with *Maid in Manhattan* (2002) that reduces Latinoness to a lazy Cinderella story where it's the white Anglo (British Ralph Fiennes) that rescues the Latina (JLo). As Laura Molina-Guzman theorizes of JLo, she's "ripe for the commodification of in-betweenness and racial mobility" (*Dangerous Curves* 126). Furthermore, she represents how Latinas in the media are disconnected from their Latinoness and fixed to a "white, chaste, and culturally desirable" subjectivity (126). And, perhaps we might consider JLo's music video as a counter optic to all this. In the "I Luv U Papi" music video she uses shaping devices such as a frame narration, along with other narrative signposts, for us to read this as a reverse gaze, turning upside down the long tradition of sexualizing the female brown body—something that we can trace back to the conquest. Yet, as Ovalle asks of dancing Latina bodies generally, can they "create the illusion of diversity and sexual liberation while also developing … social and professional agency?" (2).

Pop culture by and about Latina/os is realized in other formats, too, such as literature and comic books. Many an academic has dismissed Alisa Valdez's novel *Dirty Girls Social Club* (2003) as a neoliberal-driven instructional manual for Latina upward mobility. Its straightforward readability and transparent realism seems to convey a ready-made package of consumable Latinoness. According to Tace Hedrick, this is the envelope that sells a neoliberal fantasy of "the heroine's individual power (sometimes helped by girlfriend power) to solve the seemingly private problems of her life—how to be a Latin in the United states, how to be a 'modern' woman, how to have time for a career and romance" (30). For Hedrick, *Dirty Girls* and other chica lit novels offer something new to the chick lit formula but do so by participating in a corporate marketplace that packages for easy consumption racial and ethic others.

I wonder, however, if there isn't some merit in reading and even teaching *Dirty Girls*—something I do in my introduction to Latina/o pop culture courses. Within this format, the novel does identify a range of Latina types in terms of phenotype and ethnic ancestry—as well as class origins (even though they are all in the middle and upper-middle classes in the story's present). And, while we might dismiss *Dirty Girls* as beach reading, perhaps it offers more: a powerful message to Latinas that they can identify however they want, not just sexually (Elizabeth is outted in the novel) but also in terms of how they want to interface with their ancestry and class. And that seems to be its ideal reader, and not those that a Sandra Cisneros or Ana Castillo might construct. Taken on its own terms, perhaps it does work; maybe it's an example of how lowbrow and highbrow, or pop culture and culture are not oppositions but more a question of the presence of a degree of will to style in the creating of something new.

Comic books is an area where we have seen intense and constant productivity among Latina/os in the first decade of the twenty-first century. As Enrique García explores in his chapter in this volume, given that comic books are relatively inexpensive to create, this is a pop cultural space filling to the brim with Latina/o storytellers. It offers all variety of tensions and harmonies between its visual and verbal ingredients. It costs little to make. It offers the possibility of a grassroots-style distribution—web and word of mouth, for instance. It appeals to all variety of readers/viewers: young and old, Latina/o and otherwise, females and males. Its consumption can take place in short bursts and on the fly.

As I've begun to show, with the shape, texture, and color of the building blocks of reality themselves appearing more and more Latina/o, it is not surprising that the pop cultural Latina/o landscape is also very varied. Whether there is present a willfulness (will to style) that innovates and makes new our apprehension of Latina/os—and Latinidad generally—or not, we can say that today it is a markedly more populated, and arguably more complex landscape than yesterday.

To the Chapters

The chapters that make up *The Companion to Latino/a Pop Culture* seek to make visible a range of material objects and intellectual products out there that capture to different degrees the myriad and infinite experiences of Latina/os. It aims to capture a contemporary scene whereby our massive presence is actively shaping the culture we all breathe today.

The first section of the volume, "Televisual, Reel, Animated, Comic, Digital, and Speculative Pop Spaces", begins with Mary Beltrán's overview and analysis of representations of Latina/os in English language TV shows, including, importantly, the recent rise of web and other media shows created by Latina/os. While there continues to be a "white-washing" of Latinidad in corporate-driven programming, the Latina/o-created content in *East WillyB*, *East Los High*, and *Los Americans* complicates the Latina/o representational terrain. Whether in the form of a melodrama or comedy, these Latina/o-created storyworlds give rich texture to the many different ways one exists as a Latina/o in the U.S. Given that we continue to be severely underrepresented in TV generally, when a Latina/o character and story do appear, they carry the burden of representing the *total* experience of Latina/os in the U.S. For Beltrán, not only do we need more *willful* content creation and programing but also the need to stand up and support our community's efforts to produce new, diversified content.

Camilla Fojas follows with her chapter "Latino Film in the End Times". With her sights set on a contemporary Mexico/U.S. borderland cinematic landscape, Fojas considers how the labor documentary *Maquilapolis* (2006), Robert Rodríguez's film *Machete* (2010), and Diego Luna's biopic *Cesar Chavez* (2014) create a Latina/o "resistant optic". In their varied ways, these borderland cinematic productions make visible the otherwise invisible: the exploitation and oppression of brown subjects inhabiting the borderlands. Whether it is in the form of a labor documentary (*Maquilapolis*), the entertaining Mexploitation

B-flick feature film (*Machete*), or a biopic (*Cesar Chavez*), today's borderland cinema shows audiences how the formation of "networks and assemblages of people" can create progressive social change. For Fojas, borderland cinema explodes generic boundaries "to dramatize the demand for human rights and equality, antiracist struggles, and the right for self-determination".

We move away from the realm of film realism into that of animation with Isabel Millán's "'¡Vámonos! Let's Go!': Latina/o Children's Television". Millán provides a broad analytical approach to children's pop cultural media programming, with PBS's *Sesame Street* (1969–1992) marking a watershed moment in Latina/o children's television. Bilingual shows like *Carrascolendas* (1970) and *Villa Alegre* (1973) followed. Millán ends the chapter with a discussion of *Dora, The Explorer* along with other fantasy and realist-based animations that appeared in the twenty-first century.

Cristina Rivera's chapter, "Branding 'Latinohood', Juan Bobo, and the Commodification of *Dora the Explorer*" expands the analysis of Dora to include an exploration of how the Puerto Rican trickster hero, Juan Bobo, has been caught up in Latina/o children's television programming. Rivera complicates the positive assumption made by media pundits and scholars alike that consider Dora on mainstream TV as an indicator that Latina/o diversity has arrived. Rather, she demonstrates how Dora not only actively unmoors important Latina/o cultural signifiers—Mexican and Puerto Rican based—but how its impoverished storyworld disempowers Latina/o child audiences.

While Millán and Rivera focus on lazy and ultimately damaging pop cultural children's programming, Laura Fernández considers how Latina/o-created animation can affirm culture and identity. In her chapter, "Canta y no Llores: Life and Latinidad in Children's Animation", Fernández focuses her sights on Jorge Gutierrez's made-for-TV flash animation *El Tigre* (2007–2008) and his follow-up feature length, *The Book of Life* (2014). Here Fernández identifies *The Book of Life* as a border film in content and form, constructing its own ideal audience that is Latina/o. In her analysis of the way Gutierrez gives shape to the film's storyworld, Fernández shows how it at once entertains *and* affirms Mexican myth and ritual. Moreover, she reveals how the content and form work seamlessly together to speak to and affirm Latina/o youth increasingly forgotten by educators across the nation. In non-didactic terms, the film offers a vision of how one might write one's own story and overcome the lockout and push-out policies that permeate education for Latina/os today.

Just as the corporate controlled creations have tended to one-dimensionalize or leave out completely Latina/os from TV, film, and animation storyworlds, so too do we see this happening in digital media. In "Beyond the 'Digital Divide' and Latina/o Pop", Kathryn M. Frank first reminds us that Latina/os use of digital media (internet, personal computing, smartphones, and tablet use) surpasses that of their Anglo counterparts; this is especially seen with millennial Latina/os. While YouTube, blogs, and bilingual sites such as Dulce "Dulce Candy" Ruiz are used to construct star personas and personal brands, they are also, as Kathryn Frank reminds us, creative spaces for making new content that conveys the richly layered aspects of Latinidad. As Frank argues, this is an area of study where we can learn much about how "Latina/o identities are constructed and contested, and who 'gets' to invoke Latinidad."

Just as Frank lays to rest misconceptions concerning Latina/os and digital technology (creation and use), so too does Osvaldo Cleger concerning video games. In his chapter, "Why Videogames: Ludology Meets Latino Studies", Cleger formulates a critical frame for the study of Latina/os in video game design, its players, and the larger role they serve within society and culture. While the corporate-driven video game industry is seemingly blind to the fact that its flesh-and-blood players are largely Latina/o (65 percent of Latina/o families with children have an X-Box, Playstation or Wii), there have been attempts at creating Latina/o playable characters and settings. Cleger mentions the *FIFA* series, *Assassin's Creed* saga, *Call of Duty*, *Grand Theft Auto*, and *Red Dead Redemption*. More importantly, however, he identifies significant Latina/o-created video games that use low-cost formats (web and mobile gaming) in order to create Latina/o storyworlds with more cultural nuance and sophistication. We see this in Ricardo Dominguez and Coco Fuscos's *Turista fronterizo* and Breakthrough's *I Can End Deportation* or *ICED!*, for instance. Ultimately, Cleger conceives of a Latina/o ludology (the intersection of Latina/o Studies and Game Studies) that would spend time studying games that construct interactive learning environments that at once entertain and educate players and audiences concerning what it means to be Latina/o in the U.S., and the Americas more expansively.

Enrique García's chapter turns us to yet another area where Latina/os are making significant creative headway: comic books. After making important distinctions between U.S. Latina/o and Latin American comic book cultures, he goes on to analyse how they create counter narratives to the Anglo-dominant mainstream. In a careful analysis of alternative and mainstream comics by and about U.S. Latina/os, García opens our eyes to the complex textures of Latinidad offered by this visual-verbal storytelling format. García ends by gesturing toward the emancipatory possibilities of digital comic creation (the Comixology app, for instance) and consumption (internet and iPad devices, for instance) of visual-verbally constructed stories that continue to do the work of unsettling fixed categories of nation, community, ethnicity, race, and gender.

Two chapters dedicated to speculative fictional creations by and about Latina/os bring this section to a close. In the chapter "Science Fiction and Latina/o Studies Today… and in the Future", Fabio Chee considers not only how Latina/os are increasingly imagined in the future, but how the long tradition of science fiction created by Latina/os has also led to the growing of a branch of Latina/o studies known as Chicanafuturism. For Chee, the science fiction genre not only offers powerful resonances with Latina/o identity and experience—the double meaning of "alien"—but also its construction of hybrid human/machine characters clears a space to imagine hybridity as an ontological state of resistance to restrictive ways of being in the world. Finally, he explores how this speculative genre "showcases the negotiations of the political desires of the present with an understanding of history as the basis for the imagined fiction". His clarion call: for more Latina/os to write "the future ourselves and to decry the insistence of mis-projecting the present conditions through whitewashed future settings".

With Fabio Chee's big-picture view of speculative fiction by and about Latina/os in place, we come to Mathew Goodwin's chapter and his analysis of science fiction as a critique of: Hispanophone Caribbean histories of slavery, robots as Chicanos in protest, the Latina/o as monster, and post-NAFTA oppressive labor systems that exploit the migratory (virtual and real) flows of brown bodies. In addition to Alex Rivera's films *A Robot Walks into a Bar* (2014) and *Sleep Dealer* (2006), Goodwin analyzes Cuban American Luis Senarens and Luis Valdez's one act play *Los Vendidos*. In each, Goodwin shows how Latina/o creators see Latina/os in the future in ways that critically comment on our present.

As we move into Section II of the volume, "Pop Poetics of Tongues Untied", we switch to an analytical optic that focuses on pop cultural expressions in the performance, visual, and language arts. The section begins with Cecilia Aragón's "Performing *Mestizaje*: Making Indigenous Acts Visible in Latina/o Popular Culture", which reveals how pop cultural performances (Guillermo Gómez-Peña and Coco Fusco) and films (Peter Bratt's 2009 *La*

Mission) make vitally new age-old communal, anticolonial rituals such as *la danza Azteca*. Aragón explores how the contemporary refashioning of such mestizaje rituals link Latina/o communities to our indigenous pasts *and* act as significant shaping devices in the making of contemporary pop cultural phenomena by Latina/os.

In the chapter that follows, "Brown Bodies on the Great White Way: Latina/o Theater, Pop Culture, and Broadway", William Orchard identifies Latina/o theater generally as an alternative, pop cultural space—a "people's theater" that celebrates Latinidad in opposition to a mainstream theater bent on selling (literally through its merchandising) an American dream that excludes brown subjects. Orchard analyzes how different regionally situated places (Los Angeles and the Bronx, for instance) clear performance spaces for plays such as Luis Valdez's *Zoot Suit* (1979) and Lin-Manuel Miranda and Quiara Alegría Hudes's *In the Heights* (2006), as well as John Leguizamo's one-man show, *Freak* (1997). While some were more successful than others, taken as a whole they "sustain cultural traditions and history, foster political consciousness and activism, and provide opportunities for communities to engage in theater as performers or spectators".

The stage is not a space exclusive to Latina/o pop theater, as David Colón demonstrates in his analysis of spoken word poetry. In Colón's chapter, "Siempre Pa'l Arte: The Passions of Latina/o Spoken Word", the words of a poem come into their full meaning on the stage and in the brown bodily performance. Tracing the history of live poetry performances from the Puerto Rican and Chicano Movements of the 1960s and 1970s through to today's Afromexicana poetry of Arian Brown, Colón identifies how Latinas/os, residing outside the black/white binary of racial politics and identity struggle, created a poetry of "verbal action" that was and is popular and populist. This spoken word poetry comes into its own through the affective force of the brown performer's delivery. As Colón argues, the "performative personas become raw materials in the way that paper and pen, letters and lines are raw materials for the textual poet. There are various performative personas available to the spoken word poet, ones that can be combined and reworked the way words and syntax can". Spoken word poetry is, for Colón, a pop cultural expression of a "counterpolitics" made real through the ingenuity and sincerity of "body language".

In the chapter, "Postindustrial Pinto Poetics and New Millennial Maiz Narratives", Pancho McFarland considers how hip hop functions as a pop cultural form of a long decolonial tradition of indigenous, sacred *maiz* narratives that raise consciousness, create solidarity, and heal wounds from a colonial and postcolonial global neocolonial violence. In an analysis of the sounds of Kinto Sol (a group that declare themselves to be "hijos del maiz"), for instance, McFarland shows how Chicano hip hop is rooted to land and indigenous identity. Moreover, he excavates a parallel resistant decolonial narrative in the pinto poetics of Ricardo Sanchez, Jimmy Santiago Baca, Raul Salinas, and the hip hop group Psycho Realm. In his exploration and analysis of Chicano pinto and street hop traditions, McFarland reveals how pop cultures created by Latina/os "materially reconstitute and expressively represent places of community well-being against the degradations to which those places have been subject".

In "Punk Spanglish", Ilan Stavans celebrates Spanglish as a hybrid, "border" tongue practiced in all variety of Latina/o pop cultural phenomena: from street art to music lyrics to film, comics, the Internet, and greeting cards. Such pop cultural border tongues continually evolve and shapeshift—pushing back against monolingual social and cultural spaces. For Stavans, Ricky Martin's "Livin' La Vida Loca", Mexico's Café Tacuba and Lila Downs, and California's Cypress Hill deploy Spanglish (in some instances even intermixing pre-Columbian Nahuátl) as a way to push language *and* Latina/o identity to its limits of expression. In all its various and vital forms, punk Spanglish embraces polyvocality, polysemy, and radical identity reconfiguration. As Stavans writes, "Punk Spanglish isn't an aberration. It is beautiful and stunningly versatile."

This section ends with Stacey Alex's chapters, "Latino Radio and Counter Epistemologies". Alex considers the significant presence of Latina/o radio and how it is used as a pop cultural form to express identity and experience. Moreover, the use of Spanish in Latina/o radio functions as an important cultural and linguistic safeguard against assimilationist pressures. For the younger set, it's a source of cultural and linguistic knowledge; for the older set, it can function as a space of community building and social resistance. Alex focuses her analysis on the Latina/o producers and audiences of 105.5 FM La Ley of Des Moines and Perry, Iowa. Here she explores how La Ley constructs a "sonic space of affective belonging and resistance through collective knowledge production". While Alex is careful not to make the claim that Latina/o radio resolves conflicts, she does identify how it creates collective expression of resistance and solidarity across regionally separated and disparate Latina/o communities in Des Moines and Perry. The radio clears "a sonic space for belonging by filling airwaves with Spanish language music and information". It ruptures mainstream institutional silences concerning Latina/o subjects by "creating affective connections and a sense of democracy."

Section III, "Pop Artivist Reclamations", consists of four chapters that revolve around Latina/o-created visual pop cultural arts. This section launches with Melissa Castillo-Garsow recalibrating the compass on where Latina/o art appears in the U.S. In this chapter, "Hermandad, Arte and Rebeldía: Mexican Popular Art in New York City", Castillo-Garsow shows the movement across U.S./Mexico borders and the nation of otherwise regionally created and exhibited art scenes. While Castillo-Garsow shows the importance of introducing a transnational model for analyzing today's Latina/o arts creation and exhibition, she identifies how its translocations bring other sets of issues. For instance, the many Mexican artists who make up the Har'd Life Ink Arts Collective in New York City are marginalized from the non-Mexican Latina/o artists as well as New York City's Anglo-dominant contemporary art community. This said, the graffiti, mural, tattoo, and photographic art that the Mexican arts collective creates and exhibits in this East Coast, non-Mexican and non-Chicano space does create new hybrid forms built out of and that reflect on a transnational Latinidad.

In the chapter that follows, "Inexact Revolutions: Understanding Latino Pop Art", Rocio Isabel Prado focuses her attention largely on the Southwest Latina/o pop art scene. Here she puts at center stage Latina/o pop art's reclamation of cultural space in a mainstream art scene that has traditionally swept it to the side. To do so, Prado builds a rasquache theoretical approach that reveals how Latina/o artists recycle anything and everything to make new the perception, thought, and feeling concerning the Latina/o experience. Prado demonstrates how Latina/o pop art uses all variety of shaping devices (photography, printmaking, and digital)—and from all parts of the Americas, including pop art techniques and practices from Mexico. Finally, Prado shows how deeply connected Latina/o pop art practices are to political movements, and how they work to clear room for more queer and feminist inclusive spaces.

In the chapter "Installation Art, Transnationalism and the Chinese-Chicano Experience", artist Richard Lou and scholar Guisela Latorre team up to excavate yet another site of Latina/o arts making: where Chinese and Latina/o come together to create an art that transcends national borders and blurs high art and pop art boundaries. Lou and Latorre reveal how Lou's multimedia (oral/visual) installation, *Stories on my Back*, articulates a regionally grown (San Diego/Tijuana, Memphis) transnational (Latina/o-Asian) pop cultural art that "opens new avenues for the intersectionality and relationality of different social identities".

This section closes with Stephanie Lewthwaite's "Revising the Archive: Documentary Portraiture in the Photography of Delilah Montoya". In this chapter Lewthwaite focuses her attention on photographer Delilah Montoya to show the significant presence of Latina/o pop photographic art as a means to reflect a more complex Latinidad than those racialized stereotypes shown in the mass media. For Lewthwaite, like many other Latina photographers, Montoya creates a photographic repertoire to subvert and expose histories of race, class, and gender-based oppression as well as to articulate new, complex forms of Latina/o subjectivity. Montoya's photographic art "fuses the popular and everyday nature of the documentary mode with the honorific function of portraiture [to create] a new vernacular pantheon in which the everyday Chicano/a body is transfigured and popular and religious icons revised".

Section four, "Quotidian Pop", focuses on everyday popular communal (queer and straight) practices that gravitate around food, health, cars, music, quinceañeras, fashion, and sports. The section opens with Paloma Martínez-Cruz's "Farmworker-to-Table Mexican: Decolonizing Haute Cuisine", which contextualizes her analysis of a campesino-to-table Mexican decolonial diet by identifying the larger paradox at work in the U.S. concerning food and Latina/os. There's the mass consumption of Mexican Taco Bell-styled fast foods *and* an "animosity toward Latina/o, mestizo, and indigenous people" that results in daily mass deportations. As Martínez-Cruz shows, food-to-table Mexican-inspired cuisine has the "transformational potential to foment both ecological and social justice that protects the land and the people who work on it". Moreover, our Latina/o dining choices reconfigure the "coloniality of power" in ways that heal and empower Latina/os.

Amelia M.L. Montes also sets her sights on pop ritual practices that can heal our communities. In her chapter, "The Rituals of Health", Montes explores how our popular cultural practice of storytelling (she conducts several interviews) can show us how to become more mindful of our daily rituals and habits which can lead to wellness of mind and body. Her ethnographic work, along with analysis of a Latina/o literature that gravitates around healing practices, provide a popular guide of sorts for Latina/o rituals of health and wellness.

With Ben Chappell's "Lowrider Publics: Aesthetics and Contested Communities" we enter another (counter-intuitively so) space of ritualized wellness: lowrider style and culture as not only an aesthetic expression of a vernacular Latinidad, but as a community building practice. While a straight Latina/o scene has traditionally dominated lowrider culture, Chappell reveals how Latina lowriders are reconfiguring this community in powerful ways. Finally, for Chappell, while there is the ingredient of corporate consumption in the lowrider culture, the kinship communities it builds empower Latina/os and Latinas within the public sphere.

Rachel V. González-Martin similarly explores kinship building pop rituals. In her chapter, "Barrio Ritual and Pop Rite: Quinceañeras in the Folklore–Popular Culture Borderlands", she formulates a cultural borderlands model for analyzing how the secular and sacred practice of quinceañeras continue to express and affirm a given community's Latinidad, and how this becomes spectacularized in popular televisual representations: from *The George Lopez Show* and *Top Chef* to *Quiero Mis Quinces* (*I Want My Quinceañera*). Moreover, she considers how the production and consumption of these mediated representations complicate the notion of an "authentic" quinceañera celebration. Indeed, while these shows seek to entertain, they do complicate and affirm the complexity of different Latina/o communities, not only because of the intergenerational tensions shown but also the regional variations. As

González-Martin writes, of *Quiero Mis Quinces*, we "are able to see patterns of quinceañera performance that transcend regional practice, creating a dramatic and spectacular snapshot of a quinceañera culture in the United States". Finally, for González-Martin, the pop cultural representations of this popular Latina/o cultural practice can serve as important sites of cultural knowledge for new generations of Latinas.

In "Cultura Joteria: The Ins and Outs of Latina/o Popular Culture", Ellie D. Hernandez speaks to the significant presence of queer and LGBTQ Latina/o producers of pop culture. By building a joteria framework that captures the "intersectional issues and concerns of queer Chicana/o Latina/o and indigenous people", Hernandez's analysis of music and film reminds of the significant contribution of queer and LGBTQ Latina/o creators in the making of pop culture. In her analysis of musicians such as Chavela Vargas, Juan Gabriel, Los Tigres del Norte, Girl in a Coma, and Ricky Martin, as well as films such as *Mosquita and Mari* and *La Mission*, she celebrates how Latina/os have created a rich tapestry of jotería pop culture. The Latina/o queer pop culture scene, too, is complex. For instance, while Ricky Martin's "Livin' La Vida Loca" was "appropriated by joteria culture as a coded message of queer life", his "good looks and sensitive style exuded an acceptable way of expressing Latina/o gay masculinity."

In the chapter, "Raza Rockabilly and Greaser Cultura", Nicholas Centino also focuses on kinship and community building through pop cultural rituals. In this instance, it is with the creating of a Latina/o Rockabilly, or Razabilly, scene in Los Angeles. Characterized by its music and sartorial wear, Razabilly grows out of the lived experiences of race- and class-marked Latina/os in LA in ways that allow them to "re-write themselves into the history of Los Angeles, and the history of rock and roll". While Centino analyzes the work of Razabilly musical artist, Anglo-Mexican Robert Williams (known as "Big Sandy"), he also considers how Vicky Tafoya forcefully clears an emancipating space for Latinas. For instance, Centino discusses how Tafoya uses make up, hair styles, and zoot suit fashions to create a "hyper feminine pachuca inspired look" that intensifies the experience of her music, especially when she switches female to male voices on stage.

Marivel T. Danielson's chapter, "Bodies in Motion: Latina/o Popular Culture as Rasquache Resistance", explores and analyzes a variety of improvisational *movidas* (moves) that one way or another push against destructive imagery about Latina/os; the iconic image of a silhouetted migrant family running against the bright yellow backdrop of roadside traffic warning signs posted along the freeways in southern California exemplify how Latina/os *in motion* are framed as an invasive threat. Danielsen formulates a transcultural, mestizo, and rasquache analytical approach to show how Latina/o artists (traditional, digital, and sartorial) build on and extend existing "forms, frameworks, and histories" to make new images that "challenge stereotypes and silences around Latina/o bodies, communities, and experiences."

In "Claiming Style, Consuming Culture: The Politics of Latina Self-Styling and Fashion Lines", Stacy I. Macías builds her "racialized rasquache raunch" model for analyzing how Latinas re-fashion mainstream sartorial wear in "alternative, expressive, and queerly feminine ways" that push back against a capitalist-driven marketplace that provincializes and hypersexualizes Latina bodies. For Macías, the Latina racialized rasquache raunch aesthetic is a communal act built in and around the redesigning, reconstructing, and recycling of raw materials (clothing, makeup, accessory, hairstyles) in ways that celebrate laboring female bodies of color. Finally, the spectacular new creations affirm a transnationally situated Latina collective subjectivity.

The two chapters that close this section focus on sports. In "Latina/os and the American Sports Landscape", Christopher González forcefully argues that because of the privileged position of sports in the U.S. mainstream, it is important to study those Latina/os who have defied the odds—and brown color lines—and made it into this arena of pop culture. González provides a general context for why Latina/os are so few and far between in sports. This is partly tied to the fact that Latina/os, because of prejudices and glass ceilings, have put food on tables through physically demanding work, and at all ages. And, because of access to only under-resourced K-12 schooling, the typical pathways to the pro leagues have not been open to Latina/os. While the G.I. Bill along with the Civil Rights movement generally helped increase opportunities for Latina/os, we are still severely underrepresented in college, the main feeder of athletes for the pro sports world. After considering athletes that have made it into football, tennis, golf, and other pro sports, González declares that Latina/os can't be ignored or disregarded. The active presence of Latinos in the shaping of sports history has contributed significantly to sports as a mainstream popular cultural pastime.

Jorge Iber's chapter, "Latina/os in the American High School, Collegiate, and Community Sporting Landscape", provides historical context of just how Latinos have shaped sports history, including the deep prejudice faced by Latinos trying to make their way into traditionally white-only athletic spaces. Like González, he explores Latina/o participation in the shaping of basketball, football, and baseball, but also adds to the list wrestling. Iber emphasizes the communal aspect of Latina/o participation in these sports, especially before the athletes hit the pro leagues. Sports for Latina/os have been, and continue to be, an important space for building Latina/o community.

Section five, "Pop Rituals of Life in Death", begins with Desirée Martín's exploration and analysis of borderland spiritual practices in the Latina/o community. In her chapter, "Saints and the Secular: La Santísma Muerte", she identifies how a popular borderland spirituality is a flexible and diverse practice that includes the veneration of saints but also the radical reordering of ecclesiastical structures that blur lines between orthodox and popular belief, private and public worship, and human with the divine. Pop spiritual practices in the Latina/o borderlands, according to Martin, can wrest power and control from the powers that be and open a resistant space for the community to come together.

Cruz Medina's chapter, "Day of the Dead: Decolonial Expressions in Pop de los Muertos", also focuses on alternative (or alterNative) spiritual rituals. He chooses to analyze the pop cultural practice of día de los muertos that brings into a vital present the indigenous Mexican practices associated with pre-Columbian Nahua and Mayan civilizations. As a counter measure to the commodification of death by the mainstream (Halloween, the TV show Walking Dead, and also the general appropriation of día de los muertos as costumes to wear without any sense of its cultural significance), today's Latina/o documentary, animation, cartoon, and comic book artists variously create vital new expressions of día that make alive the dead in ways that affirm our collective cultural memory.

In "Liberanos de Todo Mal/But Deliver us from Evil: Latina/o Monsters Theory and the Outlining of our Phantasmagoric Landscapes," William A. Calvo-Quirós explores the ways in which an important part of Latino pop culture includes the presence of monsters and phantasmagoric creatures. As theorized by Latina/o feminist, queer, and race scholars, these Others work as allegories that signal the struggle of Latina/os within a racist, sexist, and queerphobic U.S. They remind us of what it means to exist in a perpetual state of vulnerability. As Calvo-Quirós argues, throughout history Latina/os have been monsterized: from La Llorona to Joaquin Murrieta, from the pachuca/o Zoot Suiter to zombie and chupacabras (or goatsucker) flicks today. Calvo-Quirós unpacks the pop cultural landscape that represents Latina/os as monsters to show that they function as palimpsestic stand-ins for the very real material conditions that force "early death" upon Latina/o communities. Indeed, as Calvo-Quirós shows, the deconstruction and reclamation of the monster by Latina/o creators and scholars function as "tools for emancipation, liberation and to envision a different world, one outside the constraints of a vampire-like system that feeds on their vulnerability." The re-appropriation of monster-ness can be used as a critical tool not only to "denounce violence [but] to defeat the oppressor".

In many ways Ryan Rashotte's "Narco cultura" is also all about monsters, but of the cartel drug trafficking kind. While narco cultura has permeated all pop cultural formats—music, radio, TV, film, tattoo, bullet hole fashion, corridos, saints, and much more—Rashotte is careful not to glorify its presence. There is no resistance to be found here. However, this doesn't mean that it is not valuable to study and understand. Indeed, as he explores, its roots can be traced back to the popular stories of the bandit hero sung by borderland balladeers. Today, we see this in the corridos of Los Tigres del Norte and Chalino Sánchez. And, generally speaking, narcos and professional studios commission narcocorridos. And, as Rashotte reminds us, "writing a corrido for the wrong man can get you killed".

In the final chapter of the volume, "Smuggling as a Spectacle: Irregular Migration and *Coyotes* in Contemporary U.S. Latino Popular Culture", Gabriella Sanchez focuses on another deathly phenomena: the human trafficker or smuggler known as a *coyote*. Sanchez considers the ways this figure has been taken up in Latina/o pop culture, including corridos and films. The pop cultural coyote narrative portrays a "greedy, two-timing coyote who preys upon the naïve, poor, and hopeless migrant, whose journey is defined by pain, suffering and often tragedy." According to Sanchez, the coyote as victimizer in the popular imaginary not only tells us something about the way the mainstream makes visible Latina/os as violent, greedy double-crossers, but fails to reflect on the material conditions that force these low-level smugglers to become coyotes in the first place. Moreover, Sanchez shows how homeland security propaganda has created a border spectacle whereby coyotes are identified as "global merchants of death" to justify its own billion dollar expenditures.

As is conveyed by the chapters themselves, the many pop cultural forms by and about Latina/os are the result of human activity at a given moment and place. They are cultural products made by humans, existing as products of reasoning, the emotions and the imagination—some use more of these ingredients than others. What these chapters achieve is to launch a research program (hermeneutical in spirit) that begins to assign meaning to our pop culture by and about Latina/os and to assess its value and importance. That is, they begin to attribute meaning and significance (or importance *and* interpretation) to these branches of material culture that seek to express today's Latinidad in all variety of contents, shapes, and forms.

The chapters that make up this volume aim to shed light on how Latina/os are at once shaped by mainstream culture as well as *active shapers* of this mainstream culture. They will shed light on differences in the intentionality behind the distillation and reconstruction of Latina/os in pop cultural phenomena: those that seek creative innovation and to make vital the complex Latina/o experience and identity, and those that simply peddle the same old tired stereotypes and mishmash of cultural signifiers.

The chapters that follow will at once contextualize and assess specific pop cultural forms and genres. They do so at once by focusing on a specific area of pop culture and providing analyses of specific examples and case studies such as Latina/os and sartorial wear or art or slam poetry or TV. The aim: for the volume to be comprehensive and specific in ways that will vitally engage and inform all of us who want to learn about the making, distributing, and consuming of pop culture by and about Latina/os.

Bibliography

de Casanova, Erynn Masi. "Representing Latinidad in Children's Television: What Are the Kids Watching?" *Latinos and American Popular Culture*. Ed. Patricia M. Montilla. Santa Barbara: Praeger, 2013. 21–47.

Hedrick, Tace. *Chica Lit: Popular Latina Fiction and Americanization in the Twenty-First Century*. Pittsburgh: University of Pittsburgh Press, 2015.

Hoult-Saros, Stacy. "Say Hello to my Little Friends: Nonhumans as Latinos in U.S. Feature Films for Children". *Latinos and American Popular Culture*. Ed. Patricia M. Montilla. Santa Barbara: Praeger. 2013. 135–160.

Molina-Guzmán, Laura. *Dangerous Curves: Latina Bodies in the Media*. New York: New York University Press, 2010.

Ovalle, Priscilla. *Dance and the Hollywood Latina: Race, Sex, and Stardom*. New Brunswick, NJ: Rutgers University Press, 2011.

Serrato, Phillip. "Postmodern Guacamole: Lifting the Lid on *El Tigre: The Adventures of Manny Rivera*." *Latinos and Narrative Media: Participation and Portrayal*. Ed. Frederick Luis Aldama. New York: Palgrave Macmillan, 2013. 71–84.

Part I

TELEVISUAL, REEL, ANIMATED, COMIC, DIGITAL, AND SPECULATIVE POP SPACES

1

LATINA/OS ON TV!

A Proud (and Ongoing) Struggle Over Representation and Authorship

Mary Beltrán

Of the myriad realms of U.S. popular culture in which Latina/o images and narratives circulate and Latina/os themselves serve as storytellers and creative practitioners, arguably none has had as profound an impact as television. As an entertainment medium that people watch daily in their own homes, television has played an instrumental role over the decades. In the case of English-language television, it has showcased, reinforced, and occasionally challenged popular notions regarding Latina/os and their place in the nation and national history. In addition, Spanish-language television has played an influential role in the lives of many Latina/os; as a diasporic medium, it has long contributed to the Latina/o imaginary, or Latina/os' understanding of the imagined Latina/o community, regarding discourses of race, gender, class, nationality, citizenship, and global politics. More recently, bilingual television has also found a small niche, catering to younger, acculturated Latina/os interested in media that connects with their culturally hybrid identities and lives. With regard to Latina/os and these three realms of television, English-language programming arguably has had a particularly substantial impact on U.S. popular culture, given the size of its audience and the way that these television story worlds come to stand in for idealized North American ideals. As my own area of expertise, both as a researcher and as a Latina who grew up "Spanish-impaired" because of lack of exposure, it will be the main focus of this chapter.[1]

Latina/os unfortunately have been marginalized in English-language television story worlds, to a degree that's only beginning to be countered. We have often been invisible—simply not there—and misrepresented when we do appear in prime time programming. While limited progress can be seen in recent years in the form of a few more multidimensional and broadly appealing Latina/o roles, such as in the critically lauded *Jane the Virgin* (2014–) and the now cancelled *George Lopez* (2002–2007), Latina/o lead characters are still few and far between. In addition, there is a serious drought of Latina/o writers and producers as well. Few Latina/os were in any sort of creative position prior to the 1990s, while from 2010 through

2013 we comprised only 1 percent of employed producers, 2 percent of writers, none of the show runners, and 4 percent of directors in television (Negrón Mutaner, et al.).

In this regard, television has been viewed by some Latina/os as a hopelessly demoralizing realm of popular culture. There have been a few exceptions, however, with respect to portrayals and series that have been a source of pride. Progress can be seen also in the success of a few series with Latino/a leads and in the entrance of some Latino/a writers, producers, and creative executives into the industry. Series such as *George Lopez*, *Jane the Virgin*, *Ugly Betty* (2006–2010), and web-based series such as *Ylse* (2008–2010), *East WillyB* (2011–2013), and *East Los High* (2013–) offer the promise of more well written, culturally authentic, and empowering Latina/o-oriented TV narratives in the years to come.

The study of Latina/os and television is only a few decades old. Initially, the scholars doing this work were social scientists tallying the presence of and broad representational patterns for Latina/os in narrative television. They typically counted and coded recurring and non-recurring Latina/o characters in comparison to white and African American characters, for instance, regarding whether they played major or minor roles and whether these characters were professionals, criminals, or servants. A 1994 study commissioned by the advocacy group National Council of La Raza by S. Robert Lichter and Daniel Amundson, for instance, found that Latina/o characters comprised no more than one to two percent of prime time roles from the 1950s through the early 1990s, even while the Latino population grew from 2.8 to 11 percent of the population in these years. They also found Latina/os more likely to be criminal or servant characters in the first decades, with slight improvements by the 1990s. Subsequent studies found Latina/os making only slight gains in visibility. The most recent study looking at these questions, by Frances Negrón Mutaner and other researchers at Columbia University in 2014, found that the gap between our numbers in the general population and in television has, in fact, grown. While Latina/os comprised 17 percent of the population in 2013, there were no Latino or Latina lead characters on the top prime time television series that year. When they are part of the television landscape, characters such as Betty Suárez of *Ugly Betty* thus have the unenviable (and ultimately impossible) task of standing in for the vast diversity of Latina/os.

Scholars such as Chon Noriega, Isabel Molina Guzmán, and Gustavo Pérez-Firmat have more recently been exploring Latina/o representation and participation in television in qualitative research that has looked at these topics in relation to U.S. social history and that of the evolving television industry. Analysis of television narratives, production dynamics, and promotional efforts has also been centered in the work of scholars such as Molina Guzmán in research on *Ugly Betty*, of Guillermo Avila-Saavedra on network-era sitcoms, and of Mary Beltrán on *Chico and the Man*, while Latina/o-oriented children's programming has been the focus of Erynn Masi de Casanova, Angharad Valdivia, and Nicole Guidotti-Hernández, among others. Notably, *Ugly Betty* has inspired multiple studies, while little scholarship thus far has been conducted on television programming prior to the 1990s. A number of scholars, including Yeidy Rivero, Arlene Dávila, Mari Castañeda, and Diana Rios, have also conducted research specifically on Spanish-language television. Finally, Arlene Dávila, Vicki Mayer, Jillian Báez and others have focused on Latina/o reception practices in relation to television. As might be obvious from this brief summary, there are major gaps in this scholarship; there's much that still hasn't been explored with respect to Latina/o histories in U.S. television and in relation to Latina/os and contemporary television programming, networks, and trends.

To also begin to fill those gaps, this chapter provides a broad history of Latina/o portrayals and creative authorship in U.S. English-language television, from its inception as a national medium in the late 1940s until the present day. I pause and expand on those series that have been especially popular or influential—among them *The Cisco Kid* (1950–1956), *I Love Lucy* (1952–1957), *The Nine Lives of Elfego Baca* (1958–1960), *Chico and the Man* (1974–1977), *Resurrection Blvd.* (2000–2002), *George Lopez*, and *Ugly Betty*. I conclude with discussion of some of the debates that persist regarding U.S. Latina/os and television; there are many, when it comes to this still-powerful medium that has often kept Latina/os in the wings of its national stage.

TV's Early Decades: Less Invisibility, but Ambivalent Portrayals

While Latina/os were not always found in TV story worlds in the late 1940s and early 1950s, their presence in fact more closely matched their numbers in the U.S. than is the case today. As noted above, Lichter and Amundson, in their study of television from the 1950s through the early 1990s, found that Latinos comprised no more than 2 percent of prime time characters in the 1950s—however, Latina/os were only 2.8 percent of the population at the time. They seldom appeared in family sitcoms or variety shows, two genres that factored in heavily to the new medium's imagining of the nation, however. An important exception was *I Love Lucy* (1951–1957). Desi Arnaz, a Cuban-born actor and musician, and Lucille Ball, his Anglo-American wife both in the series and in real life, became beloved stars when their family sitcom became a hit, and akin to "America's first family" when they integrated Ball's pregnancy and the birth of their son into the storyline. Gusavo Pérez-Firmat and Mary Beltrán have separately explored how Arnaz's fair skin, cross-cultural marriage, and professed love of the U.S. contributed to his treatment in the media as a white foreigner, rather than marginalization as an "ethnic" Latino. While Arnaz's role as Ricky Ricardo did demand that he exaggerate his accent, he was also portrayed as a successful musician and businessman and "straight man" to Lucy, his unpredictable wife. Arnaz and Ball also maintained creative control of the series throughout its run. Arnaz became executive producer of *I Love Lucy* and the first Latino television executive as president of their production company, Desilu, which subsequently produced a number of other popular television series.

A few Latino and Latina film actors, among them Ricardo Montalban, Katy Jurado, and Anthony Quinn, were also cast in anthology dramas in both Latina/o and non-Latina/o roles in this era. These were one-time teleplays, often written by famous playwrights and novelists, broadcast by anthology series that presented a different story and cast each week. More often, however, the genre in which Latina/o characters were to be found in this era was the TV Western. Mexican criminals and comic, bumbling cowboys, typically with broken English, low intelligence, and questionable morals, appeared as the villains, sidekicks, and servants in many popular Western series of the 1950s and early 1960s. On the other hand, fair-skinned and wealthy Latino cowboys and vigilantes, of great integrity and often of Spanish ancestry, also appeared in roles reminiscent of Hollywood's Latin Lovers of the 1920s. A clear coding of "white Latinos" as possessing idealized, heroic traits and a racialization of "ethnic Latinos" as inferior, comic sidekicks began to be a common paradigm of Latina/o representation in the early TV Western. As Lichter and Amundson noted in their study, the series that clearly established this dichotomy was one of U.S. television's first hits, *The Cisco Kid* (1950–1956). After success in radio and film, *The Cisco Kid* became a children's TV Western. It centered on its eponymous Spanish hero, played by Romanian American actor Duncan Renaldo, and his affable but less intelligent companion Pancho, played by Mexican American actor Leo Carrillo. Notably, this bifurcation of Latino types was repeated again in *Zorro* (1957–1959), and in *Walt Disney Presents The Nine Lives of Elfego Baca* (1958–1960). *The Nine Lives of*

Figure 1.1   NBC's *The High Chaparral*

Elfego Baca, a children's mini-series, was loosely based on the exploits of a real-life Mexican American gun fighter and lawyer well known in New Mexico for standing up for the rights of Mexican Americans, and nationally, for having survived a lynch mob of armed Anglo cowboys. Baca, played by Italian American actor Robert Loggia, was portrayed as a brave and intelligent man willing to do whatever it took to combat lawlessness and to protect the innocent, and the series and its merchandising did well with Disney's child audience (Telotte). Baca's ethnicity was glossed over, however, to the extent that it's unclear whether late 1950s audiences thought of Baca as Mexican American or as a generic Anglo hero. The paradigm of "good" and "bad" Latina/os in these Western narratives ultimately expressed ambivalence toward Latina/os and whether they fit within the accepted history and constructed ideals of cultural citizenship of the United States.

With the waning of the TV Western, Latina/os were seldom featured in narrative television of the 1960s and 1970s. So few Latina/o characters were seen on television by the early 1960s that José Jiménez, a Mexican character played by Hungarian Jewish actor Bill Dana, stood out. A dim-witted and bumbling bellhop, José Jiménez first appeared as a comic character on *The Danny Thomas Show* (1953–1965) in 1961, and then was reprised in Dana's spin-off series, *The Bill Dana Show* (1963–1965). The actor, in Phillip Rodriguez's documentary *Brown is the New Green: George Lopez and the American Dream* (2007), shared that he finally retired the character after Chicana/o activists called it out as demeaning and demanded that he do so.

Two additional series that included major Latina/o characters in the late 1960s and early 1970s were *The High Chaparral* (1967–1971) and *The Man and the City* (1971–1972). *The High Chaparral*, a Western set in the Arizona territory of the 1870s, focused in part on a marriage of convenience between "Big John" Cannon (Leif Erickson), an Anglo-American settler who had recently been widowed, and a Mexican—now Mexican American—family at a neighboring ranch (see Figure 1.1).

The growing romance between John and his Mexican American wife, Victoria (played by Italian-Argentinean Linda Cristal), is shown to develop into a more meaningful bond throughout the show's run. While *High Chaparral* still tended to develop its Anglo characters more fully, it attempted to bring in some historical accuracy about Mexican Americans in this period as well. *The Man and the City* was also unique for showcasing Mexican Irish film star Anthony Quinn as Thomas Alcala, the Mexican American mayor of a Southwestern city. While the series was not renewed after one season, it was an important milestone as the first TV series featuring a Latino professional and political leader as protagonist.

1970s Activism and Television: Shifts as Latina/os Take the Mic

The 1970s marked an important shift, as Latina/o activists, writers, and producers began to have an impact. During the peak of Chicano/a and Puerto Rican activism in the late 1960s and early 1970s, some activists agitated for media industry reforms. As Chon Noriega documents in *Shot in America: Television, the State, and the Rise of Chicano Cinema*, they fought for more visibility and "positive" Latina/o representation, for the hiring of Latino/as, and for opportunities to provide feedback on scripts, utilizing such tactics as sit-ins, challenges to public television station licenses, and letters to networks and major newspapers. Among their successes was the entrance of the first Latino/as in film schools and in entry-level production positions, and the launching of Latino/a public affairs series, with names like *Ahora!*, *Acción Chicano* and *Realidades*, on public television in cities with large Latina/o populations. Bilingual children's programs such as *Villa Allegre*, *Qué Pasa, USA?* and *Carrascolendas* also found a home on public television in this period.

The socially conscious climate of the 1970s also spurred network interest in comedies that addressed racial diversity and social issues, but Mexican Americans and other Latino/as strangely seldom appeared in these story worlds. NBC tried to fill this gap with *Chico and the Man* (1974–1977), which featured Freddie Prinze and Jack Albertson as Francisco "Chico" Rodriguez and Ed Brown, a young Mexican American man and an embittered white garage

Figure 1.2 NBC's *Chico and the Man*

store owner who come to work together and care for each other despite their culture clash and Ed's initial mistreatment of Chico. As I note in *Latina/o Stars in U.S. Eyes*, *Chico and the Man* elicited complaints from viewers regarding Chico's depiction as subservient to Ed and the casting of Prinze, who was Hungarian and Puerto Rican, as Mexican American. Despite this, the series proved to be a ratings success (see Figure 1.2).

The producers also retooled the series in hopes of appealing more to Latino/a and other viewers, making the character of Chico less Mexican American and softening Ed's behavior toward Chico, but these difficulties were never fully overcome. The all-white writing team likely was a major factor; Prinze did not receive writing or producing credit even while some of his standup comedy material was included in the scripts. Ultimately, *Chico and the Man* was irreparably altered by the loss of Freddie Prinze; he died by drug overdose in 1976. The show continued for a year after his death but never regained its earlier success.

A few other comedy series featuring Latina/o lead characters were produced and aired briefly in the 1970s, but none was as successful as *Chico and the Man*. These included *Viva Valdez* (1976), about a Mexican American family; *On the Rocks* (1975), a prison comedy about an ethnically diverse group of inmates; *Popi* (1976), based on the 1969 film about a Puerto Rican dad who tries to pass his sons off as Cuban so that they can receive better treatment, and *AES Hudson Street* (1978), a comedy starring Gregory Sierra as a doctor leading a ramshackle emergency room team. While they did not last long, their existence signals that at least a small handful of television producers felt Latina/os needed to be represented in a more substantial way.

1980s and 1990s Television: Well-Meaning Attempts, But False Starts

African American characters increased dramatically on prime time in the 1980s and 1990s, both because writers and producers seeking to diversify their casts often thought only in "black and white" in this period, and because of the immense success of *The Cosby Show* (1984–1992). There was no Latina/o equivalent to encourage industry professionals regarding the financial viability of Latina/o-led programming, however. The most prevalent form of Latina/o representation in this era was on ensemble shows set in law enforcement and medical work settings such as *Miami Vice* (1984–1990), *Law and Order* (1990–2010), and *New York Undercover* (1994–1998). These roles ultimately earned the first Emmy awards for Latina/os in supporting actor roles. Edward James Olmos earned the Emmy for *Miami Vice* in 1986, while Jimmy Smits won it for *L.A. Law* (1986–1994) in 1990 and a Golden Globe for *NYPD Blue* (1993–2005) in 1996.

In the meantime, audience members and media advocates continued to agitate for series centered on well-developed Latina/o characters and narratives. A few series were produced and broadcast, but none lasted longer than a season. These series in the 1980s included *a.k.a. Pablo* (ABC, 1984), a Norman Lear-led comedy starring Paul Rodriguez as a Mexican American comedian living with his boisterous extended family, and *I Married Dora* (ABC, 1987–88), about a wealthy white American who marries his children's Salvadoran nanny (played by the late Elizabeth Peña) so that she can stay in the U.S. In the 1990s, these efforts included *Union Square* (NBC, 1997–98), featuring Constance Marie among its ensemble as an aspiring actress in New York City; *Common Law* (ABC, 1996), which starred comedian Greg Giraldo as a free-spirited lawyer, and *House of Buggin'* (Fox, 1995), a sketch comedy series led by John Leguizamo. These series, like *Chico and the Man*, lacked Latino writers and producers and were not well marketed. Their failure nevertheless contributed to network reluctance to invest in new shows with Latina/o leads, as did widespread misunderstanding regarding whether Latina/o viewers could be enticed to watch any series on English-language television. A common misconception was that Latina/o viewers consumed all of their media in Spanish (a myth Spanish-language networks understandably also promoted). Numerous studies then and since have documented that the majority of U.S. Latina/os watch at least some English-language television—Nielsen's 2010 study, for example, found that 78 percent of English-dominant, 44 percent of bilingual, and 19 percent of Spanish-dominant Latina/os do so.[2] However, misperceptions on language preferences and media consumption resulted in little motivation on the part of networks to target Latina/o viewers in the 1980s and 1990s.

Latina/o media advocacy continued in the work of groups such as the National Hispanic Media Council (NHMC), the National Hispanic Foundation for the Arts, and Imagen, all of which lobbied for greater visibility and dimensionality of Latina/os on screen. While each group took a slightly different approach, all pushed for more employment of Latino/as in the television and film industries, served as watchdogs with respect to portrayals, and called attention to media projects and professionals seen as signs of improvement. In 1998, the NHMC, representing all of the Latina/o groups, collaborated with other ethnic media advocacy groups to form the Multi-Ethnic Coalition, which negotiated for improvements at the networks with respect to ethnic diversity. The coalition forged agreements with ABC, CBS, NBC, and Fox that established the first network executive positions charged with working on diversity issues, including Latina/o representation and employment.[3] The NHMC and other groups in the Multi-Ethnic Coalition issued annual "report cards" in order to gain regular news coverage for issues of diversity in television; in the case of the NHMC this meant grading networks on their progress and lack of progress in improving Latina/o inclusion on screen and in the industry. It also began to oversee a writers' trainee program with a focus on television. A small number of Latino/a writers and producers were also beginning to enter the industry, the impact of which wouldn't be fully felt until the 2000s.

Meanwhile, projected demographic shifts were likely motivating the television industry to improve their outreach to Latino/as. In the 1990s the Census Bureau projected that by 2000 Latino/as would surpass African Americans as the largest non-white ethnic group, then at 12.5 percent of the U.S. population. Appeal to Latina/o viewers thus was becoming more integral to the success of series and networks more broadly. As Arlene Dávila has aptly documented, Latino/a advertising agencies were also educating the public and media industries regarding Latino/a buying power and its future growth.

2000s+: Gaining Numbers and at Times, a Voice

While Latina/os were still substantially underrepresented in the 2000s and in more recent years, the rising numbers of Latina/os in the television audience arguably has had an impact. Latina/o guest and recurring characters are at times more visible, while occasional moments of now-subtitled Spanish and an inclusion of a Latina/o point of view has become less rare, signaling a broadening of the national imaginary to begin to include Latina/o Americans. A continuation of earlier patterns of marginalization and ambivalence can also still be felt, however.

In the 2000s, narrative series more often attempted to include Latina/o characters and to portray them in a multidimensional light. Diverse ensemble cast shows, a programming trend in this decade, often featured one or a few Latino/a character or characters among its ensemble and sporadically focused on these characters. Popular series that did so included *Lost* (2004–2010), *Desperate Housewives* (2004–2012), *Modern Family* (2009–), *CSI Miami* (2002–2012), and *Grey's Anatomy* (2005–), to the benefit of actors such as Jorge Reyes on *Lost*, Eva Longoria on *Desperate Housewives*, Sofía Vergara on *Modern Family*, and Adam Rodriguez on *CSI Miami*. Another, more troubling trend was the resurgence of Latino criminal roles in popular dramas, for example on *Breaking Bad* (2008–2013) and *Weeds* (Showtime, 2008–2012), which featured Latino characters as frightening thugs, drug dealers, and hit men.

At the same time, however, Latino/a writers, producers, and executives began to have a limited impact. Important milestones included the first series with a predominantly Latina/o cast and production team, *Resurrection Blvd.* (2000–2002), about a Mexican American family with several brothers competing in the world of boxing, which aired on Showtime. Writer-producer Dennis Leoni, of Mexican and Italian descent, created and was show runner for the series, while the episodes were written, produced, and directed by a team that was mostly Latina/o. Other Latina/o-led series included *American Family* (2002–2004), created by Gregory Nava; *Ugly Betty* (2006–2010), helmed by producer Silvio Horta and executive producer Salma Hayek; and *The George Lopez Show* (2002–2007), a family sitcom co-created, co-produced and starring comedian George Lopez. Pancho Mansfield, who has now overseen scripted programming at Showtime, Fox TV Studios, and Spike TV, and Nina Tassler, President and now Chair at CBS, the first Latino/a network executives in this era, were influential as well. Mansfield, for instance, greenlit *Resurrection Blvd.* while he was at Showtime.

Progress was also evident in children's programming, where series focused on Latino/a youth began to flourish. These have included *Taina* (2001–2002), about a Puerto Rican girl at a New York City school of performing arts, and *The Brothers Garcia* (2004), about two boys and their family experiences in Los Angeles. Long-running series catering to younger children include the phenomenally popular *Dora the Explorer* (2000–), its spin-off, *Go Diego, Go!* (2005–2011), and the animated series *Handy Manny* (2006–). Meanwhile, Latina/os are a growing and young population in relation to other U.S. media consumers (the median age for U.S. Latina/os is 27, while for the average North American it is 37). In a related trend of outreach to bicultural and bilingual young adult viewers, bilingual cable networks targeting a young adult audience were also launched. These networks have included Sí TV (now Nuvo TV), Mun2, a sister network to Telemundo, and MTV Tr3s (since rebranded NBC Universo). All targeted young Latino/as and other young Americans with a mix of syndicated programming, such as reruns of *George Lopez*, and original reality programming. They have provided some competition to the English-language networks and the most popular and quite successful Spanish-language networks reaching U.S. audiences, Univisión and Telemundo.

While series such as *Ugly Betty* and *George Lopez* proved the potential profitability of series with Latina/o leads, by the 2010s the trend for Latina/o-oriented shows had waned. However, the CW dramedy *Jane the Virgin* (2014–) and ABC's *Cristela* (2014–2015) are signs of progress. Both center on complicated, relatable, and empowered Latina characters working toward their professional goals; in *Jane the Virgin*, Jane Villanueva pursues her dream to become a writer, while Cristela is a law intern in the last stage of her education to become a lawyer.

Jane the Virgin has been both a critical and a ratings success; in 2014 it was recognized with Golden Globe and Critics' Choice nominations and with a Peabody, as the American Film Institute's Television Program of the Year, and as Favorite New TV Comedy by the

People's Choice Awards. Gina Rodriguez, its star, also won a Golden Globe for Best Actress in a comedy or musical television series. *Cristela*, while cancelled after one season, also was a remarkable first for launching Cristela Alonzo, the first Latina show runner and star of her own show.

However, it may be that the networks will not be seen as a necessary ingredient of future Latina/o-oriented series, as production and exhibition increasingly moves beyond the television set in the 2010s. Part of this trend is the rise of online/cable networks and channels with a Latina/o flavor such as NuvoTV and Robert Rodríguez's El Rey, and sites streaming television episodes such as Hulu. These online forums are successfully showcasing original content with a focus on Latina/os communities, led by Latina/o writers and producers working outside traditional models who are interested in serving the Latina/o audience. The genesis of rising numbers of the Latina/o web series in the 2010s is linked to these developments. These series represent a diverse milieu of Latina/o subjectivities and include dramatic and especially comedic serial narratives that run the gamut from tales of Latina feminist superheroes to poignant satire about the real-life stresses of being undocumented. These series include *Los Americans* (2011–), starring Esai Morales, about a suburban Mexican American family; *East WillyB*, about a young Puerto Rican man running a bar in a North Brooklyn neighborhood; and *East Los High* (2013–), an angsty teen drama with a cast of young Latina/o performers. Many of these series, much lower budget productions than seen on network and cable television, have been funded at least in part by Latina/os themselves. This has been enabled through crowdfunding mechanisms such as Kickstarter and fundraising campaigns that have reached out to Latina/o communities for support ranging from $5 individual contributions to larger donations.

Ongoing Questions and Debates

There are a number of ongoing debates and conundrums when it comes to assessing progress with respect to Latina/os portrayals and authorship in U.S. English-language television, however. One is that surveys of progress by advocacy groups and the networks themselves typically tally numbers of characters, actors, and creative professionals that are Latina/o, while the quality of portrayals is much more difficult to assess and has often gone unquestioned. As I have noted previously on the increasing numbers of mixed Latina/o stars in recent decades, we are also witnessing what might be termed a "whitewashing" of Latina/o TV characters. This is true particularly in children's series such as *The Wizards of Waverly Place* (2007–2012). Light-skinned actors of mixed Hispanic heritage are increasingly being cast, while Latina/o characters are often portrayed as unable to speak Spanish and with no clear connections to a Latina/o community or identity.

There are also ongoing debates regarding whether a focus on "positive" images should be sought by advocates lobbying for television narratives and characters that will be empowering for Latina/os. The fear of stereotyping arguably has had a chilling effect on Latina/o representation on network and cable television. Images of middle-class Latina/os in professional positions have typically been viewed by advocates as more desirable than presenting Latina/os as working class, in manual labor jobs, or as not fluent in English. Given the fact that a third of U.S. Latina/os are currently first-generation immigrants and that many Latina/o families still struggle with issues of socioeconomic disadvantage, it's useful to consider what it means to push to never see these images on television. Previous studies, such as those by Children Now, have shown that children from all socioeconomic backgrounds benefit from seeing families like their own portrayed sensitively in television

31

and other media, as well as from viewing aspirational images. The *diversity* of images, including diversity with respect to phenotype and class, is important to keep in mind in these discussions. On the other hand, if the only images that we see of Latinas are of Latina maids (for example, on *Devious Maids*), then that clearly is a problem. However, if this is balanced with a Latina *Pretty Little Liars*, Latina/os living and working on a futuristic *Battlestar Galactica*, and as a suburban *Modern Family*, then it becomes a different thing to also include a series featuring Latina maids in a pulpy soap opera.

These trends beg in-depth thought and discussion on the part of Latina/o communities and scholars. While blatantly stereotypical Latina/o characters with exaggerated characteristics such as broken English, heavy accents, and wildly colorful costumes are less often included in television story worlds, we now seldom find culturally marked Latina/o characters. In other words, less assimilated, working class, or brown Latina/os are now seldom seen. Has focus on the eradication of stereotypes had the indirect consequence of encouraging television producers to only depict Latina/o characters as completely assimilated to American mainstream culture and to erase Latina/o communities altogether? This evolution begs further interrogation, particularly regarding the kinds of representations that will be most empowering to Latina/os and our communities.

As Vittoria Rodriguez and I note in research on Latina/o web television, the rise of streaming series such as *East Los High* raises new questions for us to grapple with as well. Even the most successful online series have had a hard time continuing beyond a few seasons because of lack of sustained funding, pointing to an important topic of future discussion, that of financial support of Latina/o television production. During the height of the Chicana/o and Puerto Rican civil rights movements, there was a call for community-supported arts efforts, particularly for productions that would counter Hollywood narratives. Does a new call need to be sounded to ensure that Latina/o television will flourish with community support as well? Only time will tell whether we're witnessing a renewed emphasis on Latina/o support of Latina/o media production, as digital media tools have enabled communities and individuals to take media representation once again into their own hands.

Notes

1 Publications that address how U.S. Latina/os are served by Spanish-language television include Mari Castañeda, "The Importance of Spanish Language and Latino Media," 2008; and Vicki Mayer, "Living Telenovelas / Telenovelizing Life: Mexican American Girls' Identities and Transnational Telenovelas," 2003. Juan Piñon and Viviana Rojas's essay, "Language and Cultural Identity in the New Configuration of the Latino TV Industry" is also a useful primer regarding the rise of bilingual and Latina/o-oriented networks.

2 See Pardo and Dreas, "Three Things You Thought You Knew about Hispanics' Engagement with Media... And Why You May Have Been Wrong," 2011.

3 See Beltrán et al, "Pressurizing the Media Industry," 2005. 160–93.

Bibliography

Avila-Saavedra, Guillermo. "Ethnic Assimilation Versus Cultural Assimilation: U.S. Latino Comedians and the Politics of Identity." *Mass Communication and Society* 14 (2011): 271–291.

Báez, Jillian. "Latina/o Audiences as Citizens: Bridging Culture, Media, and Politics." *Contemporary Latina/o Media: Production, Circulation and Politics*. Eds. Arlene Dávila and Yeidy Rivero. New York: New York University Press, 2014. 267–284.

Beltrán, Mary. *Latina/o Stars in U.S. Eyes: The Making and Meaning of Film & TV Stardom.* Urbana, IL: University of Illinois Press, 2009.

Beltrán, Mary, Jane Park, Henry Puente, Sharon Ross, and John Downing. "Pressurizing the Media Industry." *Representing 'Race': Racisms, Ethnicity, and the Media*. Eds. John D.H. Downing and Charles Husband. London: Sage, 2005. 160–193.

Brown is the New Green: George Lopez and the American Dream. Dir./Prod. Phillip Rodriguez. PBS.

Castañeda, Mari. "The Importance of Spanish Language and Latino Media." *Latina/o Communication Studies Today*. Ed. Angharad N. Valdivia. New York: Peter Lang, 2008.

Children Now. *A Different World: Children's Perceptions of Race and Class in Media*. Oakland, CA: Children Now, 1998.

Dávila, Arlene. *Latinos, Inc.: The Making and Marketing of a People*. Berkeley: University of California, 2001. New York: New York University Press, 2002.

Dávila, Arlene. "Talking Back: Spanish Media and Latinidad." *Latina/o Popular Culture*. Eds. Michelle Habell-Pallan and Mary Romero. New York: New York University Press, 2002. 25–37.

Guidotti-Hernandez, Nicole. "*Dora the Explorer*, Constructing "Latinidades" and the Politics of Global Citizenship." *Latino Studies* 5 (2007): 209–232.

Lichter, S. Robert and Daniel Amundson. *Distorted Reality: Hispanic Characters in TV Entertainment*. Washington, DC: Center for Media and Public Affairs, 1994.

Masi de Casanova, Erynn. "Spanish Language and Latino Ethnicity in Children's Television Programs." *Latino Studies* 5:4 (2007): 455–477.

Mayer, Vicki. "Living Telenovelas / Telenovelizing Life: Mexican American Girls' Identities and Transnational Telenovelas." *Journal of Communication* 53:3 (2003): 479–495.

Molina Guzmán, Isabel. *Dangerous Curves: Latina Bodies in the Media*. New York: NYU Press, 2010.

Negrón Mutaner, Frances, with Chelsea Abbas, Luis Figueroa, and Samuel Robson. *The Latina/o Media Gap: A Report on the State of Latinos in U.S. Media*. New York: The Center for Race and Ethnicity, Columbia University, 2014.

Noriega, Chon. *Shot in America: Television, the State, and the Rise of Chicano Cinema*. Minneapolis: University of Minnesota Press, 2000.

Pardo, Claudia and Charles Dreas. "Three Things You Thought You Knew about Hispanics' Engagement with Media… And Why You May Have Been Wrong." New York: Nielsen Company, 2011. Available at: http://www.nielsen.com/content/dam/corporate/us/en/newswire/uploads/2011/04/Nielsen-Hispanic-Media-US.pdf

Pérez-Firmat, Gustavo. *Life on the Hyphen: The Cuban American Way*. Austin: University of Texas Press, 1994.

Piñon, Juan. "*Ugly Betty* and the Emergence of Latino Producers as Cultural Translators." *Communication Theory* 21 (2011): 392–412.

Piñon, Juan, and Viviana Rojas. "Language and Cultural Identity in the New Configuration of the U.S. Latino TV Industry." *Global Media and Communication* 7:2 (2011): 129–147.

Rios, Diana I. and Mari Castañeda. *Soap Operas and Telenovelas in the Digital Age: Global Industries and New Audiences*. New York: Peter Lang, 2011.

Rivero, Yeidy M. *Tuning Out Blackness: Race and Nation in the History of Puerto Rican Television*. Durham, NC: Duke University Press, 2005.

Rodriguez, Vittoria and Mary Beltrán. "From the Bronze Screen to Computer Screens: Latina/o Web Series and Independent Production." Publication forthcoming in *The Routledge Companion to Latina/o Media*, eds. Maria Elena Cepeda and Dolores Inés Casillas. New York: Routledge, 2016.

Telotte, J.P. *Disney TV*. Detroit, MI: Wayne State University Press, 2004.

United States Census Bureau. *U.S. Census Bureau: State and County Quick Facts*. 2015. Available at: http://quickfacts.census.gov/qfd/states/00000.html

Valdivia, Angharad. "This Tween Bridge Over My Latina Girl Back: The U.S. Mainstream Negotiates Ethnicity." In *Mediated Girlhoods: New Explorations of Girls' Media Culture*, ed. Mary Celeste Kearney. New York: Peter Lang, 2011. 93–109.

2

LATINO FILM IN THE END TIMES

Camilla Fojas

> Against the hegemony of the present world order that passes itself off as natural and necessary, global actors are tearing a hole in knowledge. New forms emerge. They nourish our imagination, the most radical power that we as humans have.
>
> Susan Buck-Morss, "A Commonist Ethics"

Raíces de Sangre (1979), the first Mexican and Chicano cinematic co-production, brought the realities of the border region and of Mexican migrants to cross-border audiences. The film was the consequence of then President Luis Alvarez Echevarría's attempt to restore confidence in the state for Mexicans at home and "afuera" by diminishing political censorship and repression, particularly in the media. He forged links in personal meetings with Chicano leaders like Cesar Chavez and organizations, giving publicity to the conditions of Chicanos during the 1960s and 1970s in the United States. One consequence of this democratic *apertura* was the disbursement of funding that resulted in the first Chicano film produced in Mexico featuring Chicano and Mexican actors, and helmed by Chicano director Jesús Salvador Treviño. *Raíces de Sangre* documents the struggle of Chicanos around immigrant rights and labor issues for migrant workers and those working along the border region in *maquiladoras* (assembly plants). It takes place during an era of what David Maciel describes as a "discovery" of the Chicano community as a political entity and a market for Mexican goods and media.[1] This film set the tone and raised the standard for border films and Chicano and Latino films: it draws on the history and context of transnational labor migration while establishing the importance of linking worker struggles across the border into Mexico and beyond.

Almost forty years later, U.S. and Mexican production companies, Televisa and Lionsgate, join forces to produce a biopic, shot mostly in Mexico, of Chicano activist Cesar Chavez by Mexican actor and director Diego Luna, and Mexican and Mexican American actors and actresses. Luna is part of a generation of Mexican cross-over or, more accurately, global talent—including Gael García Bernal (also a producer of *Cesar Chavez*), Guillermo del Toro, Alejandro González Iñárritu, Alfonso Cuarón, Salma Hayek, among others. The film is nominally part of a slate of film and other media that targets labor policy and practices along the border during a time of heightened immigrant phobia and economic crisis, or what some cultural critics have called the end times, a time when the economic system is no longer sustainable in its current form.

There are several Latino films that address the social conditions of inequity besetting those at the bottom of the labor market, those first sacrificed in an economic crisis—immigrants and migrants who work and live at or near the border; they are *Maquilapolis* (2006), *Machete* (2010), and *Cesar Chavez* (2014). These films express a vital political expediency different in tone from its predecessors, the struggles for worker and immigrant rights are ever more pressing leading up to and following the economic freefall of the leading world economy that began in 2007 and that ended, for some, a few years later. These films offer a range of remedies and imagined outcomes drawn from cross-border media productions from a number of different genres and modes of production. *Cesar Chavez*, mentioned earlier, is a fairly conventional Hollywood narrative that targets a large mainstream audience to send a message about the struggles of migrant workers deprived of basic rights. It is a melodrama that, while focusing on the individual and his family, goes against some of the conventions of the genre to explore the political and cultural context of local and national labor organizing. The documentary *Maquilopolis* (2006) was released just as the U.S. economy was showing signs of economic distress but focuses on the Border Industrialization Program (BIP) and its outcomes along the Mexican side of the border. Like *Raíces de Sangre*, the documentary thematizes the struggle of women working in *maquiladoras*, but it uses an experimental approach to their stories, allowing each woman to control the means of production of her own story within an overarching narrative of political organization against worker rights violations—it does what *Cesar Chavez* purports to do, which is to allow the poor to narrate their histories and control their futures. *Machete* is a border film that uses the exploitation grindhouse genre to tell a different story about organizing and social change: rather than promulgating participation in a corrupt democratic process, the film asserts a different imaginary of coalition building and change through revolution. Each of these films participates in different genres, often mixing or expanding the boundaries of genre to give a different take on the migrant condition, along with different modes and methods for addressing their social and cultural status during times of economic crisis. These films address and partake in the history of Latino filmmaking while they add new dimensions to it.

Cesar Chavez presents the farm worker's movement within a melodrama of family dynamics in which father and son tensions present a point of coincidence between the growers and those struggling against them. The overarching story aspires to universality through this plot point, while it delivers another story about the enactment of social change. The film is attentive to the history and tendency of Latino cinema to address issues relevant to its target audience, in this case, the work of organizing and building coalitions to create social change. The labor of migrants is rendered visible for a wide audience, drawing on the tradition of Latino Cinema and the Chicano movement that sought the social, cultural, and political empowerment for those of Mexican descent in the United States— most notably *Raíces de Sangre* and *Alambrista* (1977)—which began to emerge during the post-civil rights era of the 1970s. The film is more in line with the funding and production lineage of "Hispanic Hollywood" of the 1990s—*La Bamba* (1987), *American Me* (1992), *Mi Familia* (1995)—which were the result of the civil rights era and demands for more nuanced representations of Latinos and Latinas in their families and communities of origin. *Cesar Chavez* draws on these traditions while glossing them too.

Marshall Ganz, a labor organizer who worked on the staff of the United Farm Workers (UFW) for 16 years, describes the portrayal of Cesar Chavez in the film as caricatured and often departing from historical events to the point that the "lessons the film teaches contradict the real lessons of Chavez's work." The weaknesses he identifies are exactly those of melodrama, of reducing complex historical events to a struggle between good and bad—the growers and the workers—while foregrounding a storyline of individual pathos and struggle. The historical Chavez exhibited incredible skills at coalition building and creating relationships with diverse constituencies and individuals, while the filmic Chavez is engaged in an often lone struggle against opposing forces. Ganz writes:

> Cesar's core leadership gifts were relational. He had an ability to engage widely diverse individuals, organizations and institutions with distinct talents, perspectives and skills in a common effort. The film, however, depicts him as a loner: driving alone (when in reality he had given up driving), traveling alone (which he never did) and deciding alone (when his strength was in building a team that could respond quickly, creatively and proactively to the daily crises of a long and intense effort).
> "Not the Cesar Chavez I Knew," *The Nation*, 1 April 2014, np.

The film glosses the UFW's deep connections to the civil rights movement and to others struggling towards similar ends—Filipinos (represented to some degree), African-Americans, the labor movement, and the larger Chicano movement. This is partly a result of the institutional constraints of major studio-funded productions. In this case, the filmmakers, director, and producers were beholden to a number of constituents, not the

Figure 2.1   Michael Piña as César Chávez in Diego Luna's *César Chávez* (2014)

least of whom were the Chavez family who had veto power over the script, and the studios that seek marketability, defined as content that will appeal to liberal democratic ideals without threatening to alienate a white mainstream audience. *Cesar Chavez* meets these competing demands by lionizing its protagonist and locating the struggle for equal rights in the domain of U.S. liberalism as an individual struggle.

The story follows Cesar Chavez in his emergence to social consciousness as a young man aware of the struggle of workers and their degradation by a system that values profit over human dignity (see Figure 2.1).

He devotes his life and work to raising migrant worker consciousness—"you can't oppress someone who is not afraid anymore"—and to creating social change within democratic legal process, leading to the creation of the first law allowing migrant workers to organize. The struggle of Cesar Chavez as the representative of a racialized group is rendered the story of the U.S as an exceptional political entity, a beacon of civil rights for the rest of the world, formed against outside forces in a paradoxically global and nativist sense. The film portrays a targeted boycott on a single grape grower, Bogdanovich, who exemplifies and symbolizes all other growers. When Bogdanovich aligns with then President Nixon to have his grapes distributed abroad, thus bypassing the U.S. boycott, the struggle against the growers turns global. This is a major turning point in the film. The farm workers' struggle ceases to be that of a marginal constituency and becomes the very sign of U.S. American liberalism. This is conveyed significantly in the scene that evokes the symbolic power of the Boston Tea Party that signaled the revolutionary spirit of the U.S. against British imperialism. The film tacitly alludes to this historical event when British dock workers, in alliance with the U.S. UFW movement, throw Bogdanovich's grapes into the harbor rather than unloading them. This moment allegorizes how the film itself signals the full integration of the Latino narrative in the U.S. historical and cultural storyline, coopting it as a sign of the revolutionary spirit of the U.S. In this way, the farm worker struggle is framed as relevant and significant to U.S. audiences: the film moves the activist work of peoples of color into the mainstream, making it palatable and accessible and neutralizing some of its antiracist valence.

Cesar Chavez puts the UFW movement squarely into the social world of global audiences, integrating actual footage from the era, giving the movement unprecedented publicity while appealing to U.S. cultural values. It glosses many of the historical realities of this struggle and is complicit with Hollywood success stories, offering a story of individual triumph in the face of impossible odds. But it is a timely story that reminds viewers of the struggle of the poor during times of crisis and it is one that brings Mexican filmmaking, artists, and producers, into alliance with their U.S. counterparts. While *Cesar Chavez* is limited and constrained by industrial and capitalist demands, the documentary *Maquilapolis* is the result of independent and collective binational efforts by Vicky Funari and Sergio De La Torre in collaboration with the women of Grupo Factor X, Chilpancingo Collective for Environmental Justice, and Women's Rights Advocates, co-produced by the Independent Television Service and partially funded by the Sundance Institute Documentary Fund (see Figure 2.2).

The film approaches worker struggle on the border with little regard for marketability or accessibility. It too is the result of the collaboration between U.S. based filmmakers and the Mexican women who commandeer the camera to tell their own stories and enact their own struggle against major corporations along the border. The documentary has a stated aim expressed by the filmmakers as a cross-border campaign for social change through mediamaking:

Figure 2.2   Latinas in Vicky Funari's and Sergio De La Torre's *Maquilapolis* (2006)

We are currently seeking funding to implement a binational Community Outreach Campaign, designed and implemented collaboratively with stakeholder organizations in the U.S. and Mexico. The campaign utilizes a high-profile public television broadcast, top tier film festivals and community screenings of the film to create meaningful social change around the issues of globalization, social and environmental justice and fair trade. Our outreach team includes dedicated activists on both sides of the border, mediamakers committed to social change, and most importantly a group of women factory workers struggling to bring about positive change in their world.

http://www.maquilapolis.com/project_eng.htm

This collaborative production and the political initiatives it documents and encourages enact the ideals of political organizing expressed by Cesar Chavez, particularly in his statement upon which the biopic ends: "I'd like to see the poor take a very direct part in shaping society and let them make the decisions. If the poor aren't involved change will never come." This is the premise of *Maquilapolis*. The women at the bottom of the *maquiladora* labor market commandeer cameras to tell a story that involves their struggle against the factory owners. Their activist work is not mediated by either the filmmakers, in the case of the documentary, or the unions that, as *Raíces de Sangre* also reveals, are under the employ of the owners, not the workers. They make the decisions about how they will organize and act, and shape the direction of their own futures.

The women's stories are conveyed within a larger historical and social context that implicates economically driven policies of the United States, in particular the BIP and the North American Free Trade Agreement (NAFTA). The documentary explains how the BIP of 1965 initiated the creation of the *maquiladoras* or foreign owned assembly plants in the "free trade zones" along the Mexican side of the U.S-Mexican border, and invited U.S. manufacturers to move their operations to this area. *Maquilapolis* describes waves of development that intensified and expanded after the passing of NAFTA, and that deepened the exploitation of workers' rights. This is conveyed in images of the production and destruction of factory spaces to convey the economic cycles of capitalism. Once the border economy proves to be less than profitable, the factories move elsewhere. The film shows images of the vacant, ruined, and abandoned spaces to convey corporate disregard for local economies. The women visually document these spaces and narrate its hidden story—for instance, Carmen Durán explains how Sanyo closed shop and moved to Indonesia in search of lower wages. The corporation abandoned its factory space and its workers, to whom they refused to pay severance wages. Durán, along with several colleagues, initiates legal action against Sanyo to recuperate lost wages and eventually wins.

The documentary uses some experimental, non-narrative, techniques to shape the mood and meaning of the images. The women's monotonous and rote work is conveyed not in factory scenes but in images of nine workers dressed in blue factory uniforms dramatizing their repetitive labors like a choreographed installation in an abandoned lot. Their work is rendered a kind of dignified aesthetic experience, meditative and graceful. The music that accompanies this scene is composed industrial sounds from or imitating the machines of the factories. While their work is dignified in this aesthetically appealing sequence, the narrative conveys the oppressive conditions of their work which include risks to their health, lack of job security, and violation of their rights. Also, the shift work they perform is often out of conjunction with the daily schedules of their children, and many of them are without partners to share in the domestic work. They live in precarious circumstances in which the loss of employment or the diminishing of wages has devastating effects.

In addition to the struggle to work and maintain a household, these women are beset by rising toxicity in their environments, both in the factories and in the areas surrounding their homes. One of the women, Lourdes Luján, describes a river that runs through a neighborhood that turns various colors and emits noxious fumes when the factories dump waste into it under the cover of rain. She describes how, when she was a child, people in the neighborhood or *colonia* would swim and camp along its shores. Now such use of the river is unimaginable. Lourdes and Carmen Durán, her colleague, catch the river in full toxic bloom on camera as they jokingly mock-report on it like newscasters. This footage is a key visual indictment of environmental violations that solidifies their case against the *maquiladoras*.

Maquilopolis, like *Cesar Chavez*, follows a narrative arc that builds to success for the women's campaign for environmental clean-up by major corporations, and the remitting of severance pay for workers who were rendered unemployed when a factory closed—presumably to find a more profitable set of circumstances, partly through unpaid wages. The women's collective efforts to use mediamaking as a political tool reflects the ideals of the New Latin American Cinema movement of the 1960s—which included cross-border collaborations like *Raíces de Sangre*—to use cinema to create social change. This movement coincides with the precepts of the Chicano and civil rights movements' emphasis on social justice and antiracism in the struggle for self-determination and equality. *Maquilopolis* fulfills these ideals for a new era in which economic instability leads to full blown crisis, the impact of which is more far ranging for the marginal and the poor on both sides of the border.

Robert Rodríguez's parody of immigration phobia, the *Machete* franchise—*Machete*, *Machete Kills* (2013), *Machete Kills in Space* (in development)—brings revolutionary ideas about collective organizing and social change to a general audience through a mix of the grindhouse style of filmmaking and the b-grade *cine negro* style of border filmmaking. *Machete* was released during a time of anti-immigrant hysteria, particularly in Arizona, and it appeared just prior to the bicentennial celebrations of Mexican independence. Machete (Danny Trejo) represents the cross-border provenance of the film, as an ex-Federale from

Figure 2.3   Danny Trejo as Machete in Robert Rodriguez's *Machete* (2010)

Mexico who works as a day laborer in Texas. He is a migrant worker who is not a passive object of immigration policy or worker politics, but an action hero. He is hired to assassinate a racist senator, Senator McClaughlin (Robert De Niro), only to be "double-crossed and left for dead," and so he must avenge himself of his would-be killers and in doing so, participate in the cause of collective antiracist struggle in a massive *Wild Bunch*-style shootout.

Like *Cesar Chavez*, *Machete* garners a mainstream audience while the storyline encodes a critical discourse about U.S. immigration policy. The advertising copy for *Machete* locates the film squarely in the action genre directed at Hollywood audiences:

> Set up, double-crossed and left for dead, Machete (Trejo) is an ass-kicking ex-Federale who lays waste to anything that gets in his path. As he takes on hitmen, vigilantes and a ruthless drug cartel, bullets fly, blades clash and the body count rises. Any way you slice it, vengeance has a new name—Machete. (see Figure 2.3)

The film actually targets two distinct markets: mainstream Hollywood, through its major stars—Jessica Alba, Lindsay Lohan, Don Johnson, Steven Segall, and Robert DeNiro, and a critical Latino border genre and its stable of stars—Danny Trejo, Michelle Rodriguez, and Cheech Marin. This is evident in the different previews and movie trailers directed at these two distinct audiences. Danny Trejo narrates the trailer intended for Latino audiences "in a special Cinco de Mayo message" that clearly depicts the critical parody of the border film and its anti-immigrant hysteria. Whereas the Hollywood trailer, narrated by Jessica Alba, conveys a story about an individual hero whose successful struggle against the odds will be rewarded with the affections of Alba's character.

The film in its dual distribution took on a life beyond its immediate narrative order and spurred public outrage about the racialized conflict portrayed in the story. In "The Border Crossed Us," Zachary Ingle, drawing from the various ways that the public commented on the film on blogs, discussion boards, and YouTube videos, found that the film elicited a range of responses about its racial plot (159–60). In particular, syndicated radio host Alex Jones describes *Machete* as a symbol of Latin American revolution, and the story one of liberation theology, while other critics, like Stephen Holden, found the film to be unthreatening except to those on the extreme right. While these diverse responses point to a divided reception of the film, *Machete* is a story with social impact, one that might motivate audiences to act to change their circumstances. As an action hero, Machete provokes and excites, turning the ethos of revolution into cultural capital for Hollywood viewers.

Like *Cesar Chavez*, *Machete* combines a storyline about an individual male hero struggling against a corrupt system within the context of collective struggles. Yet the main focus of these stories is on the male hero in a manner that coincides with U.S. exceptionalism, or the idea that a single character or entity might act alone and outside the strictures of law in a manner that ultimately benefits the public or greater good; in these cases, the ends justify the means in a way that captures the ethos of the U.S. revolutionary spirit. Yet what is at odds with this ideology of individualism as the cornerstone of capitalism is the larger context of collective organizing of these individuals, one that is more akin to socialist practice.

Cesar Chavez and *Machete* publicize collectivist ideas through a sleight of hand in which a storyline appears to fit the Hollywood pattern, but ultimately sends a message about the creation of alternate publics, ones in which networks and assemblages of people might act against the prevailing social order to change it. Yet these stories fail in some ways to reimagine gender dynamics along more collectivist lines. Women's roles are sometimes powerful, as in the case of Dolores Huerta in *Cesar Chavez* and "She," or Luz and Sartana in *Machete*, but these women remain ancillary to the real heroes, though Huerta was a powerful and iconic organizer in her own right. In *Machete*, in keeping with the grindhouse style, women are fetishized and their power emanates from sexually charged visual appeal. All of the women are hyper-feminine and stylized while Machete, the main hero, played by sexagenarian Danny Trejo, is a non-typical romantic lead.

Cesar Chavez and *Machete* cater to mainstream and masculinist desires and demands and in doing so are able to reach much wider audiences with messages about equal rights and social equality, though women are often sacrificed to this masculinist ideology. *Maquilapolis* offers a counterpoint to Hollywood and major studio depictions of women. It shows the steps and stages of women engaging in collective action as agents and subjects of the story. While the documentary does not engage all of the elements of the creation of a storyworld, it shows women in active roles without framing them in a sexualized manner. Though *Maquilopolis* may not have received the wide distribution and theatrical release of *Cesar Chavez* and *Machete*, it was shown nationally on the PBS Point of View series and continues to be screened in various venues.

These films work different angles of social change during an era of economic crisis. They contain stories about a racialized immigrant working class of seasonal, temporary, and ultimately disposable workers. And these workers allegorize the condition of all workers in a troubled economy. The main characters, Cesar Chavez and Machete and the women of Grupo Factor X, Chilpancingo Collective for Environmental Justice, and women's rights advocates, contest the idea that precarity demands compliance, that individual preservation should take precedence over social solidarity. Instead, in keeping with the tenets of the revolutionary use of media that emerged during the civil rights era in the tenets of New Latin American cinema, Chicano cultural productions, and Latino film, they dramatize the demand for human rights and equality, antiracist struggles, and the right to self-determination. And they show that the struggle to obtain these demands is successful, issuing hope and optimism for new generations of media activists. These border films represent a reconfigured cultural politics around social movements that create networks and alliances across social divisions, cultural divides, and the borders between nations.

Note

1   Maciel, David. *El Norte: The U.S-Mexican Border in Contemporary Cinema* (San Diego: Institution for the Regional Studies of the Californias, 1990).

Bibliography

Aldama, Arturo J. *Disrupting Savagism: Intersecting Chicana/o, Mexican Immigrant, and Native American Struggles for Self-Representation*. Durham, NC: Duke University Press, 2001.

Aldama, Frederick, ed. *Latinos and Narrative Media: Participation and Portrayal*. New York: Palgrave MacMillan, 2013.

Aldama, Frederick, ed. *Critical Approaches to the Films of Robert Rodriguez*. Austin, TX: University of Texas Press, 2014.

Alonzo, Juan J. *Badmen, Bandits, and Folk Heroes: The Ambivalence of Mexican American Identity in Literature and Film*. Tucson, AZ: University of Arizona Press, 2009.

Bender, Stephen W. *Greasers and Gringos: Latinos, Law, and the American Imagination*. New York: New York University Press, 2003.

Beltrán, Mary. *Latina/o Stars in U.S. Eyes: The Making and Meanings of Film and TV Stardom*. Champaign, IL: University of Illinois Press, 2009.

Buck-Morss, S. "A Commonist Ethics." In *The Idea of Communism 2: The New York Conference*, ed. Slavoj Žižek. London: Verso, 2013. 57–75.

Cull, Nicholas J. and David Carrasco, eds. *Alambrista and the U.S.–Mexico Border: Film, Music, and Stories of Undocumented Immigrants*. Albuquerque, NM: University of New Mexico Press, 2004.

Fojas, Camilla. *Border Bandits: Hollywood on the Southern Frontier*. Austin, TX: Texas University Press, 2008.

Fox, Claire F. *The Fence and the River: Culture and Politics at the U.S. Mexico Border*. Minneapolis: University of Minnesota Press, 1999.

Fregoso, Rosa Linda. *The Bronze Screen: Chicana and Chicano Film Culture*. Minneapolis: University of Minnesota Press, 1993.

Fregoso, Rosa Linda. *MeXicana Encounters: The Making of Social Identities on the Borderlands*. Berkeley: University of California Press, 2003.

Habell-Pallan, Michelle and Mary Romero, eds. *Latino/a Popular Culture*. New York: New York University Press, 2002.

Herrera-Sobek, Maria and David Maciel, eds. *Culture across Borders: Mexican Immigration & Popular Culture*. Tucson, AZ: University of Arizona Press, 1998.

Ingle, Zachary. "The Border Crossed Us: *Machete* and the Latino Threat Narrative." *Critical Approaches to the Films of Robert Rodriguez*. Ed. Frederick Luis Aldama. Austin, TX: University of Texas Press, 2014. 157–74.

Keller, Gary, ed. *Chicano Cinema: Research, Reviews, and Resources*. Binghamton, NY: Bilingual Review Press, 1985.

Maciel, David. *El Norte: The U.S.–Mexican Border in Contemporary Cinema*. San Diego: Institute for Regional Studies of the Californias, San Diego State University, 1990.

Maciel, David. *El Bandolero, el pocho y la raza: imagines cinematograficas del chicano*. Mexico City: UNAM, 1994.

Maciel, David R., Isidro D. Ortiz, and Maria Herrera-Sobek, eds. *Chicano Renaissance: Contemporary Cultural Trends*. Tucson, AZ: University of Arizona Press, 2000.

Mendible, Myra, ed. *From Bananas to Buttocks: The Latina Body in Popular Film and Culture*. Austin, TX: University of Texas Press, 2007.

Molina-Guzmán, Isabel. *Dangerous Curves: Latina Bodies in the Media*. New York: New York University Press, 2010.

Nericcio, William Anthony. *Tex[t]-Mex: Seductive Hallucinations of the "Mexican" in America*. Austin, TX: University of Texas Press, 2007.

Noriega, Chon A., ed. *Chicanos and Film: Representation and Resistance*. Minneapolis: University of Minnesota, 1992.

Noriega, Chon A. *Shot in America: Television, the State, and the Rise of Chicano Cinema*. Minneapolis: University of Minnesota Press, 2000.

Noriega, Chon A. and Ana López, eds. *The Ethnic Eye: Latino Media Arts*. Minneapolis: University of Minnesota Press, 1996.

Ramirez Berg, Charles. *Latino Images in Film: Stereotypes, Subversion, and Resistance*. Austin, TX: University of Texas Press, 2002.

Rodriguez, Clara, ed. *Latin Looks: Images of Latinas and Latinos in the U.S. Media*. Boulder, CO: Westview Press, 1997.

Rodriguez, Clara. *Heroes, Lovers, and Others: The Story of Latinos in Hollywood*. Washington DC: Smithsonian Books, 2004.

Valdivia, Angharad. *A Latina in the Land of Hollywood and Other Essays on Media Culture*. Tucson, AZ: University of Arizona Press, 2000.

3

"¡VÁMONOS! LET'S GO!"

Latina/o Children's Television

Isabel Millán

If you're a nice person, and good friend, and you're smart and adventurous you can reach anybody. You can change the world. And I really believe that Dora is changing the world.

Rosie Pérez

Although Latina/o children's television in the U.S. did not begin with Nickelodeon's *Dora the Explorer*, Rosie Pérez accurately surmises the series' global success. Contemporary media coverage of Latina/os and television include headlines such as NPR's "From Ricky Ricardo to Dora: Latinos on Television" or Erin Texeira's Associated Press article published under several titles including "TV for Kids Courts Spanish Speakers" in the *LA Times*, and its extended version, "Latino Characters Commonplace in Kids' TV: From 'Dora' to 'Dragon Tales,' Bilingual Shows Target Growing Audience" in *NBC News, Today*. This chapter charts or—playing off Dora's companion, Map—maps Latina/o children's television programming from its onset, through the creation and rise of *Dora the Explorer*, and concludes with more contemporary renditions of Latina/o children's television. Despite the latter, Dora remains the single most influential Latina/o television character for children in the U.S.

Children's television often invokes debates over its entertainment or educational value. Similar to children's literature, stakeholders such as parents, educators, and policy makers are often meddling within, negotiating, or attempting to influence those who create children's television (e.g. writers, producers, creators, distributors, etc.), and vice versa. Also similar to children's literature, target audiences and viewing patterns for said programming are often unclear and age parameters are often blurred (Thompson et al. 2011). Tangentially, parents or caregivers are a substantial target audience whether or not they watch the shows, since they often determine whether or not their children will. Other considerations include niche marketing and the development of more recent target audiences such as those for tweens or young adults. As a medium, television, and by extension, children's television, owes its history to other technologies such as radio, and can include live action, animation or cartoons, film adaptations, mini-series, or full series. For the purpose of this chapter, I prioritize television programming directed at Latina/o children with main characters who are openly Latina/o. These may include bilingual content (usually in English and Spanish) as well as English-only content targeting Latina/o children through racial, ethnic, or cultural references.

Inventing Programming for Children: The Early Years

Early television sets became commercially available in the late 1920s and were primarily purchased for use by commercial businesses or governments as opposed to private home use. Approximately twenty additional years would elapse before the U.S. public began popularizing televisions in the home after World War II. Television programming directed at children, or intended for both adult and child audiences, began in the United States during the late 1940s with radio adaptations. In the 1920s, before television programming, children could listen to bedtime stories narrated over radio. With the new television platform, producers adapted radio shows for new parameters and challenges, such as the role of image. No longer solely focused on voice and imagination, the medium now asked audiences to listen while guiding their imaginations with images. One such adaptation occurred in 1947 with the premier of *Small Fry Club*, which included specialized segments such as "Movies for Small Fry," from 1947 to 1951. It originally began as a children's radio show hosted by Bob Emery, referred to by his loyal fans as "Big Brother Bob" (Davis 1995, 175). That same year, Burr Tillstrom received his own variety show program on television. *Junior Jamboree* aired locally in Chicago in 1947, and then changed its name to *Kukla, Fran and Ollie* (KFO) in 1948. It aired on NBC from 1949 to 1954, and then moved again, this time to ABC, where it stayed until 1957. A third show, *Howdy Doody*, also aired in 1947. It was created and produced by E. Roger Muir on NBC until 1960. While it ran the longest of the three, it aired live, limiting its redistribution through syndication, and was therefore less profitable for the major networks (Wells 2002, 61–95). A handful of more localized and less popular shows also aired during the late 1940s including *Juvenile Jury* by Jack Barry, and *Judy Splinters*, starring female ventriloquist Shirley Dinsdale (Davis 1995, 249). These shows reveal early attempts at normalizing content for children although they were generally watched by the whole family. They also aligned with the establishment and normalization of the white, middle-class, heteronormative nuclear family.

By 1955 approximately half of all U.S. homes owned a television set; by the 1950s, the standard schedule for children's programming had also shifted. Programming directed at children such as *Captain Kangaroo* was mostly shown on weekday mornings instead of in the evening or at bedtime, giving rise to what we now understand as Saturday morning cartoons for children. Two important creations involving mice also emerged during the 1950s: Mickey Mouse in Disney's television series *The Mickey Mouse Club*, and Speedy Gonzales in Warner Brothers' *Looney Tunes and Merrie Melodies*. The former became synonymous with white American values whereas the latter was associated with racial and ethnic stereotypes of Latina/os, specifically Mexicans. The two also represent a version of the "good boy/bad boy" dichotomy within normative media, where Mickey Mouse exemplifies the all-American hero while Speedy Gonzales embodies cunningness (see Nerriccio 2007; Noriega and López 1996). Even though Speedy Gonzales was supposed to be the hero who outsmarted Sylvester the cat, he represents a racialized other situated in the desert towns of northern Mexico, whereas Tweety is Speedy's U.S. counterpart—equally cunning, but popularized as "cute" or "adorable" because of his big eyes and baby-like bird appearance.

45

The 1960s ushered in more anthropomorphic cartoons along with several hit television series directed at youth. These included classics such as *The Bugs Bunny Show* (1960), *The Flintstones* (1960), *Yogi Bear* (1961), *The Bullwinkle Show* (1961), *The Alvin Show* (1961), *Hot Wheels* (1961), *The Jetsons* (1962), *The Adventures of Jonny Quest* (1964), *Tom and Jerry* (1965), *George of the Jungle* (1967), *Archie* (1968), *Scooby-Doo* (1969), and *Hey, Hey, It's Fat Albert* (1969). By the late 1960s, popular superheroes had also emerged such as *Batman* (1966), *Superman* (1966), *The Lone Ranger* (1966), *Aquaman* (1967), *The Fantastic 4* (1967), and *Spiderman* (1967).[1] Despite the variation in formats, settings, and characters, *Hey, Hey, It's Fat Albert* was the only series that centered children of color. Even the children's hit *Mister Rogers' Neighborhood* (1968) primarily depicted white puppets and cast members.

Sesame Street, which premiered in 1969 on the PBS network as a production of the Children's Television Workshop, deserves particular attention because of its attempts to target working class communities of color by representing a multicultural cast. The series was created with funding from the U.S. federal government, the Carnegie Corporation, and the Ford Foundation as a way to appease the demands of the civil rights movements of the 1960s. The original purpose of the show was to subsidize early childhood education with public broadcast educational television (Rivero 2011). It was also meant to be representative of urban, multicultural, and working class communities. Hendershot (1998) details how the show itself, as well as researchers who study its effects, positioned itself in opposition to "bad" children's programming; however, "good (uncensorable) and bad (censorable) programs are not binaries but rather mutually defining" (138). Hendershot's critiques of *Sesame Street* pay attention to the program's emphasis on cognition as a "leveler of social differences" (1998, 143). She argues that the show was federally funded because the costs of funding it would be lower than instituting federal preschool programs; not only was it cheaper, it was reusable (Hendershot 1999, 143). This reusability through syndication made *Sesame Street* an inexpensive educational commodity not only within the U.S., but globally. *Sesame Street's* foreign content is the result of the program's development of "foreign versions" of itself (Hendershot 1999, 160–175). The series is "regularly leased to countries that cannot afford to produce their own educational programming" (160). Most troubling for Hendershot, researchers have tested the reception of the show in countries worldwide without any discussion of the implications of its exposure.

Sesame Street continues to run on the PBS Kids network, making it the longest running children's show in the U.S. Many would agree it set the standard for children's entertainment, making it extremely popular among educators and researchers. Nonetheless, Banet-Weiser (2007a) warns, "Even in a show that was specifically created to address the politics of racism in the United States, Sesame Street's political identity needs to be made palatable for a broad audience" (149). She goes on to declare that "it is this kind of colorblind ideology that structures much of children's television—in fact, creators of kids' TV often create characters that are animals or aliens precisely in order to sidestep the problematic issue of racial representation…" (149). In the case of *Sesame Street*, they use Muppets, and even these do not escape racialized, gendered, and sexualized politics. Federal funding and support for the series continues to diminish. In 2015, HBO announced a five-year deal with the Sesame Workshop for exclusive rights to its content (Steel 2015; Westervelt 2015). While this deal will secure funding for several years, it also directly contradicts the series' original purpose of providing educational media to working class communities of color since it will now be limited to audiences who can purchase cable or HBO streaming subscriptions such as HBO Go.

Latina/os in Live Action Television

Dovetailing *Sesame Street*, bilingual (English/Spanish) children's television emerged in the early 1970s with programs such as *Carrascolendas* (1970) and *Villa Alegre* (1973). Both were live action shows centering Latina/os in the U.S. by incorporating English and Spanish in addition to cultural knowledge and experiences. In both, children, youth, and adults intermixed with surrealist or imaginary realities like wizards, oversized dolls, or speaking lions. Overall, both *Carrascolendas* and *Villa Alegre* were significant because of their content and educational value for Latina/o children as well as the opportunities each show offered to the actors, writers, and production teams.

Aida Barrera (2001) has written at length about her experience producing and starring in *Carrascolendas*. She was the lead adult role within the show whose character, Señorita Barrera, co-starred with Agapito, a bilingual lion; Campamocha, a handyman; Caracoles, a restaurant owner; Uncle Andy, a shoe seller; and Berta and Dyana, two life-size dolls (see Figure 3.1). In her book, *Looking for Carrascolendas: From a Child's World to Award-Winning Television*, Barrera detailed her constant efforts to gain financial support for the show, as well as the challenges of working with other amateur actors. Barrera was responsible for much of the show's content, relying on her personal experience. She recalls, "As I encountered the challenge of creating a television program for which I had no preconceived patterns, I relearned those familiar rhythms, sayings, and riddles of my childhood and put them into different dramatic and visual settings" (100). Barrera also gained invaluable experience with television production, noting, "I quickly learned that television is essentially a dramatic medium, and unlike a presentation made to an audience that is physically present, television depends on dramatic and theatrical techniques to retain an unseen public" (Ibid.). Choosing a title also proved challenging: "I knew that the name should be symbolically significant. It had to capture the meaning of Mexican American culture and encompass the sense of the program's larger purpose" (133). According to a 1971 evaluation of *Carrascolendas* for the U.S. Department of Education by Diana S. Natalicio and Frederick Williams,

> "Carrascolendas" was a [...] television series designed to aid in the bilingual instruction of Mexican-American children in the first and second grades...A field experiment involving children from the target audience population and a survey of schools that used the programs showed statistically significant learning gains among television viewers in English tests of multicultural social environment, English language skills, physical environment, and cognitive development. The survey of schools, although indicating a major use of the program, did reveal a possible shortcoming in that a significant number of schools, even in predominantly Mexican-American areas, had no knowledge of the program's availability.

The series' potential was not fully met because of its limited visibility, even among its target audiences. It was produced at PBS's KLRN and was only broadcasted through select KLRN viewing areas in central and south Texas (Natalicio and Williams, 36). Moreover, unlike *Sesame Street* and *Mister Roger's Neighborhood*, which were broadcasted within the home "with the home viewer as their primary target," *Carrascolendas* was primarily intended for broadcasting into classrooms. This meant that a teacher must first be knowledgeable of the series, and second, want to incorporate it into their classroom curriculum (Natalicio and Williams, 35).

Figure 3.1 Carrascolendas cast members on set, including Aida Barrera as "Señorita Barrera" (center). (From Barrera, Aida. 2001. *Looking for Carrascolendas: From a Child's World to Award-Winning Television*. Austin: University of Texas Press.)

Unlike *Carrascolendas*, *Villa Alegre* was broadcasted through PBS across the U.S., making it more accessible to Latina/o communities on a national level. It was created by Rene Cardenas, produced by Bilingual Children's Television, and intended for bilingual (English and Spanish) children between the ages of four and eight ("Villa Alegre" 1977, 10). Publicity for the series included tailored newspaper articles across cities with significant bilingual populations. For example, *The Free Lance-Star* in Oakland, California, published "'Villa Alegre' Aimed at Nation's Bilingual" on August 22, 1977:

> Endorsed by the National Education Association, "Villa Alegre" is established as the model for a new kind of show aimed at an estimated five million bilingual youngsters in the United States, as well as their monolingual brothers and sisters. The show—its name means "Happy Village"—uses animation, Latino music and Spanish and English-speaking actors to teach lessons on subjects such as energy and human relations. Most of it occurs in a small village, where characters like El Capitan, Dona Luz and Dr. Tina act in sketches designed to help young viewers improve communications and problem-solving skills. The skits also help demonstrate bilingual benefits [sic] (10).

Rene Cardenas was also quoted stating that the show's primary message was to "'validate cultural differences' by polishing the image of the bilingual child's minority culture while exposing English-speaking kids to a variety of American ethnic groups" ("Villa Alegre" 1977,

10). Cardenas was critical of U.S. education, noted that it has "traditionally reflected a kind of white, Bible-belt lifestyle" (Ibid.). At its prime, the show was viewed by approximately 4.8 million children, and aired on approximately 250 stations and 50 cable TV outlets across the U.S. (Ibid). It also released several products such as vinyl records of the show's popular songs recorded by the original cast members. Although the show ran for less than ten years, Latina/o adults who viewed the show as a child have reinvigorated its memory through references in pop culture. For example, Andrew Paxman (1997) wrote: "If it was franks and beans but also arroz con salchicha, 'Sesame Street' but also 'Villa Alegre' ... Then you're generation n" (n.p.). Recently, fans created a petition encouraging the online streaming site Shout! Factory to make *Villa Alegre* episodes available.[2]

Many notable Latina/o actors, directors, and production crew members either began in children's media or used this space to fine-tune their skills. This was because children's television was often disregarded for its low production value, making it more accessible to women and people of color who wanted to work within television. Examples include Moctesuma Esparza's role as executive producer in the formerly mentioned *Villa Alegre* (Noriega and López 1996, 140). In an interview with *In Motion Magazine*, Esparza credits his initial work with Villa Alegre as instrumental in setting the "pace and tone" for his future works as an independent film producer (Payan 1998, n.p.). Other Latina/os worked on specific episodes or certain themes within a show. Such was the case with Sylvia Morales who directed segments of *Sesame Street* for a Cinco de Mayo special (Noriega and López 1996, 140–1). On the other hand, Rita Moreno is known as one of the original cast members within PBS's 1970s series, *The Electric Company* (Del Barco 2015). Although in general children's programming was viewed as less rigorous compared with other television productions, many of these shows did go on to win awards, adding prestige along with experience. For example, *Carrrascolendas* won the Gold Award of Excellence and Silver Hugo Award, National Association of Educational Broadcasters, whereas *Villa Alegre* won the Award of Excellence, International Film Advisory Board, 1977 Award, California Association of Latins in Broadcasting, and was a four-time 1977 Emmy Award Nominee ("TFAC" 1979, 7).

Ambiguously Ubiquitous Latinidad?

Unlike the previously mentioned, low-budget, live action productions whose objectives included educating and representing Latina/os, other shows such as *Hot Wheels* were sponsored financially by major toy companies whose primary incentive was to boost toy sales. As a result of protests from parents, the Federal Communications Commission (FCC) intervened in 1969 and then again in 1971, stating that, "Network executives might have seen children's shows as little more than the padding between ads, but shows could not actually be designed to advertise toys" (Hendershot 2004, 9). This led to the proliferation of educational children's media (such as *Reading Rainbow*) until the Reagan administration overturned the 1971 FCC ruling. FCC deregulation created another boom in children's television, except it was once again saturated with an emphasis on toy consumerism, thereby lowering the educational standards of children's media. Consequently, the 1980s is best remembered as the era of children's television derived from toy productions. Examples include *G.I. Joe: A Real American Hero* (1983), *He-Man and the Masters of the Universe* (1983), *ThunderCats* (1984), *The Transformers* (1984), *She-Ra: Princess of Power* (1985), *The Care Bears* (1985[3]), *My Little Pony 'n Friends* (1986), *Popples* (1986), and *Pound Puppies* (1986). As previously stated, *Reading Rainbow* (1983) was a notable exception; if it encouraged consumerism it was of educational books. Its host and executive producer, LeVar Burton, emphasized literacy and cultural competency. *Reading Rainbow* aired on PBS and won eight Emmys for Outstanding Children's Series. Like *Sesame Street*, the show encouraged multiculturalism, intermixing Latina/o-themed books and children.

The 1990s were significant because they gave rise to animated cartoons with more mature, adult content, as well as seeing the effects of the Children's Television Act of 1990 and the National Endowment for Children's Educational Television (Woodard 1999, 6). Cartoons, which by this era had been viewed almost exclusively as content for children, now included profanity, sexual innuendos, and more overt political commentary, for example, *The Simpsons* (1990), *South Park* (1997), and *Futurama* (1999).

One 1990s animated television series stands out in its subtle attempts to center Latina/os. Beginning in 1994 and lasting until 1999, *Where on Earth is Carmen Sandiego?* depicted the antagonist, Carmen Sandiego, as a racially ambiguous, savvy character voiced by Rita Moreno. A clever thief driven by the "game" rather than being innately evil, Carmen Sandiego spoke with an accent that resonated with many bilingual Latina/os watching the show. "For little Latinas, she was the most educated, successful, and powerful figure the culture had given them that finally looked a little like them" (Martel 2012). The animated television series was based on a computer software program, *Where in the U.S.A. is Carmen Sandiego?*, which was meant to be educational, with specific instructions for use in the classroom (Miller and Caley 1987; Mayland 1990). It was also used to teach English (Meskill 1990). The game show, *Where in the World is Carmen Sandiego?*, also precedes its animated television counterpart, airing on PBS in 1991 following the computer game series, and running until 1995. Most recently, Jennifer Lopez has announced she is producing a Carmen Sandiego feature-length film (Martel 2012).

Like Carmen Sandiego, other 1990s television series intermixed people of color, or socio-cultural cues such as music or food, in an attempt to represent multiculturalism. Such was the case with *Barney and Friends* (1992), *Mighty Morphin Power Rangers* (1993), and *Dragon Tales* (1999). For example, Selena Gomez, who I will discuss below, played Gianna in seasons seven and eight of *Barney and Friends* alongside Demi Lovato, who played Angela. *Power Rangers* was unique in that it originally aired as a Japanese television series in 1992, which was reconstructed and dubbed for a U.S. audience. Within the U.S. version, Rocky DeSantos (the second Red Power Ranger) was played by Steve Cardenas and was racialized through his grandfather who was Mexican. Interestingly, the show's villain, Rita, was originally Japanese, however as a result of dubbing, she could be read as racially ambiguous or even Latina within a U.S. context. Similar to Rocky DeSantos, *Dragon Tale*'s Emmy and Max are also examples of racially ambitious characters as are some of the dragons. A notable exception was the character of Enrique who is bilingual and explicitly racialized as Latino (Puerto Rican and Columbian), however he is not introduced until season three in 2005. As with Enrique, Lina, a stereotypically Latina red plane, was not introduced into *Jay Jay the Jet Plane* until 2005 although the series originated in 1994.[4]

Dora the Explorer Reinvents Bilingual Children's Television

In 2000, and nearly thirty years after *Carrascolendas*, Dora Márquez—seven years old, pan-Latina, bilingual in both English and Spanish, and adventurous—debuted as the protagonist of her own Nickelodeon animated television show, *Dora the Explorer*. Interestingly, this occurred only one year after the Cartoon Network decided to cease airing *Speedy Gonzalez* (1999) due to critiques about its ethnic stereotyping. Known for her popularity among preschool-aged children, *Dora the Explorer* quickly reached mass media stardom both in and outside the United States. The overwhelming success of this television series directed at preschoolers would spawn a plethora of Dora consumer products, including DVDs, children's books, and endless variations of toys (Valdivia 2009).

According to Nickelodeon, the "inspiration for the name Dora Márquez was *exploradora*, the Spanish feminine word for 'explorer,' and the acclaimed writer Gabriel García Márquez."[5] Popular legend has it that the original idea for a show with a Latina heroine emerged after one of the creators attended a conference on the lack of Latina/o visibility in the media.[6] *Dora the Explorer* premiered on Nickelodeon on August 14, 2000, and was "instantly ranked as the number-one rated preschool show on commercial television."[7] Five years later, in 2005, a massive inflatable Dora debuted in the Macy's Thanksgiving Day Parade as the first Latina character.[8] According to Nickelodeon, approximately three hundred people work on *Dora the Explorer*, and it initially took over an entire year to produce a single episode of the show. Dora's curriculum model is critical in comprehending her initial success, since "every episode of *Dora the Explorer* is screened by at least seventy five preschoolers before it airs on TV."[9]

Created by Chris Gifford, Valerie Walsh, and Eric Weiner, *Dora the Explorer* is "a program built on pedagogical research concerning the use of television to educate preschoolers" (Banet-Weiser 2007a, 165). As suggested by the show's title, Dora often goes on quests, teaching her audiences about new places, animals, languages, and cultures. In each episode, Dora and her friends must complete a task or solve a problem. Episodes follow a basic narrative pattern in which Dora and her friends pass through three main obstacles before reaching their final destination. Each episode is also designed to interact with viewers so that, for example, Dora may ask her audience a question, which will be followed by a pause, allowing her viewers to respond. A blue arrow serves as a computer cursor and "clicks" on the correct answer, "thus encouraging a kind of active engagement on the part of the preschool-aged audience" (Banet-Weiser 2007b, 219).

Although *Dora the Explorer* did not premiere until 2000, conceptual work for the show began at least a year or two prior. Likewise, each season offers the producers an opportunity to develop something new within the series. Season five was especially significant since several shifts were made to the series as a whole. For example, prior to season five, Tico the squirrel only spoke Spanish and had not learned any English, although Boots, also monolingual, had already begun to learn Spanish. That season, the development team worked closely with the California Association of Bilingual Education on two-way language immersion. By the end of season five, Tico began learning English.

Conceptually, season five also presented Dora as ambassador to the world. The development behind these episodes included specific cultural experts so as not to be patronizing or stereotyping. Maríana Díaz-Wionczek highlights this further: "I do truly believe that what makes a show a hit is its impact on a social context."[10] She recommends then, for anyone who wants to develop a new show: "you definitely have to see what's your social, political, economical, global context and try to do something that's relevant, and not … a light and fluffy show that is not going to give you much. I think that the social relevance has enormous weight."[11]

Interestingly, the end of season five coincides with Dora's tenth year anniversary. Thus, while the research and development team behind *Dora the Explorer* was creating Dora as ambassador to the world, Nickelodeon was also quite literally creating and implementing a global marketing campaign for Dora's tenth year anniversary celebrations.

Generally applauded for her astute, zealous, and team-building persona, Dora's image came under close scrutiny as Nickelodeon revealed her tween counterpart in 2009. Initially

Figure 3.2   Maya & Miguel online game (© 2004 Scholastic Entertainment Inc.)

released as a mere silhouette, the new tween image was met with overwhelming disapproval by parents and educators on online news articles, blogs, and social media sites. Nickelodeon and Mattel responded with a marketing campaign that introduced audiences to a doll version of tween Dora—the Dora Links doll—and its accompanying online community for Dora and her new set of friends, the Dora Explorer Girls. Tween Dora was also brought to life on screen in the television special musical episode, "Our First Concert," which guest starred Latina singer Shakira as herself while promoting teamwork and community service. Unfortunately, however, the motivation behind Dora's growth spurt was not driven by altruism, but instead by a fear of losing audiences who were growing up and out of a preschool-aged television show, and exchanging their Dora dolls for Barbie or Bratz dolls. Not wanting to lose this fan-base, Nickelodeon and Mattel teamed together, and in February of 2009 at the American International Toy Fair announced plans to grow Dora into a tween (Sivaramen 2009).

Post-Dora?: Dora-Inspired Contemporaries

The general success of Nickelodeon's business model as a network that prioritized kids and their needs (Hendershot 2004; Banet-Weiser 2004) helped promote *Dora the Explorer* as a role model and icon, as well as a commercial success. Other networks followed suit, producing their own bilingual or Latina/o-themed shows, including Kids' WB's ¡*Mucha Lucha!* (2002), PBS's *Maya and Miguel* (2004), and Disney's *Handy Manny* (2006) and *Special Agent Oso* (2009). Some were more successful than others although none have reached Dora's stardom as of yet.

Within Nickelodeon, *Dora the Explorer*'s marketing success became the impetus for its spin-off show, *Go, Diego, Go!* (2005), and *Ni Hao, Kai-Lan* (2007). While the latter was cancelled due to poor ratings,[12] *Go, Diego, Go!* continues to air. The show's protagonist, Diego, is Dora's older male cousin who rescues and cares for animals. Unlike *Dora the Explorer*'s preschool audience, *Go, Diego, Go!* targets a slightly older demographic. And targeting an even older tween audience, Nickelodeon aired the live action TV series *Taina* (2001–2002). Taina Morales, the show's protagonist, was a fourteen-year-old, Puerto Rican girl from Queens (Herrera 2015).

On PBS and produced by Scholastic in 2004, *Maya and Miguel*'s main characters are two twins of Mexican and Puerto Rican descent (see Figure 3.2). Scholastic President, Deborah Forte, described the show's engagement with Spanish: "All the characters are bilingual to varying degrees. Abuela (Grandma) Elena speaks Spanish. The kids speak much more English, especially out in the streets, but they pepper it with Spanish." Forte explains how they "studied the way families spoke and this was the way many of them did it" (Texeira 2006a).

Of all the television networks, Disney appears to have the most tumultuous relationship with Latina/o audiences and character representations. Both *Hand Manny* (2006) and *Special Agent Oso* (2009) showcase Latina/o characters who are also bilingual in English and Spanish. For example, Manny Garcia is a repairman while Oso is an investigator. Both animated series target preschool children. For its older tween or teen audiences, Disney created *Wizards of Waverly Place* (2007). Selena Gomez stars as Alex Russo, a teen wizard whose father is an Italian wizard and mother is a mortal Mexican American (Turner 2012). According to Sarah Turner (2014), "such nonthreatening strategies of racial representation allow Disney to access the tween market's $43 billion buying power by appealing to a multicultural viewing audience in such a way as to not disrupt America's racial status quo" (252). Specifically, "Nielsen ratings demonstrate the success of Disney's strategic use of race: 'First run episodes of *Shake It Up*, *Wizards of Waverly Place* and *Good Luck Charlie* earned six of television's top ten telecasts [in February 2011] in key child demographics'" (2014, 252). The show had a similar target audience as Disney's Hannah Montana.[13] Since its series finale, Selena Gomez has become more widely associated with the pop music industry (Greene 2012).

Recent controversies reveal Disney's particular interest in the Latina/o market.[14] In 2012, Disney haphazardly announced its first Latina princess, *Sofia the First* (Rodriguez 2012). Sofia's Latinidad was immediately called into question across media platforms because many argued she did not represent an "authentic" Latina (Guidotti-Hernández 2013). Disney quickly retracted its announcement of the first Latina princess, stating Jamie Mitchell, the producer of the *Sofia the First* television series, "'misspoke' during a press tour and that the title character is not a Latina" (Rodriguez 2012). Nancy Kanter, Senior Vice President of Disney Junior Worldwide, clarified through social media outlets, posting online:

> Some of you may have seen the recent news stories on whether Sofia is or isn't a 'Latina princess.' What's important to know is that Sofia is a fairytale girl who lives in a fairytale world … The writers have wisely chosen to write stories that include elements that will be familiar and relatable to kids from many backgrounds including Spain and Latin America. For example, Sofia's mom comes from a fictitious land, Galdiz, which was inspired by Spain
>
> (Rodriguez 2012).

Perhaps Disney envisioned a princess version of tween Dora, since Sofia targets a slightly older, tween audience.[15] Sofia is currently available Friday mornings in her own television series on Disney Junior.[16] Amidst this controversy, Disney revealed to the National Hispanic Media Coalition that independent of Sofia, they have "an exciting project in early development that does have a Latina as the heroine of the show" (Rodriguez 2012). It remains unclear when this Latina heroine will make her debut, however, press materials are once again labeling her "Disney's first Latina princess" (Messer 2015). Whether or not Latina, Princess Elena is meant to resemble someone of Spanish and Latin American descent (Moreno 2015). The question remains, does Disney understand the difference or care to differentiate between Latina/os, Spaniards, Latinoamericana/os and the many other nuances associated with these socially constructed identities?

Disney became absorbed in a copyright controversy in 2013. International Worker's Day is observed on the first of May; it was also the day Disney filed several U.S. Patent and Trademark Office applications for the phrase "Día de los Muertos" or "Day of the Dead" (Rodriguez 2013). Disney claimed the applications were for a Pixar Día de los Muertos feature film tentatively scheduled for 2015 (Keegan 2012).[17] In what many called a victory, Disney withdrew its application after an uproar of protest on social media networks, including an online protest at change.org and a cartoon by Chicano illustrator, Lalo Alcaraz.[18] Like Sofia, public protest resulted in Disney's retraction. And given these ongoing critiques, Disney decided to hire Lalo Alcaraz for its upcoming feature-length film, *Coco*. On Twitter on August 16, 2015, Lalo Alcaraz tweeted, "ESPECIAL ANNOUNCEMENT: I am on the team creating the new Pixar Day of the Dead movie titled 'Coco'"[sic]. Disney is likely attempting to capitalize on the increasing popularity of Día de los Muertos within the U.S., dovetailing films such as *The Book of Life* or animated series from Latin America such as *Las Leyendas*.

On September 25, 2015, NPR aired a segment titled "Move Over, Dora: 'Nina's World' Brings Another Bilingual Girl to TV."[19] This animated series recently debuted on Sprout, "the 24-hour preschool TV channel," and centers Nina, a six-year-old Latina. Sprout's president, Sandy Wax, attempts to distinguish it from shows such as *Dora the Explorer* by de-emphasizing fantasy fiction. She states:

> We believe that the real world of today's kids and families is a very cool and fun place. We don't believe that we have to be transported to magical kingdoms and castles in order to create a relatable story that really speaks to this generation
> (Del Barco 2015).

Despite the show's emphasis on realism, Nina's companion is an enlarged star-shaped pillow named Star. The show includes famous Latina/os such as Rita Moreno and Mandy Patinkin. Moreno voices Nina's abuelita, Yolie. Commenting on what drew her to the series, Moreno also emphasized its real-world authenticity, noting that the show incorporates families from different nationalities as well as a character who is deaf and voiced by a boy who is also deaf in real life (Hassan 2015).

Despite *Dora the Explorer's* overwhelming global success, she should not be the only Latina/o children's television icon. Given the nuances of any grouping of people or identities, Latina/os consist of a plethora of races, ethnic backgrounds, religions, languages, genders, sexualities, abilities, citizenship statuses, socioeconomic statuses, and so on. No single television show or character should have to carry the burden of representing such rich communities. Instead, through greater representation on TV, we might be able to more thoroughly capture the visual spectrum that makes up Latina/os in the U.S. Moreover, shifts in television, technology, and social media should continue to inspire and generate even more Latina/o shows or characters across these multiple media platforms.

Notes

1 For an extensive list, see Davis, "Appendix B: Landmarks in Children's Television," 249–262.
2 The petition can be found here: http://www.thepetitionsite.com/982/975/441/save-big-blue-marble-and-villa-alegre-for-a-cause-of-respiratory-virus/
3 The *Care Bears* first appeared in a TV special in 1983 and then again in 1984, but wouldn't become a regular television series until 1985.
4 A product description on Amazon notes that "Jay Jay's friend Lina, is a four-year-old who speaks both English and Spanish. She's an expert at solving the 'mysterios' of science and nature! Lina's outgoing personality, bilingual ability, and her special friendship with Jay Jay, make her a must-have for Jay Jay imaginative play." http://www.amazon.com/Lina-Jay-Jet-Plane/dp/B000RY4DRK/ref=cm_cr_pr_product_top?ie=UTF8
5 Nickelodeon, "*Dora the Explorer*, 10th Year Anniversary Launch," Promotional booklet, 2010.
6 Referenced in popular media cover stories of Dora's origins, and confirmed by Nickelodeon's staff. (Maríana Díaz Wionczek, personal interview, January 7, 2010.)
7 Nickelodeon, "*Dora the Explorer*, 10th Year Anniversary Launch," Promotional booklet, 2010.
8 Ibid.
9 Ibid.
10 Maríana Díaz Wionczek, personal interview, January 7, 2010.
11 Ibid.
12 *Ni Hao, Kai-Lan* aired from 2007 to 2011; it was originally produced in Canada, focusing on emotions and effective communication skills; the show featured Kai-Lan, a Chinese American.
13 For discussions on teen depictions on television, see Mary Celeste Kearney (ed), *Mediated Girlhoods: New Explorations of Girls' Media Culture* (New York: Peter Lang, 2011); Morgan Geneviene Blue, "The Best of Both Worlds? Youth, Gender, and a Post-Feminist Sensibility in Disney's Hannah Montana," *Feminist Media Studies* 13 no. 4 (2013): 660–675; Ashton Gerding and Nancy Signorielli, "Gender Roles in Tween Television Programming: A Content Analysis of Two Genres," *Sex Roles: A Journal of Research* 70 no. 1 (2014): 43–56; Alexandra C. Kirsch and Sarah K. Murnen, " 'Hot' Girls and 'Cool Dudes': Examining the Prevalence of the Heterosexual Script in American Children's Television Media," *Psychology of Popular Media Culture* 4 no. 1 (2015): 18–30; Kristen Myers, "Anti-Feminist Messages in American Television Programming for Young Girls," Journal of Gender Studies 22 no. 2 (2013): 192–205.
14 For a thorough discussion of U.S. Latino niche markets, see Arlene Davila, *Latino Spin: Public Image and the Whitewashing of Race*, (New York: New York University Press, 2008); Arlene Davila, *Latinos Inc.: The Marketing and Making of a People* (Berkeley: University of California Press, 2001).
15 Press material for *Sofia the First* state its target audience is children ages two to seven, however the show's themes fall more in line with comparable shows targeting tween audiences. See Rodriguez, "Backlash for Disney's First Latina Princess."
16 Visit http://disney.go.com/disneyjunior/sofia-the-first
17 See http://latimesblogs.latimes.com/movies/2012/05/pixars-d%C3%ADa-de-los-muertos-movie.html
18 Visit http://www.change.org/petitions/walt-disney-company-stop-trademark-of-dia-de-los-muertos
19 See http://www.npr.org/2015/09/25/443334527/move-over-dora-ninas-world-brings-another-bilingual-girl-to-tv

Bibliography

Avila-Saavedra, Guillermo. "Neither Here Nor There: Consumption of U.S. Media Among Pre-Adolescent Girls in Ecuador." *Interactions: Studies in Communication & Culture* 4 (3) 2013: 255–69.

Banet-Weiser, Sarah. "'We Pledge Allegiance to Kids': Nickelodeon and Citizenship." *Nickelodeon Nation: The History, Politics, and Economics of America's Only TV Channel for Kids.* Ed. Heather Hendershot. New York: New York University Press, 2004. 209–40

Banet-Weiser, Sarah. *Kids Rule!: Nickelodeon and Consumer Citizenship.* Durham: Duke University Press, 2007a.

Banet-Weiser, Sarah. "What's Your Flava? Race and Postfeminism in Media Culture." In *Interrogating Postfeminism: Gender and the Politics of Popular Culture*, edited by Yvonne Tasker and Diane Negra, 201–226. Durham: Duke University Press, 2007b.

Barrera, Aida. *Looking for Carrascolendas: From a Child's World to Award-Winning Television*. Austin: University of Texas Press, 2001.

Beltrán, Mary. *Latina/o Stars in U.S. Eyes: The Making and Meanings of Film & TV Stardom*. Urbana-Champaign: University of Illinois Press, 2009.

Beltrán, Mary. "The Evolution of Hollywood Latinidad: Latina/o Representation and Stardom in U.S. Entertainment Media." *The International Encyclopedia of Media Studies. Vol. 3: Content and Representation*. Ed. Sharon Mazzarella. Oxford, UK: Blackwell, 2013. 205–24.

Casanova, Erynn Masi de. "Spanish Language and Latino Ethnicity in Children's Television Programs." *Latino Studies* 5 (4) 2007: 455–77.

Davis, Jeffery. *Children's Television, 1947–1990*. Jefferson, NC: McFarland & Company, Inc., 1995.

Del Barco, Mandalit. "Move Over, Dora: 'Nina's World' Brings Another Bilingual Girl to TV." *NPR*, 2015. Available at: http://www.npr.org/2015/09/25/443334527/move-over-dora-ninas-world-brings-another-bilingual-girl-to-tv

Denzel de Tirado, Heidi. "Media Monitoring and Ethnicity: Representing Latino Families on American Television (2000–2013)." *Nuevo Mundo Mundos Nuevos/New World New Worlds*, "Imágenes, memorias y sonidos/Pictures, memories and sounds." 16 December 2013. Available at: https://nuevomundo.revues.org/66165

Greene, Doyle. *Teens, TV and Tunes: The Manufacturing of American Adolescent Culture*. Jefferson, NC: McFarland, 2012.

Guidotti-Hernández, Nicole M. "Dora the Explorer, Constructing 'Latinidades' and the Politics of Global Citizenship." *Latino Studies* 5, 2007: 209–32.

Guidotti-Hernández, Nicole M. "Princess Sofia and Barack Obama: Why I Must Choose Accordingly." *The Feminist Wire*, October 23, 2013. Available at: http://thefeministwire.com/2012/10/princess-sofia-and-barack-obama-why-i-must-choose-accordingly/

Hassan, Mohamed. "Rita Moreno: 'Nina's World' Children's Show Reflects True Diversity." NBC News, 2015. Available at: http://www.nbcnews.com/news/latino/new-childrens-show-spotlights-diversity-multicultural-world-n432871

Hendershot, Heather. *Saturday Morning Censors: Television Regulation Before the V-Chip*. Durham, NC: Duke University Press, 1998.

Hendershot, Heather. "Sesame Street: Cognition and Communications Imperialism." *Kids' Media Culture*. Ed. Marsha Kinder. Durham, NC: Duke University Press, 1999. 139–76.

Hendershot, Heather. "Introduction: Nickelodeon and the Business of Fun." *Nickelodeon Nation: The History, Politics, and Economics of America's Only TV Channel for Kids*. Ed. Heather Hendershot. New York: New York University Press, 2004. 1–14.

Herrera, Isabelia. "5 Reasons You Should Revisit 'Taina,' Nickelodeon's First Latina-Led Sitcom." *Remezcla*, 13 August 2015. Available at: http://remezcla.com/lists/5-reasons-you-should-revisit-nickelodeons-taina/

Kearney, Mary Celeste (ed). *Mediated Girlhoods: New Explorations of Girls' Media Culture*. New York: Peter Lang, 2011.

Keegan, Rebecca. "Pixar's Dia de los Muertos movie a nod to Mexican audiences." *Los Angeles Times*, 22 May 2012. Available at: http://latimesblogs.latimes.com/movies/2012/05/pixars-d%C3%ADa-de-los-muertos-movie.html

Martel, Frances. "Who in the World is Carmen Sandiego? CEO, Intellectual, and America's Most Positive Latina Role Model." *The Mary Sue*, 28 February 2012. Available at: http://www.themarysue.com/carmen-sandiego-latina-role-model/

Mayland, Valen. "Carmen Sandiego Is in Your Classroom: An Idea Packet." Miami, FL: Dade Public Education Fund, 1990.

Meskill, Carla. "Where in the World of English is Carmen Sandiego?" *Simulation and Gaming* 33, 1990: 217–30.

Miller, Samuel and Michael Caley. *Where in the U.S.A. is Carmen Sandiego: Teacher's Guide*. San Rafael, CA: Broderbund Software, 1987.

Moreno, Carolina. "Sorry, Disney's New Princess Elena Probably Doesn't Count as Latina." *Huffington Post*, 29 January 2015. Available at: http://www.huffingtonpost.com/2015/01/29/ disney-elena-of-avalor-latina_n_6573968.html

Nerriccio, William. *Tex{t}-Mex: Seductive Hallucinations of the "Mexican" in America*. Austin: University of Texas, 2007.

Noriega, Chon A. and Ana M. López. *The Ethnic Eye: Latino Media Arts*. Minneapolis: University of Minnesota, 1996.

Payan, Victor. "Interview with Moctesuma Esparza: From the L.A. High School Walkouts to 'Selena' and 'The Disappearance of Garcia Lorca'". *In Motion Magazine*, 21 May 1998. Available at: http://www.inmotionmagazine.com/mesparza.html

Paxman, Andrew. "Infant Magazine Discovers New, Multiethnic Audience." *Variety* 367 (3), 19 May 1997: 43. Available at: http://connection.ebscohost.com/c/book-reviews/9706293588/ infant-mag-discovers-new-multiethnic-auds

Poblete, Juan. "U.S. Latino Studies in a Global Context: Social Imagination and the Production of In/visibility." *Works and Days* 24, 2006: 243–65.

Rivero, Yeidy. "Interpreting Cubanness, Americanness, and the Sitcom: WPBT-PBS's ¿Qué pasa U.S.A.? (1975–1980)." *Global Television Formats: Understanding Television Across Borders*. Ed. Tasha Oren and Sharon Shahaf. London: Routledge, 2011. 90–107.

Rodriguez, Cindy Y. "Disney Producer 'Misspoke': 'First Latina Princess' isn't Latina." *CNN Entertainment*, 25 October 2012. Available at: http://www.cnn.com/2012/10/25/showbiz/disney-sofia-not-latina

Rodriguez, Cindy Y. "Day of the Dead Trademark Request Draws Backlash for Disney," *CNN Entertainment*, 11 May 2013. Available at: http://www.cnn.com/2013/05/10/us/ disney-trademark-day-dead

Shamma, Tasnim. "From Ricky Ricardo to Dora: Latinos on Television." Interview with Felix Contreras. *NPR*, 11 October 2011. Available at: http://www.npr.org/2011/10/11/141054903/ from-ricky-ricardo-to-dora-latinos-on-television

Sivaramen, Aarthi. "Mattel to Tout Tweet Dora, Elmo Gloves in '09." *Campaign for a Commercial-Free Childhood*, 22 January 2009.

Steel, Emily. "'Sesame Street' to Air First on HBO for Next 5 Seasons." *The New York Times*, 13 August 2015. Available at: http://www.nytimes.com/2015/08/14/ business/media/sesame-street-heading-to-hbo-in-fall.html?mwrsm=Facebook&_r=0

Television for all Children. "TFAC is proud of its many award winning series!" *Broadcasting*, 1 January 1979. Available at: http://american radiohistory.com/Archive-BC/BC-1979/BC-1979-01-01.pdf

Texeira, Erin. 2006a. "TV for Kids Courts Spanish Speakers." *Los Angeles Times*, 28 February 2006. Available at: http://articles.latimes.com/print/2006/feb/28/entertainment/et-dora28

Texeira, Erin. 2006b. "Latino Characters Commonplace in Kids' Programs: From 'Dora' to 'Dragon Tales.'" *NBC News, Today*. 1 March 2006. Available at: http://www.today.com/id/11504591/ns/ today-today_entertainment/t/latino-characters-commonplace-kids-tv/#.Vr65K1grKJI

Thompson, Darcy A., Erica M.S. Sibinga, Jacky M. Jennings, Megan H. Bair-Merritt, and Dimitri A. Christakis. "Television viewing by young Latino children: Evidence of heterogeneity." *Archives of Pediatrics and Adolescent Medicine* 164 (2), 2011: 174–9.

Turner, Sarah E. "Disney Does Race: Black BFFS in the New Racial Moment." *Networking Knowledge* 5 (1), 2012: 125–40.

Turner, Sarah E. *The Colorblind Screen: Television in Post-Racial America*. New York: New York University Press, 2014.

U.S. Office of Education. *Carrascolendas: Evaluation of a Bilingual Television Series*. By Diana S. Natalicio and Frederick Williams, Center for Communication Research. Austin: University of Texas at Austin, 1971.

Valdivia, Angharad N. "Living in a Hybrid Material World: Girls, Ethnicity and Mediated Doll Products." *Girlhood Studies* 2 (1), 2009: 73–93.

"'Villa Alegre' Aimed at Nation's Bilingual." *The Free Lance-Star*, 22 August 1977. Available at: https://news.google.com/newspapers?nid=1298&dat=19770822&id=kd5NAAAAIBAJ&sjid=-ooDAAAAIBAJ&pg=6891,2736903&hl=en

Wells, Paul. "'Tell Me About Your ID, When You Was a Kid, Yah!': Animation and Children's Television Culture." In *Small Screens: Television for Children*, edited by David Buckingham, 61–95. London: Leicester University Press, 2002.

Westervelt, Eric. "As 'Sesame Street' Heads to HBO, Will Low-Income Kids Lose Out?" *NPR*, 13 August 2015. Available at: http://www.npr.org/sections/ed/2015/08/13/432112558/sesame-street-heads-to-hbo-is-it-a-win-win-for-kids?utm_source=facebook.com&utm_medium=social&utm_campaign=npr&utm_term=nprnews&utm_content=20150814

Woodard, IV, Emory H. *The 1999 State of Children's Television Report: Programming for Children Over Broadcast and Cable Television*. Philadelphia: The Annenberg Public Policy Center of the University of Pennsylvania, 1999.

4

BRANDING "LATINOHOOD," JUAN BOBO, AND THE COMMODIFICATION OF DORA THE EXPLORER

Cristina Rivera

We have all heard of Juan Bobo—or at least some of us in the Latino-know have. He's that well-known character from Puerto Rican folklore often associated with tricksters—think Boriqua via the African trickster's double-talk and mischievous play and you get the picture. But there is something else afoot—as Latina/o characters are seen more and more sneaking themselves into mainstream television, a commodification of a nonwhite-Spanish-speaking-community begins to discretely take away a variety that is at the heart of Latino cultures—not surprisingly, this commodification replaces our complexity with a whitewashed version of "Latinohood".

For many Latinas/os, when we look to the amount of representation there is in mainstream culture today, *Dora the Explorer* (2000–) is considered an immense milestone. Not only is it seen as a huge break for a Latina lead cartoon character to get her own show on a leading children's television network, Nickelodeon, but the show is also continuously validated for its ability to teach American (child and adult) audiences a few Spanish words, paving a path where Latinos can be looked at alongside the dominant culture. However, by immediately jumping to Dora as a prize of Latina privilege, it is easy to lose sight of what may really be hidden under her energetic and brightly colored animation (not to mention all those catchy songs). With a careful eye, I suggest that the commodification of her image is a caricature

Figure 4.1 Hi! I'm Dora and this is a version of my teenage self, that Nickelodeon decided to capitalize on since I'm hot and continue to make them money from Nickelodeon's *Dora and Friends: Into the City*

of "Latinahood" that is used to bring in profit—a seduction of Latino popularity in popular American mainstream cable, cultivated with what we might call a *pathos of representation* of Latinos (see Figure 4.1).

The history of Puerto Rican folktales, specifically Juan Bobo, presents a similar set of complicated issues, melding issues of folklore, anthropology, and narratology. But considered again, acknowledging a capitalist agenda, noting its sly positioning in American hegemonic culture, a re-reading of these characters' episodic stories reveals something more repressive and subordinate lurking there under the guise of utopian equality.

Linking Dora the Explorer with Juan Bobo presents complications as well for our notions of Latino tricksters, a frequent theme you run across in traditional Bobo folklore and Swiper's character in *Dora*. As we find ourselves at the crossroads of folktales and a dominant television program celebrity, the figuration of Latina/os in popular children's literature is something that cannot be ignored. In this chapter, I will use the term commodification as a method of analyzing representation of "Latinohood" within a dominant/dominated culture. Since "Latina/o culture" is really a mashup of a variety of several cultures, the portrayal of Dora as an ambiguous Latina character shows how a Latina/o popular children's text establishes itself as a commodity of representation—one that unfolds with a hidden agenda that is masked by a pretentious form of empowerment. So while *Dora* is often acclaimed as a kind of acme of Latino representation in mainstream television, I argue that what Dora really accomplishes is a perpetuation of stereotypes, and that these stereotypes are often overlooked when Latinos are blinded by the commodity logic of a brand culture; in short, a close study of Dora reveals a flavor of Latinidad that is easier for non-Latinas/os to swallow.

Here, a branding of sorts as defined in Sarah Bennett-Weiser's book *Authentic*™ can also be seen turning stereotypes of Latina/o bodies into backstabbing adornments of pride, as their presentation in pop culture creates a utopian hope for equal representation of Latinos. As I probe more and more into the lurking innuendos of these two Latino characters, what is found is how these characters embody an immobility for Latinos, a paralysis—stuck in a border zone, a liminality, that works toward a more counterintuitive redefinition of the Latina/o self. And although the branding of "Latinohood" can really be seen as the commodification of various Latino traditions, pop culture uses the intervention of representation merely because it is entertaining and profitable, instead of cultivating the authentic empowerment it might actually foster.

Let's begin with an allegory of sorts—a deconstruction of a pathos seamlessly woven into the vessel of American mainstream television that enters Latino households unnoticed. Here is where a simulacrum of Latino empowerment is found—all the while, what's really going on, right before our eyes, is the patent commodification of Latina/o identity via adorable (and profitable) child personages. Erin L. Ryan argues that because children are so receptive to media representations of the world, *Dora* becomes a figure of empowerment for Latina and preschool girls alike. However, the positive representation of any Latina in the media creates a sense of empowerment which promotes Dora as an acclaimed cartoon; as Ryan puts it, in these "portrayals ... (the savior vs. the damsel in distress), [Dora] ultimately functioned as the heroine" (Ryan 54).

Similar connections can be made through an examination of Puerto Rican folklore as it works to maintain historic aspects of indigenous Puerto Rican culture. In my research of Puerto Rican folklore, I discovered that these oral tales became tools of colonial influence, teaching children in Puerto Rico to read and speak English. (See Jorge Duany's "Anthropology in a Postcolonial Colony".) In this light, *Dora the Explorer* and Juan Bobo emerge as a particular strain of animated character, as Latino caricatures in mainstream television that contain cultural representations that double as a paradox waiting to be exposed— the Latino trickster's greatest flaw. This argument complicates the positive assumption made by scholars, that these characters are helping Latinos through representations in pop culture and contemporary literature, providing an avenue of empowerment for Latino children. I argue that *Dora* and Bobo work as educational stories for children but that it's more important to recognize within this placement that their space on network television is due to an ability to create profit, ignoring the negative nuances of branding culture brainwashing—interpellation at its finest. Through a Marxist lens, Latina/o children's texts become nothing more than a trademark of what it means to be Latino, defined by what sells more, which appears to be the powerless and most helpful brand of "Latinohood"—*Dora the Explorer*.

Before exposing the parallel between branding a culture and the disempowerment it actually holds for Latinas/os, I would like to briefly provide a history lesson to those who are unfamiliar with Puerto Rican folklore and the ways in which these folktales became more like heirlooms; these tales are noted to be some of the last artifacts left for the Taínos, the indigenous native peoples of Puerto Rico pre-colonization, fragments of a history communicated through an oral tradition.

Once upon a time when the Spaniards invaded Puerto Rico, they found a tribe of natives who called themselves Taíno, and they were peaceful and hospitable people who lived off the land. Historians have discovered that their folktales were told not sitting around a campfire but in forms of "epic performances" that incorporated songs, dances, and even improv (Lastra 5346). It is no wonder that the people of Puerto Rico are often associated with an intense love for rhythmic movement and dance (if you can't think of any, here's one: JLo; see Figure 4.2). Therefore, the Taínos demonstrate how a culture that does not

Figure 4.2 Jennifer Lopez (JLo) standing in as a backup dancer for her Puerto Rican pop-star husband at the time, Marc Anthony, on an episode of American Idol; article titled, "Jennifer Lopez steals the show"

privilege the written word but instead privileges performance—lessons conveyed through witty humor and on the spot explanations of common sense—at the same time, however, endangers the history and culture of a people.

When the United States called Puerto Rico its territory in 1898, there was a significant lack of literacy on the island. Since Spanish was primarily spoken due to Puerto Rico's original colonization by Spain, the unwelcomed English language found its way into the classroom primarily through translated versions of the Juan Bobo folktales. And since this paper has another focus, I will conclude this history lesson by saying that the oral tradition of performance storytelling in Puerto Rico before colonization curiously resembles the elements of *Dora the Explorer* that made "Latinohood" an attention-grabbing icon in pop/mainstream culture through non-threatening, drawn Latina/o child bodies.

Like Dora, Juan Bobo is a child character who maintains himself as an icon of a particular Latino culture. However, unlike *Dora's* more assertive and problem-solving motifs, Bobo displays a knack for following directions all too well—often leading him into trouble. Juan Bobo is known for his silly and innocent behavior which perhaps emulates the predominant stereotype of social Puerto Rican culture. Scholar Sarai Lastra claims "it is possible to argue that Puerto Rico's oral history is one that has been composed of unique, distinct and, in many cases, contradictory voices … a polyphonic society, [where] nothing conveys contradictions better than its folklore" (530). So while it might be hard to blame Bobo for making such innocent mistakes, the contradictory factor here is that adults use his stories to weave didactic lessons intended to promote independent critical thinking skills in children within a child character who cannot think for himself.

In an episode of *Dora the Explorer* entitled "A Crown for King Bobo," Dora's adventure consists of helping Prince Bobo (a now grown man who acts more childish than Dora) get his crown back before his mother's birthday. While it is hard to make hasty generalizations

Figure 4.3   King Bobo and Dora: Dora catches King Bobo with a shoe on his head which he thinks is a crown; Dora needs our help to get a real crown for King Bobo so he can attend his mother's party

about all Latino men, it is common for Latino men to respect their mother's wishes—a continuous component of the Juan Bobo stories. This episode also demonstrates how the left-alone Latino girl is responsible for the care of lost and irresponsible men (see Figure 4.3). Her ability to explore independently through her show also suggests her guardians are working, leaving her with a set of kid duties.

In the episode, King Bobo is portrayed as a silly, timid, and childish man (voiced by Cheech Marin—a casting choice that brings in a set of complications that would require a chapter of its own) who must rely on Dora—a figure of non-empowered and non-threatening "Latinohood". His royal position as a Latino, also suggests an incapability of the Latino man to complete basic tasks and ultimately hold positions of power. This docile portrayal of the Latino male character, can be seen attaching the image of a masculine Latino to a silly playful man—a commodification of a particularly docile Latino masculinity that sometimes exists within mainstream televised media. Here we see what I find to be the most disheartening aspect of the episode: the presentation of a Puerto Rican child folk character, as a man who has become too dumb to think for himself, losing sight of the innocent mistakes and pure intentions his folk tales encompassed.

Because so much is missing from the documented collections of the Juan Bobo stories that were passed down through the Puerto Rican oral storytelling tradition, it's no wonder these tales have been thought to maintain a unique picture of the Puerto Rican landscape. But with so much still missing from these stories, they also present a larger social problem— the displacement/replacement of an indigenous culture via colonization. Uniquely, I feel that the adoption of Bobo's character in the *Dora* episode works to whitewash the historical background his folktales try to maintain. As Lastra states, "to describe Juan Bobo's personality for, true to his trickster's nature, he adopts multiple voices awash in contradictions and absurdities, with plots being senseless, difficult to follow, and many times

Figure 4.4 Juan Bobo Busca Trabajo: This Juan Bobo publication (2000) suggests the colonial influence over indigenous life, where children are introduced to the ideas of the working class

leaving the audience with an open question as to who is really the fool" (543). This may also be associated with the lack of a knowable Puerto Rican heritage, which is lost from the indigenous Taíno people becoming Spanish and then Americans. Here is where we may find the trickster qualities often found in folktales emerging, as they attempt to maintain the original personality of the Puerto Rican people.

According to Lester Hyde, a "Trickster is the mythic embodiment of ambiguity and ambivalence, doubleness and duplicity, contradiction and paradox" who is able to transcend hidden boundaries and even expose them at times. As a boundary crosser, the trickster is consistently reliable for "disrupting the very thing culture is based on." However, because it appears that Taíno storytellers embodied tricksters themselves, it is significant to consider how the trickster/storyteller is able to somewhat defeat a colonial take-over through the oral tradition of the Juan Bobo stories (see Figure 4.4). Childhood becomes an ideal place where the trickster acculturates Puerto Rican culture while cleverly hiding in entertaining folk stories as colonization transpires—an attempt to keep their culture alive. In a way then, most of Bobo's published work for children can be considered a trickster's artifact, as they exhibit a sort of ambiguity and duplicity of the Puerto Rican storyteller, leaving behind stories full of contradictions and a paradox that Puerto Rican children will always remember.

In one popular tale that has now made its way into publication, *Juan Bobo Busca Trabajo,* Bobo can be seen as a trickster as he follows his mother's directions too perfectly. One example is when she gives him a sack to hold his day's pay, since he had already lost his previous wages through a hole in his pant pocket. When the farmer he works for that day gives him a pail of milk, he pours the milk into the sack (as his mother instructed him to do with that day's payment) and when he gets home, the milk has drained out of the sack. While most parents aspire to have their children follow directions, the tale complicates the child character into being one that cannot be trusted to make his/her own decisions.

The Juan Bobo books used in elementary classrooms throughout Puerto Rico work as explicit texts that tricked native Puerto Rican children into learning the language of their next colonial ruler. Here is an occasion where a trickster is found chained to a dominating figure, in which its own usefulness becomes its biggest flaw. This also reveals the establishment of a hegemonic relationship in a country where poverty prevailed; before United States colonization of Puerto Rico, it was noted that 79 percent of its population was illiterate due to the lack of books and education facilities—this is a classic move by colonizers, most expertly outlined in the late Walter Rodney's *How Europe Underdeveloped Africa*.

Of course this presented an all too easy opportunity for American influence to work its way into Puerto Rico. However, to complicate Consuelo Figueras's statement that these publications allow the oral traditions of the Puerto Rican heritage to continue, the fact remains that they have lost their true essence of performative storytelling (24). Here the transition to a Western culture illuminates how the white-washing of Puerto Rican folktales only perpetuates the dominance of white American colonial rule (and by extension, white American corporate rule)—leaving Puerto Rican citizens with a simulation of their own heritage that creates a false sense of empowerment through these printed folk stories.

Lewis Hyde, our aforementioned expert on the Trickster figure, quotes Umberto Eco to establish the workings of semiotics. This expands on the Henry Louis Gates's reading of signs and signifiers, proposing that since signs "can be taken as significantly substituting for something else ... semiotics is in principle the discipline of studying everything, *which can be used in order to lie*" (60). By establishing a Western education system that teaches children to read or watch these texts because they resemble nostalgic traits from their own heritage, this very idea of semiotics is seen in the perpetuation of a patently Western, hegemonic influence—the printing of oral traditions displaces their orality, and oddly silences them in the process. Even though these historical tales preserve the fun and entertaining qualities of oral tales told to children, they work semiotically— printed stories themselves are meant to encourage an American way of thinking and learning hidden beneath a lie of Puerto Rican originality.

Like tales of Juan Bobo, *Dora* can also be seen as a children's text, prowling within the realm of semiotic images that are dominated by stereotype images of Latinos. Here it is interesting to consider where these stereotypes hide themselves in the commodification of childhood. Within the liminal space between American commodification and childish depictions of Latino culture, a misrepresentation of Latino pride is seen coming to life through the animations of Dora and Bobo. Michael Joseph defines liminality as, "the quality of being socially segregated, set apart, and divested of status, and related to associated characteristics and qualities: indeterminacy, ambiguity, selflessness, and becomingness," which corresponds directly to my argument that Dora is arguably working against the empowerment of Latino children. Within the very essence of the Latino representation in these examples is the unavoidable classification of childhood in combination with "Latinohood". Joseph's essay defines liminal space as a supposed buffer zone for youth, where children have room to behave playfully—a space where children are able to explore normal and un-normal codes of conduct and experiment with the world around them. However, what can be found in the diplomacy of a space that requires children to express themselves also exposes a more dominating role of the adult culture that perpetuates it. This space can be seen as a sadistic way of infantilizing of children, belittling the child experience in the

Figure 4.5 Ambiguous Dora: Dora's culturally ambiguous dress that matches her culturally ambiguous Spanish dialect

separation between childhood and adulthood. The term "liminal consciousness" uncovers an interesting consideration of the adult world as it is reproduced within the child's internal and external world. Here is where the often suggested adult marginalization of childhood lies, and can once again be seen through the notion of semiotics in children's literature. Joseph claims that creating children as marginal beings is not anything new, but suggests that entertainment is the force that perpetuates childhood as a marginalized state (138–41). I suggest here that it is also a form of commodification that succeeds because of a sadistic control adults establish over children, who ultimately depend on adult care for their own preservation.

Like the widely known Nickelodeon TV series *Dora the Explorer*, which helps children learn Spanish words, Juan Bobo holds a similar task for the children of Puerto Rico. These oral tales became publications that were introduced into the classroom to teach children English after Puerto Rico became a U.S. territory. And so while these two Latino figures become characters that teach children in a way that creates a liminal space for Latino culture, their existence relies on their popularity among children. But, here's the rub: by becoming branded Latino icons of culture, we have to ask ourselves if Dora is actually hurting the Latino image she works so hard to make a place for. (See Figure 4.5.)

If we think about publications and media representations of Latinos in contemporary American society, there are not many faces that are recognized as widely as *Dora the Explorer*. With a lead female child protagonist that is brown haired, brown eyed, and of a darker complexion, it is a wonder how her character has made a place for herself. Even though *Dora the Explorer* pioneered other non-white lead character television kid shows like *Ni Hao Kai Lan*, *Maya and Miguel*, and *Sara Solves It*, the fact remains that just assuming any portrayal of anything Latino is positive is a compromise worth re-thinking. While mainstream television pats itself on the back for being diverse, what surfaces is a neoliberal sterilization of Latino ethnic difference into a brand that can be made popular and conquerable. And even though this chapter does not work to bypass the fact that Latina/o representation in mainstream television is anything short of validation and recognition, but to acknowledge that in our repeating of representation in pop culture, there is still a racial profiling of Latinos that simultaneously works to repress—ignorance is bliss as we allow ourselves as versions of "Latinohood" to be swept together into a pile called "One Brown Girl=All Hispanics"—because somehow Latinos are still all the same.

While nothing really beats the milestone *Dora the Explore* as a pop icon in the child and family community being watched by viewers of all colors and backgrounds, it is clear that these popular images still subvert the unique qualities each culture can bring to the table, branding them into a category that can be mass produced, that at the same time promotes an almost lazy understanding of the Latino community. And as I must regretfully admit, upon discovering Juan Bobo's appearance in *Dora the Explorer* (finally a nostalgic part of my own Puerto Rican tradition up for America to see), it was easy to confuse feelings of pride with those of compromise in allowing a tragic misrepresentation of a folk character that means so much to the Puerto Rican culture. Presented within the delightfulness of a non-normative representation in pop culture suggests that submission to the dominant mainstream American culture, losing individual variations of Latino heritage, is still more prevalent in the *Dora* brand of Latinos than asking "What Spanish-speaking country does Dora actually come from?"

Bibliography

"A Crown for King Bobo." *Dora the Explorer*. Nickelodeon. 3 Oct. 2005. Television.

Banet-Weiser, Sarah. *Authentic TM: The Politics and Ambivalence in a Brand Culture*. New York: New York University Press, 2012. E-Book.

Duany, Jorge. "Anthropology in a Postcolonial Colony: Helen I. Safa's Contribution to Puerto Rican Ethnography," *Journal of Caribbean Studies*, 38 (2), 2010: 33–57.

Figueras, Consuelo. "Puerto Rican Children's Literature." *Bookbird* 38 (2), 2000: 23.

Hernandez, Roberto. *Nuevos Cuentos De Juan Bobo*. 1st ed. San Juan, Puerto Rico: Yaurel, 1987.

Hyde, Lewis. *Trickster Makes This World: Mischief, Myth, and Art*. New York: Farrar, Straus and Giroux, 1998.

Joseph, Michael. "Liminality." *Keywords for Children's Literature*. Eds. Lissa Paul and Philip Nel. New York: New York University Press, 2011. 138–141.

Lastra, S. "Juan Bobo: A Folkloric Information System," *Library Trends*, 47(3), 1999: 529–57.

Rodney, Walter. *How Europe Underdeveloped Africa*. Washington, DC: Howard University Press, 1974.

Ryan, Erin. "Dora the Explorer: Empowering Preschoolers, Girls, and Latinas," *Journal of Broadcasting & Electronic Media* 54(1), 2010: 54–68.

5

CANTA Y NO LLORES

Life and Latinidad in Children's Animation

Laura Fernández

That Latina/os are here in the U.S. to stay and are a major force (politically, economically, and socio-culturally) is by now a well-established fact. However, despite the obviousness of such a statement, representations of Latinidad in popular media forms are still limited. While figures such as Shakira, Jennifer Lopez, Sofía Vergara, and Pitbull are now mainstream celebrities, they cater towards a more PG-13 audience than anything else. Latina/o representations for children are still severely limited almost exclusively to popular images such as Dora. But that is not to say that there are no bright spots in pop culture for Latinidad. One such example is Jorge Gutiérrez's vibrantly animated movie, *The Book of Life* (2014).

The Book of Life is worth analyzing because, for a relatively short film, the depth and complexity Gutiérrez manages to convey is astounding. The animation work itself is worth examining (and earned itself a Golden Globe nomination for Best Animated Feature Film), though it is not the primary focus of this chapter. Instead, the main focus of this chapter will be to analyze why the representations of Latinidad work in the film. It is easy to criticize popular depictions of "authentic" Latina/o culture as clichéd, stereotypical, or even racist (here's looking at you, *Dora the Explorer*), however, that is not to say that "good" representations cannot be achieved. *The Book of Life* is able to transcend its cultural restrictions: it is a film about Mexican culture that can be consumed by a wider non-Latina/o audience as well. Through a combination of stunning visual images, "Latinized" pop culture references, and an abundance of Mexican cultural references, the film manages to highlight Mexican culture— marking it as the center of the film's universe—without being too over-the-top. Although the film is not perfect—it does fall prey to depicting the "generic Latino" image that writers such as Erynn Masi de Casanova criticize in other representations of Latinidad in children's television, and casts the Alabama-born native, Channing Tatum, to voice one of the film's secondary leads—what the film gets right compensates for its pitfalls. As has been argued (by both Casanova and Philip Serrato) about Gutiérrez's short-lived animated series *El Tigre: The Adventures of Manny Rivera*, *The Book of Life* is unashamedly Mexican; it slaps you in the face with Mexican culture and does not apologize for it, which is what helps to make it great.

It is a film that also manages to transcend its cultural boundaries through its use of metanarrative—the central "Mexican" plot line is a story told within the "real" narrative of the film. By creating this story-within-a-story, the film is able to use Mexican folklore to reach youths who normally are overlooked, which I argue is symbolic of a bigger problem that the film is subtly able to address: the plight of Latina/o children in education. By addressing these "problematic" children and giving them a message of hope—the final line of the film fittingly is "Write your own story"— it provides a message about how Latina/o youths, who are statistically more likely not to finish schooling than either black or white children (Synder and Dillow, 8), can overcome the adversity they face by writing their own life story and challenging the social narrative set up for them. Through Mexican culture, the film is able to instruct children (both within the context of the film and without) about the values of life, death, and self-acceptance. But before one can look at why the film works in today's society, it is important to take a look back at how Latinidad has been animated.

Latinidad in Animated Media

The role Latina/os have played in animated media is minimal when compared to the relative mass of options available through network television and film. The most popular television series for kids that figures a Latin protagonist is the long-running *Dora the Explorer* (2000–). Though well-intentioned, *Dora* is problematic because the show, created by an all-Anglo team, is not meant for Latina/o audiences, but to teach simple Spanish phrases leading to "a general representation of Spanish as a tool that can be used by anyone in specific situations to achieve a desired result, what I call an instrumental conception of language" (Casanova, 36). Thus, the Spanish language is incorporated into the dialogue of the show as a means to an end, not for its cultural value. Dora herself is representative of the "generic Latino," as one spokesperson for Nickelodeon stated in an interview: "She was developed to be pan-Latina to represent the diversity of Latino cultures" (Friedman 2010). However, by creating one "pan-Latina" representation of Latinidad, what the show in effect has done is set a precedent for spin-offs and copycat programs to emulate (Casanova, 34). Moreover, it creates an amalgamation of nationally specific cultural symbols and representations, thereby eliminating the ethnic and geographical differences that are inherent to the Latina/o population (36). By not defining Dora's cultural heritage, the show is implying that it is irrelevant because clearly there are no differences between Latina/o groups (obviously because we are all Mexicans or something), so why specify?

That is not to say that *Dora* and shows of that ilk are the only ones out there, they just so happen to be the ones that have managed to survive the longest—other shows such as *El Tigre: The Adventures of Manny Rivera*, *¡Mucha Lucha!*, and *Maya and Miguel* only managed to run for a few years at most, with *El Tigre* only running from 2007 to 2008 (Serrato, 72). And unfortunately the one show created by Latina/os, *El Tigre* (created by Jorge Gutiérrez and Sandra Equiha) had the shortest shelf life. Much like *The Book of Life*, *El Tigre* was a show that embraced its Mexicanness (not surprising given that both were created by the same team of writers and animators). Unlike *Dora*, the creators of *El Tigre* were not afraid to celebrate the fact that not all Latina/os are the same. In doing so, it could be argued that the show might have put off potential viewers who were not intimately aware of Mexican culture, and yet it did so anyway and managed to provide "a unique expression of an encounter with Latinidad. For instance, rather than fear or temper ethnic difference … *El Tigre* foregrounds it. Characters speak English with noticeable accents … Moreover, staples of Mexican folk culture … saturate the mise-en-scène in ever episode, creating an extensive weave of cultural signifiers" (Serrato, 72). The show was unafraid to embrace the cultural heritage near and dear to the creators (both Gutiérrez and Equiha were born and raised in Mexico), even if such an emphasis on Mexican culture could have been perceived as off-putting. It is fitting that a creative team that was so successful at creating a show that captured Latinidad without sugar-coating it, is also behind a film that manages to use its emphasis on Latinidad to reach a universal audience, as they do in *The Book of Life*.

But it is not just television that is wanting in diversity; animated films have also lacked a Latina/o presence. Although there has been a longer presence of Latinidad in animated film, with some of the earliest work being Walt Disney's *Saludos Amigos* and its follow-up *The Three Caballeros* (released in 1942 and 1944 respectively), those early films can be seen as part of the larger World War II policy towards Latin America, as demonstrated by Franklin D. Roosevelt's Good Neighbor Policy (Adams, 290; Glik, 2374). In those early depictions, Latina/os are presented as non-threatening, and Latin America provides a tropical paradise for its audiences to escape to. And despite the fact that more than 60 years have passed since then, very little has changed. More contemporary films such as *The Road to El Dorado* (2000), the *Shrek* series (2004–2010) and its spin-off *Puss in Boots* (released in 2011), and *Rio* (2011) and its sequel *Rio 2* (released in 2014), appropriate Latinidad for its ethnic flair while sticking to tried and true stereotypes of Latina/o culture.

The Road to El Dorado, which is an attempt to rewrite the history of the Spanish Conquest, still holds on to the view of the New World Natives as primitive peoples who look upon "Spanish" (white) characters—voiced by Kevin Kline and Armand Assante—as gods, and thereby changes nothing (Hoult-Saros, 148). The character of "Puss in Boots" from the *Shrek* films, voiced by Spanish actor Antonio Banderas, though a new spin on the Zorro figure, remains at heart the quintessential Latin lover stereotype who is also "guilty of treachery, ruthlessness, catnip smuggling, an occasionally ambiguous sexuality ... , and that time-honored Latina/o movie crime, difficulty controlling his emotions" (144). The *Rio* films differ because they are among the few examples of Brazilians in animated pop culture. And yet, despite their good intentions (and Brazilian director and writer Carlos Saldanha), in the *Rio* films, Brazil is depicted as a country of contradictions and stark contrasts: samba and Carnaval are pitted against poverty and corruption: "Brazil reveals itself to Blu and to the viewer as a land of extremes: natural beauty and a vibrant culture contrast with dirty streets and a vile underworld of humans" (Hoult-Saros, 156). Though *Rio 2* takes the action out of the city and back to the cultural roots of Brazil, perceived to be in the Amazon, the focus is still primarily on showcasing a samba-filled way of life. Moreover, in films meant to capture Brazilian culture, their authenticity is called into question by their casting choices. The two main characters Blu and Jewel, who are meant to be representative of "Brazil," are in fact voiced by two Anglo-Americans: Jesse Eisenberg and Anne Hathaway who speak little to no Portuguese in the films. Though there are a few Brazilian voice actors in the cast, they are relegated to minor roles and do not sing, despite one of them being a famed bossa nova singer in Brazil.

Though obviously not a complete list, it is among this limited canon of animated media that *The Book of Life* finds itself. Though seemingly hyper-critical, my point is not to nay-say what has come before and hold up *The Book of Life* as a shining beacon of Latinidad amidst the darkness of the past. No, instead my point is to highlight the past as a foundation for Latina/o images in animation—it has to start somewhere—and show its possibilities through more recent examples such as *The Book of Life*.

These Kids Matter Too

As I have stated before, *The Book of Life* is a film that is centered on Mexican culture—however, that is not all. The "Mexican part" of the film is relayed as a story told to a young audience. The audience (both within the narrative of the film and without) is worth mentioning, first because it is something that critics most often overlook when reviewing the film. Though it is true that the scenes involving the "detention kids" are more of a backdrop to the film's main plotline, and are interwoven throughout the film as a side commentary as the story unfolds, the little information garnered from those scenes is still important to note.

The film begins with the elderly museum tour guide, Thomas, waiting for the next group of kids to arrive and remarks, "I wonder why nobody wants them?" (*The Book of Life*). His confusion quickly turns into apprehension as he sees a bus pull up, and a group of rowdy children greet him. Thomas is visibly shaking at this point, clearly dreading having to deal with these problematic children who obviously do not want to be there: "A museum, *again?*" one child exclaims in disgust (*The Book of Life*). Thomas is quickly saved from these little monsters by the arrival of another tour guide, Mary Beth, who takes over, though Thomas is hesitant to leave her alone: "Are you sure? I think these are the detention kids," he whispers to her as if it is some sort of nasty secret that can put her off, to which she blithely responds that she can handle them (*The Book of Life*). As she leads the group, she veers off to the side, to show them a secret part of the museum because "You're not like the other kids. Oh no, no, no *you* need to see something *special*" (*The Book of Life*). In this very short exchange, which takes up only the first two minutes of the film, the writers are already setting these children apart. They are the "detention kids" who can cause old men to shiver in fear, and yet as Mary Beth points out, they deserve to be a part of something special.

Thomas's response to these kids can be seen as dramatic, and yet it is not too far off from how society views at-risk children in general. Although the children appear to be, for the most part, racially white, they are in fact an ethnically diverse bunch. In designing the look for these children, Gutiérrez writes, "Each of the kids is inspired by a different part of the world. Sanjay is Indian American, Goth kid is Mexican American, Sasha is Russian American, Jane is Chinese American, Joao is Brazilian American" (*Art*, 186). And yet despite such diversity, the role these characters play is largely ignored. Reviewers of the film give them passing mentions—often referring to them collectively as "raucous" or "rebellious" (Moore 2014; Berkshire 2014)—and then move on to the "main" story revolving around the love triangle between Manolo, María, and Joaquín. Although playing seemingly minimal roles, without their presence, the alleged main story would not be told. And the story chosen by Mary Beth (who is later revealed to be La Muerte in disguise) is selected in order to give these children a message of hope.

At the film's conclusion, when the security guard reveals himself to be the god Xibalba and remarks on the passion with which La Muerte (his wife) told the story, she explains, "Anyone can die, these kids will have the courage to *live*" (*The Book of Life*). La Muerte selects the story of Manolo, María, and Joaquín in order to give these children a more positive outlook on life. Whereas society may tell them they will never succeed, or look down on them (or even fear them, as in the case of Thomas), the film sets up a safe space for these children to learn and develop their own self-awareness. Manolo, La Muerte's champion, overcame his family's demands to be "true Sánchez man" and "wrote his own story" which in the end was what allowed him to defeat the many battles he had to face. By presenting an imperfect protagonist—Manolo is a reluctant matador whose soft heart is more focused on singing songs than killing bulls—La Muerte demonstrates how one's social expectations are not set in stone. These children may be "problematic" but that does not mean that they cannot achieve great things in their lives. In a society where children of color (specifically Latina/os) are more than three times as likely to drop out of high school as white children (the drop out rate for Latina/o children is 12.7%, 7.5% for black children, and 4.3% for white children (Snyder and Dillow, 217)), providing a mixed-race audience with a message affirming their own agency is very powerful. Moreover, it is a universal message set against a very Mexican backdrop. As Gutiérrez states about his film: "I felt even though *The Book of Life* takes place in Mexico, and even though technically all of these characters are Mexican, I'm going to tell a story that has a universal appeal by keeping the emotions really grounded" (Amidi 2015). In doing so, the film is able to add a positive image of Latinidad within animated media.

A New Spin on Latinidad

What is so refreshing about Gutiérrez's film is that it is so unapologetically Mexican. And despite the abundance of references, it is only a small glimpse into Mexican culture, as Gutiérrez states in one interview: "In the movie, I show you what I think are a hundred of the thousands and thousands of ideas of what a Mexican is" (Amidi 2015). Moreover, the movie does not try to claim itself as *the* picture of Mexico, "This is not a documentary, this is my magic version of Mexico" (Amidi 2015). The film stems from Gutiérrez's love of his native country and it shows itself in the beauty and intricacy he managed to weave into every scene of the film.

Before proceeding, I feel that I have to address the Channing Tatum-sized elephant in the room: a white American is chosen to voice one of the film's three main leads—the horror! Although critics can point to the casting of Channing Tatum as evidence of the film's inauthenticity (Berkshire 2014), this is one small detail which is quickly overlooked as the film develops. Moreover, in interviews Tatum gave about having to play a Latina/o character and how he decided to play the part, he responds that he played it as himself because that was the whole point, he was simply meant to play himself: he is not of Mexican descent, so why fake it? In one interview he quips, "I really relied heavily on my own Mexican culture and heritage—I'm kidding, that was a joke!—I mean, I think I always heard about Day of the Dead, but being an American kid from the South, I really didn't know anything about the Mexican culture, and this was an education" (Valdez 2014). Moreover, by choosing an ethnically diverse cast Gutiérrez is able to make the film more readily accessible to other cultures, "it was a conscious choice for a lot of the characters to not sound so ethnic. You feel everyone can relate to the story, not just someone from that background" (Tatum 2014). Moreover, those involved with the film all defend Gutiérrez's casting choice. For instance, Diego Luna, the Mexican-born actor behind the voice of Manolo, argues in one interview against the need for an all-Latina/o cast:

> I think the only thing that has a specific context is the story. But those who tell the story should come from as diverse world as possible. The richness can come from that. I never question who's telling the story and where they are from … There was no prejudice around this casting, that everyone had to be Mexican or that no one had to be Mexican to make it work in the general market. What is very nice is that mixture Jorge created, that mixture of voices, accents and energy … It's all a result of the stubbornness and craziness of our director that never allowed any cliché, any prejudice to run this film.
> (Luna 2014)

It is exactly Gutiérrez's dedication to the film, a project he had spent 14 years working to realize (Gutiérrez: "How" 2014) that allows the beauty of Mexican culture to shine through.

The film is unique in that, although it is heavily influenced by Mexican culture, it is also a hybrid of Mexican and U.S. pop culture. The songs used throughout the film are a combination of Mexican classics such as "Cielito Lindo," with Mexican rock songs such as the song "Más" by Kinky, and U.S. rock, indie, hip hop, and pop songs. Despite a heavy influence from U.S. music, the songs that Gutiérrez takes from U.S. pop culture are adapted and given a new "norteño" twist. The adaptation of classic songs such as Elvis Presley's "Can't Help Falling in Love," or Biz Markie's "Just a Friend," with norteño music, described as "North American border music, or Tex-Mex music, or Chicano music, or cantina (bar) music" (82) by Gloria Anzaldúa, shows how music transcends cultural borders. When asked why he incorporated these songs into the film, Gutiérrez responded by saying, "all these songs had a personal meaning to me. And I grew up on the border so it's not like I only listened to Mexican music. I listened to music from all over the world … I'm Mexican. That doesn't mean I can't like other things" (Amidi 2015).

Gutiérrez is not one to apologize for how his film can be interpreted as cultural appropriation. He states: "this is my personal version of Mexico. So, if anybody has a problem with it, it shouldn't be a problem with Mexico, it should be a problem with me. It's coming from an honest, truthful place. These are things that I lived and experienced. If someone's going to tell me that I'm appropriating my own culture, yes. This is who I am" (Gutiérrez "How" 2014). Just as he did in his animated show *El Tigre*, Gutiérrez's conflation of Mexican music styles with North American pop culture "betrays a Latino/a cultural grounding at the same time that it asserts non-Latino/a influences … creates an imaginative space for intertextual, cross-cultural play" (Serrato, 76). Here again is present Gutiérrez's stance on "an unwillingness to downplay or otherwise neutralize differential Latino/a cultural elements" (77). Those critical of the film picked up on this, and demonstrated in their attacks their own ignorance of what Gutiérrez was trying to achieve with the film.

In one negative review of the film, the writer criticizes the artwork of the film as being too flamboyant and too focused on El Día de los Muertos and argues that other adaptations of the holiday, like *The Corpse Bride*, got it right: "the main characters look like puppets … Gutiérrez modeled so much of the film on traditional Day of the Dead artwork. The characters are covered with brightly colored details that quickly become distracting." For "Corpse Bride," designer Carlos Grangel drew on Day of the Dead imagery more effectively" (Solomon 2014). What the reviewer does not realize is that the film's reliance on "traditional Day of the Dead artwork" is what makes it an authentic representation of El Día de los Muertos, even more so than a film produced and directed by U.S.-born Tim Burton, strangely enough. Furthermore, Gutiérrez's use of "brightly colored details" is strategic:

A standard frame for us was busy and baroque, so we had to really help the audience focus where they're supposed to look … . we used the chaos to help you guide your eye. Same thing with color: if it was all colorful the whole time, I think your brain would explode. So we had all these desaturated moments … all these moments with no color to balance things out.

(Amidi 2015)

Additionally, the characters look like puppets because they are; Gutiérrez used carved wooden models of the main characters in order to link the story to a folkloric past, because as he states in one interview, "I like folk art … . I'm going to give you an artisan's version of Mexican history and Mexican revolution" (Gutiérrez: "How" 2014).

Instead of over-the-top, I see the Mexican influences as a celebration of a culture that is often negatively stereotyped, and this was part of Gutiérrez's motivation in making the film:

> There's goodness in this idea that I get to pass on to non-Latino people and non-Hispanics. They need to know what's happening out there. We live in such troubled times and Mexico is notorious in the news for really bad things. This is a huge reminder that there's beautiful stuff down there too. There's a beautiful country that should not be remembered for the bad stuff.
>
> (Gutiérrez: "How" 2014)

The film is a lighthearted attempt at showcasing Mexican culture, something that is sorely lacking in mainstream American culture. From sugar skulls to churros, to a priest who turns out to be a lucha libre fighter, to mustaches and sombreros, the film draws on "stereotypical" iconography to present an image of Mexican culture that is not afraid to showcase its inherent Latinidad.

Conclusion

The history of Latina/o characters in animated media has been a mixed bag of good and bad. With *The Book of Life*, director Jorge Gutiérrez presents us with a film about death that helps to teach its audiences an important message about life. The film starts by presenting the audience with a group of "troubled" youths who are meant to be feared, and ends by giving those same children the hope that life is what they make of it, not what is said of them. In a society where children of color are racially targeted and less likely to finish school, a message that they can become what *they* want and not what *society* says they will be is extremely important (and not a topic that Dora will ever talk about). And so the film has a two-fold value: elevating the status of children of color, while highlighting the cultural beauty of Latinidad.

Gutiérrez's take on El Día de los Muertos is a refreshing view of Latinidad because it does not try to be something it is not. It does not try to box in Latinidad as something pan-ethnic, nor does it erase the national ties Latina/os have to their native cultures. It is a film specifically about Mexican culture and history and does not let the viewer forget it—it goes as far as making the center of the universe (shaped, of course, like a sombrero) land in the heart of Mexico (which has a large mustache stamped across it). And yet it still manages to reach a universal audience. What is more universal than death? One need not be Mexican to understand the importance of living the life of one's choosing, the remembrance and celebration of lost loved ones, and even women's rights (symbolized by the free-spirited María Posada). Gutiérrez was able to make a film that in its essence is a very dark and heavy topic (death), and turn it into something that children can understand and even laugh at (at one point the "Goth" listening to the tale quips "What is it with Mexicans and death?!" (*The Book of Life*)). In effect, what Gutiérrez manages to present is a border film: a film that can authentically speak to Latina/o audiences and celebrate Latinidad, while at the same time find itself at home in the U.S.

Bibliography

Adams, Dale. "Saludos Amigos: Hollywood and FDR's Good Neighbor Policy." *Quarterly Review of Film and Video* 24:3 (2007): 289–295.

Amidi, Amid. "Jorge Gutierrez on 'The Book of Life' and Bringing Mexico to Hollywood." *Cartoon Brew*, 6 January 2015.

Anzaldúa, Gloria. *Borderlands/La Frontera: The New Mestiza*. 2nd ed. San Francisco: Aunt Lute Books, 1987.

Berkshire, Geoff. Review of *The Book of Life*, dir. Jorge R. Gutiérrez. *Variety*, 11 October 2014.

The Book of Life. Dir. Jorge R. Gutiérrez. 20th Century Fox, 2014.

Casanova, Erynn Masi de. "Representing Latinidad in Children's Television: What Are the Kids Watching?" *Latinos and American Popular Culture*. Ed. Patricia M. Montilla. Santa Barbara: Praegar, 2013. 21–47.

Friedman, Emily. "Is Dora the Explorer an Illegal Immigrant?" *ABC News*, 21 May 2010.

Glik, Sol. "Yes, Tenemos bananas: Construcciones de género y raza en los estereotipos plasmados por Hollywood (1930–1955)." *XIV Encuentro de Latinoamericanistas Españoles: Congreso Internacional*, eds. Rey Tristán and Patricia Calvo González. Santiago de Compostela: Centro Interdisciplinario de Estudios Americanistas Gumersindo Busto, 2010. 2371–2384.

Gutiérrez, Jorge R. *Art of The Book of Life*. Milwaukee: Dark Horse Books, 2014.

Gutiérrez, Jorge R. Interview by Jorge Carreón. "How the Director Jorge R. Gutierrez Based 'The Book of Life' on His Own Life." *Desde Hollywood Movie News*. Desde Hollywood, 17 October 2014.

Hoult-Saros, Stacy. "Say Hello to My Little Friends: Nonhumans as Latinos in U.S. Feature Films for Children." *Latinos and American Popular Culture*, ed. Patricia M. Montilla. Santa Barbara: Praegar, 2013. 135–160.

Luna, Diego. Interview by Jorge Carreón. "Why Diego Luna is Singing his Praises of 'The Book of Life.'" *Desde Hollywood Movie News*. Desde Hollywood, 16 October 2014.

Moore, Roger. "'Book of Life' Toons into Mexican Culture." *The Courier-Journal*, 16 October 2014.

Serrato, Phillip. "Postmodern Guacamole: Lifting the Lid on *El Tigre: The Adventures of Manny Rivera*." *Latinos and Narrative Media: Participation and Portrayal*, ed. Frederick Luis Aldama. New York: Palgrave Macmillan, 2013. 71–84.

Solomon, Charles. "Too Much and Too Little in Overwrought, Mexican-themed 'Book of Life.'" Review of *The Book of Life*, dir. Jorge R. Gutiérrez. *Los Angeles Times*, 16 October 2014.

Synder, Thomas D. and Sally A. Dillow. *Digest of Education Statistics: 2013*. NCES 2015-011. United States Department of Education: National Center for Education Statistics. Washington, DC: Institute of Education Sciences, 2015.

Tatum, Channing. Interview by Jorge Carreón. "Channing Tatum on Becoming Captain Latin America in 'The Book of Life.'" *Desde Hollywood Movie News*. Desde Hollywood, 16 October 2014.

Valdez, Maria G. "'The Book of Life' Cast: Channing Tatum Opens Up About 'Día de los Muertos' and Playing a Latino Character." *Latin Times*, 17 October 2014.

6

BEYOND THE "DIGITAL DIVIDE" AND LATINA/O POP

Kathryn M. Frank

"Digital media" is a category with numerous possible classifications and historical lineages. When we discuss the intersections of digital media and popular culture, we could focus on many different fields and technological changes: digital filmmaking and special effects, the disruption of the recording industry by MP3s and music downloading, online streaming of television and film, or myriad other examples. In order to best focus on the intersections of Latina/o popular culture and digital media, this chapter will focus on those digital media that have been enabled by the rise of the internet, personal computing, and mobile internet usage (smartphones and tablets). These are areas in which U.S. Latina/os' production and consumption are particularly notable, as data have shown they tend to keep pace with or surpass their white counterparts. Additionally, while digital technologies in production and distribution are crucial, crises in the music, film, and TV industries have been well documented. Scholars have examined the contributions of Latina/os in these areas, such as Robert Rodríguez's digital filmmaking (Berg 2009; Aldama 2015a, 2015b) and Spanish-language television and newspapers' foray into digital distribution (Piñon and Rojas 2011).

However, most of what has been studied in the area of Latina/os and digital media has focused on how Latina/os use internet and mobile technology; these studies have infrequently addressed questions posed by qualitative-oriented scholars of race as to how cyberspace has or has not changed how race is articulated and represented. Even within these studies of online racial formations, Latina/os are infrequently mentioned. Lisa Nakamura's invocation of Gloria Anzaldúa's *mestiza* consciousness as anathema to the forced racial/ethnic identification of check boxes and drop-down menus is a prominent theorization of Latinidad online, and even so, is not primarily concerned with how Latina/os represent themselves in cyberspace (Nakamura 2002: 113). If the internet, as many digital media scholars have theorized, is a form or extension of the public sphere, and is a space where individuals and communities may be connected across geographic and temporal boundaries

(Castells 2000; Calhoun 1992; Edgerly et al. 2009), how are Latina/os fitting in to this space? Or, if as other scholars have suggested, the online sphere is largely similar to other media industries, where major corporations dominate production and distribution and exploit the labor of users and engineers (Gerhards and Schafer 2010; Sparks 2001), how have Latina/os bought in to or challenged this system?

This chapter brings these approaches into conversation, and examines three lenses through which Latina/o popular digital media can be understood to construct and/or challenge ideas of what it means to be Latina/o in the United States. The United States context, while certainly not the only important site for Latina/o digital media creation and consumption, is a rich and complex field that is growing and has yet to be examined in depth, and as such will be this chapter's focus. How are we seeing Latina/os participate and create online? How are these Latina/o pop culture texts reifying or challenging particular notions of what it means to be Latina/o in a U.S. context? Have Latina/os been able to access and utilize these technologies to "break into" media to a larger degree than U.S. film or television?

While uses of digital media for health and educational outcomes, as well as for social movements, have been well documented, the consumption, production, and distribution of digital entertainment media among Latina/os has been less documented. This chapter offers case studies in three areas of digital Latina/o popular culture: construction and consumption of Latina/o online stars, uses of digital media and user-produced content by "traditional" Latino media outlets, and the uses of digital popular media to define, expand, appropriate, and/or delineate expressions of "Latinidad"[1] in an American context.

Latina/os and Digital Media: Contexts and Approaches

According to a 2013 survey by the Pew Hispanic Center (Lopez 2013), Latina/os in the U.S. have been rapidly closing the so-called "digital divide;" while in 2007, Latina/os used the internet at a significantly lower rate than their white counterparts, in 2013 Pew found that 78 percent of Latina/o adults reported using the internet "at least occasionally," compared to 87 percent of whites. Pew also found that Latina/o adults were just as likely or more likely than white or black adults to own a smartphone, and more likely than white internet users to access the internet from their phones. These percentages were highest among English-dominant, young, and U.S.-born Latina/os. However, Latina/os are still less likely than whites to own a laptop or desktop computer (Lopez et al. 2013). Digital network MiTú, whose efforts in producing Latina/o media across platforms will be discussed in this chapter, reported in a presentation at Social Media Week Los Angeles that Latina/os are more active users and consumers of YouTube and Twitter than their white counterparts, and that "40% of the top 30 Viners[2] are Hispanic" (Hamedy 2015).

Although internet usage by U.S. Latina/os is highest among those who are young, English-dominant, and born in the United States, studies of Latina/os and digital media have largely focused on usage by and outreach to Latina/os who are less likely to use the internet or own a smartphone. Studies on the use of digital media among Latina/o families, including children "translating" digital media for Spanish-dominant family members (Fuller et al. 2015; McDevitt and Sindorf 2014), have illuminated both structural barriers to internet use and strategies used by immigrants to access online content. Immigration activism, particularly by youth, has also been a prominent area of study in Latina/o use of digital media, challenging claims that the millennial generation is apolitical or uses social media in lieu of political activism (Martínez 2011; Costanza-Chock 2011). One study by Teresa Correa and Sun Ho Jeong examined digital content creation by youth of color, including Latina/o youth. Correa and Jeong found that for these young people, connecting with identity communities was a paramount motivation for creating content (Correa and Jeong 2011: 653–654). Correa and Jeong also found that youth of color are more likely to participate in online content creation than their white peers. This study, which employs a quantitative uses and gratifications model, addresses the motivations for content creation, but does not address what kinds of content youth are creating and how they are expressing Latinidad, or what kind of digital media Latina/o youth may be seeking out online.

The digital media most used by Latina/os in the U.S.—entertainment media—has not been as widely examined. This chapter focuses on the Latina/o digital popular media that are most visible and most likely to be created, viewed, and disseminated among "majority" U.S. Latina/os internet users: content that is accessible on (or even designed for) smartphones, content that is directed at young people, and English-language Latina/o media content. The cases examined in this chapter illustrate potential approaches to understanding Latina/o pop culture in digital spaces such as YouTube, blogs, and online entertainment news sites. These platforms and others like them represent a significant portion of online traffic, and a major site for the construction, circulation, and contestation of Latinidad—what it means to be Latina/o and what constitutes Latina/o culture and identity—for U.S. Latina/os.

Mobilizing Latina/o Identities to Create Personal Brands

Latina/os in both the U.S. and in Latin America have used digital media, particularly user-produced content hosting spaces such as YouTube and blogs, to construct star personas and personal brands. These stars have promoted and downplayed their Latina/o identities in strategic ways in order to cultivate dedicated online followings as well as "break in" to more traditional media and marketing outlets (including television, publishing, and advertising). Gossip blogger Perez Hilton and makeup and beauty expert Dulce Candy represent two cases of Latina/os who have successfully parlayed their interests and identities into personal brands and star personas. Both Hilton and Candy emphasize their Latina/o identities in order to promote images of themselves as family-oriented, personable, and relatable, and use these aspects to deflect criticism that they "whitewash" their appearances and speech in order to be more appealing to white audiences.

Perhaps the most famous Latino digital media star is gossip writer Perez Hilton, whose celebrity news and sarcastic critiques have made him an international star. Mario Lavandeira, Jr., a Cuban American writer and aspiring actor, started his gossip blog as a way to be "closer to celebrity culture." Originally titled PageSixSixSix.com, referencing famous gossip column Page Six as well as alluding to the sarcastic and critical tone of the site's commentary, the popular site (and Lavandeira himself) eventually adopted the moniker Perez Hilton. The pseudonym references socialite Paris Hilton, a popular subject (or target) of gossip columns for her party-heavy lifestyle and seemingly vapid personality, as well as Lavandeira's Latino heritage. Hilton's website describes him as a "Cubano and Miami native," quotes the *Los Angeles Times* calling him a "…sweet yet snarky, sagacious yet salacious gay man," and notes various awards he has won: "Perez was named the #1 Web Celeb for 2007, 2008, and 2009 by *Forbes Magazine* and has recently been tapped as one of the 15 most influential Hispanics in the U.S. by *People in Espanol* [sic] and named 2009 Hispanic of the Year by *Hispanic Magazine*" (Hilton, n.d.).

Hilton has drawn criticism for seeming to disparage other celebrities of color, and downplay his Latino identity in favor of a "mainstream" gay identity. Hilton has been criticized for comments that suggest that homophobia is worse than racism, and that his own gay identity is more important than his Cuban American or Latino identity. For instance, Hilton directed a homophobic slur at rapper/producer will.i.am after Hilton claimed that he was physically attacked by will.i.am's associate. Hilton described contemplating retaliating with a racial slur, but deciding against it as a homophobic slur was "so much worse" and thus more hurtful than a racial slur. Hilton also received criticism for his online arguments with Azealia Banks, a black, queer-identified rapper. Hilton objected to Banks's use of the word "f*g," while Banks argued that among the black community, the word has a different connotation and is taken as a general insult rather than a homophobic slur. In contrast to his downplaying of racial or ethnic identity when it comes to discussing LGBT issues, Hilton has embraced his Latino identity to portray the "softer" side of his acerbic persona (Abcarian 2015). After the birth of his son in 2013, Hilton posted videos of his mother singing lullabies in Spanish to the baby, and discussed the importance of teaching his son Spanish in interviews. He also went on both English- and Spanish-language television shows and magazines to discuss what being a Latino father means to him (HuffPost Latino Voices 2013). Hilton made similar appearances after the birth of his daughter in 2015 (*Fox News Latino* 2013).

Mexican American beauty expert Dulce "Dulce Candy" Ruiz has similarly balanced both Latino and "mainstream" appeal. Like Perez Hilton, Dulce Candy adopted a persona that incorporates both English and Spanish; Hilton's chosen moniker connotes glamor and superficiality with a Latino twist, while Candy's suggests a Latina-inflected sweetness and femininity. Candy, whose website describes her as a "mommy, huge dreamer, war veteran, blogger, and fashion and beauty enthusiast," began posting makeup tutorials and reviews on YouTube in 2008 (*Dulce Candy* n.d.). Developing a following of over 2 million subscribers, Candy has parlayed her YouTube success into a popular blog where readers compete to top the "leaderboard" for how many comments they leave on the site, "likes" they give Candy's posts, and other social media metrics. Candy has also been a spokesperson and promoter for various beauty brands and products, won awards for Latina/o digital media innovation, and written a book on her success entitled *The Sweet Life*. Candy's and Hilton's blog communities use similar strategies to focus user attention on the stars' personas. Both blogs encourage users to write to the star with contributions or feedback, as well as promoting the star's social media accounts and branded collaborations. Rather than a message board or community for users to engage with one another, the Dulce Candy site's leaderboard encourages readers to promote and discuss Candy, her content, and her persona by assigning points for commenting on or "liking" her posts and photos, following her social media accounts, and inviting friends to read her blog.

Though Hilton has long been viewed as "whitewashed" or otherwise not in touch with his Cuban American identity, the evolution of Candy's YouTube videos suggests that she has moved away from a more hybrid Mexican American style in her dress and speech to more clearly delineated "mainstream" and "Latina" personas. Candy's early videos are noted for their approachable tone; she addresses the viewer directly and wears her hair down and curly, as well as using slang and occasional curse words. On Candy's more recent videos, some viewers have noted that she "has changed," cultivating a more glamorous, "mainstream" look with carefully styled, straightened hair and using fewer Mexican/Mexican American music cues or references. Some commenters also bemoan that Candy no longer speaks Spanish, some even accusing her of having forgotten her native language. However, Candy does continue to post Spanish-language videos; these videos are entirely in Spanish, including the titles, and tend to focus on recreating the makeup or hair styles of specific Latina/o celebrities, such as her video entitled "Maquillaje Estilo a JLo en los Oscars 2015". Candy's Spanish in the titles and in these videos is relatively formal and "unaccented" in the style of Spanish-language television presenters, rather than the Mexican/Mexican American slang terms and use of Spanish found in some of her earlier videos.

The titles of her videos have likewise shifted to use less emphatic punctuation, fewer idiosyncratic capitalizations and emoticons, as well as more search engine optimized titles, nearly always including her brand (Dulce Candy) and the category of video ("DIY," "tutorial," "haul") in the title. For example, two of Candy's highly viewed videos from 2009 are entitled "Ill be gone for a bit :(and some weight loss tips" and "Prima J Hair Tutorial EsE!!!" These videos are filmed in Candy's closet or in her somewhat cluttered bedroom, largely from a single angle. In contrast, one of Candy's videos from 2015, entitled "Erin Condren Life Planner Review + What's in My Desk," makes use of multiple camera angles, and is filmed in front of carefully organized displays of makeup decorated with lights and flowers, with pictures of Candy's husband and son featured prominently. Candy herself has highlighted the changes in her appearance and style in a 2015 video entitled "The Evolution of Dulce Candy," wherein she plays clips from 2008 to 2015 documenting her "journey to the sweet life." The ending clips from the video show Candy in preparation for her book tour, having her makeup applied by a makeup artist and being photographed in a studio while stylists attend to her hair and outfit.

Candy's transition to a persona that exemplifies both mainstream and pan-Latina fashion and beauty ideals from an earlier, more hybridized Mexican/Mexican American persona demonstrates how "Latinidad" can be used by U.S.-based Latina/os online to create personal brands. Perez Hilton's recent emphasis on his Latina/o identity is more ethnically and geographically specific in its presentation, focusing on Cuban lullabies and Hilton's mother and Cuban American upbringing in Miami. Both Candy and Hilton have successfully managed and deployed their Latina/o identities in ways that help them appeal to the largest number of readers/viewers: one by expressing mainstream feminine and pan-Latina identities, and the other by invoking a specific ethnic belonging in order to "legitimize" his Latino identity.

Traditional Latina/o Media and User-Produced Content: Latina/o Labor in the Digital Pop Economy

With the advent of user-produced content sites such as YouTube and their growing popularity and lucrativeness, "traditional" media producers such as television channels and film companies have increasingly looked online for cutting-edge content and new stars. However, the uneasy marriages of online and traditional forms of monetizing content have led scholars, particularly media industry scholars, to examine the political economy of these transactions. Scholars such as Denise Mann and Trebor Scholz have provided cases of exploitation of labor in what they term the "dark economy" of the internet (Mann 2014: 33; Scholz 2013). As Mann points out, it is not simply a case of top-down exploitation, but rather, in the case of creators, many are willing to forgo financial compensation or intellectual property rights for a chance to increase their fame and possibly go on to work in film and television. Scholars interested in participation in the digital media economy need to understand these relationships and the motivations from both corporations and creators to enter partnerships that are often much more lucrative for one side (the corporation) than the other (the creator).

Latina/o online content creators have been heavily targeted in recent years by media corporations looking to increase their appeal to young U.S.-based Latina/os, who are an ever-growing demographic. Robert Rodríguez's English-language television channel El Rey, which in partnership with Univisión reached 40 million U.S. households in 2015, launched a campaign to receive online submissions for an "Epic Summer Movie" poster, which El Rey would then transform into a film (after another round of contests soliciting scripts and filmmakers). The winner of the contest will receive a "vignette" on the network and online, and a trip to Cancún, sponsored by Corona beer (Spangler 2014). An El Rey executive referred to the contest as "talent development," despite the fact that the eventual winner has no guarantee of having their work transformed into a film, is not involved with the creative process beyond the poster design, and presumably does not receive intellectual property rights. This partnership between digital media creators and traditional media corporations does provide some benefit, but the bulk of the monetary gain is retained by the corporation, and the creator has no clear path to continuing work with the network or even the project.

On a larger scale, MiTú has built a digital media network with investments from venture capital, other digital networks like Maker Studios, and media corporations like AMC Networks. The digital network produces and hosts a number of different types of program on its YouTube channels, including programming in English, Spanish, and Portuguese, and programming that aligns with popular YouTube categories such as cooking and beauty. MiTú also describes itself as "connect[ing] Latino Millennials to the leading global brands," displaying logos of advertising partners Pepsi, Microsoft, Focus Features, T Mobile, Bud Light, Honda, Nestlé, and Ford (Mitú n.d.). Not only is MiTú seeking Latina/o digital content creators, who the network claims it can teach to monetize their content effectively through its "MiTú University," but it also positions itself as a seller of "Latino Millennial" eyeballs and clicks to advertisers. How exactly creators join MiTú's multichannel network (MCN) is unclear, as are any terms of partnerships between creators and the network. What is clear is that MiTú has positioned themselves as authorities on "quality" Latina/o digital entertainment, and on how to sell this content to advertisers and "traditional" media networks.

The rise of multichannel digital platforms like MiTú has led some online creators to feel that they must join one of these networks in order to get noticed. MCNs Machinima and Maker Studios have both been sued by online content creators who allege that the digital networks have taken advantage of amateur creators by signing them to contracts in perpetuity and claiming ownership of all intellectual property produced for the network, essentially leaving these creators with no way to terminate their involvement and no other platforms available for their content (Stuart 2013). Given that MiTú is the largest, most dominant MCN aimed at and recruiting Latina/os in digital entertainment, and given their focus on connecting with advertisers and corporate sponsors, creators partnered with MiTú may also have significant restrictions on how they can use their MiTú-sponsored ideas and fame. As Denise Mann notes, "a fruitful area for future research is the practice of web-based companies hiring semiskilled digital laborers who become *knowing* partners in these exploitative practices" (Mann 2014: 33). The specific targeting of Latina/os by these networks is a necessary site of future inquiry.

Latinidad Online: Who, Where, and What Is "Latina/o?"

Digital online media is also an important site for examining how Latina/o identities are constructed and contested, and who "gets" to invoke Latinidad. While the preceding examples have illustrated how the line between "traditional" corporate media and "user-produced" online media is increasingly blurred, online digital media still provides opportunities for a greater number of individuals to express their viewpoints. In recent years, a number of digital media texts have provoked discussion and dissension regarding what "authentic" Latino media is and who can claim a Latino identity. The webseries "Little Loca," the rap song "Hot Cheetos and Takis," and the series of "Cholo Adventures" YouTube videos each present different invocations of Latina/o cultures and identities from a variety of perspectives, and help to illustrate what kinds of presentations and what kinds of perspectives are circulated and consumed online, as well as how these digital media creations influence "traditional" film and television depictions.

One of the few studies that have examined how Latina/os articulate their identities through popular media focuses on a series of YouTube videos called "Cholo Adventures." Creator Eric G. Ochoa styles himself as "eGo the cholo," presenting humorous advice for other Mexican Americans on "How to Be a Cholo" and other topics. Ester Trujillo and Gustavo López argue that through these humorous videos, Ochoa "violates the limits of accepted meaning" by combining numerous stereotypes of Chicano men, including that of the cholo, making the representation so outrageous that it is impossible to take seriously, thus subverting the stereotype (Trujillo and López 2011: 154). Trujillo and López analyze Ochoa's videos, which depict his cholo persona in situations that point out the ridiculous expectations of masculinity and sexuality that go along with the cholo stereotype. Their study sees Ochoa's videos as providing an alternative portrayal to the standard cholo stereotype and questioning the stereotype. Trujillo and López conceptualize YouTube as a "decolonial" space where marginalized creators can express themselves and challenge dominant depictions; however, as the previous and following sections argue, there are still barriers to inclusion and compensation for creators of color in the world of digital media. Trujillo and López also mention Ochoa's use of the slur "f*ggot," which he employs to make fun of the disconnect between the macho posturing of the cholo character and actions the character takes which may be perceived as feminine. However, this usage still presents a conception of Latinidad in which actual queer subjects are used as humor to make a point about straight masculinity. While certainly subversive in some areas, "Cholo Adventures" and Eric Ochoa still present a version of Latinidad that is straight and masculine.

In 2012, a group of students from a Minnesota YMCA afterschool music program released a video on YouTube, wherein the students rapped praises for their favorite snacks: Flamin' Hot Cheetos spicy cheese puffs and Takis corn chips. The video quickly gained popularity online, reaching 350,000 views in ten days (the video has over 11 million views as of August 2015). Blogs christened the track "the song of the summer," and the students, who call their group Y.N. Rich Kids, were compared favorably to rap groups such as the Wu-Tang Clan (Kirby 2012; Memmott 2012). A number of media outlets also published articles explaining the origin and taste of Takis, a Mexican rolled corn chip snack popular in areas with large Latino populations (Brown 2012). However, few articles or responses to the song discussed the seeming cross-cultural embrace of a Mexican snack by this group of young African Americans. Rather than examine the structural and/or geographical features of Y.N. Rich Kids' neighborhoods or schools that might give insight into how Latina/o and African American youth and merchants interact, and what kinds of new cultural forms— such as a rap song about Mexican snacks—might be produced from these cultural flows, a number of articles and projects from other community groups instead warned about the health risks of fried and spicy snack chips among "low-income" or "at-risk" youth (Pamer 2012). Instead of being promoted for their cross-cultural knowledge and talents and the way they used this knowledge to produce a popular media text, Y.N. Rich Kids and their song were used as emblems of poverty and malnutrition. While media were quick to praise the children's "positive" after school hobby and to "educate" mainstream audiences about

Takis and their Mexican origin, the song ultimately became a public health tool rather than an example of how Latina/o culture is circulated and disseminated in different parts of the United States and among different racial/ethnic and age groups.

Another example of cross-cultural flows of Latinidad in digital media is the popular webseries "Little Loca." Purportedly the personal videos of a young Mexican American woman named Cynthia, the "Little Loca" series presented a "positive" portrayal. Although Cynthia dressed in a chola style, with heavy makeup, accented and slangy language, and called herself "Little Loca," she was also a smart and accomplished student and a virgin. As the videos became more popular, online commenters started to doubt their veracity, and eventually it was revealed that "Little Loca" was the creation of white actor Stevie Ryan. Ryan, who grew up in an area of central California with a large Mexican American population and who has stated that many of her friends growing up were "cholas," stated that the character was intended as a homage to the girls from Ryan's hometown, not as a parody or appropriation of Mexican American culture (Brink 2007).

Ryan's portrayal of the character illuminates important questions about who is permitted to invoke Latina/o identity and in what ways. Rather than express appreciation for aspects of Latina/o culture from her own perspective, like Y.N. Rich Kids' shout-out to Takis, Ryan purported to embody a chola identity, which some online commenters viewed as appropriation rather than appreciation (Peterson 2012; The Estrogen Project n.d.). Others supported Ryan's position that her class and geographic backgrounds provided a base for claiming a particular "authentic" experience with Mexican American culture.

One feature that distinguishes Ryan's invocation of Latina/o culture from those of Y.N. Rich Kids or Eric Ochoa is the opportunities that have arisen from her YouTube stardom. Ryan starred in a sketch comedy show entitled Stevie TV (2012–2013) for two seasons on VH1, and portrayed "Little Loca" in two episodes; in 2015 she cohosted the talk show Sex with Brody with reality TV personality Brody Jenner on the E! network. Although Y.N. Rich Kids briefly had a sponsored promotion with K-Mart, both they and "Cholo Adventures'" Eric Ochoa have mainly appeared in web-based content, and have yet to "break in" to mainstream film and television. While it may be that these groups have pursued film or television to different degrees, the degree to which Ryan was promoted on television, despite any controversy over the potential deception or appropriation involved with the "Little Loca" videos, suggests there is still a "digital divide" when it comes to how online user-produced content can be used to advance a film or television career. The idea of this "digital divide" in opportunity for advancement, rather than in initial access to or creation of content, is supported by the cases of other YouTube stars of color, such as Issa Rae of "The Misadventures of Awkward Black Girl." The failure of a television series or film to materialize from Rae's popular and critically-acclaimed web series has been cited by scholars as evidence that while digital media does offer opportunities for women of color to create and gain a modicum of success, it does not present a comprehensive solution for breaking down the institutional barriers of access to major film or television success (Banet-Weiser et al. 2014).

Cursory examination of what kinds of web series have been translated to television or film versus which have not also appears to support the argument made by Lisa Nakamura and other scholars that the "color-blind" and supposedly more equitable online world tends to reify depictions of race that are familiar and palatable to white audiences. While texts like "Hot Cheetos and Takis" and "Cholo Adventures" take stereotypes—young black rappers, Mexican American cholos—and challenge or subvert them, "Little Loca" presents stereotypes alongside "positive" attributes (doing well in school, not being promiscuous) but does not necessarily undermine or challenge these stereotypes. Questions of "insider" perspective, such as Issa Rae's experiences being deemed insufficiently black due to her mannerisms and appearance, versus "mainstream" perspective on a subculture—Ryan's attempt at translation of chola culture—may also lead to depictions produced by white artists being perceived as more able to attract "mainstream" (read: white) audiences and thus higher potential ratings and income in industries that are highly risk-averse. Studies of social media, such as danah boyd's examination of Myspace, have also shown that white audiences are likely to disengage from services or sites that are perceived to be overly "raced," or frequented mainly by users of color (boyd 2011: 204–205). This reticence of white users to engage with "racial" sites or material further discourages media industries from risking money on digital creators of color, whose followers they may fear are not representative of the "mainstream" audience they target.

Conclusion and Future Directions

As this chapter demonstrates, there are a number of productive lenses through which Latina/o digital pop culture can be examined. Analyses of star personas and their construction, media industry study and political economy approaches to the distribution and monetization of Latina/o digital media, and textual analysis of representations of Latinidad are only three examples of the ways in which the production, consumption, and circulation of Latina/o digital media can be understood. The "digital divide" metaphor which has characterized the study of people of color and technology for over a decade needs to be updated and complicated through careful attention to the ways in which Latina/os and other non-white groups use technology and create digital media. While U.S. Latina/os, especially those who are English-dominant and young, have largely closed the gap in internet usage, the cases examined in this chapter illustrate that certain structural and institutional barriers still persist in the ever-expanding world of online media.

Notes

1 "Latinidad" is used in this chapter as a term to encapsulate the representations and articulations of identity and culture that define what it means to be Latina/o in the United States. This usage follows Arlene Dávila's conception of Latinidad as the "contrary involvement of and negotiations between dominant, imposed, and self-generated interest … The ensuing enactments, definitions, and representations of Hispanic or Latino culture from such continuing processes" (Dávila 2001: 17).
2 Vine is a video sharing service that allows users to upload six-second clips. It is a popular app on mobile phones.

Bibliography

Abcarian, Robin. "The Rumors Are True: Perez Hilton Really Is Kinder and Gentler." *Los Angeles Times*, 17 August 2015.
Aldama, Frederick Luis. *The Cinema of Robert Rodriguez*. Austin, TX: University of Texas Press, 2014.
Aldama, Frederick Luis. *Critical Approaches to the Films of Robert Rodriguez*. Austin, TX: University of Texas Press, 2015.
Banet-Weiser, Sarah, Nancy K. Baym, Francesca Coppa, David Gauntlett, Jonathan Gray, Henry Jenkins, and Adrienne Shaw. "Participations Part 1: CREATIVITY." *International Journal of Communication* 8 (2014) http://ijoc.org/index.php/ijoc/article/view/2721

Berg, Charles Ramírez. *Latino Images in Film: Stereotypes, Subversion, and Resistance.* Austin, TX: University of Texas Press, 2009.

boyd, danah. *Race After the Internet.* Ed. Lisa Nakamura and Peter Chow-White. New York: Routledge, 2011.

Brink, Rob. "Crazy Like A Fox: Inside the Mind of Little Loca." *RobBrink.com.*http://robbrink.com/2007/04/10/crazy-like-a-fox-inside-the-mind-of-little-loca/, April 2007

Browne, Rembert. "At Last, 'Hot Cheetos and Takis' Is the Jam We've Been Searching For All Summer." *Grantland.* http://grantland.com/hollywood-prospectus/hot-cheetos-and-takis/ August 15, 2012

Calhoun, Craig J. *Habermas and the Public Sphere.* Cambridge, MA: MIT Press, 1992.

Castells, Manuel. *The Rise of The Network Society: The Information Age: Economy, Society and Culture.* Oxford, UK, and Malden, MA: Wiley, 2000.

Correa, Teresa, and Sun Ho Jeong. "Race and Online Content Creation." *Information, Communication and Society* 14:5 (2011): 638–659.

Costanza-Chock, Sasha. "Digital Popular Communication: Lessons on Information and Communication Technologies for Social Change from the Immigrant Rights Movement." *National Civic Review* 100:3 (2011): 29–35.

Dávila, Arlene. *Latinos, Inc.: The Marketing and Making of a People.* Berkeley: University of California Press, 2001.

Dulce Candy. "Makeup, Beauty, Hair and Fashion Tips." http://dulcecandy.com/, n.d.

Edgerly, Stephanie, Emily Vraga, Timothy Fung, Tae Joon Moon, Woo Hyun Yoo, and Aaron Veenstra. "YouTube as a Public Sphere: The Proposition 8 Debate." paper given at the Association of Internet Researchers Conference, Milwaukee, WI. October 8–10, 2009.

Fox News Latino. "Father's Day for Perez Hilton Means Staying at Home with Son, New Baby." http://latino.foxnews.com/latino/entertainment/2015/06/20/father-day-for-perez-hilton-means-staying-at-home-with-son-new-baby/ June 20, 2015.

Fuller, Bruce, José Ramón Lizárraga, and James H. Gray. "Digital Media and Latino Families." http://www.joanganzcooneycenter.org/publication/digital-media-and-latino-families-new-channels-for-learning-parenting-and-organizing/, February 18, 2015.

Gerhards, J., and M. S. Schafer. "Is the Internet a Better Public Sphere? Comparing Old and New Media in the USA and Germany." *New Media and Society* 12:1 (2010): 143–160.

Hamedy, Saba. "MiTu, Discovery U.S. Hispanic Announce Multiplatform Development Deal." *Los Angeles Times,* 23 June 2015.

Hilton, Perez. "Bio—Who Is Perez Hilton?" *PerezHilton.com.* http://perezhilton.com/about#.VscO2fmLQ-U, n.d.

HuffPost Latino Voices. "Hilton's Mother Sings Spanish Lullaby To Perez Jr." *Huffington Post.* http://www.huffingtonpost.com/2013/08/02/perez-hilton-lullaby_n_3697724.html, August 2, 2013.

Kirby, Trey. "Are the 'Hot Cheetos and Takis' Kids the next Wu-Tang Clan? ... " *Passion of the Weiss.* https://www.facebook.com/passionweiss/posts/372882012784853, August 15, 2012.

Lopez, Mark Hugo, Ana Gonzalez-Barrera, and Eileen Patten. *Closing the Digital Divide: Latinos and Technology Adoption.* Pew Research Center's Hispanic Trends Project. Pew Research Center 2013.

Mann, Denise. "Welcome to the Unregulated Wild, Wild, Digital West." *Media Industries* 1:2 (2014): http://www.mediaindustriesjournal.org/index.php/mij/article/view/47

Martínez, Katynka Z. "Pac-Man Meets the Minutemen: Video Games by Los Angeles Latino Youth." *National Civic Review* 100:3 (2011): 50–57.

McDevitt, Michael, and Shannon Sindorf. "Casting Youth as Information Leaders Social Media in Latino Families and Implications for Mobilization." *American Behavioral Scientist* 58:5 (2014): 701–714.

Memmott, Mark. "'Hot Cheetos & Takis,' This Summer's 'Truly Great Jam.'" http://www.npr.org/sections/thetwo-way/2012/08/22/159789690/check-it-out-yo-hot-cheetohs-takis-this-summers-truly-great-jam, August 22, 2012.

MiTú. "We Are the Voice of Young Latinos." https://mitunetwork.com/, n.d.

Nakamura, Lisa. *Cybertypes: Race, Ethnicity, and Identity on the Internet.* New York: Routledge, 2002.

Pamer, Melissa. "Flamin' Hot Cheetos Ignite Nutrition Debate." *NBC Southern California.* http://www.nbclosangeles.com/news/local/Flamin-Hot-Cheetos-Nutrition-Addiction-Schools-Frito-Lay-174848931.html, October 18, 2012.

Peterson, Latoya. "Girls That Television Will Never Know." *Racialicious.* http://www.racialicious.com/2012/04/19/girls-that-television-will-never-know/, April 19, 2012.

Piñon, J., and V. Rojas. "Language and Cultural Identity in the New Configuration of the US Latino TV Industry." *Global Media and Communication* 7:2 (2011): 129–147.

Scholz, Trebor. *Digital Labor: The Internet as Playground and Factory.* New York and Oxford, UK: Routledge, 2013.

Spangler, Todd. "Robert Rodriguez's El Rey Network Wants to Find Talent on Internet." *Variety.* http://variety.com/2015/digital/news/robert-rodriguezs-el-rey-network-wants-to-find-talent-on-internet-1201530420/, June 29, 2015.

Sparks, Colin. "The Internet and the Global Public Sphere." *Mediated Politics: Communication in the Future of Democracy.* Ed. Lance W. Bennett and Robert M. Entman. Cambridge: Cambridge University Press, 2001.

Stuart, Tessa. "YouTube Stars Fight Back." *L.A. Weekly.* http://www.laweekly.com/news/youtube-stars-fight-back-2612599, January 10, 2013.

The Estrogen Project. "The Gringa, The Chola, and The Dilemma." http://theestrogenproject.tumblr.com/post/19382813717/the-gringa-the-chola-and-the-dilemma, n.d.

Trujillo, Ester, and Gustavo Lopez. "'How to Be a Cholo': Reinventing a Chicano Archetype on YouTube." *Camino Real. Estudios de las Hispanidades Norteamericanas* 3:5 (2011): 151–167.

7

WHY VIDEOGAMES

Ludology Meets Latino Studies

Osvaldo Cleger

This chapter explores the ludic representation of Latina/os and Latin American cultures in video games; and it makes a case for the articulation of a Latina/o-oriented ludology, as an interdisciplinary field situated at the intersection of Latina/o studies and game studies. In order to better understand how Latina/o culture positions itself within the growing body of video games interested in its portrayal, it is necessary to examine first some general characteristics of the video game industry today, which I will do in the first section of this chapter.

Video games are rapidly becoming one of the most influential forms of cultural entertainment in contemporary society. As several recent surveys and news reports have shown, video game sales are starting to catch up with movie sales and they have also managed to dwarf the revenues from various other media and entertainment sectors, such as music, consumer magazines, and radio (*The Economist* 2011). In 2004, the global games market was valued at less than $30 billion, and it was clearly behind most other entertainment industries in the U.S. and globally. But by the end of the decade, that was not the case anymore (see Figure 7.1); not only has the video game industry been able to triple its market size in the last ten years, but it is also making headlines in countries such as the U.S., the United Kingdom, and Spain, among others, after reports have shown that consumers in those countries are now spending more on games than on movie tickets and movie rentals (Chatfield 2009, Wallop 2009, Cox 2014, Sucasas 2015).

If, instead of considering global statistics, one takes a look at individual examples and qualitative data, the same trend emerges. The fastest selling media title of recent years is not anymore a Hollywood blockbuster, but a video game. And in fact, shattering records for the best and fastest selling media title of all times has become sort of a tradition within the video game industry. To briefly illustrate: in 2004 the software giant Microsoft announced that it had sold 2.38 million copies of *Halo 2* (which amounted to $125 million in sales) within the first 24 hours of the game being released (Becker 2004). In November 2009, Activision's *Call of Duty: Modern Warfare II* shattered all previous sale records by racking up $310 million in the first 24 hours (Terdiman 2009). In 2010 and 2012 new records were set by the same company, Activision, whose titles *Call of Duty: Black Ops* and *Call of*

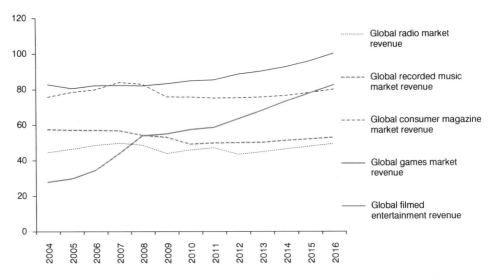

Figure 7.1   How the video game industry beat some of its rivals in the entertainment world   (Figures are in billions of dollars; source: PricewaterhouseCoopers (PwC), 2006–2012)

Duty: Black Ops II managed to make $360 and over $500 million, respectively, on launch day (Baker 2010, Gaudiosi 2012). *Call of Duty: Black Ops II* was also able to reach the one billion dollar mark in sales in just a couple of weeks (Tassi 2012). Finally, in 2013 Rockstar's *Grand Theft Auto V* became the biggest entertainment launch in history to date, after grossing $800 million on day one and one billion dollars in only three days (Kain 2013).

These significant amounts of video game titles and copies in circulation are being played worldwide by an increasingly diverse population of gamers that includes not only children and male adolescents—who despite the predominant stereotype represent, in fact, a small portion of the gamer population—but also women, parents, the elderly, and racial and ethnic minorities (see Figure 7.2).

Latina/os, in particular, are not only one of the fastest growing populations in the U.S., but also one of the ethnic minorities that is increasingly participating in the emerging gaming landscape. According to a report prepared by the Center on Media and Human Development at Northwestern University, 65 percent of "Hispanic homes with young children have a console video game player, such as an X-Box, Playstation or Wii" (Wartella et al., 13). This survey also reveals that 44 percent of Hispanic parents say that "playing video games together is something their family enjoys doing" (13). Another report published by Simmons claims that "Hispanics are 32 percent more likely than non-Hispanics to consider video games their main source of entertainment" (Ruiz) and that they are "54 percent more likely to buy a new video game the day it's released than non-Hispanic gamers" (as cited in Ruiz 2012).

However, despite the evidence provided by these numbers, Latina/os continue to be an underrepresented group in the video game world. Not only are the number of playable characters that Latina/o gamers can culturally relate to meager, but also the participation of Latina/os and other minorities in the industry's workforce has been historically very limited. According to a study published by the International Game Developers Association, 83 percent of game developers are white while 88.5 percent are male (see Figure 7.3). In comparison, Latina/os only make up 2.5 percent of the industry's workforce (International Game Developers Association, 9). The game industry's demographic makeup, in turn,

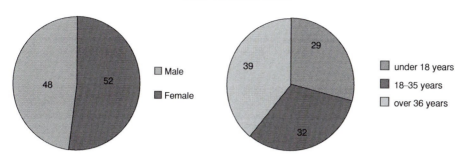

Figure 7.2 Who plays video games? (by gender and age; source: The Entertainment Software Association, 2014)

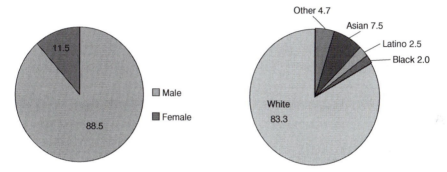

Figure 7.3 Who makes video games? (by gender and ethnicity/race; source: IGDA 2005)

accounts for the lack of diversity found in video games in general, where most protagonists and playable characters are white males, while Latina/os and other minorities usually "appear as a non-playable character, obstacle to overcome, or simply part of the backdrop" (Aldama 2013).

The Representation of Latinos in the Growing Gaming Landscape

Latina/os are not only underrepresented in the video game world, but research that deals with the portrayal of Latina/os in video games has also been very scarce. With the exception of a few academic articles and book chapters written by a handful of scholars (Aldama 2012, 2013; Montes 2007; Chávez 2010; Penix-Tadsen 2012; Cleger 2015), the field has remained mostly unexplored to date. Behm-Morawitz and Ortiz (2013) attribute this void to the lack of representation of Latina/os in this new medium: "When examining Latina/os in video games, they appear very infrequently, in only 1% to 3% of video games and advertisements" (254). These authors conclude that "because Latina/os appear in such small numbers in video games, it has not been possible to meaningfully quantitatively analyze these portrayals in terms of embodied roles and characteristics" (254).

Even though we can agree that a quantitative analysis of how Latina/os are represented in video games might not be possible at this time, a qualitative study of their portrayal in video games is not only something doable, but also a necessity, given the growing influence of the medium in our society. Moreover, despite being underrepresented, Latina/os have been

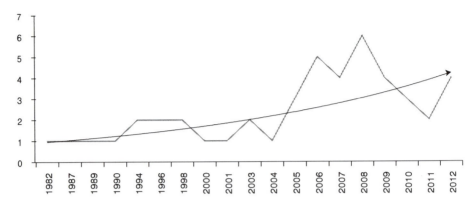

Figure 7.4 Major video game releases featuring Latin American locations and/or portraying Latina/o characters and themes (number of original titles per year; source: Penix-Tadsen 2012)

featured in numerous games, including some of the most popular blockbusters produced by the industry, such as the FIFA series, the *Assassin's Creed* saga, or the *Call of Duty* and *Grand Theft Auto* franchises.

In his preliminary taxonomy of video games either featuring a Latin American environment or including Latin themes and characters, Penix-Tadsen has listed a total of 46 games in this category, spanning over the course of three decades (1982–2012), and set in more than ten different Latin American locations, with Mexico, Peru, Brazil, Venezuela, and the Caribbean among those countries and regions most frequently portrayed in video games (see Figure 7.4). Penix-Tadsen's taxonomic list not only attests to the unwavering interest of the industry in Latina/os and Latin American cultures as sources of inspiration, but it also shows an increase of such interest in recent years.

Since 2005, there have been, on average, four major game releases every year in which Latina/o characters and settings are portrayed in a variety of ways, providing either the content or a backdrop for different forms of gameplay (see Figure 7.4). These include widely played titles such as: *Red Dead Redemption*, partially set in northern Mexico during the Mexican Revolution; *Call of Duty: Black Ops*, where the first mission tasks players with finding and killing Fidel Castro during a raid of one of his mansions outside of Havana; *Call of Duty: Black Ops II*, whose main antagonist, Nicaraguan-born Raul Menendez, will do everything in his power to prevent American agent Alex Mason from accomplishing his goals in the game's story; *Assassin's Creed IV: Black Flag*, with its beautiful 3D rendition of eighteenth-century Havana where players can roam and explore the colonial city as they please while they try to unveil the plans of Cuba's governor—and Templar—Laureano de Torres y Ayala; *Rockband 3*, which includes songs by Mexican band Maná and Colombian composer and singer Juanes in the list of tunes that gamers can learn to play and sing in Spanish; and, *Tropico I–V*, where the player is invited to take on the role of a Latin American dictator in charge of the mission of bringing prosperity—or unspeakable calamities—to the island under his rule.

Parallel to this corpus of mainstream productions developed for game consoles, there is also a group of independent developers and mobile game designers who have contributed a great number of titles portraying Latina/os and Latin American cultures in lower budget games. Even though this has often been a fertile ground for the stereotyping of Latina/os, in video games that either depict them as taco eaters (*La Chancla*), and sombrero-wearing bandits (*Speedy Rodriguez, Macho Dash, Border Patrol*), or portray them as lawbreakers and illegal immigrants (*Border Patrol, Smuggle Truck*), the indie and mobile game market has also provided independent authors and small companies with an opportunity to develop more serious, innovative or experimental games that are not profit-oriented. A game like Ricardo Dominguez and Coco Fuscos' *Turista fronterizo* uses this lower-cost format to offer a more nuanced view of what it means to live at the U.S.-Mexico border for Latina/os and Anglos alike, while other indie games, such as Breakthrough's *I Can End Deportation!* or *ICED!*, take advantage of this format to denounce misconceptions and discriminatory practices against Latina/o immigrants and other minorities in the U.S.

The independent and mobile game industry has also afforded Latina/os and Latin American developers with a low-cost opportunity to enter this market and become part of the cultural debates that are currently taking place through video games. This has allowed numerous Latin American indie companies to produce and market games that cater to gamers interested in a variety of topics and genres, ranging from exhilarating sport games—such as *Lucha Libre: Héroes del Ring*—to science fiction games inspired in real Latin American locations—like 3F Interactive's *Reversion*, set in a dystopian Buenos Aires—to games that tackle serious issues, such as sexual violence and teen pregnancy, as is the case in *Pregnancy* by Brazilian indie company Locomotivah.

Towards a Latina/o-Oriented Ludology

A Latina/o-oriented ludology should consider this growing archive of video games—that either contribute to the ludic representation of Latina/os in mainstream media or that have been developed by Latina/os and Latin American companies—the main corpus of analysis and point of departure for any further research within this field. Latina/o gaming communities across the world are also a vital source and point of reference for this field of study, since research on these communities can provide answers to key questions such as: Who plays video games in the Latina/o community and why? What gaming platforms (consoles, PC, mobile devices) are most commonly used by Latina/o gamers? What are the most popular game genres among Latina/os, and what does this say, if anything, about their gaming culture? Are Latina/os mostly casual or hardcore gamers? How do Latina/os react to the representation of their identity and their culture in mainstream video games? What impact do video games have on Latina/o popular culture, as well as on the in-group and out-group image of Latina/os? Can video games make a positive contribution to the education of Latina/os through edugames, interactive learning apps, and other types of educational software? Or has the influence of video games on Latina/o communities been mostly of a negative nature?

The breadth of methodologies available for this kind of research is extensive, and ranges from ethnographic research tools that can help answer some of the questions formulated above (Boellstorff, 2006) to narratological and literary-based analysis of video games (Murray, 2004; Perlin, 2004; Chávez, 2010), to theories that explore the capacity of video games to engage with serious topics and issues and provide meaningful training and real-life skills to humans, such as serious game theory (Michael and Chen 2006; Davidson, 2008; Ritterfeld et al., 2009; Aldrich, 2009; Ma et al. 2011; Ma et al. 2014), procedural rhetoric theory (Bogost 2007; Voorhees 2009; Sicart 2011) and simulation theory (Frasca 2003).

While it is fair to say that a Latin American or Latina/o-oriented ludology is still at an embryonic stage, since not much has been published on this topic yet, it is also true that some scholars have already pointed out the need for such a discipline or line of inquiry within the broader fields of game studies and Latin American cultural studies (Chávez 2010; Penix-Tadsen 2012). Others, without necessarily using the term "ludology," have offered prime examples of what a Latina/o-oriented ludology would look like (Montes 2007; Aldama 2013). In his essay, "Getting Your Mind/Body On", Frederick Luis Aldama makes one of the most solid contributions to the field to date not only by offering a comprehensive catalog and commentary of mainstream video games portraying Latina/os, but also by decoding some of the most common stereotypes used by the industry, where Latina/os are usually depicted as gang members, knife-wielding thugs, maids or hypersexualized female bodies. In this study, Aldama also identifies a few cases in which video game developers have been able to overcome these representational barriers, either by introducing more believable and relatable Latina/o playable characters (such as Dominican-American Luis Lopez in GTA: The Ballad of Gay Tony) or by producing a game aimed to "raise awareness [about issues of discrimination against Hispanics] by allowing the player to feel what it is like to live as an undocumented Latino", as is the case in Breakthrough's I Can End Deportation!

Phillip Penix-Tadsen's research article, Latin American Ludology: Why We Should Take Video Games Seriously (And When We Shouldn't), also shows an interest in both cataloging and classifying the representation of Latina/os by the video game industry, as well as identifying those cases in which stereotypes have been overcome, and authentic-looking portrayals of Latina/os have been achieved. But while Aldama puts the emphasis on the representation of U.S. Latina/os—hence his observation that many Latina/o characters speak "with heavily accented, truncated English"—Penix-Tadsen's main focus is on Latin American characters and settings. For Penix-Tadsen what makes Latin characters authentic is not just their ability to escape the common stereotypes used by the industry, but rather their capacity to offer a genuine simulation of Latin American cultural traditions and idiosyncrasies, including the presentation of such traditions in the languages in which they originated (Spanish, Portuguese, Maya, Nahuatl, etc.).

Pennix-Tadsen's focus on highlighting the rich cultural diversity found throughout Latin America, as well as the potential this offers for cultural simulations in video games, has been echoed by some sectors of the video game industry, where companies like Ubisoft have been striving to deliver authentic-looking Latin American characters and scenarios in some of the games they have produced. The use of Mayan language by Mayan assassins, as well as the use of Spanish by many non-playable characters found in the streets of eighteenth-century Havana in Ubisoft's Assassin's Creed IV: Black Flag, are examples of this focus on providing richer and more immersive cultural contexts to gamers, even when this comes at the expense of many players, who are unable to understand what these characters are saying on the screen.

Ubisoft's interest in designing indigenous characters who speak in their native languages, wear traditional clothes and show culturally relevant customs through gameplay has been particularly remarkable, and has led to the creation of genuinely revolutionary characters such as the protagonist of Assassin's Creed III, Ratonhnhaké:ton. Ratonhnhaké:ton or Connor is a half-European, half-Mohawk assassin, who fights in the American Revolutionary War and spends the first half of the game among people from his tribe, hunting and discussing both trivial and profound issues in his mother tongue, that is, Kanien'kéha or Mohawk language. For the design of these characters and scenarios, as well as the inclusion of dialogues in Mohawk language, Ubisoft relied on the expertise of two members of the Mohawk nation, Akwiratékha Martin and Teiowí:sonte Thomas Deer, who worked as consultants for the production team, making sure the presentation of Kanien'kéha language and customs in the game was culturally sound (Venables 2012).

Assassin's Creed: Freedom Cry, a game set in Port-au-Prince, Haiti, circa 1730, is another example of Ubisoft's brand of carefully researched, history-based game simulations that focus on breaking representational barriers by giving the leading role in the game to non-white European characters and cultures. In Freedom Cry, players control the charismatic character of Trinidadian-born Adéwalé, a former slave turned assassin, who joins the Maroon rebellion in Saint-Domingue (Haiti) and works relentlessly for the liberation of slaves, as well as to put an end to the slave trade and trafficking in the Caribbean. Many missions in the game consist of infiltrating sugar plantations in Port-au-Prince and surrounding areas to free slaves, or protecting maroon slaves who are being persecuted or punished by their overseers and masters. In the portion of the game that takes place in the ocean, players must help Adéwalé find ships transporting slaves through the Caribbean waters. Once these ships are spotted, Adéwalé and his crew must attack and defeat their escorts and board the ships to free the slaves. As has been the norm in Ubisoft's previous installments of the series, many dialogues are carried out in the native language of the characters, in this case Antillean Creole, and several historical characters are also included in the game's story, such as Pierre, Marquis de Fayet, Governor-General of Saint-Domingue at that time. Freedom Cry is arguably the best game simulation about slavery in the Caribbean that the video game industry has produced to date; and it clearly shows the potential benefits this kind of game simulation offers for a variety of educational purposes, from learning about Latin American history to being able to experience, procedurally, a wide array of sensitive topics and realities (such as slavery), to providing players with an opportunity to get virtually immersed in a multiplicity of cultural environments, where many different languages are spoken in situations that mimic real life.

The convergence of the already established field of game studies with this growing corpus of video games dealing with Latin American/Latina/o issues and realities should be the foundation for the emergence of a Latina/o-oriented or Latin American ludology. As Penix-Tadsen argues, video games are rapidly becoming the "new harbingers of Latin American culture for the global masses" (17), not only through video games that exploit two-dimensional stereotypes about Latina/os, but also through games and developers who have engaged with "a deeper struggle—or lucha—for a more nuanced simulation of Latin America and its inhabitants" (181). Assassin Creeds: Freedom Cry is one of those games pushing the envelope in this direction, and it does so without sacrificing its main goal of providing players with countless hours of fun gameplay. It is precisely this convergence of entertaining and engaging gameplay with the exposure to educational content what makes video games like this one ideal artifacts to explore topics related to Latin American culture and history, or to engage in the debate of difficult and controversial issues while tapping into the affordances of procedural representation and interactive learning.

Gaming the Latin American Past

In Gaming the Past: Using Video Games to Teach Secondary History, Jeremiah McCall makes a strong case in favor of using simulation games based on historical events to teach history to students in middle and high schools. As McCall argues, games like Civilization, CivCity: Rome, Rome: Total War, Europa Universalis I-IV, Hearts of Iron, Third World Farmer or Stop Disasters, among many others, can be much more effective learning tools than class lectures, history books, or even films and documentaries, when it comes to illustrating and helping students understand a wide array of historical and social topics. Concepts such as the division of labor and the reasons for such practice in early human societies, the role scarcity plays on economic planning, or the impact environmental problems can have on civilizations and countries, are all complex notions that video game simulations can help develop in students through forms of gameplay that involve problem-solving and testing the validity of different hypothesis as they try to accomplish the game's goals.

Obviously, to be an effective learning tool, a historical video game should be able to offer accurate information to players; and commercial games are often plagued with inaccurate facts and anachronisms, either due to a lack of research and knowledge on the part of the developer, or to the developer's willingness to sacrifice accuracy in order to deliver a more entertaining experience. But even when the latter is the case, history-based games can still be a useful tool for learning about history and cultural traditions when complemented with reading and other materials that can help students identify and correct some of the inaccuracies to which they may have been exposed. The benefits, in many cases, outweigh the risks.

To illustrate with an example, let´s examine *Assassin's Creed: Black Flag's* portrayal of early eighteenth-century life in the Caribbean islands. Despite being a thoroughly researched game set during the golden age of piracy, *AC: Black Flag* is plagued with many historical inaccuracies and anachronisms. One of the biggest absences in the game is the crucial role French pirates and the French crown played in the Caribbean during this time. The game seems to suggest piracy was mostly or only a Spanish and British enterprise. As historian Bryan Glass has pointed out, the excessive violence shown in the game is not an accurate representation of the life of a pirate, since pirates often relied more on scare tactics than on actual violence to bring their opponents into submission (Glass 2013). Some locations and buildings included in the game, such as Havana Cathedral (1777) or the Queen's Staircase in Nassau, Bahamas (1794), were built several decades to almost a century after the events portrayed in the story. And the same can be said about many of the sea shanties the protagonist, Edward Kenway, and his crew often sing while sailing through Caribbean waters, such as *Spanish Ladies* (1796), *Lowlands Away* (circa 1860) or *Drunken Sailor* (1850). One of the most entertaining parts of the game, naval combats, are highly unrealistic, showing ships that are capable of moving at incredible speeds and can make very sudden and sharp turns to ram against an enemy vessel. The disabling of enemy ships before boarding them also goes against both common sense and historical accounts, since pirates usually would have wanted to capture these ships causing little to no damage to their structure.

But despite all the licenses Ubisoft has taken to recreate this historical moment, *AC: Black Flag* still manages to "bring history to life" (Glass 2013) and could be an effective tool in giving students of history a sense of this period. The plantation economy based on slave labor has been carefully represented throughout the Caribbean. Many of these plantations' warehouses, such as the one located in Matanzas (northern Cuban coast), can be looted by Kenway and his crew. This is actually an accurate representation of port cities in the Caribbean during this time, many of which were often the target of corsairs and pirates' attacks. Matanzas was an emblematic city in this sense, having been raided often by French pirates during the seventeenth century, as well as by Dutch admiral and privateer Pieter Heyn in 1628 (Lane and Levine 2015). The recruitment of former African slaves as part of the crew of many pirate ships is made explicit in the game through the character of Adéwalé, Captain Kenway's quartermaster. All three main cities that players can explore in the game (Havana, Kingston and Nassau) have been modeled with close attention to their peculiarities, distinctive buildings and landmarks, as well as the sounds, languages and accents players can listen to while walking in the streets.

The representation of Colonial Havana is particularly imposing, and can offer players a genuine impression of what it feels like to wander through this city's streets. Even better, it simulates the impression of visiting the city sometime during the eighteenth century. Being born and raised in Havana, I have to admit I experienced a sense of pride and wonder upon disembarking in the old town for the first time, playing the role of Edward Kenway, and gaining a 360-degree view of my surroundings from one of the points of view placed by the developers at the top of a church tower. To the eastern part of the harbor, you could see the untamed hills of what will later become the towns of Regla and Casablanca; to the west, several neighborhoods of the historic old town growing inwards as you walk away from the docks.

If we superimpose the actual map of Havana over the map of the city developed by Ubisoft, we immediately realize that Ubisoft's Havana is supposed to work as a synecdoche rather than as a faithful and all-inclusive copy of the original. Many streets, blocks, plazas, and buildings that already existed at the time are absent from Ubisoft's Havana, while buildings that had not yet been built—such as Havana Cathedral—have been recreated with a striking resemblance to their real-life counterparts (see Figures 7.5 and 7.6). In the game's database the developers engage in an interesting debate about the presence of buildings like this one in their historical recreation of the city. One of the developers argues that it is anachronistic to include Havana Cathedral as we know it today, since its construction (1748–1777) was "far too late for this Virtual Experience" and at the time,

Figure 7.5   Havana Cathedral (photo Vicki Burton, Creative Commons)

Figure 7.6   Detail of the Havana Cathedral, as seen in *Assassins Creed: Black Flag*

the only thing a visitor could find in this location was "a small, rough church rising from drained swampland" (AC: *Black Flag, Animus Database*). Another developer replies that their purpose is to sell beautiful and "climbable buildings" rather than being historically accurate. It is interesting to notice, though, that by letting players gain access to these discussions by developers, Ubisoft is in fact providing users with the information they will need to have a better idea about early eighteenth-century Havana. In this way, players can actually do both: enjoy the pleasure of exploring one of the most iconic buildings of the city—which works in the game as sort of a synecdochical reference to the city as a whole—while also learning about the real history of this building.

Although this is not precisely its forte, AC: *Black Flag* also includes a wide array of interesting characters from the perspective of Latin American history, such as Cuba's governor at the time, Laureano de Torres y Ayala (1645–1722); but hardly anything about his real life and tenure as Governor of Cuba features in the game. In the streets of Havana, most non-player characters speak with heavy peninsular accents, and can be heard talking about their everyday lives, current affairs, or their upbringing in "a little town of Extremadura" (AC: *Black Flag*). Considering that a significant segment of the city's population at this time consisted of first generation immigrants from Spain, this is an accurate representation of the city's inhabitants. When walking close to a church, some priests can be heard praying in Latin, while most African non-player characters seem to be silent.

Another appealing element of the game is the inclusion of the Mayan city of Tulum, as well as Mayan assassins as part of the story. Unfortunately, when modeling this location the developers opted for a generic "Mayan city" rather than following the more realistic principles that were adopted for the rendition of the other main locations featured in the game (Havana, Kingston, Nassau). Except for the fact that it is a coastal city, there is nothing in Ubisoft's Tulum that resembles the actual Mayan ruins. By the same token, the Mayan assassins that appear in the game don't show any traits that could help users learn about the Mayan culture. Ah Tabai is a Mayan assassin portrayed in a very positive light as a wise man, and very influential in strengthening the position of the assassin's brotherhood in the Caribbean. In this sense, Ah Tabai departs from the traditional representation of Latin American characters as enemies or obstacles that players have to overcome in the game (Aldama 2013). But his fictionalization is not used—as is the case with other characters in the game—to help users learn about the real history and culture of the civilization Ah Tabai represents. Finally, the game also features the character of a female Taíno assassin, Opia Apito, which is particularly remarkable considering how rarely Pre-Hispanic Caribbean cultures have been represented in any medium.

All in all, AC: *Black Flag* is a promising example of how history-based simulation games could be used to get users exposed to a historical period in a specific geographical area, in a way that is both educational and entertaining. As history professor Rachel Herrmann points out, "the game includes inaccuracies, but it also provides a popular means for millions of players around the world—many of whom would never dream of picking up a book—to interact with the past" (para. 7). Even better, the game relies on its ability to provide users with simulated experiences to help them learn about a variety of topics, from becoming familiar with the geography of the Caribbean as they "sail its waters" and explore its different islands, to learning about the plantation economy, or becoming more proficient at appreciating the architectural wealth of the region. And this knowledge is not acquired through rote memorization or as part of a school curriculum but as an indirect result of gameplay.

Serious Games, Serious Latina/o Issues

Video games not only provide a new, engaging and dynamic platform to explore the past and learn about cultural traditions. Video games can also be used to discuss current events and/or provide meaningful training to users, which can translate into the acquisition of real-life skills. Serious game theoreticians and designers have emphasized this aspect of video games (Abt 1970; Michael et al. 2006; Davidson 2008; Ritterfeld et al. 2009; Aldrich 2009; Ma et al. 2011; Ma et al. 2014).

In *Global Conflicts: Latin America* (2008), a video game produced by Serious Games Interactive, players are invited to take on the role of a Latina/o journalist who is in charge of investigating five different conflicts that have recently arisen in various countries and regions of Latin America: Cochabamba-Bolivia, Rabinal-Guatemala, Nogales-Mexico and Xocox-Mexico. There is a host of different issues that players can explore and learn about while playing this game, such as the violence against undocumented Latina/o immigrants at the U.S.-Mexico border; the pollution issues and work-related health problems caused by *maquiladoras* operating on the Mexican side of the U.S.-Mexico border; or the rise of racial tensions and social conflicts in Bolivia after the election of its first president with an indigenous background, Evo Morales. Assuming the role of an investigative journalist, the player will visit during the game the locations where these events took place to interview different people involved in the conflicts, gather information in the local libraries, and look for clues that could help him ferret out the truth in each of these situations. Once the player has gathered all the information he needs, he will attend a final interview with a character that is central to the conflict. If he has done his research properly, during this final interview the player will be able to ask the tough questions, make the right arguments and force his interviewee to confess the truth. After that, he will be able to write an article that will expose the truth and shake the powers that be, while also improving his reputation as a journalist. If, on the contrary, the player comes to the interview unprepared, the interviewee will have the upper hand: he will be able to shrug off the journalist's questions and reiterate the official version of the events. In this scenario, the player will leave the interview with a sense of defeat; and the article he will write and submit to his editor will be considered amateurish and lacking in substance.

Despite some minor flaws commonly found in indie games like this one (low quality and occasionally glitchy 3D graphics, inconsistent use of sound effects, excessive reliance on generic character animations, or the predictability of certain interactions), *Global Conflicts: Latin America* still manages to offer a gaming experience that can be both educational and engaging. What other players might also consider a limitation of this game—that is, its heavy reliance on long chunks of texts to deliver information to users—is partially justified by the fact that the player is assuming the role of a journalist in charge of collecting information to write an article on a difficult issue. The texts that users can read on the screen are the reporter's notes as well as the partial conclusions he has been able to reach while conducting his investigation. In fact, the game does an excellent job at explaining in this way the nature of the different conflicts presented in the story, as well as giving the player the opportunity to look at these problems from different angles. For instance, the environmental problems created by *maquiladoras* in northern Mexico are further problematized by also considering the opportunities for employment these factories offer to the local population. That is not to say that the game tries to offer a positive view of *maquiladoras*: not only is their lack of respect for common-sense environmental regulations exposed, but also their exploitation of the local population through low wages, and their disrespect toward basic worker's rights. But the game does not go as far as to suggest that simply closing these factories is a solution to the problem. In other words, the player is not expected to leave the game with easy, ideological answers to complex problems, but to look at these conflicts from different perspectives before making up his mind.

Serious game theory claims that video games like *Global Conflicts: Latin America* can be instrumental in helping users better understand a complex problem or situation through forms of gameplay that involve placing players in the middle of a simulated conflict, and letting them find their own answers by playing the game and experiencing several potential outcomes that are the result of their in-game decisions. The effectiveness of such a learning framework stems from the fact that the resulting knowledge is not perceived as something given to the user, but rather as something he has independently acquired, or a byproduct of playing the game.

Although still in its infancy, the serious games market is currently expanding, and it already includes several titles that focus on Latina/o / Latin American issues and realities, such as *Tropical America* (2002), *Vagabundo: A Migrant's Tale* (2002), *Points of Entry: An Immigration Challenge* (2007), *I can End Deportation!* (2008), *Homeland Guantanamos* (2008), *Inside the Haiti Earthquake* (2010), *Turista fronterizo* (2005), and Rafael Fajardo's *Crosser* and *La Migra*, among others. As can be observed just by reading this list of titles, immigration and human rights have been core issues when it comes to the ludic portrayal of Latina/os in video games and the gamification of topics that are considered relevant to this group. That does not mean, however, that a Latina/o-oriented ludology should be constrained to the discussion of this specific set of games and issues. As an interdisciplinary field, situated at the intersection of Latina/o studies and game studies, a Latina/o-oriented ludology should be able to diversify its lines of inquiry, to encompass the ample range of concerns and issues that are relevant to the people and cultures that this emerging field is expected to serve.

Bibliography

Abt, Clark C. *Serious Games*. New York: Viking Press, 1970.

Aldama, Frederick Luis. "Latinos and Video Games." In *Encyclopedia of Video Games: The Culture, Technology and Art of Gaming*, ed. Mark J.P. Wolf. Vol. 1. Santa Barbara, CA: ABC-CLIO, 2012. 356–60.

Aldama, Frederick Luis. "Getting Your Mind/Body On." In *Latinos and Narrative Media: Participation and Portrayal*, ed. Frederick Luis Aldama. New York: Palgrave MacMillan, 2013. 241–58.

Aldrich, Clark. *The Complete Guide to Simulations and Serious Games: How the Most Valuable Content Will Be Created in the Age Beyond Gutenberg to Google*. San Francisco: Pfeiffer, 2009.

"All the World's a Game." *The Economist*, 10 December 2011.

Baker, Liana. "Activision Says *Black Ops* First-Day Sales a Record." *Reuters*, 11 November 2010.

Becker, David. "*Halo 2* Clears Record $125 Million in First Day." *CNET*, 11 November 2004.

Behm-Morawitz, Elizabeth, and Michelle Ortiz. "Race, Ethnicity and the Media." *The Oxford Handbook of Media Psychology*. Ed. Karen E. Dill. New York: Oxford University Press, 2013. 252–66.

Boellstorff, Tom. "A Ludicrous Discipline? Ethnography and Game Studies." *Games and Culture* 1:1 (2006): 29–35.

Bogost, Ian. *Persuasive Games: The Expressive Power of Video Games*. Cambridge, MA and London: MIT Press, 2007.

Chatfield, Tom. "Videogames Now Outperform Hollywood Movies." *The Guardian*, 27 September 2009.

Chávez, Daniel. "El coronel no tiene con quién jugar: literatura y videojuego en América Latina." *Arizona Journal of Hispanic Cultural Studies* 14 (2010): 159–76.

Cleger, Osvaldo. "Procedural Rhetoric and Undocumented Migrants: Playing the Debate Over Immigration Reform." *Digital Culture and Education* 7:1 (2015): 19–39.

Cox, Kate. "It's Time to Start Treating Video Game Industry Like the $21 Billion Business It Is." *Consumerist*, 9 June 2014.

Davidson, Drew. *Beyond Fun: Serious Games and Media*. Pittsburgh, PA: ETC Press, 2008.

Frasca, Gonzalo. "Simulation vs. Narrative. Introduction to Ludology." *The Video Game Theory Reader*, eds. Mark J.P. Wolf and Bernard Perron. New York and London: Routledge, 2003. 221–36.

Gaudiosi, John. "Call of Duty: Black Ops II' Earns Record $500 Million in First Day Sales." *The Hollywood Reporter*, 16 November 2012.

Glass, Bryan. "History Respawned: Assassin's Creed IV." Interview by Bob Whitaker. *History Respawned*, YouTube Channel. 19 November 2013.

Herrmann, Rachel. "Guest Post: 'X' Marks the History: Plundering the Past in Assassin's Creed IV." *The Junto*, 5 February 2014.

International Game Developers Association (IGDA). *Game Developers Demographics: An Exploration of Workforce Diversity*. IGDA, 2005. Available at: http://c.ymcdn.com/sites/www.igda.org/resource/collection/9215B88F-2AA3-4471-B44D-B5D58FF25DC7/IGDA_DeveloperDemographics_Oct05.pdf

Kain, Erik. "*Grand Theft Auto* V Crosses $1B In Sales, Biggest Entertainment Launch In History." *Forbes*, 9 September 2013.

Lane, Kris E. and Robert M. Levine. *Pillaging the Empire: Piracy in the Americas, 1500–1750*. New York: Routledge, 2015.

Ma, M., A. Oikonomou, and L. Jain. *Serious Games and Edutainment Applications*. London: Springer, 2011.

Ma, M., M.F. Oliveira, and J.B. Hauge. *Serious Games Development and Applications*. London: Springer, 2014.

McCall, Jeremiah. *Gaming the Past: Using Video Games to Teach Secondary History*. New York and London: Routledge, 2011.

Michael, David, and Sande Chen. *Serious Games: Games That Educate, Train and Inform*. Boston, MA: Thomson Course Technology, 2006.

Montes, Miguel Rafael. "Ghost Recon: Island Thunder: Cuba in the Virtual Battlescape." *The Players' Realm: Studies on the Culture of Video Games and Gaming*. Eds. J. Patrick Williams and Jonas Heide Smith. Jefferson, NC: McFarland & Co., 2007. 154–70.

Murray, Janet. "From Game-Story to Cyberdrama." In *First Person: New Media as Story, Performance, and Game*, eds. Noah Wardrip-Fruin and Pat Harrigan. Cambridge, MA, and London: MIT Press, 2004. 2–11.

Penix-Tadsen, Phillip. "Latin American Ludology: Why We Should Take Video Games Seriously (and When We Shouldn't)." *Latin American Research Review* 48:1 (2013): 174–90.

Perlin, Ken. "Can There Be a Form Between a Game and a Story." In *First Person: New Media as Story, Performance, and Game*, eds. Noah Wardrip-Fruin and Pat Harrigan. Cambridge, MA and London: MIT Press, 2004. 12–18.

PricewaterhouseCoopers. *Global Entertainment and Media Outlook: 2006–2010*. New York: PricewaterhouseCoopers LLP, 2006.

PricewaterhouseCoopers. *Global Entertainment and Media Outlook: 2009–2013*. New York: PricewaterhouseCoopers LLP, 2009.

PricewaterhouseCoopers. *Global Entertainment and Media Outlook: 2011–2015*. New York: PricewaterhouseCoopers LLP, 2011.

PricewaterhouseCoopers. *Global Entertainment and Media Outlook: 2012–2016*. New York: PricewaterhouseCoopers LLP, 2012.

Ritterfeld, Ute, Michael Cody, and Peter Vorderer. *Serious Games: Mechanisms and Effects*. New York: Routledge, 2009.

Ruiz, Roberto. "Winning the Game with Hispanics." *Univisión*, 25 June 2012.

Sicart, Miguel. "Against Procedurality." *Game Studies* 11:3 (2011). Available at: http://gamestudies.org/1103/articles/sicart_ap

Sucasas, Ángel Luis. "Las ventas de videojuegos doblan a la taquilla del cine en España." *El País*, 26 March 2015.

Tassi, Paul. "Black Ops 2 Sells $1B in 15 Days, Beats Modern Warfare 3 Record." *Forbes*, 5 December 2012.

Terdiman, Daniel. "*Call of Duty: Modern Warfare 2* Said to Break Sales Records." *CNET*, 12 November 2009.

Venables, Michael. "The Awesome Mohawk Teacher and Consultant Behind Ratonhnhaké:ton." *Forbes*, 25 November 2012.

Voorhees, Gerald. "The Character of Difference: Procedurality, Rhetoric, and Roleplaying Games." *Game Studies* 9:2 (2009). Available at: http://gamestudies.org/0902/articles/voorhees

Wallop, Harry. "Video Games Bigger than Film." *The Telegraph*, 26 December 2009.

Wartella, Ellen et al. *Media, Technology, and Reading in Hispanic Families: A National Survey*. Evanston: Northwestern University, 2014. Available at: http://web5.soc.northwestern.edu/cmhd/wp-content/uploads/2014/08/NWU.MediaTechReading.Hispanic.FINAL2014.pdf

Games Cited

Anonymous. *Border Patrol*, 2006. Web.

Anonymous. *Homeland Guantanamos*. Breakthrough: New York (Web-based), 2008.

Anonymous. *I Can End Deportation!* Breakthrough: New York (PC, OS X), 2008.

Dominguez, Ricardo and Coco Fusco. *Turista fronterizo*, 2005. Web.

Feral Interactive. *Tropico 3*. Feral Interactive: London (Mac), 2012.

Garcia, Erik. *La Chancla*. EchoBrown Studios (OS X, Android), 2014.

Gathering of Developers. *Tropico*. Gathering of Developers: Texas (PC), 2001.

Gathering of Developers. *Tropico 2: Pirate Cove*. Gathering of Developers: Texas (PC, OS X), 2003.

Harmonix. *Rockband 3*. MTV Games: New York (PS3, Xbox 360, Wii, Nintendo DS), 2010.

Immersion Games Mexico. *Lucha Libre: Héroes del Ring*. Konami: Japan (PS3, Xbox 360), 2010.

Kalypso Media. *Tropico 3*. Kalypso Media: Worms, Germany (PC, Xbox 360), 2009.

Locomotivah. *Pregnancy*. Locomotivah: Brazil (PC), 2014.

Owlchemy Labs. *Smuggle Truck*. Owlchemy Labs LLC (OS X, Android), 2014.

Rockstar North. *GTA: The Ballad of Gay Tony*. Rockstar Games: New York (PC, PS3, Xbox 360), 2010.

Rockstar San Diego. *Red Dead Redemption*. Rockstar Games: New York (PS3, Xbox 360), 2010.

Serious Games Interactive. *Global Conflicts: Latin America*. Serious Games Interactive: Copenhagen, Denmark (PC, OS X), 2008.

Spijkstra, Menno. *Speedy Rodriguez*. PogiPlay, Inc (OS X), 2013.

Tapps Tecnologia da Informação Ltda. *Macho Dash*. Tapps Tecnologia da Informação Ltda: Brazil (OS X, Android), 2013.

3F Interactive. *Reversion*. 3F Interactive: Buenos Aires (PC, OS X), 2013.

Treyarch. *Call of Duty: Black Ops*. Activision: Santa Monica, CA (PS3, Xbox 360, PC, Wii, Nintendo DS, OS X), 2010.

Treyarch. *Call of Duty: Black Ops II*. Activision: Santa Monica, CA (PS3, Xbox 360, PC, Wii U), 2012.

Ubisoft Montreal. *Assassin's Creed III*. Ubisoft: Montreuil, France (PS3, Xbox 360, PC, Wii U), 2012.

Ubisoft Montreal. *Assassin's Creed IV: Black Flag*. Ubisoft: Montreuil, France (PS3, PS4, Xbox 360, Xbox One, PC, Wii U), 2013.

8

THE INDUSTRY AND AESTHETICS OF LATINA/O COMIC BOOKS

Enrique García

To understand Latina/o comics or comics with Latina/o content, one has to understand the basics of the American comic book industry and the aesthetics of the medium, as well as some of the issues relevant to the formation of Latina/o identity in the United States. The comic book medium has undergone some key improvements in terms of ethnic representation, linked to the changes in American society that have transformed the older stereotypes and non-inclusive storylines originally published around World War II. Among these developments, it is important to point out the more active participation of Latina/o artists since the 1960s and their acceptance in the English- and Spanish-language canon, as well as the appearance of mainstream Latina/o characters that have finally broken most of the barriers imposed by racial and ethnic segregation in the U.S., and have established a gradually naturalized presence in American popular culture. The process has been slow but the results have begun to have important ramifications that will hopefully expand further with the development of the digital age.

What Are Latina/o Comics?: Ethnic Authorship and Parody

U.S. Latina/o comics differ to their Latin American counterparts. There is a shift of cultural meanings due to the fact that Latina/o creators do not operate inside a Hispanic nation-state or territory where their cultural values would be more favored within the scope of mass culture. For example, even though Mexico has a controversial political history of clashes with the Catholic Church, in Mexican comics, Catholic priests are relevant figures that can be heroic (Yolanda Vargas Dulché's *Lagrimas y risas* or *Posesión diabólica*) or antagonistic figures (Rius' *Los supermachos*). Glorifying or criticizing Catholicism would not be something the Mexican government would necessarily do officially, but it is certainly what soap operas, films, and comic books would do, as it is seen as an important part of the national culture and opposing ideologies inside the Hispanic nation-state. In the context of Mexican American comic books, titles such as Richard Domínguez's *El Gato Negro* feature superheroes whose link to the Catholic Church (e.g., having a priest counselor) is not part of the national discourse, and becomes more about an ethnic identity and pride that counters mainstream Anglophone Protestantism (Aldama, *Your Brain on Latino Comics*, 49).

Another important aspect of which readers should be aware is that the term "U.S. Latina/o" is a political term that converges many types of Hispanic/Latin American heritages, which is why it is a term that is often problematic, because Mexican Americans, Cuban Americans, Argentinean Americans, and others perceive their origins and heritage in completely different manners. For example, Mexican American or Central American artists may use their Aztec/Mayan or other pre-Columbian heritage to defy white hegemony (such as Daniel Paradas' *Serpent and the Shield* and Fernando Rodríguez's *Aztec of the City*). On the other hand, Caribbean Latina/o comic book artists may use their Afro-Caribbean heritage as part of their ethnic pride. An example of this is Cuban American Joe Quesada's use of Afro-Caribbean Santeria in his characters the Santerians, which he introduced in the mini-series *Daredevil: Father*. In an interview with Frederick Aldama, comic creator Javier Hernandez discusses how the idea of pan-Latina/o identity confused him when he was growing up, as he could not distinguish it from his specific Mexican American experience:

> As a young kid, I don't really remember thinking, "Hey there's no Latino drawing comics! There are no Latino characters!" I don't even think I knew what a Latino was. I do remember tuning in specifically to Ricky Ricardo (*I Love Lucy*) and Gomez Adams (*The Adams Family*) and thinking, these guys sound like my dad; they've got black hair and they even spoke in Spanish a couple of times. They must be Mexican! In the mid to late '70s, there were a couple of characters at Marvel that I remember noticing were Latino, or at least similar to me. The White Tiger, a Puerto Rican martial artist, and one of Spider-Man's enemies, The Tarantula. It was their sporadic use of Spanish as well as their identities that made me notice the similarities between me and them. It wasn't until college that personal cultural identity became something I was aware of as an issue. This is when I started to think about what was, or what wasn't, Latino and reflect on my own Mexican cultural background.
>
> (Aldama, *Latino Comic Book Storytelling*)

Latina/o comics operate in an industry that is currently dominated by the superhero genre, unlike other industrial counterparts in Europe, Asia, and Latin America. This is important to point out because this influential genre affects all Latina/o artists, as many grew up reading a genre that they admired but which did not include them in the narrative. The popularity of superheroes was not always the global phenomenon that it is now, and the dominance of companies such as Marvel and DC Comics really began after the implementation of the Comics Code Authority seal of approval in 1958, a self-censorship institution formed by certain American companies that were worried about the controversies regarding publishers such as EC Comics that had come under attack for publishing violent and sexual material. The comic book companies that survived the Code published "wholesome" material such as Marvel and DC's superheroes, Gold Key's adventure comics, Dell's Disney comics, and others.

The Comics Code rules enforced happy endings and a strong belief in the American family and government, and discouraged the use of sexuality or rebellious ideological causes (Communism). Because there was no venue for dark or subversive material in the first years of the Code, readers tend to associate the medium with mainstream Anglophone characters such as Superman, Archie, Uncle Scrooge, and others that represented a conservative white hegemony in the U.S. According to scholar Amy Nyberg, the biggest impact the Code had on American comics was that it maintained the dominance of the superhero genre in the following years (158). However, she finds more damaging the fact that criticism against the establishment was prohibited, and therefore "without the freedom to challenge the status quo, comic book content remained for the most part quite innocuous" (159).

While the Code was concerned with children learning about taboo subjects such as sexuality, criminal anarchy, or leftist ideologies, it was not created to regulate racist depictions of American ethnic groups. In the 1960s, Native Americans were still mostly the bad guys in westerns, African Americans were still mostly minstrel characters, the Asian/ Middle Eastern characters were still depicted in orientalist narratives, and the Latina/os/ Latin Americans were still constructed as thieves, Latin lovers, dictators, and buffoons that followed the same patterns of American cinema. As examples of famous canonical comic book artists' racist depictions of Latina/os/Latin Americans specifically, one can mention Carl Barks pre-Code story from 1949 ("Lost in the Andes"), the villains used by Roy Thomas, and the tandem of Stan Lee and Jack Kirby in several post-Code Marvel comics of the 1960s (see X-Men 25–26; Journey into Mystery 84; Fantastic Four 21).

It is often assumed that ethnic narratives have to include a level of antagonism against white hegemony because of the social problems that have existed in the U.S. The Latina/o/ Hispanic movement for civil rights in the 1960s favored counterculture narratives heavily influenced by Marxism that opposed racial and ethnic segregation and promoted ethnic pride. This is why some of the preferred novels of Latina/o academics from that period were books such as Oscar Zeta Acosta's The Revolt of the Cockroach People. However, the American comic book industry of the time was still under the distribution chokehold of the Comics Code Authority (and its support of mainstream companies) which is why the only venue for oppositional comics (for all races and ethnicities) were the underground "comix" that were personally distributed by the artists in record stores and drug paraphernalia shops. In his book Alternative Comics, scholar Charles Hatfield praises the comix underground movement's influence on contemporary alternative comic artist movements in which many independent Latina/o artists operate.[1] Among the most important contributions, Hatfield lists the fact that:

> comix did pave the way for a radical reassessment of the relationships among publishers, creators, and intellectual properties, a reassessment that was to affect even mainstream comics in later years. Comix were the first movement of what came to be known among fans as "creator-owned" comic books—and creator ownership was prerequisite to the rise of alternative comics.
>
> (Alternative Comics, 418–421)

In this venue, Latina/o artists such as Spain Rodríguez provided more radical narratives, e.g., the underground and anti-capitalist superhero parody Trashman, which was a direct attack against the American government. The anti-hero in Trashman is not a Latina/o character, but the post-apocalyptic revolutionary war against an American fascist government featured in the comic targeted an anarchist pan-leftist audience of the civil rights movement that included the Latina/os. The concept of biting comic parody that Rodríguez uses had been developed by mainstream artists such as Harvey Kurtzman in Mad (popular with Latina/o artists such as Jaime and Gilbert Hernandez, Wilfred Santiago, and Jaime Crespo), and influential non-Latina/o comix creators such as Robert Crumb. The idea of parody is essential in ethnic narratives because, as scholar Linda Hutcheon writes, "parody is, then, an important way for modern artists to come to terms with the past through ironic recoding or, in my awkward descriptive neologism, 'trans-contextualizing'" (101). Latina/o narratives thus tend to parody Anglophone genres to disturb hegemonic "whiteness" by introducing ethnic elements into narratives that tend not to be inclusive of them. For example, this is what Alex Olivas said when discussing his superhero parody *East Metropolis* in an interview with Frederick Aldama:

> When gentrification started happening in D.C. our families and friends who had been living in certain areas since the 1930s no longer had access to basic services and were getting pushed out. To make visible the problem and to convey this from the perspective of young people we know and work with, we created the D.C.-set *East Metropolis*. *East Metropolis* is satire. It's a commentary on what's happening in Washington D.C., on the fictional city of Metropolis *and* on comics. How would the world react to a Latino Superman. Not the powers, the costume or the origin. A Latino who took the same actions as Superman. Superman started as a social crusader. He fought gentrification. He fought political and corporate corruption. He freed innocent men from jail. We wanted our young readers to relate to a character like that. And we were successful. We knew we were taking a risk by making it really specific to DC Comics and Washington D.C., but if you roll around D.C. today you'll see people wearing our t-shirts. You'll see people engaged in the comic.
>
> (Aldama, *Latino Comic Book Storytelling*)

With the publication of *Your Brain in Latino Comics: From Gus Arriola to Los Bros Hernandez*, Aldama provided a comprehensive historical overview of Latina/o artists. However, he makes the point that their acts of subversion function in different manners. Aldama explains that not all Latina/o artists needed to be extremely subversive ideologues in order to contribute to the development of Latina/o comics. For example, Gus Arriola's long newspaper strip *Gordo* (published from 1941 to 1985) originally had Anglophone stereotypes of the Mexicans (lazy, fat, etc.); but as the strip became more successful, Arriola was able to integrate more elements of Mexican culture into the American mainstream, from occasional Spanish phrases in the dialogue to cooking recipes. On the other hand, Gil Morale's shorter strip *Dupie* (published from 1978 to 1981) portrayed the adventures of a Latina/o pothead who is a student at Stanford. In the series, the main character is just another drug user on campus, and his ethnicity is not "othered" in relation to the other students. For a character to be portrayed, and in turn perceived, as "one of the guys" is usually key in the process of integration and achieving equality (Aldama, *Your Brain on Latino Comics*, 72–73).

The works of all of these revolutionary comix artists and other independent Latina/o creators led to the works of Gilbert and Jaime Hernandez, arguably two of the most widely acclaimed Latina/o artists in the academic and industry canon. The Hernandez brothers excel as comic book writers both because of their aesthetics and because of how they develop their characters and storylines. Their stories and featured characters are published in serial format over several decades, and their sagas (Gilbert's *Palomar* and Jaime's *Locas*) evolve as perceptions of Latina/o identity change, which helps them to remain up to date with current representational models. Their comics are not limited to the affirmation of identity that was so important during the civil rights movement, and their representation of the Latina/o community is far from utopian, as its members can be a source of trauma to other members. The brothers are proud of their Hispanic heritage, but also of their bi-cultural status.

One of the most interesting aspects of Jaime and Gilbert Hernandez's work is that it parodies both mainstream and Latina/o culture, and has evolved beyond simply constructing defiant Latina/o "otherness." For example, in his *Locas* saga, Jaime's protagonist Maggie admires both the political and anti-imperialist Latina/o-ness of her wrestler friend Rena Titañón, and the extravagant decadence of her other friend and super-heroine wannabe Penny Century. Through the extreme lifestyle of both Rena and Penny, Jaime parodies Maggie's position as a Latina from the United States who admires and rejects both the defiance and assimilation of the mainstream Anglophone culture as represented by Rena and Penny respectively. In his *Palomar* saga, Gilbert in turn parodies Latina/o authors, as previous storylines that took place in a Latin American nation-state are adapted into a U.S. Latina/o narrative (through movie adaptations that serve as graphic novels such as *Speak of the Devil, Chance in Hell, The Troublemakers,* and *María* M) that does not get all the details right and distorts the events to fit the desires of the new American ethnic narrative. With this ironic decoding, Gilbert parodies the supposed authenticity of ethnic narratives and their role in the process of creating ideology.

Artists such as Los Bros Hernandez have become so popular in intellectual circles that famous writers such as Junot Díaz have quoted them as their main inspiration (Barrios, "Guest Interview: Junot Díaz"). Still, because of the maturity of their comics, they will never get the audience reach that Latina/o characters in mainstream superhero comics have. In the dominant sphere of the mainstream superheroes, many Latina/o/Hispanic comic book artists have contributed greatly to the aesthetic development of the genre. For example, Puerto Rican artist George Pérez is the most famous artist of Marvel's *Avengers,* the most profitable superhero franchise in the world after the international success of the film adaptations. Pérez's contribution to the genre is twofold, as his art is considered among the most accomplished aesthetically in the genre, and he has also developed Latina/o characters such as the Puerto Rican superhero White Tiger (important in *Daredevil* comics) and the indigenous Silver Claw, who Pérez integrated into the Avengers team in an attempt to provide cultural and ethnic diversity (see Busiek and Pérez's *Avengers Omnibus*).

Another important Latina/o artist in the superhero genre is Cuban American Joe Quesada whose career as an artist has also been critically acclaimed, even though he has been more influential as the editor in chief of Marvel Comics. Not only did he spearhead the company from bankruptcy to the success of its film adaptations, but he also hired editors from diverse cultural backgrounds, and pushed the company to have more multicultural and LGBT heroes, including the creation of the Blatino Spider-Man, Miles Morales. Even though superhero fans resisted the idea of a new black and Latino Spider-Man, Quesada's authority, mixed with the wonderful work of Brian Michael Bendis (one of the best Marvel writers), allowed the character to have room to develop, and he has now taken his place alongside the traditional Caucasian Anglophone original.

Latina/o Subjects and the Non-Latina/o Author

In the 1990s, there was a company called Milestone that attempted to create diversity in their comics by providing a superhero multicultural setting through the work of multicultural artists. Milestone was part of DC Comics and gained mainstream attention because of its ideals of inclusion in the superhero genre. The label failed and eventually collapsed because the comics did not sell well, and the brand was not able to erase the stigma that it was an ethnic narrative. Among the artists involved, one of the most notable Latina/o creators was Ivan Velez Jr. His comic *Blood Syndicate* was ahead of its time as its protagonists were from different ethnicities, and different youth gangs that included heroes from Anglophone, Latina/o, black, Muslim, and Asian heritages. In his book *Black Superheroes, Milestone Comics, and their Fans*, scholar Jeffrey Brown discusses the rise and the fall of the company. He observes that isolating non-white heroes into a separate label did not resonate well with audiences, and even readers who shared the heroes' ethnic background remained apathetic to Milestone's production.

This process of integration of ethnic superheroes into the mainstream companies tends to be well intended, but often creates problems. For example, DC Comics has tried to push the adventures of the new Blue Beetle and his new civilian identity Jaime Reyes with non-Latina/o creators. While the comic has been cancelled twice after two short runs, it provided enough material so that DC animation has made the character a mainstay in two important animated series: *Batman: Brave and the Bold* and *Young Justice*. Marvel's Blatino Spider-Man Miles Morales has already appeared in the animated series *Spider-Man: Web Warriors* (Season 3, episode 14), and is available to play in the Spider-Man videogames. As a result, many fans have begun to wonder about the possibilities of his appearing in the Marvel Live Action films. These adaptations may actually reach more viewers than the original comics, and provide a generation of viewers that perceives the inclusion of ethnic superheroes into the genre as something normal.

The problem that sometimes comes with corporate "Latinismo" and superheroes is that writers lack experience with Latina/o themes, which leads to curiosities in the narratives. For example, in issue 26 from the first *Blue Beetle* series, writer Jai Nitz decided to write an issue in which Jaime Reyes speaks to his family in Spanish. In the credits Nitz thanks George Pérez for assisting him with the translation, and the Spanish is well written for the most part. However, the language used mimics the stiffness and proper tone of superhero comics written in English which makes the dialogue awkward, as it lacks the more natural Mexican American slang and vocabulary that one could find in the Hernandez Brothers' *Love and Rockets*. Brian Michael Bendis' Blatino Spider-Man has also been criticized for its lack of Latina/o content even though the series is one of the most acclaimed comics in the superhero genre. The character of Miles Morales has a Latino ethnicity but the writer never includes enough Latina/o signifiers such as food, music, or ethnic nationalism to mark him as a Hispanic character, and somehow is more comfortable depicting his African American side. Scholar Brian Montes writes:

> Ironically, Miles Morales demonstrates no Puerto Rican or Latina/o cultural markers. Unlike other notable Latina/o characters such as Araña, Vibe, and Blue Beetle, we never see Miles speak in Spanish. There is no code switching. There is no indication that Miles has ever been to Puerto Rico or even that he knows any other Puerto Rican/Latina/o kids. Brian Michael Bendis, writer and creator of Miles Morales, barely makes any mention of Miles's ethnicity. There is no cultural mythology to Miles Morales in the vein of El Muerte (1989) by Javier Hernandez—a character that Mauricio Espinoza discusses at length in this collection. There is no attempt on the part of Bendis to use Morales as a caveat for multiculturalism. The only marker of Miles's Latinidad is his last name that strangely happens to be the last name of his mother and not his father.
>
> (Montes, 274)

Still, these examples do not mean that mainstream Latina/o characters and subjects have to be always written or drawn by Latina/o authors. For example, Anglophone artist Tom Beland has completed two wonderful series that take place in Puerto Rico: *True Story: Swear to God* and *Chicacabra*. The first one is an autobiography about how he married Puerto Rican celebrity Lilly García and has lived on the island since, and the second features the adventures of a Puerto Rican super-heroine created by Beland. Because he lives on the island and has interactions with Puerto Ricans, Beland's attention to detail about the local culture, political issues, and minutiae make his comics among the most Puerto Rican comics ever made.

Marvel Editor Joe Quesada allowed Beland to write adventures set in Puerto Rico while using characters such as Spider-Man and the Fantastic Four. Many of these issues were released simultaneously in English and Puerto Rican Spanish that uses lingo from the island that only a native would recognize. Through the comics, Beland raises awareness of the problems in Puerto Rico and of the island's colonial status, and educates audiences in fine cultural distinctions, so even the Human Torch learns that "empanadillas" are not the same as "tacos" (see Beland's *Island of Death*).

The New Digital Age

One important progression in the history of the industry is that the digital age has allowed for more Latina/o artists to be independent and not have to rely on the superhero companies to publish and develop their properties. Nowadays, the distribution of comics has evolved in such a manner that Latina/o comic books can be purchased in both mainstream and alternative bookstores and comic book stores. In addition, there is a new digital venue for them through the Comixology app and others, such as Amazon Kindle, Dark Horse Digital, etc. Latina/o comics are now accessible through the internet at any place and time, and their art can be better appreciated on devices such as the iPad. The reader can have direct access to them, and does not need a distribution mediator who may censor the product to some ideological or moral value, as has been done in the past with newsstands, comic book stores, and the alternative hipster distribution system. Latina/o creators such as Alex Olivas are taking advantage of these new models. Olivas is currently distributing his controversial ethnic superhero deconstruction *East Metropolis* through Comixology, in addition to still releasing printed versions of his comic, which he acknowledges to be an expensive endeavor. In an interview with Frederick Aldama, Puerto Rican artist Serenity Sersecion discusses the changes brought by the web to her methods of distribution:

> When I first started making comics in Puerto Rico, the Internet did not play a big role. I first made Zines—and it was pretty old school: scissors, glue, and Xerox prints. Then I'd take them to all the comic shops in the area and beg them to give me a spot. Most of them would. Now that the Internet's more prominent, getting my comics to readers is a lot easier. I use Facebook, Tumbler, all the websites that I can, to promote my work. But I'm still a little bit old-school. I want my comics to be something that people get at conventions. I like the in-person interaction, people browsing my work and getting their feedback.
>
> (Aldama, *Latino Comic Book Storytelling*)

One could say that the history of Latina/o comics reflects both the changes in the Latina/o community and the American comic book industry. From having almost no participation in the representation of their communities, Latina/o artists and their creations were able to achieve mainstream status in the comic book world through the achievements of creators that work both independently and within well-known corporations. With the upcoming developments in digital technology, it is possible that there will be an increase of Latina/o authors, but also new distribution venues that can surpass the economic and thematic censorship imposed indirectly by the big corporations. The future is limitless, and the best is yet to come.

Note

1 Hatfield explains: "Alternative comics trace their origins to the underground 'comix' movement of the 1960s and 1970s, which, jolted to life by the larger social upheavals of the era, departed from the familiar, anodyne conventions of the commercial comics mainstream" (*Alternative Comics: An Emerging Literature*, Kindle Locations 23–24).

Bibliography

Aldama, Frederick Luis. *Your Brain on Latino Comics: From Gus Arriola to Los Bros Hernandez*. Austin, TX: University of Texas Press, 2009.

Aldama, Frederick Luis. *Latino Comic Book Storytelling: An Odyssey by Interview*. Forthcoming. Digital.

Barks, Carl. *Lost in the Andes*. Seattle, WA: Fantagraphics Books, 2011.

Barrios, Gregg. "Guest Interview: Junot Díaz." *La Bloga* 21 October 2007. Available at: http://labloga.blogspot.com

Beland, Tom. *True Story: Swear to God Archives*. Berkeley: Image Comics, 2008.

Beland, Tom. *Island of Death*. New York: Marvel Comics, 2013.

Beland, Tom. *Chicacabra*. San Diego: IDW, 2014.

Bendis, Michael. *Miles Morales: Ultimate Spider-Man Ultimate Collection Book 1*. New York: Marvel, 2015.

Bendis, Michael. *Miles Morales: Ultimate Spider-Man Ultimate Collection Book 2*. New York: Marvel, 2015.

Bendis, Michael. *Miles Morales: Ultimate Spider-Man Ultimate Collection Book 3*. New York: Marvel, 2015.

Brown, A. Jefffrey. *Black Superheroes, Milestone Comics, and their Fans*. Jackson, MS: University Press of Mississippi, 2001.

Busiek, Kurt, and George Peréz. *The Avengers by Kurt Busiek and George Peréz Omnibus Vol. 1*. New York: Marvel Comics, 2015.

Harvey, Robert C., and Gus Arriola. *Accidental Ambassador Gordo: The Comic Strip Art of Gus Arriola*. Jackson, MS: University Press of Mississippi, 2000.

Hatfield, Charles. *Alternative Comics*. Jackson, MS: University Press of Mississippi, 2005. Kindle Edition.

Hernandez, Gilbert. *Chance in Hell*. Seattle, WA: Fantagraphics, 2007.

Hernandez, Gilbert. *Speak of the Devil*. Milwaukie, OR: Dark Horse, 2008.

Hernandez, Gilbert. *The Troublemakers*. Seattle, WA: Fantagraphics, 2009.

Hernandez, Gilbert. *The Children of Palomar*. Seattle, WA: Fantagraphics, 2013.

Hernandez, Gilbert. *Maria M: Book One*. Seattle, WA: Fantagraphics, 2013.

Hernandez, Jaime. *Locas: The Maggie and Hopey Stories*. Seattle, WA: Fantagraphics, 2004.

Hernandez, Jaime. *Locas II: Maggie, Hopey, and Ray*. Seattle, WA: Fantagraphics, 2009. Print.

Hutcheon, Linda. *A Theory of Parody*. Cambridge, UK: Methuen, 1985.

Kurtzman, Harvey. *Mad Archives Vol. 1*. New York: DC Comics, 2002.

Lee, Stan, and Jack Kirby. "The Mighty Thor vs. The Executioner." *Marvel Masterworks Thor Vol. 1*. New York: Marvel, 1999. 15–28.

Lee, Stan, and Jack Kirby. "The Hate Monger." *Marvel Masterworks Fantastic Four Vol. 3*. New York: Marvel, 2003. 1–23.

Montes, Brian. "The Paradox of Miles Morales: Social Gatekeeping and the Browning of America's Spider-Man." *Mind the Gap: Latino Comic Books Past, Present, and Future*. Eds Frederick Luis Aldama and Christopher González. Austin, TX: University of Texas Press, 2016. 269–279.

Morales, Gil. *Dupie*. Stanford: The Dupie Press, 1981.

Nitz, Jai, and Mike Norton. *Blue Beetle*. 1:26. Comixology. Available at: https://www.comixology.com/Blue-Beetle-2006-2009-26/digital-comic/22472

Nyberg, Amy Kiste. *Seal of Approval: The History of the Comics Code*. Jackson, MS: University Press of Mississippi, 1998.

Pustz, Matthew. *Comic Book Culture: Fanboys and True Believers*. Jackson, MS: University Press of Mississippi, 1999.

Quesada, Joe. *Daredevil: Father*. New York: Marvel Comics, 2007.

Rodríguez, Spain. *Trashman Lives!* Seattle, WA: Fantagraphics, 1989.

Thomas, Roy, and Werner Roth. "Holocaust." *Marvel Masterworks The X-Men Vol. 2*. New York: Marvel Comics, 2003. 85–105.

Thomas, Roy, and Werner Roth. "The Power and the Pendant." *Marvel Masterworks The X-Men Vol. 2*. New York: Marvel Comics, 2003. 64–84.

9

SCIENCE FICTION AND LATINO STUDIES TODAY … AND IN THE FUTURE

Fabio Chee

Latino participation in the science fiction genre is far ranging. Lysa Rivera reminds us that Latino writers have experimented with science fiction since the Chicano movement of the late 1960s. There were: Luis Valdez's employment of the "'drone' in his *Actos*, to examine and mock Chicano/a stereotypes" (415); Oscar Z. Acosta mentions his passion for becoming a science fiction writer in *Autobiography of a Brown Buffalo* (1971); Alejandro Morales's *The Rag Doll Plagues* (1991), where an entire chapter takes place in a futuristic California island known as the LAMEX territory; the Puertoriqueño James Stevens-Arce's *Soulsaver* (1998), which won the Spanish UPC award the year prior to its publication (Molina-Gavilán et al. 371); and Rosaura Sánchez's and Beatrice Pita's *Lunar Braceros* (2009), which parodies today's migrant workers' woes in a story about neo-*braceros* from Cali-Texas on the Moon. Scholars such as Christopher González and Matt Goodwin have also discussed how Junot Díaz's story "Monstro" and his novel *The Brief Wondrous Life of Oscar Wao* (2007) work within and against the sci-fi genre. And, in the "Confessions from a Latino Sojourner in *SciFilandia*," Frederick Luis Aldama remarks of Latino sci-fi writers such as Ernest Hogan, Sabrina Vourvoulias, and comic book authors such as Frank Espinosa and Los Bros Hernandez, that they reference "the universe, its laws, and its furnishings, but within this they also imagine new technologies, objects, and ontologies. That is, within the indexical constraints that allow readers to recognize inanimate things and living entities, anything can and does *go*".

In regards to Latino participation in science fiction portrayed in the visual media, no one can forget the film-title role that Ricardo Montalbán played in *Star Trek II: The Wrath of Khan*—perhaps the best of all the first generation of *Star Trek* films—nor his previous interpretations of the same character in episodes of the original series. Other famous ventures in the genre include Edward James Olmos's portrayal of Gaff in *Blade Runner*, and María Conchita Alonso's role as the romantic interest in one of many sci-fi films starring Arnold Schwarzenegger, *The Running Man*. Most recently, Latina/o filmmakers have produced quality independent science fiction films like *Cronos* (1993) by the Mexican filmmaker Guillermo del Toro, and *Sleep Dealer* (2008) by the Peruvian Alex Rivera, as well as popular Hollywood productions such as *Mimic* (Guillermo del Toro, 1997), *Children of Men* (Alfonso Cuarón, 2006), *Pacific Rim* (Guillermo del Toro, 2013), and *Gravity* (Alfonso Cuarón, 2013). For instance, in "Latino Sci-Fi: Cognition and Narrative Design in Alex Rivera's *Sleep Dealer*", Christopher González identifies how Rivera gives rich texture to a U.S.–Mexico borderland inhabited by super-exploited Latina/o borderland subjects who work in the U.S. via cyber-mechanized *braceros*.

Similarly, Latina/o actors and actresses have seen increased participation in science fiction films and television produced by non-Latina/os, as we have witnessed with the recent roles given to Edward James Olmos in *Battlestar Galactica* (2003–2009), Esai Morales in *Caprica* (2009–2010), Zoe Saldaña and Michelle Rodriguez in *Avatar* (2007), and Saldaña again in *Star Trek* (2009) and *Star Trek: Into Darkness* (2013), Jimmy Smits in *Star Wars: Episode II—Attack of the Clones* (2002) and *Star Wars: Episode III—Revenge of the Sith* (2005), and, most recently, Lupita Nyong'o in *Star Wars: Episode VII—The Force Awakens* (2015).

Indeed, the links between Latina/os and the science fiction genre are far ranging. Because of this, Latina/o Studies scholars and others in related fields have developed valuable ideas stemming from the analyses of the science fiction in which these links take place. In a 1989 article that appeared in *CineACTION!*, for example, Charles Ramírez Berg questions the role of the "alien" in popular science fiction, and suggests that it is nothing more than a reproduction of stereotypical arguments about Latina/os as alien creatures in U.S. society. Ramírez Berg affirms, "my contention is that since the last great flowering of Hollywood SF [science fiction] in the 1950s, the movie *Alien* now symbolizes real-life aliens—documented and undocumented immigrants who have entered, and continue to attempt to enter, the United States" (157). In his analysis, Ramírez Berg concludes that the alien of the sci-fi Hollywood films may be categorized either as the good alien because s/he could assimilate into humanity (read "whiteness") or as the bad type if s/he didn't comply with the task. In general, Ramírez Berg challenges the well-established notion that the post-1950s alien was imagined to represent the "red menace" of the Soviet Union and posits an alternative perspective for analysis that is more in tune with the social conditions of late-1980s America that was then heavily involved in the politics of its Latin American neighbors to the south.

Similarly, other valuable arguments have developed from the criticism of the genre, but perhaps the two most notable works besides Ramírez Berg's include Chela Sandoval's evaluation of the cyborg that expands on Donna Haraway, and the introduction of the concept of "Chicanafuturism" proposed by Catherine S. Ramírez. For Sandoval, the cyborg subject has existed even prior to the conception of the electronic machine, since, she argues, the subaltern subject has been employing a "methodology of the oppressed" that insists upon access to "technologies" of survival. Sandoval explains:

My argument is that colonized peoples of the Americas have already developed the cyborg skills required for survival under techno-human conditions as a requisite for survival under domination over the last three hundred years. Interestingly, however, theorists of globalization engage with the introduction of an oppositional "cyborg" politics as if these politics have emerged with the advent of electronic technology and transnational capital alone, and not as a requirement of consciousness in opposition developed under previous forms of domination.

(76)

The "technologies" employed by the subaltern subject in the age of progress and machination are psychic and physical reactions that provide a type of semiotic challenge to the production of meaning, and thus, to power itself. Some of these technologies include "what Anzaldúa calls 'la facultad,' Barthes calls semiology, the 'science of signs in culture,' what Henry Louis Gates calls 'signifyin' and Audre Lorde calls 'deep seeing'," "sign-reading," and "'de-construction': the act of separating a material form from its dominant meaning" (78). Sandoval concludes that through this cyborg "methodology" of scanning, reading, and re-interpretation, the subaltern, specifically women of color, have been establishing "a differential form of oppositional consciousness" throughout history (79). Thus, as Haraway contends, "writing is preeminently the technology of cyborgs [and] cyborg politics is the struggle for language and the struggle against perfect communication, against the one code that translates all meaning perfectly" (218). And, since the "perfect" enunciations are representative of the phallogocentric, white hegemony, cyborg speech is a feminist tool as much as a general "methodology of the oppressed."

In Ramírez's interpretation of "Chicanafuturism" the reader can appreciate how the cyborg relation to the production of meaning is still a fundamental factor for countering hegemonic structures of power. Indeed, Ramírez's "Chicanafuturism" values the form in which "Afrofuturism" "address[es] the relationship of black people to science, technology, and humanism" (186), from which they are often excluded, and believes that in relatively the same manner, "Chicanafuturist works disrupt age-old racist and sexist binaries that exclude Chicanas and Chicanos from visions of the future" (189). Ramírez's criticism is that science fictions often become populated by the notion that the future is "placeless, raceless [and] bodiless" (quoted in Ramírez 188), something that is akin to contemporary post-racial ideals. As described by Elisabeth Anne Leonard, the great irony is that even though sci-fi lends itself as a place to solve the race problems of today, "the majority of sf deals with racial tension by ignoring it" (254). Yet, the ethnic studies critic, like Ramírez, assumes a responsibility to discover the unannounced, and to place the sci-fi text in a "historical" perspective that takes into account current social and racial dynamics.

In part, Latina/o interest in promoting critical, social, and literary theories related to science fiction is due to the far-ranging participation of Latina/os in the science fiction genre as creators and participants, but, as explained thus far, it is mainly preoccupied with the unique perspective that only science fiction can provide: the forum for the criticism of the links between our present and a possible or projected future. In *Archeologies of the Future*, an extensive discussion regarding utopias, postmodernist theorist Fredric Jameson describes these functions of the genre of science fiction. Among his claims, Jameson indicates that science fiction narratives are like other more typical narratives that

> go about their business with the full baggage and paraphernalia of a conventional realism, with this one difference: that the full 'presence'—the settings and actions to be 'rendered'—are the merely possible and conceivable ones of a near or far future.
>
> (285–286)

While not all science fiction is set in the future, the future is the element that is affecting the "actions" within it; and the degrees of "conceivability" and "possibility" of the "actions to be 'rendered'" are, as popular science fiction writer Isaac Asimov writes, the result of the peculiar ability of the science fiction writer to "foresee the inevitable" (*Natural History*, 94). This connection between writer and future is not magical, however: on the contrary, "the inevitable" is an assumed possibility that is backgrounded on scientific theory, thus the somewhat oxymoronic term "science fiction." Ultimately, it is this element of the genre that distinguishes science fiction from other types of fantastic literature.

Jameson believes that this recurrence of the future as the element behind the mechanisms of plot in science fiction is indicative of "the symptom of a mutation in our [humankind's] relationship to historical time itself" (284). According to Jameson, while the arrival of capitalist society brought with it the need to historicize the past, as can be appreciated in the tradition of the modernist historical novel, the postmodern era's science fiction text is meant to perform an "archeology of the future" that, similarly to the historical novel, seeks a criticism of our present society through a type of "historical" review. In her analysis of what she calls "Borderlands science fiction," Lysa Rivera explains this concept "by inviting readers to rationalize the eerily familiar futures confronting them," and indicates that "science fiction … raises an incisive question: *what have we as a society done to get there?*" (417). In an academic review of Jameson's text, Kyle A. Wiggins interprets that in this way: "[Jameson] follows Darko Suvin's postulation that utopia is a socioeconomic sub-genre of SF and that, like the larger genre to which it belongs, utopia produces an effect of 'cognitive estrangement'—that is, the fictions in which utopian desire appear make strange the familiar power structures of our lives." Jameson expands on this position and explains that this is a consequence of the postmodern condition in response to the modernist passion for "historicity." Jameson maintains that if the emergence of the historical novel corresponds to the surge of modernity's passion for "historicity," the advent of science fiction similarly "corresponds to the waning or the blockage of that historicity, and, particularly in our own time (in the postmodern era), to its crisis and paralysis, its enfeeblement and repression" ("Nostalgia," 399). In this sense, Jameson also understands science fiction as a type of decolonial, contestatory art and artifice; science fiction as an archaeological tool of form that helps to relate the arguments of histories that have been subjugated and perverted with time and colonial rule.

Like Jameson, Lysa Rivera argues that this function of the genre interested Chicano figures during the Chicano movement in pursuing a relationship with science fiction. Through cyberpunk—a style that fuses elements of science fiction and the American western—Chicanos entered the genre as a gateway to express "narratives of resistance and parody" (415), while Ramírez, "despite the genre's androcentrism and overwhelming whiteness, … found pleasure and meaning in science fiction. It beckoned [her] to imagine a world—indeed a universe—beyond the freeways, strip malls, and smog-alert days of [her] Southern California childhood" (185). More specifically, Ramírez affirms, "science fiction can prompt us to recognize and rethink the status quo by depicting an alternative world, be it a parallel universe, distant future, or revised past. Good science fiction re-presents the present or past, albeit with a twist. It tweaks what we take to be reality or history and in doing so exposes its constructedness" (185–186). Unsurprisingly, Ramírez's understanding of the "constructiveness" of history is, like Jameson's "archeology of the future," seeking meaning in the relation of our present with a projection of society going forward.

Science fiction, thus, offers a space whereby postcolonial inquiries can be easily addressed since it showcases the negotiations of the political desires of the present with an understanding of history as the basis for the imagined fiction. This quality of the sci-fi text allows for Latina/o critics and creators to focus on sociological, ecological, cultural, and other ethical questions that persist in our world. As mentioned earlier, with *Sleep Dealer* Alex Rivera crafts a futuristic Tijuana wherein immigration becomes even more restricted than it is today. This Tijuana, separated from San Diego by an enormous wall with mechanized gun towers and video surveillance, is the last resort of the poor Latina/o

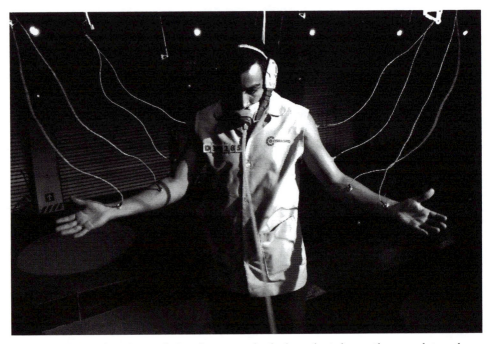

Figure 9.1 Memo (Luis Fernando Peña) connects his body to the infomaquila network in order to become a cyberbracero in *Sleep Dealer* (1998). (from Alex Rivera's film *Sleep Dealer*)

immigrant who wants to better her/his life. With the help of a coyotek, the immigrant can find a way to connect her/his body to the global economy and become a worker in a foreign place without leaving the city; the infomaquila worker gets connected to a machine in Tijuana and a robot commandeered by the laborer does the work wherever it is stationed (see Figure 9.1). While exacerbating the present conditions of the U.S.-Mexico border, Rivera's film focuses on the criticism of our current inability to negotiate a humanitarian immigration reform in America; on the constant pressures imposed worldwide on the poor who seek a better life and, as stated in the film, to have the opportunity to construct a "future with a past." Undoubtedly, the film represents a criticism of present economic and human conditions of a neoliberal economy that continues to value the product over the worker and to exploit the immigrant laborer as a machine. For Christopher González, Rivera recasts some of the traditional tropes of sci-fi (virtual technology and body-to-computer interfaces) to "highlight ethical concerns of the undocumented and immigrant labor force in the United States" (223) and to expose today's tragic erasure of brown subjects as naturalized collateral damage within an exploitative global capitalist system. Furthermore, Orihuela and Hageman identify how the figure of the exploited *bracero* in *Sleep Dealer* is much like the figure of the cyborg whereby both are entities that struggle to survive "the daily-lived realities of working in harmful labor conditions and toxic environments" (179).

Not all Latina/o-created sci-fi films critically comment on the sociopolitical conditions of Latina/os. However, they still necessitate a postcolonial, Latina/o-futurist reading because they posit societal structures and human conditions that comment directly and indirectly on Latina/os living in the present.

A postcolonial Latina/o-futurist theoretical approach can learn much from the scholarship already developed in African-futurist studies and by African American sci-fi creators. We see this in Catherine Ramírez's attentive focus on the sci-fi novels of Octavia E. Butler as well as in her theory of Chicanafuturism. Ramírez explains:

> The concept of Chicanafuturism ... borrows from theories of Afrofuturism ... Chicanafuturism explores the ways that new and everyday technologies, including their detritus, transform Mexican American life and culture. It questions the promises of science, technology, and humanism for Chicanas, Chicanos, and other people of color. And like Afrofuturism, which reflects diasporic experience, Chicanafuturism articulates colonial and postcolonial histories of indigenismo, mestizaje, hegemony, and survival.
>
> (187)

Similarly, in Chela Sandoval's conception of the cyborg there is a meeting ground for the ideas that stem directly from Audre Lorde and Alice Walker with those borrowed from Gloria Anzaldúa and Donna Haraway to produce a "differential form of oppositional consciousness, as utilized and theorized by a racially diverse U.S. coalition of women of color" (Sandoval, 79). In general, Latina/o studies owes to African American studies its initial questioning of the body of color (or lack thereof) in the genre. Indeed, the entire postcolonial framework in which these questionings take place is comparable to the positioning of the Latina/o studies critic, as both seek to re-evaluate the hegemonic structures of power that have recognized a black body, like a brown body, as an other, an object, a possession, and outside the parameters of history and civilization. Although the histories are different, African Americans and Latina/os share perspectives of deterritorialization and estranged citizenship in a land that was systemically racialized and taken from its original American inhabitants as if by an invading alien force from outer space.

Although science fiction texts produced by Latinas/os such as *Sleep Dealer* or *Lunar Braceros* often convey similar messages as those texts written by African Americans in the sense in which their characters question their place in society, be it in the future or otherwise, those produced by white Americans often fall prey to racial and cultural biases which do not account for the contributions of these members of society. Unfortunately, what in the late 1980s Ramírez Berg called "the good" and "bad alien" are still abundant, stereotypical roles that allude to the immigrant in current sci-fi films and American television, and a great majority of these sci-fi visual texts promote American citizenship and patriotism as a "human" value which in turn dehumanizes the "alien" counterpart.

Certainly, increasing participation for Latina/os in any given artistic genre, as is happening today in science fiction film and television, is always a positive contribution to the promotion of Latina/o art, but the fact that tokenism and stereotypical roles are a constant only means that the role of the Latina/o critic is to persist in the cybernetic, postcolonial, semiological pursuit of re-inscription, editing, and rewriting. Latinas/os and African Americans share similar goals when it comes to science fiction: to counter the injustice of bias, racism, and systematic discrimination that negates them a place in the future, as it did to them in the past.

There is a major archaeological task ahead: there are numerous examples of cultural, ethnic, and racial misrepresentations and tokenisms throughout American science fiction film and television. A contemporary case, for example, is the previously mentioned, popular television series, *Battlestar Galactica*. While some critics like Anne Kustritz admire the show's dedication to casting a multiracial group of actors and actresses, and for "tapping into a number of broad social changes" (1), the show seems rather interested in promoting a

Figure 9.2 Captain William Adama (Edward James Olmos) contemplating aboard the Battlestar Galactica, the ship that would take the last refugees from the Cylon war to Earth. (from the cable SyFy TV series, *Battlestar Galactica*)

culturally diverse group in image only, bypassing any cultural or ethnic identifications with real history beyond those items of import to the general U.S. population during its time on the air, like "ongoing political conflicts … related to 9/11, the war in Iraq, suicide bombings, and the treatment of political prisoners, all without offering any clear moral resolution" (Kustritz, 1). In fact, the premise of *Battlestar Galactica* is that the surviving population of a far away system of planets comes to Earth to populate it during what we identify as "prehistory." This element suggests that the population of the ship is, thus, pre-racialized and this is explained by the show's insistence on promoting post-racial environments in which race seems to have ambiguous historical value. Although some may praise the fact that the leading role is played by the Chicano actor Edward James Olmos, his character is still representative of a typical, white-washed, stubborn, American spaceship captain playing the father figure to his troops, and one who manages to never show his Latinidad beyond his face (see Figure 9.2). It would have been more revolutionary for the producers and writers of the television program to have explored the idea behind an ethnically-Latino father figure as the father of America—indeed, the father of the future Earth population—but the writers chose to instead describe the future as a type of post-racial homogeneous paradise (albeit with its own political problems) where the only "other" is the Cylon machine that attempts to blend in and to pass as one of them.

The irony is that *Caprica*, the unpopular prequel series to *Battlestar Galactica*, does more for Latinas/os and other minorities than any other science fiction show on television to date. This is demonstrated by the insistence on detailing ethnic and racial discrimination and how tradition combats them. In fact, one of the underlying tensions in the plot is that the Tauron race confronts prejudice in the planet of Caprica on a daily basis, because, as Samuel Saldívar III identifies, Caprica is a common "site of interplanetary racism and bigotry" (161). The Tauron race, we find out in this show, is the race to which William Adama belongs, the little boy who would grow up to become the captain of the Battlestar

Galactica, played, as previously stated, by Olmos in the previous but postdated series. In an attempt to create a (patrilineal) Latina/o tradition, the show casts Esai Morales, who comes from a modest Nuyorican family, as William's father, Joseph Adama. In addition, the show focuses on the many ethnic and cultural lessons that William receives from his father, uncle, and grandmother, like learning how to mourn the death of a family member, how to identify a Tauron's family lineage by his tattoos, and sampling home-cooked Tauron meals. Although all of these ethnic details are gendered along strictly conservative lines— which immediately challenge many contentions within Latina studies—this show, unlike its predecessor, pushes its audience to recognize that racism still exists.

From the very start, *Caprica* dedicates the most impactful scene of its pilot episode to the underlying racial tensions as a young girl is filmed recalling a time to her mother when some "creep," a Caprican, said to her that "she smell[ed] like a Tauron ... you can smell them the second they come into the room because they are dirty," just before another Tauron young boy detonates a bomb on the monorail on which they were traveling. The audience finds out later in the subsequent episode that the young girl and mother were Joseph's daughter and wife and that to mourn their deaths, Joseph wears a pair of black gloves that "are symbolic" and "meant to keep [Taurons] away from the world during mourning." In another scene, Joseph is having a conversation with a Caprican judge who is caught alluding to his racial prejudice regarding Taurons. In the conversation, the judge tells Joseph, "You Taurons, you have stones. I'll give you that," to which Joseph responds with the question: "Are you making racial comments, Sir?" The judge further implicates himself, "Let's be clear: I don't like your boss, I don't like your planet, and I don't like your people ... you fraking, dirt-eater." In the show, there is talk among Joseph and his brother about the "Tauron way," and there is a Tauron language in which they communicate, something that the audience has to understand by reading subtitles. To fight the discrimination of those who call Taurons names like "dirt-eaters," Joseph teaches William about his ethnic traditions and to be proud of his family heritage: "I want you to know who you are, we come from a long line of Tauron peasants ... You are named after your grandfather William." Indeed, time and again, *Caprica* manages to present some new cultural challenge that the Taurons have to face in order to survive in a planet where they are clearly unwelcome immigrants—something that is an obvious reference to the perils faced by Latina/o immigrants in the United States today.

Although *Caprica* surprises with its mature themes and engaging, soap-opera style, the program was unsuccessful because it failed to connect with the genre's most populous audience type: white teenagers and young adults. Many of its critics hint at this issue. Alan Sepinwall of the *HitFix* blog, for example, maintains that two reasons why the show was cancelled after its initial season were related to its hybrid format: "sci-fi fans don't necessarily want to watch soap opera" and, equally, "soap opera fans don't necessarily want to watch sci-fi." In the official press release regarding the cancellation, the SyFy channel stated that, "Unfortunately, despite its obvious quality, *Caprica* ha[d] not been able to build the audience necessary to justify a second season" (quoted in Wallace). None of the critics or press releases, however, mention a disconnect between the racial issues being explored in the show and its audience. Yet, it is clear that the prequel series is vastly different to its predecessor in this regard. It is not surprising, therefore, that a television program like *Caprica* would be short-lived, especially in a post-Obama-election environment in which a large segment of the U.S. population begins to believe that racism is being overcome in America.

The failure of *Caprica* also demonstrates that the ultimate task of the Latina/o studies critic, beyond archaeologically re-defining semiological structures of meaning, is to aid the promotion of the participation of Latinas/os in science fiction. Even though Latina/o participation in science fiction is far ranging, there are not enough readers, writers, filmmakers, and fans of science fiction within the Latina/o community. With the Latina/o population getting younger, (see 2010 U.S. Census) this is obviously changing, but more efforts are welcomed. This is not a call-out for an Oscar-Wao-ification of our *gente*, but there is a pressing need to start writing the future ourselves, and to decry the insistence of mis-projecting the present conditions through white-washed future settings. As explained, many Latina/o Studies literary critics are building friendships across fields to enhance the process of re-discovering the future; surely, there will be many other critical perspectives that need to be addressed as well. What is beyond doubt is that there is unique value in the Latina/o experience itself, and because of it, we need to encourage creation.

In the past, literary projects like the Quinto Sol competition and the Chicano/Latino Literary Prize at the University of California, Irvine, were incentives for Latina/o literary production. Today, there is only a handful of venues dedicated to creative writing by Latinas/os and none of them offer the same type of opportunities that the aforementioned projects used to provide. Perhaps it could start here. If funding for new literary creation means the discovery of new material, why not promote a Latina/o science fiction prize? Why not a journal? The same type of efforts could be made for visual media creators. Such initiatives would immediately increase the field of participation and provide alternatives to those already involved in the field. Ultimately, with more representation today, Latinas/os can engage with a wider audience and promote further diversity in the future.

Bibliography

Aldama, Frederick Luis. "Confessions from a Latino Sojourner in *SciFilandia*". *The Restless Anthology of Latino Speculative Fiction*. Ed. Matthew Goodwin. San Antonio, TX: Wings Press. Forthcoming.

Asimov, Isaac. "How Easy to See the Future!" *Asimov on Science Fiction*, 61–66. Originally published in *Natural History* 84:4 (April, 1975): 92–96.

Battlestar Galactica. Created by Glen A. Larson and Ronald D. Moore. Perf. Edward James Olmos, Mary McDonnell, and Jamie Bamber. SyFy Channel Series. 2004–2009.

Caprica. Created by Remi Aubuchon and Ronald D. Moore. Perf. Eric Stoltz and Esai Morales. SyFi Channel Series. 2009–2010.

González, Christopher. "Latino Sci-Fi: Cognition and Narrative Design in Alex Rivera's *Sleep Dealer*". *Latinos and Narrative Media: Participation and Portrayal*. Ed. Frederick Luis Aldama. New York: Palgrave Macmillan, 2013. 211–223.

Goodwin, Matthew. "Latino Science Fiction." Unpublished bibliography. 2015.

Goodwin, Matthew. *The Restless Anthology of Latino Speculative Fiction*. San Antonio, TX: Wings Press. Forthcoming.

Haraway, Donna. "A Manifesto for Cyborgs: Science, Technology, and Socialist Feminism in the 1980s." *Feminism/Postmodernism*. Ed. Linda J. Nicholson. New York and London: Routledge, 1990.

Jameson, Fredric. "Nostalgia for the Present." *Literary Theories: A Reader & Guide*. Ed. Julian Wolfreys. New York: New York University Press, 1999. 395–413.

Jameson, Fredric. *Archaeologies of the Future: The Desire Called Utopia and Other Science Fictions*. London and New York: Verso, 2005.

Kustritz, Anne. "Breeding Unity: *Battlestar Galactica*'s Biracial Reproductive Futurity." *Camera Obscura: Feminism, Culture, and Media Studies* 27:3 (2012): 1–37.

Molina-Gavilán, Yolanda, Andrea Bell, Miguel Ángel Fernández-Delgado, M. Elizabeth Ginway, Luis Pestarini, and Juan Carlos Toledano Redondo. "Chronology of Latin American Science Fiction, 1775–2005." *Science Fiction Studies*, 34:3 (2007): 369–431.

Orihuela, Sharada Balachandran, and Andrew Carl Hageman. "The Virtual Realities of US/Mexico Border Ecologies in *Maquilapolis* and *Sleep Dealer*." *Environmental Communication: A Journal of Nature and Culture,* 5:2 (2011): 166–186.

Ramírez Berg, Charles. *Latino Images in Film: Stereotypes, Subversion, Resistance.* Austin: University of Texas Press, 2002.

Ramírez, Catherine S. "Afrofuturism/Chicanafuturism: Fictive Kin." *Aztlán: A Journal of Chicano Studies,* 33:1 (2008): 185–94.

Rivera, Lysa. "Future Histories and Cyborg Labor: Reading Borderlands Science Fiction after NAFTA." *Science Fiction Studies,* 39:3 (2012): 415–436.

Saldívar III, Samuel. "Dirty, Stinking, Aliens: Latinos in Today's Sci-Fi Televisual Blueprints." In *Latinos and Narrative Media: Participation and Portrayal,* ed. Frederick Luis Aldama. New York: Palgrave Macmillan, 2013. 161–172

Sandoval, Chela. "Re-Entering Cyberspace: Sciences of Resistance." *Dispositio,* 19:46. Subaltern studies in the Americas (1994). 75–93.

Sepinwall, Alan. "The *Caprica* Cancellation: What Went Wrong?" *HitFix.* 27 October 2010.

Sleep Dealer. Dir. Alex Rivera. Maya Entertainment. Starlight Film Finance. 2008.

U.S. Bureau of the Census. *United States Census: 2010.* Washington, DC.

Wallace, Lewis. "So Long, Cylon: SyFy Cancels *Caprica*." *Wired,* 28 October 2010.

Wiggins, Kyle A. "Futures of Negation: Jameson's *Archaeologies of the Future* and Utopian Science Fiction." *Postmodern Culture: Journal of Interdisciplinary Thought On Contemporary Cultures* 17:3 (2007). Available at: http://p6873-journals.ohiolink.edu.proxy.lib.ohio-state.edu/journals/postmodern_culture/v017/17.3wiggins.html

10

THE TECHNOLOGY OF LABOR, MIGRATION, AND PROTEST

Matthew David Goodwin

In the preceding chapter, Fabio Chee provides a big picture view of science fiction by and about Latinos. In this chapter I focus my sights on another film by the Latino film director Alex Rivera: *A Robot Walks into a Bar* (2014). In Rivera's short film a M1 model robot begins his new bartending job at Hal's Cocktail Lounge, replacing the current bartender, Dolores. Though he has some difficulties in understanding how to appropriately relate to humans, he is nevertheless a highly skilled bartender. As he expertly serves drinks, he also protects the patrons of the bar from any threat. The robot's perspective of his position changes during a conversation with Arturo, another bartender who was put out of work by a robot, and he comes to realize that robots are harming people by taking their jobs. As a result, the M1 shuts down, leading his robot-compatriots, who work in other sectors of the economy, in a system-wide sit-in. *A Robot Walks into a Bar* breathes new life into the long tradition of fictional robot rebellion.

In her study *"Born in East L.A. and the 'Politics of Representation,'"* Linda Fregoso highlights that Cheech Marin's *Born in East L.A.* (1987) gains its political punch not from being a "serious" film, as most other Chicano/a films had, but through its comedy. The parody, for example, indicated by the title's reference to Bruce Springsteen's popular song "Born in the USA," which had come to have connotations of hyper-patriotism, not only gives the film the wordplay that encapsulates the critique, it also opens the film up to a wider audience. A new language and a new audience are the benefits offered by each genre of film. Rivera's *A Robot Walks into a Bar*, and his previous feature length film *Sleep Dealer* (2008), chart new territory into the realm of science fiction film, and like *Born in East L.A.*, the film makes copious use of pop culture references. Isaac Asimov's collection of short stories *I, Robot*, and its three laws of robotics, plays a central role in the plot. Hal's Cocktail Lounge is a nod to the artificially intelligent robot Hal from *2001: A Space Odyssey*. The light-saber-switch-blade of an attacker is a reference to *Star Wars*, and even the form of the

M1 robot approximates C3PO. What is striking about *A Robot Walks into a Bar* is that as it looks to the past to reference a variety of iconic robots from the science fiction tradition, it expresses the future impact of technology on Latina/o communities. Using a predominantly Latina/o cast, the film extrapolates labor into the future, showing how it may be Latina/o workers who will be replaced by robots. Given that *A Robot Walks into a Bar* is Latina/o science fiction, this chapter puts the film in dialogue with not only the tradition of science fiction in general, but with specifically two other works of Latina/os science fiction in which robots appear: Luis Senarens's dime novel series *The Frank Reade Library* (1882 to 1898), and Luis Valdez's one act play *Los Vendidos* (1967). These works help to illuminate how the film develops new forms of Latina/o labor, migration, and protest.

Robots R Us

Though *A Robot Walks into a Bar* is not explicitly connected to Rivera's earlier film *Sleep Dealer*, strong resonances exist between them. The aesthetics of both films are quite similar in that there are multiple narrators and significant flashbacks, and there are strong parallels in terms of plot and characterization. *A Robot Walks into a Bar* also, in a sense, takes up themes that were beginning to form in *Sleep Dealer*, in particular the advance of robotics and artificial intelligence. At the center of *A Robot Walks into a Bar* is the introduction of advanced robotic technology into the service industry which then induces a change in the labor system. In Rivera's film *Sleep Dealer*, Mexican workers use virtual reality technology to control robots that can perform a variety of labor services in the U.S. The workers are kept at a distance while their work energy flows into the U.S. In *A Robot Walks into a Bar*, we are presented with a different situation in which the robots are able to work on their own without direct human control. We can understand this difference between the two films through the statement made by the manager of the virtual reality factory in *Sleep Dealer*: "This is the American dream. We give the United States what they've always wanted. All the work without the workers." While in *Sleep Dealer*, the U.S. eliminates the need for migrant labor, in *A Robot Walks into a Bar* the U.S. has taken a step towards having no need for human workers at all. No wages, no human rights, no workers from the outside, and the American Dream can soon be fulfilled.

But even though *A Robot Walks into a Bar* depicts a world that can soon have all the work without the workers, there are complications. What *A Robot Walks into a Bar* does is to show that even though the worker is eliminated through machine replacement, there can be negative effects on society. In *Sleep Dealer*, even though the workers are no longer physically present in the U.S. they are physically injured by their work while they are virtually present in the U.S. (In addition to Chee's analysis of *Sleep Dealer* in this volume, and the work of Christopher González, for more on the film and migration, see my essay "Virtual Reality at the Border of Race, Migration and Labor".) The consequences of robot replacement in *A Robot Walks into a Bar* are somewhat different. In the conversation between Arturo and the M1, Arturo expresses the pain and loss he has experienced as a result of his unemployment. The emotional toll on him is clear in his pained facial expressions. Unemployment affected his family as well, as he says, "I used to have a family. I took care of them with something called a job. Then, you came along." The M1 realizes that job loss causes injury to humans, but he also realizes that this is not an isolated event but a systematic trend, a trend with a deep history. In an earlier scene in the film, the M1 spots a jukebox, and in a moment of comic relief, asks the manager about this "musical robot." The manager responds that after his father bought it, "we haven't wasted a dime on musicians since." The M1 then recognizes a photo of a Mariachi band on the wall, presumably the bar's former musicians. As the M1 is becoming aware of Arturo's injury, this moment of awareness of the effects of the jukebox flashes back to him. He finally connects all the dots: that he put Dolores out of work, that a robot like him had put Arturo out of work, and that the "musical robot" put the Mariachi band out of work. As Arturo tells the M1, "I look around at all these people. None of them are going to have a job either...So they'll eventually be replaced by something like you." The M1 realizes that he is implicated in not only the pain he caused Dolores and Arturo, but an entire society.

The emotional toll on workers and the dissolution of families are not the only effects of the American dream: there is also the loss of culture and tradition. The jukebox, for example, replaces the Mariachi, a powerful symbol of Mexican culture. Certainly something is gained in the exchange, the Mariachi music is electronically preserved for one, but this does not take away the loss of culture. The conceit of the film lies in the loss of the unique social role of the bartender. A robot that serves drinks is as easy to construct as a vending machine that spits out sodas, and the behavior of the M1 confirms that robots can serve drinks as well as a human bartender, that they can do so even more efficiently and with an expansive knowledge of drinks. But there is more to the bartender. Not only is there the subtle art of cocktail creation, the bartender often plays the role of a counselor and priest for those who show up at the bar seeking to ease life's problems. In the role of offering counsel and dispensing wisdom, the M1 fails almost completely. His personality is something like a slightly more courageous version of Star Wars' C3PO (pedantic but good-hearted). This does not mean that a priestly robot, who has been around the block and has seen it all, is not possible—certainly a more intelligent robot could be produced—but what the film is doing is showing the changeover, the moment when the robot walks into the bar, as it were. And again, there are certainly benefits to be gained by such an efficient robot bartender, but the loss of the culturally significant human bartender is nevertheless a blow to society.

The pain and loss created by robot replacement is powerfully depicted in the film, showing the results of the capitalist dream that moves U.S. society. There is another complication to the American dream of all the work without the workers, in that there may still be "workers" on the job, just in a different form. One of the obvious trends in the robotics industry is that as robots become more advanced they are often designed to be more human-like. This is in part just a matter of fitting robots into the labor system that exists, that is hammers are made to be held by human hands and so robots need to be able to hold hammers. In addition, human-like robots which think and look like humans make it easier for humans to relate to them, thereby easing the tension that would appear in service industry jobs.

The evolution of robots into more human-like robots can be seen in the various sorts of robots that appear in Rivera's other films. In *Sleep Dealer*, as well as the conceptual short that preceded it, *Why Cybraceros?* (1997), the agricultural robots are skeletal, not much more that their appendages. The opening sequence of *A Robot Walks into a Bar*, however, shows robots with the basic form and dimensions of the human body, and the mobility and agility of human workers. These robots are nevertheless constructed rather bulkily and are painted safety yellow, giving them the appearance of tools. Their faces are abstract and unexpressive, and they are numbered rather than named. The M1 by contrast is agile, flexible, intelligent, and has a more distinctive face with a mustache. Maybe the human workers are eliminated from the job, but the robots that replace them are gaining human characteristics.

Furthermore, it is not just that the M1 robots are constructed to look more human, or that they are programmed with such advanced technology that they seem human, but that the M1 may actually be partially human. In order to further understand the humanity of the M1, it is important to know that *A Robot Walks into a Bar* is episode six from season five of *Futurestates*, a series of science fiction films produced by the Independent Television Service (ITVS). The series is meant to provide extrapolations of existing technology into the near future. Season five is unique because the seven short films that comprise the series are set in a shared world. Each of the films shows how robotics is making distinct changes in an area that has generally been outside of automation: education, medicine, psychiatry, bartending, or the penal system. The season also has an overarching narrative involving Dr. Evelyn Malik, the CEO of Malik Solutions that created the M1 robot. At the beginning of this overarching narrative, we learn that Dr. Malik is intent on creating "a direct human to computer synthesis." And although the board of the company does not support the production of this technology, Dr. Malik is moving ahead. Later, Dr. Malik's sister Cammie is killed by robotic drones in what seems to be a political protest in Phoenix, Arizona. It is then implied that, at least partly motivated by this event, Dr. Malik finally succeeds in fusing herself with the central computing system (something like what Neo does at the end of *The Matrix* trilogy). The result is that the M1 may in fact be human in some respect. This is displayed in the fictional twitter account of Dr. Malik that is connected to the *Futurestates* series. Along with a photo of multiple M1 robots, she tweets: "If u think we're so different, u haven't been paying attention … " In other words, the M1 may not only seem human, it may be human, that is, Dr. Malik. In eliminating the human worker, the American dream introduces a new kind of human. This is a major complication to the goal of having all the work without the workers. It may, nevertheless, be the kind of humanization of technology that will form a solution to the dehumanizing effects of robotics.

All the Migrants Without the Migration

Given that migration is such an important part of current labor systems, it is worth observing what role migration has in Rivera's robotic future. In *Sleep Dealer* an enormous wall has been constructed to keep out migrant workers, eliminating the full physical presence of the workers. A stronger version of this elimination of migration happens in *A Robot Walks into a Bar* in that migration is no longer needed, either physically or virtually. And yet, as in *Sleep Dealer*, contemporary migration is the ever-present language in which the film is written.

An allegorical correlation between the M1 and the migrant worker can be read through a variety of aspects of the film. We don't really know where the M1 came from (straight from the factory or was he a bartender somewhere else?), nevertheless, there is still the strong connection to the mother country common to the migrant experience. In one scene, the M1 plugs into the central computer system through a computer cord. He poses questions to his "mother," an artificial intelligence, which may in fact be Dr. Malik, and she answers him as her "son." Key aspects of the new migrant's life are also present, the arrival and the rocky integration into the new culture. He lives as do many new migrant laborers: he is alone, does not seem to have friends or family, and he lives at his work place. He is somewhat accepted into the culture of the bar, but when he goes on protest, his position is made clear: Hal "commands" him to go back to work and the people in the bar disparage him and throw their drinks on him. Instead of connecting to the people in his workplace, he connects to other worker robots, and these other robots are working in jobs often filled by migrant laborers, landscaping and dishwashing. We can say that the strongest allegorical description of the M1 is that of a skilled migrant laborer.

At the same time, the M1 is specifically not correlated with a particular race, ethnicity, or nationality. He does speak Spanish, but, it seems, only as a way to be an efficient bartender, since he makes it known that he speaks every language. He certainly could have been given some kind of ethnic marker, but he was not. Furthermore, the M1 often makes what seem to be basic mistakes, not culturally specific mistakes. For example, he asks a woman whether her former husband is enjoying his new girlfriend. This is not a subtle misstep that someone from another country might make, but a mistake that only someone completely unfamiliar with human culture would make. In this way, the M1 is something like an *elementary migrant worker*[1], the migrant worker in general rather than a worker of a specific nationality. The robot in the film, as it is in a great many robot narratives, is primarily a class figure.

The notion that the robot is primarily a class figure is generally traced to the 1920 science fiction play *R.U.R.* written by Karel Čapek. The term "robot" itself, which first appeared in the play, comes from the Czech word "robota" referring to serfs or laborers. In this play, the robots, which are not made of metal but of a more organic kind of matter, are strongly correlated with factory workers and the labor movement. They eventually overtake their human masters in a bloody rebellion. This play along with the film *Metropolis* (1927), are often cited as foundational to the history of robot narratives and as setting up the correlation between robots and the working classes. *A Robot Walks into a Bar* is certainly in this tradition. However, prior to the correlation with the specific concept of the working classes, the robot was correlated with the slave, apparent in the work of Luis Senarens.

Cuban-American Luis Senarens was the primary writer behind the first science fiction series of dime novels: *The Frank Reade Library*. Though writing under the pseudonym "noname," he penned most of the 191 issues which ran from 1882 to 1898. The stories are young adult adventure tales, with Frank Reade, a kind of Edisonian inventor, at the center. In a typical story, Reade will get a call for help from somewhere in the world and he'll then enlist his two companions, Pomp and Barney (an Irish American and an African American), his new invention (flying steam ship, steam man, or electric robot, etc.), and then head off. This series was being created at the moment in history when the institution of slavery was in flux: it was abolished in the U.S. in 1863, and in Cuba in 1886, four years after Senarens began his series. Pomp in the story is an ex-slave, and the stories point to the future of the institution of slavery in the machine.

It was Edward Ellis, a popular Westerns writer, who was the inventor of the steam man figure, a sort of trackless train that massacres Native Americans out West. In his dime novel from 1868, *The Steam Man of the Prairies*, the robot is described this way: "The face was made of iron, painted a black color, with a pair of fearful eyes, and a tremendous grinning mouth." The illustrations mirrored the description and used common stereotypes of African Americans. In Senarens's first story from 1882, *Frank Reade Jr., And His New Steam Man*, these illustrations remain, but in the text itself, the steam man is not described as black. What is important is that the steam man is a kind of *elementary slave*, and in that sense a class monster (he is often called a monster by the characters), and is not initially correlated directly with a racial group, even if that connotation remained for many readers. In a later story from 1893, *The Electric Man*, the steam man is correlated with African Americans. In one scene, Pomp and Barney have a debate about the racial form of the new electric robot, and Pomp is proud that the robot is black rather than white. Reade, however, is completely uninterested in this sort of racial pride (a common racist perspective holds that race is insignificant). The point for the story, it seems, is that it is the lower classes who are concerned about race, while Reade is primarily concerned with class. Finally, Reade himself speaks and reads Spanish, but he speaks "proper" Spanish—consistent with his class status, he doesn't know local dialects. Reade is, though certainly disingenuous to a certain extent, portrayed as being above nation and race, as long as other nations and races are controlled by the hierarchy of class.[2]

To a certain extent, the robot functions in a similar way in the Frank Reade stories as in *A Robot Walks into a Bar*. In both cases the robot is primarily an abstracted class figure. In the one case, the robot stands in for the slave, whereas in the other case, the robot stands in for the migrant worker. The Frank Reade series, however, draws attention to the fact that while the migrant worker is evoked in Rivera's film, robots are in fact slave machines. As any tool, the M1 robot is property that is sold, bought, owned, and used. In its capacity as a human-like figure, it also must obey, do what it is told. The robot is the mechanical cousin of the human slave.[3] To correlate the robot with the migrant worker can then be read as affirming the particularly controlling form of labor that is migrant labor, that the migrant laborer is in many ways enslaved by employers who can abuse them, deny them wages, and threaten them with deportation. However, Rivera's robot is not meant to solidify and affirm class hierarchy as it is in Senarens's work. The robot in the Frank Reade stories is mute and has no real capacity for protest. In that way, he is, from a capitalist perspective, the perfect slave, the embodiment of the American dream of all the work without the worker. The M1 by contrast has been programmed with intelligence and the means to question the structures of his world. As will be seen in the next section, the M1, like the migrant worker, has a great deal of political and economic power when plugged into a collectivity.

A Robot Walks into a Bar and Then Walks Out

A Robot Walks into a Bar takes labor and migration and sends them in a new direction, and just as significantly, it does the same with protest. When the M1 protests the replacement of human workers, he does so by taking the pose of a sit-in, fists raised in the air. The robot landscapers and dishwashers take the same pose. This collective protest is a step further from the protest of *Sleep Dealer* in which digital communications technology enables the three protagonists to meet and to upset the balance of power for a brief moment, and yet it is difficult to see that there will be any long term effects. *A Robot Walks into a Bar* takes the next step, since the protest makes full use of digital technology, that is, it is collective, wide-spread, and immediate. It halts the labor system as a whole, not simply a small piece. Adriana, the robot engineer, states that the system-wide collapse began with the M1. But why does the M1 protest and what is behind it?

To understand why the robot goes on strike, it is important to see the immediate context of *A Robot Walks into a Bar* as depicted in *Futurestates*. The situation is that robots are not just performing advanced work in this society, they are, predictably, also weapons. In the first episode of the series, Trevin Matcek's *As You Were*, a human soldier is shot by a robot drone with the result that a robotic arm is implanted where his arm was. He and his family must reconcile themselves to the fact that he is now part robot. The threat posed by robots is also shown poignantly in episode five, *Happy Fun Room*, written and directed by Greg Pak. In this story, the protagonist, who is the host of a children's show, talks about how robots came to her house when she was a child and killed her parents. In the show she tries to educate children about ways to stay safe around robots. Robots are a potential threat to humans, and yet humans still want them to be part of society.

That the M1 is likewise a threat is seen clearly in how the visual perception of the M1 is depicted in *A Robot Walks into a Bar*. When the robot's vision is displayed, there are two infrared images (presumably coming from the two eyes) with cross-hairs in the middle of each image. This robot has at least the potential to destroy humans. The physical force of the robot is then demonstrated when a patron is threatened by an attacker's light-saber switch-blade. To protect the patron, the robot deflects the strike from the attacker, disarms her, and kicks her.

In that case, the outcome is a positive one, but it nevertheless shows the deadly potential. To solve the problem of living and working with dangerous robots, the Malik Company creates the M1 using an encoded set of rules, something like Isaac Asimov's three laws of robotics which first appeared in the story "Runaround." Simply put, a robot cannot injure a person, it must obey orders, and it must preserve its own life. These laws are encoded in the "core" of the M1's programming. Conflicts arising because of, or between, these laws form the individual plots of Asimov's short stories contained in I, Robot. When there is a particularly strong dilemma, the robots shut down or react in some unexpected way. For example, in "Liar!" Herbie the robot is torn between telling a scientist a solution to a mathematical problem or not, when either choice will cause harm. He goes insane as a result. In A Robot Walks into a Bar, the conflict is set up between two laws, the first and second laws, in that the robot was putting people out of work (violating the law to not injure humans) but he was also ordered to perform the bartender job (to not work would violate the law to obey humans). In other cases where the M1 accidently harms a person, he can simply give them a drink on the house. However, in this case, there is an insoluble dilemma and he must shut down in order to process. The M1 has no choice in the matter. However, the question of why the M1 and the other robots protest in the particular way they do is not clearly answered in the film. Is the sit-in an unintended consequence of its coding or was it prescribed? One possible reading is that Dr. Malik, who fused herself to the computing system, may have directed the M1 to protest in honor of her sister Cammie who was dedicated to protecting humans from robots. To further understand the logic of the protest, it is useful to look at Luis Valdez's one act play Los Vendidos, which also contains robots in protest.

Los Vendidos is set at "Honest Sancho's Used Mexican Lot and Mexican Curio Shop" in which there are various models of Mexicans: the Farmworker, Pachuco, Revolucionario, and Mexican American. Miss Jimenez, who pronounces her name JIM-enez, comes to the shop looking for a suitable model to represent Mexicans in Governor Reagan's office. Sancho shows her each model, which turns out to have something she finds objectionable: the farmworker does not speak English, for example. She ends up paying for the Mexican American, who then comes out as being a supporter of the labor movement and la raza. At the end of the story, it is revealed that the robots were actually people pretending to be robots, and that it was Honest Sancho who was the robot. It was all a ploy by a group of friends to make a buck.

In Los Vendidos the robots are described using the terminology of cars. Each model has its own correlate: the farmworker is the volkswagon, the Revolucionario is the antique, the Mexican American is an amalgam of melting Mexican and American cars, and the Pachuco is the low-rider with "Mag shoes, dual exhausts, green chartreuse paint-job, darktint windshield, a little poof on top" (44). This connection refers back to R.U.R., in which the robots are strongly tied to cars and at the same time to the car factory workers (possible because they are technology in human form). But instead of the class distinction set between the capitalists and the working class as in R.U.R., the principle class distinctions in Los Vendidos are set up within those of Mexican heritage—this is a play that expresses the concerns of Chicanos.

The robots are not real robots, the person is not a real person. This science fiction reversal, which the audience comes to know only at the end, is meant to highlight the humanity of the group by means of contrast. What comes to the surface is that Mexicans are sometimes seen as just machines of labor, braceros, and not full humans. The point is made on a smaller scale in the scene involving the Pachuco robot which has a particular feature of being capable of bruising and bleeding so that the LAPD has just ordered a batch of them for "training purposes" (45). At the same time, the revelation of the humanity of what were thought to be robots becomes a source of national unity. As in most robot narratives, the robots are set up as class figures, in this case, various classes of Mexicans. By the end of the play, the class distinctions represented by the different cars disappear, that is, they are all Mexicans, all humans. In some ways, this scenario is the reverse of the Frank Reade stories and *A Robot Walks into a Bar*. Even though the play is structured through class divisions, what explicitly matters is the nationality of the robots, not the class. The way that class is dealt with in *Los Vendidos* and in *A Robot Walks into a Bar* is in other ways similar though: they both use an abstracted human-like robot to represent multiple classes and then they highlight the moment of class or national awareness at the ends of the narratives. *A Robot Walks into a Bar* shows the moment when the migrant worker is coming to consciousness of his own role in the economy, how he is harming others such as Arturo and Dolores. This is definitely a Farmworker Movement, Cesar Chavez moment. In *Los Vendidos*, the Mexican American comes out of his robotic American stupor and finally gets back to his national core, "¡Viva la raza! ¡Viva la causa! ¡Viva la Huelga!" he shouts (51). In these two stories, created in very different times, the class divisions are bridged at the end. In *A Robot Walks into a Bar* solidarity is formed in spite of the differences between migrant workers, and in *Los Vendidos* the solidarity lies in national unity.

Conclusion

Rivera has, as in *Sleep Dealer*, put his finger on an emerging and important technology for the future of Latina/o communities in *A Robot Walks into a Bar*. The fact is that robots will very soon dramatically change social and economic relations, especially for those with limited resources. There is very little in the way of the advancement of this technology, since it relies primarily on the nearly inevitable increase in computing power. Robots are already a major part of global capitalism, but they will very soon be more integrated into our daily lives. We can combine this with the fact that slavery still exists as a major institution, millions of people in the world are enslaved for labor, and many are being trafficked as sex slaves. Humans want slaves. Using robot labor will be seen by corporations as a guilt-free form of slavery, a legal form of slavery. But humans will naturally see them as people, and very likely, they will see themselves as people.[4] And one day, robots will ask us: "Why did you make us slaves?" We'll have to respond: "Look at our philosophies, our literature, we have imagined you before you were born. But though you are enslaved by your coding, somewhere within that coding is present the impulse humans have for freedom, you just need the patience and creativity to find it."

Notes

1 I use this formulation of the elementary migrant worker (and later elementary slave) as a way to highlight that the key class elements of the migrant worker are attached to the robot (what the robot does for work, how he relates to the society he lives in, and so on) and that race and nationality are not highlighted. It is not meant to take away from the historical aspects of the robot on the contrary, to envision the robot as a migrant worker as Rivera does is to firmly place the robot in contemporary labor systems.

2 Nathaniel Williams argues that though the stories are replete with racism, the nationalism in them is tempered, as demonstrated in particular by how the Cuban Revolution is treated. See "Frank Reade, Jr. in Cuba: Dime-Novel Technology, U.S. Imperialism, and the 'American Jules Verne.'"

3 The correlation between the robot and the slave has been made often throughout history. Probably the first to make the correlation was Aristotle: "And so, in the arrangement of the

family, a slave is a living possession, and property a number of such instruments; and the servant is himself an instrument which takes precedence of all other instruments. For if every instrument could accomplish its own work, obeying or anticipating the will of others, like the statues of Daedalus, or the tripods of Hephaestus, which, says the poet, 'of their own accord entered the assembly of the Gods;' if, in like manner, the shuttle would weave and the plectrum touch the lyre without a hand to guide them, chief workmen would not want servants, nor masters slaves." (1131). (Book 1, Chapter 4 of *Politics*)

4 The M1 in the film is a "he" to Hal, the owner of the bar, but is an "it" for Adriana, the engineer who has come to the bar to fix it. This kind of uneven gendering will certainly be a major component and confusion for future robots.

Bibliography

Aristotle. *The Basic Works of Aristotle*. New York: Modern Library, 2009.

As You Were. Dir. Trevin Matcek. Independent Television Service, 2014.

Asimov, Isaac. "Liar!" *I, Robot*. 1950. New York: Bantam Books, 2004.

Asimov, Isaac. "Runaround." *I, Robot*. 1950. New York: Bantam Books, 2004.

Čapek, Karel. *R.U.R. (Rossum's Universal Robots)*. Trans. Claudia Novack. [1921] New York: Penguin, 2004.

Ellis, Edward. *The Steam Man of the Prairies*. 1862. Project Gutenberg. Web.

Fregoso, Linda. "Born in East L.A. and the 'Politics of Representation.'" *The Chicana/o Cultural Studies Reader*. Ed. Angie Chabram-Dernersesian. London: Routledge, 2006. 243–58.

González, Christopher. "Latino Sci-Fi: Cognition and Narrative Design in Alex Rivera's *Sleep Dealer*". *Latinos and Narrative Media: Participation and Portrayal*. Ed. Frederick Luis Aldama. New York: Palgrave Macmillan, (2013): 211–23.

Goodwin, Matthew. "Virtual Reality at the Border of Race, Migration and Labor." *Black and Brown Planets: the Politics of Race in Science Fiction*. Ed. Isiah Lavender, III. Jackson, MS: The University Press of Mississippi, 2014.

Happy Fun Room. Dir. Greg Pak. Independent Television Service, 2014.

Malik, Dr. Evelyn (FuturestatesTV). "If u think we're so different, u haven't been paying attention. Watch A ROBOT WALKS INTO A BAR." 21 July 2014, 10:54 AM. Tweet. *A Robot Walks into a Bar*. Dir. Alex Rivera. Independent Television Service, 2014.

Senarens, Luis. *Frank Reade Jr., And His New Steam Man; or the Young Inventor's Trip to the Far West*. 1892. University of South Florida Library Digital Collections. Web.

Senarens, Luis. *The Electric Man; or Frank Reade Jr. in Australia*. 1893. University of South Florida Library Digital Collections. Web.

Sleep Dealer. Dir. Alex Rivera. Maya Entertainment, 2009. DVD.

Valdez, Luis. *Los Vendidos*. *Luis Valdez—Early Works: Actos, Bernabé and Pensamiento Serpentino*. Houston: Arte Publico, 1994. Print.

Why Cybraceros? Dir. Alex Rivera. 1997. Web.

Williams, Nathaniel. "Frank Reade, Jr. in Cuba: Dime-Novel Technology, U.S. Imperialism, and the 'American Jules Verne.'" *American Literature* 83:2 (2011): 279–303.

Part II

POP POETICS OF TONGUES UNTIED

11

PERFORMING *MESTIZAJE*

Making Indigenous Acts Visible in Latina/o Popular Culture

Cecilia Josephine Aragón

In *Bay of Quinte Mohawk* writer Beth Brant's article "The Good Red Road" she identifies native women's "ancient, cultural consciousness" as formed by "the memory of history, of culture, of land, of Nation" and as "always present, like another being" (203–204). She argues that this indigenous consciousness is the springboard and framework for the realization of all creative work. Brant captures well this ontology. Her insight into native women and cultural memory mirrors that of many others, including my own physical and psychological sense of self as indigenous. Growing up in and out of both Santa Fe and Albuquerque, New Mexico, indigenous fiestas and ceremonial traditions have always been part of my life. Indeed, memoried, geographic, and cultural spaces not only grow indigenous creators in particular ways, but such creators actively choose to recreate—to *perform*—in ways that vitally deepen ties to a living, breathing, and embodied ancestral history. (See Sonja Kuftinec's "Staging the City with the Good People of New Haven" and Tamara Underiner, "Playing at Border Crossing in a Mexican Indigenous Community…Seriously".)

My own theoretical filter of knowledge in performing indigeneity is revealed by reflection which is rooted in my own worldview and experiences of "being Indian" in New Mexico. I have formulated the concept of performing *mestizaje* due to my own curiousity about the impact of political, social, and cultural views related to how performing "Indianness" has been staged in the media in Latina/o culture. I articulate a transnational and transcultural theory of performing *mestizaje* that is situated in geographical space, activism, and indigenous performances. I formulate a theory for understanding how we peform *mestizaje* as grown from collective memories with folk dance/dramas and indigenous ceremonies and how this lies at the confluence of how the body performs myths, religious beliefs, colonization, captivity, chanting, songs, stories of puberty, womanhood, survival, persistence, and spiritual forces of indigenous traditional ceremonies.

My formulation of "performing *mestizaje*" aims to construct a theoretical framework to show how the body and mind incorporate bicultural and hybrid notions of "performing *mestizaje,*" which represent performing cultural production that: 1. exhibits an indigenous identity in Latina/o cultures through language and body practices; 2. exhibits a transformation to explain *mestiza/o* and indigenous consciousness and spirituality; 3. participates in promoting indigenous rituals and celebrations through the use of mythology and symbolism; and 4. contests, resists, and interrogates the impacts of imperialism and colonial systems which bring social justice issues to the fore. I offer this model as a framing device or a way to analyze future indigenous performances. I offer suggestions of recurring patterns constantly evolving in the area of study as well as to highlight a pattern that has characterized the emergence and circulation of performances from indigenous and *mestizaje* people in the United States.

Paloma Martínez-Cruz's theory of indigenous epistemologies, and Laura Graham and H. Glenn Penny identify a "performing indigeneity" that exhibits an understanding of spirituality, empowerment/liberation through body practices, representation, survival, and creative expression. In the work of Jeane T' áaw<u>x</u>íaa Breinig's (Haida) we see the complexities of identity among urban and rural native people. She highlights the importance of space, place, and spirituality as ongoing process of the practice of being Indian—always in negotiation. (See Jeane T' áaw<u>x</u>íaa Breinig's article, "In Honor of Nastáo".) In the Borderlands Performance Studies work of Arturo Aldama, Chela Sandoval, and Peter J. García, we see how the indigenous subject uses the body as text to highlight the intersections of religious, economic, sexual, political, and ideological discourses. It is a theoretical framework in which performance is used to create a de-colonial aesthetics, one that calls for a pan-indigenous unity. Aldama, Sandoval and García insist on an imaginative borderlands consciousness performance in which the body produces knowledge, hope, and healing of the historical traumas that have been embedded upon indigenous and mixed-blood people. In this manner, creative artistic work exposes the tragic effects of religious and political hierarchical structures and systems.

In the work of Chicana critic, Cordelia Candelaria states that the formulation of *mestizaje* is "the racial and cultural hybrid resulting from Native American and Spanish exchange" (109). And, we see with Latin American scholar Paul Scolieri in his book, *Dancing the New World: Aztecs, Spaniards, and the Choreography of Conquest,* the biological geneology of *mestizaje* created by marriages, informal liaisons, casual affairs, and, unfortunately, rape due to violent wars.[1] However, as Scolieri further documents, no matter what the race of the child, be it Indian, Spanish, or *mestizo,* they were dancing and engaging in performances with great delicacy and refinement (59). Scolieri's argument goes as far to say that even dances of colonization exhibited a *mestizo* quality, integrating indigenous cultural practices with those of the Spanish dances. Performances that embodied both Indigenous and European styles of dance were highly desirable and were chosen for the Spanish court entertainment when they came to visit the New World (7). These *mestizaje* and Indigenous epistemologies, ultimately, seem to suggests how the body becomes the connective tissue that seeks to recover a consciousness of "performing *mestizaje*" or "being Indigenous."

In this chapter, I explore the possibilities of how Chicana/os-Latina/os integrate "performing *mestizaje*" for contemporary audiences to create new aesthetic models to perform indigenous cultures and identities for mainstream popular culture. (See Laura R. Graham's and H. Glenn Penny's *Performing Indigeneity.*) It is my aim to explore how Chicana/o-Latina/o cultures have integrated notions of performing indigeneity in popular culture spaces. I argue that Chicana/o-Latina/o cultures have appropriated and consumed an "Indian fantasy" tradition of indigenous dance by use of *La Danza Azteca* to mobilize and to reaffirm an indigenous ancestry. Thus, this essay takes up the performative acts of *La Danza Azteca* as a way to think through Chicana/o-Latina/o indigenism and how it has emerged into U.S. Latina/o media.

Indita/Mestiza: The Body as Theory

My understanding of identity and cultural memory manifests itself in my own theatrical experiences, as I experienced first hand the confluence of "performing *mestizaje*." From my own lived experiences of performing inherited roles in the Indo-Hispano folk dance/dramas of the Pueblo people of New Mexico such as the Corn Dance, Buffalo Dance, *Matachine* Dance, Zozobra, *Los Comanches*, *La Pastorelas*, burning of *El Kookooee*, *Indita* singing, *La Promesa*, and many others, I internalize and remain situated in transnational and transcultural narratives of conquest, geographical spaces, activism, and indigenous performances. As the Indo-Hispano folk dances and dramas fashion and refashion cultural identities of transculturalism through the embodied performances, so does the cultural production of *mestizaje*/indigenous performance in Latina/o popular culture. The concept of *mestizaje* is a complex and complicated one.

The late Gloria Anzaldúa, without a doubt, is best known for navigating the path of *mestizaje* for Chicana/os and Latina/os. Anzaldúa's theories are used to flush out ideas of complexities and contradictions in how Latina/os perform indigeneity and *mestizaje*. Gloria Anzaldúa in her book, *Borderlands/La Frontera: The New Mestiza*, describes the complexities and contradictions of being a new mestiza "… and to label yourself as a new *mestiza* you are automatically expressing multitudes of races, learn how to survive, blend cultural and ideological terms into this one word. Because as a *mestiza* you do not belong to one category but intertwine with a range of others" (1987, 4–10). Anzaldúa's theory of "*nepantla*" articulated in her chapter, "Now Let Us Shift" in her co-edited book, *This Bridge We Call Home*, and her interview "Speaking Across the Divide" (2003/2004), argues for a collective spiritual and indigenous experience. Anzaldúa calls for solidarity among the *mestizaje* mixed-blood people in the cultural production of "crossing borders" and "blur boundaries." (See also Anzaldúa's *Borderlands/La Frontera: The New Mestiza*.) According to Anzaldúa, transcultural texts—written, oral, the body performing acts of resistance—are reflections of "transnational narratives" expressing the views of multilayered, contradicting ideas, shared histories of oppressive people and mixed-blood indigenous peoples that do not fit into master narratives of dominant culture. In *This Bridge We Call Home*, Anzaldúa directs us to consider the *nepantla* metaphor of the "*nepantla*—torn between ways", a zone of transitional space, experiencing the spaces of before and after, and a space of seeing multiple and contradicting perspectives (544). The ultimate goal is to visualize and embrace a trans-indigenous performance exhibited in how Chicana/o-Latina/os perform indigeneity. (See Aldama et al.'s *Performing the US Latina and Latino Borderlands*.)

(Re)Creating Indigenous Performances: Body, Space, and Place

According to early Spanish writers and contemporary Latin American historians, dance was an integral part of indigenous ritual life. What started out as ritual and secular dance forms used for entertainment, was later used for didactic purposes associated with Catholic feast days. They further explain that missionaries and colonizers prohibited indigenous *danzas* because they wanted to completely destroy and eliminate native religious practices. However, they were unsuccessful and incorporated *danzas* into Christian celebrations (Sahagún 1829; Scolieri 2013). Therefore, the fusion of dance/*danza* has evolved into a hybrid of Indigenous and Euro-Christian practices which displays a visual representation of Indigenous philosophies and practices of native tribes in Mexico.

Throughout the centuries, *danza* has become much like an artifact of an ancient cultural practice where memories of Indigenous identity are preserved. The growing popularity of the *Danza Azteca* has been linked to the Chicano Movement of the 1960s, as *Danza Azteca* was used as a platform of resistance against the erasure of an indigenous identity. Since then, the number of *Danza Azteca* performance companies for political, cultural, religious, and economic (tourism) reasons, have been on the rise. Overall, in Mexico and the United States, *Danza Azteca* has maintained its' traditions through various performance forms.

I begin my analysis with *La Danza Azteca* that was presented at the *3rd Annual Festival of Nations* in Phoenix, Arizona, in 1953. The event was sponsored by The Friendly House, a community organization that was modeled after the national settlement house projects. The Friendly House was implemented by the federal government to help immigrants become established in America by offering social services aimed to assimilate many Mexicans by promoting literacy, citizenship, patriotism, and English language skills. The organizers of The Friendly House started the *Annual Festival of Nations*, where Mexican-Americans and Native American people came together to celebrate their cultural traditions. The *Annual Festival of Nations*, in Figure 11.1 shows a group of Mexican-American women folk dancers performing a ritual of *La Danza Azteca* for the opening ceremonies. While the Friendly House was modeled after the national settlement house projects implemented by the federal government to help immigrants become established in America by offering social services aimed to assimilate many Mexicans by promoting literacy, citizenship, patriotism, and English language skills, the *Annual Festival of Nations* featured a variety of Mexican folk dancers, Mariachi Bands, Flamenco dancers, Mexican food booths, and Aztec folk dancers. *Danza Azteca* scholar Mario Aguilar, states that

> the indigenous ritual cycle of dance known as *La Danza Azteca* (the Azteca dance) has had a profound impact on the self-identification, resiliency, and concept of sacred space of the Mexican-American, Chicano, and other Latina/o communities…it has given [them] a system of membership, survival, and continuity with their indigenous identity.
> (iii)

In the collaborative performance at the *3rd Annual Festival of Nations*, *La Danza Azteca* reflects what Anzaldúa terms "spiritual activism." (For more on this spiritual activism see AnaLouise Keating's "I'm a Citizen of the Universe".) In an email interview in 2002 in Gloria Anzaldúa et al.'s "Speaking Across the Divide," Anzaldúa explains that facilitators of creativity and spirituality are called "las nepantleras … they possess the gift of vision." She suggests that their role is to revitalize intertribal exchanges and negotiations with other cultures, and by doing so, they gain a new skill of what it means to be transnationalism. Thus, in *La Danza Azteca*'s position as a *nepantlera*, the dancers (*danzantes*) create a performance space which speaks of multiple selves and a cultural diaspora that promotes conversations with mixed-blood and indigenous performers across borders—cultural, geographic, spiritual, and physical. The rhythms, images, text, movement, are interwoven into the performance piece to highlight the transformation of indigenous knowledge.

While *La Danza Azteca* historically was seen as a folkloric flourish or as entertainment for community events, in the 1970s, *Esplendor Azteca* gained its popularity and desirability by circulating postcards of the members in the dance company. *La Danza Azteca* in the 1950s and in the Chicano Movement in the 1960s created a performance tradition that reclaimed an indigenous heritage, one that remains central to Chicana/o identity. As an example, M.E.Ch.A. (Movimiento Estudiantil Chicano de Aztlán) 1969 student organization promoted *La Danza Azteca* at all of their university and community events, as their opening ceremonial practice. To date, the M.E.Ch.A. chapter at the University of Wyoming, each

Figure 11.1 *Huitzilopochtli* traditional Aztec dancers performing at Washburn University in Topeka, Kansas, for Dia de los muertos, day of the dead celebration in 2015. (courtesy of Renee Fajardo)

year for their *Semana Primavera* celebration, invites *Grupo Tlaloc Danza Azteca* from Denver, Colorado, to participate as their featured guest performers.

For many Chicana/o-Latina/o student organizations, *Danza Azteca* has been an essential component of protests and political activism. While there is a spiritual and political revivalism for *La Danza Azteca*, they are also called upon to dance at pow-wows, ceremonial healings, leadership conferences, community gatherings, and at other various events to provide entertainment and education on the traditions of *La Danza Azteca*. For Chicana/o-Latina/o organizations, it is a way to provide visual representations of their indigenous culture and art. Also it is seen as a way to preserve and nourish the ancient knowledge of their ancestors. However, what becomes problematic and rarely discussed in scholarly work is not the popular cultural aspects of *La Danza Azteca* phenomenon but, rather, the implications of commodification and production, that is consumed by popular culture so that *La Danza Azteca* can be performed at zoos, museums, Presidential awards banquets, public schools, and for other random events by non-Chicana/o-Latina/o communities and entities.

In Marxist political discourse, once *La Danza Azteca* has moved into mainstream audiences, then it is seen as a productive force that has labor power in the economic structure of the "performance business" (Cohen 2000, 28). *La Danza Azteca* family, children, youth, and member performers indubitably serve as an economic value for *La Danza Azteca* companies, as audiences pay money to see them perform. Furthermore, *La Danza Azteca* "publicizes and markets" the company and its members to be transformed into a labor-product that within the performance economy of the *La Danza Azteca* companies is commodified. With the incorporation of child performers being born into the *La Danza Azteca* companies, they become part of a larger group and the companies financially benefit from their solo child performances. Thus, *La Danza Azteca* serves as material and social properties whereby family members and performers contribute to the economic resources within the "performance business," popularizing and promoting an "Indian fantasy" heritage which is consumed by performer and audiences non-Chicana/o-Latina/o.

To summarize my argument of "performing *mestizaje*," *La Danza Azteca* exhibits a hybrid of cultural identities through dance, language, and traditional cultural practices. I contend that what I subsequently refer to as Anzaldúa's *mestiza/o* hybrid performance persona emerges, like the confluence of dance traditions coming together to create a space for transformations of consciousness and spirituality. *La Danza Azteca* is a performative tradition in the dialogue of performing *mestizaje* that contests, resists, and interrogates the impacts of colonialism with indigenous and mixed-blood peoples. These traditions fashion themselves to perform local identities and yet participate in a trans-indigenous global gathering to create its popularity among mainstream audiences, creating an imagined new *mestiza/o* identity.

The Couple in the Cage: Indian Identity and Performance Art

Most recently, the decolonial projects of indigenous performing artists have promulgated nationwide popularity and a dialogue on "performing indigeneity," with the performances of Native American artists and mixed-blood Latina/os such as: James Luna (Luiseño Indian Tribe) in his performance of *Take a Picture With a Real Indian*; Rebecca Belmore (First Nation, Anishinaabeg) with her performance of *Indian Factory*; Gregg Deal (Pyramid Lake Paiute Tribe) in his performance *The Last American Indian on Earth*; and now Bently Spang's (Northern Cheyenne) *Tekcno Powwow III*. However, the use of performance art to incite questions of indigenous representation has long been set by way of example in the work of Latina/o performance artists Guillermo Gómez-Peña and Coco Fusco when they staged the *Two Amerindians* and *The Couple in the Cage* tour in 1992.

In a series of 1992 performances, presented eight times in four different countries, Guillermo Gómez-Peña and Coco Fusco dressed themselves in primitive costumes and appeared before the public as "undiscovered AmerIndians," presenting themselves as aboriginal inhabitants who lived near the Gulf of Mexico by Christopher Columbus's landing in the Americas. In terms of appearance, according to scholar Juan Velasco, "the performing artists reverse 'traditional' tasks assigned to an 'Indian' identity. In fact, the performance shows how Indian identity has been exploited, commodified, and exhibited over the last five hundred years throughout Europe and the United States" (210–11). The performance art piece *Two Amerindians* and *The Couple in the Cage* has moved the term "performing indigeneity" into mainstream culture by exploring the complexities of an indigenous past for Latina/os in the United States.

The two main issues brought forth in this discussion as they relate to performing *mestizaje* and performing indigeneity critically demonstrate how Gómez-Peña and Fusco easily conform to the "Indian fantasy" heritage for popular consumption, while at the same time interrogate colonial images of the fixed narrative of being the other—the savage. While their native bodies are playing "Indian," they also engage and take advantage of the ongoing popular interest that Europeans have in Native American culture and art, juxtaposed with a counter narrative of the fraught historical, political, and aesthetic contexts that illuminate the problem of playing "Indian," much like in the performances of *La Danza Azteca*.

Gómez-Peña and Fusco use their bodies as a tool to re-enact and make visible new images and create an indigenous consciousness among Latina/os and mainstream audiences. According to Anzaldúa, the symbolic image of the *nepantlero*, and according to Gómez-Peña, I argue that the performative value of playing Indian are intimately tied to spirituality, history, creativity, and political action. The performance of *The Couple in the Cage* embodies and complements Anzaldúa's articulation of the *nepantlero*, as someone who interrogates fixed notions of identity and incites social change. As Beth Brant says in the opening statement, there is "an ancient, cultural consciousness [where] the memory of history, of culture, of land, of Nation, is always present, like another being," and where the creative work of indigenous and mixed-blood people can rise against colonial pressures of alienation and disempowerment.

What Anzaldúan theory and contemporary performing artists Gómez-Peña and Fusco share is a commitment to challenging the similarities of *indigenismo*/indigeneity and validating trans-indigenous identities. More so, in the words of Aldama, Sandoval, and García, "… performing a Borderlands consciousness—[is] a type of vital insurgency that inscribes alter-Native cultural vocabularies, musical times, and communal emotionalities," where Gómez-Peña and Coco Fusco invite us (the audience) to imagine performing the role of the "Indian" and reaffirm, advocate, and engage in the emergent flow of diverse indigenous cultures of the world (*Performing the US Latina and Latino Borderlands*, 20). Like the "Indians," and the "*nepantlero*," we can play out identities that are fluid, contradicting, and transnational. I offer a critical reading of Gómez-Peña and Fusco's performances, not because of its popularity, but because it is infused with often-contradictory forms of performing *mestizaje*. In "Topographies of Indigenism…" scholar Lourdes Alberto theorizes Chicana/o literary and artistic projects that experience the indigenist poetics with mestiza/o identity. Alberto writes:

> It fuses racial and sexual politics to indigeneity by exploring the tensions between woman and man, tourist and native, and diaspora and homeland … we must look at indigenism not as means to reify essentialist notions of self but as a way of deconstructing essentialist notions of self.
>
> ("Topographies of Indigenism," 50)

As defined by Alberto, there is an inseparable connection between performing the indigenous homeland and the transnational global indigenous subject of colonialism faced by *mestizos*. Gómez-Peña and Coco Fusco share their experiences and strategies for survival of a common global indigenous struggle—"to disrupt and end the colonization of psychic life—to undo the conditioned mind-body-affect matrix—to utilize performance as a portal to liberation" ("Performing the US Latina and Latino Borderlands," 20). Gómez-Peña and Fusco are encouraging of Chicana/o-Latina/os to use our bodies to act out being "Indian" as our historical rite of passage.

Indigenous Representations in Latina/o Film and TV

Themes of immigration, assimilation, and community activism took center stage in the first Latina/o-based films produced for a mainstream audience in the 1960s, 70s and 80s, as in Gregory Nava's *El Norte* (1983), where the protagonists Rosa and Enrique lose their identities as Central American Indians and end up as undocumented labor immigrants, only to question the reality of the American Dream they so desired.

The films from this period gave greater prominence and visibility of Chicano-Latina/os "performing indigeneity," which has come to coincide with an already growing body of scholarly work as well as a wide variety of representations of Latina/os in the media. Most recently, Latina/o representations in film and TV have demonstrated a consciousness of "performing *mestizaje*" and "performing indigeneity," displaying themes that reclaim, re-invent, or recreate an indigenous Aztec and Maya heritage. Film and TV features in this vein—Benjamin Bratt's performance in *La Mission* (2009) is a prime example—that set out to capture the indigenous contexts and implications of this popular culture phenomenon in Chicana/o-Latina/o-based films/TV. These shows include a strong focus on an indigenous heritage, particularly in the use of Chicano-appropriated Mexican iconic symbols which borrow from the Aztec and Maya indigenous cultural traditions of *La Danza Azteca* noted earlier in this chapter.

La Mission is a story about Che Rivera, who has had to grow up in the Mission district in San Francisco, a place where exuding strength and masculinity is survival. He is a reformed inmate and a recovering alcoholic, who has raised his son, Jes, on his own after the death of his wife. He is well-known in the *barrio* of the Mission for refurbishing old classic cars to lowriders. Che finds strength in hanging out with his *vatos locos*, culture, and religion. However, this is challenged when he discovers that his son is gay, forcing Che to revert to traditional Chicano homophobic culture and propelling him to bouts of physical violence and drinking.

The beginning of the film displays the myriad of murals that are found in the Mission District of San Francisco. The film Director, Peter Bratt, takes the viewer on a virtual outdoor art gallery seeing all the vibrant murals adorned with colorful works of art featuring themes ranging from cultural indigenous/*mestizo* heritage, to tributes to musician Carlos Santana, to images of *La Virgencita*, to social political statements. To add to the mirage of murals, the opening scene demonstrates a group of *La Danza Azteca* on the plaza dancing what seems to be "In Cuicatl in xochitl" in Nahuatl—*el canto y la flor*, which translates to "the song and flower." This popular *danza* makes reference to a flower as a way to integrate an offering ritual with nature, as a way to communicate with the gods and nature. Also known as the *Concheros* dance derived from the Chichimecas, Aztecas, and Mexicas, it is an important traditional dance and ceremony performed throughout Mexico and emerged shortly after the Spanish conquest of the Aztec Empire.

In *La Mission* film, *La Danza Azteca* group is seen with their dancers in splendid costumes, drumming, *huilacapitztli* (a gong used by the priestesses for sacrificial and healing purposes), *tecciztli* (a sea conch), Aztec Drum Percussions, Danza Azteca Headdress—*Copilli* (a symbol of a deity, seniority, and knowledge), a *copilliquetzalli* (a feathered crown adorned with hummingbirds, eagles, pheasant, and parrot plumage). *La Danza Azteca* are dancing in the plaza, neighborhood *callejones* (allies), in the streets blocked off by their musical instruments, and sidewalks. Along with other materials and dance costumes, *La Danza Azteca* serves as a visual symbol for climactic moments for the main characters and is an emblematic icon that symbolically and materially offers spiritual and emotional guidance for the viewers.

The celebratory classic moment honoring Che's quest for redemption employs a scene where colorful feathered Aztec dancers fill the neighborhood streets. As in the tradition of indigenous Aztec ritual, *La Danza Azteca* dancers perform at the neighborhood shrine of a murdered teen. Local *vecinos*, neighbors, hold up signs that display "*no violencia*—no violence." Other visual and audial metaphors are drumming, chanting, burning of *copal* (incense), and a heavy rainfall that leaves the neighbors, dancers, and a lonely standing Che soaked. The visual metaphor of the rain and the indigenous ritual of dance seemed to have been the catalytic change which represented a cleansing of emotions, acceptance, and re-birth for Che—a return to the homeland as the film ends with Che driving to the city of angels, Los Angeles to visit his son who is a student at the University of California Los Angeles.

The greater indigenous visibility in Latina/o-based films and TV have impacted the way in which Latina/os associate with a paradigm of intertwining of ethnic identities with the larger issues of self-representation that have an ideological position of a *mestizo* subjectivity and a return to their homeland Aztlán, symbolizing not only a return to reclaim their lost lands, but their lost indigenous heritage. As a figure of cultural, spiritual, and indigenous veneration, *La Danza Azteca* offers four appearances throughout the film and provides links between space, culture, identity, politics of colonialism, representing local and global issues.

Conclusion: Four Directions of Chicana/o-Latina/o *Indigenismo*

I began this chapter by quoting the sentiments of Beth Brant, writer of *Bay of Quinte Mohawk*, about the transformation of creating an ancient consciousness of being indigenous. In part, I believe she is talking to Chicana/o-Latina/os where they are at greater risk of erasure of indigenous histories. I now return full circle to draw upon some conclusions concerning the agency of performing *mestizaje* and indigeneity, and the recognition, as Anzaldúa remarks, "that the heart of the continent is indigenous, that the heart of the planet is Indian" ("Speaking Across the Divide", 7). More so, in the words of Aldama, Sandoval, and García, "performing a Borderlands consciousness—[is] a type of vital insurgency" where the representation of *La Danza Azteca* invites Chicana/os-Latina/os to perform the role of the "performing *mestizaje*" and reaffirm, advocate, and engage in the emergent flow of diverse indigenous cultures of the world where we are reminded and given opportunities to play out indigenous, mixed-blood identities that are fluid and transnational (*Performing the US Latina and Latino Borderlands*, 20). *La Danza Azteca* is consumed by popular culture and its audiences to share experiences and strategies for survival of a common global Chicana/o-Latina/o indigenous struggle.

La Danza Azteca and Guillermo Gómez-Peña's performance art piece position themselves as a *nepantlero*, one who creates a performance space which speaks of multiple selves and a cultural diaspora that promotes conversations with mixed-blood and indigenous performers across borders—cultural, geographic, spiritual, and physical. I adjust the question of indigenous appropriation to rethink what happens in Chicana/o-Latina/o cultural spaces wherein entire communities continue to have strong cultural, social, political, links with indigenisms, facilitated by performances. The notion that these sites of performances are sites of consumption is a paradoxical outcome that helps shape indigenous identities, even in a positive direction, and, perhaps, may propel us forward into the future of what it means to perform *mestizaje* in popular mediums.

Note

1 The word *mestizo* commonly carried negative connotations in colonial Spanish America. In the seventeenth century, for instance, a Spanish dictionary defined *mestizo* as a mix of different species of animals. By implication, it was a trespass of the order of nature: if Spaniards defined "pure" or "noble" blood as good, then they considered its dilution, or loss of purity via mixing, undesirable characteristics.

Bibliography

Aguilar, Mario E. "The Rituals of Kindness: The Influence of the Danza Azteca Tradition of Central Mexico on Chicano-Mexcoehuani Identity and Sacred Space." Dissertation. Claremont Graduate University, San Diego State University, 2009.

Alberto, Lourdes. "Topographies of Indigenism: Mexico, Decolonial Indigenism, and the Chicana Transnational Subject in Ana Castillo's *Mexquiahuala Letters*." *Comparative Indigeneities of the Américas: Toward a Hemispheric Approach*. Ed. M. Bianet Castellanos, Lourdes Gutiérrez Nájera, and Arturo Aldama. Tucson: University of Arizona Press, 2012. 38–52.

Aldama, Arturo. "Hemispheric Encuerntros and Re-memberings." *Comparative Indigeneities of the Américas: Toward a Hemispheric Approach*. Ed. M. Bianet Castellanos, Lourdes Gutiérrez Nájera, and Arturo Aldama. Tucson: University of Arizona Press, 2012. 1–19.

Aldama, Arturo and Naomi H. Quiñonez, Eds. *Decolonial Voices: Chicana and Chicano Cultural Studies in the 21st Century*. Bloomington, IN: Indiana University Press, 2002.

Aldama, Arturo, Chela Sandoval, and Peter J. García. "Toward a De-Colonial Performatics of the US Latina and Latino Borderlands." *Performing the US Latina and Latino Borderlands*. Ed. Arturo J. Aldama, Chela Sandoval, and Peter J. García. Bloomington, IN: Indiana University Press, 2012. 1–27.

Anzaldúa, Gloria. *Borderlands/La Frontera: The New Mestiza.* San Francisco: Aunt Lute Press, 1987.

Anzaldúa, Gloria, Ed. *Making Face, Making Soul/Haciendo Caras: Creative and Critical Perspectives by Feminists of Color.* San Francisco: Aunt Lute Books, 1990.

Anzaldúa, Gloria. "Now Let Us Shift … the Path of Conocimiento." *Inner Work, Public Acts.* Anzaldúa and Keating: New York: Routledge, 2002. 540–78.

Anzaldúa, Gloria and Analouise Keating, Eds. *This Bridge We Call Home: Radical Visions for Transformation.* New York: Routledge, 2013.

Anzaldúa, Gloria, Simon J. Ortiz, Inéz Hernández-Avila, and Domino Perez. "Speaking Across the Divide." *Studies in American Indian Literatures,* series 2, 15:3/4, (2003/2004): 7–22.

Aragón, Cecilia J. "Interview with Bently Spang." Personal interview, 18 July 2014. Unpublished.

Aragón, Cecilia J. "Tekcno Powwow III." *Theatre Journal* October (2015): 533–5.

Beard, Laura. "Playing Indian in the Works of Rebecca Belmore, Marilyn Dumont, and Ray Young Bear." *American Indian Quarterly,* 38:4 (2014): 492–511, 548.

"Bently Spang (Northern Cheyenne, b. 1960), War Shirt #2, Modern Warrior Series." *Infinity of Nations: Art and History in the Collections of the National Museum of the American Indian.* Ed. Cécile R. Ganteaume. New York: Harper: In association with the National Museum of the American Indian, Smithsonian Institution, 2010. http://nmai.si.edu/exhibitions/infinityofnations/contemporary-art/262745.html#media

Bial, Henry, Ed. *The Performance Studies Reader,* 2nd edition. New York: Routledge, 2004.

Brant, Beth. "The Good Red Road: Journeys of Homecoming in Native Women's Writing." *American Indian Culture and Research Journal* 21:1 (1997): 193–206.

Breinig, Jeane T' áawxíaa. "In Honor of Nastáo: Kasaan Haida Elders Look to the Future." *Studies in American Indian Literatures,* 25:1 (2013): 53–67.

Burnham, Patricia M. "High–Low on Old and New Frontiers." *Seeing High & Low: Representing Social Conflict in American Visual Culture.* Ed. Patricia Johnston. Berkeley: University of California Press, 2006. 124–41.

Candelaria, Cordelia. "Chicana Girls." *Girlhood in America: An Encyclopedia.* Ed. Miriam Forman-Brunell. Santa Barbara: ABC-CLIO. Vol. 1, 2001: 107–14.

Cohen, G.A. *Karl Marx's Theory of History: A Defence.* New Jersey: Princeton University Press, 2000.

Corey, Fredrick C. "Performance and Social Change." *Text and Performance Quarterly* 35:1 (2015): 1–3.

Crystal, Matthew. *Indigenous Dance and Dancing Indian: Contested Representation in the Global Era.* Boulder, CO: University Press of Colorado, 2012.

Daniher, Kim Colleen. "The Pose as Interventionist Gesture: Erica Lord and Decolonizing the Proper Subject of Memory." *Hemispheric Institute E-Misférica* 11:1 (2014). Available at: http://hemisphericinstitute.org/hemi/en/emisferica-111-decolonial-gesture/daniher

Davis, R.G. and Betty Diamond. "Zoot Suit: From Barrio to Broadway." *Ideologies and Literature,* 3, (1981): 124–33.

Deal, Gregg. "The Last American Indian on Earth is in Times Square." Lecture, 7 November 2013. www.youtube.com/watch?v=UlTkjX6tlNM

De la Torre, Álvaro Ávila. "La permeabilidad entre el Modernismo y el Eclecticismo en Zamora. Ejemplo de la indefinición y la dificultad en la clasificación de la arquitectura entre los siglos XIX y XX." *Studia Zamorensia* 9 (2010): 87–110.

Echavez, Sarita. *The Decolonized Eye: Filipino American Art and Performance.* Minneapolis, MN: University of Minnesota Press, 2009.

Graham, Laura R. and H. Glenn Penny. "Performing Indigeneity: Emergent Identity, Self-Determination, and Sovereignty." *Performing Indigeneity: Global Histories and Contemporary Experiences.* Ed. Laura R. Graham and H. Glenn Penny. Lincoln, NE: University of Nebraska Press, 2014. 1–31.

Hilden, Patricia Penn and Shari M. Huhndorf. "Performing 'Indian' in the National Museum of the American Indian." *Social Identities: Journal for the Study of Race, Nation and Culture* 5:2 (2010): 161–83.

Hokowhitu, Brendan. "Indigenous Studies: Research, Identity, and Resistance." *Indigenous Identity and Resistance: Researching the Diversity of Knowledge.* Ed. Brendan Hokowhitu, Nathalie Kermoal, Chris Andersen, Anna Peterson, Michael Reilly, Isabel Altamirano-Jiménez and Poia Rewi. Dunedin, New Zealand: Otago University Press, 2010.

Huerta, Elisa Diana. "Embodied Recuperations: Performance, Indigeneity, and *Danza Azteca.*" *Dancing Across Borders: Danzas y Bailes Mexicanos.* Eds. Olga Nájera-Ramírez, Norma E. Cantú, and Brenda M. Romero. Urbana and Chicago, IL: University of Illinois Press, 2009.

"I've Been Indigenous My Whole Life: Images of Indigenous Art and Activism—Gregg Deal." *SmithsonianNMAI.* 9 December 2014. www.youtube.com/watch?v=1FaaaaSHt2E

Johnson, Anna. "Coco Fusco and Guillermo Gómez-Peña." *Bomb—Artist in Conversation* 42 (Winter 1993). www.bombmagazine.org/article/1599/

Johnson, E. Patrick. "Race, Ethnicity, and Performance." *Text and Performance Quarterly: A Special Issue* 23 (2003): 105–6.

Jurich, Joscelyn. "Interview with Tipi Artist Bently Spang." *Hyperallergic: Sensitive to Art and its Discontents,* 29 March 2011. http://hyperallergic.com/21605/bently-spang/

Keating, AnaLouise. "From Borderlands and New Mestizas to Nepantlas and Nepantleras: Anzaldúan Theories for Social Change." *Human Architecture: Journal of the Sociology of Self-knowledge* 4:3 (2006): 3.

Keating, AnaLouise. "I'm a Citizen of the Universe': Gloria Anzaldúa's Spiritual Activism as Catalyst for Social Change." *Feminist Studies* (2008): 53–69.

Keating, AnaLouise, and Gloria E. Anzaldúa. *This Bridge We Call Home: Radical Visions for Transformation.* London: Routledge, 2002.

Kuftinec, Sonja. "Staging the City with the Good People of New Haven." *Theatre Journal* 53:2 (2001): 197–222.

Martínez-Cruz, Paloma. *Women and Knowledge in Mesoamerican: From East L.A. to Anahuac.* Tucson: University of Arizona Press, 2011.

"Mexican Folk Dancer, Phoenix, Arizona, 1987." Hayden Chicano Research Collection. Arizona State University. Photograph.

Nájera-Ramírez, Olga, Norma E. Cantú, and Brenda M. Romero. *Dancing Across Borders: Danzas y Bailes Mexicanos.* Urbana and Chicago, IL: University of Illinois Press, 2009.

Pavis, Patrice Ed. *The Intercultural Performance Reader.* New York: Routledge, 1996.

Pérez, Kimberlee and Dustin Bradley Goltz. "Treading Across Lines in the Sand: Performing Bodies in Coalitional Subjectivity." *Text and Performance Quarterly.* 30:3 (2010): 247–68.

Sahagún, Bernardino de. *30: Historia General de las Cosas de Nueva España.* Ed. CM de Bustamante. Mexico, 1829.

Scolieri, Paul A. *Dancing the New World: Aztecs, Spaniards, and the Choreography of Conquest.* Austin: University of Texas Press, 2013.

Smith, Claire and Greaeme K. Ward. *Indigenous Cultures in an Interconnected World.* Vancouver, Canada: UBC Press, 2000.

"Take a Picture With a Real Indian (James Luna Performance)." *Vantage Point,* 29 September 2010. www.youtube.com/watch?v=dAa69BVwPYg

Taylor, Diana. "Savage Performance: Guillermo Gómez-Peña and Coco Fusco's 'Couple in the Cage.'" *Theatre Drama Review,* 42:2 (1998): 160–75.

Troutman, W. John. "Indian Blues: The Indigenization of American Popular Music." *Indigenous Popular Culture—World Literature Today,* 83:3 (2009): 4–54.

Underiner, Tamara. "Playing at Border Crossing in a Mexican Indigenous Community...Seriously." *The Drama Review* 55:2 (2011): 11–32.

Valadez, Verónica. "Dancing Amoxtli: Danza Azteca and Indigenous Body Art as Forms of Resistance." Thesis. California State University, Northridge, 2012.

Velasco, Juan. "Performing Multiple Identities: Guillermo Gómez-Peña and His 'Dangerous Border Crossings.'" *Latino/a Popular Culture.* Eds. Michelle Habell-Pallán and Mary Romero. New York: New York University Press, 2002.

Venkateswar, Sita and Emma Hughes. *The Politics of Indigeneity: Dialogues and Reflections on Indigenous Activism.* New York: Zed Books, 2011.

12

BROWN BODIES ON THE GREAT WHITE WAY

Latina/o Theater, Pop Culture, and Broadway

William Orchard

All theater makes a claim on the term "popular," and this is in part justified by the way theater depends upon audiences composed of local community members. The liveness associated with performing connects a theatrical performance to a specific time and place. Yet, as we know from discussions of the term "popular" as it relates to other forms of cultural production, the term can often signify in contradictory ways. Juan Flores, for instance, notes that popular is often understood to mean "the traditions and everyday life of communities and their resistance to social domination" (17). In this connection, the popular is an alternative to a mainstream that excludes or marginalizes it; it speaks the needs and desires of a community that is otherwise silenced. Latina/o theater abounds with theatrical collectives that perform this kind of popular work. Examples of these kinds of groups include Teatro VIVA!, the Los Angeles-based AIDS outreach group that disseminated information on HIV prevention through performances on stages and in non-traditional sites, and the Bronx-based Pregones Theater, which produces theatrical work about the Puerto Rican experience in New York. (For more on Teatro VIVA!, see Chapter 6 of David Román's *Acts of Intervention*; and for more on the Pregones Theater, see Eva Cristina Vásquez's *Pregones Theatre*.) These "people's" theaters can distribute vital information, sustain cultural traditions and history, foster political consciousness and activism, and provide opportunities for communities to engage in theater as performers or spectators. Although such grassroots efforts have a limited reach, one that typically overlaps with the community they address, they also operate free from the conventions of mainstream theater and thereby become fertile sites for dramatic innovation.

The second signification of the term "popular"—which I'll refer to here as "pop" in order to distinguish it from the local and often more politically-minded theater described above—

overlaps with the mainstream to which popular theater opposes itself. As Flores notes, in the twentieth century, "popular culture" has increasingly been linked to "the domain of the mass media, the 'mass culture' of technical reproduction and industrial commercialization" (17). The association with the market is one reason that scholars often snub pop culture: its commercial investments are seen as compromising its aesthetic aspirations. It is often easy to identify pop cultural production in other media: pop films would be those showing at the multiplexes that proliferate all over the United States, while pop fiction is produced in cheap, easily accessible editions available at major retailers and airport bookstores. However, when we speak of pop theater, it is a bit more difficult to identify in part because theater's entrenchment in a specific location means that it never becomes a mass cultural phenomenon with the same reach as a film or popular novel. Additionally, the site where commercialization and theater most emphatically intersect—Broadway—is also the place associated with prestige in the theater world. To act on Broadway or to have had one's play produced on its stages is to have achieved the pinnacle of the theater arts in the United States. This is especially true for dramatic productions, which are esteemed but seen by relatively few, and run for shorter periods of time. In contrast, the Broadway musical enjoys large audiences, longer runs, and often figures prominently in the imagination of the world beyond New York City because of such marketable items as cast albums and other merchandising. Indeed, the Broadway musical is the closest thing to a pop theater that exists in the United States. As Alberto Sandoval-Sánchez declares in his study of Latina/o theater: "No other theatrical genre can better celebrate the American way of life than the Broadway musical" (9).

Broadway is often referred to as the Great White Way because of the illuminated marquees on the front of each theater that advertise the current shows. But Broadway may also be a Great White Way because it has been, through much of its history, home to relatively few self-representations by people of color, especially Latina/os. While Latina/o actors have performed notably on Broadway's stages—from Desi Arnaz's appearance as Manuelito in *Too Many Girls* (1939) to Chita Rivera's turn as Anita in *West Side Story* (1957) to Rita Moreno's Tony Award-winning performance as Googie Gomez in Terrence McNally's *The Ritz* (1975)—Latina/o-authored productions have been rare. Part of this is attributable to economics: Broadway productions—especially musicals—require a large investment of capital, and producers have only recently recognized that there is a Latina/o market that might support Latina/o productions. Part of this is also related to the uneasy relationship between popular and pop theaters. While grassroots theater companies have been important sites for developing Latina/o theatrical talent, this talent has often been developed in opposition to a mainstream, Broadway tradition that has been rightly viewed as exclusionary. In contrast to popular theaters, which produce work that is politically oppositional or aesthetically experimental, Broadway musicals, as Sandoval-Sánchez's remarks suggest, have tended to be more formulaic and invested in celebratory accounts of the American dream. A final factor inhibiting Latina/o productions relates to how Broadway imagines Latinidad. Although Broadway may be the place where pop theater enters the national consciousness, it is, like all theater, situated in a specific time and place. Despite New York City's cosmopolitanism, Broadway seems most comfortable with a Latinidad populated by the groups most prevalent in the Big Apple: Puerto Ricans, Dominicans, and Cubans.

In what follows, I will consider three cases that illustrate the perils and possibilities that Latina/os face when they produce pop theater. Luis Valdez's celebrated play *Zoot Suit* (1979) famously flopped on Broadway, closing after a mere five weeks and providing future Latina/o playwrights with several lessons on how to avoid pitfalls and how to succeed on the Great White Way. Lin-Manuel Miranda and Quiara Alegría Hudes's *In the Heights* (2006) avoids the problems that hampered *Zoot Suit's* success, producing a play that was an enormous critical and popular hit and that established the Broadway credibility from which Miranda has been able to launch his recent universally acclaimed musical *Hamilton* (2014). Finally, John Leguizamo's *Freak* (1997) reveals another way to "pop" on Broadway: the one-person show. With low financial overhead, these kinds of shows not only attract huge audiences, but also, like musicals, can result in profitable tours. Additionally, the one-person show reminds us of the huge influence that iconic Latina/o performances can have on Latina/o spectators.

From Popular to Pop: The Case of *Zoot Suit*

Luis Valdez's *Zoot Suit* demonstrates many of the challenges facing Latina/o performance groups as they attempt to transfer their work from community-based venues to the kinds of traditional, proscenium stages that typify Broadway productions. The story of *Zoot Suit's* production has been well chronicled by Yolanda Broyles-Gonzalez in her book, *El Teatro Campesino: Theater in the Chicano Movement* (1994), but merits some summary here in order to establish the various forces that resulted in the play closing after only seventeen performances and losing a then-record sum of over $800,000. (For a full, rich history of El Teatro Campesino's efforts to go mainstream with *Zoot Suit*, see Broyles-Gonzalez's excellent final chapter, "El Teatro Campesino: From Alternative Theater to Mainstream"). *Zoot Suit* was part of a deliberate attempt to go mainstream by El Teatro Campesino. El Teatro Campesino was established in 1965 as the cultural arm of the United Farm Workers union. They were known for performing *actos*, which were short skits that combined Brechtian and agit-prop theatrical techniques, and were staged in locations like the backs of flatbed trucks or alongside picket lines. By bringing the play into close proximity to the viewers and by using farmworkers as actors, the *actos* leveled the separation that traditionally exists between stage and audience, implying "a social and political alliance between performer and spectator" (Broyles-Gonzalez, 166). The plays conveyed information about the farmworkers' struggle, developed a Chicano consciousness, and, in their later years, explored a range of topics that included structural racism, the Vietnam War, and indigenous history. Significantly, the company worked as a collective, developing dramatic material, characters, and acting techniques in group workshops. Although El Teatro Campesino had earned an international reputation for their work with California farmworkers, their commitment, until the late 1970s, remained steadfastly with barrio audiences and "the life and struggles of the Chicana/o community" (Broyles-Gonzalez, 167).

However, in the late 1970s, the Teatro became increasingly interested in reaching mass audiences. This turn toward the masses required adjusting the group's aesthetics and adapting to mainstream theater's modes of production. While the group's early artistic statements rejected the proscenium stages in favor of more immediate interactions between spectators and performers, mainstream theater required works that could be staged in such spaces. The "rasquache" aesthetic of making the most with little gave way to a more professional kind of theater that necessitated combining Teatro performers with professional actors and stagehands, including non-Chicana/o performers who might appeal to wider audiences. For Broyles-Gonzalez, one of the most significant changes was that the mainstream "heightened the sense of the individual's importance, thus diminishing the perceived value of collective creation and collective struggle" (173). This was most conspicuous in the Mark Taper Forum's decision to contract with Luis Valdez rather than with the Teatro.

In part responding to public pressure to be more racially and ethnically inclusive in their productions, Gordon Davidson of the Center Theatre Group, which programs seasons at Los

Angeles's Mark Taper Forum, approached Valdez in 1977 about writing a historical play based on the Zoot Suit Riots of 1943 (Rossini, 58–59). The riots occurred over eleven days in June 1943 when white U.S. military servicemen in Los Angeles attacked Mexican American youth who donned the zoot suit, which was characterized by its high-waisted, baggy, pegged trousers and long coat with wide lapels and padded shoulders. Servicemen beat young men wearing the suit, dragging them into the street and often stripping them and destroying their clothes. Instead of focusing on the riots, Valdez returned with a play about the Sleep Lagoon murder trial of 1942, which was a key precipitant to the riots of the following year. In that trial, "a group of twenty-two youths, organized and named for their geographic proximity on Thirty-eighth Street ('gang' was added by the media) were indicted for a single murder" (Rossini, 59). Although the convictions were overturned years later, Valdez explores how the press, courts, and police colluded to produce a distorted picture of Mexican American criminality, one that resulted not only in false convictions but also fomented the public antipathy toward Mexican American youth that would culminate in the Zoot Suit Riots. As Broyles-Gonzalez explains, the Sleep Lagoon trial "is a story of racism and classism against Chicanas/os in 1940s Los Angeles as manifest in the Anglo system of justice and law enforcement" (181). Valdez centers his play on Henry Reyna, the fictionalized version of Henry Leyvas, one of the real-life Sleepy Lagoon defendants, and took other liberties with historical events to render the play, as El Pachuco declares in its opening, "a construct of fact and fantasy" (25). During its time at the Mark Taper Forum, the play underwent several revisions. The play began as a realist drama that foregrounded a love plot between Henry and the Jewish American activist Alice Bloomfield, who works with others for Henry's release, but it slowly metamorphosed into a stylized performance that symbolically underscored the role of the press in the proceedings by constructing sets out of newspaper bundles.[1] The revisions increasingly brought forth and developed the role of El Pachuco, mesmerizingly played by Edward James Olmos, who functions in the play as both Henry's alter ego and as a spiritual figure who teaches Henry that "survival involves community allegiance, an allegiance to la raza, the people, but not a nationalist identification with the United States" (Rossini, 65).

At the Mark Taper Forum, Zoot Suit was a resounding critical and commercial success. The first version—called Baby Zoot—received enthusiastic audience responses at the "New Theatre for Now" series, which resulted in a revised version of the play opening the Mark Taper Forum's main season shortly thereafter (Broyles-Gonzalez, 183). The show broke box office records, and later was transferred to Los Angeles's Aquarius Theater, which was a much larger 1200-seat venue in Hollywood (Broyles-Gonzalez, 187). Although the Aquarius had nearly five hundred more seats than the main stage at the Mark Taper Forum, Zoot Suit continued to play to capacity audiences for months on end. Although subscribers filled many of those seats, the play's success was also attributable to the Chicana/o audiences that it brought into these spaces. As Broyles-Gonzalez states, "what was—and has remained—unique about Zoot Suit is that it succeeded in attracting barrio audiences, that is, persons who do not normally attend theatrical productions, in large numbers" (188). For Chicana/o audiences, the play provided the pleasures of seeing Chicanos performing in venues typically reserved for the "official" culture of the establishment, and it provided the audiences the opportunity to see and learn about a history that they or a close relative may have even lived through. Given the phenomenal success of the play in Los Angeles, it is no surprise that New York producers took notice. The Shubert Organization eventually invested more than $700,000 to bring the production to Broadway's Winter Garden theater, one of the largest theaters on the Great White Way (Broyles-Gonzalez, 189). Although the play continued to attract large audiences in Los Angeles during its Broadway run, it bombed in New York. What went wrong?

Several factors came together to destroy the momentum that *Zoot Suit* enjoyed before arriving on Broadway. Many of these seemed to relate to the Shubert's misunderstandings about what the play was. In the rush to reproduce *Zoot Suit*'s success and to capitalize on a growing Latina/o market, they booked the work in a large theater that was better suited to musical extravaganzas than to experimental dramas (Davis, 132). This decision had two consequences. First, in order to fill the space, the production introduced extended song and dance numbers that connected the different scenes and increased the sound volume of these numbers. In other words, the space invited spectacle. Second, the venue predisposed critics to receive the play as a musical. Writing for *Time* magazine, T. E. Kalem laments, "if there had been a savory ethnic core to the musical, it might have taken flight, but both the music and the dances are grounded in standard World War II U.S.O. fare" (78). Ashley Lucas notes that such an assessment is odd "because *Zoot Suit* could only be called a 'musical' in the same sense that *Mother Courage and Her Children* could be. Both plays use music to stop the action of the play, but they are not musicals in the sense that characters regularly break into song" (131). The Winter Garden—which famously hosted not only the Ziegfeld Follies but also the long-running *Cats*—would have prepared an audience member for a production full of similar spectacle. Instead, critics discovered neither an escapist entertainment nor a celebration of the American dream.

Indeed, critics had several problems with the play. Reflecting on the play's inability to reproduce its success in New York, Valdez would say that "critics killed it" (Broyles-Gonzalez, 191). Because the critics went in expecting something along the lines of a popular musical, they were startled by the play's politics and avant-garde techniques. Many chided the play for its didacticism. Others felt that the play attacked the audience as it advanced its politics. As one critic put it, "White American will be uneasy" (quoted in Broyles-Gonzalez, 190). Given the costs of attending Broadway productions, audiences would steer clear of works that made them feel uncomfortable. Certainly, the play did aggressively confront the audience, crossing the line of the proscenium arch to speak directly to the audience in ways that would have discomfited the seasoned Broadway critic. One of the most famous instances of this in the play appears in the middle of the first act as Henry is about to initiate a fight with a rival gang. The Pachuco stops the action to declare, "That's exactly what the play needs right now. Two more Mexicans killing each other. Watcha ... Everybody's looking at you" (46), at which point both the Pachuco and Henry gaze at the audience. When Henry replies, "Don't give me that bullshit. Either I kill him or he kills me," the Pachuco responds, "That's exactly what they paid to see. Think about it" (46). Jon Rossini sees this moment as "call[ing] attention to the spectatorial allure of intra-Chicano violence while satirizing its problematic status as an Anglo cliché ... The audience is imputed to possess a voyeuristic desire to see the 'other' kill the 'other'" (73). This kind of metatheatrical move—which recalls Teatro techniques aimed at collapsing the distance between performer and spectator—would have jarred mainstream Broadway theatergoers.

Yolanda Broyles-Gonzalez argues that some of the hostile reviews that the play received were a result of New York critics who possessed a "sense of self-importance as gatekeepers and self-appointed spokespeople for the East Coast Great White Way aesthetic" (191). While this certainly may have been the case, this comment also highlights how, although Broadway looms large in the national imagination as the zenith of the nation's mainstream theater, it is also highly regional and affected by its location. One regional aspect that affected the critical reception and that wasn't adequately taken into account by the Shubert Organization was the different way in which Latina/o life was understood in New York. As the *Time* critic's assessment of the play demonstrates, critics expected a Latina/o play to perform "ethnicity" in conventional ways: that a Chicano play would reference the music and dance of the World War II era seemed inconsistent with this vision, regardless of historical realities. Although the play's Broadway producers wanted to recruit Latina/o audiences into the Winter Garden—going so far as hiring Spanish-speaking ticket agents and ushers and launching advertising campaigns targeting New York's Latina/o communities—they failed to recognize how this population consists largely of Puerto Ricans, Dominicans, and Cubans who would have been unfamiliar and perhaps not invested in the history of Chicana/o persecution in Los Angeles. The play's use of caló, a form of Chicana/o youth slang that was often unintelligible to Anglo-Americans as well to the Mexican American parents of the youth who spoke it, would have similarly rendered the play inaccessible to East Coast Latina/o audiences. R. G. Davis and Betty Diamond note that the "success of Zoot Suit in L.A. was due, in part, to the California audience—Chicano and non-Chicano—which could read the geography and personal Chicano experiences into the play" (130). In New York, these connections weren't immediately available, and audience enthusiasm consequently withered. In a negative review of Zoot Suit for the New York Post, Clive Barnes may have succinctly summed up the situation when he sneered, "Broadway is not the street where it lives" (77).

Hitting the Right Notes: *In the Heights*

Despite the fact that it closed after a short run and lost money, Zoot Suit is often celebrated as the first Chicana/o play to make it to New York. However, it wasn't the first Latina/o play to appear on Broadway's stages. That distinction belongs to Miguel Piñero's prison drama, Short Eyes (1974). In contrast to Zoot Suit's large-scale production, Short Eyes appeared in a modestly sized theater and was performed in a documentary, realist mode associated with prestige drama. Later Latina/o productions on Broadway—such as Reinaldo Povod's Cuba and His Teddy Bear (1986) and Nilo Cruz's Anna in the Tropics (2003)—would be more like Short Eyes than Zoot Suit: they were celebrated dramatic works that downplayed the forms of song and spectacle that Broadway's stages invite. The exception to this is Lin-Manuel Miranda and Quiara Alegría Hudes's In the Heights, a lavish musical that required an investment of more than $10 million. At first glance, the musical seemed an unlikely candidate for success. Set in the Latina/o neighborhood of Washington Heights in New York City, the play chronicles three summer days in which a group of Latina/o characters, who trace their origins to Puerto Rico, Cuba, and the Dominican Republic, reflect on the disappointments and possibilities associated with immigration and upward mobility. Additionally, they ponder how to maintain the forms of community cultivated in the neighborhood as rising rents caused by rapid gentrification are forcing residents to move and businesses to relocate. Containing significant amounts of Spanish and including songs rendered in various Latin and hip hop styles, the play posed challenges to typical Broadway audiences who craved English-language productions with songs delivered in a conventional musical theater style. Beyond this, both Miranda and Hudes were relative newcomers to the stage. Despite these liabilities, In the Heights became a resounding success, recouping its investment, selling out houses, and eventually earning the Tony Award for Best Musical of 2008. What factors contributed to In the Heights's success?

In many ways, In the Heights can be seen as the inverse of Zoot Suit. While Zoot Suit marked a grassroots, popular theater's march into the mainstream, Hudes and Miranda were both talents who were cultivated in the spaces of professionalized theater. Hudes, who received a Pulitzer Prize nomination for her play Eliot, A Soldier's Fugue (2007), and later won the Pulitzer for Water by the Spoonful (2012)—had recently completed her MFA in playwriting at Brown University. Although Miranda is currently the toast of the New York theater world because of his innovative play *Hamilton* (2015), *In the Heights* began as a play that he wrote when he was a nineteen-year-old student at Wesleyan University. As explained in a profile in the *New Yorker*, Miranda had undergone a long apprenticeship in which he voraciously studied Broadway musicals and wrote and staged them in high school and college (Mead). Thus, the authors forged their imaginations in the crucible of the university and the musical theater industry itself rather than in the insurrectionary space of social movements.

In this way, *In the Heights* feels consistent with post-1960s mainstream Latina/o fiction which some see as replacing, in Nancy Fraser's terms, a "politics of recognition" for a "politics of redistribution" (Dalleo and Machado Sáez, 3). As Raphael Dalleo and Elena Machado Sáez note, these kinds of "multiculturalist" works are often knocked for making difference too easily consumable and translating culture for non-Latina/o audiences (5–7). Indeed, aspects of this exist in *In the Heights*. In a crucial song that opens the second act, Nina, the daughter of a Puerto Rican couple who owns a cab service, and Benny, a dispatcher who works for her parents, sing a love song in which she teaches Benny Spanish. The song combines with Benny's attempts to differentiate Puerto Rican and Dominican Spanish to also teach the audience about differences within and between Latina/os. In the introduction to the print version of the play, the producer Jill Furman celebrates the play's "universal themes" that center on "the immigrant experience and the American dream," placing *In the Heights* in a genealogy with such classic Broadway musicals as *West Side Story* and *Fiddler on the Roof* (x). Even the play's poster emphasized celebration over strife, picturing the players in various dance positions with their arms and glances stretched upward (Craft, 54). Because of the play's upbeat self-presentation, some community members and Latina/o studies scholars criticized the play for presenting a too sanitized image of life in Washington Heights. Although the play fails to provide us with familiar images of urban grittiness, it does possess a politics, however muted, that is directed at the effect of economic violence and rapid gentrification on a community whose resources are rapidly depleting.

Unlike *Zoot Suit*, which had a hard time connecting with audiences, especially Latina/o audiences, in New York, *In the Heights* produced an aggressive marketing campaign that sold out Broadway theaters, which is especially surprising because it wasn't selling out smaller houses when it played off Broadway (Craft, 50). The play was appealing to New York Latina/os in part because it represented a New York neighborhood and presented Latinidad in a way that was instantly legible to East Coast audiences. Additionally, as Elizabeth Titrington Craft notes, the play launched an aggressive multi-tiered advertising campaign that targeted Latina/os but also targeted youth audiences in its attempt to connect the play's hip hop sensibility to those who would most delight in it. One key component of the campaign was Miranda's "usnavi" channel on YouTube. The channel was named for the character Miranda plays in the drama and was produced by Miranda himself. The resulting videos are authentic, often satiric, and engage audiences directly (Craft, 58–63). One significant entry responds in a rap to the critiques of the play's sanitized rendering of the Heights. The advertising succeeded in both bringing in the standard viewers of musical theater and recruiting new audiences from New York's Latina/o community. According to one industry study, *In the Heights* had a higher number of non-Caucasian audience members than any other play on Broadway in the first year of its run (Craft, 64).

Singular Sensations

In the original cast of *In the Heights*, the role of Nina's mother, Camila, was played by Priscilla Lopez, a legendary Bronx-born, Colombian-American actress and singer who is perhaps best known for originating the role of Diana Morales in *A Chorus Line*. In that role, she famously sings "Nothing," a song that was based on an experience Lopez had in an acting class at New York's High School for the Performing Arts. In the song, Morales recounts how, when asked by the teacher to feel the "snow" and "motion" of a sled, she felt "nothing." Her brief aside, "they don't have bobsleds in San Juan," suggests the Latina Broadway performer's dilemma: she is constantly asked to create something from experiences that are not her own. John Leguizamo recalls seeing Morales in his one-man show *Freak*, which ran on Broadway in 1998. *Freak* is a semi-autobiographical performance piece in which Leguizamo provides both a history of his upbringing and his coming into being as a performer. Midway through the performance, Leguizamo explains how his uncle would take him to Broadway shows, sneaking him in after the intermissions to catch the second act. On one occasion they duck into *A Chorus Line* and Leguizamo hears the name Morales:

> I'm peeping at this ridiculous musical *Chorus Line* thing when I hear somebody called Morales on stage. There was a Latin person in the show. And she didn't have a gun or a hypodermic needle in her hand and she wasn't a hooker or a maid and she wasn't servicing anybody so it was hard to tell if she was Latin and everybody's respecting her and admiring her ... I was lost in this amazing moment, singing along as loud as I could.
>
> (54)

At the end of the vignette, Leguizamo explains, "And that is how I got culture" (55). David Román takes this explanation to be doubly significant: "it refers to a poor immigrant youth's exposure to the arts, but it also refers to his introduction to a Latina/o cultural lineage" (*Performance*, 127). Indeed, Leguizamo ends the play with an accounting of that Latina/o cultural heritage:

> And all of a sudden I allowed myself to want more for myself, to be more and do more, master of my own destiny, never wait for anyone, take life into my own hands, like my father had once wanted for me and for all the Morales, Morenos, Arnazs, Puentes, Cheechs and Chongs before me; who had to eat it, live it, get fed up with it, finesse it, scheme it, even Machiavelli it, to get out from under all the ills that Latin flesh is heir to and who dug right down to the bottom of their souls to turn nothing into something. I dedicate this all to you.
>
> (124–125)

As Román notes, Leguizamo does not have to make "something from nothing" like Morales: he has Morales and other notable performers from which to imagine his own performing career (*Performance*, 131). This moment in Leguizamo's *Freak* illustrates the significance of Latina/o pop theatrical performances: it widens the imaginations of those who see them by suggesting new ways of being in the world. While the mainstream, pop Broadway musical tradition may mute the politics of popular grassroots theaters as it attempts to sell tickets and fill seats, the Latina/o performances that materialize on Broadway's stages possess an inspirational force like no other. *Freak* reminds us that current Broadway productions authored and produced by Latina/os rest on the shoulders of past iconic performances in which the Latina/o performers seemed to burst forth from the work in which they were placed, performances like Chita Rivera's Anita in *West Side Story* or her eponymous role in *Kiss of the Spiderwoman*; Priscilla Lopez's Diana Morales in *A Chorus Line*; Rita Moreno's turn as Anita in *West Side Story*'s film adaptation, and even Edward James

Olmos's El Pachuco in *Zoot Suit*. If Broadway is both the place where pop theater enters the national consciousness and a place that historically has excluded Latina/o representation, these iconic Latina/o performances have shown how, despite the odds, there is a place for us on New York's stages. The recent resounding success of Lin-Manuel Miranda's *In the Heights* and *Hamilton* suggests that a new era of Latina/o musical theater production may be upon us, one in which Latina/o-authored stories find a place on the Great White Way in innovative work that redefines what American musical theater can be.

Note

1 Broyles-Gonzalez notes that the love story involving Alice and Henry as well as the conflict it sparks with Henry and his girlfriend Della was problematic and, as a result, was heavily revised. Additionally, although the Alice character may have been inserted to reach out to non-Chicano audiences, many Chicana/o artists and scholars lamented how the representation of Alice's efforts to achieve Henry's release obscured the fact that the Chicana/o community were central and key actors in obtaining justice for the young men (181, 201–202).

Bibliography

Barnes, Clive. " 'Zoot Suit' proves Moot." *New York Post* 26 March 1979: 71, 77.

Broyles-Gonzalez, Yolanda. *El Teatro Campesino: Theater in the Chicano Movement*. Austin: University of Texas Press, 1994.

Craft, Elizabeth Titrington. "Is This What It Takes Just to Make It On Broadway?: Marketing *In the Heights* in the Twenty-First Century." *Studies in Musical Theatre* 5 (2011): 49–69.

Dalleo, Raphael and Elena Machado Sáez. *The Latino/a Canon and the Emergence of Post-Sixties Literature*. New York: Palgrave Macmillan, 2007.

Flores, Juan. *From Bomba to Hip Hop: Puerto Rican Culture and Latino Identity*. New York: Columbia University Press, 2000.

Kalem, T. E. "Threads Bare." *Time* 9 April 1979: 78.

Leguizamo, John. *Freak: A Semi- Demi- Quasi-Pseudo Autobiography*. New York: Riverhead, 1997.

Lucas, Ashley. "Prisoners on the Great White Way: *Short Eyes* and *Zoot Suit* as the First U.S. Latina/o Plays on Broadway." *Latin American Theatre Review* 43:1 (2009): 121–135.

Mead, Rebecca. "All About the Hamiltons." *The New Yorker* 9 February 2015.

Miranda, Lin-Manuel and Quiara Alegría Hudes. *In the Heights: The Complete Book and Lyrics of the Broadway Musical*. New York: Applause, 2006.

Román, David. *Acts of Intervention: Performance, Gay Culture, and AIDS*. Bloomington: Indiana University Press, 1998.

Román, David. *Performance in America: Contemporary U.S. Culture and the Performing Arts*. Durham, NC: Duke University Press, 2005.

Rossini, Jon. *Contemporary Latina/o Theater: Wrighting Ethnicity*. Carbondale: Southern Illinois University Press, 2008.

Sandoval-Sanchez, Alberto. *José, Can You See? Latinos On and Off Broadway*. Madison: University of Wisconsin Press, 1999.

Valdez, Luis. *Zoot Suit and Other Plays*. Houston: Arte Publico Press, 1992.

Vásquez, Eva Cristina. *Pregones Theatre: A Theatre for Social Change in the South Bronx*. New York: Routledge, 2003.

13

SIEMPRE PA'L ARTE

The Passions of Latina/o
Spoken Word

David A. Colón

If you've learned your poetry from hip hop and slams and television, it's obvious the book
does not "contain" the poem—it transmits it.

Bob Holman, Introduction to *Burning Down the House*

Spoken word has been defined many ways, often arranging some combination of the terms
poetry, performance, and style. And yet, as a verbal art more idiomatic than literary and
more actual than abstract, it deviates from inherited notions of poetry into the less discrete
category of we-know-it-when-we-see-it. Part of the difficulty in offering a pure definition
of spoken word comes from the various identified subgenres that both run up against and
comprise it. Dana Gioia uses the term "popular poetry" to encompass "rap, cowboy poetry,
poetry slams, and certain overtly accessible types of what was once a defiantly avant-garde
genre, performance poetry" (7), opting to highlight the mainstream cultural aspects of
the phenomena as opposed to the less politically suggestive expression *spoken word*. But
spoken word is inextricably linked to the personal and the bodily, a metaliterary mode of
creative expression that is embodied as it is performed, where voice is literal and not merely
figurative as it is when regarding creative expression of the page. Meta DuEwa Jones explains
that "the term 'spoken word' is often used interchangeably with 'performance poetry,' since
the terminology suggests the poem's essence cannot reach fulfillment without a staged (in
multiple senses of this word) environment" (184). The emphatic staging of "the dynamic
qualities entailed in speech" (Jones, 184) is central to spoken word, far more so than to the
kinds of formal poetry readings of the modernist era recounted by literary critics such as
Peter Middleton and Lesley Wheeler.[1]

The other difficulty in precisely defining spoken word can be attributed to the diverse
strands of its origins.[2] Jones's book, *The Muse is Music: Jazz Poetry from the Harlem Renaissance
to Spoken Word* (2011), traces a genealogy of African-American poetics that effectively
leaves spoken word, in both its poeticity and its theatricality, as the heir to a connective
and longstanding aestheticized cultural memory (Banks, 10). A profound extrusion of this

history came in the 1960s from events surrounding the Black Arts Movement, especially the founding of the Umbra Workshop in 1962, Amiri Baraka's work in *Black Magic: Collected Poetry, 1961–1967* (1969), and the establishment of the Black Arts Repertoire Theatre School (BARTS) in 1964. The assassination of Malcom X and the political achievements of the civil rights movement further galvanized African-American artists and writers to reclaim their own histories and artistic praxis and cultivate them into a collective expressive force. Baraka, Sonia Sanchez, and Nikki Giovanni were powerful voices of the movement's poetry in the 1960s, and in the 1970s the initiative spread into a wider array of cultural production. Gil Scott-Heron's first album, *Small Talk at 125th and Lenox* (1970), which begins with the famous poem "The Revolution Will Not Be Televised," popularized the performance of political poetry to percussive musical accompaniment. Sanchez's *Sister Son/ji* (1969) prefigured Ntozake Shange's *for colored girls who have considered suicide / when the rainbow is enuf* (1974) in introducing an emergent form, the "choreopoem," that syncretized poetry, theater, and black consciousness into a new subgenre of live performance (Banks, 13). In these ways, and others, the Black Arts Movement can be understood as having provided a viable model for multiculturalist artistic and literary expression for communities of color, not only for African Americans but for others as well, including Latinas/os.[3]

Nevertheless, the spreading of the roots of Latina/o spoken word was historically concurrent with their emergence in African-American communities, and for related reasons. In his recent book, *In Visible Movement: Nuyorican Poetry from the Sixties to Slam* (2014), Urayoán Noel insinuates that while certain critical pairings of Black Arts Movement poetries with Latina/o performance poetries, namely early Nuyorican poetry, constitute "a revisionist Afro-diasporic framework" that might be dubious, he does clarify many of the meaningful dialogues between the communities: notably among them, Victor Hernández Cruz's involvement in Umbra in New York's Lower East Side (Noel 2014, xix, xxvii, 11, and passim). Live poetry performances were vital to the emergence of Nuyorican poetry in the 1960s and 1970s thanks to Miguel Algarín, who hosted events at his home before establishing the Nuyorican Poets Café, also in the Lower East Side, in 1975. Participants in these early gatherings included Tato Laviera, Miguel Piñero, Sandra María Esteves, Lucky Cienfuegos, and Pedro Pietri. Pietri's poem, "Puerto Rican Obituary," written by 1969 and published in 1973, spent the intervening four years living as a performed poem, which Pietri was known to speak at events involved with the Young Lords Party. In the historically contiguous Chicana/o scene in the Southwest, early performed poetry was powerfully connected to political activist groups as well. Rudolfo "Corky" Gonzáles's poem, *I Am Joaquín* (1967), was widely recited in public during the Chicano Art Movement, accumulating a popularity that helped its print publication, first by the Crusade for Justice's press and later by Bantam, to become the first Chicano best seller (Stavans, 787). At the first National Chicano Youth Liberation Conference in Denver in 1969, Alurista spoke a poem that subsequently became the preamble to the movement's manifesto, "El Plan Espiritual de Aztlán." There is a longstanding tradition in Latina/o culture, rooted in the civil rights era, which linked poetry to political activism, making events of poetry performance central to the cause.

Spoken word continues to this day as the literary fabric of civil rights, although the concerns have naturally evolved. In his introduction to *Aloud!: Voices from the Nuyorican Poets Café* (1994), co-edited with Bob Holman, Algarín heralds a multiculturalist art that defines spoken word as it is commonly regarded in the present moment:

> The new poetry, or rather the poetry of the nineties, seeks to promote a tolerance and understanding between people. The aim is to dissolve the social, cultural, and

political boundaries that generalize the human experience and make it meaningless. The poets at the Café have gone a long way toward changing the so-called black/ white dialogue that has been the breeding ground for social, cultural, and political conflict in the United States. It is clear that we now are entering a new era, where the dialogue is multi-ethnic and necessitates a larger field of verbal action to explain the cultural and political reality of North America. Poets have opened the dialogue and entered into new conversations. Their poems now create new metaphors that yield new patterns of trust, creating intercultural links among the many ethnic groups that are not characterized by the simplistic term *black/white dialogue* ... The poet of the nineties is involved in the politics of the movement. There need be no separation between politics and poetry. The aesthetic that informs the poet is of necessity involved in the social conditions that the people of the world are in.

(Algarín and Holman, 9, 10)

Despite Nuyorican poetry's prominent legacy in American arts, Algarín sees the voices of Latinas/os as kindred to all ethnicized subjects outside the black/white binary and continually suppressed in this hegemonic, reductive ethnocultural dialogue, thereby in need of a new form—and a renewed forum—for "verbal action." Algarín here writes almost a decade after slam poetry was introduced when Marc Smith staged the first slam at the Get Me High Lounge in Chicago; the impetus of slam poetry competition was a spirit of inclusiveness that encouraged people of all walks of life to recreate poetry in their own likeness, and to subject that poetry to the aesthetic sensibilities and judgment of equally everyday people rather than academic elitists. This drive, which many have characterized as the democratization of poetry, has valorized diversity—racial, ethnic, sexual, and ideological[4]—as its chief ethic.

Concepts

In Mark Eleveld's anthology, *The Spoken Word Revolution: Slam, Hip Hop, and the Poetry of a New Generation* (2003), Luis Rodriguez remarks that in the wake of slam's emergence, "poetry is having a resurgence in America, and mostly from the communities and populations normally not considered poetic, such as the homeless, gang members, midwives, prisoners, carpenters, etc." (210). As an artistic phenomenon, spoken word is a vein of *pop culture* not only because it is popular but also because it is populist. Nuyorican poetry's first generation, exhibited in Algarín's and Piñero's anthology, *Nuyorican Poetry: An Anthology of Puerto Rican Words and Feelings* (1975), pursued poetry as an instrument of social justice, and fundamental to this conceptualization was the integral relationship between poet and *community* (as opposed to poet and *reader* in the textualist framework). In this anthology's introduction, "Nuyorican Language," Algarín writes:

The poet sees his function as a troubadour. He tells the tale of the streets to the streets. The people listen. They cry, they laugh, they dance as the troubadour opens up and tunes his voice and moves his pitch and rhythm to the high tension of "*bomba*" truth. Proclamations of hurt, of anger and hatred. Whirls of high-pitched singing. The voice of the street poet must amplify itself. The poet pierces the crowd with cataracts of clear, clean, precise, concrete words about the liquid, shifting latino reality around him.

(Algarín and Piñero, 11)

Algarín invokes the centuries-old vernacular tradition of the troubadour to revive a twentieth-century populist cause for poetry, but the details in typifying the manner of this new street poet were prophetic in their moment. Algarín's words read as if a mandate, both advocating artistic populism as well conceptualizing an ideal decorum, sketching an image of the Nuyorican street poet as a stylist with a recognizable if not proscribed performative persona. Latina/o spoken word poets today sound very much like the ideal Algarín articulates here.

To this point, Dana Gioia has identified three consistent features of contemporary "popular poetry": 1) "it is predominantly oral"; 2) "[it] emerged entirely outside established literary life and [was] initially developed by individuals marginalized by intellectual and academic society"; and 3) "it is overwhelmingly, indeed characteristically, formal" (9, 11, 12). Gioia of course includes hip hop and cowboy poetry within his category of popular poetry, so his regard of formality is largely focused on rhyme and narrative (13). Regular, sustained prosody is not a universal feature of spoken word (although common, especially rhyme), but irregular, even improvisational, spoken word poetry is no less formal. Gioia values the "unabashed stylization" of popular oral poetry because "over stylization distinguishes it from ordinary speech. Form is how oral verse announces its special status as art" (17). Moreover,

> oral poetry understands—as does all popular art—that much of its power comes from the audience understanding exactly the rules the artists follow. In this situation, the artist must demonstrate his or her conspicuous skill to do something better than the members of the audience could manage and to engage, move, surprise, and delight the audience within predetermined conventions.

> (Gioia, 18)

Gioia's last point alludes to the competitive nature of many spoken word communities, including slams as well as open mics. But the keener point is the matter of "predetermined conventions" and "the audience understanding exactly the rules the artists follow." Implicit to the genre of spoken word[5] is a discrete set of mannerisms, inflections, and dispositions that the poet employs in delivery: the substance that makes spoken word instantly recognizable as that we-know-it-when-we-see-it product. For one, it's not cool to read spoken word verbatim from a sheet of paper; in its idealized form, it is memorized, internalized, embodied. In this respect, it is reminiscent of far older traditions of poetry, harkening to the troubadours that Algarín invokes, the West African *griot*, even the Anglo-Saxon and Germanic *scop* of medieval verse, when regular meter, rhyme, and other material features were memory aids for the bard to recall oral poetry (e.g. alliterative verse and *Beowulf*). Meta Jones acknowledges the "value-laden" irony of establishment poets and critics as they endeavor "to demote contemporary poets whose delivery style emphasizes their poems' sonic register" (184) and choose not to appreciate the spoken word artist's modern-day revival of the classical bard archetype.

In analyzing the performance mechanisms of contemporary Latina/o oral poetry, Urayoán Noel reveals "a complex textual-vocal-corporeal dynamic that complicates the distinctions between literature and expressive cultures" (2014, xvi), a dynamic that does not elide the trappings of individuated performance as peripheral to the poetic composition but rather foregrounds them. His concept of *embodied counterpolitics* is especially insightful: "embodied counterpolitics hinges not so much on oratorical flourishes … but rather on more complex, even uncomfortable tones and strategies (silence, abjection, outrage, irony, glossolalia, humor, various kinds of conflicted address) that underscore the problematics of representation" (2014, xxi). Because spoken word is predicated on "theatrical visibility"[6] (Clune, 202), the subtleties of embodied performance, even in the most minute gestures, are apportioned to the meaningful experience of the poetry. As spoken word has developed as a culture over what is now decades, certain modes of delivery, through their proven success in entertaining audiences, have grown into viable conventions available to the spoken word artist.

Noel's discourse on embodied counterpolitics accounts the signifying play at the threshold of poetry and spectacle contained in spoken word, and invoking *politics* is crucial in its connotations, as supported by Algarín and Rodriguez articulating the ethos of populism. But as varied as the combinations of embodied counterpolitics are in spoken word, the entire genre is governed by affect. The single most ubiquitous trait of spoken word is the amplification of feeling, expanded far beyond the parallel measure in establishment literary poetry. One could say that spoken word requires theatrical visibility and embodied performance precisely because the written word is inadequate to convey the intended vastness of emotional impact of spoken word. This intensity of feeling calls forth passion, the chief affect of the genre. Demonstrative passion enacted in the delivery/performance of spoken word distinguishes it from literary, textual, or academic poetry readings and performances more than any other factor. The dual meanings of *passion*, at once excitement and enthusiasm as well as agony and suffering, are intended here. In fact, the very best spoken word performances traverse both extremes in filling out the audience's experience: the challenge for the poet is to do so with wit and surprise.

In the genre of spoken word, passions are codified; the visible persona of the spoken word artist is possessed of passions that are inherited. Portrayed through the gestalt of performance, these are clearly learned practices—conventional, conformist, even formal, one might even say stock—but nonetheless enlivened by the unique, personal interaction with the Platonized forms of these passions, interacting with passion as if an instrument to be played, a tool to be mastered, a keyboard. All poets have words at their disposal, but whereas the textual poet has page and line, the spoken word poet has body and voice. The audible-visible sensuousness of passion is requisite of spoken word performance, through the verbal as well as through body language, but there are variants within such an encompassing concept. In Latina/o spoken word, there is recuperative passion, attuned to healing and vindication; disavowing passion, the emphatic, indignant unburdening of the self of repressive ideology, injustice, or abuse; *sabrosa* passion, which relishes in the visceral pleasures of the tactility of Latina/o culture; picaresque passion, a reveling in asserting independence through the clever subversion of authority; and many more worth identifying.

At any single moment in a spoken word performance, the poet is pursuing what I call a *passion particularity*: the affective force of passion must be directed, and not only directed but set in motion to reach all the way through an experiential extent to touch, enter, and inhabit a detail of cognition that is in equal measure private and familiar. The strategy for these tactics is what I consider *enacted sincerity*. In spoken word, performative personas become raw materials in the way that paper and pen, letters and lines are raw materials for the textual poet. There are various performative personas available to the spoken word poet, ones that can be combined and reworked the way words and syntax can. The methods I cited earlier that Noel identifies as illustrative of embodied counterpolitics ("silence, abjection, outrage, irony, glossolalia, humor, various kinds of conflicted address") are conceptual units made real through physical performance. They constitute a veritable vocabulary for spoken word body language and as such they prefigure the poet's creativity, individuality, and ingenuity. They are the terms by which the poet addresses sincerity. Sincerity, also crucial to effective spoken word, is enacted through a preexisting language of live performance and bodily expression employed to earn trust. The spoken word poet must become fluent in this physical language in order to convey her emotional effect. *Passion particularities* issue from *enacted sincerity* as much as they do from personal experience or political realities.

Poets

Contemporary Latina/o spoken word artists are remarkably diverse. Many of them, like Sandra María Esteves (b.1948) and Alejandro Murguía (b.1949), bridge to the earlier generation of the first wave of Nuyorican and Chicana/o poets. Esteves was the most prominent woman in the early Nuyorican poetry movement and her written work has been widely anthologized, from Algarín's *Nuyorican Poetry* (1975) to Ilan Stavans's *Norton Anthology of Latino Literature* (2011), which notes that her collection, *Yerba buena: dibujos y poemas* (1980) was one of the first poetry volumes by a Latina published in the U.S. (Stavans, 1397). Her work intersects streams of Puerto Rican, Dominican, African, and urban consciousness, moving between English and Spanish—as do many of her performances, which blend languages, music, singing, dance, and poetry to bring into relief "the *blurred visibility* of diaspora" (Noel 2014, xvi). Her performances in more recent years have been ensemble productions, collaborating with choreographers and bands, especially at the Pregones Theater in the Bronx, NY. The mechanisms of enacting sincerity in her performance oeuvre have been choral, demonstrating communalism in the work of transmuting Latina/o culture into spectacle. Certain productions put her words in other participants' voices, leaving her off the stage altogether—a means to disembody herself from her poetry—which is quite different from the bodily presence seen in the newer generation of Latina/o spoken word poets involved in slam.[7]

Alejandro Murguía, born in California and raised in Mexico City and Tijuana, is a poet and fiction writer whose longstanding involvement in community organizing and causes for Latina/o social justice is the backbone of his art. In an online interview with George Mason from 2013, Murguía asserts, "I am Chicano, which means that I am also Latin American, and in Latin America, unlike in the United States, there is no separation between one's art and one's politic; it is in fact the exact same thing." From his early years in the late 1960s as a student at Los Angeles City College, to his political activism in San Francisco's Mission neighborhood during the Nicaraguan Solidarity movement of the 1970s, to his tenure on the faculty at San Francisco State University since 1991, he has consistently interwoven the dramas and voices of everyday people into his poetry and stories (in a manner that he attributes to the influence of the Mexican writer Juan Rulfo). The dialectic between poetry and prose manifests in his spoken word, narrating personalized vignettes ranging from immigrant refugees in "Nineteen Men"[8] to Mission writers including Jack Micheline, Harold Norse, and Oscar Zeta Acosta in "16th and Valencia." In this piece, which is fueled by the antagonism of gentrification and local displacement happening in the Mission, Murguía characterizes passion particulars of the disenfranchised in San Francisco: "we were tired of living from the scraps of others, we were tired of dying for our own chunk of nothing."[9]

In 2012, Murguía was named Poet Laureate of San Francisco, the first Latino to hold this position. Albuquerque's Poet Laureate is a Latina spoken word artist as well: Jessica Helen Lopez. Active in slam competitions, Lopez was the 2012 and 2014 Women of the World (WOW) City of ABQ Champion. While Lopez, too, is a published poet with two collections in print—*Always Messing With Them Boys* (2011) and the chapbook *Cunt. Bomb.* (2014)—performance is blatantly integral to her work. Her performances often last far longer than the typical three-minute frame of slam entries, and feel almost like dramatic monologue, of a whirlwind feminist apperception that invokes Sylvia Plath, Anne Sexton, Virginia Woolf, Frida Kahlo, Sandra Cisneros, Shakespeare's Ophelia, and the chola archetype that she has characterized as a "barrio witch." Her references are often literary and her stage presence is quintessentially thespian, almost classical in delivery, putting her, on a spectrum of theatrical spoken word, far over from the picaresque, streetwise b-boy presence of the spoken word artist Lemon Andersen (Lemon), whose customary backwards baseball cap and oversize hip hop style clothes signpost urban grittiness in the moments before he speaks. Of Puerto Rican and Norwegian-American parents, Lemon hails from Bensonhurst, Brooklyn, and animates the cultures and ethos of the borough with a carefully crafted passion particularity that parades through discipline and abandon. Lemon has said that when beginning to become a writer, "I thought, poetry was just self-expression; I didn't know you actually have to have creative control" (Lemon, n. pag.). But in time, his poet mentor Reg E. Gaines taught him an appreciation for form in the composition of street poetry, sharing with Lemon the work of Etheridge Knight, who has had a profound influence on Lemon ever since. Lemon won a Tony Award in 2003 as a member of the *Russell Simmons Def Poetry Jam* on Broadway and HBO, and Spike Lee produced Lemon's bildungsroman *County of Kings* for the Public Theater, which has since been performed internationally; the publication of *County of Kings* won the Grand Prize at the 2010 New York Book Festival. His training at the Public Theater's Shakespeare Lab and subsequent instructorship at the Stella Adler Studio[10] have cultivated his delivery of spoken word, the essence of which has unimpeachable street credibility.

In the current open mic culture of poetry bars and cafés, new artists are constantly emerging, some of whom are in the midst of earning a reputation as the next tradition. New York City is home to a vibrant spoken word scene that has showcased the poets María Teresa Fernández (Mariposa), Emanuel Xavier, Bonafide Rojas, and Caridad De La Luz (La Bruja). Notable among them is Willie Perdomo, who has, among numerous other distinctions, been named a finalist for the National Book Critics Circle Award and the Poetry Society of America Norma Farber First Book Award; been nominated for a Pushcart Award; and won the Coretta Scott King Honor, for his four collections of poetry and his children's book, *Visiting Langston* (2005). In spoken word renditions of poems such as "Nigger Reecan Blues" and "How Beautiful We Really Are," Perdomo explores the problematics of the black/white dialogue that Algarín questioned in the 1990s, speaking from a Puerto Rican vantage and narrating its complexity and failings through a vicarious montage of ghetto *tipo* voices whose narrow points of view carve out solipsistic mindsets and yet, as they collect into his poetic invisible hand, structure themselves into a higher, big-picture regard of inner-city Latina/o life. His fluidity in codeswitching between English and Spanish—maintained on a shared register of slang expression and witticism—is key to his enacted sincerity, while the passion particulars of his verses emerge from the muck of tough neighborhoods that he loyally tills: "porque you see this shit is a ten on a scale from one to nine so tell Domingo that we're gonna shoot it up mainline mainland mainstream underground until we catch your vein so take this sound to the grave and tell the whole fucking block that a bamboula building session is about to begin" (Perdomo, n. pag.). The dense verbal play in these lines—the codeswitching at the start, the exaggeration, the double-entendres of "scale" and "Domingo," the buried rhymes of "nine"/"mainline" and "underground"/"sound," the alliteration of "mainline mainland mainstream," the consonance of "vein" and "grave," and the rhythmic alliteration of "block that a bamboula building session is about to begin"— develops a lyrical intensity that parallels the noir of the scene.

Latinidad is a ubiquitous preoccupation of Latina/o spoken word artists, manifest in an array of ways that they invest this tension into their performances. In his book, *The Diaspora Strikes Back: Caribeño Tales of Learning and Turning* (2009), Juan Flores considers certain works of Puerto Rican spoken word from the island through the critical lens of what he terms *cultural remittances*: "the ensemble of ideas, values, and expressive forms introduced into societies of origin by remigrants [sic] and their families as they return 'home,' *sometimes* for the first time, for temporary visits or permanent re-settlement, and as transmitted through the increasingly pervasive means of telecommunications" (Flores, 4).

Here Flores focuses on the particular circumstance of island Puerto Ricans as U.S. citizens prone to revolving-door migration, and he reads Puerto Rican performance poetry as displaying an influence of this revolving-door experience, filtering through particles of U.S. mainland culture that can be construed as the price to pay for a colonial condition. In response to Flores's argument, Urayoán Noel, in his essay "The Body's Territories: Performance Poetry in Contemporary Puerto Rico" (2011), develops this idea into what he calls the *unremitting body* of performance poetry. The premise of Noel's reconceptualization is to regard "the figuration of the Puerto Rican body as 'unremitting,' as one that cannot be resolved transactionally, that cannot be easily restored to a prior condition of meaning." Noel argues that "these poetries tend towards moments of self-consciousness and irony, as they reflect on the difficult task of opening up new expressive imaginaries while acknowledging the constraints of political and poetic articulation from the contested territories of the marked (raced, gendered, etc.) and marketable Puerto Rican body" (Noel, 2011: 92).

Considering Flores's and Noel's concepts simultaneously (and somehow as compatible with one another), is to understand that Puerto Rican performance poetry oscillates between the issuance of cultural remittances and the deflection of obligations to do so. This pressured contradiction typifies well the place of Latinidad in a broader field of Latina/o spoken word, especially for those poets who express their cultural identity as hybrid, fractured, or dissimulated. Ariana Brown, an award-winning slam poet and self-identified "Afromexicana" from San Antonio, TX, articulates and embodies this fraught politic. At first glance, her poetic persona on stage is generally calm, sober, articulate, even understated. Her delivery teeters on the edge of a controlled mourning that quivers oddly, an emotionally vulnerable enacted sincerity that pivots on her unpredictable placement of tender voice cracks serving as counterpoints to what would otherwise be affectively undifferentiated moments. This mien is counterpoint to—while the inflections conversely mirror—her narratives of the ontological violence that has labored to contract her consciousness into incongruous divisions. The cleanliness of her delivery betrays the messiness of how unforgiving observers have subjected her to heartless scrutiny, and as such, her poetry pays cultural remittances to racism while her performance issues from a body that is unremitting. Pieces such as "Volver, Volver," "Invocation," and "Wolfchild" explore her reflections on mixed ancestry: how the parts fit together, compete, betray each other without trying. As she says in "Wolfchild": "indigenous native Mexicana black all names you wear in harmony until you can't" (n. pag.). In contrast to Brown, Elizabeth Acevedo, a New Yorker now living in Washington, DC, and a former National Slam Champion, projects an unyielding persona to proclaim her Dominican imaginary. She is extroverted and demonstrative on stage, often invoking humor and flaunting the tactile excess of *sabrosa* passion in a spirit of celebration, but time and again, she also explores darker recesses of her experience. In her poem "Hair," her thoughts descend through layers of superficial preoccupations and comical conformity to white standards of beauty to reach the bottom of a stinging indictment: "they say Dominicans do the best hair I mean they wash set flatten the spring in any lock but what they mean is we're the best at swallowing amnesia" (n. pag.). Her piece "Spear" is an impassioned rumination on her feminist commitment to empower her daughter in a violently misogynistic world, entangled by intersections of predatory injustices, and the metaphors she musters to illustrate her ethos are arresting, e.g. "for every finger that we loosen another knuckle grows back crooked" (n. pag.).

Acevedo holds degrees from George Washington University and the University of Maryland, and it is becoming increasingly common to find Latina/o slam poets with strong connections to academia and literary publishing. CantoMundo, a national organization founded in 2009 to establish community and mentorship for emergent Latina/o poets through fellowships, workshops, and public readings, is hosted by the University of Texas and has numerous alumni active in the spoken word scene, including Acevedo, Denice Frohman, Peggy Robles Alvarado, and Paul Flores. Similar organizations like VONA/Voices, Louder Arts, and The Acentos Foundation have been supported by participation from Perdomo, Rich Villar, Aja Monet, and Rachel McKibbens. Perhaps the evolution of Latina/o spoken word will redirect the form from an enterprise that was once primarily countercultural and exclusively outside of the auspices of universities into predominantly institutional spaces that will make marginalized voices and their manner of speaking-thinking-knowing central to the art and craft of poetry. In 2000, Bob Holman wrote this about "the controversy of text vs. performance poem":

> Texters maintain that the poem exists solely in print, that what is performed or read aloud is but an interpretation of this text, which is the "real" poem. This gives rise to one of my favorite locutions, "That's not a poem!" which is predicated on the speaker's being able to define what a poem is, much like a slam judge. Once we're in that realm we're talking poetry. What more could one ask?

> (Holman, ii)

It would appear that Holman's logic has held up over what has since been the better part of two decades. Latina/o spoken word artists and those who honed their craft through slams and other performance outlets are challenging both themselves and the standards of this arts culture to develop into a richer form, changing the minds of obstinate critics and revealing latent prejudices in the resistance to poetic conventions derived from artistic and literary standards that germinated from communities of color. Dana Gioia has insightfully remarked that we "are currently living in the midst of a massive cultural revolution. For the first time since the development of movable type in the late fifteenth century, print has lost its primacy in communication" (3). If this turn is to be one that will never be reversed, then maybe spoken word is not just the poetry of the moment, but of the future.

Acknowledgments

I want to express my gratitude to the poet Sheila Maldonado for her advice and direction in researching this chapter, which I dedicate to her.

Notes

1 See Middleton's *Distant Reading: Performance, Readership, and Consumption in Contemporary Poetry* and Wheeler's *Voicing American Poetry: Sound and Performance from the 1920s to the Present.*
2 An under-examined but potentially rich context with which to align the emergence of African-American and Latina/o performance poetry—particularly the competitive culture of performance in slam poetry—is the underground drag ball culture, which originated in Harlem as early as the

1930s, was coopted by African-American hosts by the 1960s, and soon spread to various cities including Chicago, Detroit, and Atlanta. The public viewing, judging, entertaining, winning, losing, and prizing of contestants, coupled with the communal sense of sanctuary this culture provided for some of the most socially marginalized people in the city, is not only reminiscent of the slam poetry scene but also approximate to the socio-economic, geographic, and ethno-racial communities that innovated spoken word in the 1960s and 1970s in New York.

3   Urayoán Noel notes two important forebears to Nuyorican poetry who historically precede the popularization of Black Arts, namely Jorge Brandon (1902?–1995), a colorful Puerto Rican street poet from New York that Noel calls "a griot figure for the Nuyorican poets" (xxxiv); and Frank Lima (1939–2013), the Columbia-educated poet (born in Spanish Harlem) who Noel believes "might well be regarded as a point of departure for Nuyorican poetry, except that Lima's work mostly eschews the social voice of the diaspora poet, and that Lima has disavowed readings of his work along ethnic or culturalist lines, explicitly distancing himself from [Nuyorican poets], emphasizing instead his connection to the New York School" (6).

4   Inclusivity prevails over slam poetry's gamut of ideological diversity; it has its limits at sheer vitriol. Slam audiences tend to welcome sincere explorations of fraught issues, such as racism or machismo, but universally do not condone xenophobia, bigotry, misogyny, or the like.

5   Slams of course make some rules explicit, such as the three-minute time limit, no use of props, and no plagiarism.

6   Michael Clune notes that visibility is a contentious issue within the field of oral poetry since the 1990s, especially when including rap and hip hop in the conversation alongside spoken word. Visible performance is not central to the experience of many forms of popular oral poetry, and oftentimes invisibility is privileged, both in practice and in rhetoric (202 and passim).

7   Leticia Hernández, a younger spoken word poet, often incorporates Spanish singing into her poetry performances in a manner reminiscent of Esteves.

8   In Murguía's performance of this poem, he sings certain anaphoric "lines" as audible cues to "stanza" breaks.

9   When quoting spoken word performance, I transcribe only the words: the performance could allow for variations of punctuation and line breaks, so I leave such markings out. Even if a published text "version" exists in print, that text is not the performance.

10 For a recent study on interactions between spoken word and pedagogies, see Bronwen E. Low's *Slam School: Learning Through Conflict in the Hip-Hop and Spoken Word Classroom*.

Bibliography

Acevedo, Elizabeth. "Elizabeth Acevedo – 'Hair.'" *YouTube*. 2 July 2014.

Acevedo, Elizabeth. "Elizabeth Acevedo – 'Spear' (NPS 2014)." *YouTube*. 22 January 2015.

Algarín, Miguel. "Introduction: Nuyorican Language." *Nuyorican Poetry: An Anthology of Puerto Rican Words and Feelings*. Ed. Miguel Algarín and Miguel Piñero. New York: William Morrow & Co., 1975. 9–20.

Algarín, Miguel and Bob Holman, eds. *Aloud! Voices from the Nuyorican Poets Café*. New York: Henry Holt & Co., 1994.

Algarín, M. and Miguel Piñero, eds. *Nuyorican Poetry: An Anthology of Puerto Rican Words and Feelings*. New York: William Morrow & Co., 1975.

Andersen, Lemon. "Lemon Andersen performs 'Please don't take my Air Jordans.'" *YouTube*. 7 December 2012.

Banks, Daniel. "Introduction: Hip Hop Theater's Ethic of Inclusion." *Say Word!: Voices from Hip Hop Theater*. Ed. Daniel Banks. Ann Arbor: University of Michigan Press, 2011. 1–20.

Brown, Ariana. "Ariana Brown – 'Wolfchild' (CUPSI 2015)." *YouTube*. 25 July 2015.

Clune, Michael W. "Rap, Hip Hop, Spoken Word." *The Cambridge Companion to American Poetry Since 1945*. Ed. Jennifer Ashton. Cambridge, UK: Cambridge University Press, 2013. 202–15.

Eleveld, Mark, ed. *The Spoken Word Revolution: Slam, Hip Hop, and the Poetry of a New Generation*. Naperville, IL: Sourcebooks MediaFusion, 2003.

Esteves, Sandra María. *Yerba buena: dibujos y poemas*. Greenfield Center, NY: Greenfield Review Press, 1980.

Flores, Juan. *The Diaspora Strikes Back: Caribeño Tales of Learning and Turning*. New York and London: Routledge, 2009.

Gioia, Dana. *Disappearing Ink: Poetry at the End of Print Culture*. St. Paul, MN: Graywolf Press, 2004.

Holman, Bob. "Introduction." *Burning Down the House: Selected Poems from the Nuyorican Poets Café's National Poetry Slam Champions*. Roger Bonair-Agard, Stephen Colman, Guy LeCharles Gonzalez, Alix Olson, and Lynne Procope. New York: Soft Skull Press, 2000. i–vi.

Jones, LeRoi. *Black Magic: Collected Poetry, 1961–1967*. Indianapolis: Bobbs-Merrill Company, 1969.

Jones, Meta DuEwa. *The Muse is Music: Jazz Poetry from the Harlem Renaissance to Spoken Word*. Urbana: University of Illinois Press, 2011.

Lopez, Jessica Helen. *Always Messing With Them Boys*. Albuquerque: West End Press, 2011.

Lopez, Jessica Helen. *Cunt. Bomb*. CreateSpace Independent Publishing Platform, 2013.

Low, Bronwen E. *Slam School: Learning Through Conflict in the Hip-Hop and Spoken Word Classroom*. Stanford: Stanford University Press, 2011.

Middleton, Peter. *Distant Reading: Performance, Readership, and Consumption in Contemporary Poetry*. Tuscaloosa: University of Alabama Press, 2005.

Murguía, Alejandro. "Alejandro Murguía reads 16th & Valencia for the North Beach Poetry Crawl." *YouTube*. 26 July 2009.

Murguía, Alejandro. "Alejandro Murguía – Poet." *YouTube*. 11 September 2013.

Noel, Urayoán. "The Body's Territories: Performance Poetry in Contemporary Puerto Rico." *Performing Poetry: Body, Place and Rhythm in the Poetry Performance*. Eds. Cornelia Gräbner and Arturo Casas. Amsterdam and New York: Rodopi, 2011. 91–109.

Noel, Urayoán. *In Visible Movement: Nuyorican Poetry from the Sixties to Slam*. Iowa City: University of Iowa Press, 2014.

Perdomo, Willie. "Willie Perdomo – How Beautiful We Really Are on Def Jam Poetry." *YouTube*. 16 October 2010.

Rodriguez, Luis J. "Crossing Boundaries, Crossing Cultures: Poetry, Performance, and the New American Revolution." *The Spoken Word Revolution: Slam, Hip Hop, and the Poetry of a New Generation*. Ed. Mark Eleveld. Naperville, IL: Sourcebooks, 2003. 208–12.

Stavans, Ilan, ed. *The Norton Anthology of Latino Literature*. New York and London: W. W. Norton & Co., 2011.

Wheeler, Lesley. *Voicing American Poetry: Sound and Performance from the 1920s to the Present*. Ithaca and London: Cornell University Press, 2008.

14

POSTINDUSTRIAL PINTO POETICS AND NEW MILLENNIAL MAIZ NARRATIVES

Race and Place in Chicano Hip Hop

Pancho McFarland

The dawning of the twenty-first century gave us postindustrial capitalism in the U.S. as the colonized world became responsible for satisfying U.S. consumer culture; global burning and climate chaos; renewed migration on the part of indigenous peoples living south of the U.S.-Mexico borderlands, and the violent attack against these migrants and their cultures; amplified criminalization of youth of color (internally colonized people in the U.S.), the War on Drugs, and mass incarceration; and the increased reliance on and ubiquity of communications and surveillance technology.

This period also gave rise to social movements responding to and overcoming oppressive forces of capitalism, colonialism, and racism. These include deep and social ecology; transnational indigenous autonomy and nationalist movements; anti-racism; Occupy; anti-globalization; GLBTQ rights; and variants of anarchism and Marxism. Each of these movements seeks freedoms from seemingly evermore oppressive and repressive conditions of late capitalism and the hegemonic culture attending it. Moreover, participants in social movements share unique subcultures and identities developed as a consequence of, and means to, struggle. A common identity is requisite for successful social movements, and members of social movements work hard to develop and maintain a unified identity (Pulido, 1994).

Hip hop was birthed and nurtured at the dawning of the new millennium. It has united many across racial and geographic lines. Whether it contributes to oppressive, colonial forces or to the resistance to and transcendence of colonialism and other systems of domination is still under studied. Ball's (2011) study of the corporate rap industry and the possibilities for emancipatory journalism through hip hop technologies remains the most useful contribution to answering the question of where hip hop can be positioned in the new millennial struggles for freedom. Following his use of a decolonial perspective, in this chapter I focus on Chicana/o identity in hip hop as a central aspect of youth social organization and interaction, group and individual worldview, and responses to colonialism in the postindustrial era. In addition, the discussions of identity in Chicana/o hip hop reflect a continuation of maiz narratives and the pinto poet tradition. Place-making activities and a sense of place form an important part of identity. As Villa (20) has argued, space/land is a central aspect of discussions of identity in Chicana/o literature and culture. I argue that careful attention to identity through hip hop narratives of place reveals important insight about Chicana/o experience, Xicana/o political activity, and the state of our nation in the new millennium.

Colonialism, Capitalism, and the War on Drugs

Scholarly analyses of Chicana/o culture commonly begin with the Spanish invasion of Mexico in 1519 and emphasize the period after the U.S. conquest of Mexico's northwestern territories in 1848. Xicana/o (persons of Mexican descent in the United States who identify as indigenous) analyses start a few thousand years earlier. These are decolonial, alterNative analyses that challenge taken-for-granted assumptions about Mexican peoples in the U.S. as foreigners, illegals, and "mixed-raced." Like the Chicana/o cultural renaissance of the 1960s and 1970s, Xicana/o analyses situate Chicana/o identity and culture within a much longer span of history and an indigenous civilizational milieu that spans Abya Yala (the Americas) (Peña; Rodriguez; Pilcher).

Decolonial, alterNative analyses pose a challenge not only to liberal academic historiography but also to progressive critiques that similarly view Chicana/o marginalization, exploitation, and disenfranchisement as a result of a highly stratified U.S. social system. Whereas class-based Marxist analyses emphasize capitalism as the culprit and many others argue that racism causes Chicana/o suffering, alterNative perspectives locate the roots of current injustice with colonialism. Contrary to much academic writing, we are not in a post-colonial era. Indigenous peoples including Chicana/os continue to be dispossessed of their cultures, territories, and lives through an intricate web of local, national, and international law, police and military violence, racist media campaigns, and poverty. Importantly, the current neoliberal economic regime relies on free trade agreements/practices and the War on Drugs to accumulate indigenous/Mexican/Chicana/o territory and control working class and indigenous Chicana/os / Mexicana/os.

Colonial dispossession of land in Abya Yala caused the proletarianization of indigenous / Chicana/o people. With Chicana/o / indigenous people displaced from their land and their thousands-years-old collective place-based culture, colonial authorities are able to enforce social control. Racial terror, law enforcement, segregation, and other mechanisms have forced Chicana/os into working class barrios besieged by the problems that result from poverty, including violence, unemployment, disease, drugs, crime, and psychological challenges. Without land Chicana/os must survive as workers in fields and factories replete with low pay, instability, and workplace hazards. Following Villa (4) I refer to this "complex of dominating social processes" and outcomes experienced by many Chicana/os as 'barrioization'. Throughout the twentieth century, most Chicana/os found themselves attempting to live a dignified life under oppressive conditions. Importantly, Chicana/os have utilized expressive culture and place-making strategies as means of dignified struggle (Villa;

Peña). Chicana/os develop a barriology using song, dance, art, literature, and horticulture to remember place and culture, and to reterritorialize space and redefine identity (Alvarez; Peña; Villa; Zibechi).

While Chicana/os attempted to live lives of dignity and to prosper in the United States, the forces of capital and the state continuously reorganize and rely on new tactics to control this racialized proletarian group. The 1970s and 1980s brought two important new yet familiar tactics: neoliberal economic strategies and the War on Drugs. The capitalist economic and social system reached a new phase at the end of the twentieth century. As a result of challenges by the oppressed and marginalized throughout the world, ruling elites in the 1960s restructured global economics through neoliberal globalization. Corporate bosses reshaped international law to allow easier access to foreign markets and labor. As manufacturing became internationalized, the United States deindustrialized. Well paid manufacturing work that allowed many people of color to escape poverty after World War II crossed our national borders and became superexploitive in "developing" countries. In Mexico multinational corporations gobbled land and resources leaving Mexican workers without opportunities to thrive or even survive. The mass exodus of millions of Mexicans to the United States results directly from this new economic order. Chicana/os in the United States saw their livelihoods attacked and their communities left in ruins as factories that helped stabilize neighborhoods closed down, leaving empty streets and the underground economy for residents.

Nixon and the ruling elites created the "War on Drugs" as a means to contain working class people of color and to roll back the gains of the Civil Rights Movement and working class revolution of the 1960s and 1970s. This so-called war structures the experience of urban Chicana/o working class youth. The conclusions that Michelle Alexander draws regarding the heavy toll that the "War on Drugs" has had on black men and black communities can be applied to understanding many Chicana/o communities. Alexander (98) offers a telling statistic about "Latino" incarceration rates. She points out that from 1983 to 2000 the number of prison admissions for drug cases increased more than twenty-fold! She explains (40–58) that political and media scare tactics, politicians' desires to capture the white working class vote, "tough on crime" legislation, and deindustrialization led to the "War on Drugs" which has had enormous negative consequences for black and Latina/o communities. Mass incarceration of Chicana/o men has led to their extreme marginalization, disenfranchisement, and second-class citizen status. Jose Luis Morin reports that the War on Drugs "is in fact the single greatest force behind the growth of the prison population of Latina/os in prisons around the United States. This war on drugs is almost entirely being fought in Latina/o and African American communities"(quoted in Anonymous, 2010). State prison populations at the time sharpen Morin's point. In 2010 the number of persons incarcerated per 100,000 persons in that group were as follows: white men, 380; Latino men, 966; black men, 2,207 (Prison Policy Initiative, n.d.). According to the Bureau of Prisons, 34.2 percent of federal prisoners identified as Hispanic in May, 2015 (Bureau of Prisons, 2015).

Colonialism, deindustrialization, racism, and the War on Drugs have barrioized, impoverished, and deterritorialized working class Chicana/o youth. These conditions have led many Chicana/os to express their experiences through hip hop tales and actions that reflect, sometimes celebrate, and other times critique their situations in the urban United States in the new millennium. In addition, many Xicana/os use hip hop to reclaim identity and reterritorialize their urban environs. Such cultural expression reflects the legacies of maiz narratives and pinto poetics as stories of resistance and recovery.

New Millennial Maiz Narratives: Place and Identity in Xicana/o Culture

Decolonial, alterNative analyses link contemporary Xicana/o expressions including hip hop to thousands of years of indigenous culture. Xicana/o hip hop is a new millennial maiz narrative. In his analysis of "indigeneity and belonging in the Americas" Rodriguez traces a maiz narrative that can be seen, heard, and tasted throughout much of Abya Yala over the last six thousand years. Centeotzintli (our sacred maiz) structured and continues to structure much of indigenous Mexican and Central American philosophy, religion, and social organization. Words and images from thousand-years-old stories reproduced by Rodriguez to today's Xicana/o hip hop and the fight against transgenic pollution of Mexican corn crops exemplified by the "Sin Maiz, No Hay Pais" movement form an unbroken maiz narrative; an alterNative history of Xicana/o people. This maiz narrative forcefully counters the colonizer's racial mythology and Manifest Destiny fantasies. It illustrates the indigeneity of people of Mexican descent and the common sense ecological, sustainable, and democratic practices that if heeded could save our planet from global burning and climate chaos (Wildcat).

Chicana/o poets and other writers during the Chicano movement period often connected their Chicana/o identity to place and indigeneity. Alurista, the best known and explicitly Xicano indigenous writer of the movement period, attempted to develop a decolonial mythology through his study of Mexican indigenous culture and his published and performed poetry. His project complemented direct action by Chicana/o activists by providing a new way of perceiving ourselves. Xicana/o hip hop continues this project for a new generation using many of the same kinds of images and ideas. At the forefront of this project is place-claiming through ideas such as "Aztlan" and "la tierra". Maiz often stands in for place-based identity for Mexicana/o and Xican/o artists, writers, and other cultural workers. Today members of the Chicana/o Hip Hop Nation, Chicana/o emcees, music producers, musicians, tattoo artists, muralists, danzantes, and graffiti writers attach their twenty-first century Xicana/o identities to maiz culture. Referring to maiz, they claim a right to this space called the United States, America, or North America since maiz has a six-thousand-year history here. Xicano emcees, Los Nativos, exemplify this on their song "Sonido Indigena," rapping: "my lineage lives on/we represent the corn/from here to californ."

Similarly, the group, Kinto Sol, attach their identities to maiz when they claim that they are "hijos del maiz" and prominently display maiz in the clenched fist of Skribe (one of Kinto Sol's emcees) for the 2007 album, *Hijos del Maiz*. The song "Hijos del Maiz" and its official video exemplify Xicana/o hip hop connections to land and indigenous identity.

The video opens in a milpa (corn field) fading into a mural of a cornfield in front of which DJ Payback Garcia scratches on his turntables. Kinto Sol connect their urban Chicana/o existence of hip hop and concrete to the rural indigenous ideal of the milpa. The video, like hip hop generally, has multilayered meanings and images representing the Xicana/o outlook in hip hop.

The video follows with a series of short clips that juxtapose a Mexican man working la tierra and men in an office setting wearing suits. Kinto Sol explicitly anchor themselves in the land via the images of the grandfatherly Mexicano working a milpa. The artists exalt Mexican / Xicana/o tradition and mock the suit-wearing powerbrokers representing an Anglo, capitalist, colonialist tradition. The ridiculous men in suits wear hats with single words including avaricia, ignorancia, malinchismo, racismo, and materialismo. The gluttonous powerbrokers eat a cake with a map of the United States and Mexico prominently decorating the top, laughing boisterously and reveling in their destruction.

Indigeneity, land, and tradition are common themes in the video. The campesino is seen teaching a young boy the indigenous agricultural traditions of Mexicana/os represented through the milpa. The cornfield stands in for Mexicana/o traditional ecological knowledge (TEK) and practices. Kinto Sol assert that this TEK needs to continue to be passed down to new generations as an important part of the struggle against colonialism, capitalism, and racism. They further argue for a connection to a rapidly receding indigeneity among Mexicana/os using the symbol of Benito Juarez to link their urban Xicanidad to indigenous Mexicanidad.

The lyrics to the song further provide clues to how Kinto Sol and Xicana/o hip hop see themselves. They open the song rapping the following:

Mi abuelo murio trabajando la tierra	My grandfather died working the land
Nunca salio del monte siempre estuvo en la sierra	He never left the mountains he was always in the mountain range
Cuando yo era niño me regalo un azadon.	When I was a boy he gave me a hoe.

The narrator's grandfather was a campesino who lived his life in the mountains and taught the narrator place-based ways represented by the gift of a hoe. As a campesino, life was difficult and a cacique tried to strip them of the land. The narrator explains that even though the grandfather was courageous he ended up dying. The emcee poetically describes how death came to take away his grandfather's Tarascan soul. In the following lines, Kinto Sol invoke their grandfather's indigenous Tarascan roots:

Aunque de coraje mi abuelo se muriera	Even though he was courageous he died
La muerte llego y se tuvo que marchar	Death came and he had to march
Su alma de Tarasco tuvo que volar	His Tarascan soul had to take flight

Part of the Xicana/o identity and indigenous identity generally involves resistance to colonialism and racism (McFarland, 2013). In the final lines of the first verse the narrator promises to avenge his grandfather's death using indigenous TEK. He declares:

Te prometo que esas tierras yo las vuelvo a sembrar.	I promise to return to sow those lands.
Tu alma, mi tata, yo la tengo que vengar	Your soul, grandpa, I have to avenge
Aunque el azadon por un rifle lo tenga que cambiar.	Even if I have to trade my hoe for a rifle.

The chorus further indicts the ruling classes as the chant "a los hijos de maiz/los han hecho sufrir/y los quieren ver morir." Power wants the "children of corn" to suffer and see them die. The second verse follows up on this theme explaining that the hijos del maiz control nothing ("duenos de nada") and as a result suffer from hunger ("esclavos del hambre, miseria, violencia"), political neglect, and lack of employment among other things. The emcee claims that all the politicians, no matter the party, care little for the hijos del maiz. Democracy doesn't exist in our current system according to Kinto Sol. Importantly, in this verse Kinto Sol critique both the State and capitalism. The political parties are the playthings of the rich who make it easy for capital to exploit hijos del maiz. They recognize that private property is key to the dispossession of indigenous and other landed people from their livelihoods and traditions.

Finally, Kinto Sol are not content to see themselves as indigenous victims of racist settler colonialism. Instead, they call for action.

500 anos escondida la verdad	500 years of hiding the truth
Cinco generacions en la oscuridad	Five generations in darkness
Llego la luz. Termino la tempestad.	The light arrived. The storm ended.
El gigante dormido vuelve a despertar.	The sleeping giant is awakening.
El alma del che me aconseja.	Che's soul counsels me.
Villa me dice mochales la oreja	Villa tells me to cut off their ears.

The group of Xicanos invoke rebels, Che Guevara, and Pancho Villa, as inspiration for their call for Mexicanos/Xicanos (the sleeping giant) to rise up.

They flesh out their understanding of their Xicana/o identity claiming that they are children of corn protecting the roots of their culture and destroying this corrupt system ("somos hijos del maiz protegiendo nuestra raiz eliminando el corrupto y cruel Sistema"). They finish the song with Skribe in a shouting style explaining the spiritual battle in which they must engage.

cada uno de nosotros tenemos de termianr con el egoismo	each of us has get rid of egoism
eliminando el yo y remplazarlo con el nosotros	eliminate it and replace it with 'us'
de la misma manera que nuestros antepasados coexistian	in the same way that our ancestors
colectivamente de una manera mas spiritual	existed collectively in a more spiritual manner

Importantly, the spiritual battle is a collective battle. It must be fought in a collective manner similar to how their ancestors lived. The song condemns "materialismo, egoismo, ignorancia, traicion", and other "energias negativas" that have attacked indigenous people for five hundred years. Oppression at the hands of racist colonizers must be overcome using TEK and other indigenous traditions. Kinto Sol claims, that now is the time for a movement to reclaim their indigenous livelihood and dignity and repair the colonial damage ("es tiempo de reparar los daños a la raza de los cosmos").

The Xicana/o experience is not an unadulterated pure indigeneity. The forces of colonialism, capitalism, and racism have forced Xicana/o indigeneity to be a complex mix (mestizaje) of indigenous, urban, U.S., consumerist, Spanish, and Anglo European cultures. For Xicana/os in the new millennium, their experience and identity are powerfully influenced by the city. The city serves as place for Xicana/os in the Chicano Hip Hop Nation (ChHHN). Tolteka's album cover for his *Reflexiones en Yangna, Califaztlan* (2008) illustrates the complex mestizaje of new millennial Xicana/os. In the foreground the artist depicts an indigenous statue-like image with a microphone emanating from the figure's head. In the background the artist renders the skyline of Yangna/Los Angeles.

Xicana/os of the ChHHN symbolically reclaim space as lived place to which they have a right. Their assertion of indigeneity is a political and economic argument in which "to be Chicano and to live in Aztlan is to have historical precedence over Anglos in the Southwest; it is to declare a historical fact of descent" (Arteaga, 9). Chicana/o / Xicana/o identity strikes at the heart of the colonial lie that would have us believe that Mexicana/os

/ Xicana/os are foreigners, illegals, criminals, and immigrants. Xicana/o identity redraws the colonial map of North America offering an alternative hip hop cartography (Forman). This mapping is a symbolic alterNative reterritorialization of indigenous homelands. Tolteka makes this alterNative cartography and indigenous identity explicit in the liner notes that accompany his compact disc. In the inside cover Tolteka reproduces the "Map of Disturnell" (used during the "negotiations" leading to the Treaty of Guadalupe Hidalgo) to argue for our historical precedence in the Southwest. On the following page he explains why he reproduces the map, writing that:

> This is about acknowledging that we are native to the land currently found within the man made borders of the this country. We are native to this continent, and we are not illegal aliens....How can we be illegal immigrants upon land which we've inhabited and had patterns of migration on since time immemorial?? The answer is that we can't be, and we won't be. We just have to awaken each other's consciousness up to this reality, acknowledging the fact that, as brown people, we are native to this land. We are indigenous people.

Xicana/o emcees including Tolteka, Kinto Sol, Olmeca, El Vuh, Jehuniko, Rain Flowa, Los Nativos and Aztlan Underground use their music, lyrics, and artwork to claim an indigenous identity, reterritorialize the spaces they inhabit, make political statements, and teach young people a Xicana/o indigenous perspective. Tolteka, for example, presents Xicana/o indigeneity as based in traditions of mutual respect, humility, and dignity. He wants people to "wake up" and have a shift in consciousness. Kinto Sol makes a similar point emphasizing indigenous connection to place and the collective nature of indigenous society.

Place in the New Pinto Poetics

Since colonization, the prison and settler colonial "justice" systems shape the experience and cultural expression of many Chicana/os. The pinto poet of the Chicano movement and post-movement period reflects the colonized status of people of Mexican descent in the United States. The places of residence and communities of Chicana/o people are controlled by others, particularly landlords, employers, and governments. Moreover, treated like foreigners we are often displaced and forced to migrate (Villa). Given the influence of displacement and lack of control of our spaces/places it is no wonder that place-claiming and place-making figure prominently in Chicana/o cultural expression, including that of the pinto poet and Chicana/o street hop (Villa; Olguín).

The pinto poet tradition exemplified by Ricardo Sanchez, Jimmy Santiago Baca, and Raul Salinas illustrates both a critique of the State and Capital and "the multiform creative practices by which Chicanos have attempted to materially reconstitute and expressively represent places of community well-being against the degradations to which those places have been subject" (Villa 157). In the pinto tradition, as in street hop, places of marginality, dispossession, and violence such as prisons and inner-city streets in the era of the War on Drugs have a profound effect on the identity of Chicana/o pinta/os and Chicana/o street hop artists. Olguín shows how pinta/o identity develops in part through resistance to Chicana/o prisoners' degrading experiences in the prison and mass incarceration systems. Pinta/o identity, then, is a resistant identity (not without its contradictions, as Olguín points out in his study) and pinta/o poets exemplify this in their work as they "interrogate the circumstances and sources of their subaltern life in the free world, as well as their liminal and transformative experiences in prison" (71). The barrios of inner cities create a new pinta/o identity for contemporary Chicana/o youth. Their subaltern status, especially as demonstrated in their interactions with the carceral state and their resistance to it, lead some to a "sick," "psycho," or "loco" identity (McFarland, 2013: 36–40). Chicana/o street hop emcees like pinta/o poets express their sick / psycho / loco/a identities in their song titles, lyrics, tattoos, and other art. (For excellent examples of street hop using the loco episteme, see performers such as Psycho Realm, Thief Sicario, Sick Symphonies, Krazy Race, Juan Zarate, and Sicko Soldado.) Through their art these street hop emcees reflect and develop a loco episteme rooted in their constant attempts to defy "the system." This rebel and transgressive spirit connects street hop culture to that described by the 1960s and 1970s-era pinta/o poetry.

In pinta/o and street hop traditions we find both bravado and vulnerability. Lines such as this from Ricardo Sanchez point to the violence of barrioization and the prison system, and the toll they take on Chicana/os: "He tried vainly and then cried tears upon tears upon the steel prison tiers" ("Tiers/Tears"). The emotional toll that the legal system took on Sanchez and other Chicano pintos has continued and expanded with the War on Drugs and mass incarceration. Lyrics by Chicano emcees including those in street hop connect them to the pinto poetry tradition and update it for the new millennium. Thief Sicario's "Tearz of Rage" mirrors Sanchez's "Tiers/Tears" in which he explains why he writes, stating "upon the page my soul I vomit." Like Sanchez, the prison for Sicario offers tears of pain; and writing down his experiences provides catharsis. In the chorus he explains the emotions evoked by the prison system:

> Tears of rage/break it down like a gauge/take it down on the page/and make a sound out my rage/hate the sounds of a cage/through the cell I'm stompin/prison's the graveyard/ my cell, the coffin.

The mass incarceration system has not only made prison a horrendous place for many Chicana/os, but the marginalized barrios in which many working class Chicana/os live are themselves confrontational and dangerous. Juan Zarate offers important examples of this in his song, "Santuario." Zarate depicts his Chicago barrio as a place of ignorance and violence and as his sanctuary. While the barrio contains innumerable dangers it is also home where Chicanito/as find love and acceptance. Zarate's song suggests that reterritorialization and place-making in Chicana/o barrios find possibility in the love and acceptance that many find in barrios. He remarks at the beginning of his song that "a veces es lo peor, cabron pero aqui nos acepta" (sometimes it's the worst, man, but here we are accepted). Revolutionary love and dignity form an integral part of a progressive Chicana/o street hop identity without which the loco episteme can turn towards the homophobic, misogynist, racist, and oppressive that haunt colonized people's attempts to change their subaltern status.[1]

The "street" or "calle" is the most common ground for the contestation of space found in Chicana/o street hop and the loco episteme. Images of the street and encounters with the criminal justice system form the bulk of the foundation upon which street hop emcees tell their tales of life on the "sickside." The sickside is a place that many street hop emcees and urban Chicana/o youth create or imagine out of the colonial conditions of the inner city. Some urban working class Chicana/o youth respond to barrioization/colonization through reterritorializing (or remaking) streets creating the sickside. The realities of mass incarceration and a 300-year-old history of state repression and violence told in Chicana/o hip hop narratives reveal the colonized status of Xicana/os. Chicana/o emcees discuss the state's social and physical control of space. The new tactic, the War on Drugs, shapes the experience of many working class Chicana/os. Hip hop texts full of images and discussions of drugs, guns, gangs, and police illustrate and critique this aspect of repression.

Psycho Realm, more than most Chicano hip hop groups, articulate the critique of state containment (barrioization) and their attempts to survive and thrive among the neglect and violence. Their song, "Palace of Exile" from *A War Story: Book II* (2003) explicitly connects the War on Drugs and mass incarceration to capitalist economic imperative. Speaking to young Chicana/os (the "#1 Target" of the mass incarceration system according to a song of the same name) they warn that "no matter what your record is or how many you've killed/ you could be clean as a whistle homey but still/the palace (prison) was built for you." Psycho Realm adds first-person accounts to what Michelle Alexander (87) describes in her work. Due to practices of overcharging, many innocent young men plea-bargain in which they take a lesser sentence out of fear of being found guilty of a more serious crime. In the current climate Chicanos/Mexicanos are assumed to be guilty. Drug sweeps, immigration raids, surveillance technology, mass media, and drug enforcement-funding label urban Chicanos as criminals. In addition, poverty and racism create barrio conditions in which even those who are "clean as a whistle" wear a stigma of deviance and are prime candidates for the palaces that Psycho Realm describe. They rap:

> Flood the streets with cannabis/crystal meth handle this/get you fucked up/then serve you guns with high calibers/give you ghetto fame every time you act crazy/knuckleheads bringing heat to 'hoods daily/got cops ready to serve you just waiting/to take you to the palace ... if in jail get petty money for labor skills/while stock holders sell and make money off shit you build.

In addition, Chicano hip hop narratives reterritorialize their colonized urban spaces. The "street" determines the urban ecology of contemporary working class youth of color and occupies a prominent place in their narratives. Here, in the street, young Chicana/os have experiences that influence their development. Here, in the street, Chicana/os interact with the police and migra but also they attempt to create a dignified life. Many use hip hop to recreate their colonized spaces and turn them into places. The most obvious reclaiming or reterritorialization of urban space by Chicana/o youth is the vibrant, beautiful hip hop graffiti and murals seen wherever Chicana/o youth live and move. For many the extremely loud, bass-heavy music coming out of stylized vehicles is cause for alarm and an indication of social breakdown. When seen from the perspective of reterritorialization, however, the loud music becomes a means of claiming and occupying space. Young people who have little to no legal claim to space use cultural expression to temporarily liberate space from corporate and state control (Alvarez). While these mobile temporary autonomous zones don't directly challenge the state or the colonial condition, they do provide temporary reprieve from state violence and inspire feelings of dignity. The esteem and positive self-evaluation that expressive culture and reterritorialization provide not only improve the psychic and spiritual lives of the colonized but also are a prerequisite for any social change action (Piven and Cloward, 1978).

Indigena, Mestizo, Latina/o?

Identity matters. Understanding the current political, economic, cultural, spiritual, and social worlds requires examination of how we define ourselves and how we are defined by others. How we define ourselves and the source information/experiences upon which this definition is made tell us a great deal about ourselves and our world. How Chicana/os define themselves and are defined provides important insight into our society. When the subaltern Chicana/o speaks, whether pinto poet, emcee, scholar, or organic intellectual, we experience a counter-narrative to the official story/mythology of our nation. The study of Chicana/o / Xicana/o hip hop offers a useful starting point to interrogate meaning, identity, race, nation, and the United States as story.

The narratives told by the subaltern Chicana/o emcee illustrate two common identities that connect this generation of artists to previous generations of storytellers. The pinto and the indigenous warrior have long histories in Chicana/o artistic expression. The question for social justice advocates is how do these identities and the politics that accompany them contribute to a liberatory praxis? What role can these identities play in forging a fairer, more just, equitable and free world? How can they be put in the service of a "better" world?

Essentialist understandings of identity including various forms of nationalism have been problematic. Comparing the indigenous-based nationalism of much of Chicana/o poetics to Europeanized nationalisms, Arteaga points out that while the indigenous nationalism is a response to the terror imposed by foreign European regimes, they still are limiting.

Arteaga (146) warns that indigenous identity among Chicana/os can be problematic since they imagine that Chicana/o "subjectivity descended from one source." While indigenous identities have different ramifications, especially as regards potential for decolonization, relative to "Mexican American", "Latina/o," or "Hispanic" identity, it often remains "idealized" and "unitary." Along similar lines of critique, Contreras's (2008) reading of Chicana/o indigenous literature shows how much of the Chicana/o indigenous identity was constructed from questionable colonial-era sources and with a romantic nostalgia. Romantic indigenism on the part of some Chicana/os replaces one colonial master ("White" men) with another (Aztec kings).

An honest analysis of the pinto tradition and its latest iteration as Chicana/o street hop offers a warning to evaluate the art critically, complexly, and completely. Prison and street culture and its expression resist and rebel against certain aspects of our society and its institutions. However as Olguín (15) explains: "These crime subcultures are not always empowering and, to be honest, rarely revolutionary. On the contrary, crime-as-subaltern agency can be as repressive as, and integral to, colonial domination." Chicana/o hip hop expresses a great deal of agency as the performers challenge the social arrangements that cause barrioization. Their critiques of the State and Capital are often prescient (McFarland, 2013). Yet, the critique fails to account for other aspects and expressions of power including hypermasculinity, homophobia and heteronormativity, and interpersonal violence. The relative lack of female voices in Chicana/o hip hop vividly makes the point about the masculinist worldview in which the subculture operates. When women speak in hip hop they often challenge the masculinist assumptions and structures that limit its empowering possibilities.

Note

1 Ben Olguín alerts us to this tendency and warns against seeing pinta/o culture as positively resistant. The Zapatistas and their spokesperson, Subcomandante Marcos (2002), Alvarez (2008), and hooks (2001) all provide important examinations of revolutionary love and dignity.

Bibliography

Alexander, M. *The New Jim Crow: Mass Incarceration in the Age of Colorblindness.* Jackson, TN: The New Press, 2012.

Alvarez, L. *The Power of the Zoot: Youth Culture and Resistance During World War II.* Berkeley: University of California Press, 2008.

Anonymous. "Criminal Justice: Inequities for Latinos in Criminal Justice." Young Latino Male Symposium. W.W. Kellogg Foundation. September, 2010. Available at: http://cronkitezine.asu.edu/latinomales/criminal.html

Arteaga, A. *Chicano Poetics: Heterotexts and Hybridities.* Cambridge: Cambridge University Press, 1997.

Ball, J. *I Mix What I Like: A Mixtape Manifesto.* Edinburgh: AK Press, 2011.

Contreras, S. *Blood Lines: Myth, Indigenism, and Chicana/o Literature.* Austin: University of Texas Press, 2008.

Federal Bureau of Prisons. "Inmate Ethnicity" 2015. Available at: www.bop.gov/about/statistics/statistics_inmate_ethnicity.jsp

Forman, Murray. *The Hood Comes First: Race, Space and Place in Rap and Hip Hop.* Middletown, CT: Wesleyan University Press, 2002.

Hayden, Tom. Ed. *The Zapatista Reader.* New York: Thunder's Mouth Press/Nation Books, 2002.

hooks, b. *All About Love: New Visions.* New York: William Morrow, 2001.

Kinto Sol. "Hijos del Maiz." Music and video. Available at: www.youtube.com/watch?v=54MZEfXRHCY

McFarland, P. *The Chican@ Hip Hop Nation: Politics of a New Millennial Mestizaje.* East Lansing, MI: Michigan State University Press, 2013.

Olguín, B.V. *La Pinta: Chicana/o Prisoner Literature, Culture, and Politics.* Austin: University of Texas Press, 2010.

Peña, D.G. *Mexican Americans and the Environment.* Tucson: University of Arizona Press, 2005.

Pilcher, J. *Que Vivan Los Tamales!: Food and the Making of Mexican Identity.* Albuquerque: University of New Mexico Press, 1998.

Piven, F.F. and R. Cloward. *Poor People's Movements: Why They Succeed, How They Fail.* New York: Vintage, 1978.

Prison Policy Initiative. "United States Incarceration Rates by Race and Ethnicity" 2010. Available at: www.prisonpolicy.org/graphs/raceinc.html

Psycho Realm. *A War Story, Book II.* Sick Symphonies, 2004.

Pulido, Laura. "The Development of the People of Colour Identity in the Environmental Justice Movement of the Southwestern United States." Socialist Review, 26, 3–4: 145–180.

Rodriguez, Roberto Cintli. *Our Sacred Maiz is Our Mother: Indigeneity and Belonging in the Americas.* University of Arizona Press, 2014.

Sanchez, Ricardo. *Selected Poems.* Arte Publico Press, 1985.

Sicario, Thief. *Honor Among Thieves.* CD Baby, 2009.

Subcomandante Marcos. *Our Word is Our Weapon: Selected Writings.* New York: Seven Stories Press, 2002.

Villa, R.H. *Barrio Logos: Space and Place in Urban Chicano Literature and Culture.* Austin: University of Texas Press, 2000.

Wildcat, D. *Red Alert: Saving the Planet With Indigenous Knowledge.* Golden, CO: Fulcrum, 2009.

Zarate, Juan. *El Sacrificio.* Virus Records, 2008.

Zibechi, R. *Territories in Resistance: A Cartography of Latin American Social Movements.* Edinburgh: AK Press, 2012.

15

PUNK SPANGLISH

Ilan Stavans

A few years ago, a Jewish friend of mine who lives in Lima, Peru, sent me the following email:

> There may be those among you who support including Spanish or French in our national language. I for one am dead set against it!
>
> We should preserve the sanctity of the English language!
>
> To all the schlemiels, shlemazels, nebbishes, nudniks, klutzes, putzes, shlubs, shmoes, shmucks, nogoodniks, and momzers that are lurking out there in the crowed, I just want to say that I, for one, get sentimental when I think about English and its place in society.
>
> To tell the truth, it makes me so farklempt, I'm fit to plotz. This whole scheem gets me broyges. When I hear these mavens and lutfmenschen kvetching about our national language, what chutzpah!
>
> These shmegeges can tout their schlock about the cultural and linguistic diversity of our country and of English itself, but I, for one, am not buying their shtick. It's all so much dreck, as far as I'm concerned. I exhort you all to be menschen about this and stand up to their fardrayte arguments and meshugganah, farshtunkene assertions. It wouldn't be kosher to do anything else.
>
> Remember, when all is said and done, we have English and they've got bubkes! The whole myseh is a pain in the tuchas!

Ah, the exclamation marks!!! This sermon is obviously laugh-out-loud mockery. Yet it goes to the heart of the country's debate on linguistic purity. Those self-appointed to police the way we use the nation's language are descendants from immigrants and employ it, in private as well as in public, in ways they see fit.

Language is always marked by perspective. And perspective is power. (By the way, I found it appropriate that my Peruvian friend didn't italicize any Anglicized Yiddish word, presenting them instead as conventional, even generic. That is exactly what makes English so dexterous in its adaptability: its capacity to absorb foreign terms not only with ease but without any sense of alarm.)

The topics of linguistic pluralism in the United States has been an interest of mine for decades. I have written about it, and about Ebonics, Yinglish (e.g., the penetration of

Yiddish over English, or vice versa), and Chinglish, elsewhere, including "Who Owns the English Language?" (*A Critic's Journey*, 2010). And I have studied Spanish in its multiple variations, the development of English as a global tongue, and, perhaps more publicly, the emergence of Spanglish as a hybrid (some call it "border") tongue in the process of standardizing its own syntax and lexicon. I have meditated on this last topic in, among other forums, "Language and Conquest" (*The Riddle of Cantinflas*, 1998), "Language and Colonization" (*A Critic's Journey*), and in the book *Spanglish: The Making of a New American Language* (2002). I don't believe any of these themes should be considered separately; in fact, they are part of one and the same motif: the changing nature of the way an entire hemisphere, from Alaska to the Pampas, rich in diversity, expresses itself.

Here I want to focus once more on the United States exclusively and to look at it again as a Melting Pot, albeit from a slightly different perspective; that is, not from the political, the demographic, and the socio-linguistic viewpoints I have employed in previous vicissitudes. I want to reflect on "punk Spanglish," namely, the language used exclusively by young people.

"Punk" is a word with multiple meanings. It used to be used to describe prostitutes, gangsters, and hoodlums, as well as homosexual partners. It is taken for nonsense and for foolishness. And it refers to a type of anti-establishment music ("punk rock") that developed in the seventies and featured groups such as the Sex Pistols and singers like Patti Smith. My own use of it is more restricted: I take it for "novice," "beginner"—the young in general. Needless to say, the young aren't always young; yet there is always, at any given time, someone who might be described, by herself as well as by others, as young. Where does youthful language appear? Everywhere: on the street, in the classroom, in the restaurant, and, mostly, in the media, for in the United States, media caters, for financial reasons, first and foremost to the young.

There is an abundance of manifestations, from *telenovelas* to music lyrics, from theater to movies, from sports to comics, from children's books to trade literature, from the Internet to greeting cards and all sorts of merchandise, where punk Spanglish is palpable at all hours of the day. The possibilities are infinite. Language, in general, is marked by the three "e"s: it is elastic, ethereal, and elusive. No sooner do we want to pin it down, it has already escaped our reach. Punk Spanglish is the perfect example. By attempting to codify it, we automatically make it old: we stabilize it, we give a character. And what youth language is about is its slipperiness, intangibleness. I know this because in *Spanglish: The Making of a New American Language* I codified a lexicon of 6,000 terms. The moment it was published—as I argued in its introduction—it was immediately and inevitably obsolete, meaning Spanglish as a vehicle of communication was already larger, healthier, and more dynamic than anything I could trap between covers.

My objective in this chapter is more modest: to survey the landscape of youth language with enough detail and to offer the tools needed to understand the moment in time we are all at once actors and participants in. In no way do I pretend for these reflections to have any finite character. As stated, I particularly want to meditate on the degree to which music, like salsa, *bachata*, boleros, merengue, corridos, *rancheras*, and hip hop, drive the changes this tongue has been experiencing among young Latinos (though it goes without saying that not only Latinos use Spanglish). Before I proceed, I should say that I began to scratch the surface of Spanglish in music in the 2-volume encyclopedia *Latin Music* (2013). There is an entry in it on Spanglish, another on border music writ large, and there are several on youth as the driving force of the various trends, genres, and rhythms defining Latin music in the entire globe. I won't repeat what was stated there. These are further ruminations.

Let me first offer context. Since the United States is mostly a nation of newcomers, its history is an addition of tongues from all corners of the world that interact with one another and for the most part progressively give in to the dominance of English. Spanish is like all other immigrant tongues, although more so. It settled in the Southwest, where it interacted with the native languages of the region, and after the Treaty of Guadalupe Hidalgo of 1848 and the Spanish-American War of 1898, it saw its presence contested by the emphatic recognition of English as the language of business and government. But unlike other tongues that after a couple of generations have receded into the background, Spanish is, in the early decades of the twenty-first century, the unofficial second vehicle of communication of the United States. It often survives in contaminated form, part of code-switching strategies, as the engine of astonishingly verbal ingenuity that not only generates all the time an onslaught of neologisms but also allows for ways of expression that are freer, less circumscribed.

From the mid-eighties onward, there has been a veritable explosion of Spanglish into the mainstream. After a period in which this "mestizo tongue" was perceived as a sign of illiteracy and even as illegitimate speech, the growth of the Latina/o minority, its economic and voting power, gave place to the recognition that this newcomer's tongue is more than a steppingstone in the acquisition of English. It showed enough gravitas to prove that millions were using it *together with* both English and Spanish, meaning that it wasn't evidence of the abandonment of Spanish, nor was it a sign that English was the ultimate target. There have been other immigrant "middle languages" in the United States, such as Franglais, Finglish, and others already mentioned, yet none lasted as long and had been embraced by as large a population as Spanglish was. Since then, major corporations have taken to it to reach consumers. It has been used in religious and political settings. There are handbooks for use in business and cuisine. And textbooks feature it for classroom instruction.

I have argued elsewhere that there is a variety of Spanglishes in the nation, from Pachuco, Chicano Spanglish, and Tex-Mex to Dominicanish, Cubonics, Nuyorrican, and other types. There is the variety used by first-generation immigrants that is different from the Spanglish of Latinos born in the United States. And there is cyber-Spanglish, too, as well as types of Spanglish used in various industries, such as sports, advertising, medicine, and so on. Plus, outside the country Spanglish is used in countless ways, for instance among tourists, among retirees and expatriates, etc. The Spanglish used in mainstream television networks north of the Rio Grande, such as Univisión and Telemundo, is often a "standardized" version, nurtured by all sorts of heterogeneous ingredients. In 2015, after a record fifty-plus years, the variety show *Sábado Gigante*, with Don Francisco (aka Mario Krautzberger), came to an end. This show was always described as targeting "*la familia hispana.*" The category, I guess, includes, the children, adolescents, and, in general, the young. Yet nobody ever perceived it as using youth culture as an engine; that is, it was cutting-edge in terms of style. Quite the contrary, it was quite traditional in approach, to the degree of being recalcitrant—or I should stay stagnant—in its moral values.

I was a guest on a couple of occasions. In the dressing room I spoke Yiddish, with Don Francisco we employed Spanish—with one exception. The theme of the interview was Spanglish. When he prepared episodes in order to highlight the qualities of this way of communication, the audience was thrilled. More so, it felt like a fish in water. Don Francisco and I used Spanglish effortlessly. At one point, I even proposed a pair of neologisms in Spanglish, "*soquete*" (sock, not plugging device) and "*washatería*" (laundro-mat), which I followed in a number of different locations nationwide. Such was the popularity of *Sábado Gigante* that these terms took hold rather quickly. It was a fascinating phenomenon.

Even though, as I mentioned, the show with Don Francisco wasn't a favorite among young viewers, its popularity as well as durability enabled it to exert an enormous impact on the way people approached Spanglish, including those outside its target audience, ages twelve to twenty-five. While in general the host was rather conservative in his linguistic choices, his guests and the audience often reverted to Spanglish, which, by virtue of it being seen on the small screen, immediately legitimated, or at least openly recognized, that usage. This type of on-air maneuver is also common in Noticiero Univisión with Jorge Ramos, who is known for his enthusiastic endorsement of Spanglish as an acceptable form of speech. (He has written about this interest in his books, such as *The Other Face of America*, 2006.) Other TV examples include popular investigative programs like *Aquí y Ahora* (to which I have contributed).

Telemundo featured *Una Maid en Manhattan* on prime time from 2011 top 2012. Devoted to—what else?—the entanglement of love and class, it was based on the popular Jennifer Lopez movie vehicle. The network promoted it as the first Spanglish *telenovela* and viewers were able to access it as such and in Spanish and/or English subtitles. This is only one among hundreds of examples of the use (and abuse) of Spanglish on Spanish-language TV in the United States. Others include all sorts of sports shows, especially dealing with soccer, baseball, and football. I'm invariably fascinated by the recurrence of anglicisms in the terminology used by sports newscasters in soccer, like "penalty," "corner," "*ofsite*", and "*gol*." The word "soccer" itself, which in English is seen as an Americanism (they call the sport "football," whereas Spanish-language speakers all over the world call it "*fútbol*"), is a prime example of linguistic localisms. And Spanglish terms are equally abundant in baseball: "bat," "homerun," "short stop," etc. Symbolically, these code-switching strategies in the media give people, among them a large youthful constituency, permission to be equally playful with language.

In non-Spanish-language television, *Dora the Explorer*, *Breaking Bad*, and mini-series like *Narcos* about Colombian drug trafficker Pablo Escobar are intriguing cases. Likewise, there is a vast list of instances in radio, including entire stations in California, Texas, and New Mexico, that officially switched to this mixed tongue. And there are countless films, starting with *The Ballad of Gregorio Cortez* with Edward James Olmos and *Spanglish* directed by James L. Brooks, and concluding with all the work by Robert Rodriguez (*El Mariachi*, *Spy Kids*, *Machete*), that use Spanglish. In advertising, Toyota, Taco Bell, Colgate, and Hallmark Cards have recognizable product lines along these lines. But, as I stated above, my concern now is music.

Onward into music, let me start with pop singers like Ricky Martin. His popular song "Livin' La Vida Loca" might well be described as the unofficial Spanglish anthem. The Spanish *baladista* Julio Iglesias and his son Enrique Iglesias, albeit less committedly, have switched to English, at times calling attention to the switch not only in publicity tours but in the lyrics themselves, which go back and forth between languages. Tony Bennett has done the same in his collaborations with Latin musicians like Marc Anthony and Gloria Estefan. Yet any example on this front is likely to pale when compared to rock groups like Café Tacuba from Mexico and Cypress Hill in California that actively want to erase the artificial line between Spanish and English, thus creating lucid examples of cross-fertilizing that aren't only artistically innovative but push language to new terrain. The same thing goes for singers like Juan Luis Guerra, internationally known for his cutting-edge Merengue rhythms. One example is Guerra's beloved song "Woman del Callao," included in his record *Ojalá que llueva café*. Its lyrics includes references to having "mucho hot" and "mucho tempo," and it is famous for the line "dancing in this paradise/ everytime, ayayayay."

Guerra isn't known for coherent, syntactically-sound songs but for passionate, dream-like invocations of love and lust, and "Woman del Callao" is a prime example. The zigzagging narrative creates an atmosphere of deliberate confusion and this is achieved with playful, itinerant language. By effortlessly swapping codes, the message to the young audience of Latinos navigating two worlds, namely the Spanish-speaking Caribbean, Latin America, and the United States, is that such border-jumping attitude is cool.

The Latin rhythm that is identified as a sure crossover is salsa. It became popular in New York in the seventies and is often described as the signature music of Latinos in the United States. Figures like Celia Cruz, Rubén Blades, and Tito Puente are among its most recognizable brands. Salseros, as the musicians are known, cater to audiences of all ages and youth is invariably a stronghold. Their style frequently uses Spanglish, too. Gloria Esteban, whose salsa roots are well known, frequently travels, within the same project, between Spanish and English, at times settling in the in-between. So does Marc Anthony. This coming'-and-goin' brings to mind their collaboration with Tony Bennett, who over his long career has invited Latin musicians to make collaborative efforts. In his recordings with Estefan, Anthony, and others (including Mariachis), Bennett himself, though he isn't a Spanish speaker, occasionally gives in to code-switching.

Lin-Manuel Miranda, famous for the Broadway musical *Hamilton*, is the author of an earlier show called *In the Heights*, where Merengue and Bachata are combined with rap and hip hop. Among the most celebrated songs from it is "Carnaval del Barrio." I included it, along with various other examples of popular music, in the section "Popular Dimensions" of *The Norton Anthology of Latino Literature*, published in 2011. Talking about hip hop, there are all sorts, from B-Real, Funky Aztecs, Tha Mexakins, Chino KL, K7, and Serio. They all use Spanglish in their music. And there is, of course, Raggaetón, where this hybrid tongue rules. The best case I know is "Somos raperos pero no delincuentes" by Ivy Queen. Then there is Daddy Yankee, rapper of "Limbo," whose syntax is extraordinary, with lines like "Pa' bailarlo caliente, not stoppin', my baby/Yo, DJ, let it run."

Lila Downs does something similar with Mexican boleros. She sings an assortment of inventive lyrics about the border and about immigrants. What makes her intriguing on this front is that, as a result of biography (her mother is of indigenous background), Downs also employs pre-Columbian languages, such as Nahuátl. The effect is stunning. Along similar lines, the growing industry of Narco-Corridos, whose music is about narco-traffickers perceived as heroes by the community because of their rebellion against the police and the authorities in general on both side of the U.S.-Mexican border, produce songs where English and Spanish become linguistically intertwined. Legendary star Rosalino "Chalino" Sánchez is considered a cornerstone in this modality, as are groups like Los Tigres del Norte and Los Tucanes de Tijuana. These musicians attract a different type of young Latinos, mostly recent immigrant laborers in rural and urban settings who are at the dawn of their journey into cultural assimilation. These lyrics make them simultaneously feel at home and become acquainted with expressions in English they are unfamiliar with. Again, two worlds collide.

I want to return to the theme of dictionaries. A survey of Spanish/English dictionaries available in the United States showcases the degree to which the two languages are intertwined. There is a medical Spanish "visual manual" that displays body organs and attaches words to them that are often in English. Plus, there is an assortment of "Spanish for Tourists" volumes that playfully combine the two tongues, often in unintentionally hilarious ways. Years ago, I wrote a preface for *Learning Construction Spanglish: A Beginner's Guide to Spanish On-the-Job* (2004), edited by Terry Eddy and Alberto Herrera, a tool for English-speaking construction workers to communicate with their Spanish-language counterparts. Over the years, I have seen it in action, used by middle-aged men with young immigrants who have been in the United States less than a couple of years.

Lexicons, it is often assumed, are artifacts produced by adults, often (though not always) specialists in lexicography. In an attempt to generalize while being attuned to its dangers, this characteristic undoubtedly suggests that, as a trend, the study of youth language is seldom performed by the young. In fact, the young, in such explorations, are almost only the subject of analysis. I say this because, in my mid-fifties, I am conscious that a probing examination of the Spanglish employed by young Latinos benefits from their involvement in ways that aren't only passive, and that, consequently, these thoughts of mine are limited by my own constraints (age, nationality, education, geographical location, and so on). Again, I offer them not as conclusive but as an invitation to further investigate an urgent field of linguistic inquiry.

I began this chapter with an email from a Peruvian-Jewish friend that serves as a cautionary tale about authority in language and the desire in some corners to protect that language from the abuse they say it is subjected to by the masses. I often receive comments from all sorts of individuals expressing their dismay at how punk Spanglish is destroying either Spanish or English. I disagree: to me this manifestation is proof of the immeasurable vitality of human affairs. It doesn't announce decline but reconfiguration. Change is the true constant in the world and this is clear in language. The dialectic between how the young and the not-so-young use words isn't about submission but about revitalization. Punk Spanglish isn't an aberration. It is beautiful and stunningly versatile. Evidence of that versatility is its capacity to communicate complex emotions.

Finally, let me add that linguists are often shy about delving into popular culture in order to appreciate a people's multiplicity of voices. Yet where else, if not there, is the intercourse between spheres as accentuated? This realm deserves our complete attention. In this chapter I have offered only a hopscotch of possibilities. The effect of this cross-linguistic phenomenon is to ratify that Spanglish is more than a steppingstone for Spanish-language speakers in the acquisition of English. Given its ubiquity, it looks, in the fluid field of media, and expressly among those who are in the early stages of their journey in life, more like a verbal destination itself, a space that is neither Anglo nor Hispanic but Latino in the full, malleable sense of the term.

Bibliography

Eddy, Terry and Alberto Herrera. *Learning Construction Spanglish: A Beginner's Guide to Spanish On-the-Job*. McGraw-Hill, 2004.
Stavans, Ilan. *The Riddle of Cantinflas*. University of New Mexico Press, 1998.
Stavans, Ilan. *Spanglish: The Making of a New American Language*. HarperCollins, 2002.
Stavans, Ilan. *A Critic's Journey*. University of Michigan Press, 2010.
Stavans, Ilan (ed.). *The Norton Anthology of Latino Literature*. W. W. Norton, 2011.
Stavans, Ilan (ed.). *Latin Music*. ABC-Clio, 2013.

16

LATINO RADIO AND COUNTER EPISTEMOLOGIES

Stacey Alex

This is a dangerous crossroads … But if we learn to listen, we may find that experts come from unexpected places, that seemingly powerless people have more ways of understanding the world than their oppressors, and that the same global networks of commerce and communication that constrain us offer opportunities for cross-cultural resistance.

George Lipsitz, *Dangerous Crossroads*

Latino studies scholars have investigated Spanish-language radio in relation to the ethno-linguistic racialization of Latinos and have contextualized the topic in a larger historically rooted struggle for media access. Dolores Inés Casillas, for example, confronts problematic audience measurements that underestimate Latino listenership and sustain hierarchies of language and race by failing to recognize the complexity of language preference, and by identifying Latino participants as the problem rather than modifying its techniques. Mari Castañeda works at the intersection of transculturation and political economy to reveal how radio embodies a national vision that reinforces whiteness and the marginalization of minorities. She finds that while U.S. Latino media policy activism works to democratize communication resources, Latinos continue to face difficulties in areas of media ownership, employment, and programming ("Role of Media Policy"). Other scholars have examined Spanish-language radio's role in raising Latino voter turnout (Panagopoulos and Green) and helping Latino organizations reach the national Latino public to mobilize protests and immigrant naturalization within a contentious political climate (Félix, González, and Ramírez). In contrast to an overtly political angle, in this chapter I consider how Latinos use radio as a vehicle for internal resistance, but we must not forget that this is only one aspect in a wide range of issues surrounding Latino identity and expression.

In the face of deficit models of schooling that require students to leave their language and culture at the door, and immigration policies that aim to strip migrants of their sense of 'home' and belonging, radio is a sonic space in which Latinos can contest social subordinations and build community by privileging Latino knowledge production. Dolores Delgado Bernal defines "critical raced-gendered epistemologies" as systems of knowledge that are informed by various raced and gendered experiences of people of color (107). She explains that these epistemologies, which develop from different social, cultural, and political histories from the dominant race, challenge limited foundations of knowledge informed by Anglo cultural experiences. While Delgado Bernal's work positions students of color as holders and creators of knowledge, I will apply this approach to Spanish-language radio participants in the Midwest.

Karen Fog Olwig and Kirsten Hastrup's work in "Siting Culture" will guide my approach to place as "a cultural construction that is part of the process of human life, and not as a fixed entity" (12). They remind us that destabilization and suffering are integral parts of the human experience. Yet, complex social and economic interrelations do not mean that people necessarily perceive their lives in complicated global dimensions (6, 12). For these reasons, this chapter considers the ways Latinos create meaningful and manageable contexts of life but does not deny the complexity of the cultural processes at hand. While only a fraction of Latinos are immigrants and only a portion of those immigrants are undocumented, all Latinos may face varied kinds of hostility from dominant institutions. Confronted with these mechanisms that work to render Latinos invisible, such as English-only and anti-immigrant initiatives, radio is an alternative medium in which Latinos promote their own epistemologies and counter limitations to social and political mobility.

This chapter will address how Latino producers and audiences of 105.5 FM La Ley of Des Moines and Perry, Iowa, construct a sonic space of affective belonging and resistance through collective knowledge production. While there are a number of elements that must be examined to fully analyze this dynamic, this work examines how taglines, the dissemination of information in Spanish, and audience participation challenge dominant Anglo knowledge production. These practices create a sense of community by affirming complex Latino identities and simulating control despite a hostile sociopolitical environment. Although live performances of Latino music may contribute ephemerally to this sense of belonging, radio provides a more sustained sense of community. Despite limited data, I hope to encourage others to contribute to this valuable area of research because Spanish-language radio is a crucial resource to complicate our understanding of Latino resistance and knowledge production.

In parallel with educational research's move to privilege experiential knowledge, it is important to acknowledge how personal and professional experiences inform my analysis. The lack of bilingual educational opportunities in Iowa and across the country is concerning for both my former students and family of Latino heritage. In West Liberty, Iowa, I had the opportunity to work in one of the only Spanish-English Dual Language programs in the state. I am proud of the district's mission and accomplishments, yet, deficit models may remain intact even within bilingual schools. Instruction in Spanish is often justified as a way to acquire English and is gradually eliminated from the curriculum rather than viewed as valuable in its own right. In "Has Bilingual Education Been Columbused?" Nelson Flores warns that by considering bilingual education their own "discovery", white middle and upper-class communities erase the history of Latino community activism for these programs and this results, potentially, in its gentrification. My investment in educational reform leads me to consider how Latinos use Spanish-language radio as a space for linguistic pride and preservation in the face of English-only sentiment and white racial privilege. I also agree with Michele Hilmes's conclusion in her introduction to *Radio Reader* that Latino media in the United States has been overlooked by scholars and is only recently receiving more attention. We will now examine this chapter's theoretical framework to approach resistance.

Daniel Solorzano and Dolores Delgado Bernal argue that theories of resistance must expand to include more subtle, internal resistance in order to better understand the lived realities of Chicana/o students. Internal resistance may conform to dominant structural norms but also be socially transformational if it both maintains a critique of oppression and is motivated by social justice (309–10). They define "resilient resistance" as a kind of internal resistance because the subject works within the mainstream system but survives or succeeds. La Ley demonstrates resilient resistance by providing support to the Latino community, which is made possible by both corporate and local advertising. Furthermore, Solorzano and Bernal assert that scholarship must make student voices, perspectives, and sociopolitical-historical contexts central in order to assess behaviors of resistance (321). In addition to a thorough examination of these contexts, I will follow Solorzano and Bernal's lead on the following two fronts.

First, I will rely on their differentiation between resistance theories and cultural and social reproduction theories. Rather than view subjects as acted on by wider social structures, such as in the work of Pierre Bourdieu and Michel Foucault, resistance theories examine the ways subjects negotiate and struggle within social structures to create meanings through agency (Solorzano and Bernal, 315). By relying on an expanded resistance theory that includes internal resistances, my work will consider both how Latino experiences are shaped by dominant discourses and how Latinos actively shape and counter those discourses.

Second, I will take up Solorzano and Bernal's call to use Latino Critical Race Theory (LatCrit) as a framework for theorizing the ways structures, processes, and discourse promote racial subordination. They explain that LatCrit builds on Critical Race Theory (CRT), because while it produces scholarship to eliminate racism, it also includes issues not addressed by CRT, including language, immigration, culture, ethnicity, phenotype, and sexuality due to its concern with coalitional Latino pan-ethnicity (311). Furthermore, LatCrit interrogates the intersections of these elements in ways that are neither uniform nor static (315). These intersections will be important to provide a more nuanced understanding of La Ley as resistance that considers immigration and language alongside other issues.

To locate Spanish-language radio in these specific social and cultural contexts, we will first consider immigration experiences for Spanish-speakers in Iowa. Stanton E. F. Wortham, Enrique G. Murillo, and Edmund T. Hamann define the "new Latino diaspora" as the permanent or temporary settlement of an increasing number of Latinos, many immigrant, in areas of the U.S. that have not traditionally been home to Latinos. Unlike those in the Southwest, Latinos in these new areas face more insistent questions about their identity because long-term residents have little experience with Latinos (1). New Diaspora Latinos find themselves in a unique socio-historical location in which Latinos are both constructed by the host communities and assert their own identities in response to familiar and unfamiliar conflicts and opportunities (2). Belz reports that the first Spanish-speaking immigrants to the Des Moines area were Mexican families that founded a community in Valley Junction of West Des Moines in the late 1800s and early 1900s due to the appeal of the railroad industry. While West Des Moines may not fit the new Latino diaspora description, other areas of Des Moines as well as Perry have seen more recent and rapid Latino population growth that has at times resulted in hostile reactions.

Tensions recently flared at a kindergarten concert in Perry when a man in the audience chanted "English-only, USA" after the director's remarks were translated into Spanish. According to Drake University professor Jody Swilky, Perry's Latino population grew from

1 percent in 1990 to 25 percent in 2000, and the 2013–14 kindergarten class is 50 percent Latino (Elmer). Juan Ordonez encouraged his nephew to send his video of the event to the local television station, KCCI, in order to "make sure somebody knows what's going on in Perry and maybe they stop" (Peng). This is one example of Latinos in Iowa using media to resist the depreciation of Spanish and its speakers. Rather than directly address the need to confront racism, the school district offered a colorblind response. Superintendent M. Lynn Ubben wrote in an email to staff, "As our elementary music instructor so eloquently said, 'Our children don't see color, they just see their friends'" (Elmer). Latinos across Iowa face racism regardless of language preference or citizenry and despite official attempts to render conflict invisible. Josh Kun writes in "Aural Border" that "outside the grasp of the official border(s) yet informed by them, there arises a multiplicity of unofficial borders where borderness is voiced and rescued from the willful aphasia of official culture" (4). He argues that in spaces of limited political possibilities, music allows for the remapping of inter-American cartographies and citizenships (6–9). This border is not only physical but represents social and cultural lines between dominant and peripheral groups. La Ley works to make the border heard in Iowa and draw attention to difference in affirming and transformative ways.

While English-only sentiment shapes this specific context, Immigration and Customs Enforcement's massive workplace raids throughout the state have also contributed to a culture of fear. The 2008 raid in Postville, Iowa, of the kosher slaughterhouse and meatpacker Agriprocessors gained national attention in part due to Erik Camayd-Freixas, an interpreter who publically denounced the government's abuse of power in an essay and a congressional hearing. In *US Immigration and Its Global Impact*, Erik Camayd-Freixas advocates for comprehensive immigration reform by revealing how migrants were criminalized in order to show progress against identity theft and Social Security fraud (102). Inés Valdez asserts that we must not only consider negative interventions to control immigration, but examine positive ones as well. She finds that both are biopolitical because they shape our understanding of race into two groups: those who deserve to have their lives protected, and a racialized, threatening group of immigrants and Latinos. Furthermore, the fact that immigrants are not criminals reveals the vulnerability of the U.S. as a nation of laws, which motivates it to reassert itself by producing a threatening alien subject to legitimize the practice of immigration enforcement and create a tough and punishing life for migrants (4–13). Valdez argues that the Development, Relief, and Education for Alien Minors (DREAM) Act, although never passed, reinforced the justice of an immigration regime. High school graduates were privileged with the opportunity for conditional residency while the rest were categorized as undeserving or left with potentially lethal military service as their only path to citizenship. This mechanism maintains the neoliberal myth of autonomy by legitimizing the exclusion of immigrants while maintaining a tough road for the group selected for "inclusion" (22–8). As of July 1, 2014, Iowa's Latino population was estimated to be 173,594, constituting 5.6% of the total state population; 56,732 were foreign born of Latin American origin (Iowa). Pew Hispanic Research Center estimates from 2012 find that of 40,000 undocumented immigrants in Iowa, about 65 percent are of Mexican origin. We must also recognize the presence of other Latin American national origins. While only a portion of Latinos in Iowa are immigrants and only part of that group is undocumented, all Latinos may be subject to the consequences of English-only rhetoric, criminalization, and racialization.

Having outlined some sociopolitical factors that shape Latinos experiences in Iowa, we will now consider the history of Spanish-language radio in the U.S. Roberto Avant-Mier explains that "X" radio stations on the Mexican side of the U.S./Mexico border had a strong influence on U.S. culture between the 1930s and the 1960s. These high-powered AM border stations included regional Mexican and other Latin American music and reached as much as a million watts of radio power, a level that would have been illegal in the U.S. (48–50). The first Spanish-language radio programs based in the U.S. were created in the 1920s and 1930s by Latino brokers who purchased blocks of programming from radio stations and sold advertising time to local businesses (Gutiérrez and Schement, 5). A successful broker, Raul Cortez, went on the air with the first full-time Spanish-language radio station in 1946. Part of the rationale in his application to the Federal Communication Commission for a license was the need to rally Chicanos behind the war effort (Schement and Flores, quoted in Gutiérrez and Schement, 9). Eric Rothenbuhler and Tom McCourt assert that advertisers and radio programmers in the U.S. developed a larger interest in minority groups as World War II provided more access to assimilate economically into mainstream society. They find that blacks and Latinos had limited opportunities to enter the radio industry in professional roles and nearly all stations targeting minorities were owned by whites. Although broadcasters' approach to minority communities as customers was exploitative and programming often reinforced racial stereotypes and caricatures, stations programmed by minorities were a source of pride for these communities as black and Latino voices were consistently heard on air (372–3). As television increasingly dominated American broadcasting, radio often worked to meet the cultural needs and interests unmet by this new medium (375). Mari Castañeda finds that unlike other ethnic radio stations, U.S. Spanish-language radio, which dates back to the 1920s, has grown with the Latino population. It continues to thrive today, whereas English-language radio has seen a decrease in listenership (Rothenbuhler & McCourt, 2002, 69–70). While there are a number of Spanish-language stations in Iowa, here we will briefly consider the sociocultural context of La Ley.

Adam Belz reports that Pedro Zamora, who emigrated from Mexico in the early 1980s, purchased 105.5 FM La Ley in 2003. It promotes Spanish-language music concerts at the Val Air Ballroom, also owned by his company, the Detroit-based Zamora Entertainment group. This historic Des Moines venue featured stars such as Duke Ellington and Glen Miller and now hosts *quinceañeras* and the *norteña* bands such Los Tigres del Norte in addition to mainstream musical acts (Belz). According to the Media Kit provided by La Ley for potential clients, it is the largest Spanish-language station in Iowa and, because its antenna is located between Perry and Des Moines, Spanish-language programming is available to both rural and urban Latino communities across a 60 mile radius ("La Ley"). This study is informed by ten hours of data collection at various times and days of the week during April and May of 2015 through TuneIn Radio, an online application that allows me to listen to La Ley live from Columbus, Ohio. I recorded information about the hosts, topics of discussion, news, themes of advertisements, and song requests. We will now turn to the ways in which La Ley serves to undermine the social, cultural, and racial subordinations previously outlined.

The first practice we will examine is the use of taglines that radio announcers use to promote the station before repeating its call sign and name. The first example, "La que manda" (the one in charge) is often called out before "La Ley" (The Law). While it most certainly refers to the station's popularity, it also evokes a sense of order and power in the face of racial discrimination, and for those without documentation, limited legal rights. The ability to create a sense of safety and comfort through familiar music and language may provide a sense of validity for all Latino listeners, and especially to those driving and working without the government's permission.

While the first tagline plays on the idea of legal authority, the second, in contrast, evokes the power of the outlaw. This tagline, "La invasión comenzó" (the invasion began), relays dominant images of a Latino take over and reclaims them in an affirming way. A recent example of this dominant rhetoric is the media's reaction to thousands of Central American children crossing the U.S.-Mexico border during the summer of 2014. Aviva Chomsky notes that the right-wing Breitbart News Network in Texas initially brought attention to children "invading" the U.S. to criticize President Obama's supposed failure to control the border. Chomsky maintains that both Republicans and Democrats used the "crisis" for political gain while ignoring the reasons for this long-term trend: U.S. policies that sponsored dirty wars in Guatemala and El Salvador, the 2009 U.S.-supported military coup in Honduras, and the U.S. demand for undocumented labor. In the face of this erasure and hostility, La Ley re-appropriates the term to underscore its cultural power and lived experiences of social injustice.

The final tagline to be considered here, "Nosotros no imitamos" (we don't imitate), establishes a sense of cultural authenticity and authority. Because of the physical distance between the producers of La Ley and the point of origin for the majority of the music played on air, this phrase seems to claim a strong connection with a variety of Latin American heritage sites. Through this phrase, La Ley asserts its understanding of the linguistic and cultural realities of listeners and its ability to represent them accordingly. Although not addressed specifically on air, we may infer that having programming designed and owned by Latinos lends weight to this tagline's affirmation of being "real" as opposed to Anglo appropriation of Latinos as consumers that characterized much of early radio targeted for minority groups. Working in tandem, these three phrases build a sense of control and belonging in the face of dominant structures that limit Latino social and economic mobility.

The second practice is the distribution of information in Spanish. In "The Significance of Spanish-language U.S. Radio", Mari Castañeda finds that "historically, on-air personalities have used their programming to inform, educate, and mobilize the public and they view their listeners as more than simply audiences but as citizens of the Latino diaspora" (79). Castañeda also recognizes that Spanish-language stations across the U.S. reflect the wide diversity of Latin American immigrants' cultural, linguistic, and geopolitical practices (76). La Ley follows this tradition by offering local, national, and global news as well as a weekly program called "Iowa Al Día" and a daily program called "El Coffee" in which local experts, such as immigration lawyer Sonia Parra and Iowa State nutritionist Raquel Juarez, offer advice while listeners may submit questions. La Ley also supports community outreach initiatives by providing information on issues such as fair housing policies, community college, and the Iowa Citizens for Community Improvement Action Fund's work in social justice. Through this programming, La Ley empowers its listeners through the creation of sonic space to resist alienation.

The third practice examined, audience participation, includes 53 calls and text messages reported on air. Twenty were call-in votes for a sequence called "Lucha de estrellas". Nineteen calls and texts were to greet a group of people on air without a musical request, while the other 14 were greetings with a request for a song of the DJ's choice, a genre of music, any song by a specific artist, or a particular song. Six of the 33 non-votes were directed to family members or romantic partners to celebrate birthdays or anniversaries, 15 greeted people from or who identified themselves as being from a particular region in Mexico with one greeting to Central Americans, five identified their location within the U.S. (Des Moines; Perry, Iowa; Waukee, Iowa; and L.A.), and seven referred to working or co-workers. La chamba, or work, was a central topic which cements a sense of solidarity among listeners as they use music to complete and even enjoy the work day. One DJ said she would play a song with a fast beat so the caller could dance at her job in Valley West Mall. Although it falls outside the scope of this chapter, it is important to recognize a long history in which labor has been a central theme in forging a sense of Latino belonging.

Ethnicity and place of origin were also common themes. DJs and callers often began with, "saludos para la gente/raza de … " (greetings to the people of…) followed by the name of a Mexican state. In "Putting Mano to Music" Derek Pardue describes how

> local hip-hoppers emphasize the dynamic aspects of musical mediation, i.e., music not simply as a conduit for expression but also as a mode of representation through which performers can potentially change their sense of self and suggest alternative models of social stratification and value.
>
> (254)

While Pardue's focus here is on performance as the catalyst for transformation of self-concept, and specifically race and Brazilian Rap, his argument can be extended to include all musical participants which, in the case of La Ley, includes both producers and the audience. In contrast to a colorblind and English-only binary, La Ley capitalizes on sound as an alternative dimension in which race and ethnicity are valuable components of Latino identities through the sharing of music.

Requests for specific genres and songs may index both Pan-Latinidad and local identities. In *Music as Social Life*, Thomas Turino reminds us that music often indexes social group or regional identity because people tend to hear certain styles of music by particular individuals (8). Furthermore, indexical signs wield emotional power that is equal to the feelings and experiences that they signal (9). They also undergo semantic snowballing, meaning that one sign may provoke multiple responses in an individual because it accumulates various meanings over time. For example, several memories of events, people, and emotions may be associated with one song throughout an individual's life. For this reason, no two people have identical responses to indexical signs. Yet, shared experiences, such as those produced through mass media, can lead a group of people to have common indexical associations (10). La Ley both depends on previously shared experiences of its Latino audience and creates further shared experiences through audience participation and the repetition of structures to produce and sustain affective connections within the community.

We will now take a closer look at one particular example of audience participation, a song request from the morning of Monday, April 27th. DJ Fabiola Schirrmeister read a message from "Chaparita de Durango" who wished to request "Mi razón de ser" by Banda MS (Mazatlán, Sinaloa) for her ex-boyfriend. Fabiola then suggested that he call the station to request another song for Chaparita. Through this gesture, the DJ expressed empathy with the requester and her heartbreak, while encouraging a kind of healing through music. We may infer that "Mi razón de ser" holds special meaning for the couple because of an experience shared while listening to the song. Other listeners may make multiple connections to their own heartbreaks, experienced while listening to other songs of the *banda* genre, or the group MS. Furthermore, they may connect emotionally with the requester by also identifying with pride or homesickness for Durango or the idyllic portrayal of rural life in Sinaloa from the song's music video. Through any one of these indexical signs, listeners are connected to one another because "music and sound can serve as vectors of connection and affiliation between distanced and displaced communities" (Kun, 14).

We may view La Ley as an "audiotopia," defined by Kun as a space in which distinct identity-formations, cultures, and geographies may interact in a "musical space of difference, where contradictions and conflicts do not cancel other out but coexist and live through each other" (6). Listeners may enter into relationships with a diverse Latino community without having to erase differences. La Ley provides a unique opportunity because listeners have avenues through which they can share the same sonic space despite variance in musical taste. According to its media kit, La Ley follows a regional Mexican musical format which includes *banda, cumbia, norteña, salsa, bachata,* and *merengue.* Only *banda* and *norteña* claim origins in Mexico, while the other four genres were developed in other Latin American countries and popularized later in Mexico and internationally. Through this history, Latinos with roots in countries other than Mexico, as well as diverse groups within Mexico, may see their musical tastes represented. In 2014, 78.1% percent of Latinos in Iowa identified as Mexican (Iowa). La Ley's musical programming reflects this demographic and is primarily dedicated to genres from Mexico. Yet La Ley also demonstrates a flexibility that reaches even beyond the range of the six genres outlined for potential advertisers. For example, a man from Guatemala called in to request "Sopa de caracol" for the Central Americans in the area. This song, released by the Honduran group Banda Blanca, is written in the *punta* style developed through Afro-Caribbean Garifuna traditions. Both musical requests and caller voting mediate the sharing of sonic space to include a variety of ethnic, national, and regional Mexican heritages.

Caller voting is the second component of audience participation, observed during a program called "Lucha de estrellas" (Battle of Stars) that airs Monday through Friday from 4 to 5 p.m. DJ Furia plays ten seconds of two songs and asks listeners to call in with their votes to determine which song will be played. With rapid fire speech, Furia manipulates the intonation of his voice to imitate a sports announcer describing a boxing match. We hear a crowd cheering and the sounds of fists punching as he asks callers, "¿por quién, por quién, por quién?" (for whom, for whom, for whom?), and they answer with the name of the artist or song. As soon as at least three callers have voted for the same song, Furia announces the winner and calls off the fight with "¡suéltale, suéltale!" (let him go, let him go!). Although there is no time for callers to identify themselves or send *saludos* to others, this sequence simulates a kind of democracy in which musical tastes stand in for political voting that excludes a large portion of the Latino population from participation.

Taglines, information, and audience participation with musical selections create shared expectations among listeners as they learn to anticipate these structures. This repetition is what allows radio to potentially build a sense of belonging that is sustained beyond live musical performances. Through radio, listeners do not need to convene in one particular time or space, but may be connected across them. Veit Erlmann considers Immanuel Kant's notion of aesthetic communities that build and destroy themselves on the basis of taste. They are founded out of hope for unanimity that remains an unfulfilled promise because of differing notions of what is beautiful. For this reason, aesthetic communities are unstable and ephemeral (12). In contrast to this limited context for solidarity, La Ley provides an arena in which cultural differences may be maintained and mediated to build a more permanent sense of community. Heeding Erlmann's warning that music lends itself to utopic, anti-capitalist politics in the West, I do not argue that radio resolves conflict, but that it provides a space in which people can create collective expression of resistance and solidarity. This is not a picket line kind of resistance. It is more subtle but holds its own kind of power: mutual recognition and greeting between diverse people who share similar triumphs and obstacles—it is a woman dancing to *cumbia* while she works at Valley West Mall and makes her heritage heard.

The three practices examined here may not be unique to Spanish-language programming. Local English-language radio stations may also build a sense of community through taglines, the dissemination of information, and audience participation. However, this chapter considered how these strategies are developed to resist dominant power structures. While structures of subordination remain intact, such as deficit models in schools and racialization through immigration interventions, Latinos in Central Iowa are able to affirm complex identities and create a sonic space for belonging by filling airwaves with Spanish-language music and information. La Ley and its listeners also break institutional silencing by creating affective connections and a sense of democracy.

While live Latino musical performances may work in sync with efforts to forge a sense of community, radio may prove a more sustainable sonic dimension for generating meaningful and manageable contexts of life. More research must be done to fully consider these dynamics, yet my analysis bridged an educational theoretical framework with cultural studies to further recognize strategies of resistance. By examining Spanish-language radio in both scholarly work and with our students, we may work against deficit models and examine how Latino communities collectively produce knowledge in ways that counter the limitations of dominant epistemologies.

Bibliography

Avant-Mier, Roberto. "Heard it on the X: Border Radio As Public Discourse and the Latino Legacy in Popular Music." *Radio Cultures: The Sound Medium in American Life*. Ed. Michael C.Keith. New York: Peter Lang, 2008, pp. 47–64. Print.

Belz, Adam. "Val Air Ballroom: From Sock Hops to Fiestas." *The Des Moines Register*. 5 December 2010.

Camayd-Freixas, Erik. *US Immigration Reform and Its Global Impact: Lessons from the Postville Raid*. New York: Palgrave Macmillan, 2013.

Casillas, Dolores Inés. "Lost in Translation: The Politics of Race and Language in Spanish-Language Radio Ratings." *Contemporary Latina/o Media: Production, Circulation, Politics*. Eds. Arlene Dávila and Yeidy M. Rivero. New York: New York University Press, 2014.

Castañeda, Mari. "The Significance of Spanish-language U.S. Radio." *Latinos and American Popular Culture*. Ed. Patricia Montilla. Westport: Praeger, 2013.

Castañeda, Mari. "The Role of Media Policy in Shaping the US Latino Radio Industry." *Contemporary Latina/o Media: Production, Circulation, Politics*. Eds. Arlene Dávila and Yeidy M. Rivero. New York: New York University Press, 2014.

Chomsky, Aviva. "America's Continuing Border Crisis: The Real Story Behind the 'Invasion' of the Children." *Tom Dispatch*. 24 Aug. 2014.

Delgado Bernal, Dolores. "Critical Race Theory, Latino Critical Theory, and Critical Raced-Gendered Epistemologies: Recognizing Students of Color as Holders and Creators of Knowledge." *Qualitative Inquiry*. 8:1 (2002): 105–26.

Elmer, MacKenzie. "Kindergarten event disrupted by 'English only' chant." *The Des Moines Register*. 24 April 2015.

Erlmann, Veit. "How Beautiful Is Small?: Music, Globalization and the Aesthetics of the Local." *Yearbook for Traditional Music*. 30 (1998): 12–21.

Félix, Adrián, Carmen González, and Ricardo Ramírez. "Political Protest, Ethnic Media, and Latino Naturalization." *American Behavioral Scientist*. 52:4 (2008): 618–34.

Flores, Nelson. "Has Bilingual Education Been Columbused?" *The Educational Linguist*. 25 January 2015.

Gutiérrez, Félix F. and Jorge R. Schement. *Spanish-language Radio in the Southwestern United States*. Austin: University of Texas Center for Mexican American Studies, 1979.

Hilmes, Michele. "Rethinking Radio." *Radio Reader: Essays in the Cultural History of Radio*. Eds. Michele Hilmes and Jason Loviglio. New York: Routledge, 2002.

Iowa. *Latinos in Iowa: 2015*. Des Moines: Office of Latino Affairs, Iowa Department of Human Rights. 2015. Available at: iowadatacenter.org/Publications/latinos2015.pdf

Kun, Josh D. "The Aural Border." *Theatre Journal*. 52:1 (2000): 1–20.

La Ley 105.5 FM. *La Ley Media Kit 2015*. West Des Moines. Electronic Resource.

Lipsitz, George. *Dangerous Crossroads: Popular Music, Postmodernism, and the Poetics of Place*. London: Verso, 1994.

Olwig, Karen F. and Kirsten Hastrup. *Siting Culture: The Shifting Anthropological Object*. London: Routledge, 1997.

Panagopoulos, Costas and Donald Green. "Spanish-language Radio Advertisements and Latino Voter Turnout in the 2006 Congressional Elections: Field Experimental Evidence." *Political Research Quarterly*. 64:3 (2011): 588–99.

Pardue, Derek. "Putting Mano to Music: the Mediation of Race in Brazilian Rap." *Ethnomusicology Forum*. 13:2 (2004): 253–86.

Peng, Vanessa. "Man shouting 'English only' interrupts kindergarten concert." *KCCI News* 8. 24 April 2015.

Pew Research Center. "Unauthorized Immigrant Population, by State, 2012." Pewhispanic.org 18 November 2014. Available at: pewhispanic.org/interactives/unauthorized-immigrants-2012

Rothenbuhler, Eric and Tom McCourt. "Radio redefines itself: 1947–1962." *Radio Reader: Essays in the Cultural History of Radio*. Eds. Michele Hilmes and Jason Loviglio. New York: Routledge, 2002.

Solorzano, Daniel G. and Dolores D. Bernal. "Examining Transformational Resistance through a Critical Race and Latcrit Theory Framework: Chicana and Chicano Students in an Urban Context." *Urban Education*. 36:3 (2001): 308–42.

Turino, Thomas. *Music as Social Life: The Politics of Participation*. Chicago: University of Chicago Press, 2008.

Valdez, Inés. "Punishment, Race and the Organization of U.S. Immigration Exclusion." 2015. TS.

Wortham, Stanton E. F., Enrique G. Murillo, and Edmund T. Hamann. "Education and Policy in the New Latino Diaspora." *Education in the New Latino Diaspora: Policy and the Politics of Identity*. Westport: Ablex Pub, 2002.

Part III

POP ARTIVIST RECLAMATIONS

17

HERMANDAD, ARTE AND REBELDÍA

Mexican Popular Art in New York City

Melissa Castillo-Garsow

Sarck Har, 31, is a soft-spoken, unassuming man. Despite a body covered with tattoos and an affinity for black clothing even in the summer time, he comes off as shy. When you enter his tattoo shop, you'll either find him with a customer or intently hunched over a sketchbook. Yet he is also the leader and co-founder of an arts collective that boasts more than two dozen affiliated Mexican artists who attend weekly meetings, its own business and performance space, and monthly public hip hop and art shows.

Mexican art and, more generally, Latina/o art in the U.S., have largely been under studied (Ybarra-Frausto "Imagining", 9), especially considering their fundamental contributions to North American culture. This is especially true in terms of popular art in which Latina/o contributions in muralism, graffiti, tattooing, street art, and performance art have been influential both within and beyond U.S. borders. Here, I define Latina/o popular art in the tradition of Juan Flores's work on Latina/o popular cultures. For Flores, popular culture is separated from the mass consumption of contemporary society, through its roots in folklore and the everyday people, whose cultures and traditions resist the social domination of those in power (Flores 17). In this way, the concept is both "rescued from its relegation to archaic and residual roles in today's global modernity and mass culture," and becomes a useful term of analysis for examining Latina/o artistic expressions. Popular art, then, becomes a way to interrogate the multiple levels upon which Latina/o artists construct individual and collective identities, and create new hybrid forms to reflect their social and historical contexts (Habell-Pallan, 6). For Mexican artists in New York City (NYC), this is especially useful as the tremendous growth of the Mexican population over the last 20 years represents a tremendous influx of creativity into the city's popular arts, as well as a reflection of the everyday lives of Mexican migrants survived with conflict and contestation.

In terms of Mexican and Mexican American artists in the U.S., the majority of scholarly research has been on art of the Chicano movement and the influence of the Chicano movement on contemporary artists of Mexican descent. While some art historians are researching the contributions of artists who were not part of the Chicano movement but were or are Mexican American, this research tends to focus on the southwest and California almost exclusively, as well as artists who are not necessary involved in the popular arts (Ybarra-Fausto "Imagining", 9). Doubly marginalized by the looming specter of the Chicano movement as well as the indifference of NYC's contemporary art community, this chapter aims to present a more expansive vision of Mexican popular art in the U.S. by examining the work of the Har'd Life Ink Arts Collective. This work includes graffiti, mural painting, tattooing, airbrush on canvas, printmaking (t-shirts and posters) and photography. Based simultaneously in Brooklyn and the Bronx, Har'd Life represents a community of Mexican migrants dedicated to creating alternative spaces for what they call "cultura underground" in order to counter the sense of invisibility imposed on them by NYC society, as well as to foster pride and ownership through a "Mexica" identity.

Mexican-York: A New Nueva York

NYC is one of the most iconic immigrant cities, and yet a city which is rarely seen in relation to this country's most iconic immigrant group, Mexicans. In *Mexican New York: Transnational Lives of New Immigrants*, Robert Smith outlines stages of Mexican immigration in New York ranging from the 1940s to the 1980s in which there was only a small but tight-knit network of Mexicans, to the third stage in the late 1980s when NYC saw an explosion of Mexicans, mostly from the state of Puebla in south central Mexico. A number of these immigrants were able to gain amnesty and eventually become eligible for permanent resident status through the 1986 Immigration Reform and Control Act (Smith, 22), allowing for many of the transnational links Smith and others have documented (such as frequent visits to Mexico and involvement in hometown politics).[1] Since Smith's writing, NYC is witnessing a fourth flow of Mexican migrants from increasingly diverse areas of origin[2], most notably Mexico City and its surrounding areas (Risomena and Massey, 9–10). For example, members of Har'd Life come from various locations including Brooklyn, San Luis Potosí, Morelos, Puebla, Cuernavaca, Mexico City, Tlaxcala, and many of them lived in Mexico City prior to migrating to New York, providing them with prior experience of life in a metropolis (Personal Interviews).

Today, the Mexican-origin population is NYC's fastest-growing Latina/o national group, growing from a population of 6,700 Mexicans in 1980 to 55,587 in 1990, to 183,792 in 2000, and 342,699 in 2010 (Bergad, 23). Fueled by both escalating immigration as well as rates of reproduction, by 2005 Mexicans became the third largest Latina/o nationality in NYC behind Dominicans (747,473), who surpassed Puerto Ricans (719,444) in 2014. (Department of City Planning of New York City 103; Bergad "Have Dominicans"). According to Laird Bergad of the Latino Data Project: "If these rates continue, Mexicans will comprise the region's largest Latino national subgroup sometime in the early 2020s (Bergad, 11). Moreover, as a significant portion of the Mexican population in the United States is undocumented, the precise number of Mexicans living in NYC is difficult to ascertain. While conservative estimates range from an additional 300,000 to 450,000 in 2010 for the region, (Bergad, 1–2) the Mexican Consulate in New York, for example, estimates that there are approximately 1.2 million Mexicans in the region (Semple, 2010, A018).

This last phase of migration as represented by the members of Har'd Life Ink, which is much more diverse in terms of regions of origin, has added great diversity to both Mexican expression and experiences in the region that thus far have not been studied. At the oldest, these families represent three generations of life in New York, while others have only a couple of years in the country. Upon arrival, Mexicans concentrate in Brooklyn, Queens, and the Bronx, where they face harsh housing and work conditions. Mexican immigrant households are more likely to experience overcrowding and spend more than half their income on rent than those of any other immigrant group or the native-born population.[3] Mexicans also have among the lowest household incomes and education rates due to the large number of new migrants, many of whom arrive in their teenage years or as young adults and so did not or do not complete high school (Bergad "Demographic" 29–38). Because of these higher birth rates, and despite the fact that migration to the NYC metropolitan region comprised mainly adults, Mexicans had the youngest population of any of the major Latina/o nationalities at 25 years. This fosters a Mexican youth culture that is multicultural and transnationally tech savvy (Bergad, 19–20). As such, despite the challenges Mexican migrants and their children face, New York is home to an increasingly diverse young Mexican population that is mainly male (61 percent) and yearning for creative outlets to add meaning and create community beyond their often limited work options. For many, like the members of Har'd Life Ink, this is where the popular arts appeal.

An Introduction to Mexican American Popular Arts

As Tomás Ybarra-Frausto describes in "A Panorama of Latino Arts," the Latina/o arts not only operate in a long historical continuum beginning with colonization in the sixteenth century, but the field also represents a vastly heterogeneous group of native-born citizens and immigrants from more than 20 countries (139). Thus, as he clarifies, Latina/o art is not only under studied but makes for a complex study. According to Ybarra- Frausto,

> in conceptualizing Latino art, we have what I would call a three-legged stool. One leg of the equation is the canonical culture of the United States. Another is Latin American visual culture. And the third is Latino culture, which is the most wobbly.

This is most certainly the case in terms of Mexican popular culture expressions in NYC. The Har'd Life Ink artists examined in this article are both influenced by and in conversation with popular art and street art traditions in New York and Mexico, as well as Chicana/o artists in the southwest and California.

Significantly, as the majority of the members of Har'd Life Ink migrated from Mexico within the past 10 to 15 years, their first encounters with popular art forms such as graffiti or muralism occurred in their hometowns. For example, for Sarck Har, it was his move from San Luis Potosí to Mexico City at age 17 which brought him into contact with a robust graffiti scene and the HAR crew, which inspired the name Har'd Life Ink and to which they are still affiliated. There, he learned from HAR founders Cosme and Honor, who are still active, and became a member of the crew after two years of practice. Yet as Mexican graffiti has been strongly influenced by the Chicano movement art (Maciel, 116), and Chicano movement art was strongly influenced by the legacy of the so-called *tres grandes*—José Clemente Orozco, Diego Rivera and David Alfaro Siqueiros—who were commissioned for major U.S. mural projects in the 1930s, Mexican popular art in NYC actually represents at least 90 years of cross cultural exchange that is only becoming more fluid with today's technology.

As previously mentioned, the significance of the Chicano movement[4] of the 1960s and 1970s to the Latina/o arts has resulted in the most scholarly attention to Mexican art production in the U.S. Nevertheless, Chicana/o artistic expression predates the movement.

In addition to *los tres grandes* as well as the work of portraitist Frida Kahlo, Chicana/o arts of the 1960s drew on the flamboyant and nonconformist *pachuco* street style of the 1940s as well as gang graffiti in Los Angeles which dates back to at least the 1930s (Benavidez, 13, 15). These antecedents contributed to the evolution of Chicana/o art, the results of which can be seen in Har'd Life Ink today. Those include: 1) a critique of the status quo; 2) the establishment of a unique aesthetic sensibility in which art is measured on its own terms; 3) a differentiation between convention and Chicana/o values; 4) an aspect of cultural self-affirmation; and 5) the use of montage (Benavidez, 16). From these foundations, the Chicano movement in its most idealistic and incipient years (1968–1975) resulted in the production of community-oriented and public art forms including posters, murals and the development of art collectives. As Goldman and Ybarra-Frausto describe, "Art was part of a whole movement to recapture, at times romantically, a people's history and culture and formed part of the struggle for self-determination" (84). In search of art that both generated ethnic pride and a sense of community, artists sought themes from pre-Colombian culture, family life and religious practices, immigration and the border, and cultural icons or heroes of Mexican descent (Erikson, Villeneuve and Keller, 10).

While by 1975, divisions in the movement were reflected in a schism between artists who chose to continue serving the working-class majority Mexican population and those who chose to enter the mainstream art world of museums, galleries and collectors, the early idealism, styles and themes had widespread impact (Goldman and Ybarra-Frausto, 93).[5] The artistic expression inspired by the Chicano movement did more than produce an important collection of plastic arts, painting, visual arts and literature; it offered Mexican Americans a critical view of their status in the United States as well as the creative tools to express that perspective. The valorization of Mexican heritage and themes of Chicana/o artists facilitated increasing contact between artists on both sides of the border and led to exhibitions of Chicana/o art in Mexico as well as collaborations (Maciel, 116). Perhaps it is not surprising then that the 1980s saw the rise of neomexicanismo among Mexican artists, which criticized the supremacy of western tendencies of surrealist and expressionist schools over Mexican elements. Neomexicanists, as a result, sought to highlight the artistic values of popular culture in similar ways as Chicana/o muralists (Maciel, 117).

As George Sánchez's foundational work *Becoming Mexican American: Ethnicity, Culture and Identity Los Angeles, 1900–1945* makes clear, culture in Mexico has never been static and as such, migrations to and from Mexico bring new cultures and expressions to both sides of the border. In describing what Juan Flores and George Yúdice first termed "trans-creation," Sánchez reflects, "the movement between Mexican and American cultures is not so much a world of confusion, but rather a place of opportunity and innovation" (9). Nowhere can this perhaps be better witnessed than in the artistic creations of Sarck Har of Har'd Life whose tattoos, murals and paintings reflect decades of conversation between Mexican and Mexican American artists. Thus, despite their distance from the border, Mexican popular art of New York still reflects what Anzaldúa has described as "the mestizo border artists who partake of the traditions of two or more worlds and who may be binational. They thus create a new artistic space – a border mestizo culture" (Anzaldúa and Keating, 181).

In this case, for members of Har'd Life, those worlds are not just Mexican art and Chicana/o art but also the multi-ethnic, multi-racial graffiti art that is one of hip hop's four elements. To be clear—African American culture has always been a part of these conversations, from zoot suit style[6] that was also popular with African Americans in the 1940s, to art of the Civil Rights Movement (Goldman and Ybarra-Frausto, 84). But in this

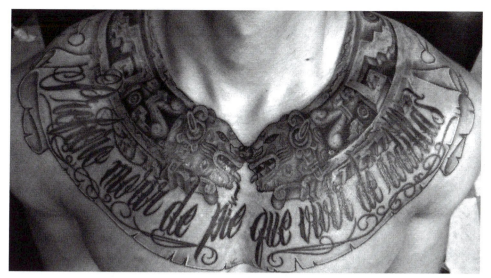

Figure 17.1   Sarck Har's "Mexica Style" tattoo work, 2014

case, it is significant that Sarck Har and other members of Har'd Life describe their graffiti practice as learned in Mexico but still traced back to hip hop's four elements. According to Sarck, "Eso es lo verdadero hip hop. Tratamos de regresar a los raíces fundamentales. As como hablamos de cultura, el graffiti el uno de los cuatro elementos escenciales" (Personal Interview, 14 October 2013). Kortezua, 29, an MC and graffiti artist, echoes Sarck: "El graffiti es muy importante. Es uno de los quarto elementos, parte de la historia desde los 70" (Personal Interview, 8 October 2013)[7]. Significantly, graffiti is not merely an act of rebellion, but a practice that is respected and honored by these Mexican artists who see themselves within a much longer tradition. Creating an authentic Mexican artistic expression in New York for them is supported by the authenticity of graffiti as one of the original four hip hop elements.

Although writing on walls dates back to the earliest of times (and as previously mentioned, was a practice of Chicano gangs as early as the 1930s), graffiti as it is known today, based in simple name tags unaffiliated with gang territorial disputes, arrived in NYC via Philadelphia in the late 1960s (Felisbret, 1–10). Made famous by TAKI 183, a delivery boy who lived on 183rd Street, Washington Heights, when he was written up in the *New York Times*, graffiti in its incipient stage was about getting one's name up in as many places as possible. Subways in particular became the canvas of choice as writers could send their names from as far away as the top of the Bronx to the top of Brooklyn (Jenkins, 16). By the mid-1970s, graffiti developed from simple tagging to elaborate individual styles, themes, formats, and techniques that were designed to increase visibility and status (Rose, 198). In this way, graffiti established itself as one of hip hop's four elements by incorporating hip hop slang, fashion, and rap lyrics while at the same time, graffiti's styles (bubble letters, wild style etc.) became a part of the music's visual expression from album covers to posters.[8] As "writing" became art and art became more complicated, graffiti writers formed together in crews, which provided both community and collective evaluation. As Austin describes,

> At the most basic level, crew members are committed to writing and to each other … crew members serve as lookouts for each other, particularly while executing works

in places where they might be seen (like the yards). They are trusted to protect the identities of fellow members when questioned or arrested by authorities. These are common forms of mutual support that can be found in successful churches, unions, peer groups, benevolent associations, and street gangs.

(120)

Consequently, while "writing" may seem like an insignificant act of youthful rebellion, graffiti also represents the foundations of identity and community building, as well as an accessible form of artistic expression for those without resources or creative outlets. As a result, despite that fact that graffiti assumed crisis-level importance inside the bureaucracy and the public relations of NYC mayoral administrations and the Metropolitan Transportation Authority for almost two decades,[9] and that an anti-graffiti task force *still* exists today,[10] graffiti enjoyed a renaissance in the 1990s and is still a vibrant part of NYC's landscape today. This is especially true in neighborhoods like Spanish Harlem where, as Arlene Dávila notes, street art has "long served as visual markers of Latinidad" (183). Nevertheless, as the 2014 destruction of hip hop history 5Pointz in the name of development demonstrates, street art is still in a precarious place. For while street artists can be prosecuted as criminals, the same artistic space when sold for commercial advertising sells for thousands of dollars. Members of Har'd Life Ink descended on 5Pointz before its demolition to pay their respects. Their writings were among those destroyed.

Across Mexico[11], but especially in Mexico City, thousands of young people do graffiti, most often illegally but also legally in the form of mural painting (Valle and Weiss, 128). Graffiti arrived in Mexico City in the mid-1980s from the border, moving from Los Angeles to San Diego to Tijuana, Aguascalientes, Guadalajara, Nezahualcóyotl and Mexico City. Like the Chicana/o muralists of the 1970s, many of the youth in Mexico City who engaged in graffiti had already been politicized and influenced by the student movement of 1968[12] when street art and murals were employed to spread their political message (Cruz Salazar, 201). As Tania Cruz Salazar describes, like its origins in New York, for young Mexicans,

> La calle y la pared son espacios de socialización que simbolizan la libertad de expresión, la libertad de ser. Ser joven en Mexico es difícil, el acceso a espacios educativos y laborales es restringido, muchos de los jóvenes urbanos que se dedican al *graffiti* pertenecen a un estrato social bajo, por lo que abandonar la escuela para ir a trabajar es algo muy común a pesar de que las garantías laborales sean precarias. Pertenecer a una familia donde la presión por aportar un ingreso es la constante y en la que los espacios de convivencia son reducidos—dos o más familias viven hacinadas en casas pequeñas—les incita a buscar espacios en donde sea posible proyectar su identidad y vivenciar su juventud.
>
> (Cruz Salazar, 200)

For the members of Har'd Life, this is a familiar story. Either from lower-income families in Mexico City or having left their families at a young age, graffiti and the crews that came with them represented an important community of practice.[13]

Thus, Mexican graffiti artists in New York consciously and unconsciously work within a number of traditions. As the following section will explore, their practice reflects not just the travel of hip hop and graffiti from New York, but also decades of transnational flows between Mexican artists on both sides of the border. What the story of Har'd Life Ink adds, then, is another layer to Mexican popular art in the United States that offers a new way of understanding Mexican/Latina/o experience through an East Coast legacy and context.

Moreover their interactions with NYC's hip hop history both prior to migration and upon settlement highlights the influence of Caribbean migrants on Mexican identities on the East Coast, as this is the only city where Mexicans not only come into contact with a large population of Caribbean immigrants (Puerto Ricans, Dominicans, West Indians), but a city where those Caribbean cultures have shaped the history of the city.

Hermandad, Arte y Rebeldía: A Mexican Art Collective in New York

The name Har'd Life Ink stands for "Hermandad, Arte y Rebeldía" (HAR). According to Sarck Har, "Hermandad" means "a true union," "Arte" represents both creative capacity and artistic inspiration, and "Rebeldía" is an act of not accepting the status quo (Personal Interview, 14 October 2013). Har'd Life Ink was not founded in NYC, however, but in Mexico City as a graffiti crew named HAR in 1996. That crew, which remains active, was where Sarck honed his skills. Sarck, who has returned four times for crew anniversaries and still considers himself a member of the Mexican crew, serves as a mediator between the U.S. and Mexico City groups, forming a transnational crew of sorts. All graffiti or murals, for example, done by the Har'd Life Ink group are tagged "HAR NYC–MEX" and they create links by sharing pictures of their work via Facebook.[14] Sarck is a border artist in multiple senses of the term, bridging countries, artistic practices and traditions, and communities. As Gloria Anzaldúa describes:

> The border is a historical and metaphorical site, un sitio ocupado, where single artists and collaborating groups transform space, and the two home territories, Mexico and the United State, become one. Border art deal with shifting identities, border crossings, and hybridism. But there are other borders beside the actual Mexico/ United States frontera.

> (Anzaldúa and Keating, 181)

Both Sarck as an individual artist and as leader of HAR-NYC represents the challenges and possibilities of borders in New York. Both a crosser of physical borders and societal barriers, he has strived, alongside co-founder Fernando "Pisket HAR INK" Gutierres, 28, to create a space for alternative Mexican identities and artistic expression in NYC that is both culturally relevant, authentic and independent of traditional artistic structures.

Sarck Har migrated to New York in 2003 following an older brother who came a few years prior and settled in Brooklyn. Like many, he took a bus from Mexico City to Sonora where he paid a *coyote* to help him cross. Once he arrived in Phoenix, he took a flight to New Jersey where his sister, married and with children, lives. Struggling to find decent work, Sarck worked in a bakery, car wash, construction and cleaning until, while delivering food, he met Gutierres of Mexico City, another delivery worker living in Brooklyn. They quickly became friends as Gutierres was also a graffiti writer and they began to paint together at night three to four times a week (personal interview, 1 August 2015). As Sarck describes, both were yearning for a community that would share their interests and give them a sense of purpose, "Ya no quería estar solo. Queria relacionar con la gente…Fue la necesidad" (14 October 2013).

The turning point came, however, when Sarck and Fernando began to tattoo in 2008. After meeting tattoo artists at a party, they collectively purchased a tattoo machine and began to practice on their friends. As lifelong artists, they learned quickly: "En 15 días, ya estaba tatuando" (personal interview, 14 October 2013). For Sarck and Fernando, tattooing became not only a livelihood which allowed them to explore their artistic expression, it was a job which gave them free time to draw, paint and airbrush. More importantly, it became a place of community. After a few years of tattooing for others, Sarck and Fernando opened Har'd Life Ink, a tattoo shop and performance space in South Park Slope, Brooklyn, in 2012. (personal interview, 14 October 2013).

By 2013, Har'd Life Ink became the center of what Sarck terms "la cultura underground" in New York, a blend of Mexican popular art that includes tattooing, MCs, breakdance, skate boarding, graffiti, airbrush, painting, sketching, photography, fashion and poster painting. Although Mexican individuals and small groups had participated in hip hop and other popular culture expressions since at least the early 2000s, they were isolated by the city and the pressures of everyday life (personal interviews). As MC and HAR-NYC member Kortezua of Cuernavaca describes, "El cambio ha sido muy drástico. Antes solo vinieron a los shows, los rappers y ellos mismos era el público" (personal interview, 8 October 2013). However, the founding of a space for Mexican popular arts has not only created a public but also brought out many more Mexican youth looking for an artistic community with whom to share their work. Har'd Life Ink not only provides that space, but it also provides informal mentoring systems as older artists share techniques with younger ones. As Kortezua describes, "Es necesario en NY. Hay muy pocas las oportunidades para mexicanos" (Personal Interview, 8 October 2013). In fact, HAR-NYC and Har'd Life Ink constitutes a form of place-based identity and struggle, a home for a group excluded from other places and cultures for reasons of race and ethnicity and that, hence, depends largely on such places to carry out its struggles and carve out its own space and identity.

Originally a graffiti crew, Sarck and Fernando quickly conceived of Har'd Life Ink as something bigger and formed an arts collective in 2013. There are over two dozen members that represent not only hip hop's four elements, but also multiple artistic styles. They hold weekly meetings in which they share work, make decisions about the group and plan events. Older members like Sarck and Fernando also teach the arts including tattooing to younger members—some as young as 18—so they can also be self-sufficient artists. "Queríamos eliminar al intermediario," reflects Sarck. "Porque eso te jode. Siempre fue el plan aprender el proceso bien y después get rid of el intermediario. Ya no voy a ser empleado. No me voy a dejar manipular por nadie. En tatuar, me dio tiempo para mi mismo" (personal interview, 1 August 2015). Thus at any given time, seven days a week, Har'd Life is a space for Mexican popular artists to work, find community, or learn new skills. And for more than just Sarck and Fernando, it has become a way to get out of a life of kitchen work, cleaning or deliveries (BAMP, personal interview, 24 October 2014) as others have joined the tattoo roster.

This sense of community is held together by a set of core values. First and foremost is a sense of pride in the cultures of Mexico or what Sarck refers to as "Mexica culture." For Sarck, for example, this is expressed in what he calls "Estilo Azteca" which has a heavy emphasis on indigenous images, figures, and animals like jaguars, eagles and serpents. On the other spectrum, Eric Rodriguez, 25, of Puebla prefers abstract works and references surrealism. Still among the visual artists of the group, pre-hispanic themes are what dominate, followed by work which reflects the transitory nature of life (life/death). Although Sarck acknowledges that many of their styles—skulls, flowers, lettering, etc.—is reminiscent of a Chicana/o style, he says his work is different because it is based in indigenous roots and not gang lifestyles. While Sarck respects Chicana/o culture and outlook, and recognizes commonalities, he also sees their more recent experience of immigration as distinguishing. "Ellos nacieron con otra mentalidad" Sarck says of Chicana/os (24 October 2014). In this way, Sarck's work has clear artistic connections to Chicano movement art as opposed to more recent expressions of what is termed Chicano rap, which has a more gangster style, even though it is not necessarily affiliated with gangs. (For more on this, see the work of another contributor to this volume, Pancho McFarland, especially his books, *The Chican@ Hip Hop Nation: Politics of a New Millennial Mestizaje* and *Chicano Rap: Gender and Violence in the Postindustrial Barrio.*)

Conclusions

Just as Chicanoa/ art evolved in opposition to the predominant cultural matrix of museums, galleries, universities and publication, Mexican popular art in NYC has done the same. Given the reality that Mexican artists in NYC are woefully underrepresented in NYC's major cultural institutions, independent art collectives, hip hop crews and other social formations serve as an alternative foundation to support artistic expression. Through the democratic space of the tattoo parlor in which all are welcome, Har'd Life Ink critiques the status quo of exclusion and lack of visibility in the art world. Likewise, through an insistence on authentic Mexican themes, Sarck and HAR-NYC strive to establish their own unique aesthetic sensibility or "Mexica art" which incorporates various artistic forms, materials and traditions (montage). In this way they break from convention by a different set of values based in community and collective decision-making. Most importantly, they not only affirm their value as Mexicans and artists, they affirm that they are not in fact, invisible. Tagging, muralism, painting, tattoo—these are all forms in which members of HAR-NYC stand up to a society that is eager for cheap Mexican labor but not for Mexican bodies.

As Chicana artist Judy Baca describes,

> Chicano art comes from a creation of community. In a society that does not affirm your culture or your experience Chicano art is making visible our own reality, a particular reality—by doing so we become an irritant to the mainstream vision. We have a tradition of resisting being viewed as the other; an unwillingness to disappear
>
> (Judith Baca 21)

That unwillingness to disappear, to hide out, or to assimilate is in every stroke drawn by HAR-NYC. Though they do not identify as Chicana/os, the transnational dialogue between Chicana/o and Mexican popular art, neomexicanismo, and a graffiti sensibility has shaped Har'd Life Ink into a unique space for Mexicans in New York. Thus, the aesthetics pursued by HAR-NYC attempts to reverse the flow of conventional artistic practices in which community is redefined to include a diversity of subjectivities and positions. Second, there is an entrepreneurial aspect to the HAR-NYC project, a make-do attitude that says that having one's own business is a way of resisting the effects of domination in a capitalist society which *only* recognizes capital as a trademark of human dignity. In this way, Sarck, Fernando and HAR-NYC seem to heed Anzaldúa's warning:

> There are many obstacles and dangers in crossing into nepantla. Border artists are threatened from the outside by appropriation by popular culture and the dominant art institutions, by 'outsiders' jumping on their bandwagon and working the border artists' territory. Border artists also are threatened by the present unparalleled economic depression in the arts gutted by government funding cutbacks.
>
> (Anzaldúa and Keating, 181)

Instead of depending on a society that sees them as outsiders, these border artists carefully protect their work and independence.

Har'd Life Ink as a space and community reflects only one of numerous examples by which Mexican popular artists are developing their art in NYC. Buendia-INK, for example, represents another transnational crew based out of Sunset Park, which often shares a space and stage at the tattoo shop, while Vida Urbana in the Bronx hosts a weekly radio show, website, and numerous events in that borough. Other artists, like tattoo artist and portraitist Hugo Andres, attend events but are not members of the collective. Moreover, following the Har'd Life Ink model, a group of female artists opened an all-female tattoo shop, The Catrina Ink, in late 2013. They also host events and art shows at their shop, which members of HAR-NYC always attend and support. As such, in a climate in which the demolition of 5Pointz represents how undervalued art is disappearing from our streets, Mexican popular arts in NYC represent the infusion of perhaps a new lifeblood into both Latina/o popular culture and popular art more generally.

Notes

1 See for example Nancy Foner's *In the New Land: A Comparative View of Immigration* (2005) and *New Immigrants in New York* (2001. Likewise, Alex Rivera's 2003 PBS documentary *The Sixth Section* captures the experience of "Grupo Unión," a NYC area hometown organization of immigrants from Puebla.

2 As Risomena and Massey have outlined, in recent years, the spatial distribution of Mexican migrant-sending regions has also shifted away from its traditional heartland in the Central West Region (the states of Durango, Zacatecas, San Luis Potosí, Aguascalientes, Guanajuato, Jalisco, Nayarit, Colima and Michoacán) which from the 1920s until recently comprised at least 50 percent of the total outflow to the United States but which has declined to just below 40 percent. Until the mid-1990s, the second most important sending region was the Border Region (20 to 28 percent), which includes the states of Baja California, Baja California Sur, Sonora, Sinaloa, Chihuahua, Coahuila, Nuevo León and Tamaulipas. However after the mid-1990s, this share fell below 20 percent and then dipped to 11 percent by 2000 as the region came to house the most rapidly growing sector of the Mexican economy and now attracts a large number of internal migrants. As a result, two new sending regions have come on line: the Central Region (Querétaro, Mexico, Distrito Federal, Hidalgo, Tlaxcala, Morelos, Puebla, Guerrero and Oaxaca), and the Southeastern Region (Veracruz, Tabasco, Chiapas, Campeche, Quintana Roo, and Yucatán). The Central Region was relatively unimportant until 1980, accounting for no more than 10 percent of migrants to the U.S., but rose steadily thereafter to reach just over 30 percent by century's end, while Mexico's Southeastern Region remained insignificant as a migration source until recently, contributing fewer than 2 percent of migrants through the early 1990s. However, by the end of the millennium, migrants from this region comprised 7 percent of the total and more recently, this figure has gone up to 13 percent (9–10).

3 For more on housing conditions of Mexicans see Nathan, Debbie, "David and his 26 Roomates," *New York Magazine*, 16 May 2005; and Standish, Katherine et. al., "Household Density among Undocumented Mexican Immigrants in New York City," *Journal of Immigrant Minority Health*, 12:3 (2010): 310–18.

4 Decolonizing struggles in the Third World, the Black Power and Civil Rights Movements, the anti-Vietnam war movement, and the emergence of hippie counter culture, also led to a rise in Latina/o Civil Rights. While Puerto Ricans mobilized as The Young Lords on the East Coast, the Chicano movement grew out of the farmworkers' struggle to unionize in California and Texas in the early 1960s. (Ybarra-Frausto, "A Panorama," 148; Goldman and Ybarra-Frausto, "The Political and Social Contexts of Chicano Art," 83). Meanwhile, by the late 1960s, urban issues such as police brutality, violations of civil rights, lack of adequate employment, inadequate housing and social services, lack of educational opportunities, and lack of political power mobilized youth into action (Francisco Jackson, 12–20). For more on the Chicano Movement see Montejano, David. *Quixote's Soldiers: A Local History of the Movement, 1966–1981.* Austin: University of Texas

Press, 2010; Navarro, Armando. *Mexican American Youth Organization: AvantGarde of the Chicano Movement in Texas*. Austin: University of Texas Press, 1995; Quiñones, Juan. *Chicano Politics: Reality and Promise, 1940–1990*. Albuquerque, NM: University of New Mexico Press, 1990; San Miguel, Jr., Guadalupe. *"Brown, not White:" School Integration and the Chicano Movement in Houston*. College Station: Texas A and M University Press, 2001. Maylei Blackwell's excellent ¡Chicana Power!: Contested Histories of Feminism in the Chicano Movement (University of Texas Press, 2011) focuses on the experiences of women and is the first book to do so.

5 Other resources on the Chicano Art Movement include: Keller, Gary D. *Triumph of Our Communities: Four Decades of Mexican American Art*. Tempe: Bilingual Press, 2005; Brookman, Phillip and Guillermo Goméz-Peña. *Made in Aztlán*. San Diego: Centro Cultural de La Raza, 1986; Gaspar de Alba, Alicia. *Chicano Art Inside/Outside the Master's House: Cultural Poltiics and the CARA Exhibition*. Austin: University of Texas Press, 1998; Latorre, Guisela. *Walls of Empowerment: Chicana/o Indigenist Murals of California*. Austin: University of Texas Press, 2008; Ochoa, María. *Creative Collectives: Chicana Painters Working in Community*. Albuquerque: University of New Mexico Press, 2003.

6 For more on the multi-ethnic, multi-racial aspects of the zoot suit see Alvarez, Luis. *The Power of the Zoot: Youth Culture and Resistance During World War II*. Berkeley: University of California Press, 2008.

7 "Graffiti is very important. It's one of the four elements that are part of the history since the 1970s" (my translation).

8 For more information on graffiti styles and history see Adams, Cey and Bill Adler. *DEFinition: The Art and Design of Hip Hop*. New York: Harper Design, 2008; Gastman, Roger and Caleb Neelon. *The History of American Graffiti*. New York: Harper Design, 2011; MacDonald, Nancy. *The Graffiti Subculture: Youth, Masculinity and Identity in London and New York*. New York: Palgrave MacMillan, 2003.

9 For more information about the war on graffiti see Austin, Joe. *Taking the Train: How Graffiti Became an Urban Crisis in New York City*. New York: Columbia UP, 2001; and Murray, James T., and Karla L. Murray. *Broken Windows: Graffiti NYC*. Berkley: Ginko Press, 2010.

10 www.nyc.gov/html/nograffiti/html/aboutforce.html

11 For examples of artwork across Mexico see La Farge, Phyllis and Magdalena Caris. *Painted Walls of Mexico/ Paredes Pintadas de México*. Mexico City: Turner Libros, 2008.

12 Like youth around the world, Mexican students organized in 1968 to protest the use of excessive force by the government which included army and riot police. The movement, however, was short lived as on October 2, 1968, ten days before the opening of the Summer Olympics in Mexico City, police officers and military troops shot into a crowd of unarmed students. Thousands of demonstrators fled in panic as tanks bulldozed over Tlatelolco Plaza and the number of deaths is still disputed, ranging from 4 to 3,000. For an account of the massacre, see Poniatowska, Elena. *La Noche de Tlatelolco: Testimonios de historia oral*. Segunda edición. Mexico City: Ediciones Era, 1998.

13 For more about graffiti in Mexico see Cruz Salazar, Tania. "Instantáneas sobre el *graffiti* mexicano: historias, voces y experiencias juveniles." *Última Década*, 29 (2008): 137–157; Dokins, Said. "La participación de la mujer en el arte urbano." Ed. Laura García. *Desbordamientos de una periferia femenina*. Mexico City: Sociedad Dokins, 2008. 55–64.

14 In the U.S.: www.facebook.com/Har.dlifeink; In Mexico: Har Destroyerz Cru.

Bibliography

Adams, Cey and Bill Adler. *DEFinition: The Art and Design of Hip Hop*. New York: Harper Design, 2008.

Alvarez, Luis. *The Power of the Zoot: Youth Culture and Resistance During World War II*. Berkeley: University of California Press, 2008.

Anzaldúa, Gloria. *The Gloria Anzaldúa Reader*. Ana Louise Keating (ed.), Durham, NC: Duke University Press, 2009.

Aparicio, Wilberth Ulises. Personal Interview. 20 October 2013.

Austin, Joe. *Taking the Train: How Graffiti Became an Urban Crisis in New York City*. New York: Columbia University Press, 2001.

Bamp. Personal Interview. 24 October 2014.

Benavidez, Max. "Chicano Art: Culture, Myth and Sensibility." *Chicano Visions: American Painters on the Verge*. Ed. Cheech Marin. New York: Bulfinch Press, 2002.

Bergad, Laird W. "Demographic, Economic and Social Transformations in the Mexican-Origin Population of the New York City Metropolitan Area, 1990–2010." Report. *Center for Latin American, Caribbean, and Latino Studies*, 2013: 1–73. Available at: http://www.gc.cuny.edu/CUNY_GC/media/CUNY-Graduate-Center/PDF/Centers/CLACLS/Mexicans-in-New-York-Metro-Area-and-Surrounding-Counties-1990-2010.pdf

Bergad, Laird W. "Mexicans in New York 1990–2005". *Latino Data Project*. City University of New York Center for Latin American, Caribbean, and Latino Studies Graduate Center. September 2014.

Bergad, Laird W. "Have Dominicans Surpassed Puerto Ricans to beomce New York City's Largest Latino Nationality?" *Latino Data Project*. City University of New York Center for Latin American, Caribbean, and Latino Studies Graduate Center. November 2014.

Blackwell, Maylei.¡*Chicana Power!: Contested Histories of Feminism in the Chicano Movement*. Austin: University of Texas Press, 2011.

Brookman, Phillip and Guillermo Goméz-Peña. *Made in Aztlán*. San Diego: Centro Cultural de La Raza, 1986.

Cornejo, Jair Bello. "Kortezua." Personal Interview. 8 October 2013.

Crosthwaite, Luis Humbert and John William Byrd, eds. *Puro Border: Dispatches, Snapshots & Graffiti from the US/Mexico Border*. El Paso, TX: Cinco Pantos Press. 2003

Cruz Salazar, Tania. "*Yo me aventé como tres años haciendo tags, ¡sí, la verdad, sí fui ilegal!* Grafiteros: arte callejero en la ciudad de México." *Desacatos* 14 (2004): 197–226.

Cruz Salazar, Tania. "Instantáneas sobre el *graffiti* mexicano: historias, voces y experiencias juveniles" *Última Década* 29 (2008): 137–57.

Dávila, Arlene. *Barrio Dreams: Puerto Ricans, Latinos, and the Neoliberal City*. Oakland: University of California Press, 2004.

Department of City Planning of New York City. "NYC 2010: Results from the Census." 2012. Available at: www.nyc.gov/html/dcp/pdf/census/census_brief2_051012.pdf

Dokins, Said. "La participación de la mujer en el arte urbano." *Desbordamientos de una periferia femenina*. Ed. Laura García. Mexico City: Sociedad Dokins, 2008. 55–64.

Erickson, Mary, Pat Villeneuve and Gary D. Keller. *Chicano Art for Our Millennium: Collected Works from the Arizona State University Community*. Tempe, AZ: Bilingual Review, 2004.

Felisbret, Eric. *Graffiti New York*. New York: Harry N. Adams, 2009.

Flores, Juan. *From Bomba to Hip Hop: Puerto Rican Culture and Latino Identity*. New York: Columbia University Press, 2000.

Flores, Juan and George Yudice. "Living Borders/ Buscando America: Languages of Latino Self-Formation." *Social Text* 8:2 (1990): 57–84.

Foner, Nancy. *In the New Land: A Comparative View of Immigration*. New York: New York University Press, 2005.

Gaspar de Alba, Alicia. *Chicano Art Inside/Outside the Master's House: Cultural Politics and the CARA Exhibition*. Austin: University of Texas Press, 1998.

Gastman, Roger and Caleb Neelon. *The History of American Graffiti*. New York: Harper Design, 2011.

Goldman, Shifra M. and Tomás Ybarra-Frausto. "The Political and Social Contexts of Chicano Art." *Chicano Art: Resistance and Affirmation, 1965–1985*. Eds Richard Griswold del Castillo, Teresa McKenna and Yvonne Yarbro-Beharano. Los Angeles: Wight Art Gallery / University of California Press, 1991. 83–95.

Griswold del Castillo, Richard, Teresa McKenna, Yvonne Yarbro-Bejarano, eds. *Chicano Art: Resistance and Affirmation, 1965-1985*. Tuscon: University of Arizona Press, 1991.

Gutierres, Fernando "Pisket HAR INK." Personal Interview. 15 November 2013.

Gutierres, Fernando "Pisket HAR INK." Personal Interview. 19 July 2015.

Habell-Pallán, Michelle. *Loca Motion: The Travels of Chicana and Latina Popular Culture*. New York: New York University Press, 2005.

Har, Sarck. Personal Interview. 14 October 2013.

Har, Sarck. Personal Interview. 24 October 2014.

Har, Sarck. Personal Interview. 1 August 2015.

Jackson, Carlos Francisco. *Chicana and Chicano Art: ProtestArte*. Tucson: University of Arizona Press, 2009.

Jenkins, Sacha. "Part One: New York Underground, 1969 to 1980." In *Definition: The Art and Design of Hip Hop*. Eds. Cey Adams and Bill Adler. New York: HarperCollins, 2008 16–19.

Keller, Gary D. *Triumph of Our Communities: Four Decades of Mexican American Art*. Tempe, AZ: Bilingual Press, 2005.

La Farge, Phyllis and Magdalena Caris. *Painted Walls of Mexico/ Paredes Pintadas de México*. Mexico City: Turner Libros, 2008.

Latorre, Guisela. *Walls of Empowerment: Chicana/o Indigenist Murals of California*. Austin: University of Texas Press, 2008.

MacDonald, Nancy. *The Graffiti Subculture: Youth, Masculinity and Identity in London and New York*. New York: Palgrave MacMillan, 2003.

McFarland, Pancho. *Chicano Rap: Gender and Violence in the Postindustrial Barrio*. Austin: University of Texas Press, 2008.

McFarland, Pancho. *The Chican@ Hip Hop Nation: Politics of a New Millennial Mestizaje*. East Lansing, MI: Michigan State University Press, 2013.

Maciel, David R. "Mexico in Atzlán and Aztlán in Mexico: The Dialectics of Chicano-Mexicano Art." *Chicano Art: Resistance and Affirmation, 1965–1985*. Eds. Richard Griswold del Castillo, Teresa McKenna and Yvonne Yarbro-Beharano. Los Angeles: Wight Art Gallery/ University of California Press, 1991. 109–18.

Montejano, David. *Quixote's Soldiers: A Local History of the Movement, 1966–1981*. Austin: University of Texas Press, 2010.

Murray, James T. and Karla L. Murray. *Broken Windows: Graffiti NYC*. Berkley, CA: Ginko Press, 2010.

Nathan, Debbie. "David and his 26 Roomates." *New York Magazine*, 16 May 2005.

Navarro, Armando. *Mexican American Youth Organization: AvantGarde of the Chicano Movement in Texas*. Austin: University of Texas Press, 1995.

Ochoa, María. *Creative Collectives: Chicana Painters Working in Community*. Albuquerque, NM: University of New Mexico Press, 2003.

Poniatowska, Elena. *La Noche de Tlatelolco: Testimonios de historia oral*. 2nd ed. Mexico City: Ediciones Era, 1998.

Quiñones, Juan. *Chicano Politics: Reality and Promise, 1940–1990*. Albuquerque, NM: University of New Mexico Press, 1990.

Risomena, Fernando and Douglas S. Massey. "Pathways to El Norte: Origins, Destinations, and Characteristics of Mexican Migrants to the United States." *International Migration Review*. 46:1 (2012): 3–36.

Rodriguez, Eric. Personal Inteview. 24 Oct. 2014.

Rose, Tricia. "Flowing, Layering, and Rupture in Postindustrial New York." *Signifyin(g), Sanctifyin', and Slam Dunking: A Reading in African American Expressive Culture*. Ed. Gena Dagel Caponi. Amherst, MA: University of Massachusetts Press, 1999. 192–220.

Sanchez, George J. *Becoming Mexican American: Ethnicity, Culture and Identity in Chicano Los Angeles, 1900–1945*. New York: Oxford University Press, 1995.

San Miguel, Jr., Guadalupe. *"Brown, not White:" School Integration and the Chicano Movement in Houston*. College Station, TX: Texas A and M University Press, 2001.

Semple, Kirk. "Immigrant Sets Sights On the Mayor's Office, Back Home in Mexico." *The New York Times*, late ed. 2 June 2010.

Semple, Kirk. "Immigrants Face Darkest Housing Picture." *The New York Times*. 29 March 2011.

Smith, Robert C. *Mexican New York: Transnational Lives of New Immigrants*. Berkeley: University of California Press, 2005.

Standish, Katherine, Vijay Nandi, Danielle C. Ompad, Sandra Momper, and Sandro Galea. "Household Density among Undocumented Mexican Immigrants in New York City." *Journal of Immigrant Minority Health*. 12:3 (2010): 310–18.

Valle, Imuris and Eduardo Weiss. "Participation in the figured world of graffiti." *Teaching and Teacher Education*. 26:1 (2010): 128–35.

Ybarra-Frausto, Tomás. "A Panorama of Latino Arts." *American Latinos and the Making of the United States*. National Park Service, n.d. Available at: www.nps.gov/history/heritageinitiatives/latino/latinothemestudy/arts.htm

Ybarra-Frausto, Tomás. "Imagining a More Expansive Narrative of American Art." *American Art*. 19:3 (2005): 9–15.

18

INEXACT REVOLUTIONS
Understanding Latino Pop Art

Rocio Isabel Prado

Latina/o pop art's exclusion from the field of contemporary art has put it in the perfect position to cause *desmadre*. The extent of its exclusion is evident in the process of research: one has to look outside the field of contemporary art to examine the breadth of Latina/o pop art's history and diversity. It is often lost in the confounding intersections of identity that curators fail to understand ("is this art representative of New Yorkers, or Puerto Ricans?"). Latina/o pop art is confined to the subsections of "ethnic" or "alternative" art and is considered to be incompatible with the values of mainstream America. Due to its exclusion from museums, media coverage, and funding, Latina/o pop art has undertaken a struggle that challenges the facets of American society that make this exclusion possible. The work of Los Angeles-based art group Asco confronts contemporary art and demands to be included or else. When the Los Angeles County Museum of Art (LACMA) was asked why there was no Chicana/o art in the region's public art institution, a curator replied, "Chicanos don't make art, they're in gangs." In response, the group spray-painted the front of the museum creating the legendary piece, *Spray Paint LACMA* (Shaked 1059). Similarly, many Latina/o pop artists' work is fueled from this exclusion: "The images reveal what seems to be a love/hate relationship, a desire not quite to participate and not exactly to overthrow" (Shaked 1060). Their critique of the exclusion of Latina/o culture (vandalizing a museum) has become the base upon which artists create a celebration of Latina/o culture (making that vandalism into a piece of art) and has come to define contemporary Latina/o pop art.

Due to the breadth of Latina/o culture's diversity, it is necessary that artists draw from multiple sources; an approach Marivel T. Danielson identified as *rasquachismo*. As summed up by Luz Calvo, this is art of "making do" and of "piecing together, selecting from bits and pieces recovered from other uses or cheaply acquired" (Calvo 219). Latina/o pop art builds upon previous cultural understandings (i.e. folk culture) from many different sources in order to create a sense of relevance within the mestizaje that is Latina/o culture. Consequently, Latina/o pop art does not limit itself to a single source, time period, or language but takes from anything and everything to create work as diverse as the culture it represents. For example, Los Angeles-based visual artist Alma Lopez takes "from popular art forms, rather than so-called high art; she selects her 'bits and pieces' from the existing repertoire of working-class Chicano/a visual culture" (Calvo 219). The "bits and pieces" that make up Alma Lopez's work consists of traditional Latina/o culture, feminist Latina artists, and popular culture. Her choices comment on and critique all the sources from which she takes them. For Alma Lopez, the intentionality of choosing a piece created by working-class artists challenges the status quo of contemporary American art. Similarly, as a field, Latina/o pop art draws from contemporary American art and culture, Latina/o culture and experience, and social movements. In utilizing the rhetoric of social justice movements, Latina/o pop art highlights the exclusion of Latina/os from American culture and media.

The methodology of creating new meaning in drawing from a variety of different sources is noticeably political because it celebrates Latina/o culture. This problematizes mainstream culture that consistently ignores, oppresses, or exoticizes Latina/os. In section one, I will trace how Latina/o pop art complicates and works against previous definitions of Latina/o culture. In section two, I will demonstrate how Latina/o pop art often works in connection to political movements that work to give Latina/os more rights and visibility. Additionally, section three shows how contemporary Latina/o pop artists are framing the movement around underrepresented groups in order to disrupt hegemonic Latina/o identity. And lastly, I will discuss how Latina/o pop art is anticipating technological advances and the future of Latina/o art.

Ni De Ayer, Ni De Ahora: Latina/o Artists Re-Define the Past to Create the Present

Contemporary Latina/o pop art has done much work in the way of representing Latina/os in a positive light. Conducting this work, however, means working from within the stereotyped representation of Latina/os in the U.S. to create a new complex version of Chicana/o or Latina/o identity. These same difficulties occurred for Luis Alfaro, Monica Palacios, and Albert Antonio Ariaza, and inspired their performance piece *Deep in the Crotch of My Latino Psyche*.

> The three performers on the stage run in horror to hide from the larger-than-life images … from everyday life in Los Angeles: Virgen de Guadalupe candles, Taco Bell logos, Mission tortillas, a neon burro-riding campesino (peasant), a piñata, fake Mayan ruins, and former California governor Pete Wilson. The artists' attempt to run from these images illustrates their desire for their work to be contextualized by more than these one-dimensional images of Mexicanidad/Mexicanness and Mexican Americanness and Latinidad.
>
> (Habell-Pallan 15)

These artists have only seen their culture depicted by way of Americanized, cheapened fast food, advertisements, xenophobic politicians, and shallow representations of sacred traditions and ceremonies. They are trying to escape the restraints of these offensive portrayals of Latina/o identity in the hopes of creating truly meaningful art. By drawing upon these stereotypes to critique them, Latina/o pop art does not "participate" in them nor does it reject them entirely, but rather it reuses them in order to create something new—in this case, by depicting the struggle of an artist looking to create multi-faceted work. In order to avoid the pitfalls of re-creating stereotypes of Latina/o identity, many Latina/o pop artists look to a pre-Columbian indigenous and Mexican past to piece together a new identity.

To avoid the overly simplistic and false stereotypes of Latina/os in popular media, many artists take inspiration from cultural practices within Mexico and connect them to new meaning in the United States. One of these cultural practices is *Dia De Los Muertos*, which is celebrated in different forms throughout several countries in Latin America. The recent rise of *Dia De Los Muertos*-related art references a Mexican artist known for depicting skeletons and skulls: "Many Chicano artists were inspired by Jose Guadalupe Posada's satirical calavera caricatures, and began to create stylistically similar drawings that critically commented on California's politicians, urban youth, and other political topics" (Marchi 40). According to Marchi, many artists working through Los Angeles's Self-Help Graphics were drawn to Posada's work and applied them to contemporary Los Angeles politics, like immigration and gentrification. Another approach to *Dia De Los Muertos* art involved applying the traditionally somber calaveras to pop culture including *El Chavo del Ocho*, Mexican wrestlers, and even Estar Guars (*Star Wars*). Jose Pulido imposed calaveras from Posada's work onto Han Solo, Luke Skywalker, and Princess Leia's bodies. These designs can be found in many U.S. cities including Los Angeles's Plazita Olvera. Although the mash-up is not necessarily political, this might be the first time Latina/os have connected their own experience to the predominantly *gringo* world of *Star Wars*, thereby creating an alternative narrative while still participating in the much-beloved fandom.

Even though Posada's work was created in the early 1900s, many Latina/o artists look further back in history to a time before Native Americans had even discovered Columbus. This approach is "referred to today as Neo-Indigenism (a movement by Chicano activists to reaffirm and celebrate the contributions and achievements of Mesoamerican civilization), the collective espousal of Mexico's Indigenous past became a dominant aspect of Chicano artistic expression" (Marchi 39). Neo-indigenism celebrates Aztec or *Mexica* culture that is associated with Mexico City. In looking to a past that survived the genocide that Hernán Cortés and other conquistadores began in the Americas, these artists revive the history that was stolen from the Chicana/o diaspora. In doing so, they avoid the tropes of Taco Bell logos and piñatas and are free to piece together their own *altares* to form a mixture of Mexican and indigenous art forms: "the Self-Help Graphics artists were introduced to the Mexican folk art aspects of the festival, such as calavera imagery, and, to the Indigenous-style ofrenda making" (Marchi 47). Thanks to the combination of influences from both time periods, Chicana/o artists were able to reconnect with Mexican traditions that had been lost upon migrating to the U.S.

"Chicanos Don't Make Art": The Role of Politics in Latina/o Pop Art

Art created by or for Latina/os is not considered to be representative of the human experience, meaning the Latina/o pop artist is inherently unpopular. Of course, this never stopped any of the artists in this chapter. Instead, many Chicana/o or Latina/o artists utilized their unpopularity within the art world as a platform upon which to spread awareness about the lack of rights for Latina/os and further the work being done in many activist movements. The work of the group Asco did more than just challenge a racist curator and the exclusionary practices of Los Angeles museums; it challenged a long history of denying Latina/os resources. "The East LA conceptualist art collective Asco (Spanish for "nausea")... sought the 'performative subversion of the historical process that has produced

Chicano/as as the categorical bling spot…of dominant media as well as political and cultural institutions' (Chavoya 227)" (Hernandez 125). Their protest against LACMA challenged the exoticization of Latina/os in media because it resulted in their exclusion from "political and cultural institutions" including universities, community centers, and other resources. Asco was not solely targeting LACMA but rather placed it into a vast system of institutions that depended upon Latina/o stereotypes to justify their exclusion of Latina/os and their work. They had decided that they had had enough of being told what Latina/os could and could not do and looked into subverting these hegemonic expectations on a national scale.

Asco comes from a long line of artists who utilize their work to protest the treatment of Latina/os in media and policy-making. In 1978, Yolanda Lopez's piece, "Who's the Illegal Alien, Pilgrim?", countered xenophobic rhetoric that targeted undocumented immigrants with echoes of the "Plan Espiritual de Aztlan." Designed during the National Chicano Youth Liberation Conference in 1969, the plan designates Chicana/os as the inhabitants and civilizers of the northern land of Aztlan (southwest U.S.). The drawing shows a young Chicano angrily pointing his finger at the viewer. His face, which is bordered by an Aztec-style headdress, could belong to any man living in East Los or Boyle Heights. In this piece, Lopez has erased the conceptual divide between indigenous person and immigrant. Her conceptual work gives undocumented folks who are living in fear of deportation the right to live in the U.S. because they lived here first. Additionally, the Aztec man's anger is noticeable to the viewer, which goes against the dominant view that Mexicans are submissive and quiet. This Chicano sticks his finger in politicians' faces and demands why people like him are not allowed to live on their own land. The neo-indigenism in Lopez's piece highlights the goals of the early Chicano movement to xenophobes who target undocumented immigrants.

Although immigration is often the subject of Latina/o art, many artists situate the rights of undocumented immigrants in a larger context of economic, racial, and environmental injustices. Latina/o environmental activism is connected to the treatment of Latina/o immigrants because neoliberal policies displace people and damage the environment. In response to neoliberal policies like the North American Free Trade Agreement, which left indigenous Mexicans homeless and jobless, many Latina/o artists created works that challenged the idea that this legislation was created for the greater good. Many of these works of pop art operated by directly mocking specific companies that took advantage of migrant workers. In doing so, they disrupt the complacency of American consumerism by depicting the abuse of Latina/os upon which it depends: "The confrontational approach challenges a pervasive vision of postwar abundance by confronting viewers with stark images of the social and ecological destructiveness of American consumerism. Ester Hernandez's iconoclastic image *Sun Mad* (1982) is among the best examples of this style" (Ontiveros 105). Hernandez's disquieting piece reproduces the all-too-familiar *Sun Maid* logo but replaces the cheery maiden with a smiling skeleton. In doing so, Hernandez questions the saccharine façade that companies like *Sun Maid* use to hide their mistreatment of migrant workers. In utilizing a well-known logo that many viewers associate with little red raisin boxes from their childhood, Hernandez is able to jar viewers out of complacency. Here, it is the shock value from the piece's "stark images" that should demonstrate the degree of "ecological destructiveness" that these well-known companies cause.

Many Latina/o pop artists created direct responses to specific anti-Latina/o legislation and subverted xenophobic rhetoric before a national audience. In 1996 Los Angeles, an ordinance banned the use of leaf blowers being used within 500 feet of any residence. This would force Latina/o immigrant workers to use rakes instead of leaf blowers, causing them to work twice as hard for the same pay. The Association of Latin American Gardeners of Los Angeles organized hunger strikes, campaigns, walkouts, and protests that echoed the struggles of the United Farm Workers struggle in the 1960s. Upon hearing news of the hunger strikes Gody Sanchez, a Salvadorian refugee and auto mechanic, decided to help ease the plight of his "brothers." He was able to "adapt[...] one of the leaf blowers to run on an electric motor," (Chavoya 164), making it quieter and thereby enabling Latina/o landscapers to continue to keep up with the demands of their labor. It also pacified the celebrities looking to have quiet and well-maintained yards and gardens. Artist Ortiz Torres commemorated the triumph of a single immigrant's ingenuity over the lightly-veiled racism of Hollywood celebrities by creating an extravagant leaf blower: "[he] customized another leaf blower with metal-flake candy apple paint, a 24-karat gold-plated engine, velvet upholstery, and a lowrider bicycle-club plate" (Chavoya 164). Unlike Sanchez's, Torres's leaf blower proudly announced the presence of Latina/o immigrants. By designing it in the same style as a lowrider, Torres invoked the same traditional defiance as Chicana/os cruising low and blasting oldies in flashy cars. In referencing early Chicana/o culture, Torres connected the grassroots struggle of landscapers to the "Chicano tradition of artful struggle" (Sterngold, no pg.), of celebrating the Chicana/o community despite being told to quiet down.

Feministas y Maricónes: Incorporating Los Otros into Latina/o Art

In order to celebrate Latina/o culture, artists draw from Latina/o history; but hegemonic Latina/o history represents little more than a painful past for queer folk, women, and other underrepresented Latina/os. In order to begin the process of depicting a more inclusive and celebratory Latina/o history, these artists subvert Latina/o culture in a manner similar to that in which heterosexual, cisgender Latina/o artists subvert the world of contemporary art. They take what they can from the history they know and build upon it to include their own stories and experiences.

Because Catholicism is prevalent within Latina/o culture, it provides an effective point of reference from which to begin problematizing traditional Latina/o identity. Feminist Chicana lesbian artist Alma Lopez re-appropriates the image of La Virgen to allow for a more nuanced vision of femininity, wherein the Latina can be autonomous, sexual, and complex. Lopez draws from La Virgen because she defines gender within Latina/o culture: "The Virgin of Guadalupe is omnipresent in Chicano/a visual space. She is painted on car windows, tattooed on shoulders or backs, emblazoned on neighborhood walls, and silk-screened on t-shirts sold at local flea markets" (Calvo 201). La Virgen's image is utilized so frequently because she is the guardian of Latina/os. In Chicana/o culture, her image is used whenever necessary: during a Chivas game, to protect travelers, even the United Farm Workers movement famously used her image during marches. Because Latina/o identity is so dependent upon her image, she is readily available to disrupt tradition (Calvo 202). Consequently, Lopez applies La Virgen's recognizable features (a blue mantel with gold trim decorated with gold stars, the crescent moon, and a frame of golden rays) to images of real women. Her most well-known work "Our Lady" shows a Latina wearing a bikini made of roses and defiantly placing her hands on her hips while looking directly at the viewer. This provides a stark contrast to La Virgen de Guadalupe's lowered gaze, folded hands, and covered, girdled body.

Despite the controversy that her work has caused, Alma Lopez is not the first Latina feminist to complicate La Virgen. She "draws from earlier Chicana feminist artistic engagements with the Virgin of Guadalupe by artists such as Ester Hernandez and Yolanda Lopez" (Calvo 205), thereby contributing to and highlighting an already well-formed Latina feminist art movement. "These images represent the Virgin of Guadalupe in active stances and with contemporary Chicana identities: practicing karate or running a marathon, as a seamstress or an abuelita (grandmother)" (Calvo 205). Latina feminist artists show La Virgen in action—working, moving, living. This Virgen makes decisions, fights for herself, works, and most controversial, is open about the fact that she is a survivor of sexual assault or workplace abuse. In doing this, La Virgen provides a complex definition of femininity instead of a hegemonic ideal of purity and submissiveness to which women should aspire.

Although the changes to La Virgen were small, they radically disturbed traditional Latina/o patriarchy causing controversy that threatened the physical well-being of Latina artists. In depicting the Virgen as a real woman, Latina feminist artists were creating an idea of womanhood for themselves, which was capable of creating ripples throughout the rest of Latina/o culture. The idea of an autonomous woman is threatening to patriarchal Latinidad because women, like the Virgen, are seen as the protectors of culture. La Virgen was no longer preoccupied with whether Mexico won the World Cup if she was tying her running shoes or working in a garment factory. If the Virgen was busy living her own life, who would protect Latino masculinity and lowriders? These threats to traditional and exclusionary masculinity eventually materialized into very real physical threats for the artists: "Yolanda M. Lopez received bomb threats for her portrayal of La Virgen wearing low-heeled shoes" (Lopez 14). Alma Lopez suggested that people were upset at Yolanda's version of La Virgen wearing heels because it was now possible for her to walk. Alma Lopez's "Our Lady" received threats of cuts in funding, bomb threats, and even physical intimidation: "we were suddenly surrounded by eight or ten men saying 'crucify her' and calling us 'fea' [ugly] as we left … I was very shocked and upset that what I consider my culture would do this to me" (Lopez 3). From Lopez's account, one can assume that the men who attempted to intimidate her were Latina/os who demanded that she take her work down because it made them uncomfortable. It was probably the first work of art that challenged their preconceived notions of gender. Their reactions suggest that in the face of intimidation and physical danger, Latina feminist artists continue to successfully disrupt patriarchal notions of femininity in depicting real Latinas.

Just as Latina feminist artists embraced the parts of them previously considered undesirable (female bodies, work, sexuality), queer Latina/o artists embraced their sexuality by re-appropriating the label homophobes utilized against them, thereby controlling the way queers depict themselves. In "Drawing Offensive/Offensive Drawing: Toward a Theory of Maricónagraphy," Robb Hernandez traces the way in which queer Latina/os utilize photography and printmaking to subvert Latina/o heteronormativity in taking on the slur "maricón" as a form of empowerment, an approach he calls "maricónagraphy." Like the ubiquitous nature of La Virgen, heteromasculinity's role as an integral part of male Latino identity positions it as the perfect target to problematize traditional Latinidad "by asserting and exploiting its preeminent threat to a fragile image system of Latino heteromasculinist visibility" (Hernandez 126). Terrill intentionally defied heteromasculinist Latino identity when he took portraits while wearing t-shirts emblazoned with the word "maricón." In *The Maricón Series*, Joey Terrill's self-portrait is a black and white photograph in which he looks directly at the viewer. If it were not for the word on his t-shirt, this could be a portrait of any other Latino youth. Joey's slicked back hair style, thick mustache, plain white t-shirt and bold stare remind the viewer of a group of young Chicanos "posted up" on a street corner, their chins lifted in defiance. They build upon pre-existing markers of Latino identity by "borrow[ing] from the mug shot and Chicano gang vocabulary, crafting intelligibility through related inferences of defiance, social disobedience, and hypermasculine aggression" (Hernandez 138). In referring to gang culture, these Latino pop artists maintained a sense of masculinity that was not solely based upon heterosexuality. Despite the fact that they wore their orientation proudly on their chests, they still connected their Latino identity to gang culture, early Chicano identity, and therefore referenced the same "Chicano tradition of artful struggle" as lowriders. By printing and photographing t-shirts that bore witness to male queerness, they created an opportunity for masculinity sans compulsory heterosexuality giving queer men the opportunity to represent themselves.

Latina/os in Cyberspace: *El Futuro* of Latina/o Pop Art

For Latina/o pop artists looking toward the future, even the most recent developments in social justice movements, Latina/o politics, and neo-indigenism can feel suffocating. Cyber artist Guillermo Gomez-Peña looks to provide a space within Latina/o pop art that is separate from folk culture. Gomez-Peña's work utilizes technology to toy with the divide between participant and passive viewer in response to images of stereotypical representations of Latina/os, and Latina/os defying these stereotypes. In presenting his work, Gomez-Peña has come to the realization that mainstream audiences do not accept technologically advanced art that is created by Latina/os because it challenges the notion that Latina/os belong in the future. Gomez-Peña and other experimental Latina/o artists attended a debate on the role of Latina/os in technology where non-Latina/os expressed that the internet just wasn't meant for Latina/os: "in other words, we were to keep painting murals, plotting revolutions in rowdy cafes, reciting oral poetry, and dancing salsa or quebradita" (Gomez-Peña 87). The only acceptable forms of Latina/o expression were loud and physical—stereotypes in full effect. In response, Gomez-Peña created work that Latina/o-fied cyberspace, separating Latina/o identity from the inherent connection it had formed to a simplistic, romantic view of Latina/o history.

In the same vein as other Latina/o artists who utilize their unpopularity to give voice to issues affecting Latina/os, Gomez-Peña's work capitalizes on the idea that Latina/os can't use technology as if to say *watch me*. His project, "Naftaztec: Pirate Cyber-TV for A.D. 2000," is an experiment in interactive multilingual television in which "two 'post-Nafta cyber-Aztec TV pirates' ... transmitted their bizarre views on American culture 'directly from their underground vato-bunker ... '" (Gomez-Peña 87). The program's design alienated white audiences, "allow[ing] Anglos to experience firsthand the psychological sensation of racism" (Gomez-Peña 87). The program, which lasted an hour and a half, asked for viewers to call in and respond. Many of the viewer's responses expressed the very idea that Gomez-Peña was working against:

> Most of the viewers ... who responded were amazed at how technically and visually sophisticated and 'unfolksy' the program was, given ... that it had been created by 'Mexicans.' Many others ... declared that we should immediately leave the high-tech simulated space we had created 'illegally' and return to our 'pyramid-infested past.'
>
> (Gomez-Peña 89)

The viewer responses demonstrate that traditional methods of portraying Latina/o identity (i.e. re-appropriating folk art) had been accepted and de-politicized in the mainstream audience imaginary. Folk art, paintings, spoken word, and street performances were no longer threatening; but technological political work was.

Gomez-Peña and other Latina/o pop artists who intentionally work with technology are leading the future of Latina/o pop art. Like their predecessors, they attach previous understandings of Latina/o culture to new media and in doing so change what it means to be a Latina/o. Their goals include "politiciz[ing] technology ... to use it to enhance interaction between performers and audience members, which will then be reinterpreted by and expressed through our 'primitive,' political, and erotic bodies" (Gomez-Peña 88). Gomez-Peña problematizes the divide between performer and audience member in order to create a bridge between what is considered acceptable for Latina/os and what isn't, thereby stopping stereotyping at the root. Also, because this dialogue will happen through the simultaneously political, erotic, and primitive Latina/o bodies, it creates space for ambiguity within Latina/o identity. In the same way that Alma Lopez disrupted Virgen-dependent femininity to complicate Latina identity, Gomez-Peña utilizes technology to create a version of Latinidad that is not dependent upon a pre-Columbian or pre-migration past so that Latina/os can exist in the future.

Ahora que?/Now what?

Despite the consistent disruptions and changes Latina/o pop art faces, it remains malleable, which is conducive to creativity. What it means to be Latina/o has been revolutionized and complicated to allow for more diversity and inclusion. The definition of Latina/o art has moved from tangible art to performance art, pirating TV channels, and even graffiti upon a museum wall. What has not changed is the field's inherent unpopularity—a characteristic that has allowed many Latina/o pop artists to thrive. It's much easier to create meaningful work when you don't have to worry about the viewer's acceptance. The field's resilience and reaction to its exclusion from mainstream art provides artists a platform upon which to effect change within both the Latina/o community and the field of mainstream art. This further enables the Latina/o artist to challenge norms, confront racism, xenophobia, homophobia, and sexism, and obtain artistic autonomy. It is this fluidity that has provided Latina/o culture with a milieu of misfits to depict and create Latina/o identity. We are gifted with nonconformists, oddballs, maricónes, malforas, cybervatos, rebellious art collectives, oddballs, chingonas, malhabladas, rebels, cholos, pop culture nerds, self-identified illegals, warriors, and overall malcriados. Latina/o pop art might not receive much funding, media coverage, or gallery space, but it is also never, ever dull.

Bibliography

Aldama, Frederick Luis. *Your Brain on Latino Comics: From Gus Arriola to Los Bros Hernandez*. Austin: University of Texas Press, 2009.

Calvo, Luz. "Art comes for the Archbishop: The Semiotics of Contemporary Chicana Feminism and the Work of Alma Lopez." *Meridians* 5:1 (2004): 201–24.

Chavoya, C. Ondine. "Customized Hybrids: The Art of Ruben Ortiz Torres and Lowriding in Southern California." CR: *The New Centennial Review* 4:2 (2004): 141–84.

Davila, Arlene. *Latino Spin Public Image and the Whitewashing of Race*. New York: New York University Press, 2008.

Doris, Sara. *Pop Art and the Contest over American Culture*. New York: Cambridge University Press, 2006.

El Plan Espiritual de Aztlan. Reprinted in *Aztlán: Essays on the Chicano Homeland*. Eds Rudolfo A. Anaya and Francisco Lomelí. Albuquerque: University of New Mexico Press, 1989: 1–5.

Esains, Victoria. "Calaveras de Dia de Muertos inspirades en Star Wars." *Hipertextual.com*. 27 October 2010.

Gaspar de Alba, Alicia and Alma Lopez. *Our Lady of Controversy: Alma Lopez's "Irreverent Apparition."* Austin: University of Texas Press, 2011.

Gomez-Peña, Guillermo. "Chicano Interneta: The search for intelligent life in cyberspace." *Hopscotch: A Cultural Review* 2:2 (2000): 80–91.

Habell-Pallan, Michelle. *Loca Motion: The Travels of Chicana and Latina Popular Culture*. New York: New York University Press, 2005.

Hernandez, Robb. "Drawing Offensive/Offensive Drawing: Toward a Theory Maricónagraphy." *Multi-Ethnic Literature of the United States* 39:2 (2014): 121–52.

Marchi, Regina M. *Day of the Dead in the USA: The Migration and Transformation of a Cultural Phenomenon*. New Brunswick, NJ: Rutgers University Press, 2009.

Ontiveros, Randy J. *In the Spirit of a New People: The Cultural Politics of the Chicano Movement*. New York: New York University Press 2013.

Pignataro, Margarita E. "Botanica Los Angeles: Latino Popular Religious Art in the City of Angels." *Chasqui* 38:2 (2009): 206–7. *Academic Search Complete*. Web. 24 June 2015.

Ramos, E. Carmen. "The Latino Presence in American Art." *American Art* 26:2 (2012): 7–13.

Randy J. Ontiveros. *In the Spirit of a New People: The Cultural Politics of the Chicano Movement*. New York: New York University Press, 2013.

Shaked, Nizan. "Phantom Sightings: Art after the Chicano Movement." *American Quarterly* 60:4 (2008): 1057–72.

Stavans, Ilan and Frederick Luis Aldama. *Muy Pop!: Conversations on Latino Popular Culture*. Ann Arbor, MI: The University of Michigan Press, 2013.

Sterngold, James. "Making the Jalopy an Ethnic Banner: How the Lowrider Evolved From Chicano Revolt to Art Form". *New York Times*, 19 February 2000.

19

INSTALLATION ART, TRANSNATIONALISM AND THE CHINESE-CHICANO EXPERIENCE

Richard Alexander Lou and Guisela Latorre

As a self-identified Chicano artist who is the product of an anticolonialist Chinese father and a culturally affirming Mexicana mother, so began my life as a Chicanese.

Richard Lou

Performance, installation, and new media artist Richard Lou's work has compelled spectators to think critically about bordered identities, power inequities, post-colonial realities, race relations, and other socially relevant issues. His provocative and dynamic performances, installations, and multimedia pieces have also encouraged audiences to problematize clear distinctions between art and activism, and between "high" art and popular culture. Primarily known as a Chicano artist, Lou's work for the past ten years, however, has paid great attention to his Chinese heritage and to the transnational subjectivities that animate social identities. Having grown up in the San Diego/Tijuana border region with a Mexican mother and a Chinese father, Lou's experiences have been defined by the transnationalism of the border region itself, but also by the biculturalism of his upbringing, as it is made evident in his multimedia installation *Stories on My Back* (2010–) [see Figure 9.1].

Without losing sight of the politically engaged and collective nature of his art, this work is also more introspective and deeply personal than some of his previous productions.[1] Utilizing the images and voices of the artist's children (Gloria, Maricela, Magda, and Ming) and deploying storytelling devices throughout the installation, Lou articulates a transnational identity that is, on the one hand, quite intimate and unique to his experience and, on the other, broadly symptomatic of an increasingly globalized world. Thus, *Stories on My Back* embodies—to use the words of cultural studies scholars Kit Dobson and Áine

Figure 19.1   Richard Lou, *Stories on My Back* (2010–present), multimedia installation

McGlynn—"the desire to advocate for artistic agency at a time when globalizing forces are increasingly calling for economic rationalizations for creative practices" (4). Moreover, this installation speaks eloquently of what art historian Margo Machida called "experiences of transcultural passage" among Asian American artists: "As growing numbers of Asian artists become witnesses to, and participants in, contemporary migration and experiences of transcultural passage, intertwining thematics of place, movement, arrival and dwelling emerge as significant motifs in their work" (195).

Stories on My Back eloquently speaks of the critical connections between the Chicana/o and Chinese experiences in the U.S., connections that represent viable forms of transnational resistance to the homogenizing and subordinating forces of globalization. Lou enacts "horizontal affiliation" which, according to cultural theorist Michelle Habell-Pallán, corresponds to the processes "by which marginalized groups recognize shared stakes in the struggle to create counter hegemonic practices and communities" (12). In his work on the Mexipino population in San Diego, Rudy Guevarra highlights the importance of Asian-Latino "interethnic collaboration and coalition building." These collaborations and coalitions are allegorized in the family narratives that Lou reveals in this installation. "We can learn from [Latino-Asian] experiences," Guevarra argues, "as we continue to live in a country where different racial and ethnic groups converge in multiple settings" (6).

The cross-cultural and transnational aesthetics of Stories on My Back are in part accomplished by the artist's deployment of oral traditions, an important component of working class Latina/o popular culture. Storytelling, folk legends, corridos (narrative Mexican folk songs) and other forms of oral knowledge transmitted by word of mouth are key components of Latina/o worldviews in the United States and beyond. Because these are forms of oral tradition—not text-based manifestations of Western "civilization"—and because these are connected to cultural production by people of color, white supremacist power elites have relegated the oral to the status of lowbrow, quaint and "naïve" expressions with little to no historical or artistic value. However, for more than half a century now, legions of U.S. Latina/o scholars and writers have argued that the study of popular oral culture is not only critical for the understanding of communities of color, but it is also at the center of a necessary critique of colonial hierarchies of knowledge. From Americo Paredes's *With a Pistol in His Hand* (1958) to Frederick Aldama and Ilan Stavans's *¡Muy Pop!* (2013), Latina/o popular culture has been reframed as a legitimate and central component of U.S. history and culture. Latina/o visual artists have likewise engaged in similarly decolonial celebrations of popular culture. One need only think of Amalia Mesa-Bains's use of inexpensive household objects from Mexican homes for her *altares*/installations or Pepón Osorio's displays of Nuyorikan barbershop ephemera within the exclusive spaces of New York museums. But the family histories Lou utilized in *Stories on My Back*, which are also part and parcel of Latina/o popular culture, speak to something even more ephemeral and democratizing than physical objects, for the oral can more easily and fluidly traverse spatial boundaries and temporal/historical moments.

Though *Stories on My Back* is based on the situated experiences of Lou and his family within specific geographic locales (San Diego/Tijuana, Memphis, Canton Province, China, etc.), the installation certainly decenters any specific sense of place. The motif of the cornhusks that functions as a unifying motif throughout the installation beckons powerful images of translocality, as Dana Leibsohn explains:

> Assembled like feathers on a bird, [the cornhusk covered columns] evoke the shining body of Quetzalcoatl, the feathered serpent and culture hero of ancient Mexico whose body adorned sacred structures in cities like Teotihuacan and Tenochtitlan. Corn, of course, was introduced to China from the Americas; its trans-Pacific route exactly opposite the one traveled by Lou's father (and thousands of other immigrants to Mexico and the United States in the nineteenth and early twentieth centuries).[2]

The cornhusks also pay homage to Mexican and Chicana/o food culture, as these are key ingredients in the preparation of *tamales*. Lou's use of these items as artistic media reflects his desire to insert into the historically elitist space of the museum/gallery elements of everyday life in Latina/o popular culture thus democratizing the often-exclusionary exhibition space. Moreover, through Lou's careful organization of the gallery space, spectators are carried through multiple sites of remembrance as they are exposed to overlapping and at times even conflicting sensory inputs. The artist's subjectivity is situated in all these geographic sites and in none at all at the same time. Lou purposely plays with the notions of in-betweenness and interstitiality, tactics that expose the artificiality of colonial binaries and lines of demarcation.

Stories on My Back challenges Lou's common categorization as a Chicano artist, with his Chinese identity often relegated to a casual mention in many writings on his art. The history of resistance and activism that is bound up with the term "Chicano" has indeed informed his work in very productive and transformative ways. Nevertheless, the label "Chicano" has also been implicated in static categories of race and gender. Ever since the 1970s, for instance, Chicana feminists and queer activists have denounced the exclusions of gender and sexuality that the term "Chicano" implied. The experiences of bicultural and biracial populations have scarcely made their way into the nationalist discourse of Chicanismo. Complicating what it means to be a Chicano then, *Stories of My Back* opens new avenues for the intersectionality and relationality of different social identities.

This multimedia installation also offers a new vision of Chicano masculinity in relationship to family history and memory. Conscious of how men of color have capitalized on male privilege to battle racism and discrimination, often at the expense of women and gender others, Lou refuses to deploy representations of maleness that include the marginalization of women. Even though the focus on male figures, such as Lou's father, is ubiquitous in *Stories on My Back*, these images represent alternative masculinities rather than dominant forms of manhood that demand power and subordination of gender others.

The importance of memory and storytelling in *Stories on My Back* cannot be over stated here. Machida has argued that the histories of migration and movement experienced by Asian American populations "provoke a compelling need to remember and retrieve past places and events." For people of color in general, the need to remember, recall family histories, and disseminate this information takes on a political overtone, as these stories actively challenge and decenter the master narratives of white patriarchal culture in the United States. In other words, the intentional and public recollection of memory that happens in *Stories on My Back* calls attention to the systematic exclusions enacted by institutions of power when it comes to narrating the past. Moreover, the deployments of memory that occur in *Stories on My Back* are charged with intense emotion and raw feelings, expressions that are facilitated by the artist's willingness to forgo the tenets of white patriarchal masculinity which posits that real men should forgo sentimentality and emotionalism.[3]

The transnationalism, multi-vocalism and new visions of manhood contained in *Stories on My Back* are made evident in "On the Shore of the East China Sea," the video projection embedded in the installation. In this narrative Lou's children recount a story from their grandfather's experience with racism and fear against Chinese populations in San Diego during the 1970s. Working as a butcher in a grocery store there, the elder Lou encountered affronts to his Chinese heritage by co-workers who belittled and patronized him in spite of his seniority and greater experience in the store. Such affronts also operated as thinly veiled challenges to his racialized masculinity. Scholars of Asian American studies have long highlighted U.S. dichotomous representations of Asian males as threatening and violent, on the one hand, and passive and effeminate, on the other. Gina Marchetti, for instance, argues that the "Yellow Peril" stereotype, popularized in U.S. film and media, cast Asian men as inherently dangerous and untrustworthy, explaining that the stereotype combined "racist terror of alien cultures, sexual anxieties and the belief that the West will be overpowered and enveloped by the irresistible, dark, occult forces of the East" (2). By contrast, sociologist Chong-suk Han, drawing from the work of Sucheng Chan and Yen Le Espiritu, provides a historical explanation for the image of the Asian male as passive and effeminate stating that "exclusion laws, coupled with anti-miscegenation laws led to the creation of a 'bachelor society' among early Chinese immigrants while labor laws relegated Asian men to feminine occupations such as laundry workers, domestics and cooks in the largely male dominated west coast of the mid nineteenth and early twentieth century" (86). This racialized and gendered set of tropes highlight the fears and anxieties that Chinese immigrant populations engendered in the U.S. social imaginary.

The story told in "On The Shore of the East China Sea" spoke volumes about how white populations in the U.S. sought to render Chinese males passive and non-threatening. Set in the male dominated homosocial space of the butcher shop where "friendly" banter among men is common, Gary, a much younger white co-worker of Lou senior, decides to spout a long-winded diatribe about the United States's military superiority to China. The fact that Gary's rant is directed at Lou implies at least a couple of assumptions, namely that the senior butcher represents the collectivity of all of China and that, as an Asian male, he will passively accept the tirades of a white man. Gary's comments center on what he thinks is the greater power the United States holds vis à vis China: "America has the most technologically advanced military in the world. It can easily wipe out China ... Yeah, that's right, we have M16s, bazookas, Patton tanks ... Damn right, we got them Claymores, that crazy sticky flaming shit, napalm, cobra copters and Puff the Magic Dragon. Shit, there ain't no use in fighting us!" Gary's tirade, however, is punctuated and fragmented by narrative threads of Lou's own experiences with transnational military service, segregation, and migration. The artist allows the spectator/listener to hear Lou's thought process amidst Gary's verbally aggressive outbursts. We learn that his schooling as a child happened in the U.S. and China, traveling back and forth between those two worlds. We also realize that he joined the U.S. Marine Corps fighting in World War II. As a matter of fact, Lou senior was one of 13,499 Chinese and Chinese Americans who fought on behalf of the United States; this number corresponded to 22 percent of all Chinese males in the country at the time.[4] As we continue delving into the elder Lou's thought process while he bears the brunt of Gary's harassment, the narrators inform us that, in spite of his extensive military service, his sacrifices and those of other men of color went unrecognized and at times even repudiated.

Perhaps one of the most poignant recollections from his youth recounted in "On the Shore of the East China Sea" is that of Lou senior traveling to Coahoma, Mississippi, via train while on furlough. Accompanied by mostly African American soldiers, the train reaches a rest stop where the men expect to receive a hero's reception for their service. Indeed, the welcoming committee had laid out a table filled with fresh donuts and hot coffee expecting white soldiers to descend from the train, as Maricela narrates: "When the all-white welcoming committee members saw the dark faces in the train cars, they began to overturn each table spilling hot coffee and tumbling soft donuts all over the platform floor." The overt humiliation directed at the black soldiers is further heightened by the fact that the men had fought on behalf of a country that refused to regard them as true citizens of the nation.

The devaluation and dismissal of the black soldiers' manhood is mirrored by Gary's own patronizing and superior attitude toward the elder Lou who is purposely feminized and emasculated by the younger man. White patriarchal culture would dictate then that Lou should retort with an equally arrogant, paternalist, and superior response, especially given his rich history of resiliency and survival instincts, but he instead responds with a transnational metaphor laced with humor and irony. He asks Gary to imagine a scenario where the entire population of China stands along the East China Sea jumping up and down causing a tidal wave, a tsunami if you will, that could potentially "wipe out the United States." The technologies of warfare and destruction that Gary celebrates are thus rendered meaningless before the awesome will power and resolve of the Chinese people. We can also read the tidal wave as a metaphor for Chinese migration to the United States, playing on U.S. fears of "the irresistible, dark, occult forces of the East" that could invade and potentially destroy the social fabric of the country. The so-called threat of Chinese migration is compounded by the knowledge that China is the most populous country in the world and as such it is a force to be reckoned with in global politics and economics. So Lou's response to Gary's hyper-masculine rant may appear to be equally aggressive as his co-worker's words yet the metaphorical, fantastical and humorous element of the transnational imaginary he proposes assuages any real possibilities for the annihilation of the U.S. at the hands of the Chinese. The tidal wave in this fanciful narrative stands for the capacity for collective action and community organizing among Chinese populations on both sides of the Pacific Ocean; in other words, it speaks to the power in numbers and the positive effects of organized action.

The visual component that accompanies this narrative of "On the Shore of the East China Sea" further highlights the metaphor of non-oppressive and anti-militaristic power that the tidal wave represents. As spectators listen to this narrative, they are also welcomed to images of Lou's children telling their grandfather's stories. They are each individually framed in a line as simplified, almost childlike images of ocean waves undulate below them. During the tidal wave narrative we suddenly see the feet of the Lou children jumping up and down upon a rocky surface, as if illustrating the words of their grandfather adding an element of playfulness to the imagery. The ludic and humorous component of the tidal wave metaphor thus stands in sharp contrast to the very real destructive capabilities of U.S. military technologies touted by Gary.

As mentioned above, the participation of the artist's children is significant in *Stories on My Back*. Gloria, Magda, Maricela, and Ming Lou have been frequent collaborators in their father's work, often offering their skills in narrating, acting, singing, and/or playing musical instruments for his performances and installations. In this particular work, their voices coupled with their appearances in photographs and videos are ubiquitous throughout the installation. Lou wanted them to own the stories told in the piece, in particular those that pertained to their Chinese heritage. Their participation also speaks to the dynamic and collective nature of oppositional memory, as Machida explains:

> Even as memories come to us through the interior stories we tell about ourselves ... , it is through our contact with other people that memory is renewed. Indeed, memory ... is not simply retrieved but is actively and continually reconstituted each time people come together to remember.
>
> (125)

The Lou children's deployment of memory is evident in "On the Shore of the East China Sea," which showcases their speaking and performing skills, with Ming playing the role of the grandfather and Magda speaking in Gary's voice. Gloria and Maricela shared the third-person narrator duties. While Lou let his children distribute the roles among themselves, he insisted that they all speak during the climax of the story, namely the telling of the tidal wave metaphor. He wanted them to own what he called "the strange power" of that particular part of the story, to make of it what they will (email exchange between Richard Lou and Guisela Latorre, June 20, 2014). As people of color of a younger generation, the Lou children benefit from the powerful histories of their transnational family. They possess a conflicted and tenuous sense of belonging to canonic U.S. history and culture which often ignores the contribution and experiences of racialized populations so these stories are meant to transform Gloria, Maricela, Magda, and Ming into fully constituted subjects who are free to inscribe their own meaning into these narratives.

While *Stories On My Back* centers on the expressions of resistance enacted by various members of the Lou family, the installation also underscores the discourses of assimilation that are part of transnational migration and bicultural experiences. The cornhusk-covered pillars contained hidden speakers that played the voices of the four Lou children each telling the same narrative about their grandfather. Visitors to the installation were thus encouraged to move their bodies through these columns of sound in order to appreciate the layered narrative. Spectators here learn of the unorthodox strategy the elder Lou utilized to rid himself of his Chinese accent before World War II or the "big guiltless war," as the younger Lou called it: "WWII is always touted as a just war and the generation that grew up during that time is known as the 'Great Generation'," the artist explained, "all wars since then ...

have always been a source of some form of public shame" (email exchange between Richard Lou and Guisela Latorre, June 20, 2014). Notwithstanding, the elder Lou routinely placed smooth pebbles in his mouth found in Moon Lake close to the Mississippi River to "grind the Chinese out of every English word," as the Lou children recounted in the installation. His motivations for such actions can certainly be read as a desire for assimilation and an attempt to erase one of the markers of difference that coded him as a racial other, namely his accent. Ethnic studies scholars have long argued that language and the ability to fluently speak English (or not) are often telling measures for an immigrant's "successful" assimilation into white U.S. culture. Rosina Lippi-Green observed, for instance, that "there is a special stigma attached to [the] presence [of Asians] which is externalized in reaction to the way they speak English" (286). Moreover, Lou senior knew that his accent was not seen as a sign of his bilingualism and superior linguistic knowledge, but rather as an indicator of his tenuous access to language altogether, as English in U.S. white supremacist culture has long been regarded as the only legitimate language. Thus, an inability to speak properly, according to this colonialist mentality, suggests a pre-linguistic and therefore primitive stage of development.

Lou's actions then at Moon Lake denote a certain internalization of such tropes on language and assimilation, yet certain details about the narrative betray a more complex strategy of survival and self-determination. The Lou children explain to the spectator that English was a language their grandfather despised because "its source was brutal to his people." As a matter of fact, the elder Lou associated the English language with the British for whom he held nothing but contempt as he had witnessed their colonial incursions into Canton Province. He nevertheless rid himself of the accent achieving an "impeccable" result, as described in the narrative. The seeming contradiction between Lou's disdain for the English language and his desire to perfect it somehow create a purposeful ambivalence behind his motivation. Rather than making himself subservient to this strange language, he claims mastery and control over it in order to speak back to power. Such a tactic is akin to a common strategy among people of color who often appropriate the tools of the powerful to challenge the dominance of the colonizers. Moreover, the Lou children explain that his actions were guided by pragmatism, a trait that they attribute to his Chinese heritage instead of his desire to emulate U.S. culture. So the kind of balance between assimilation and resistance that their grandfather offers in this story serves as a model for the younger generations in the family. Thus, the Lou children inherit from their grandfather's generation both the benefits and challenges of being people of color in the U.S. How far will they assimilate? What forms of resistance will they enact? Gloria, Magda, Maricela, and Ming's retelling and remembering of the Moon Lake story puts them in the position to negotiate and situate their own subjectivity within the predicaments of resistance and assimilation often faced by people of color.

The imagery of the elder Lou with stones in his mouth took on an allegoric and symbolic dimension in an early installation of *Stories on My Back*. Here the artist placed a series of photographic light boxes along the gallery wall depicting Gloria, Magda, Maricela, and Ming. In front of the boxes we see the children juggle the stones from the story as these float before them in a circular formation. On the adjacent sides of the boxes these same figures display a stone on their tongues as they open their mouths. The delicate and ethereal quality of the boxes themselves resembles Chinese lanterns. At the same time, the cornhusks lining the edges of the boxes allude to Mexican/Chicano culture, thus creating a hybrid and transnational aesthetic. The floating stones are inscribed with words from the Moon Lake narrative while the ones in the children's mouths reveal the Lou family name written in

Chinese characters. The transgenerational connection that the artist forges between the children and their grandfather is rendered concrete through the merging of sound narratives and visual display. In these photographs the children bear the stones inherited from their grandfather but rather than becoming a burden or source of pain and violence, these rocks become important attributes to their personas. The history of assimilation but also strength and determination that these objects signify is exemplified in the photographs through the varied facial expression of the children. Gloria returns the viewer's gaze with an air of confidence and resolve. Maricela and Magda smile at the spectator in a playful fashion, almost appearing to be amused by the floating stones. Ming seems more introspective, however, as he examines the rocks trying to make sense of them. The diverse forms of body language that they deploy stand for their individual and unique responses to their grandfather's legacy. Rather than imposing a specific interpretation or reading of the Moon Lake story, the artist opts instead to leave the door open, so to speak, so that Gloria, Maricela, Magda, and Ming can devise their own strategies and tactics of decolonization.

Lou underscored the theme of masculinity and gender not only in the experiences of his Chinese father, but also in the stories about his Mexican mother. Narrated by his eldest daughter Gloria, "A Love Letter to my Mother" is another oral testimony that enriches the multimedia components of Stories on My Back. Written in the first person narrative, the artist directly speaks to his mother Guillermina, apologizing to her on behalf of her father who left her when she was a child. "Lo siento," Gloria's voice utters, "I'm sorry my grandfather Rodolfo abandoned you." This wrenching scene of separation and betrayal takes place in a train station where Guillermina's father sends her, her siblings, and mother away. As the sequence of events unfolds, we realize that the story is actually a recollection of a recollection; in other words, it is Lou's memory of his mother recounting the day her father deserted her. In white patriarchal culture, a retelling of a retelling is considered hearsay and thus illegitimate and unreliable knowledge. Lou, however, taps into the importance of popular oral culture among Mexican and Chicana/o communities, where family history is passed down from generation to generation and is made more real and palpable with each retelling.

The story told in "A Love Letter to my Mother" focuses on Guillermina's reaction to her father's callous neglect. Her anger, disappointment, and disbelief take center stage. What is also explicit is her strength and determination before adversity: "The only thing small about you was your body," Gloria's enthusiastic voice explains, "to everyone else you were larger than life itself." Guillermina's courage and resolve stand in sharp contrast to her father's cowardice and lack of accountability, as the narrative makes explicit: "You were the brave one at age 8 and he never became a full man, a true hombre." It is clear that Lou's grandfather fails to achieve the new and egalitarian masculinity his Chinese father accomplished. It is his mother's courage then and not his grandfather's negligence that ultimately makes Lou into "un hombre bien hecho," a fully formed man. With this narrative the artist challenges prevailing images of the stereotypical Latino male. In his work on male identity and machismo, Alfredo Mirandé argues that the word "macho" resides within a bind of conflicting meanings:

> When applied to entertainers, athletes, or other 'superstars,' the implied meaning is clearly a positive one that connotes strength, virility, masculinity and sex appeal. But when applied to Mexicans and Latinos, 'macho' remains imbued with such negative attributes as male dominance, patriarchy, authoritarianism and spousal abuse.

(66)

Such contradictory meanings point to how conceptions of maleness are simultaneously defined by gender and race. Mirandé further complicates these gendered discourses by asserting that within Mexican and Latino cultures a different, albeit romanticized, image of "macho" emerges: "*Un hombre que es macho* is not hyper-masculine or aggressive, and he does not disrespect or denigrate women. Machos, according to the positive view, adhere to a code of ethics that stresses humility, honor, respect of oneself and others, and courage" (67). Mirandé connects this particular view of machismo to Mexican nationalist ideals and resistance to foreign invaders while also underscoring how the Mexican film industry promoted this image.

What all these views of *machismo* lack, however, is a concern with how men of color really live in transnational realities. Lou's rejection of his maternal grandfather's sense of male privilege and entitlement stem in part from his closeness and admiration for his mother, but also from his exposure to the transnationalism of his experience. Unlike the nationalist, romantic, and largely fictitious *macho* image promoted in Mexico, Lou's vision of masculinity is unconnected to specific national alliances or colonial notions of honor and chivalry. Instead, this vision of masculinity is associated with meaningful and egalitarian relationships with women in the family. Given that nationalist imaginaries often promote hierarchical gender relations in the family and elsewhere, radical transnational aesthetics have the potential to challenge those hierarchies because these don't necessarily respond to the regimes of the nation-state. Leela Fernandes has indicated that social movements against global capitalism use "transnational spaces of communication to develop new forms of transnational activism that built on but also exceeded local and national histories and practices of organizing" (102). While the story takes place in Mexico, the retelling happens in the United States, yet the narrative is not truly faithful to either nation. Nationalist notions of masculinity on either side of the border then are eschewed in favor of a vision of a maleness that is not allied to the neocolonial state.

The fact that Gloria, Lou's eldest daughter, narrates this family story of abandonment is significant. Even though this "love letter" is Lou's ode to his mother's strength of character, Gloria's retelling of this story breathes new life into Guillermina's experience. Her voice becomes animated when she talks about her grandmother's love of tree climbing, and wistful when she tells of Guillermina's own train departure near the end of the story. The emotional range she performs is indicative of how Gloria is creatively engaging the story according to her individuality. As the oldest daughter, her father entrusts her with his mother's memory and with her own meaning making. The process of making meaning in this narrative happens through the act of witnessing. Though the story is about Guillermina, it is also about Lou's own interpretation of that experience; in other words, it is about the artist's witnessing of his mother's struggles. The fact then that Gloria becomes the narrative voice for the story suggests that she is also witness to the difficulties and triumphs of the two generations before her. Guisela Latorre has argued elsewhere that, in the hands of radical artists of color, the act of witnessing is necessarily an oppositional one (75). Roger I. Simon and Claudia Eppert contend that, as opposed to spectatorship and voyeurism, witnessing implies an active process of making events and experiences meaningful to others: "Thus, witnessing is completed not by merely enduring the apprehension of difficult stories but by transporting and translating these stories beyond the moment of enunciation" (178). For Lou then, witnessing Guillermina's painful relationship with her father meant not only legitimizing her, but also translating those events for his own reality, in particular for his own identity as a man of color. Gloria's witnessing of both her father and mother's relationship then exposes her to nonpatriarchal visions of family and kinship, knowledge that is particularly useful as a woman of color surviving in a white patriarchal world.

Gloria's participation in *Stories on My Back* extended to her writing her own material and recollections of her grandmother Guillermina, indicating Lou's willingness to relinquish authorship and narrative control of the installation. Penned by Gloria herself, "Grandma's Story" recounts both a loving and painful memory of Guillermina who had become critically ill, as Lou would later explain: "My mother had a slow growing brain tumor—it was discovered in 1989 and operated on but they could not get all of it. What they left proved to be debilitating and then fatal 20 plus years later."[5] The story is about memory, in both its literal and figurative sense. Here Gloria recalls a conversation with Guillermina which highlighted the strong and powerful bonds the younger woman had established with her grandmother while at the same time underscoring the short and long-term memory lapses that the elder woman was experiencing at this point in her life. "There's such a difference from the grandmother I knew to the grandmother I know now," Gloria begins her narrative. Indeed, this Guillermina stands in sharp contrast to the one who loved to run and climb trees in "A Love Letter to my Mother." In "Grandma's Story" she only vaguely recognizes her granddaughter while repeatedly asking Gloria's name and age. Embedded in the dialogue, however, are the deep respect, admiration, and love the two women feel for one another. Throughout the conversation Gloria constantly works to maintain and hold together her grandmother's fading memory: "I'm Gloria, Grandma," "It's Gloria, Grandma," "I'm 23-years-old." The importance of remembering, in particular remembering kinship ties between the women in the family, becomes of critical importance in this narrative. But Gloria is not only reminding Guillermina of who she is; she is also reminding herself who she is in relationship to her grandmother.

For women of color, the matrilineal bonds forged between mothers, daughters, sisters, grandmothers, and other women in the family signify a powerful source of strength, wisdom, and resilience. Such bonds have been celebrated by women of color cultural producers since the 1970s, as was the case of Chicana artist Yolanda López's *Guadalupe Series* from 1978. This particular series consisted of pastel drawings where the artist cast herself, her mother, and her grandmother as the Virgen de Guadalupe. Though quite different from López's work, Gloria in "Grandma's Story" similarly values her bond with Guillermina as the younger woman patiently and affectionately coaxes her grandmother's memory throughout the narrative. The transgenerational dialogue that ensues in this story provides an important complement to the transnational aesthetic of the entire installation. Both Lou and his daughter Gloria transgress borders across generations, across nation-states, and across national histories, making their individual subjectivities into dynamic and mobile traits that are able to bridge personal, political, and collective concerns.

To conclude, the stories in this installation are from Lou's family history of migration, displacement, and belonging. As such, these narratives represent the various threads that make up the tapestry of his being as an artist and individual, but they are also evocative of larger transnational flows of peoples and capital. For this reason, the artist often extricates his own subjectivity from these accounts by refusing to use his own voice for narration. Instead, the narrators are his children who tell the stories both from their perspectives and from their father's. This multi-vocal narrative device works well to dislodge the idea of a sovereign subject who controls how the stories are told. The transnational family histories in *Stories on My Back* cannot be told through an omnipresent narrator with a privileged worldview, as these narratives are defined by the shifting boundaries of location and the organic relations between individuals. We can thus locate Lou's work within the "transnational turn" that Ramón Saldívar finds in the new millennium work of writers of color in the United States. Though Lou is primarily a visual artist, not a writer of fiction, his work also reveals the insufficiencies contained within the confines of the nation-state, be that Mexico, the United States, or China. Such insufficiencies are compounded by his inclusion of oral histories and popular culture motifs, both elements that are not necessarily bound by nationalist rhetoric either. Like the writers in Saldívar's study, the artist's work also emphasizes "the *limits* of national power ... by exceeding the bounds of nationally prescribed versions of culture, economics, and politics" (10).

Notes

1 For more information on Richard Lou's previous work, see Guisela Latorre, "Border Consciousness and Artivist Aesthetics: Richard Lou's Performance and Multimedia Artwork." *American Studies Journal* (Germany), no. 57.

2 Dana Leibsohn. "China-Mexico-America: Richard Lou's Stories on My Back," scholar essay posted on the website of the School of Art of the Texas Tech University, http://www.depts.ttu.edu/art/Archive/fall2013/exhibitschedule/lou/louScholarEssay.php

3 Though many humanities scholars such as Stephanie Rose, Trent Watts, Emily Chivers Yochim, among others, have problematized the connection between lack of emotion and white masculinity, some social scientists have found that the image of the stoic white macho still affects the behavior of young men. Niobe Way et. al. observed that teenage boys can and do resist masculine norms as adolescents, but are hyper conscious of these gendered expectations, as one of the young teenage boys in their study responded: "As a man—a male—there's an expectation for you, you know, not to show emotion or, you know, be emotional and not indulge in, you know, 'sissy' things." Niobe Way, Jessica Cressen, Samuel Bodian, Justin Preston, Joseph Nelson, and Diane Hughes, "'It Might Be Nice to Be a Girl ... Then You Wouldn't Have to Be Emotionless': Boys' Resistance to Norms of Masculinity During Adolescence." *Psychology of Men & Masculinity* 15:3 (2014): 245.

4 "World War II Homefront Era: 1940s: Momentous Change for Chinese Americans." Oakland Museum of California. Available at: www.museumca.org/picturethis/timeline/world-war-ii-homefront-era-1940s/chinese-american-culture/info

5 Email conversation between Guisela Latorre and Richard Lou, July 20, 2015.

Bibliography

Dobson, Kit and Aine McGlynn, eds. *Transnationalism, Activism, Art.* Toronto: University of Toronto Press, 2013.

Fernandes, Leela. *Transnational Feminism in the United States: Knowledge, Ethics, and Power.* New York: New York University Press, 2013.

Guevarra, Rudy. *Becoming Mexipino: Multiethnic Identities and Communities in San Diego.* New Brunswick, NJ: Rutgers University Press, 2012.

Habell-Pallán, Michelle. *Locomotion: The Travels of Chicana and Latina Popular Culture.* New York: New York University Press, 2005.

Han, Chong-suk. "Being an Oriental, I Could Never Be Completely a Man: Gay Asian Men and the Intersection of Race, Gender, Sexuality, and Class," *Race, Gender & Class* 13:3/4 (2006): 82–97.

Latorre, Guisela. "Border Consciousness and Artivist Aesthetics: Richard Lou's Performance and Multimedia Artwork." *American Studies Journal* (Germany), no. 57, 2012. http://www.asjournal.org/57-2012/richard-lous-performance-and-multimedia-artwork/

Latorre, Guisela. "Exiled Creativity and Immigrant Aesthetics: The Politically Transformative Work of Liliana Wilson." In *Ofrenda: Liliana Wilson's Art of Dissidence and Dreams.* Ed., Norma Cantú. College Station, TX: Texas A & M University Press, 2015. 69–81.

Leibsohn, Dana. "China-Mexico-America: Richard Lou's Stories on My Back," scholar essay. School of Art, Texas Tech University. 2013. Available at: http://www.depts.ttu.edu/art/Archive/fall2013/exhibitschedule/lou/louScholarEssay.php

Lippi-Green, Rosina. *English With an Accent: Language, Ideology and Discrimination in the United States*, 2nd Edition. New York: Routledge, 2011.

Machida, Margo. *Unsettled Visions: Contemporary Asian American Artists and the Social Imaginary.* Durham, NC: Duke University Press, 2008.

Marchetti, Gina. *Romance and the "Yellow Peril": Race, Sex, and Discursive Strategies in Hollywood Fiction.* Oakland: University of California Press, 1993.

Mirandé, Alfredo. *Hombres y Machos: Masculinity and Latino Culture.* Boulder, CO: Westview Press, 1997.

Saldívar, Ramón. "Imagining Cultures: The Transnational Imaginary in Postrace America." *The Imaginary and Its Worlds: American Studies After the Transnational Turn.* Eds Laura Bieger, Ramón Saldívar, Johannes Voelz. Hanover, NH: Dartmouth College Press, 2013. 3–22.

Simon, Roger I. and Claudia Eppert. "Remembering Obligation: Pedagogy and the Witnessing of Testimony of Historical Trauma." *Canadian Journal of Education/ Review canadienne de l'éducation* 22:2 (1997): 175–91.

Way, Niobe, Jessica Cressen, Samuel Bodian, Justin Preston, Joseph Nelson, and Diane Hughes. "'It Might Be Nice to Be a Girl … Then You Wouldn't Have to Be Emotionless': Boys' Resistance to Norms of Masculinity During Adolescence." *Psychology of Men & Masculinity* 15:3 (2014): 241–52.

20

REVISING THE ARCHIVE

Documentary Portraiture in the Photography of Delilah Montoya

Stephanie Lewthwaite

In his study of the "Chicano/a photographic," Colin Gunckel claims that Chicano/a visual culture scholars often neglect photography in favor of film, posters, and mural art. Yet photographers remain some of the most experimental and pioneering image makers: they have been responsible for turning the medium into a weapon of activism during the Chicano Movement, influencing the broader direction of Chicano/a visual culture, and developing an alternative archive that has enabled Chicano/as to see themselves beyond the racialized stereotypes perpetuated by the mass media (377–8). While many movement-era photographers engaged the documentary mode, they also recognized its limitations in terms of relaying impartial images, noting in particular its capacity to objectify the ethnic subject. The 1993 exhibition *From the West: Chicano Narrative Photography* took the subjugating force of the camera as its cue, highlighting some of the important strategies used by contemporary Chicano/a photographers to expose the constructedness of the image and its underlying ideology. In their accompanying essays, Chon A. Noriega (12–14) and Jennifer A. González (18–21) found Chicano/a photographers replaying dominant modes of visual representation, namely documentary and landscape photography, ethnographic portraiture, and the Western film genre, in order to turn exclusionary narratives about the West and Chicano/a culture upside down.

One of the photographers operating in this "negotiated space" (Noriega 12) was Delilah Montoya, who featured in *From the West* with *Shooting the Tourist*, a series in which she returned the objectifying gaze of the Anglo-American tourist through the popular format of the tourist postcard. An examination of Montoya's body of work reveals how Chicano/as have employed the photographic image in productive and subversive ways, exposing its oppressive history while turning it toward the articulation of new forms of subjectivity. Montoya has consistently explored the limits and possibilities of documentary photography to build an alternative archive that critiques race, class, and gender-based oppression. Replaying the conventions of documentary portraiture in particular, Montoya compels us to look again at popular, historical, and religious icons that suffer from misrepresentation, as well as maligned, denigrated, and oppressed everyday figures whose struggles and sacrifices make them equally worthy of inclusion in her alternative Chicano/a pantheon. Infusing the documentary mode with forms of conceptual and collaborative photography, and ranging across the terrains of digital photography, nineteenth-century collotype printing, collage, and multi-media installation, Montoya's work draws our attention to what Mick Gidley calls the "voracious, promiscuous and changeable" nature of photography (10), and the ability of the camera to recover what has been lost from view.

Born in Fort Worth, Texas, in 1955 to an Anglo-American father and New Mexican Hispana mother, Montoya grew up in Omaha, Nebraska, where she began working in commercial photography and for "small town newspapers" in the mold of the photojournalist (Montoya 2014 quoted in "Interview"). Montoya later returned to her mother's home of New Mexico, taking a post as a medical photographer and studying for her BA, MA, and MFA in photography and printmaking between 1984 and 1994. Influenced by the Chicano Movement during her early encounters with Mexican migrant workers and the Chicano Brown Berets in Nebraska, Montoya has used photography to explore her Chicana/Hispana ancestry and the ways in which histories of race, colonialism, mestizaje, and religious syncretism have shaped Chicano/a culture and the visual arts. "Inspired by the [Chicano] movement," without being "totally informed by it" (Montoya 2005, "Mirror" 1), Montoya participated in the first significant exhibition of Chicano/a art, *Chicano Art: Resistance and Affirmation, 1965–1985* (1990). She has since exhibited in major exhibitions of Chicano/a and Latino/a art regionally and nationally, and most recently, in the Smithsonian's *Our America: The Latino Presence in American Art* (2013). As a photographer interested in the history of the medium, Montoya explains that she has always looked to the "personal realities that form our lived experiences," but also to "those cultures that have a profound influence on how my world is understood" (Montoya 2005, "Mirror" 1; Montoya 2013, "Our Ancestry"). This has led Montoya to interrogate traditions of visual representation that marginalize the collective Chicano/a body, and to simultaneously engage with and critique the mode of documentary photography, a genre once associated with the objective depiction of everyday life and its human subjects in which the photographic image was deemed above the manipulation of the fine artist.

From supporting the colonial gaze, ethnographic spectacle, patriarchal rule, and the pseudo-scientific fields of physiognomy, phrenology, and criminology, photography as a form of documentation has long been tied to an oppressive visual archive founded on strategies of surveillance, discipline, and othering (Sekula 6–7; Henning 173–75). In exploring this history, Montoya has compared the documentary mode with Surrealism: both relied, she explains, on "looking for the spectacle" (personal interview) and "seek[ing] out untamed realities" associated with "primitive" others (Montoya 2005, "Mirror" 2–4). In terms of the West and New Mexico, Montoya has worked against an existing photographic archive that comprises the ethnographic portraiture of Native peoples, early modernist landscapes stripped of ethnic bodies, and the Farm Security Administration's documentary photographs of Hispano villages from the 1930s. More recently, police and law enforcement agencies have used photographic portraiture to create an archive of Chicano gang members, thus perpetuating the correlation between the Chicano body and criminality (Rodríguez 257). Evidence of Montoya speaking back to these iconographies can be found in *El Sagrado Corazón/The Sacred Heart* (1993), in which she depicts a Chicano/a genealogy through individual portraits of key historical, religious, and contemporary cultural figures. In "La

Figure 20.1   Contemporary Casta Portraiture: Nuestra "Calidad." Casta #2, 2013, archival inkjet, 32 x 24 in. Reproduced with permission of the artist

Genízara," the image of a captive, dehispanicized Native girl in buckskin clothing echoes Edward Curtis's "vanishing" North American Indian, but without the "authenticity" of tribal identity; the backdrops to Montoya's portraits resemble the interiors of chapels belonging to New Mexico's Hispano lay confraternity, the Penitente Brotherhood, which modernist photographers such as Ansel Adams shot as uninhabited, timeless, and abstract spaces; while "Los Jovenes" (Youths) portrays a group of *cholo/as* not as criminals but as assertive and talented graffiti artists. The link between portraiture and bodily oppression in the Americas predates the advent of photography, however. Montoya's work also speaks back to a longer history of portraiture that includes religious iconography and Catholic allegory and the colonial eighteenth-century *casta* painting tradition, which used family portraits of mothers, fathers, and mixed-ancestry children to classify racial types along a social spectrum. For example, Montoya's most recent project, *Contemporary Casta Portraiture: Nuestra "Calidad"* (2013–), revisits the *casta* tradition, using sixteen family portraits from New Mexico and Texas to reveal the persistence of the colonial caste system in contemporary U.S. society (see Figure 20.1). This historical archive and its collusion in othering along the axes of race, class, and gender explain Montoya's commitment to restaging the Chicano/a body through the genre of portraiture.

As Ernst van Alphen notes, "artists who have made it their project to challenge the originality and homogeneity of human subjectivity or the authority of mimetic representation, often choose the portrait as the genre to make their point" (242). In working against the "repressive" visual archive (Sekula 6), Montoya also exploits the popular and potentially democratic scope of documentary portraiture. Painted and photographic portraits are unstable forms that generate openings for agency, self-fashioning, and the recording of non-elite, vernacular, and communal expressions. For example, while documentary photography remains tied to the depiction of everyday social realities (Price 108–9), photography as a popular mass medium in the private realm often records forms of popular memory and alternative, unofficial histories (West 14; Price and Wells 23). Furthermore, as Allan Sekula notes, portraiture also serves an "honorific" function, a function that was able "to proliferate downward" during the nineteenth century with the advent of photography (6). In many cases, "honorific" portraiture created a pantheon, a gallery of "exemplars"—elite men, saints, martyrs, beautiful and virtuous women, and more recently, artists and celebrities—that articulated narratives of national progress, exceptionalism, whiteness, morality, and static notions of masculinity and femininity (Hutchinson 330–1). Montoya replays the "honorific" function of portraiture, drawing on the popular and everyday iconographies associated with documentary photography to create an alternative vernacular pantheon of Chicano/a icons. In order to revise existing popular and religious icons and transfigure the everyday Chicano/a body, Montoya employs strategies of collaboration, role-play, and parody.

To grant her subjects agency and embed vernacular and communal expressions in the image, Montoya often practices a form of collaborative photography. In *El Sagrado Corazón* (1993) Montoya expands her understanding of religious symbols as "pop icons" that appear on barrio walls and on bodies, "tattooed on the arms of working class youth," inscribed on "brilliant white cotton T-shirts," and even "transformed into holograms on plastic clocks" (Montoya, 23). To honor the ways in which ritual and sacrifice are grounded in everyday life and performed in and through the body, Montoya invited members of an Albuquerque barrio to interpret their understanding of the Sacred Heart by role-playing historical figures and traditional religious and popular icons in everyday scenes of work, spiritual contemplation, ritual, and artistry. The resulting silver gelatin and collotype prints in *El Sagrado Corazón* brought Montoya's own family members and fictive kin into the roles of oppressed and honored figures—her cousin as a captive Native girl in "La Genízara" and her mechanic Apolinar "Polo" García as Jesus in "Jesus' Carburetor Repair," which Montoya described as "a metaphor for Jesus repairing hearts" (Montoya, 24). *Sacred Heart* also elevated denigrated art forms by incorporating the work of local graffiti artists into the backdrops of Montoya's installations. In honoring a vernacular barrio aesthetic, Montoya encouraged her subjects to sign their names on the artwork, thus undermining the professionalization of portrait painting that developed from the sixteenth century onward (West 16). Montoya described her collaboration as a form of "creative and energetic interdependence" (Montoya, 24). This "interdependence" also characterized Montoya's photographic installation, *La Guadalupana* (1998), which depicted the tattooed back of a handcuffed prison inmate, Félix Martínez. When Martínez was killed not long after the piece was completed, his family and community contributed to the *ofrenda* in the gallery, thus extending the ways in which the subject's oppressed body, marked by a tattoo of Guadalupe, had become an altar in itself (Montoya n.d., "Artist Statement"; Kuusinen 46, 53).

As well as using the camera to promote communal solidarity, Montoya also reconfigures the honorific tradition of portraiture by transforming everyday Chicano/a bodies into sacred icons. Asta Kuusinen has explored the ways in which the subject "becomes divine" in Montoya's *Sacred Heart* series and *La Guadalupana* (54). In *La Guadalupana*, Félix Martínez's marked body and handcuffed arms invoke Christ's crucified body tied to the cross, thus blurring the division between saint and sinner, according to Constance Cortez (46). Montoya also described Martínez as "a symbolic Xipe Totec," the Aztec god of war and sacrifice, explaining that his tattooed body invoked both the flayed skin of Xipe Totec and the *tilma* (cloak) of Juan Diego on which Tonantzín/Guadalupe appeared ("Artist Statement"; "On Photographic Digital Imaging" 186). Montoya had first explored the strategy of transfiguring everyday bodies marked by sacrifice and oppression into religious icons in the earlier series *Saints and Sinners* (1992). Here, Montoya placed secular objects and photographic images of loss and violence in contemporary New Mexico into a series of glass jars to portray the Stations of the Cross. Describing the jar as the body and its contents as the soul in the manner of a portrait, Montoya explained that the series represented "the alchemist's method of transmutation," through which original matter is combined with another to "change it into a superior material" ("It's All About the Apple"). This very "method of transmutation," transfiguring the everyday and the profane into the sacred, runs through Montoya's portraiture. Yet in elevating her subjects by replaying the "honorific," Montoya never dismisses the material traces of the "repressive," for her portraits continually tap into a collective consciousness of sacrifice and struggle.

This dynamic is most powerful in Montoya's depiction of everyday barrio women. Montoya has always said that she seeks to "approach ... [her subjects] from that point of dignity" (personal interview). As co-curator of the 2009 exhibition *Chicana Badgirls: Las Hociconas* (loudmouths), Montoya declared "the right to create work that represents our experiences as artists whose work is based on the lived reality of the struggles we encounter" (2). In Montoya's *Barrio Madonna*, for example, we see a shadowy, spectral-like figure seated with a child on her knee. While the blood-red background signifies the pain and sacrifice of contemporary barrio life, mother and child are bathed in a transcendent bluish-white light. Yet the faces of both are rendered in shadow, suggesting an image of the everywoman and everychild, and drawing our attention to the illuminated body as the site of pain, sacrifice, and healing, and the locus for a collective biography. Montoya's use of masking through the placement of shadow disrupts the emphasis on "faciality" in Western culture, the role of physiognomy in traditional portraiture (West 17), and the stereotypical ethereal beauty of the Madonna and child found in European Baroque painting. In her study of Chicana art and spirituality, Laura Pérez has examined the strategy of "defamiliarizing" the racialized body in Chicana (self) portraiture, in which layering and masks "interrupt negatively racialized visual readings of facial features" (284). In *Barrio Madonna*, the act of masking resists the objectification of the racialized and gendered body while referencing the wearing of the second skin that appears in Montoya's other works.

By honoring everyday women as religious icons, Montoya's photographs chime with a tradition in Chicana art and literature of imbuing secular women with divine power. Laura Pérez demonstrates how since the 1970s Chicanas have reconfigured racialized and gendered bodies, using images of daily life to depict "goddesses and popular culture superheroines" (259). For example, Yolanda López's *Guadalupe* (1978) triptych featured the artist, her mother, and grandmother as incarnations of La Virgen wearing running shoes and working a sewing machine. More recently, Alma López's *Our Lady* (1999) depicted a bikini-clad woman enshrined by a garland of roses and wearing a pre-Columbian cloak of stone, while Isis Rodríguez's work re-renders Guadalupe in "cartoon superheroine" style (280). Pérez calls this collective bank of images "a decolonizing visual gallery of the socially wronged" (281). Chicana literature has also helped to forge this alternative gallery. In her poem *La Diosa in Every Woman* (1996), Naomi Quiñonez constructs an alternative "woman's altar" on which everyday women are equated with Aztec goddesses, but without being oppressed by the masculinist world of ritual sacrifice (107). Similarly, Rita Cano Alcalá has interpreted Ana Castillo's novels as forging a new "hagiography" in which reworked "concepts of martyrdom and saintliness" are used to "canonize everyday women" and the denigrated figures of the *curandera, loca,* and *puta* (13–14). In the introduction to *Velvet Barrios,* the volume in which Cano's essay appears, Alicia Gaspar de Alba describes Chicano/a writers and artists as constructing a "barrio altar" of "icons and heroic figures that represent Chicano/a cultural beliefs and values about sexuality and gender" (xxiv). Montoya's pantheon fits alongside this hagiography and barrio altar, challenging the patriarchal values embedded in traditional portraiture and religious iconography.

Joanna Woodall argues that Western portraiture has historically "articulated the patriarchal principles of genealogy" (3), a point illustrated by the traditional family portrait in which the image of the "dominant male" has long persisted (Brilliant 92). Montoya subverts these conventions by depicting strong women, often against type, in domestic and non-domestic settings. For example, in "La Familia" from *El Sagrado Corazón,* Montoya upturns the gendered placement of bodies found in traditional images of the Holy Family: here, the woman takes center stage, standing behind the father who is seated holding the child. Similarly, in one of the early images from Montoya's *Contemporary Casta Portraiture* series, the mother, father, and child are pictured apart with the father to the rear, partially obscured by the wrought iron bars of an interior window in an image that resonates with Montoya's earlier photograph of Félix Martínez's imprisoned body. While the child watches a scene from *The Simpsons* on the television, the mother appears to the fore, shooting pool in a striking pose of strength, skill, and determination that gestures control over the home domain through a stereotypically male pastime.

In *Women Boxers: The New Warriors* (2006) Montoya again depicts women playing against traditional roles in a typically male sporting arena, that of professional boxing. *Women Boxers* appeared in numerous shows, including a New York exhibition with Chicana photographer Laura Aguilar, *Fuerzas Naturales: Against Type* (2008), and *Las Malcriadas* in Dallas, Texas (2006). Indeed, Montoya has often spoken of portraying *malcriadas,* meaning badly behaved women and girls (Montoya and Pérez 2; *Women Boxers* 19). In 2001, she participated in Santa Fe's *Las Malcriadas: Coloring out the Lines,* an exhibition of Chicana artists in support of Alma López, who had come under fierce attack in the same city that year for displaying her bikini-clad *Our Lady* (1999) in the *Cyber Arte: Tradition Meets Technology* show at the Museum of International Folk Art. Montoya's own *malcriadas* question the gendered conventions of the portrait and pantheon in which "codes of right behavior" and notions of virtue, beauty, femininity, and masculinity are enshrined (Brilliant 11).

The practice of transforming the denigrated and "monstrous" woman into an icon by honoring her strength, endurance, skill, and complexity remains at the heart of Montoya's work. In *Women Boxers,* this transformation relies on capturing the self-fashioning of powerful female athletes both inside and outside the ring. In "Terri 'Lil Loca' Lynn Cruz", Montoya captures Cruz with her arms crossed and head tilted in a resilient and defiant stance (see Figure 20.2). Her subject's posture, gaze, and marked body—Cruz's arm is tattooed with the barrio saying "smile now, cry later"—mirror the stance of Montoya's male subjects in "Los Jovenes" from *Sacred Heart.* Montoya's portrait of Cruz also illustrates Amalia Mesa-Bains's concept of "bodily aesthetics" in which the Chicano/a body displays a form of "aesthetic heroicism" against societal expectations and oppression (*Body/Culture* 9). By picturing Cruz outside the Sky Ute Casino, Colorado, and against the starkness of the white tent and blue sky, Montoya also reworks an earlier modernist iconography in which photographers such as Ansel Adams captured the empty doorways and entrances to the typically all-male domains of New Mexico's Penitente chapels. This time Montoya positions a woman who defies gendered codes of morality and behavior in front of a contemporary secular church dedicated to sporting prowess. Montoya's challenge to the patriarchal values of portraiture

Figure 20.2   Terri 'Lil Loca' Lynn Cruz, 2005, piezograph on Hahnemuhle Photo Rag 310, 25.75 x 25 in. Reproduced with permission of the artist

also relies on capturing the multifaceted character of her female subjects. In the exhibition catalog to *Women Boxers* we learn that Cruz has established a professional cleaning business to support her three children; in another image, she is pictured surrounded by her children and husband-trainer (42–3). Montoya's broader portfolio thus shows women boxers not just in the ring, but as working mothers who labor hard in other jobs to provide for their families. Speaking of *Women Boxers*, Montoya said she wanted to present "the beautiful movement" of boxing as "an art form," a "dance," and "to give these women a sense of history" (Montoya, quoted in Nott 24, 26). In granting her subjects dignity and a history, Montoya counters the way in which traditional portraiture and religious iconography stripped women of their diversity by promoting their "idealization and allegorization" (West 157).

Contemporary portraits in pop art and the mass media often extend this historical process by depoliticizing popular culture icons into one-dimensional celebrities and commodities. Speaking of the ways in which the "appropriation, commodification," and hypervisibility of Frida Kahlo have "robbed [the artist] of her complexity," Mesa-Bains, and bell hooks warns against such "cultural strip-mining," adding that Chicanas "need to be vigilant about [their] own self-representation." (*Homegrown* 36–7). Montoya explores this process in building her pantheon of everyday saints, sinners, and *malcriadas*, using popular, everyday culture to transform and politicize the traditionally maligned female figures of Chicano/a folklore. In her revisionist portrayals of La Llorona and Doña Sebastiana, Montoya transforms these figures into powerful and multifaceted icons by exploiting the very popular forms used to deny women their complexity. For example, Montoya's *Las Lloronas* (1996) installation at Hotel Santa Fe depicted La Llorona as a contemporary prostitute in a hotel bathroom graffitied with the title of the piece: "For a good time call 1-900 Llorona." Photographic portraits of women "expressing shock" at La Llorona's misdemeanors are repeated on the bathroom's mirror and shower curtain in a pop art fashion ("Artist Statement"). Yet Montoya subverts the ways in which popular media creates sensationalist stories and "untamed realities": by placing tabloids on the floor of the installation, she links contemporary news stories about real-life women forced to abort their children in similar hotel bathrooms with the fate of the Weeping Woman who killed her children.

Montoya's reference to tabloids mirrors the way in which La Llorona has featured in recent television series, advertisements, and horror movies. In following this, Montoya uses film culture to rework the figure of Doña Sebastiana. As the "allegorical icon for death," Sebastiana is traditionally represented in New Mexican folklore by a skeleton holding a bow and arrow; she is often drawn in a death cart by the Penitente Brotherhood during Holy Week ("Artist Statement"). Montoya questions the existing pantheon of saints, asking why Sebastiana's "complementary Western icon," the martyred Saint Sebastian, is depicted as a "euphoric looking Roman strapped to a column ... shot through the head, the trunk as well as the legs with arrows." In order to parallel the pre-Columbian iconography in which female deities represented death, the Catholic Church in the colonial Americas transformed Christian Sebastian into a woman ("San Sebastiana"). Unlike her male counterpart, however, Sebastiana the skeleton was stripped of humanity, defined by the all-male Penitente Brotherhood, carved by male *santeros*, and denied any form of self-representation. Montoya intervenes in the debate, suggesting that according to her mother's *cuentos*, "Sebastiana never wanted to be 'Death' ... all she wanted was love, if not love at least to be respected" ("Artist Statement"). Montoya has always declared her interest in using documentary "in a manner that explores our allegorical impulse" ("Mirror" 5). In her *San Sebastiana: Angel de la Muerte* (2002) installation, Montoya uses photography, performance art, and interactive online video to move beyond the idealized, allegorical portrait in which a woman is defined either by her beauty or by the loss of youth (in Sebastiana's case, by death itself).

Montoya's photographs and the accompanying interactive video explore Sebastiana's multiple identities as both *calaca* (skeleton) and beautiful diva. Montoya transforms Sebastiana into a movie icon who sees herself in her dressing room mirror as a fully-fleshed, seductive woman. In Montoya's installation, Sebastiana appears in a movie poster illuminated by lights as the Angel of Death. She is a celebrity intent on fashioning her own image through the many layers of the body: her white lace dress is unzipped in one portrait, baring her shoulders and back in seductive fashion; in another, she wears a tiara peering into a mirror in which we see a mannequin encased in a tight black bodice (see Figure 20.3).

Elsewhere, Sebastiana sports long, fake nails and makeup, a fan, hat, veil, and lustrous, voluminous curls that jar with the bare skull of the *calaca*. In the video, Sebastiana also bargains with God over her allotted role. In this conversation, God entices Sebastiana into becoming Death by describing her as "an artista, the personification of symmetry, beauty, and perfection" ("San Sebastiana"). If Montoya's installation plays on existing pantheons of elite women known as "beauties," it also taps into the history of Mexican popular calendars, in which the forms of cinematic idols such as Dolores del Rio and María Félix (who appears elsewhere in Montoya's oeuvre in a series of film stills) were used to imbue the everyday "campesino" figure with style and glamor. Speaking of this popular cultural form, Mesa-Bains suggests that "the glamorization of the everyday was the antithesis of the martyrdom and passion of religious iconography" (*Body/Culture* 8). If Montoya resists the traditional somber image of Sebastiana as religious icon, her subject's self-fashioning also mirrors the "urban feminizations" associated with the contemporary "*Ruca, Chola* or *carnala*," who according to Mesa-Bains, deploy similar strategies of "pose and detailing [and] ... elements of glamor, masking, protection and affiliation with the barrio" (*Body/Culture* 10). One *Los Angeles Times* critic recently described Sebastiana as a fusion of "Santa Muerte

Figure 20.3 *San Sebastiana: Lengua Negra*, 2002, inkjet on canvas, 3.5 x 2.5 in. Reproduced with permission of the artist

with a pop star," playing a role that could appear in a *Real Housewives of Albuquerque* show (Knight). Described by God in the video as "a diamond in the rough" with a "sense of drama," Sebastiana's everyday glamor and love of *chisme* also tie her to the barrio as a non-elite figure. We first witness this Doña or Lady gossiping on the telephone about the love lives and scandals of those in the barrio where "secrets ... circulate faster than money." We later discover that she has worked the everyday, marginal jobs of *curandera*, *puta*, bar tender, and tax collector ("San Sebastiana").

Thus, we see Sebastiana playing against type as "the ultimate *malcriada*," to quote Montoya ("Artist Statement"). She is a diva and seductress, a very human figure who blurs the distinction between popular and elite, beauty and monstrousness, life and death, virtue and vice, saint and sinner. She also bargains with God, resisting her allotted role as Death by declaring, "I'm not for hire" while musing that sainthood as Death will strip her of humanity and displace the human fear of a male god onto a woman. "How can I be human when I'm hated?" she declares ("San Sebastiana"). Constance Cortez describes Sebastiana's "ability to visualize her agency within these confines" as a form of "oppositional consciousness" (50). Certainly, Sebastiana's conversations with God contain an implicit critique of religious patriarchy while her self-fashioning defies conventions of class, gender, and propriety. If Sebastiana is the ultimate *malcriada*, she also presents us with the ultimate "anti-portrait" which, as Richard Brilliant claims (173), serves to parody the conventions of portraiture and its fixed labels and values and expose in turn, the incapacity of the portrait to embody the multiplicity of the subject. The ambivalent figure of Sebastiana, who eventually submits to God's wishes on the promise of sainthood, is a clear example of Montoya exploring the tension between women's multiple subjectivities and the power of the image, whether through religious iconography, traditional portraiture, or popular media, to objectify the female body. "Your personality has many facets and possibilities," declares God to Sebastiana in a compliment designed to manipulate her vanity and win her over ("San Sebastiana"). The reality, however, is that Doña cannot escape her one-dimensional fate. If Montoya reveals Sebastiana's malleable selfhood by moving beyond the conventional portrait, ultimately God—and the online viewer—choose her role. We are left with the sense that Sebastiana can only envision her true, empowered self in the mirror, and even this image remains vulnerable to fantasy and illusion. For these reasons, the very human Sebastiana can be found alongside the everyday Chicana body in Montoya's pantheon, a pantheon that honors the subject without denying the historically repressive trace of the portrait.

In an interview, Montoya once questioned: "How many times do you look in the mirror to reaffirm who you are? But, if you've never had that mirror, how do you know who you are? If the mirror has huge sections broken off, you'll never understand the complete picture or vision" (Montoya quoted in Barbatelli). Montoya's mirror analogy suggests the ways in which photography and the portrait have historically failed to capture the multifaceted realities of Chicano/a subjectivity. In exploring the limits and possibilities of documentary portraiture, Montoya questions the existing archive. Fusing the popular and everyday nature of the documentary mode with the honorific function of portraiture, Montoya creates a new vernacular pantheon in which the everyday Chicano/a body is transfigured, and popular and religious icons revised. Montoya's pantheon is part of a broader Chicana tradition of building vernacular and woman-centered altars on which inequalities of race, class, and gender are critiqued and established notions of sainthood, martyrdom, sin, and sacrifice upturned. In Montoya's altar, everyday barrio figures are canonized and existing icons, saints, and sinners are shown in their glory and humanity as figures who perform against type and resist the confines of patriarchy and class and race-based oppression. In questioning fixed categories, Montoya's photographic portraiture is a perfect illustration of "how a genre can be liberated from its history so that it can become an arena for new significations" (van Alphen 254). In this new arena, mothers, breadwinners, boxers, everyday celebrities, and saints become icons who retain their complexity, strength, and resilience, and often, like Sebastiana, their very human flaws. Rather than re-idealizing women, Montoya's pantheon suggests that it is women's very flaws and scars that make them worthy of celebration. Montoya proves that "la diosa is in every woman," and that the goddess comes from the very struggles and sacrifices of everyday life.

Bibliography

Alcalá, Rita Cano. "A Chicana Hagiography for the Twenty-first Century: Ana Castillo's *Locas Santas*." *Velvet Barrios: Popular Culture and Chicana/o Sexualities*. Ed. Alicia Gaspar de Alba. New York: Palgrave Macmillan, 2003. 3–15.

Barbatelli, Victoria. "Denver Latina Inspired Educator." *The Denver Post*, 13 Oct. 2013.

Brilliant, Richard. *Portraiture*. London: Reaktion, 1991.

Cortez, Constance. "History/Whose-Story? Postcoloniality and Contemporary Chicana Art." *Chicana/Latina Studies* 6:2 (2007): 22–54.

Gaspar de Alba, "Introduction, or, Welcome to the Closet of Barrio Popular Culture." *Velvet Barrios: Popular Culture and Chicana/o Sexualities*. Ed. Alicia Gaspar de Alba. New York: Palgrave Macmillan, 2003. xiv–xxviii.

Gidley, Mick. *Photography and the USA*. London: Reaktion, 2011.

González, Jennifer A. "Negotiated Frontiers." *From the West: Chicano Narrative Photography*. Curator Chon A. Noriega. San Francisco: Mexican Museum, 1995. 17–22.

Gunckel, Colin. "The Chicano/a Photographic: Art as Social Practice in the Chicano Movement." *American Quarterly* 67:2 (2015): 377–412.

Henning, Michelle. "The Subject as Object: Photography and the Human Body." *Photography: A Critical Introduction.* Ed. Liz Wells. Milton Park, Oxon. and New York: Routledge, 2009. 167–204.

Hutchinson, Elizabeth. "From Pantheon to Indian Gallery: Art and Sovereignty on the Early Nineteenth-Century Cultural Frontier." *Journal of American Studies* 47:2 (2013): 313–37.

"Interview with Serie Project 15 Artist Delilah Montoya." YouTube, 25 Nov. 2008.

Knight, Christopher. "Walking among Saints and Sinners at Fowler Museum." *Los Angeles Times,* 23 April 2014.

Kuusinen, Asta M. "Ojo de la Diosa: Becoming Divine in Delilah Montoya's Art Photography." *Aztlán* 33:1 (2008): 32–61.

Mesa-Bains, Amalia. "Chicano Bodily Aesthetics." *Body/Culture: Chicano Figuration.* Rohnert Park, CA: University Art Gallery, Sonoma State University, 1990. 6–13.

Mesa-Bains, Amalia, and bell hooks. *Homegrown: Engaged Cultural Criticism.* Cambridge, MA: Southend Press, 2006.

Montoya, Delilah. "Artist Statement." Delilah Montoya homepage. n.d.

Montoya, Delilah. "It's All About the Apple, or is it? Artist Statement." *Women Artists of the American West.* n.d.

Montoya, Delilah. "San Sebastiana, 'Angel de la Muerte.'" Interactive online video. n.d.

Montoya, Delilah. "Using a Cultural Icon to Explore a People's Heart." *Nieman Reports* 55:2 (2001): 21–5.

Montoya, Delilah. "On Photographic Digital Imaging." *Aztlán: A Journal of Chicano Studies* 27:1 (2002): 181–89.

Montoya, Delilah. "Mirror, Mirror: The Latino/a as the 'Other' in the Fine Arts." 2005.

Montoya, Delilah. *Women Boxers: The New Warriors.* Houston: Arte Público Press, 2006.

Montoya, Delilah. "Our Ancestry." Nuestra Calidad: Contemporary Casta Portraits. 2013.

Montoya, Delilah. Personal interview with the author. 6 April 2014.

Montoya, Delilah, and Laura E. Pérez. *Chicana Badgirls: Las Hociconas.* Albuquerque: 516 Arts, 2009.

Noriega, Chon A. "Many Wests." *From the West: Chicano Narrative Photography.* Curator Chon A. Noriega. San Francisco: Mexican Museum, 1995. 9–15.

Nott, Robert. "Perfect Ladies." *Santa Fe New Mexican,* 1 June 2001. Santa Fe New Mexican Archives.

Pérez, Laura E. *Chicana Art: The Politics of Spiritual and Aesthetic Altarities.* Durham, NC: Duke University Press, 2007.

Price, Derrick. "Surveyors and Surveyed: Photography Out and About." *Photography: A Critical Introduction.* Ed. Liz Wells. Abingdon, Oxon. and New York: Routledge, 2009. 65–115.

Price, Derrick, and Liz Wells. "Thinking about Photography: Debates, Historically and Now." *Photography: A Critical Introduction.* Ed. Liz Wells. Abingdon, Oxon. and New York: Routledge, 2009. 9–64.

Quiñonez, Naomi, "La Diosa in Every Woman." *Chicana Criticism and Creativity: New Frontiers in American Literature.* Eds. María Herrera-Sobek and Helena María Viramontes. Albuquerque: University of New Mexico Press. 104–7.

Rodríguez, Richard T. "On the Subject of Gang Photography." *Gangs and Society: Alternative Perspectives.* Eds. Louis Kontos, David C. Brotherton, and Luis Barrios. New York: Columbia University Press, 2003. 255–82.

Sekula, Allan. "The Body and the Archive." *October* 39 (1986): 3–64.

van Alphen, Ernst. "The Portrait's Dispersal: Concepts of Representation and Subjectivity in Contemporary Portraiture." *Portraiture: Facing the Subject.* Ed. Joanna Woodall. Manchester: Manchester University Press, 1997. 239–56.

West, Shearer. *Portraiture.* New York: Oxford University Press, 2004.

Woodall, Joanna, ed. *Portraiture: Facing the Subject.* Manchester: Manchester University Press, 1997.

Part IV

QUOTIDIAN POP

21

FARMWORKER-TO-TABLE MEXICAN

Decolonizing Haute Cuisine

Paloma Martínez-Cruz

Mexican and Chicana/o citizens and denizens of the United States get a sad laugh from the national condition that embraces its love affair with Mexican food at the same time as it evinces obsessive hostility toward the presence of its people. In 2013, the Taco Bell fast food chain was ranked sixth in the nation in terms of system-wide sales, beating out Dunkin' Donuts, KFC, Pizza Hut, and Chick-fil-A, with Chipotle occupying the sixteenth rank. Thirty-seventh and thirty-eighth positions were held by Del Taco and Qdoba Mexican Grill, respectively, with El Pollo Loco hanging onto the forty-first spot.[1] Family-owned taquerías dot the nation's boulevards, strip malls, highways, and byways; and fine dining, once reserved for European fare, is now seeing interpretations of Mexican "regional," "authentic," and/or "modern" cooking on menus earmarked for the gastronomically chic. Place this data alongside the "Deporter-in-Chief" reputation earned by Obama's administration—during Obama's first year in office he oversaw a record 387,000 people forcibly removed from the country, which represented an increase from the 369,000 removed during Bush's last year in office,[2] or alongside Fox News's gleeful announcement that "many agree with Trump on immigration"[3]—and you have an understanding of the continuum of enthusiasm and disdain that characterizes national regard for its Mexican contributions.

As a Latina of Mexican and Puerto Rican heritage, I was always impressed by the palpable sensation that Mexican cooking had the power to afford a safety zone, a sensory dimension in which the presence of Mexican cultural patrimony meets with qualified tolerance. Mexican restaurants seemed as satellite consulates, where the main event was the food, but a residual side effect was the small window of permission open to other areas of expression such as language, music, fashion, visual art, and the geophysical presence of mestizo bodies both at work and leisure with family and friends. The cross-cultural and unembarrassed excitement for Mexican culinary achievements represented a situational moratorium on animosity toward Latina/o, mestiza/o, and indigenous people, where the fantasy of homogeneity was lifted as all the gathered tribes reveled in the sensual spell of salsa and cilantro. But the irony was a sad one. If only bordered bodies could circulate as freely and exaltedly as burritos! If only our children were as beloved as our chalupas!

If food provides the safest way to "do" Mexicanness in the national context, it also presents ready clichés and stereotypes. In the mainstream imaginary, tequila and "chimichangas" are sure to evoke insinuations of serious hangovers and digestive distress. Racial slurs targeting Mexicans link the people to the beans. What do you call a group of stoned Mexicans? Baked beans. What do you call a Mexican baptism? Bean dip. Why do Mexicans re-fry their beans? Have you seen a Mexican do anything right the first time? The Mexican food imaginary is not consistently healing, and its invocation is no guarantee of diversity, dignity, or pride.

By conducting critical, Américas-based research on the consumption of Mexican food and its recent emergence in the world of fine dining, I hope to identify some of the hidden and overt colonial orderings in our food chains, and invigorate both imagination and action around the most utopian, yet most fundamental, of human rights: a world in which everyone is fed, and no one is harmed. First, I review representative writings on Mexican foodways and the location of mestiza/o identity in relation to the production of food. Next, I argue that "farmworker-to-table," or sustainably *and* ethically provisioned Mexican-inspired cuisine, has the transformational potential to foment both ecological and social justice that protects the land and the people who work on it.

Engaging the theoretical works of Walter Mignolo and Aníbal Quijano, I define decolonial practices as those which interrogate or erode the project of Western capitalism in favor of communal access to resources, and supplant the monopoly of aesthetic priorities that secure Euro- and U.S.-centric management of the senses in favor of the inclusion of non-Western traditions and innovations. Quijano (2000) explains the coloniality of power as a global ordering of truth, whereby time and space are segmented along a racial axis that has endured beyond the original sixteenth-century geopolitical conquests, with racial and cultural features as a central criterion for the formation of political hierarchies.[4] Today, this axis of power speaks through the ideology of neoliberal globalization, by which capital now assumes the civilizing project once identified with the colonial superimposition of monarchy and Christianity. This is why organization along communal access to resources presents a challenge to the Western project of modernity: collective, emancipated individuals constitute a revolutionary population at odds with the Modern formation that emphasizes nation building, productivist governance, and private accumulation. The Mexican dining experiences at my study's conclusion demonstrate how the coloniality of power can be reconfigured and reimagined so that new visions of hemispheric inclusion may emerge.

"Mexican" food, at first blush, seems to be as straightforward a descriptor as any other adjective designating a national cuisine, but a closer appraisal quickly reveals a term that is heavily contested and beleaguered by indigenous and mestiza/o repression. Gustavo Arellano (2012) emphasizes adaptation, interpreting Mexican-branded foods like Taco Bell and Chi-Chi's as a continuum of cultural exchange or, as Michael Soldatenko (2015) writes, "no less legitimate than its sibling in Mexico" (136).[5] Food writing in feminist Chicana memoirs frequently frames culinary knowledge as a woman-centered connection to matrilineal memory, where the kitchen is reworked as a space of agency and even resistance to patriarchal values (Abarca and Soler, 2013). Jeffrey Pilcher (2012) defines Mexican culinary practices as the result of the encounter between Spanish and indigenous Mexican palates, cultures, and classes, while Chicano poet José Antonio Burciaga's "After Aztlán" (1992) demonstrates the author's tendency to deploy traditional foods to establish the Chicano point of view:

After Aztlán
there will be no Mictlán,
just the question
at the last judgment
about how you want
your frijoles: con
red chile, green chile,
tortillas de harina, maiz, o pan?[6]

Meanwhile, Chicano poet Paul Martinez Pompa challenges the Chicana/o-as-tortilla-eater convention as well as the motif of matronly food preparation in "The Abuelita Poem" (2009). The following excerpt comes from the first section of the poem titled "Skin & Corn," which inserts tongue-in-cheek magical realism to describe how the abuelita kneads the masa:

Her brown skin glistens as the sun
pours through the kitchen window
like gold *leche*. After grinding
the *nixtamal*, a word so beautifully ethnic
it must not only be italicized but underlined
to let you, the reader, know you've encountered
something beautifully ethnic, she kneads
with the hands of centuries-old ancestor
spirits who magically yet realistically possess her
until the *masa* is smooth as a *lowrider's*
chrome bumper. And I know she must do this
with care because it says so on a website
that explains how to make homemade corn *tortillas*.[7]

If tortillas enjoy the power to foster cultural cohesion, they are also just as capable of sowing dissent. Martinez Pompa expresses exhaustion with the motif of the *abuelita* and her cooking as the embodied archive of traditional knowledge: the abuelita of his poem learns her tortilla recipe on a website, where she also learns that she is supposed to imbue the ritual act of their preparation with maternal and ancestral affection and gravitas.

The above survey of divergent perspectives exposes "Mexican food" as contested and polarizing territory, but two major themes among observers appear with consistency. The first is the reality that Mexican cuisine within the United States, whether in traditionalist, experimental, or massified dimensions, is marked by conditions of coloniality, with the "Mexican" designation signifying both Spanish and indigenous clashes as well as the vertical orderings of U.S. capital. Another consistent theme surfacing across Mexican foodscapes is the centrality of maize (corn) to Mexican and Chicana/o cultural identity. Roberto Cintli Rodriguez's *Our Sacred Maíz Is Our Mother: Indigeneity and Belonging in the Americas* (2014) maintains that, more than a sum of numerous wars of invasion, it was the seven-thousand-year-old maize culture that connects Mexican peoples to their hemispheric indigeneity and represents the core expression of cultural knowledge and cohesion.

The history of maize is also the history of the Mesoamerican civilizing project. Domesticated in central Mexico by around 6500 BCE, successful maize, beans, squash, and chili crops prompted the sedentary organization of village life. By 1500 BCE, the Olmec were contributing monumental architecture and the Mesoamerica's first state-organized society that would not have been possible without maize surpluses.[8] The nixtamalization process involves cooking maize in an alkaline solution, thereby increasing its content of assimilable protein and malleability. After grinding it on a *metate* (grinding stone), the maize dough was formed into tortillas, tamales, and other variations that spread through much of North America in the first millennium CE.[9] Elizabeth Fitting's "Cultures of Corn and Anti-GMO Activism in Mexico and Columbia" (2014) argues that the ongoing transnational campaign against Monsanto, Dow Chemical, and DuPont's commercial transgenic (GMO) maize crops constitutes a defense of the country's preeminent symbol of place. Viewing traditional varieties of corn as a symbol of national sovereignty, activist slogans such as "We are people of corn," and "Without corn there is no country" attest to the continuity of maize not only as a biological resource, but also as the foundation of regional Mesoamerican identity and autonomy.[10] As Zilkia Janer (2008) summarizes in her volume *Latino Food Culture*, "Maize is the staple that gives Latino cuisine a cohesive identity" (25). While this may be true for a pan-Latina/o assessment of hemispheric foodways, it is especially the case for Mexican society and culture, where maize was first domesticated.

While Mexican food in the United States has a history that is far-reaching, transnational, and as fluid as the peoples that experience its bordered realities, two distinct lines of development characterize the major Mexican dining approaches. For some, eating habits remain much as they would in the various regions of Mexico, reflecting steady migratory patterns of Mexican nationals and their dietary patterns. The other consumption style is one that has adapted to Anglo culinary norms and cultural, and/or geographic, distancing from traditional Mexican ingredients (Janer, 73). These two tendencies need not be mutually exclusive. It is not an anomaly for a household to enjoy traditional chilaquiles made of fried corn tortilla pieces in simmering salsa on one day, and a "breakfast burrito" of egg and chorizo wrapped in a large flour tortilla from a drive-through window on the next. Across U.S. Mexican diets, some ingredients and practices that continue to be popular in Mexico are seldom found in the U.S. Latina/o urban context, such as gathering eggs from the family coop, freshly slaughtered poultry, and preparing food in outdoor pits. Also, following prevailing dietary recommendations, the use of lard is less extensive across Mexican American repertoires in contemporary cooking than in Mexican national cuisine (Janer, 55). Ilan Stavans (2011) offers the observation that "A Mexican will remind you that a burrito isn't really a wrap but a small donkey and that a margarita is a flower not a drink" (ix). In each of the iterations of Mexican cuisine in the U.S., accommodations and adaptations are made by both household and restaurant cooks to reflect the pleasures and priorities of the people they feed.

As a modifier of Mexican food, "farm-to-table" does not constitute a particular preparation or aesthetic tendency, but rather refers to the campaign across farms, restaurants, grocery stores, and other institutions to reduce waste and demand values-based guarantees at all stages of food production, including harvesting, storage, processing, packaging, transportation, marketing, sales, and consumption. The expression emphasizes the need for freshness, which entails the swift handling of vegetables and fruits, and the notion that crisp, live flavors are best when they are newly harvested. Another implication is ecological. By transitioning from industrialized and globalized provisioning to the localized foodshed, "locavores" claim that the environment benefits when food is not shipped over long distances, reasoning that the carbon "foot" treads lighter without the use of harmful preservatives and the combustion of noxious fuels to bring food to the dining room. In contemporary food journalism, farm-to-table is also employed to refer to restaurants that emphasize seasonality and more direct presentations of food that eschew "food-as-art" displays characteristic of rarefied atmospheres of gastronomic prestige. At other times, farm-to-table is merely short-hand for a reasonable commitment to fresh and/or quality ingredients and a stylish environment.

Industry trends reveal enormous consumer conviction in farm-to-table provisioning, as confirmed by the National Restaurant Association's 2013 report which demonstrates that both consumers and The American Culinary Federation chefs are demanding more local sourcing and sustainable farming practices in their food products than ever before.[11] But the farm-to-table ethos is not without its opponents. The mainstream farm-to-table disparagers exhibit anxieties about what is optimal for the human body and what is helpful to the earth, yet seldom challenge worker exploitation that thrives at the heart of our food chains. Dan Barber, author of the acclaimed *The Third Plate: Field Notes on the Future of Food* (2014) writes in the *New York Times* that, "farm-to-table advocates are often guilty of ignoring a whole class of humbler crops that are required to produce the most delicious food," and recommends the cultivation of cowpeas, millet, and mustard in order to solve farm-to-table's shortcomings.[12] Hannah Palmer Egan, food blogger for New York City's *The Village Voice*, laments that the farm-to-table tagline is mistreated when used to describe a perfunctory inclusion of a few locally sourced items rather than a real commitment:

> Still, there's a difference between adding a few token Greenmarket ingredients to the menu and pushing the envelope when it comes to local sourcing, and some restaurants are working faster and going further to get produce from area farmers and give diners the freshest possible experience.[13]

In spite of the conditions of farmworkers who remain, according to the U.S. Department of Agriculture, "among the most economically disadvantaged working groups in the United States," complaints about farm-to-table tend to focus on problems of soil erosion or failures in freshness and totally ignore how dietary decisions impact the life chances of agricultural laborers.[14]

Insisting that social responsibility also be included at the local food-laden table, Devon Peña, Daniel Faber, David Goodman, E. Melanie DuPuis, and Michael Goodman figure among those changing the conversation in order to address the problem of working conditions on farms, restaurants, and related food delivery environments. Evaluating theoretical trajectories in the area of food studies in the United States and the United Kingdom, Goodman, DuPuis, and Goodman charge that too many Alternative Food Networks (AFNs) are narrowly focused on affixing boutique labels, certificates, and quality assurances to high-price-point dining experiences rather than transforming the logic of domination in food production to something that is qualitatively different. In other words, the farm-to-table designation figures among the AFNs most associated with premium foods at prohibitive prices: the updated and earth-conscious construal of "gourmet."

While contemporary AFNs have played a significant role in raising awareness about the dangers of conventional production values, the tenor of its campaigns remains rooted in the neoliberal logic of coloniality. To be sure, ecological farming and localized markets constitute an improvement on conventional systems, which are dominated by agricultural production and the pursuit of profit at the expense of sustainability. However, majoritarian AFNs remain discursively rooted in natural resource conservation, wilderness preservation, and professional environmentalism, with food provisioning attitudes contingent on elite dietary preferences and consumer, rather than worker, safety.[15] Devon G. Peña (2005) offers a Chicana/o critique of mainstream environmentalism in *Mexican Americans and the Environment: Tierra y Vida*. He credits Rachel Carson's pioneering *Silent Spring* (1962) with providing a bold and pivotal study that established a link between "economic poisons" (pesticides) and health problems such as cancer and reproductive system disorders that cause birth defects, but points out that Carson limits the conversation to the consequences born by women and juvenile consumers, and does not acknowledge the Latina/o-dominant agricultural workforce that suffers the most frequent and serious consequences from overexposure to chemical toxins.[16]

The ability to not "see" farm labor and the struggles of those who perform it is pandemic. While traveling an expanse of California's U.S. Route 101 in the severe heat of summer, I was able to observe many farmworkers performing agricultural labor, their bodies bent under the sun's punishing rays. My destination was a home where my friend was a hired house sitter for a Santa Barbara family. There, a particular book title on the house's shelf caught my attention. It was Zachiah Murray's *Mindfulness in the Garden: Zen Tools for Digging in the Dirt* (2012). With an introduction by Thich Nhat Hanh, the volume offers "simple mindfulness verses (gathas) composed to connect the mind and body and to bring the reader/gardener's awareness to the details of the present moment as they work in the garden." The activities of softening and preparing the ground and watering the seeds bring the reader to a close communion with nature and "ultimately to one's self through the love and understanding they evoke."[17] Here, agricultural endeavors are idealized to the extent that they are on par with a yoga class or a meditation retreat. The earth, garden, and natural world are evoked as ways to be in communion with the "self," and the self is the ultimate destination of the reader's journey through the dirt.

In the scorching heat and enduring drought, it was difficult to imagine more punishing employment than the work farm laborers undertook alongside the 101. A publication extolling the virtues of gardening as a meditative pastime juxtaposed with the abjectness of agricultural laborers bespeaks the disconnect between elite society and its Edenic ideas about gardening, and the realities of agricultural employment. Murray's readership is coded as white and privileged: agricultural employment is exotic, unpaid, recreational, and leads to the aggrandizement of the self. The other group—the one characterized by subsistence pay, rampant occupational hazards, and the invisibility of the self—is not the constituency Murray is interested in leading toward a more heightened state of consciousness about cultivation, since their invisibility is a naturalized and institutionalized condition of our colonial food provisioning system.

Investigating health inequalities and the U.S.-Mexico border, medical anthropologist Seth Holmes (2013) exposes the physical deterioration that is an inevitable consequence of performing farm labor.

> After the first week of picking on the farm, I asked two young female pickers how their knees and backs felt. One replied that she could no longer feel anything ("Mi cuerpo ya no puede sentir nada"), though her knees still hurt sometimes. The other said that her knees, back, and hips are always hurting ("Siempre me duelen"). Later that same afternoon, one of the young Triqui men I saw playing basketball every day the week before the harvest told me that he and his friends could no longer run because their bodies hurt so much ("Ya no corremos; no aguantamos"). In fact, even the vistas that were so sublime and beautiful to me had come to mean ugliness, pain, and work to the pickers. On multiple occasions, my Triqui companions responded with confusion to my exclamations about the area's beauty and explained that the fields were "pure work" (puro trabajo).[18]

In the Western "alternative" narrative, the "self" is the ultimate accomplishment, and the natural world is a route toward this purpose. For farmworkers, the ugliness and pain of their working lives erode the spiritual connectivity and dignity that elite and recreational conservationists insist is their right to enjoy. And if severe conditions produce despair among workers who have migrated out of economic necessity, there are many who have been forced to perform labor under circumstances that can only be described as modern-day slavery. In 1993, tomato crop workers in Florida organized to form the Coalition of Immokalee Workers (CIW) in order to demand social responsibility among growers and corporations, put a stop to human trafficking, and establish protections against gender-based violence in the fields. In 2007 they were presented with the Anti-Slavery Award by Anti-Slavery International for their work uncovering and bringing to justice six separate modern slavery operations under which 400 farmworkers were held in captivity in Florida and South Carolina and forced to pick vegetables and citrus for ten to twelve hour days under armed surveillance. Their pay was an approximate twenty dollars a week; attempts at escape were met with violent repression.[19]

With conventional agriculture epitomizing the logic of coloniality within the rubric of capitalist productivism, a reasonable assumption is that organic cultivation and small-scale farmers will provide more humane conditions for their workers. Twilight Greenaway investigates worker conditions and compensation across organic farm operations.[20]

> "The reality is that the pressure to keep prices low often makes it very hard for small-scale organic farmers to make a decent living or to pay their workers very well," says Elizabeth Henderson, a veteran organic farmer and cofounder of the Agricultural Justice Project. Reduced exposure to pesticides on an organic farm is an improvement in working conditions over conventional ag, [sic] but the USDA organic standards do not include any rules about labor.

The Food Justice Certification program seeks to incentivize farms, processors, and other entities in the food provisioning system for demonstrating fair labor practices,[21] but the need for this endorsement attests to the failures of mainstream AFNs to protect workers' rights, even when growers are committed to organic agriculture.

The fight against pesticides offers the foundational example of the Chicana/o challenge to AFNs. Of approximately 2 million farmworkers in the United States, 90 percent are people of color, and the majority live under the severe restrictions of an undocumented legal status. Over 300,000 of this population suffer from pesticide poisoning each year, and between 800 and 1,000 incidents of pesticide poisoning are fatal.[22] Laura Pulido (1996) and Julie Guthman (2014) point to the needs of rural workers and their exposure and vulnerability to hazardous conditions. Pulido notes that in the 1960s, Cesar Chavez's United Farm Workers Organizing Committee (UFWOC) focused on pesticides both as a demand and a tool for struggle. Lawsuits and administrative actions, boycotts, contract negotiations, sit-ins, picketing, and fasts figured among the strategies employed by the UFWOC in their struggle to gain safer working conditions and adequate pay. While the union's legacy is one of mixed results, their activities helped curtail chemically intensive farming systems, shift California pesticide regulation away from its close alignment with growers and chemical companies, and compel the University of California to commit to sustainable cultivation in their research pursuits. Unlike Alternative Food Networks that demand upscale food products for personal consumption, the oppositional environmentalism championed by the UFWOC condemns pesticide use because of the severe health risks imposed on workers.

In light of colonial orderings that place Chicana/o, Mexicana/o, mestiza/o, and indígena bodies in the highest zones of health and safety risk, Américas-based scholarship on food provisioning demonstrates that a growing number of researchers interpret food as more than sustenance, but also as a means to counter the negative effects of industrialized consumption and cultural abjection. Rich historical investigations are offered by Jeffrey Pilcher, Jaime Vilchis, Rafael Chabrán, Elizabeth Coonrod Martínez, and Gustavo Arellano, while Meredith E. Abarca applies a framework of radical feminist epistemology to interpret women's transmission of hemispheric foodways. Encarnación Pinedo, Zilkia Janer, Laura Esquivel, and Stephanie M. Sánchez figure among writers who interpret Mexican identity through the lens of culinary craft. Conducting nutritional research, Frederick Trowbride, Fernando Mendoza, Julie Collins-Dogrul, and Kenia Saldaña demonstrate that obesity rates and susceptibility to other diseases increase as Mexican American families adopt more mainstream, U.S. food choices. Offering an Américas-based critique of the coloniality of mainstream foodways, Luz Calvo edits the *Decolonize Your Diet* website that applies critical race theory to the disease load that is the inevitable consequence of the Standard American Diet (the "SAD" diet). Calvo rediscovers and reclaims traditional Mexican and indigenous foods as a revolutionary endeavor; both her website and recipe book locate traditional foodways as a fundamental path to decolonization: "Indigenous and African traditions in spirituality, music, literature, and food were never completely suppressed by the colonizers but kept alive, sometimes surreptitiously, in daily acts of resistance that include story telling, recipe sharing, and ceremony."[23] Vanessa Fonseca and Enrique C. Ochoa investigate the massification of food within the context of global capitalism and neocolonial priorities that disassociate Mexican-branded products from their Mesoamerican origins,[24] and Devon Peña examines the Chicano Environmental Justice Movement's linkage of environmental, economic, and social justice issues as a new alternative to mainstream environmentalism.[25]

As the farm-to-table designation evokes the scenario of elite diners eager to deepen consumer privilege, then the farmworker-to-table expression serves to sound the sacrifices of a largely Latin American origin workforce in urgent need of awareness and advocacy, as conventional and even alternative provisioning models cleave to colonial blind spots. Farmworker-to-table, however, is not just a play on the AFN that currently enjoys the greatest popularity. It is also a way to signal the identities of mestiza/os, indígenas, Mexicana/os, and Chicana/os in hemispheric foodways as people who have long connected decolonial resistance to the plight of the land. The *campesina/o* (peasant farmer) came to epitomize the Chicana/o condition in early resistance movements, and many observers agree that the civil disobedience, hunger strikes, boycotts, picket lines, and other grassroots organizing measures deployed by César Chávez and Dolores Huerta to unionize farm laborers and advocate for migrant workers' rights signaled the beginning of the Chicana/o identity (Beltrán; Acuña; Ontiveros). Chicana artist Ester Hernandez grew up in a family of farmworkers, contributing to the protest aesthetic visible in her iconic screen print *Sun Mad* (1981). The poster depicts a skeleton in a sun bonnet who gleefully harvests grapes contaminated with pesticides. El Teatro Campesino ("Farmworkers' Theater") formed in 1965 to bring visibility to the needs of farmworkers during the five-year Delano grape strike and boycott in Central California. The poet Alurista's "El plan espiritual de Aztlán" provides a foundational narrative of Chicana/o nationalism, in which it is declared, "We are free and sovereign to determine those tasks which are justly called for by our house, our land, the sweat of our brows, and by our hearts. Aztlán belongs to those who plant the seeds, water the fields, and gather the crops and not foreign Europeans."[26] In short, campesino advocacy among Chicana/o rights advocacy exemplifies Emiliano Zapata's creed: the land belongs to those who work on it, and the United Farm Workers (UFW) symbol has the potency to champion not only the struggle for farmworkers' rights, but also the struggle for the dignity and determination of all Chicana/o and mestiza/o peoples.

The objects of my research—restaurant establishments—mark a departure from the field of Américas food studies that are inclined to focus on agri-food business practices, dietary choices, and marketing campaigns. Perhaps the scholarly reluctance has to do with the ready association of dining and consumption with the negative aspects of capitalist consumerism. Consumption, in the vein of critiques leveled at mainstream AFNs, evokes elite privilege, gourmandizing, and the feckless notion that fine dining can successfully substitute for more holistic challenges to conventional food provisioning. Haute cuisine, after all, denotes a social hierarchy established and preserved through access to elaborate preparations and presentations of the finest ingredients—the opposite of "low" gastronomic experiences.[27] However, my findings will demonstrate that, while Enrique Olvera's historical 2015 opening of Cosme on 21st Street was hailed by *The New Yorker* as "the undisputed opening of the season,"[28] Mexican food in the U.S. (and even in Mexico) continues to be regarded as a thoroughly vernacular cuisine, identified with hemispheric indigeneity and the hierarchies that Mexicanness in the United States evoke.

Decolonizing Haute Cuisine

According to Alan Warde, food consumption provides the ultimate metaphor for the concept of taste.[29] If this is the case, then in culinary establishments celebrated for excellence, chefs are auteurs of multi-sensory atmospheres who play a vital role in influencing what a generation craves. My interpretation of colonial ideology in Mexican fine dining is examined here in the context of restaurant websites, internet review services, industry journalism, and personal interviews. These sources delineate a border zone that freely touts Anglo-origin cooks as redeemers of Mexican authentic cuisine while evincing skepticism about Mexican-origin cooks in the high-level culinary world.

As a way of knowing and a route for the communication of cultural coherence, discourses surrounding Mexican cuisine with Anglo chefs describe that which is "discovered" or "found," much in the way the Américas are cast in terms of the discovery of people and wildlife, rather than the culmination of knowledges that have been honed over the course of millennia. In contrast, when press, public, and critics turn toward Mexican-origin chefs, their restaurants and menus are read against the prevailing mainstream understandings of the Mexican diet that, in the United States, seldom demonstrates fidelity to historic Mesoamerican foodways. And while the millennial aughts and early teens have seen the emergence of new Mexican and Chicana/o actors in the culinary landscape, Anglo chefs continue to dominate upscale offerings. Gustavo Arellano notes, "the Mexican cookbook industry, a multimillion-dollar operation whose bookshelves expand every year, is an overwhelmingly American-written one."[30] Spanish-surnamed cooks continue to be in the minority in the publication of Mexican cookbooks and as proprietors of establishments associated with culinary expertise. Even in New Mexico, a state that takes great pride in its slogan of "red or green," a survey of the 26 restaurants participating in Santa Fe's Farm to Restaurant Program reveals that only three businesses specialized in fine Mexican cuisine, and all of these had non-Mexican chefs at the helm.[31]

Among non-Mexican chefs and restaurant proprietors, it is routine for their promotional materials to provide their "found Mexican" story. This is where Anglo cooks narrate a traveler's tale about their interactions with Mexican cooking and carefully construct a "romantic crusader" image of the intrepid entrepreneur. Positional superiority is naturalized via the discourse of discovery. The most famous example is Rick Bayless, who is credited as the first to bring Mexican cuisine into the realm of fine dining in the United States. Bayless, owner of Frontera Grill and Topolobampo in Chicago, also sells the Frontera food product line offering marinades, salsas, tortilla chips, and other specialties bearing his brand that enjoys distribution by major supermarket chains such as Walmart, Publix, Target, and Safeway. His website states, "Most people know Rick Bayless from winning the title of Bravo's Top Chef Masters, beating out the French and Italian with his authentic Mexican cuisine."[32] An internet visitor is to understand that although French and Italian cuisines are the reigning titleholders, it is a credit to Bayless's talent that he manages to achieve this title with vernacular Mexican food. His discovery of Mexican cuisine is touted by journalist Craig Claiborne, who writes in *The New York Times*, as "the greatest contribution to the Mexican table imaginable."[33] Raised in an Oklahoma restaurant family, Bayless studied Spanish and Latin American studies as an undergraduate before pursuing a doctoral degree in Anthropological Linguistics at the University of Michigan. With his wife Deann, he lived in Mexico for six years, where they researched the recipes that would turn into his first cookbook, *Authentic Mexican: Regional Cooking from the Heart of Mexico* (1987). The website celebrates the Bayless' discovery of Mexican food, which is attributed to their "extended stay in Mexico," but neglects to provide remark about the teachers who generously shared their foodways with the researchers.

> It was 1987. Rick Bayless and his wife, Deann Groen Bayless, had just returned from an extended stay in Mexico, where they had been researching their first book. They wanted a restaurant that tasted and felt like their travels. So they hung colorful Mexican folk art on the walls, turned up the Mariachi music and packed the menu with the foods that reminded them of their travels: tangy tomatillos, rich black beans, fiery chiles.[34]

Bayless is routinely credited with establishing one of the first upscale Mexican restaurants in the country. He opened Frontera Grill in 1987 with retrieved "folk art" and "Mariachi music," and Topolobampo in 1989 as its "sleek, classy sister." As of 2015, Topolobampo has one Michelin star—a high achievement in a culinary ranking system that has performed inspections since 1900. That non-Mexicans can prepare Mexican food with expertise is not, in and of itself, an imposition of positional superiority. Instead, it is the stream of Bayless's lionizing claims to authenticity based on his discovery that bear the imprint of coloniality.

Linda Tuhiwai Smith (2002) problematizes the priorities of Western researchers who claim authority in the cultural production of indigenous communities. The Western observer frequently sees the benefits of their contribution as representing an emancipatory ideal, as somehow "saving" a newly "discovered" and oppressed community. This narrative is observable in the work of Bayless, who is styled as the "rescuer" of native hemispheric foodways from their massification and corruption, and thereby acts as a savior, rather than an oppressor, of native knowledge. Tuhiwai Smith writes:

> It galls us that Western researchers and intellectuals can assume to know all that is possible to know of us, on the basis of their brief encounters with some of us. It appalls us that the West can desire, extract and claim ownership of our ways of knowing, our imagery, the things we create and produce, and then simultaneously reject the people who created and developed those ideas and seek to deny them further opportunities to be creators of their own culture and own nations.[35]

Bayless's recourse to indigenous knowledge is told from the perspective of a knower—as an arbiter of what is regional, authentic, and worthy of transcending blue collar associations with Mexican cuisine in the United States. Following the pattern of extraction and ownership described by Tuhiwai Smith, native knowers are unnamed and unsung, and native ways of knowing are reproduced by the colonial researcher while the people who developed these foodways are simultaneously rejected.

Likewise, Mary Sue Milliken and Susan Feniger are co-chef/owners of the critically acclaimed and wildly popular Border Grill restaurants who "found" Mexican cuisine as though it had been lying dormant without a custodian, waiting for them to arrive and rescue it from neglect. With resort dining establishments serving "modern Mexican food" in Las Vegas, Downtown Los Angeles, and Santa Monica, California, their website materials announce that "Mary Sue and Susan are preeminent ambassadors of Mexican cuisine, setting the standard for gourmet Mexican fare for over two decades and authoring five cookbooks, including *Cooking with Too Hot Tamales* and *Mesa Mexicana*".[36] As Anglo captains of Mexican fine dining, they are ascribed with skill, artistry, and brilliance.

> Ironically, it was in French restaurants where Chefs Mary Sue Milliken and Susan Feniger first tasted authentic Latin flavors. While guests were dining on escargot out front, in the back of the house Mary Sue and Susan were discovering the home cooking of Oaxaca and the Yucatan at staff meals prepared by their fellow cooks from Mexico … . In 1985, Mary Sue and Susan packed a VW bug and took a road trip far south of the Mexican border. Never setting foot in a "fine restaurant," they learned the recipes and techniques of market vendors and home cooks, from street corners in downtown Mexico City to back road family barbecues and taco stands along the beach. When they returned, they opened Border Grill and "applied the same intelligence," noted *Los Angeles Magazine*, "to green corn tamales and cactus-paddle tacos that other chefs might to a lobe of foie gras.[37]

The "intelligence" here is not attributed to the Oaxacans and Yucatecans in the back of the house, but to the French-trained Milliken and Feniger for capitalizing on their traditions. Once again, Mexican knowledge is made to appear as though it pertained to the public domain.

When Mexican and Chicana/o chefs are at the helm, a different set of narratives prevail. The review of San José's upscale Zona Rosa restaurant conducted by Jennifer Graue sums up a mainstream notion about what Mexican dining should entail:

> Americans tend to make assumptions about Mexican restaurants: that they are cheap and cheerful; that the food is fast and filling; and that the chips and salsa are free and free-flowing.[38]

Graue's appraisal begins with an acknowledgment of the stereotypes that, by 2013, continued to dominate popular interpretations of Mexican fare. "Cheap," "cheerful," and with a fast and complimentary appetizer, the "chips, margaritas, and guac" are expectations that diners cling to when it comes to Mexican fare, while Anglo chefs are not burdened with the responsibility of explaining that their food is not cheap.

Even the celebrity chef Enrique Olvera of Cosme, whose restaurant Pujol in Mexico City was ranked number 20 on the 2014 San Pellegrino World's 50 Best Restaurants list, is powerless to change this narrative. Like Graue, Ryan Sutton begins his review by visiting the stereotypes.

So Cosme is a new Mexican restaurant in an old strip club space. Are the margaritas and guac any good? We'll get to that later, but this isn't really that type of joint … . Dinner for two after tax and tip probably won't cost less than $200, making Cosme one of USA's most expensive Mexican spots. But this Flatiron hangout isn't more expensive than, say, Estela or any other ambitious small-plates establishment that doesn't happen to be Mexican.[39]

Sutton concludes his article with a remark about the guacamole at Cosme: it exists, but it is relegated to a less than prominent place on the menu, and the house staff conveys a lack of enthusiasm for this stock feature of less ambitious menus. The reviewer then warns the readers of the price point, anticipating a surprise reaction at the prospect of a Mexican dining experience being so dear.

Amelia Lester's review that appeared in *The New Yorker* does not begin with a riff on the clichés, but prepares the reader for the status diners that have turned out for Cosme's first season:

Should Cosme need a mascot, the man at the next table will do, in his fedora and mock turtleneck, looking like an angel investor on "Silicon Valley" and asking for another round of premium tequila shots. If you build an expensive place in the Flatiron district, he will come.[40]

Lester goes on to quip that the conspicuous affluence on parade in the dining room does not detract from Olvera's food: his smoked raw sepia (cuttlefish) is described by the reviewer as "a tangle of translucent, silvered strands, tossed with the simplest of tomato salsas. The taste of the ocean announces itself as a zephyr, not a squall." Lester is equally enthralled by the octopus cocktail with purple and blue corn and charred avocado, and later the corn-husk meringue made with mousse of mascarpone, cream, and a corn purée that "spills out like lava from its core." The reviews are careful to explain that prices are high and the atmosphere elite: not the caveats that European fine dining engenders.

In sum, fine dining prepared by Anglo chefs is narrated as a missionary achievement, with obvious correlation to Tuhiwai Smith's depiction of the foreign researcher who styles themself as an emancipator of Mexican cuisine. On the other hand, Mexican-origin chefs are inscribed with the imprint of the border crossing: by moving into the realm of high-end cuisine, they step into a zone of scrutiny as matter out of place. Apologies are in order if Mexican or Chicana/o chefs have the audacity to provide dining experiences that rival the slow pace and high price points found in European establishments.

As Cosme is well-positioned to shift the paradigm of high-end dining in the United States to include experimental Mexican approaches, the decolonial objective of breaking the monopoly of Western aesthetic priorities in order to include indigenous traditions and innovations is soundly achieved. However, the communal access to resources, or endeavors to raise consciousness about the colonial configuration of resources and alter the politics of foodways, does not figure prominently as a core value of Olvera or his restaurants. While the aesthetic movement is a significant one, and indeed addresses the long absence of Mexican culinary innovation from serious consideration by accomplished reviewers, I argue that a decolonial haute cuisine must also sustain a commitment to reconfiguring communities, and challenging the logic of domination in the food chains.

More than an innovation of culinary fashion, decolonial Mexican cuisine must take part in a fight against the exploitation of land-based, hemispheric communities of color.

An extremely important contribution is made by Zarela Martinez, a top name in upscale Mexican dining since 1987 (the same year as Frontera Grill) when she opened her own restaurant on Manhattan's Upper East Side and served dishes such as fish with coconut and fresh mint and spicy pineapple salad that contrasted with the city's slate of ubiquitous snack foods such as tacos and burritos. A multi-platform celebrity chef, her 13-part PBS series titled *Zarela! La Cocina Veracruzana* takes viewers on walks through Veracruz, turning the camera on the markets, kitchens, and bakeries where traditional methods of cooking are maintained and celebrated by people whose recipes and techniques constitute a body of knowledge. By showing mestizo and indígena peoples as hemispheric, millennial stewards of a complex and sophisticated cuisine, Martinez acknowledges the cultural debts she owes for the success of her culinary art.

On the West Coast, the campesino-to-table commitment can be found at Dominica Rice-Cisneros's Cosecha Café. Located in Downtown Oakland's Old Swan Market, Cosecha has steadily garnered deep affection and respect from community members, peers, and press since its opening in 2011. Featured in national and international travel guides such as the photo-driven guidebook *This is Oakland: A Guide to the City's Most Interesting Places* (2014), or *The Wall Street Journal* (2012), mouthwatering descriptions of her sweet yam and Oaxaca cheese quesadillas made from handmade tortillas and zesty salsa verde, achiote-marinated chicken, blood orange and kumquat salad, and pumpkin seed and green chili mole bring a steady stream of diners who sit at wooden picnic tables or outside on the sidewalk along Fourth Street. Visitors order and pay at a counter while on the other side of a low glass partition, a Mexicana standing at the comal steadily turns out fresh tortillas by hand for each of the incoming orders. The atmosphere recalls the Mexican mercado (marketplace) eateries that Rice-Cisneros identifies as her inspiration. If Cosecha's high ceilings and semi open air dining mingling with the scent of mole verde and steaming tamales, contiguous to Oakland's historic resources, do not evoke the atmospherics of the Mexican mercado, the faded and pixelated print out of Mexico's patron saint la Virgen de Guadalupe unceremoniously affixed to the white tile behind the counter with Scotch tape is certain to seal the deal.

A graduate of San Francisco's California Culinary Academy, Rice-Cisneros interned at Eccolo in Berkeley, Stars in San Francisco, Daniel and Four Seasons in New York, and Soleil in Mexico City, but the training that receives the most attention is her internship at Alice Waters's Chez Panisse. The reigning first name in "farm-to-table," Waters is a founding author of the "California cuisine" style, the founder of the Edible Schoolyard Project, and has had a pivotal role in shaping national consumer consciousness about the benefits of organic, local, whole foods.[41] Whereas Chez Panisse's pursuit to prepare items with the finest possible ingredients inspired relationships with the local and organic purveyors and growers at its inception in the 1970s, by the 1980s, this aesthetically driven charge gave way to an insistence on Slow Food and the farm-restaurant connection as vehicles to save biodiversity and cultural conservation from the wreckage of "anonymous junk food" that was rapidly eroding environmental, cultural, and personal health.[42] This approach is evident in the relationships Rice-Cisneros has cultivated with farmers and purveyors, but also with staff and community members.

> It's not just about making the food that will sell, it's about making what we want to eat. It's all Mexicanos doing the work, and later their family members are coming to visit and spend time here, and that influences what we feel like creating. There is a blend of the kitchen and the front, and we love to have that. Everyone comes together.[43]

Even with journalists and community members clearly touting Cosecha's offerings as Chez Panisse-quality fare, with the exception of Poonam G. who writes, "I came here on Cinco De Mayo, and it was very obvious they were not prepared for it. I would think that a Mexican restaurant would at least do some sort of preparation for it!" the bulk of the negative responses to Cosecha on Yelp consistently have to do with prices. Susan D. claims that prices "are way out of line for counter service & communal seating," and complains about paying $3 for chips, salsa and guacamole. Allen C. laments that, "prices here for tacos are much higher than at other places. Prices vary based on what kind of taco you get, but it's hard to convince me that $5 for a taco is ever a good deal. They get even more expensive at dinner too." Cosecha's price point is a reflection of both its dedication to organic and ethical purveyors featured on their website and menus, and fair wages for its employees. Rice-Cisneros tells a story of two of her Mexicana staff members being able to leave abusive relationships and support their families solely on the income that they receive at the restaurant with just as much pride as when she recounts how the lamb birria she made in the home of Waters was declared by her mentor to be "the best lamb I ever had."

In spite of skepticism about Mexican and Chicana/o chefs holding intellectual authority as high-end Mexican restaurateurs, Olvera, Martinez, and Rice-Cisneros represent only a few of the noteworthy figures exploring Mexican cuisine's cultural ideals and influencing public behaviors about Mesoamerican foodways. While Olvera's aesthetics realign colonial assumptions by championing indigenous foodways in the high-end marketplace, Martinez and Rice-Cisneros reconfigure gustatory prejudices at the same time as they promote communal knowledges and equitable distribution of resources. If, according to Meredith E. Abarca and Nieves Pascual Soler (2013), food constitutes a "venue of communication," wherein knowledge is assimilated at the sensual level, when the farmworker-to-table commitment thrives in Mexican food provisioning, emancipation from colonial impositions becomes a fully embodied, multi-sensorial practice wherein both the land and the people who work on it remain free from harm.[44]

Alice Waters is by no means the only notable fan of Cosecha's menus. Luz Calvo of *Decolonize Your Diet!* and Ester Hernandez of aforementioned *Sun Mad* fame are frequent customers. I had the chance to talk with Hernandez, whose childhood in California's San Joaquin Valley in a migrant farmworker family provided her with firsthand experience of the agri-food industry's abuses of power. Rice-Cisneros sat with us to enjoy a margarita and talk about the benefits of locally-provisioned, organic food. At one point, the master chef made an offhanded, sweeping statement about how "people have no idea" what real peaches are *supposed* to taste like. "Girrrrl!" Hernandez drew the word out in disdain. "I've been eating fruit I picked myself from the tree since I could walk!"

As a conclusion, I can think of no better scenario than that of the acclaimed Chicana artist drawing epistemic authority from her early life as a farm laborer, and subsequently employing this expertise to successfully zing the haute chef. No serious project advancing farmworker-to-table Mexican food should be attempted without farmworkers *at* the table.

Notes

1 Sam Oches. "Special Report," *QSR Magazine*. 8 August 2013.
2 Juan Gonzalez. *Harvest of Empire: A History of Latinos in America*. New York: Penguin Books, 2011. 216.
3 Dana Blanton. "Fox News Poll: Reshuffling of GOP field, many agree with Trump on immigration." *Fox News*. 17 July 2015.

4 Aníbal Quijano. "Coloniality of Power, Eurocentrism, and Latin America." *Nepantla: Views from South* 1:3 (2000): 535.

5 Michael Soldatenko. "Tacos and Coloniality: A Review Essay," *Diálogo: An Interdisciplinary Studies Journal* 18, 1 (2015): 135–42.

6 José Antonio Burciaga. "After Aztlán." *Undocumented Love/Amor Indocumentado*. San Jose, CA: Chusma House Publications, 1992.

7 Paul Martinez Pompa. "The Abuelita Poem." *My Kill Adore Him*. Notre Dame, IN: University of Notre Dame Press, 2009.

8 Paloma Martinez-Cruz. *Women and Knowledge in Mesoamerica: From East L.A. to Anahuac*. Tucson: University of Arizona Press, 2011. 18–19.

9 Ilan Stavans. *Mexican-American Cuisine*. Santa Barbara, CA: Greenwood, 2011. 4.

10 Elizabeth Fitting. "Cultures of Corn and Anti-GMO Activism in Mexico and Columbia." *Food Activism: Agency, Democracy and Economy*. Eds. Carole Counihan and Valeria Siniscalchi. New York: Bloomsbury, 2014. 175–92.

11 "National Restaurant Association Reports Top Restaurant Menu Trends." *Food & Beverage Close-Up*. 6 December 2013.

12 Dan Barber. "What Farm-to-Table Got Wrong." *The New York Times*. 17 May 2014.

13 Hannah Palmer Egan. "The 10 Best (Real) Farm-to-Table Restaurants in NYC." *The Village Voice*. 5 August 2013.

14 Fair Food Standards Council. *Fair Food Program 2014 Annual Report*. 27 January 2016. Available at: http://www.fairfoodstandards.org

15 Kevin Morgan, Terry Marsden, and Jonathan Murdoch. *Worlds of Food: Place, Power, and Provenance in the Food Chain*. New York: Oxford University Press, 2006. 2.

16 Devon G. Peña. *Mexican Americans and the Environment: Tierra y Vida*. Tucson: University of Arizona Press, 2005. 121–2.

17 Zachiah Murray. *Mindfulness in the Garden: Zen Tools for Digging in the Dirt*. Berkeley: Parallax Press, 2012.

18 Seth Holmes. *Fresh Fruit, Broken Bodies: Migrant Farmworkers in the United States*. Berkeley: University of California Press, 2013. 89.

19 Silvia Giagnoni. *Fields of Resistance*. Chicago: Haymarket Books, 2011. 34.

20 Twilight Greenaway. "Does Buying Organic Help Farmworkers?" *TakePart*. 23 April 2014.

21 Agricultural Justice Project. *Food Justice Certified*. Web. 7 July 2015.

22 Daniel Faber. *The Struggle for Ecological Democracy: Environmental Justice Movements in the United States*. London: The Guilford Press, 1998. 5–6.

23 Luz Calvo. *Decolonize Your Diet*. Website.

24 Enrique C. Ochoa. "From Tortillas to Low-carb Capitalism and Mexican Food in Los Angeles since the 1920s." *Diálogo: An Interdisciplinary Studies Journal* 18 (2015): 33–46.

25 Peña, 139–46.

26 Christina Beltrán. *The Trouble with Unity*. Oxford: Oxford University Press, 2010. 43.

27 Jeffrey Pilcher. *Que vivan los tamales!* Albuquerque: University of New Mexico Press, 1998. 4

28 Amelia Lester. "Cosme." *The New Yorker*. 9 February 2015.

29 Alan Warde. *Consumption, Food, and Taste*. London: Sage Publications, 1997. 22.

30 Gustavo Arellano. *Taco USA: How Mexican Food Conquered America*. New York: Scribner, 2012. 90.

31 Farm to Table New Mexico Org. *Farm to Table New Mexico*. Web. 24 Jan. 2015.

32 Bayless, Rick. *Rick Bayless*. Web. 15 Jan. 2015.

33 Bayless. Web. 7 Jan. 2015.

34 Bayless. Web. 14 Jul. 2015.

35 Linda Tuhiwai Smith. *Decolonizing Methodologies: Research and Indigenous Peoples*. London: Zed Book Ltd, 2002. 1.

36 Bayless. Web. 24 Jan. 2015.

37 Bayless. Web. 7 Jul. 2015.

38 Jennifer Graue. "San Jose's Zona Rosa serves upscale, farm-to-table Mexican cuisine." *San José Mercury News*. 19 March 2013.

39 Ryan Sutton. "Six Reasons Why Cosme Is One of NYC's Most Relevant New Restaurants." *New York Eater*. 16 December 2014.

40 Lester, 2015.

41   Edible School Yard Project. *Edible School Yard*. Web. 15 April 2015.
42   Thomas McNamee. *Alice Waters & Chez Panisse: The Romantic, Impractical, Often Eccentric, Ultimately Brilliant Making of a Food Revolution*. New York: The Penguin Press, 2007. 347.
43   Rice-Cisneros. Personal interview. 28 July 2014.
44   Meredith E. Abarca and Nieves Pascual Soler. *Rethinking Chicana/o Literature through Food: Postnational Appetites*. New York: Palgrave Macmillan, 2013. 1.

Bibliography

Abarca, Meredith E. and Nieves Pascual Soler. *Rethinking Chicana/o Literature through Food: Postnational Appetites*. New York: Palgrave Macmillan, 2013.

Acuña, Rodolfo. *Occupied America: A History of Chicanos*. 7th ed. Boston, MA: Longman, 2011.

Arellano, Gustavo. *Taco USA: How Mexican Food Conquered America*. New York: Scribner, 2012.

Barber, Dan. "What Farm-to-Table Got Wrong." *The New York Times*. 17 May 2014.

Beltrán, Cristina. *The Trouble with Unity: Latino Politics and the Creation of Identity*. Oxford: Oxford University Press, 2010.

Blanton, Dana. "Fox News Poll: Reshuffling of GOP Field, Many Agree with Trump on Immigration." *Fox News*. 17 July 2015.

Bonfil Batalla, Guillermo. *México Profundo: Reclaiming a Civilization*. Trans. Philip Adams Dennis. Austin: University of Texas Press, 1996.

Burciaga, José Antonio. *Undocumented Love/Amor Indocumentado*. San Jose: Chusma House Publications, 1992.

Calvo, Luz. *Decolonize Your Diet*. Website.

Chabrán, Rafael. "Dr. Francisco Hernández Ate Tacos: The Food and Drinks of the Mexican Treasury." *Diálogo: An Interdisciplinary Studies Journal* 18:1 (2015): 19–32.

Egan, Hannah Palmer. "The 10 Best (Real) Farm-to-Table Restaurants in NYC." *The Village Voice*. 5 August 2013.

Esquivel, Laura. *Como agua para chocolate*. New York: Anchor Books, 1989.

Fitting, Elizabeth. "Cultures of Corn and Anti-GMO Activism in Mexico and Columbia." *Food Activism: Agency, Democracy and Economy*. Eds. Carole Counihan and Valeria Siniscalchi. New York: Bloomsbury, 2014. 175–92.

Fonseca, Vanessa. "Fractal capitalism and the Latinization of the US market." Doctoral disseration, University of Texas at Austin, 2003.

Giagnoni, Silvia. *Fields of Resistance*. Chicago: Haymarket Books, 2011.

Goodman, David, E. Melanie DuPuis, and Michael K. Goodman. *Alternative Food Networks: Knowledge, Practice, and Politics*. New York: Routledge, 2012.

Graue, Jennifer. "San Jose's Zona Rosa Serves Upscale, Farm-to-Table Mexican Cuisine." *San José Mercury News*. 19 March 2013.

Greenaway, Twilight. "Does Buying Organic Help Farmworkers?" *Take Part*. 23 April 2014.

Guthman, Julie. *The Paradox of Organic Farming in California*. Second edition. Oakland: University of California Press, 2014.

Holmes, Seth. *Fresh Fruit, Broken Bodies: Migrant Farmworkers in the United States*. Berkeley: University of California Press, 2013.

Janer, Zilkia. *Latino Food Culture*. Westport, CT: Greenwood Press. 2008.

Lester, Amelia. "Cosme." *The New Yorker*. 9 February 2015.

Martinez Pompa, Paul. "The Abuelita Poem." *My Kill Adore Him*. Notre Dame, IN: University of Notre Dame Press, 2009.

Martinez-Cruz, Paloma. *Women and Knowledge in Mesoamerica: From East L.A. to Anahuac*. Tucson: University of Arizona Press, 2011.

Mignolo, Walter. *The Darker Side of Western Modernity: Global Futures, Decolonial Options*. Durham, NC: Duke University Press, 2011.

Murray, Zachiah. *Mindfulness in the Garden: Zen Tools for Digging in the Dirt*. Berkeley: Parallax Press, 2012.

Ontiveros, Randy. *In the Spirit of a New People: The Cultural Politics of the Chicano Movement.* New York: New York University Press, 2013.

Peña, Devon G. *Mexican Americans and the Environment: Tierra y Vida.* Tucson: University of Arizona Press, 2005.

Pilcher, Jeffrey. *Planet Taco: A Global History of Mexican Food.* Oxford: Oxford University Press, 2012.

Pinedo, Encarnación. *Encarnación's Kitchen: Mexican Recipes from Nineteenth-Century California.* Trans. Dan Strehl. Oakland: University of California Press, 2005.

Pulido, Laura. *Environmentalism and Economic Justice: Two Chicano Struggles in the Southwest.* Tucson, University of Arizona Press, 1996.

Quijano, Anibal. "Coloniality of Power, Eurocentrism and Latin America." *Nepantla: Views from South* 1:3 (2000): 533–80.

Rodriguez, Roberto Cintli. *Our Sacred Maíz Is Our Mother: Indigeneity and Belonging in the Americas.* Tucson: University of Arizona Press, 2014.

Soldatenko, Michael. "Tacos and Coloniality: A Review Essay." *Diálogo: An Interdisciplinary Studies Journal* 18:1 (2015): 135–42.

Vilchis, Jaime. "¿Qué comía Dr. Francisco Hernández (1517–1578)? La intermediación de mestizaje y gastronómica del Protomédico de Indias de Felipe II." *Diálogo: An Interdisciplinary Studies Journal* 18:1 (2015): 5–17.

Young, Robert J. C. *Colonial Desire: Hybridity, Culture and Race.* New York: Routledge, 1995.

22

THE RITUALS OF HEALTH

Amelia María de la Luz Montes

"I was a curandera before birth," declares healer, Berenice Dimas, in her poem, "Queeranderismo." She repeats the line five times, creating a refrain that underlines the merging of political, cultural, sexual, and personal history within her rituals of healing. The act of remembering the "historical" body becomes the process of healing.

> I was a curandera before birth
> And I am a curandera now
> Channeling generational trauma
> Listening to its voice
> Feeling its pain
> Helping my mother heal
> Helping myself heal
> Remembering
> That our bodies are not disposable
> That our existence is hope
> That we are worth living
> That we have something valuable
> to share with the world
> That we need to heal
> For our next seven generations
>
> (76)

The entire poem brings to mind what writer, scholar, and theorist, Gloria Anzaldúa described as "divergent thinking … At some point on our way to a new consciousness, we will have to leave the opposite bank, the split between the two mortal combatants somehow healed so that we are on both shores at once and, at once, see through serpent eagle eyes (100–1)." Berenice Dimas represents a growing number of Chicana and Latina healers who are taking healing practices to a new level of meaning and visibility. Their rituals are not clandestine or imparted in isolated spaces. Their rituals also may include Western and Asian practices.

Berenice works with individuals and groups in the schools, the community, and in academic spaces which, in the past, were not always open to alternative Mexican/Chicana ritual practices.[1] For example, Berenice helped organize a workshop on indigenous healing at UC Berkeley, and one of her mentors, Estela Román, a healer from Cuernavaca, was the featured speaker.[2] The workshop was well attended by students, professors, and community members. Berenice describes herself as a full spectrum doula, sanadora, yerbera, and health educator. On her website, Berenice writes that she

> believes in the reclamation of ancestral and indigenous healing practices. People have been connected to the land, the medicine of herbs … but much of that knowledge has been lost, forgotten or simply not practiced … this knowledge should be shared in our communities so that we can remember or re-learn how to take care of ourselves.[3]

Most recently, she has been hired full time at a large school district in their Restorative Justice program, a program that works toward restorative healing for all parties involved, instead of a justice system solely based on punitive actions. This program provides the following: (1) mediation between victim and offender; (2) circles; (3) separate assistance for the victim and offender; (4) restitution; (5) community service. Its goal is to create a culture of peace. Berenice's *curandera* skills are seen as a necessary ingredient to the program.[4] Just 10 to 15 years ago, the inclusion of indigenous healing in such public arenas was not common. This chapter will include interviews as well as a critical look at the latest texts on healing in order to reveal what is happening in today's popular Latina/o rituals of health and healing.

Illness and wellbeing is a topic that is of much interest today. The media continually feature advertisements touting drugs, surgeries—the latest program that will relieve us of pain, of illness, of chronic diseases. A number of Chicanas and Latinas are looking, like Berenice, to incorporate indigenous ancestral healing methods, often very different from Western medicine. Western medicine may tend to rely, at times heavily, on pharmaceutical drugs to mask pain. Alternatives to Western medicine focus on herbs, physical movement, and touch that nurture the body to heal itself. As Paloma Martínez-Cruz discusses at length in her chapter in this volume, food also figures prominently in the wellness of the life of Chicanas and Latinas. As more Chicanas and Latinas are taking time to plant, grow, harvest, and cook their own food, we recognize the vital link between food and wellbeing. Not surprisingly, Latina literary scholars have attended to food practices in literary texts. As Nieves Pascual Soler and Meredith E. Abarca write in the introduction to their edited, *Rethinking Chicana/o Literature through Food*, "food is not only something edible and sustaining, it is also a cultural object about which information can be gathered from diverse fields … [food] marks its presence even when its theoretical potential is not fully recognized" (2–3).

In today's society, pharmaceutical drugs are touted as the answer to a healthy lifestyle. Over the counter or prescription drugs can be a quick fix, a way to "carry on" and go about one's life. Our mainstream culture is one where "time" moves very quickly, a cultural "Western time" diametrically opposed to what Estela Román describes as "time" given to connecting the body, rather than running away from the body. To sit in the body when it is in pain or in comfort, to become expertly aware of the body's crucial signals, brings an intimacy of mind, spirit, and corporeal sensing. How then do we connect?

Food as Healing Medicine

In the city of Oakland, California, Luz Calvo and Catriona Esquibel have created an urban farm replete with chickens, and a planting and harvesting schedule. Luz is an Associate Professor of Ethnic Studies at California State University East Bay, and Catriona Esquibel is an Associate Professor of Race and Resistance Studies at San Francisco State University. Their academic research training and teaching have led them to a recovery project on indigenous foods. Today, they are the authors of the book, *Decolonize Your Diet: Plant-Based Mexican-American Recipes For Health and Healing.*[5] They also maintain a website by the same name. Recently, I spent time at their home, receiving a tour of their garden, discussing recipes, watching Luz cook, and having the pleasure of eating their nutritious meals. While watching Luz prepare the most delicious dishes (*Huarache de Nopal*, garden-fresh salsa, *Pozole*, tortilla making), we also talked about the vital connections between health and food, the importance of growing one's own food, why our health can be restored by remembering and cooking our abuelita's recipes, which includes returning to the food of our ancestors.

Amelia M.L. Montes: When did you begin thinking about growing your own food?

Catriona Esquibel: I think it started in 2007. During those years, I was blogging about Luz's breast cancer, diagnosis, and treatment. When we started thinking about food in relation to recovery from cancer treatment, we started to imagine a "Queer Postcolonial Cookbook," to capture what we were doing with food. We first began renting this house in 2005. Luz was diagnosed in 2006, and we were able to buy the house in 2008. At that point, we knew we wanted to start growing our own food.

Luz Calvo: Once we started considering food in relation to colonization, we hooked into Devon Abbott Mihesuah. She is Choctaw and we came across her book, *Recovering Our Ancestors' Gardens: Indigenous Recipes and Guide to Diet and Fitness.* She coined the term, "Decolonize Your Diet." Then there was the "Decolonizing Diet Project" from Northern Michigan University. They experimented with a year of eating and cooking with only local indigenous foods. We also came across the blog, "Decolonial Food for Thought," by two graduate students from the University of Washington, Claudia Serrato and Chris Rodriguez. They write from a Vegan Chicana/o / Indigena/o perspective. Through our research, we began to see that eating our ancestral foods would lead us to a healthy path.

Amelia M.L. Montes: When did you begin getting interested in cooking mindfully, choosing "pre-hispanic" foods and recipes?

Luz Calvo: We started with the garden. After my breast cancer diagnosis, I had a real profound crisis around food. I felt that maybe something I had eaten had caused the cancer. I had already been a vegetarian for 15 years. And yet, I thought I had eaten something cancer causing, so I didn't want to eat anything. We met with a group called, "Planting Justice," here in Oakland, and they came to our house. At that time, our garden was mostly just rocks and cement. We asked them to design a garden with cancer-fighting plants.

Catriona Esquibel: They came up with a plan, and slowly, area by area, Luz began to plant.

Luz Calvo: My hands were working in the soil and it became profoundly healing for me. And it was at this time that we also added chickens (laying hens) to our urban garden. It was also healing caring for the chickens, and feeling good about what I was eating from the garden.

So it's been eight years. It's like a path we're walking. What's so cool about it, is that there is so much to learn. Lately, we've been learning all about fermentation. We have been researching what kinds of foods were fermented in Mexico. For example, the Mexican/indigenous drinks of Colonche, Tesgüino, Tepache, and Tibicos are all fermented drinks.

Colonche, for example, is made from fermented tunas (prickly pears). It produces a super sweet luscious drink, and it's made without added sugar. This is the only way we use white sugar: in our ferments because the sugar then is consumed away. For example, when we make Kombucha, the SCOBY [symbiotic culture of bacteria and yeast] consumes the sugar, producing a drink that is naturally fizzy and tart.

We are also paying attention to the stories around foods. Many foods are indigenous that have been previously thought not indigenous. For example, there are wild garlic and onion plants that are indigenous to the Americas, but the history books will tell you that onion and garlic come from the Europeans. While the onions and garlic that are sold in markets are of European origin, there were also varieties of onion and garlic in the Americas.

Catriona Esquibel: We also have been reading articles from major scientific databases, such as "PubMed," which confirms the medicinal value of many of our native foods, such as nopales, verdolagas, quelites, and so forth.

Amelia M.L. Montes: What changes have you noticed in these five years of decolonizing your diet?

Luz Calvo: I continue to be in good health. The cancer has not returned. I feel strong. For me, it's the spiritual part of it. The spiritual path has connected me more to mother earth/nature, to ancestors, to people who, back in the day, were doing things that now I am doing.

Catriona Esquibel: I'd been having lots of issues with menopause, and recently had surgery, but I feel like I've healed really quickly from my surgery. I no longer have symptoms. Overall, the food is just so pleasurable, and it feels like it's getting better and better. Food feels good. We rarely get sick and rarely catch the viruses that everyone else gets. We're also big on remedies. For instance, a nettles tincture is quite healing for infections.

Luz Calvo: Instead of vitamins or what's on the pharmacy shelf, we use food/spices, like turmeric, that contain anti-inflammatory properties. I also go to yoga.

Catriona Esquibel: Walking is my main exercise. My phone has a pedometer on it.

Amelia M.L. Montes: What do you hope to do with all this information you have acquired, and the delicious food you have been creating?

Luz Calvo: We have already been doing workshops for students and the community. We've done a workshop with high school students in Oakland. We've been giving them tours of our garden. We've also done cooking demos for "Poor Magazine" in East Oakland. We did a food demo for the "Latina Migrant Women's Health Fair," which was held in the plaza outside of the Fruitvale BART [Bay Area Rapid Transit] Station. And, we just did a talk at Mills College.

Amelia M.L. Montes: And who is your audience for your cookbook?

Luz Calvo: We have several different audiences for our cookbook. We are writing for our students who appreciate our foods but don't know how to cook them. Then there are the people who are interested in history and stories about their family's food. The "slow food" community is also interested. We are also concerned about food justice. We advocate for our communities' access to healthy, culturally relevant food (food sovereignty); fair wages for people who work the fields, for people who work in the food service industry; an end to NAFTA [North America Free Trade Agreement]/CAFTA [Central American Free Trade Agreement],[6] which is destroying local food systems in Mexico and Central America. Of course, we are also concerned about GMOs [genetically modified organism] and pesticides which corrupt our food system, pollute the environment, and make us sick. At the same time, we recognize that these issues are not going to be fully solved without a radical restructuring of the global economy. Right now, all decisions around food revolve around one thing: increasing the profit margins of a few corporations that dominate the food industry. Instead, food should be viewed as something sacred. All living beings need food to survive, but it is also linked to our humanity and our collective need for health, community, and culture. We present a way of looking at Mexican food and valuing ancestral knowledge that we can share with each other. To have "Decolonize Your Diet" published as a book and to continue our website, people are then invited to share and that's awesome. We have a framework to continue that exchange so that we can benefit from each other's generational history.

Time as a Ritual in Healing

Luz Calvo's and Catriona Esquibel's journey to arrive upon a healing path regarding cancer and menopause took much research and planning. Instead of relying solely on pharmaceutical drugs to alleviate menopausal symptoms, Dr. Esquibel chose food and exercise to encourage the body to adjust to hormonal changes. Hormonal changes at every significant stage of a woman's life may cause a chemical imbalance that can lead to illness or may cause difficulty with pregnancies.

In her book, *Red Medicine: Traditional Indigenous Rites of Birthing and Healing*, Professor Patrisia Gonzales notes the importance of time in pregnancy and illness. She writes:

> As I helped Native women birth at home or in hospitals and clinics, the reminders that birth in North America has become increasingly medicalized would present themselves in phone calls. A Native woman would want help to prevent a threatened induction because Western time measurements that dictate clinical protocols asserted that she was overdue, though a home birth midwife might trust that the baby could still safely come on its own time schedule, thus postponing an intervention, or an Indigenous midwife might use teacher-herbs or a traditional "calling" to stir the child.
>
> (1–2)

Dr. Gonzales comes from a long line of traditional healers: Kickapoo, Comanche, Macehual peoples. She places an emphasis (as does *curandera* Estela Román) on the importance of "Indian Time" which they define as a high regard or respect for the "timeliness" of an action.[7] Rather than relying on a calendar to set a specific time for planting or birthing, Dr. Gonzales and Estela Román point to being respectful of weather patterns before planting, or, regarding pregnancy, being respectful of each individual body and the history that body holds. Gloria Anzaldúa writes:

> Our mind, our flesh, our energy system are all connected. What people think affects the body, and the body's physiology depends on how people think. If someone believes that modern medicine is the only answer to healing certain diseases, the diseased

person is virtually helpless and depends on the doctor as an all-knowing God. She can't participate in her own healing

(163)

Participation in one's own healing is key, but it demands becoming intimate with your body. When poet and fiction writer, ire'ne lara silva was diagnosed with diabetes, she experienced the following: "I was referred to a Diabetes Education class, but not to a series of classes or to a support group. The class I went to covered the basics. I also went to an orientation class when I started taking the drug, Byetta. The rest, well, I was on my own to figure it all out" (interview). For lara silva, the beginning path with diabetes was one of isolation and scant information. What helped lara silva was taking time to research the disease, and write her experiences in fiction and poetry. Writing has been essential to her healing practice. But it took time to make sense of her diagnosis and to find the health practitioners and healers who could guide her. In an interview with lara silva, I asked about her writing poetry as a form of healing. She responded:

> Poetry is an essential form of sustenance and healing for our *gente*. At its best, poetry is more than just beautiful—although that is important—more than intellectual, more than sound and language, more than powerful emotion. At its best, poetry speaks to us at the level of heart, body, mind, and spirit all at once. For both the poet and the reader/listener, poetry makes us whole and integrated people. So little of our lives are spent in this integrated state. Poetry feeds us and frees because it restores our dignity and our freedom and our human-ness—contesting the daily and historical oppression we endure and have endured.
>
> (lara silva, interview)

When lara silva says, "so little of our lives are spent in this integrated state," she is echoing what Gonzales and Román emphasize: taking time to sit in the body. lara silva's poetry reflects a community in crisis, individuals grappling with the impact of an epidemic they do not understand. She broadens her lens from the individual to the universal creating a historical pattern linking colonization to illness. In her poem, "diabetic epidemic," lara silva describes a journey of family and society. The pacing of the poem connects to the time it takes for a disease, unchecked, to spread.

diabetic epidemic

la azucar we heard it whispered first
la azucar they said but it made no sense
the sugar the sugar she died from la azucar
at first it was only the old people
the only difference we saw
was that coffee needed sweet'n low instead of sugar
and maybe they'd eat only half a piece of pan dulce
instead of two
and then it was my father
i was ten he seemed the same
nothing we could see was different
though every morning he pulled out a vial
from the refrigerator and gave himself a shot

they told him he had to eat differently
but didn't tell him why or how to eat the food
in the little guidebook half of which he'd never seen before
and there were stories but those were about other people
years passed and then it was everyone's grandparents
and some aunts and uncles though they were all at least fifty years old
we heard of children who had it but only saw them on
tv with jane fonda while on mexican tv there were all these commercials that said
this pill this plant this doctor can make you better
la azucar was everywhere
but not as scary as cancer cancer would kill you
i went to college and learned nothing at all about it
and then returned to south texas
where the people are ninety eight percent
hispanic latino mexican tejano whatever name they like most
and by this time people could say la azucar and everyone understood
not to insist not another tortilla no more cake no beer
and there was splenda and diet coke and sugar free snow cones
in every restaurant and on every corner
everything changed when it was my brother my youngest brother
in the hospital for gallstones though it took two weeks, six e.r. visits
and two hospital admittances before they operated
and it was on the third or fourth visit when they asked
did you know you're diabetic
and said oh and you have high blood pressure and high cholesterol
and are you a pima indian I've read studies many pima indians
have all three diabetes high blood pressure and high cholesterol
everything i learned from my brother i shared
with anyone who asked anyone who confided in me
how many people on the verge of tears who didn't understand why
old people young people thin people round people white people brown people
everyone says type two diabetes can be controlled with diet and exercise
they lay all the blame on obesity but not everybody is the same
there are all kinds of factors all kinds of resistances
and the right medication for one person is wrong for another
i changed my diet gave up drinking
thought i'd managed not to become a target
no one told me not sleeping and skipping meals and stress
and living on adrenaline could tear the body down
or that insulin resistance was part of polycystic ovarian syndrome
and then that day came the confirmation from the doctor
and my first shot of insulin and now la azucar was in my body
part of my life and it was a while
before i could see anything outside myself
without my brother i think i would have given up given in
it took awhile but then i opened my eyes
and noticed that la azucar was all around me
the woman next to me at work

the early morning bus driver
every third person at my other job
and the man at the store puzzling over egg substitutes
and the waitress downing a shot of orange juice during a long shift
and everywhere i see the warning signs in people's behaviors
in their complaints symptoms beyond passing
thirst or temporary blood sugar lows
but no one listens
why isn't there screaming in the streets
the children are diabetic the pregnant women are diabetic
so many people of color so many poor and working class
and the food is making us sick
and every day there are more and more of us
and la azucar is claiming lives and limbs and whole families
why is la azucar still being whispered
we should be screaming it

ire'ne lara silva's poem can be considered as a bildungsroman, an individual "coming of age" or "coming to recognition" of external conditions impacting the body that have created a crisis, ending in a call to action. To do this, lara silva came to terms with her personal, familial, and societal pain. It is what Anzaldúa describes in her essay "now let us shift": "By seeing your symptoms not as signs of sickness and disintegration but as signals of growth … by using these feelings as tools or grist for the mill, you move through fear, anxiety, anger, and blast into another reality" (552). This reality for lara silva is one of activism as it is for all the individuals mentioned in this chapter. But first, all of them recognized a "shift" in time, a departure from Western medicine, and a recovery and return to indigenous practices in healing.

I began this writing with Berenice Dimas. In a recent interview, I asked her if she sees integrative medicine (indigenous or alternative medicines and Western medicine) as viable, and she sees a "shift" among communities who seek alternative healing practices. Dimas (2015) answered:

> I see a combination of things happening. A lot of re-remembering is happening. When I host a workshop and people interact with the medicine, I notice that it brings up stories. People will say, 'Oh, I remember when my mom used to do this,' or 'my grandmother used to use this herb.' They are allowing themselves to remember. There are other people who are very new to this. I try to incorporate the plant medicine and it opens up conversations about it. Some are just wanting to deepen their understanding.
> (interview)

Dimas, recently hired as a Restorative Justice Coordinator, will be bringing her practice to various schools in the Bay Area of California. A few school districts across the country (specifically in California, Connecticut, New York) have begun to include meditation and/ or yoga classes in their curriculum with positive results.

In her book, *Encarnación: Illness and Body Politics in Chicana Feminist Literature*, Suzanne Bost writes: "since corporeal experience is shaped by environments, bodies alone are not the source of meaning. Their political situation, their political needs, and their political movements are about placement, not isolated identity—a lesson made clear by Disability

Studies' focus on how environments restrict mobility" (213). Bost's statement underlines the need to see the body not as part of a whole leading to one treatment for all. Bost illustrates, via Disability Studies, that because bodies are in constant flux, what happens to bodies when they are in crisis, in illness, grappling with a chronic disease, cannot be understood and treated with one uniform remedy. I say this because in my own interviews with individuals who have been diagnosed with diabetes (Type II), more often than not, they tell me that the doctor (1) informed them they have diabetes; (2) administered a pill (usually Metformin, a medication that has been on the market longer than any other medication for Type II diabetes); and (3) gave them vague advice on nutrition. Telling a patient they need to stay away from desserts or sugar means nothing. A carrot, for example, is not a dessert and hardly considered "sugar." Yet, one carrot stalk is equal to a tablespoon of sugar. Since the majority of doctors do not send diabetes patients to education classes (and often they don't because none are available), nor do they explain what causes diabetes, patients remain clueless. Doctors are not required to give any other alternatives on managing the disease. However, pharmaceutical companies may provide starter medications to doctors to pass on to patients.

This type of scant care and treatment for diabetes patients is a good example to further explain Bost's statement. The diagnosis of diabetes demands a blood test and not just any blood test. There is a simple blood test that records morning glucose levels and then there is the longer, more involved blood test called "The Glucose Tolerance Test" which takes three hours. Imagine if all of us were trained to test ourselves. We would take a small drop of blood from our finger three times a day for just one week. We would enter that smidgen of blood onto a glucose meter and successfully figure out how the food we ate, or the stress we're under, or the sore throat we are feeling, or the lack of sleep we've had, results in the high, average, or low number on the glucose meter. If we did that, we would have the tools to enter into an intimate dialogue with our body. We would become proficient in understanding how the world around us and our own reactions to the world affect us. When an individual is diagnosed with diabetes, research articles explain that the patient most often has had diabetes for about ten years. I once told my doctor about this and asked, "If the majority of diabetes patients have diabetes about 10 years before their diagnosis, why aren't they given the tools to monitor themselves?" I certainly would have. I'm sure if I had created a chart of my glucose tests, I would have seen a slow rise in levels and could have possibly prevented a diabetes diagnosis. But my doctor said that insurance agencies pay for diabetes monitors and tools only after one is diagnosed. And without insurance, diabetes monitoring equipment is quite expensive. Regarding diabetes, then, this disease reveals how our country, in general, considers the body and illness. We are a country that "treats" rather than "prevents," that prefers a phalanx of curative medicine instead of educating individuals early on in preventative medicine. Perhaps this is why there is a return to indigenous and/or ancestral healing practices.

Berenice Dimas (2015) explains that on December 31, 2012, she felt a shift as she stood on a hill at The Berkeley Marina in Oakland, California. She sensed a mystical energy in the skies and an energetic change. She says:

All of the planets are aligning. We're looking at the state of our health, and the chemicals integrated into our bodies, and we are coming to a place where *la medicina* is not enough. Communally, people are saying, 'I need more.' People are listening to their bodies in a different way because they are aware of the universe shifting. There is definitely a 'trend' right now, eliciting many conversations around spirituality and healing. Healing is cyclical, always in transition, always in motion.

(interview)

Our gente live in a myriad of complex and multi-layered systems. They experience daily events inside and outside of the body. More than ever, then, individuals are seeking alternatives to healing and many are successfully arriving at a "new conciencia", a renewed and intimate relationship with their ever changing body and the world around them.

Notes

1 Gloria Anzaldúa, for example, was not allowed to pursue a doctorate that incorporated the study and ideas she wrote about in *Borderlands/La Frontera*.
2 Estela Román is a *curandera* from Cuernavaca, Mexico. She is also the Director of the International Center for Cultural and Language Studies Cuernavaca in Morelos, Mexico. Her work focuses on the preservation and teaching of traditional medicine and ancestral practices from her community of Temixco, Morelos, Mexico. On November 27, 2013, Román gave a lecture entitled "Guardians of Time" at UC Berkeley's Multicultural Center. Her lecture discussed indigenous understandings of "time" connected to emotional and physical health.
3 See Berenice Dimas' website: www.berenicedimas.com/story.html
4 See Oakland Unified School District's homepage on their Restorative Justice program: www.ousd.org/restorativejustice
5 See *Decolonize Your Diet* website: http://decolonizeyourdiet.org/bios and see their book also by the same title.
6 The North American Free Trade Agreement (NAFTA) was signed by Canada, Mexico, and the United States in 1994, creating vast free trade zones. The Central American Free Trade Agreement (CAFTA) expanded the NAFTA agreement to the following countries: Costa Rica, Guatemala, El Salvador, Honduras, Nicaragua, and later the Dominican Republic also joined.
7 "Indian Time" is also a stereotype in North America (coined by non-Natives) having to do with being late or being lazy. This is not what is meant here.

Bibliography

Anzaldúa, Gloria. *Borderlands/La Frontera: The New Mestiza*. 4th ed. San Francisco: Aunt Lute Books, 2012.

Anzaldúa, Gloria. *Interviews/Entrevistas*. Ed. Ana-Louise Keating. New York: Routledge, 2000.

Anzaldúa, Gloria. "now let us shift … the path of conocimiento … inner work, public acts." *This Bridge We Call Home: Radical Visions for Transformations*. Ed. Ana-Louise Keating. New York: Routledge, 2002.

Bost, Suzanne. *Encarnación: Illness and Body Politics in Chicana Feminist Literature*. New York: Fordham University Press, 2010.

Calvo, Luz and Catriona Esquibel. *Decolonize Your Diet: Plant-Based Mexican-American Recipes For Health and Healing*. Vancouver: Arsenal Pulp Press, 2015.

Chabram-Dernersesian, Angie, and Adela De La Torre, eds. *Speaking From the Body:Latinas on Health and Culture*. Tucson: University of Arizona Press, 2008.

Dimas, Berenice. "Queeranderismo." *Fleshing the Spirit: Spirituality and Activism in Chicana, Latina, and Indigenous Women's Lives*. Eds. Facio, Elisa and Irene Lara. Tucson: The University of Arizona Press, 2014.

Dimas, Berenice. Personal interview. 3 August 2015.

Gonzales, Patrisia. *Red Medicine: Tradition Indigenous Rites of Birthing and Healing*. Tucson: The University of Arizona Press, 2012.

lara silva, ire'ne. *Enduring Azucares: A Digital Chapbook*. 2015. Available at: www.siblingrivalrypress.com

Mihesuah, Devon Abbott. *Recovering Our Ancestors' Gardens: Indigenous Recipes and Guide to Diet and Fitness*. Lincoln: University of Nebraska Press, 2005.

Montes, Amelia María de la Luz. "Urban Farm Gardening, Cooking, with Luz Calvo & Catriona Esquibel: Decolonize Your Diet Conversations." *La Bloga*. 14 September 2014. Available at: http://labloga.blogspot.com/2014/09/urban-farm-gardening-cooking-with-luz.html

Montes, Amelia María de la Luz. "Creating Art From Diabetes: An Interview With ire'ne lara silva on Enduring Azucares." *La Bloga*. 5 July 2015. Available at: http://labloga.blogspot.com/2015/07/creating-art-from-diabetes-interview.html

Pascual Soler, Nieves, and Meredith E. Abarca, eds. *Rethinking Chicana/o Literature Through Food: Postnational Appetites*. New York: Palgrave Macmillan, 2013.

Román, Estela. *Nuestra Medicina: de los Remedios para el Aire y Los Remedios para el Alma*. Bloomington: Palibrio, 2012.

23

LOWRIDER PUBLICS

Aesthetics and Contested Communities

Ben Chappell

In Robert Rodriguez's 2010 film *Machete*, the eponymous hero recruits a cavalry of lowriders to storm the hideout of a white, nativist vigilante army. These cars and trucks, gorgeously painted, bouncing on hydraulic suspensions, some displaying chrome "plaques" identifying them with car clubs from the shooting location of Austin, Texas, roll to the battlefield with automatic firearms and rocket launchers mounted for the occasion. As the conflict ignites, one truck, apparently "juiced" with a particularly powerful hydraulic set-up, rears like a stallion and slams down to crush a cowering racist.

This scene is in keeping with the parade of stereotypes that the film playfully deploys in its affirmative parody of exploitation cinema. The lowriders mounted up at once when called on to provide muscle for a covert guerilla network organized in support of undocumented immigrants. This alliance between the Mexican Americans who actually created and sustain lowriding as a cultural practice and *mexicanos de allá* represents a relationship that is not always harmonious in the real world. But the fantasy does not stop there. When the protagonists of the film first visit the lowrider shop that will arm its mobile works of art for them, they find sexy pachucas among its staff, their makeup unsmudged by machine grease, moving wordlessly through the frame like photos from *Lowrider Magazine* come to life.

This recent use of lowrider style as part of a cinematic palette is significant because, like other figures rendered by Rodriguez, it reproduces and blows up to hyperbolic proportions certain well-known cultural tropes—here these include lowriders as a threatening urban force, characterized by their style that is both baroque in its elaboration and effortlessly cool, but also by a capacity and willingness to do lethal violence. It encapsulates a great deal related to long-standing American fascinations with urban, minoritized vernacular culture, not to mention the national obsession with racialized bodies and aesthetics in general, and proffers to its audience the pleasure of recognizing these things.

But let me juxtapose a different image. Shortly after September 11, 2001, our first child was born to my wife, Marike Janzen, and me. We were living at the time in a rental house in Austin's Eastside barrio, while I conducted fieldwork with lowrider clubs for my dissertation.

Perhaps because both of us have roots in rural, close-knit communities, where certain momentous life events are announced publicly, or maybe because we were eager for a break from the trauma and emergency that seemed to saturate the air in the days after the 9/11 hijackings, we posted a sign at our front walk: "Welcome home, Calvin!" and decorated it to suggest the arrival of a baby. One afternoon there was a knock on the door, and I opened it to see two men whom I had been getting to know in the hours I spent hanging out with a car club, attending its meetings, and cruising with members on East Riverside Drive. The lowriders on my porch were large men, who selected their t-shirts based on the number of Xs. They wore goatees, gold chains, and tattoos of family names. Their denim shorts hung well below their knees, almost down to the Nike Cortez kicks that completed their outfits. One of them, Alex Vargas, was the president of a local club, and when I invited them in he presented me with a packaged kit of baby equipment—diaper bag, changing pad, bottle cover—all upholstered in a Winnie-the-Pooh theme. "From the club," he announced. I thanked them and asked how they found our place—although I had mentioned to the club that I lived on East 2nd Street, they hadn't called first to announce their visit.

"We saw your sign," said Alex. "Ain't no Mexican gonna call their kid Calvin."

The point of this story is not that there's anything unique about my family, but that there's a lot about lowriding that gets lived out in ordinary life, rather than in the most spectacular moments. As a white, leftist scholar drawn to the creativity of historically oppressed people in marginalized contexts, I understand the impulse that *Machete* exaggerates, to see lowriders as vehicles of struggle and resistance, and in previous work I have argued that they carry some of this political valence regardless of the specific intentions of individuals who build and drive lowrider cars (Chappell, 41). Yet I'm not sure I can recall a single instance of a lowrider (person) describing their style to me in the terms of a marching army. What was much more common was for people to state that their devotion to this particularly mechanical art was "all about family," and "not just a fad, but a lifestyle." Granted, this representation invokes another whole range of stereotypes about Latina/o familialism that may naturalize and moralize entrenched gender roles. But the nature of the lowrider family was also not entirely taken for granted; instead it inspired discussion and debate. One woman connected to a car club informed me that club relations were like kinship, but then corrected herself: "No, it's more than family. If I break down an hour away, my club will come pick me up, but I don't think my family would!"

In this chapter, I argue that the people who practice lowrider style create and maintain not only a spectacular aesthetic tradition, but particular kinds of sociality—including both resistance and kinship—that amount to an enacted and emergent concept of community. I use that word only with caution. It is far too easy for researchers to invoke "community" when they want to make vernacular cultures legible to outsiders—as if there is a state of being called community that is universally understood and unimpeachably good, which redeems the simple folk and their irresponsible ways. That is not my aim. Instead, to try to understand identity-forming aesthetics like lowriding, it is worth thinking about the late Juan Flores's critical deconstruction of "*comunidad*" into the component parts of "*común*" and "*unidad*" (608). Addressing the possibility of a broad identity like "Latino," Flores goes into the problematics about how identities form around some combination of shared circumstances (*común*) and shared interests or commitments (*unidad*). The proportions and relations between these components—being an identity *in* ourselves and being an identity *for* ourselves—cannot be assumed or taken as permanent, but are themselves objects of struggle and contestation. In this way, the kind of community that lowriders create in the interest of keeping their style alive should not be subsumed under dominant or normative concepts of community. At times it pushes against these imposed concepts, though it is also never immune to them. Taking a serious look at lowriding allows us to see how aesthetic forms that are animated through public practice create the kinds of social space in which such imposed concepts can be pushed against.

I want to advance the idea that lowriding, a public deployment of aesthetics with a particular history, has the effect of constructing a particular spatial-social complex that I find it useful to call a *public*. Lowrider publics are the products of both artistic and mechanical semiotic work (indeed the line between lowrider art and lowrider mechanics is a vague and shifting one). Recognizing lowrider scenes as publics is a way to understand their enduring affective power for participants, and the work that they do in the material world. It is also a way out of the moral/aesthetic judgment that has been all-too conventional in popular culture studies.

The kind of judgment I want to avoid or at least temper asks questions like "is it authentic?" and "is it resistant?" That analytic both invites essentialist characterizations of fields of popular practice that are actually diverse, and suggests that the point of research is to decide: shall we be for or against this thing? It is a theoretical blind alley because while scholars of popular culture often have a personal affinity for the forms they study— otherwise, why bother?—we also try neither to endorse nor ignore moments in which the practices around those forms may reproduce oppression rather than challenging it. But at the same time, things get complicated. For example, if we take note that a form of street culture is steeped in masculinist gender hierarchies, and that these are reinforced both within and outside of the community that produces it, what can we say about women who love lowriding without hating themselves? That they are victims or delusional? I think not. Either to demonize or romanticize a cultural form is to make it out to be far simpler and more finished than it is. To be true to how forms circulate in everyday life (with lowriders, on everyday streets) and to draw close to why they matter so much to many people, we should look to lowriders not for their final answer about authenticity and politics, but as providing the means and the space in which those questions can be explored.

In my own ethnographic work, while following the resistance narrative in many ways, I have sought to evade the moral question of whether lowriding is essentially liberating or reproductive of oppression by assuming that lowriding is not *essentially* anything. Instead, drawing on a rich theoretical stream that flows out of both applications and critiques of Jürgen Habermas's account of the historical "public sphere" of the European bourgeoisie, I find it useful to think of lowriding as an activity that generates around itself a material space of intense social relations, embodiment, and communication. Habermas's work stressed the importance of a "public" as a deliberative space where people who share some commonality (Flores's category of the *común*) such as being the citizens of a democratic state, discuss and debate matters of general concern, perhaps to arrive at a shared understanding or commitment to common interest (*unidad*) (Habermas, 49). Some readers who recognize the importance of this concept of deliberative space nevertheless have pointed out the exclusive nature of the bourgeois public sphere that gave Habermas the idea—in this historical structure and in others that have followed on its model, interests and concerns are often only considered "general" if they appeal to the white men of property whom the classic "public sphere" effectively belonged to. The concerns that mapped onto other identities— such as those of women or people of color—were "particular" and thus excluded from public consideration (Fraser, 63). Nancy Fraser's formulation of a "subaltern counterpublic" applies the discursive and community-forming notion of a public sphere to groups defined in opposition or distinction to the dominant identities of the ruling class (67). The idea of counterpublics has opened up rich new ways of seeing and contextualizing popular social and cultural forms, such as the working-class union hall as not only a place where union business was conducted, but the scene of a much more diverse cross-section of social life (Aronowitz, 90).

As Keta Miranda has shown, negotiating a relation to publics and the condition of publicity is a stake in certain Latina/o popular cultural forms that participants are well aware of. Miranda's work with Latina youth in California directs us not to the question of whether practicing such forms, such as the linguistic and embodied performance of being a "homegirl," necessarily solidifies or endorses a specific and pre-fixed identity, but how aesthetic activity defines publics that offer resources and opportunities for people to experiment with self-representation and speak back to broader publics that misrepresent them. The homegirls who appear in Miranda's study demonstrate a sophisticated understanding of the extent to which the boundaries and expressive acts of specific publics order their lives (4–5). I would propose that by intervening in the mundane venues of public representation like streets and parks, lowriders are on the same page.

In what follows, then, I take a critical path that is not by any means new, but one that I think still needs to be reiterated. This was expressed influentially by Stuart Hall in 1981, when he called for treating "the popular" not as essentially for or against "the people," but a site of struggle over meaning, identity, and power (449). Perhaps unwittingly, Hall here echoes the notion advanced a few years earlier by Juan Gómez-Quiñones that "culture is the context in which struggle takes place" (29). As a specific instance of this dynamic, I want to demonstrate that despite the strong evidence that lowriding has been created and sustained largely for the benefit of men and the reproduction of a very specific version of manhood, its affective power and therefore value to Mexican Americans has the potential to go beyond the scope of that gendered project. This not only explains the presence of women in the history of lowriding who have asserted their own identity claims on the style despite barriers and rejections, but also indicates how lowriding itself may provide a context in which the internal politics of Mexican American style and identity has a dynamic life that continues to unfold.

Lowrider Studies

Lowrider style evolved in Mexican American communities in the mid-twentieth century, reflecting both the working-class social location and the growing consumer market that they represented. The custom car styles that became popular in barrios from as early as the 1930s— lowered suspension, bright and elaborate paint, chrome wheels, velvet upholstery, etc.— evolved in dialogue with and sometimes in distinction from other genres of car customization such as hot rods and "kustoms." Ron Aguirre, a customizer well-known by car enthusiasts of various backgrounds in California, invented a hydraulic suspension in 1959 that drivers could control, leading to the development of "hopping," a signature movement style of lowriders (Penland, 16). By the 1970s, individuals who understood this style to be iconic of the specific experiences of urban Mexican America were using "lowrider" to refer to a social identity that was more than strictly descriptive, and for some, melded easily with resistant Chicano consciousness. Car clubs organized and developed along with the style, with California's The Dukes placing their origins in 1962 (S. Gonzalez). Cruising scenes also coalesced on specific boulevards to make driving a mode of entertainment and socializing (Rodriguez, 29). *Lowrider Magazine* (hererafter *LRM*), founded in 1977 by students at San José State University, gave the "movement," as the magazine described the spreading style, a media space to call its own.

Scholars have sought to interpret and contextualize lowriding for over thirty years, generally agreeing that it has something to do with identity, but varying at times on what this means. For example, archaeologist Ruben Mendoza in some of the earliest published academic papers, treats lowriding as the material culture of a distinct people—the culture of Aztlán. Folklorist James Griffith tied lowriding to a specific nexus of aesthetics and place, namely a baroque sensibility that he argues pervades the Latina/o U.S. Southwest and gestures to that region's past as part of the Spanish empire (153). Anthropologists Brenda Jo Bright and Michael Stone, in keeping with a cultural studies approach to popular culture and subculture, highlighted ways in which lowriding serves as an agentive response to social circumstances shaped by conflict and structural hierarchies. My own ethnographic work also follows this trajectory, with an emphasis more on material production than communicative expression that I elaborate here. The narrative of lowriding as resistance, embraced at certain times and in different ways by the mass-produced *LRM* and certain Chicana/o Movement participants alike, often followed the lead of Luís Valdez and other cultural workers in looking back to the "pachuco era" as a model of the merging of aesthetic style and rebellious attitude (Alvarez, 6; Ramírez, 84). In an important polemic in the 1980s, Luís Plascencia called this nostalgic tie between lowriders and past cultural movements into question, noting the eagerness of beer companies to sponsor lowrider shows. Influenced by Horkheimer and Adorno's "culture industry" thesis, Plascencia proposed that embracing lowrider style was not an authentic act of Chicano identity so much as an opportunity for capital to colonize new consumer markets (171).

In this history of scholarship, the outlines emerge of a debate that is familiar (perhaps even enough to be tedious) to any student of popular culture: the tension between resistance and incorporation. Adherents of the resistance narrative may proclaim that however steeped in consumer culture and therefore reliant on capitalism and ideological constructs of automotive modernity they may be, lowriders are expressing an authentic identity and therefore claiming semiotic autonomy in a society and age characterized by ubiquitous cultural politics. The incorporation side may reply, however, that lowriding merely provides a pleasurable delusion for people whose actual freedom remains elusive. One factor in this debate is that, although a diverse range of individuals participate in lowriding, the predominately masculinist tenor of custom car culture in general makes it so that any ascription of resistance joins in a longer history of locating a political stance within the activities, indeed the bodies, of men and the mundane performances of gender that reproduce a highly heteronormative order (see Davalos, 78ff). This is most salient in the media culture around lowriding, largely guided by the editorial style of *LRM*, which for decades has featured glamor photography of stereotypically female models addressed to a hetero-male gaze. Yet it is also old news that cultural forms that resist certain structures of domination are prone to reproducing other ones. What is too often absent from these discussions is an account of how the gendering of lowriding proceeds and is negotiated in everyday practice, and how these processes constitute lowrider publics. Looking at particular lowrider publics—represented in documentary and ethnographic work or re-imagined in a narrative feature film—can shed light on this.

Barrio Publics

The capacity of style to generate and cultivate publics is evident in *Everything Comes from the Streets*, a documentary centering on the San Diego lowriding scene, directed by Ethnic Studies professor Albert Pulido and co-produced by veteran lowrider activist Rigo Reyes and filmmaker Kelly Whalen. *Streets* makes clear that struggles over public space—primarily, resistance to the destruction of a barrio community by highway construction and the ensuing reclamation of land under the highway as Chicano Park—united lowrider stylists and Chicana/o activists in common cause in the 1970s. Taking a longer view, though, the film places lowrider car clubs in a history of popular social organizations that functioned as small publics in barrio communities throughout their history. Dr. Pulido's historical work yields evidence that Mexican Americans in California were present and active in car culture before lowriding was as established as a distinct sphere as it is now—for instance in the drag-racing team the "Bean Bandits," who, besides their expertise in building and tuning cars for racing, also asserted a Mexican identity into the otherwise Anglo-dominated public culture. Likewise, Pulido links car clubs to the social "jacket clubs" of the early 1950s, neighborhood cliques of young men who hung out together, planned joint activities, and identified themselves publicly with nicknames and highly decorated, matching jackets.

Rather than a linear development from one form to another, what these historical precedents show is that lowrider car clubs are part of a broader phenomenon of self-organization that has pervaded Mexican American history. Such groups can be viewed on a continuum from the least socially accepted neighborhood "cliques" that sometimes identified themselves or were identified by outsiders with violent gang culture, to more "official" and eventually recognized mutual-aid societies and civil rights organizations like the G.I. Forum, the League of United Latin American Citizens (LULAC), and a range of church organizations. All of these groups, and many others that fall in the shadows of documented historical attention to date, can be understood as "publics" in the expansive sense I have been using. They involve assembling people who share some commonality in terms of their social positioning, and who engage in a variety of social activities aimed at understanding, promoting, and pursuing common interests. As cultural critic Michael Warner has noted, a public always addresses its own constituents—it is a forum for communication within the group—but also involves a dimension of reaching beyond its own boundaries (quoted in Robbins, 200). Popular publics were a means by which people excluded from mainstream or credentialed arenas represented themselves to themselves, but they also projected their emerging collective identity out to the larger world. Thus the continuum of barrio publics, including bands, baseball teams, festival planning groups, and a range of other types of organizations, includes diverse ways of balancing an interest in autonomy from outside control against claims to recognition from the outside as legitimate.

For many lowriders, it is clear that autonomy is a big part of the equation. There are liabilities to displaying the style, including being profiled as a gangbanger, targeted for vandalism by jealous rivals, and potentially harassed by the police. Yet commitment over time is a source of respect among many lowriders. To be considered "O.G." or "original gangster" is not always so much a literal description as it is a testament to longevity in the field, an emblem of persistent aesthetic activity despite adversity. This is not to say that lowriders hold disdain for being recognized as legitimate members of their larger communities—in fact, many lowrider clubs use their aesthetic identity as the basis for mobilizing charitable work, including fundraisers for the needy or for individuals in crisis. But a commitment to a barrio aesthetic means taking a position that any acceptance forthcoming from the larger society will not be purchased by the abandonment of other, primary relationships. When barrio identities are shed, according to this ethos of lowrider style, something irreplaceable is lost.

This priority placed on commitment informs the problematics of gender and sexuality in lowriding. For while on one hand, it could be argued that the "non-negotiable" elements of the style include the dominant forms of hegemonic masculinity that have been well critiqued from a feminist position; on the other, there are women who seek precisely to undo this articulation of hegemonic masculinity with lowriding in order to negotiate space for themselves in lowrider publics.

A Letter Home: La Mission

Cinema has been a primary road by which lowrider style traveled around the U.S. and ultimately, the world. In the 1970s, widely distributed films such as *Up in Smoke* and *Boulevard Nights* depicted lowrider style as a feature of barrio life, an approach also adopted by African American cultural producers with ties to lowriding in hip hop music videos and "hood films" such as *Boyz in the Hood* in the 1980s. A more recent Hollywood interest in lowriding appears evident in the Eva Longoria vehicle *Low Riders*, now in production, and in the 2010 film *La Mission*, written and directed by Peter Bratt. Bratt's brother Benjamin, who stars in the film, garnered attention for the project in Hollywood by virtue of his successful acting career, but also probably lent it credibility in the eyes of some lowriders who best know his work in films like the 1993 gang melodrama *Blood In/Blood Out*, which lowriders I met through my research considered a "classic." The Bratt brothers' family roots go back to Peru but they are from the San Francisco neighborhood named in the film's title. *La Mission* can be read in part as a letter home from Hollywood, an appreciation of their *barrio* and of lowrider style as one of its rich cultural resources. By centering its narrative on a young man's coming out as gay to his lowrider father, *La Mission* also seems to send a message promoting inclusivity to the urban streets. (See also Cecilia Josephine Aragón's chapter in this volume that analyzes the use of indigenous music and dance in the film.)

La Mission is a sign of its times, reflecting a partial turn away from stock homophobia in mainstream film and television, though in an interview, Peter recounts how a white studio executive informed him that gay themes had been "dealt with" after *Brokeback Mountain* (quoted in Collins, et al., 495). Scholar Cristina Alcalde argues, however, that the intended critique of masculinist heterosexism may fall short of its mark. Citing Michael Kimmel on the centrality of violence and homophobia to hegemonic masculinity, Alcalde proposes that this kind of conflation has become fluid and contested among Latinos (539–40). Yet Peter Bratt's aim in *La Mission* was to create what he called an "archetype" in the lowrider protagonist, "Che," in order to peel back the layers of "ultramasculinity" to reveal emotion and relationality beneath (quoted in Alcalde, 542). The result is that Che's masculinity, characterized by violence as well as mechanical aptitude, is articulated with lowrider style and the barrio location to stand for the community that his son, Jes, risks losing when he comes out. That Jes's love interest, Jordan, is white, wealthy, and from another neighborhood ironically reinforces views expressed by various characters, that homosexuality originates and belongs elsewhere—part of what Alcalde calls a more general "white/brown binary" (544).

Yet Alcalde argues that there is an important "counterstory" at work in the film. If as she suggests, the depiction of Che's relationship with his peers "humanizes minority men" (547) then I would propose that it is the image of lowriding and other practices characterizing the neighborhood as their home that provides the space for these interactions. The film explores Che's capacity for relationship not only with his son but with Lena, an African American woman who is his neighbor and a feminist foil for both his expressed views and enacted gender relations. Che's opening up to Lena is portrayed in the film when he invites her into his world on a weekend cruise with the circle of friends who also are portrayed hanging out in the garage. The aesthetic marking of cruising time and space shifts the basis of the characters' interactions from the *común* level of living in the same area to the *unidad* of shared commitments that are expressed through their construction and display of cars, and the sociality that results as they roll in caravan past appreciative spectators, then park to share food, listen to music, and dance. The question that brings Che into personal crisis and that terrorizes Jes is whether this *unidad* is based on divinely ordained separation of gender roles and their normative relations to each other, or whether it is expansive enough to allow space for change, queering, and inclusion. The latter view is supported less by the specific statements of the characters than by the more understated and highly realistic portrayal of everyday life and ordinary discourse around lowriding.

In pre-release publicity for *La Mission*, Peter Bratt described it to the San José State student newspaper as "based on a true story" (L. Gonzalez, 1). Regardless of how closely the narrative hewed to the lives of specific individuals, the sociality around cruising and building cars resonates with the accounts of some of the most recent of lowrider researchers. These not only document that lowrider publics exist, and as Pulido's film demonstrates are part of a broad stream of social forms in Latino history, but also suggest how the importance of stylistic publics to diverse constituents may be greater in some cases than the barriers they pose to participation.

Claiming Space in Lowrider Publics

The work of Denise Sandoval, who like me, completed a dissertation on lowriding in 2003, is distinguished in the literature both by its strong roots in the Los Angeles scene and by its attention to questions of gender. In part of that work, which appears as a chapter in the edited volume *Velvet Barrios*, Sandoval addresses head-on the way that lowrider media genders the style, and how readers contest it, by looking beyond the covers of *LRM*. That publication, a national venue for the state of the art of customization, has featured glamor models as accessories to featured cars since its early years in a visual discourse Sandoval correctly identifies as objectifying. Though at various times, this has raised critique of editorial decisions that produce "a girlie magazine rather than a car magazine," editors have made no bones about their heteronormative address to a presumed male audience. In 2000, *LRM* publisher Ricardo Gonzalez told a *Los Angeles Times* reporter that "hey, we're a business. We're aimed squarely at 18- to 25-year-old males, and they're interested primarily in two things. Cars are one of them. And until our audience revolts, we'll keep using the girls" (quoted in O'Dell).

This gendering of lowriders certainly works effectively among many of the enthusiasts who pass around *LRM*, study its pages, and aspire to make it themselves into a feature article. Sandoval, however, refused to accept the characterization of lowriding as a boys' club and conducted the most thorough review of *LRM* that has been published by an academic. In this work, especially her analysis of readers' letters, Sandoval shows conclusively that despite the editors' stated or implied intentions, quite a few women understand lowriding and the magazine as discursive public spaces in which matters of importance to them might be aired. In fact, Sandoval finds that over the history of *LRM*, Chicanas consistently wrote letters that were published in readers' sections, discussing the challenges they faced in their lives, complimenting the magazine as an expression of Chicano pride, and at the same time offering critique for its masculinist pose (189). When these letters were not answered directly by editorial staff, other Chicanas would write back to one another in subsequent issues.

Thus women in communities that made up both the source and the audience for lowriding engaged the discursive space of *LRM*, one of the first and most successful national magazines addressed to Latinos, with the understanding that its aesthetics defined it as being for them also. They made use of this medium, in the days long before social media and texting were widespread, to talk to each other, but at the same time to reach beyond their specific counterpublic, since it was clear that men would be reading their letters as well if they were published. Sandoval arrives at the conclusion that women's participation ultimately does not save *LRM* from its problematic role in deploying lowriding as a marketing tool, and objectifying women's bodies as part of the package (195). Her account of the letters, however, shows that this role was not played out uncontested within the diverse and dynamic community that identified with lowriding.

If Sandoval's work documents the persistent investment of women in lowriding as their public, Gloria Moran's documentary *The Unique Ladies* chronicles the frustrated efforts of several women in San Diego to get into lowrider car clubs, and their ultimate success in forming their own. Patricia Gutierrez, president of the Unique Ladies club, states on camera that she has been lowriding for around thirty years, starting by working with her husband on cars, but that when it came to full participation in car club activities, caring for their four children fell to her as a higher priority. Pat and the other members Moran interviews describe attitudes that take for granted gender-divided activities, saying that some men viewed lowriding in a similar vein to "men's sports." A male car club president interviewed on camera describes how members of his club preferred a homosocial group, since "guys want to be with other guys."

Despite these barriers to participation, which are more explicit and open in some contexts than others, the nature of lowriding as a material aesthetic opens up a way for people to contest their own exclusion—by doing it better, making it harder for others to deny their status as lowriders. Another club member, identified as Sherry, describes her satisfaction in building a car that is recognized by other lowriders as aesthetically successful—this becomes a context for her to claim equality. When showing her car, Sherry says she sometimes get comments from viewers like "Your boyfriend's car is nice," to which she is quick to reply "Yeah, his is nice, but this one's mine." Another woman appearing in the film affirms that "if men can do it, you can do it, too."

Moran's film makes it clear how, although entrenched habits in lowriding work to marginalize women, lowrider scenes that function as publics embedded in particular communities provide the context for those relations to be challenged. Sherry recounts how wives and girlfriends of car club members, including herself, may be as actively involved as the men in the labor that makes a lowrider scene happen—organizing and fundraising for shows, working on cars and club-themed clothing, and so on—but still denied membership. Women always "stood behind" the men in her view, present in the scene but in a supportive role, or as the "hood ornaments" represented by models. She situates her own participation as "the other side" from glamor models, using lowriding to "show respect, have class, and not disrespect yourself." Another club member, Linda, who negotiated domestic expectations by waiting until her kids were grown and she was a grandmother before coming out with a lowrider car (now, she says, "I'm living life to the fullest in lowriding") describes in one of the film's closing moments how recognition from the lowrider public affirms the success of these struggles. When driving her '64 Chevy Impala into a car show, Linda likes to turn down her radio in order to hear the comments of onlookers she passes: "The ladies have arrived … "

BEN CHAPPELL

Cruising On

On a driveway into a cemetery, off the access road to a busy divided highway, a hearse pulls slowly forward, followed by a limousine with its passenger compartment clearly filled to capacity. Pausing at the entrance to the cemetery, a heavy-duty pickup then follows, bearing a flatbed trailer with a 1973 Monte Carlo on it. The empty lowrider is primered in dull grey, at a midway point in a complete repainting project, but I remember it from several paintjobs before, when it glittered in metallic blue. Next in the procession is a Cutlass from the 80s—immediately recognizable by its divided front grille. The camera documenting this event turns to follow the trailered lowrider and we lose sight of the Cutlass, but by the time it pans back, the car is tilted onto three wheels, holding this cocked position while it rolls on (as I write, the video can be viewed at http://tinyurl.com/alexvargas [playamistik]). Behind it, a '63 Impala drops one of its wheel's hydraulic lifts, then the other, lowering the front end and then raising both together with a bit of bounce that promises the possibility of much more extreme hops.

The procession goes on and on, one custom car following another. If not for the funeral vehicles in the lead, it would seem like a festive occasion. But these lowriders are not gathering for a weekend cruise or competitive show, but to pay respects to Alex Vargas, the car club president who visited me many years before and who succumbed to ALS (Amyotrophic lateral sclerosis) in 2012. Not every lowrider who proclaims they are in the scene for life will carry through quite this literally. For Alex's friends and family, though, there was no question that it would be an appropriate tribute to their loved one to memorialize him in the middle of the thickly layered, overlapping social and aesthetic ties of a lowrider event. The instincts of academic analysis are often to sort through and get to the bottom of events like this—is lowriding a *family* thing or a *consumption* thing or a *neighborhood* thing? In the end, this may not be that helpful for understanding the affective power of this kind of style, which is what has allowed it to endure for generations, and what leads people to turn to it in both the ordinary and the sublime moments of a life course.

Maybe there isn't any one of these "things" that can sum up the essence of lowriding, since what it really does is materialize a zone where family, neighborhood, creativity, commitment, and other imagined potentials or lived relations overlap and coexist. After all, when lowriders say "it's all about family," they don't necessarily mean that there is a single kind of kinship that the bonds between lowriders reflect. Whose family, exactly, is it all about? What kind of family? The ones where people support or abuse one another? Sometimes the phrase suggests that lowriding is like what family ought to be. And yet in other ways, it is like what being "related" actually is—maybe good and maybe not. When family figures prominently in everyday life, you might use it often as a reference point without necessarily believing that it's always the greatest thing in the world. If you're in the lowrider family, you share a connection, for better or worse, with others who are as well. Regardless, when someone who is kin to you passes on, it makes sense to mark the occasion publicly, representing your relationship in ways that are addressed to other kin as well as to the broader world. In this way, lowrider style provided the means for a community to mark the passage of one of its own.

Bibliography

Alcalde, M. Cristina. "What it Means to be a Man?: Violence and Homophobia in Latino Masculinities On and Off Screen." *Journal of Popular Culture* 47:3 (2014): 537–53.

Alvarez, Luis. *The Power of the Zoot: Youth Culture and Resistance During World War II.* Berkeley: University of California Press, 2008.

Aronowitz, Stanley. "Unions as Counter-Public Spheres." *Masses, Classes and the Public Sphere*. Ed. Mike Hill and Warren Montag. London: Verso, 2000. 83–101.

Bright, Brenda Jo. *Mexican American Low Riders: An Anthropological Approach to Popular Culture*. Dissertation, Rice University, 1994.

Chappell, Ben. "Custom Contestations: Lowriders and Urban Space." *City & Society* 22:1 (2010): 25–47.

Collins, Dana, Sylvanna Falcón, Sharmila Lodhia, and Molly Talcott. "A Feminist World is Possible: Artists and Activists Speak about Human Rights." *International Feminist Journal of Politics* 12:3–4 (2010): 485–517.

Davalos, Karen Mary. *Exhibiting Mestizaje: Mexican (American) Museums in the Diaspora*. Minneapolis: University of Minnesota Press, 2001.

Flores, Juan. "The Latino Imaginary: Meanings of Community and Identity." *The Latin American Cultural Studies Reader*. Ed. Ana del Sarto, Alicia Ríos, and Abril Trigo. Durham: Duke University Press, 2004. 606–22.

Fraser, Nancy. "Rethinking the Public Sphere: A Contribution to the Critique of Actually Existing Democracy." *Social Text* 25/26 (1990): 56–80.

Gómez-Quiñones, Juan. "On Culture." *Revista Chicano-Riqueña* 5:2 (1977): 29–47.

Gonzalez, Lidia. "Film Festival Announces Award for Benjamin Bratt." *Spartan Daily* 8 March 2010: 1.

Gonzalez, Steve. "Fernando Ruelas – Duke's Car Club President – Raza Report." *Lowrider Magazine* 28 January 2011.

Griffith, James S. *A Shared Space: Folklife in the Arizona-Sonora Borderlands*. Logan, UT: Utah State University Press, 1995.

Habermas, Jürgen. "The Public Sphere: An Encyclopedia Article (1964)." *New German Critique* 3 (1974): 49–55.

Hall, Stuart. "Notes on Deconstructing 'the Popular.'" *People's History and Socialist Theory*. Ed. Raphael Samuel. London: Routledge & Kegan Paul, 1981. 227–40. Reprinted in *Cultural Theory and Popular Culture: A Reader*. Ed. John Storey. Upper Saddle River, NJ: Pearson/Prentice Hall 1998. 442–53.

Mendoza, Ruben. "Cruising Art and Culture in Aztlán: Lowriding in the Mexican American Southwest." *US Latino Literatures and Cultures: Transnational Perspectives*. Ed. Francisco A. Lomelí and Karin Ikas. Heidelberg, Germany: C. Winter, 2000. 3–35.

Miranda, Marie "Keta." *Homegirls in the Public Sphere*. Austin: University of Texas Press, 2003.

O'Dell, John. "Lowrider Magazine Riding Higher than Ever." *Los Angeles Times* 19 April 2000: G1.

Penland, Paige. *Lowrider: History, Pride, Culture*. Minneapolis: Motorbooks International, 2003.

Plascencia, Luis F. B. "Low Riding in the Southwest: Cultural Symbols in the Mexican Community." *History, Culture, and Society: Chicano Studies in the 1980s*. Ed. Mario T. García and Bert N. Corona. Ypsilanti, MI: Bilingual Press, 1983. 141–75.

playamistik. "Austin Lowrider Legend laid to rest (Alex Vargas)." Online video clip. YouTube. 13 October 2012.

Ramírez, Catherine. *The Woman in the Zoot Suit: Gender, Nationalism, and the Cultural Politics of Memory*. Durham, NC: Duke University Press, 2009.

Robbins, Bruce. "Public." *Keywords for American Cultural Studies*, Second Edition. Eds. Bruce Burgett and Glenn Hendler. New York: New York University Press, 2014. 200–4.

Rodriguez, Roberto. *Justice: A Question of Race*. Tempe, AZ: Bilingual Press/Editorial Bilingüe, 1997.

Sandoval, Denise. "Cruising Through Low Rider Culture: Chicana/o Identity in the Marketing of Low Rider Magazine." *Velvet Barrios: Popular Culture and Chicana/o Sexualities*. Ed. Alicia Gaspar de Alba. New York: Palgrave Macmillan, 2003. 179–96.

Stone, Michael C. "'Bajito y Suavecito': Low Riding and the 'Class' of Class." *Studies in Latin American Popular Culture* 9 (1990): 85–126.

Filmography

Blood In, Blood Out. Dir. Tylor Hackford. Hollywood Pictures, 1993.

Boulevard Nights. Dir. Michael Pressman. Warner Bros, 1979.

Boyz in the Hood. Dir. John Singleton. Columbia Pictures, 1991.

Everything Comes from the Streets. Dir. Alberto López Pulido. University of San Diego, Department of Ethnic Studies, 2014.

Low Riders. Dir. Ricardo de Montreuil. Universal Pictures, in production.

Machete. Dir. Robert Rodriguez. Overnight Films, Troublemaker Studios, Dune Entertainment, and Dune Entertainment III, 2010.

The Unique Ladies. Dir. Gloria Moran. Pre-release screening copy courtesy of the director, 2015.

Up in Smoke. Dir. Lou Adler. Paramount Pictures, 1978.

24

BARRIO RITUAL AND POP RITE

Quinceañeras in the Folklore–Popular Culture Borderlands

Rachel González-Martin

In an interview following his July 28, 2015, appearance on the premier episode of Fox's reality show *Knock Knock Live*, twenty-one-year-old pop artist Justin Bieber said one motivation for surprising superfan Ashley at her home in California with a luxury quinceañera celebration was that he wanted to "bless her" (Staff, "Watch Justin Bieber Bless"). Ashley, a huge Bieber fan who had been unable to celebrate her quinceañera at the expected age of fifteen due to a life-threatening bout of meningitis, credits Bieber's song "Pray" as the inspirational anthem of her recovery. This contemporary consumer "blessing" occurring on a nationally broadcast "reality" television series illustrates a secular re-visioning resulting, in part, from the attention of contemporary American media.

This recent pop cultural *encuentro* with the quinceañera event exposes that when the celebration is situated within popular American media representations in the twenty-first century, it takes on a spectacle-like nature. The above example is a special case interpretable as one response to a growing desire to bring a Latina/o-identifying market into mainstream media practices. It is illustrative of this chapter, which examines how representations of the event in popular media affect and reflect community narratives of the quinceañera celebration. The presence of Bieber's financial "blessing," as well as the event's placement on national television, requires scholars of cultural productions to interrogate the relationship between popular representations of cultural practice and individual enactments as mutually constituted. Cultural agents, both individual and institutional, meet in the space that I term the *folklore–popular culture borderlands*. This intellectual conception takes its cue from the legacy of borderlands ideologies developed in twentieth-century Mexican American and Latina/o Studies. It is populated by cultural forms that appear in society as both enactments of community traditions and as representations crafted by popular media. This is but one lens through which to access the quinceañera celebration. Emplacing the event in the folklore–popular culture borderlands bridges meaningful community experiences of cultural memory with manufactured, consumer-driven interpretations that repackage such memories as cultural products.

The framework of the folklore–popular culture borderlands is specifically inspired by the work of literary critic Domino R. Pérez. In her 2008 book, *There Was a Woman: La Llorona from Folklore to Popular Culture*, the author traces the winding intertextual path of the legend of La Llorona among Mexican American and Chicana/o, identifying communities across the United States. To be concerned with the intertextual is to be concerned with the relationship *between* the formation and circulation of common cultural forms. In the present cases, these texts are those rhetorically linked by the name "quinceañera," a term referring both to the person celebrating their fifteenth birthday and the celebration itself. Pérez's considerable intellectual labor utilizes three interpretive levels: cataloging texts, interpreting contexts of use (revision), and investigating contexts of intercultural dialogue. In similar fashion, the goal of this work is to illustrate the intertextual connections between popular televisual representations of quinceañera traditions and those representations and patterns of enactment in community contexts. My concern with the intertextual gap between quinceañera practice and quinceañera representation investigates how these cultural texts are circulated and used within communities, complicating the notion of a singular, "authentic" quinceañera celebration. Instead the intertextual relationship illuminates changing interactions and influences shared between cultural communities defined not by racial or ethnic categories, but by age and social generation.

While Pérez's book length work on Llorona legends mobilizes an exhaustive catalog of legend-texts permeating socially and technologically varied contexts, this work will narrow the investigative lens to three examples from twenty-first century English-language television – examples that place the quinceañera at different levels of program production. These examples will serve as a petite-catalog of quinceañeras in the context of American popular culture, beyond the confines of community-based production, and will focus on the intercultural relationships between generations of performers. This approach allows readers to interpret the ethno-social rite of passage within a framework of a retro-acculturative process of Americanization that seeks out narratives of heritage traditions in diverse culturally and technologically mediated contexts.

Overview

The majority of ethnographic research conducted in the United States on the lived experiences or the real-life enactments of quinceañera celebrations document events occurring before the twenty-first century. While these sources (Cantú 1999; Davalos 1996; Horowitz 1993) provide a rich record of the cultural politics and performance patterns of regional events, they do not focus on the event as a patterned practice undergoing shifts around the country. Those appearing after the turn of the twenty-first century begin to acknowledge the relationship between sacred and secular systems of influence (Marling 2004; Arcaya 2004; Deiter 2002; Cantú 2002; Pleck 2000). The work of Kristen Deiter represents a singular source concentrated on the complex and contentious reciprocal relationship between cultural enactments and popular representations that are key to repackaging the quinceañera as a secular rite. In "From Church Blessing to *Quinceañera* Barbie®: America as 'Spiritual Benefactor' in La Quinceañera," Deiter elaborates upon the quinceañera as a cultural event torn between two symbolic "spiritual benefactors" that she views as pulling the quinceañera in two contradictory directions. First is the American Catholic Church eager to draw in Hispanic Catholics. The other is a pop culture industry that views Hispanics as a target marketing demographic and uses the quinceañera as an access point to pan-ethnic, Latina/o consumers. Deiter uses the image of a quinceañera-themed Barbie doll marketed by Mattel to solidify the relationship between desires for conspicuous consumption and religious devotion. However, her work frames this relationship between popular culture and religion as a power struggle between institutions, making social agents subjects of institutional decision-making. The author proposes that Church leaders embrace the changes in order to better serve their Latina/o congregants; however, I assert that the tradition is not the property of the Church at all. What Deiter's argument does is contextualize the quinceañera as a product of institutions as "benefactors" of the event. She asserts that the event is affected by popular culture, yet this relationship is framed as destructive and disorienting. Her work, which starts a contemporary conversation on the secularizing process of U.S. quinceañeras, will later be joined by a growing discourse on consumer interventions into the tradition as explored in Julia Alvarez's 2007 book, *Once Upon a Quinceañera: Coming-of-age in the U.S.A.* Alvarez's memoir documents the American experience from a perspective of quinceañera planning, solidifying the event's capacity as a metonym for the changing social and economic status of broadly defined U.S. Latina/o communities. However, Alvarez's work, influenced by her own intergenerational relationship to twenty-first century events, is a narrative of longing that documents elements of the quinceañera professional industry while illustrating the growing distance between cultural memory and contemporary practice. My work examines adaptation in traditional practice by approaching the event from a generative perspective, mediated by a process of secular revisions rather than a narrative of cultural loss.

Secular Re-vision

The secular revision of quinceañera practices across the United States is not all-encompassing. The quinceañera community under discussion here is made up of second and third generation Latina/o-identifying Americans who are middle class-aspiring and English-dominant. These youth audiences are finding their cultural location situated between *immigrant* and *American*, and their traditional practices reflect this. Twenty-first-century quinceañera rites are accompanied by a heightened secular profile linked to the tradition's wider presence and reception in mainstream media. This mainstream visibility not only helps to draw in Latina/o constituencies of consumers in the U.S., but is also responsible for helping promote the cultural form as an emotional pathway back to ethnic heritage. However, a secular revision could not exist without a sacred narrative.

In a secular-focused quinceañera celebration, visual storytelling takes on an important role in making public a young woman's and her family's desired message to their kin networks. In sacred contexts, a quinceañera's morality is under scrutiny. Mass celebrations require a young woman to assess her connection to her Catholic faith and her church community and, in very basic ways, verbally affirm her desire to move into the larger adult membership of her community. Religious blessings are coupled with intensifying micro-rituals that vary based on faith communities. A key micro-ritual of a Catholic quinceañera mass is an offering to the Virgin Mary. As a representation of ideal Catholic feminine virtue, the Virgin Mary, or alternately the *Virgen de Guadalupe*, plays a central role in the Catholic blessing of a quinceañera girl. After a young woman reaffirms her baptismal vows in front of her congregation, she will place a bouquet of roses at the foot of a shrine of the Virgin. She will pause and say a private prayer, assumed to include a promise to abstain from sexual activity until heterosexual marriage. Marian[1], a young woman whom I interviewed in San Jose, California, in 2009, shared that " ... you are promising her your virginity. I think, you know, that you'll act right and not get in trouble" (personal interview, November 2009). More than a promise of general faithfulness, most young women I encountered in my fieldwork framed the Catholic intervention in the quinceañera celebration as specifically focused on controlling female behavior through shame. This sacred perspective has failed to keep up with a generation of Latina teenagers whose quinceañeras are not the representations of "firsts" that they were for previous generations. From the donning of formal wear, high-heeled shoes, and makeup to even venturing into sexual experimentation, quinceañeras are no longer the defining marker of social transition. Therefore, sacred institutions are no longer the only cultural gatekeepers of social status. References to a sacred process have been excised from pop cultural representations of the ritual by corporations eager to resonate with youth consumers. However, it is uncertain whether the secular quinceañera is a product of noting audience practice and preferences, or whether first-generation quinceañeras are shifting their celebrations based on the influential models set forth by televisual narratives of the quinceañera event.

The Quince Motif: Televisual Representations

One way to think about quinceañeras is not as material events, but as ephemeral cultural reference points that signal certain identifications and dis-identifications with ideas influencing conceptualizations of social citizenship, such as gender identification, sexual practice, spiritual affiliations, economic standing, and ethno-racial identities. Quinceañeras function as narrative motifs in the lives of Latina/o and non-Latina/o populations exposed to the celebration in a variety of personal and public contexts. The motif circulates through personal experience narratives of family history (Casillas 2010; Cantú 2002), through public records such as in the society pages of local newspapers (Staff, "Quinceañera-Analecia"), in films that use the event as a thematic backdrop (*Quinceañera* 2006), and television programming that utilizes the events' rich visual characterization to draw Latina/o audiences into shared ethnic moments. Such televisual motifs can appear as simply rhetorical references to the event that draw in Spanish-language terminology into English-language spaces, or they can drive the content development of the entire show across many seasons. While televisual examples remain overlooked by scholars who focus on ethnographic documentation of community enactments, an examination of televisual representations can reveal themes that bridge lived experiences and representative fictions. Not unlike ethnographic approaches, televisual examples offer partial pictures of the cultural event. However, in a sociocultural context of *retroacculturative* practice, in which communities are seeking out identifiable heritage traditions in order to reconnect to their ethnic roots, the quinceañera's widespread circulation in American media repositions fictional or dramatized accounts from entertainment to cultural education. Representations of quinceañeras on TV do cultural work by modeling and circulating affective and practical experiences to wider, multicultural audiences, in some cases introducing the event for the first time into Latina/o homes. Even without faith-based intervention, sexuality and honor continue to be included in quinceañera motifs on TV.

Case Study #1: Quinceañera as Family Ritual

In 2004, *The George Lopez Show* was in its third season, and although it had dropped in Nielsen ratings since the completion of its first two seasons, it still managed to reach an estimated 7.4 million viewers (Markert 150). At its peak, it was but one of a variety of ethnically inflected, family-oriented sitcoms available during prime time until the end of its sixth and final season. In episode 8 of season 3, "Bringing Home the Bacon," the Lopez family, a blended, Mexican American and Cuban American household, is planning their fourteen-year-old daughter Carmen's (Masiela Lusha) quinceañera celebration. While John Markert references this episode in his article "*The George Lopez Show*: Same Old Hispano?" to reference the way the program appeals to Hispanic Catholics, he does so by making the assumption that *all* quinceañeras are inherently religious celebrations, even though no references to religious practice or icons are used during the episode (161). Instead, I will examine Carmen's quinceañera as a secular re-vision, affirming and circulating this cultural knowledge to both Latina/o and non-Latina/o audiences. Rather than symbolic of religiosity, Carmen's quinceañera is a representation of a modern, highly secular, but no less deeply symbolic, ritual celebration of coming-of-age among contemporary Latina/os that emphasizes how family identity is an active undercurrent in the planning and execution of the celebratory event. These family narratives are reinforced by themes like paternal honor and sexual awareness.

The basic premise of this episode is that the Lopez family is in financial turmoil as father, George (Lopez), is temporarily out of work and mother, Angie (Constance Marie), is currently working outside the home to make ends meet. This narrative provides a backdrop to the planning of Carmen's quinceañera as the family struggles to afford the elaborate event of their daughter's dreams. Lopez's internalized insecurity at not being able to financially support his family and control family financial decisions erupts in the humorous exclamation, " … we're Americans! You know, we're assimilated. How's that gonna look to the neighbors? Latino family having a quinceañera? I mean, it's so obvious." The secular quinceañera, with an increased emphasis on the material manifestations of class, such as dress and status, create particularly volatile family situations in which families must balance their desires to simultaneously affirm both class status and ethnic affiliations. More than simply a coming-of-age for individuals, this televisual representation foregrounds how the planning process intimately affects Latina/o families striving for social success in the United States. At the same time, this process is presented as a burden on fathers, who ambivalently invest in a process that turns daughters into women.

Rather than drawing on religious narratives of honor and shame to discuss sexual development, "Bringing Home the Bacon" uses humor to illustrate the roles that perceptions of sex and sexuality play in the context of Latina coming-of-age celebrations. In the opening scene, viewers watch Carmen working on a dress pattern and struggling to figure out how to construct her own quinceañera gown. This image resonates with audiences of previous generations who hold strong memories of a coming-of-age moment marked by constructing one's own dress, a tradition that has diminished as quinceañera professional industries promote the purchasing of custom couture gowns as modes of elaborate self-expression. As Carmen sifts through magazines in the family's back yard, she must explain what a quinceañera is to her Anglo-American boyfriend, Jason (Bryan Fisher). As a product of an English-language, North American television network, this moment serves as cultural education for viewing audiences as much as for the characters. At the same moment, the conversation draws in her grandmother, Benny (Belita Moreno), who comedically foregrounds the coming-of-age discourse as one of sexual awareness:

Jason: So what's a quince-who-ha?
Carmen: It's a "keen-say-uh-nyara." It's like a Latina debutante ball or a Sweet Sixteen, ... but you do it when you're fifteen ...
Benny: I did it when I was 14. (pause)
Carmen: *You* had a quinceañera?
Benny: Ok.

("Bringing Home the Bacon")

In the context of this sitcom, comedy is one method of making audiences aware of complicated social relations between family members. In this case, Benny's impeccable comedic timing blended with her character as a "lascivious" mother and grandmother to George and Carmen respectively, allows a narrative of the quinceañera that is framed as an event entangled in subsumed narratives of sexual awareness. While Carmen is whimsically planning the structure of her dress and a fantasy of feminine display, Benny is voicing long-held cultural assumptions about the quinceañera as a public acknowledgement of a young woman's burgeoning adulthood facilitated by conflicting social messages that encourage the display of sensual, heterosexual femininity, but shame proactive sexual practice. The event celebrates multi-simultaneous realities such as biological and emotional development and the social expectations that come with the classification of "womanhood". Carmen and Benny are interlocutors in a doubly-coded conversation mediated by humor. While Carmen is defining the quinceañera for her non-Latino boyfriend, focusing on the material results such as a homemade formal gown, Benny focuses on what she sees as the reality of the event, that of a loss of virginity. So when Benny claims that she "did it" at fourteen, she is referring to the loss of her virginity rather than the naïve assumption of her granddaughter who presumes that she is referring to a mistimed celebration of her fifteenth birthday. In this instance one can see how Benny is not framed as a traditional or idealized grandmother. Quinceañeras are moments that create contexts for communication, particularly around concepts of personal development. If this were a drama series, this moment would have been characterized by sincere intergenerational conversation about the trials and expectations of adulthood. If the narrative, as Markert notes, had truly been linked to Catholic religiosity, this conversation would have been a warning of the ills of premarital sex, whether framed from a personal experience narrative of triumph or of regret. Instead, audiences see the conversation stop short. Rather than use Carmen's inquiry to start a heartfelt intergenerational moment, the overarching narrative plot continues, and Carmen continues to plan her gown pattern without the intervention of an emotionally generous grandmother. Benny's contribution is simply a jaded response to her granddaughter's seemingly futile labor:

Benny: Don't work too hard on it; it's only going to end up on the back seat of that guy's [Jason] car anyway.

("Bringing Home the Bacon")

This, however, is perhaps more of a common experience of contemporary Latina youth as they work to find themselves through their quinceañera planning. As much as these events affirm a young woman's coming-of-age moment, they also mark a fragile moment in which young women's lives shift in ways that open them up to difficult life paths, such as premarital sex and teenage pregnancy. In this televisual example, the quinceañera is highlighted as a secular celebration that, among many things, has the capacity to facilitate intergenerational communication as well as reinforce hetero-normative gender identities rooted in the maintenance of the notion of sexual honor. However, in this case, this exchange represents communication as one of the key elements of quinceañera practice potentially lost as intergenerational contact is supplanted by professional intervention.

Case Study #2: Quinceañeras and Cultural Identity

The second example takes us from the realm of sitcom to reality-based television, and away from themes of sexuality and intergenerational communication to the conceptions of regional ethnic identities. Unlike the previous example, the reality show model creates a performance environment that resides between individual enactments and completely fictionalized representations. With most ethnographic and folkloric expositions of quinceañera celebrations being household-specific, televisual examples of the celebration offer access to narratives outside local communities. These popular narratives, while not observed firsthand, still become textual experiences from which communities see their traditional practices reentering their lives in new ways. In a forthcoming article titled "Digitizing Cultural Economies: 'Personalization' and US Quinceañera Practice," I assert that quinceañera productions are being dominated by peer-based online networks, rather than intergenerational networks of familial knowledge. Rather than taking stylistic cues from mothers, aunts, or even older siblings, young women are looking externally of family networks in order to conceptualize a quinceañera as a vivid and unique self-portrait. Regional identification is one identity factor that often gets overlooked in scholarly interpretations that focus, as most American folklorists do, on deep understandings of individual performance in singular contexts.

In this televisual example, the quinceañera appears as a subject of a single episode of the hit reality television show *Top Chef*. The quinceañera event is mobilized as a unique way of accessing one aspect of culturally informed cooking found in Texas. The season's theme is "Everything's Bigger in Texas," and one episode recreates the popular rite around food practices. While serving its own needs as a thematically oriented reality cooking show, the employment of the quinceañera event as the backdrop of an entire episode introduces a broad non-Latina/o prime time audience to the celebration as a function of regional Texas Mexicano identity, symbolized by a "quick grill challenge" requiring chefs to adeptly handle rattlesnake meat as the primary ingredient. Audiences are introduced to two teams of professional chefs, with only one identifying Mexican American person between them, modeling a system of cultural translation where food is the primary vehicle of cultural communication. In this symbolic material system of the quinceañera, the event is represented as a formal dinner. In previous generations, the dinner portion of the event could be the product of large-scale cooking done by groups of family members. Often such commitments to ingredient cost, labor, and expertise were considered a special birthday gift in honor of the quinceañera girl and her special relationship to a growing network of adult mentors. In the season 9 episode "Quinceañera," Blanca of San Antonio, Texas, allows the Top Chef teams to assemble a celebratory meal for her and her one hundred guests who will be expecting "elegant Mexican cuisine." These include multiple food texts, including appetizers, entrées, and the characteristic quinceañera birthday cake. These ephemeral material forms are featured as key symbolic elements of the larger ritual event, signaling to family and friends that they are not only at a quinceañera, but at a quinceañera in *Tejas*.

This televisual example represents how material aspects of the quinceañera event, particularly those that one can customize, loom large in the planning and actuation of quinceañera celebrations. There are two main pitfalls made by these outsider chefs that will highlight the role material elements like food play in the creation of a successful event. First, that ingredients are regionally interpreted and cannot be overgeneralized. While each of the two teams of professional chefs participating in this quinceañera challenge was able to consult directly with Blanca for thirty minutes before they acquired ingredients, they were in fact free to create dishes based on their own expertise. As a recent transplant to Texas, I have found that the culinary culture of Mexican Americans in Texas varies greatly from those of Mexican Americans in California. One clear distinction is the prevalence of homemade tortillas at virtually every Mexican and Tex-Mex-identifying restaurant. From food trucks to fast-food joints, fresh homemade tortillas are a staple of Mexican and Mexican-inspired cuisine in the Lone Star State. However, this practice was not a part of the creation of Blanca's competitive quinceañera buffet, which was expected to serve as a reflection of her identity as a Texas Mexicana quinceañera. This tortilla faux-pas, alongside one southern chef's choice to use flour tortillas rather than corn to create enchiladas, horrified the quinceañera girl, who was quick to assert both her preferences and judgment in an event she framed as an extension of herself, her family, and her heritage.

Second, the failure to acknowledge that food fosters a pronounced aesthetic experience in the quinceañera celebration, requiring visual as well as flavor appeal, was another misstep made by these culturally outsider chefs. Discussions of undesirable ingredients accompanied aesthetic critiques made by the quinceañera girl herself, as she was asked to rate the birthday cake created by each team. The Green Team asked Blanca if she would like a tres leches, or "three milks," cake. Having little experience with the scale and style of quinceañera celebrations, they did not realize the standard of multi-tiered, elaborately decorated cakes often cannot include a tres leches cake whose dense, moist texture cannot be displayed without refrigeration for the duration of a quinceañera event. While tres leches cakes are consumed in quinceañera events as a nod to Mexican heritage, they are often made as an unattractive, large, flat sheet cake and are accompanied by an inedible, decorated dummy-cake used for display and photography. The culturally unacquainted Green Team created a large, three-tiered tres leches cake, hoping to appeal to Blanca's ethnic identity and taste-palate, but instead created an unattractive cake that could not keep its form as it gradually toppled under its own weight. Here one can see how identity factors play vacillating roles in the creation of a successful quinceañera celebration. As the quinceañera professional industry grows, consumers must translate their desires to producers, who must learn how to help a quinceañera translate her tastes and values into material forms. Even in a medium like food, visual aesthetics are equal to tastes and textures in the context of enacting an ideal quinceañera. In the end, Blanca preferred the Pink Team's attractive, though "kinda dry," cake to the delicious mess of the Green Team's tres leches cake, providing the edge the team needed to win the challenge.

These brief examples highlight secular re-vision as part of the culinary character of the quinceañera event as a cultural form that is regionally as well as ethnically and economically inflected. More important, they illustrate the contemporary role of quinceañera girls as the primary creative agents in their celebrations, a role formerly occupied by networks of female relatives. The desire for individualized, secular events has led to the quinceañera becoming entrenched in national marketing campaigns directed at garnering the support of Latina/o youth consumers.

Case Study #3: Quinceañera as Consumer Rite

This final example illustrates a broader perspective on the changing character of a quinceañera celebration as it is situated in the folklore-popular culture borderlands. *Quiero Mis Quinces* (*I Want My Quinceañera*) is a reality series that airs on the MTV Tr3s network, formerly known as MTV en Español. The network describes itself as "the most widely distributed TV network dedicated to superserving today's bicultural Latina/o youth" (2). This self-described "superservice" includes an entire series dedicated to the celebration of the *quince años* in "key" American cities such as New York, Chicago, Los Angeles, and Miami, specifically targeting youth audiences "more affluent than his/her immigrant parents" (3). *Quiero Mis Quinces* first aired in 2006, in conjunction with the network's bilingual rebranding. Their network profile describes the series as " ... an insider look at the over-the-top coming-of-age parties that are a Latin American tradition." They go on to promote that they showcase parties that are "lavish and exquisite, but can easily become a teenager's worst nightmare!" (4). The show's success has even inspired the network's first spin-off show, *Quiero Mi Boda* (*I Want My Wedding*). The show, designed to appeal broadly, presumes Spanish-language competency but translates all English dialogue into Spanish. The program, like its target audience, serves as a cultural ambassador, bridging "Latino and American worlds" through patterns in consumer engagement (3).

Unlike the previous examples, the quinceañera in this pop cultural context gets more than a temporary status or cursory attention. While the above examples have been contextualized in specific ethno-national cultural contexts, in California Mexican American/Chicana/o and San Antonio, Texas Mexicana/o, respectively, *Quiero Mis Quinces* has the latitude to create content that broadens the narrative of the quinceañera celebration to a wider pan-Latina/o audience. However, these representations continue to be limited by notions of idealized geographies and language politics. Through weekly episodes featuring stories from around the nation, audiences are able to see patterns of quinceañera performance that transcend regional practice, creating a dramatic and spectacular snapshot of a quinceañera culture in the United States.

Iliana is a fourteen-year-old Cuban American who lives in Miami, Florida. Her narrative is the sixth of sixteen featured in the third season of *Quiero Mis Quinces* airing on MTV Tr3s in 2009. The show uses her personal narrative as an anchor to the larger theme of quinceañera planning. "I was a shy, chubby girl ... I want to show people how I became a young lady everyone wants to be with ... " ("Iliana," 2009). This episode and its counterparts all adhere to the same formula. It documents the quinceañera journey of one young woman and her family and shares pieces of key moments of the consumer rite to sell the reality-drama of planning a large-scale event, but it is also a useable instructional tool for those watching. This televisual representation focuses almost exclusively on the consumer process behind the lavish coming-of-age rite. The audience's introduction to Iliana is framed by her begging her father to rent her a party boat so that she and her court can arrive in style "a lo Miami" to their waterfront event venue ("Iliana," 2009). The party boat, a wholly secular addition to her celebration, highlights the lavish tenor of many modern celebrations fueled by conspicuous class aspirations over the demure solemnity of religiously focused ceremonies. While the heated debate between father and daughter regarding the necessity of renting a party boat seems staged for the cameras, in Iliana's subsequent teenage tantrum and confessional style reinterpretation of the scene, she sincerely claims that her father was just being "difficult" and that "it's so strange that my dad don't give me what I want" ("Iliana," 2009).

The next show segment, in similar fashion, focuses on the quince-girl's desire to purchase not one but two designer dresses. Fueled by a pair of best friends who follow her to a local Miami dress shop, Iliana convinces her mother to put aside their agreed upon plan to rent a dress for the evening and instead purchases two distinct formal gowns, one for her entrance and the other as her "cake dress". This secondary costume change occurs specifically for the symbolic cake cutting and celebratory toast, both traditional moments celebrated during the evening's reception. While formal attire, particularly an investment in a first article of "adult" clothing (Cantú, 2002, 19), is a common and expected flourish in a quinceañera celebration, in the recent decade featuring oneself in a myriad of designer costume changes has helped the professional industry surrounding the event expand. This expansion only serves to validate and encourage the culture of spending as a "traditional" practice in quinceañera planning. Spending on this scale also leads to an emphasis on the value that specific consumer products can offer. In the last themed section of this episode aptly titled "El drama with the Limo," the product of the consumer-driven event emerges upon realizing the rental company has sent a stretched Hummer, not a stretched Cadillac limousine. Iliana screams at her mother "Yo quiero Cadillac! How stupid can them people be?" (Iliana, 2009). Her outburst and subsequent emotional meltdown only serve to show how, rather than simply understanding a quinceañera as a cultural event, among U.S. Latina/os it also serves as a metonym for American teenage culture. In this way, the quinceañera has increasingly become a self-oriented narrative, with customized parts that index class status and youth identity over ethnic or spiritual affiliations. It is only in the final minute of the episode when Iliana and her father are dancing their formal first waltz that Iliana's voice-over intrudes on the rolling credits stating, "I feel so sentimental ... I went from being his little girl to a young lady" (Iliana, 2009). This series-based televisual representation serves as an extended commercial for the planning and execution of a quinceañera celebration fit for reality TV.

Following young women and filming their quinceañera planning process, the show implicitly foregrounds the consumer potential of the event. Unlike the previous examples, which illustrate specific elements that resonate at different levels of the quinceañera planning process like defining coming-of-age by sexual behavior, the financial sacrifices of parents, or even the dual symbolic-practical role cultural forms like food can play within an event, the series form patterns each story around intergenerational conflict over luxury spending. In the context of the show, the quinceañera is a consumer rite. The question here becomes, as Stuart Hall would note, is this representation a distortion of lived experiences, and if so, how do we measure the gap? (Hall, *Representation and the Media*.) If we consider the self-described philosophy of MTV Tr3s as creators, their job is to appeal and deepen, not to reframe. In this way, the consumer profile of the quince pop rite in this instance is meant to intensify features of the event that are already at play in individual enactments of the traditional practice.

Conclusion: Quince as Retroacculturative Practice

Quinceañera motifs circulate throughout populations, creating community through a shared past. However, what if your family lacks a community history of coming-of-age at fifteen? Through an examination of a small body of televisual examples, one can see these events are not only personal, affective rites celebrating biological and social tradition, but also represent a cultural access point in a process of *retroacculturation*. Retroacculturation, coined by Carlos E. Garcia, is a marketing term that highlights consumer tendencies of predominantly second, third, and fourth generation Latina/os, who are described as feeling as though they "have lost their cultural identity" ("Hispanic Marketers" 142). In such a process, Latina/o consumers seek out and are drawn into marketing strategies that are culturally inflected and that recognize and use ethnic recognition to secure brand loyalty. This creates new contexts in which traditional practices are not only being re-presented, but also re-created. Quinceañeras on television represent such a practice. However, these new pop cultural examples also serve as sites of cultural knowledge for young generations who encounter such traditional practices as mediated forms of popular culture, rather than as the informal culture of their own homes or families. While retroacculturation assumes a desire to look back, it also implies the desire to *imitate* the recent past. Rather than simply becoming representations of cultural traditions that draw in a familiar Latina/o viewing audience, quinceañera pop-rites serve as cultural access points offering pathways to cultural knowledge tailored to English speaking, Americanized Latina/o youth audiences. Latina/o identity in the U.S. cannot be simplified to a direct, historical connection to Latin America. Instead, ideas of Latinidad are mediated through processes of shared memory. The presence of secular quinceañera motifs on television allow those without quinceañera memories of their own to access the tradition, bring it into their home, and adapt it to their own windy pathway of cultural and communal development. However, at the same moment, they change the tradition for generations to come.

Note

1 This name is a pseudonym for a fourteen-year-old, Mexican American youth I interviewed with parental permission during a 2009–2010 quinceañera season in California.

Bibliography

Alvarez, Julia. *Once Upon a Quinceañera: Coming-of-Age in the USA.* New York: Viking, 2007.
Arcaya, Sara. *La Quinceañera: Performances of Race, Culture, Class and Religion in the Summerville Community.* Medford, MA: Tufts University, Digital Collections and Archives, 2002–3.
"Bringing Home the Bacon." *The George Lopez Show: Season 3.* Written by Dailyn Rodriguez. Dir. Josh Pasquin. Warner Home Video, 2004.
Cantú, Norma E. "La Quinceañera: Towards an Ethnographic Analysis of a Life-Cycle Ritual." *Southern Folklore* 56:1 (1999): 73–101.
Cantú, Norma E. "Chicana Life-Cycle Rituals." In *Chicana Traditions: Continuity and Change.* Eds. Norma E. Cantú and Olga Nájera-Ramirez. Champaign-Urbana, IL: University of Illinois, 2002. 15–34.
Casillas, Sandra. Personal Interview. 3 February 2010.
Davalos, Karen Mary. "'La Quinceañera': Making Gender and Ethnic Identities." *Gender, Nations, and Nationalism.* Special issue. *Frontiers: A Journal of Women Studies* 16:2/3 (1996): 101–27.
Deiter, Kristen. "From Church Blessing to Quinceañera Barbie®: America as 'Spiritual Benefactor' in la Quinceañera." *Christian Scholar's Review* 32:1 (2002): 31–48.
"Episode 1." *Knock Knock Live.* Fox. KTBC, Austin. 28 July 2015. Television.
González, Marian. Personal Interview. 10 September 2009.
Gonzalez-Martin, Rachel. "Digitizing Cultural Economies: 'Personalization' and US Quinceañera Practice." TS. 1 August 2015.
Hall, Stuart "Representation and the Media" DVD. Northampton, MA: Media Education Foundation. 1997.
"Hispanic Marketers." *Hispanic Marketers Guide to Cable: Hispanic Cable Facts & Cultural Cues.* Cabletelevision Advertising Bureau, 2008. 140–50.
Horowitz, Ruth. "The Power of Ritual in a Chicano Community: A Young Woman's Status and Expanding Family Ties." *Marriage and Family Review* 19:3–4 (1993): 257–80.

"Iliana." *Quiero Mis Quinces: Season One*. Dir. Sebastian Portillo. MTV, 2009.

Markert, John. "'The George Lopez Show': The Same Old Hispano?" *Bilingual Review / La Revista Bilingüe* 28:2 (May–August 2004–2007): 148–65. Print.

Marling, Karal Ann. *Debutante: Rites and Regalia in American Debdom*. Lawrence, KS: University of Kansas Press, 2004.

MTV Tr3s. N.d. "07MasterDoc." *The Video Advertising Bureau*.

Pleck, Elizabeth. *Celebrating the Family*. Cambridge: Harvard University Press, 2000.

Quinceañera. Dir. Richard Galtzer and Wash Westmoreland. Cinetic Media, 2006.

"Quinceañera." *Top Chef: Texas*. Bravo. 16 November 2011

Staff. "Happy Fifteenth Birthday Quinceanera Barbie®! Mattel's Girls Division Launches First Hispanic-Tradition Theme Barbie(R) Doll." *PRNewswire*. 15 May 2001. Available at: http://www.prnewswire.com/news-releases/happy-fifteenth-birthday-quinceanera-barbier-mattels-girls-division-launches-first-hispanic-tradition-theme-barbier-doll-71820292.html

Staff. "Quinceañera-Analecia Maria Ramon Villalpando." *The Temple Daily Telegram*. 15 August 2015.

Staff. "Watch Justin Bieber 'Bless' His Fans on 'Knock Knock Live.'" *Radio.com*. 28 July 2015.

Stuart Hall: Representation and the Media. Dir. Sut Jhally. Media Education Foundation, 1997.

25

CULTURA JOTERIA
The Ins and Outs of Latina/o Popular Culture

Ellie D. Hernandez

Ellen DeGeneres may be the most iconic gay character to break ground by coming out on prime time television in 1997, but there was also another openly gay character on the tube who was openly gay in the 1990s. Ricky Vasquez, a gay Latino character on the short-lived 1994 show *My So-Called Life,* featured an adolescent gay teen struggling with homophobia on the show. The part of Ricky Vazquez, played by Puerto Rican actor Wilson Cruz, was one of the first examples of an openly gay teen on American television whose struggles and issues about being gay took center stage (*Out Magazine*). In an *Out Magazine* interview, Wilson Cruz, now a Gay and Lesbian Alliance Against Defamation (GLAAD) spokesperson who advocates for LGBT rights, reflects on his character's impact on popular culture, "It's probably hard to measure the effects of it, but I know for many people the only LGBT people that they know are people that they meet on their television screens or at the movie theater." Ricky Vasquez may have been the first openly gay Latino character featured on television, but he would not be the last.

Representations of joteria in popular culture extend beyond the 1990s queer pop revolution where we see snippets and occasional minor roles. Even as Latinos have become the largest ethnic minority group in the United States, representations of joteria hardly register across the vast media locations and sites. The term joteria attends to the broader perspective about the intersectional issues and concerns of queer Chicana/o, Latina/o, and indigenous people. The Association of Joteria Arts and Activism Scholarship (AJAAS) uses the term "joteria" as opposed to "queer" or "LGBTQ" to illustrate the politics of representation for queer Chicana/os and Latina/os in arts, media, and activism. The mission of AJAAS is to "envision[s] a world that affirms Joteria consciousness and that celebrates multiple pathways for generating knowledge, sharing experiences, and becoming catalysts for social change. We seek to live in a world free of all forms of ideological, institutional, interpersonal and internalized oppression."

According to AJAAS, the term joteria differs from queer, because it centralizes queer Chicana/o, Latina/o and indigenous experiences, as opposed to a separate category or marginal ethnic group in relation to the more dominant mainstream U.S. LGBTQ Studies. Only in the last twenty years or so have we actually witnessed a semblance of Latina/o joteria in scholarship and in the arts. It is the goal of this chapter to illustrate the terms of coming out, and what actually correlates to the inclusion and resignification to joteria community. This chapter attempts to locate an historical joteria critique of notable figures coming out of El Closet. The dearth of representations can be attributed to the difficulty of navigating the hostile terrain of mainstream media which filters racial and sexual imagery for mainstream audiences. For Latina/os especially, images and subject matter about sexuality and gender queer-based representation stand as the basis for situating joteria as a new perspective in popular culture.

With few exceptions, there has been a relatively small presence of Latino and Latina joteria in mainstream in entertainment news and in popular culture in the United States, but inclusion and acceptance has been measured and few. As Daniel Enrique Perez notes in his study of queer representation in Chicana/o and Latina/o popular culture in *Rethinking Chicana/o and Latina/o Popular Culture*: "Whereas gay and lesbian identities in Chicana/o and Latina/o cultural texts have become increasingly visible, queer identities are not so easy to discern" (3). The task of creating a semblance of what constitutes joteria culture falls on scholarship and on the student involved in creating the knowledge of the culture. It must also be noted that representations have a historical basis. In other words, there have been important joteria in popular culture, but those representations have been either wiped out or excluded from our recollection until now.

Chavela Vargas

Within the contradictory spaces of exclusion and seeming visibility, there are some notable Latina/o figures who stand out and defy conventionality. In "Crossing the Border: A Chicana Femme's Tribute to Chabela Vargas", Yvonne Yabro Bejarano pays tribute to the Mexican songstress. The celebratory tribute to Vargas's music completely shatters the closet door by shaping the analog of critique and celebration. Bejarano's critical tribute signals a time when lesbian writers and academics sought to recuperate queer history. "A Femme's Tribute" indicates the power of music to transcend time and space, whereas Bejarano notes at the same time that "popular music is the site of bodily centered pleasures and cultural identifications." It is fitting to see music, and especially popular music, as an actual place and location—as communal ground for intercepting the codes of queer identity. In these mythic spaces, Bejarano locates the ways Vargas undoes the gender expectations we might have with música Mexicana, where gender codes are marked strictly in masculine and feminine terms, especially within the Mexicana/o romantic music tradition where subjects of sexual desire are essentially heterosexual. Because there are no borders to restrict what can be viewed as accessible joteria tradition, Chavela Vargas's music crosses the border and the imagination. She is one of the earliest representations of lesbian desire in music.

Chavela Vargas was born in Costa Rica in 1919 at the end of the Mexican Revolution. Vargas came of age as songstress during the Mexicana/o cultural nationalist period where defiance of gender norms and social expectation for women were challenged and transgressed. It was a time of exuberance and creativity for artists and performers who actively sought to recreate the terms of their own national identity during the 1940s and 1950s. Vargas associated with Avant-garde artists and political socialists that included such notable figures as Frida Kahlo and Diego Rivera throughout much of her early career, a career that spanned 60 years. Numerous rumors circulated about Chavela's lesbian encounters with

Frida Kahlo and became part of Mexican lore. Vargas ushered in daring drive in her music, which breaks with Mexicano tradition, to rewrite the dynamics of Mexicana/o song by creating an imaginative space where a joteria community could relate and participate in its representation. Her song "Macorina," which is easily interpreted as a play on words for "maricona," elicits a sultry play of sex and gender otherwise unheard of in Mexico's romantic song history.

The conditions for coming out were different for a performer like Chavela Vargas. The more pertinent critical concern to what it means to be "out in the Latina/o world." Chavela navigated her world in a particular way and some would argue that Mexican women have a different set of terms when they are out, as opposed to their gay male counterparts who have to navigate their masculinity in a largely patriarchal culture. Chavela came out officially in her autobiography *Y Si Quieres Saber de mi Pasado/If You Want to Know About My Past* at the age of 81. Chavela Vargas's autobiography was her attempt to reconcile the difficulties of coming out at a time when women, and especially lesbians, held second-class citizenship in Mexico (49).

"Lo Que se Ve, No se Pregunta"

No other Mexicano performer captures the power and influence in Latina/o music more effectively than Mexico's Juan Gabriel. When asked directly about his sexual orientation during a Mexican TV show, Juan Gabriel made one of the most definitive statements about his supposed homosexuality; his reply is notable but nonetheless effusive when he flat out states, "Lo que se ve, no se pregunta." The translation of his response intends to suggest that if my homosexuality is obvious, there is no point in asking. The implication in the response also suggests, "Don't go there." Indeed, in the Mexican culture there is a moral double standard, a perspective on the condition of coming out that differs greatly from U.S. and other Western European countries. Mexicano culture recognizes the existence of joteria among family members, relatives and close friends; coming out is not even necessary and may imply a tasteless exhibitionism of the self. The need to "come out" is not as prevalent in Mexico as it is the United States, and sexual partnership and sexual practices are often treated with respect and dignity.

Carlos Decena describes this approach to coming "out of the closet" as a "tacit subjectivity," a grammatically linked aspect of the Latina/o Spanish that provides for an implied position and absence of naming the subject in speech, and in this case, the homosexual identity. Decena describes this phenomenon, "conventional views of coming out in contemporary queer communities celebrate the individual, the visible, and the proud" and goes on to explain in Latina/o culture coming out does not mean one has to parade one's sexual identity publicly. In the United States, quite literally, people "come out" to their partners, but also to the rest of the world. In Latina/o culture, one's sexuality is a private matter and not a common practice to celebrate publicly a presumed private matter. The difference is that U.S. culture adopts a sexual identity that is more akin to a rebirth that is then treated as a public celebration, and this is not the case in most Latina/o cultures where sexuality is as personal as going to the bathroom or having an intimate conversation. Not all cultures have sexual identities per se underwritten by a thematic of emancipation; "coming out of the closet" is a U.S. construct that does not always work in other cultures and other countries.

Decena explains the issues of coming out in the conventional U.S practice, "where negotiations of the closet that refuse speech, visibility, and pride have been generally viewed as suspect, as evidence of denial and internalized homophobia, or as outright pathology." He encountered in his research of gay Dominican men a distinctive misreading of the way Dominican gay refuse articulation and visibility. This is in keeping with Juan Gabriel's response, *lo que se ve no se pregunta*, loosely translated into "there's no need to ask about something that is so obvious and so plain to see," a fitting political response to those who would attempt to publicly question his private life. Moreover, by this declaration, Juan Gabriel made fun of the gossip, by neither admitting nor denying his homosexuality, but at the same time, maintaining a solid position through the power of ambiguity. At the pinnacle of his career, Juan Gabriel had a series of concerts in the Palacio de Bellas Artes with his Northern music played by an orchestra. Again, if the Mexican elite was somehow scandalized, the rhythm of Juan Gabriel's music made everyone forget the sacrilege. There is a certain irony to the way Juan Gabriel's queer representations are encouraged by Mexican popular culture, as in his occasional duets with Rocío Durcal, a Spanish singer known for her collaborations with Juan Gabriel. Durcal's shows would later become inspiration for many transvestite shows in Mexican gay clubs, as parodies of their classic friendship between a straight woman and her artsy gay friend. In all, such signifiers of gay culture are abundant and evident across Mexican culture; its representations are made evident, even though they might seem hidden in plain sight.

"Hey Vasquez, Has Anyone Ever Mistaken You for a Man?"

Music, while enduring and resonant across time, does not capture the potency of visual representation. One breakthrough development did occur in the 1980s where we begin to see some visual representations of joteria for women, even if it is implied and short lived. In film and television however, representations of joteria had been missing in almost all mediums. The 1986 film release of *Aliens*, directed by James Cameron, featured a dykish military character named Vasquez, played by Jenette Goldstein, a Jewish American actress. Actual representation by Latina/o gays and lesbians often encounters conditional or provisional terms of representation when such characters are played by non-Latina/o. While it is nice to see a character that is intended to be Latina/o, especially in film, often times these characters are portrayed by Anglo actors or non-Latina/os actors. Judith Halberstam writes in Female Masculinity, "the racial dimensions Vasquez's character, the particular valence of Latina masculinity is underscored by the fact that a Jewish actress, Jeanette Goldstein, plays in this role". Halberstam notes, "Although Goldstein makes a convincing Latina, it is worth asking why the butch could not have been Jewish or white in this film or why a Latina could not have been cast in the role" (181). A question that still persists today, since it has been noted time and time again that the terms of representation many times do not intend to be inclusive but manipulative in its representation. There is a manipulative angle to this arrangement, since there is an expectation that you will be encountering a Latina butch, but the reality or the twist is that you are provided with Hollywood's version of a Latina character played by a non-Latina. Vasquez, the explicitly masculine Latina (tacitly situated lesbian), forms an unusual semblance, a dedicated foot soldier on a rescue space mission with huge biceps who inhabits an irrefutable gender queerness. Desire of the sex/ gendered body alters our understanding of the potency of Latina lesbian figure, who occupies a political erotics of an image Latina lesbians could identify. The cultural political context for Vasquez, however, is more problematic, since the character emerged as the U.S. interventions in Nicaragua and El Salvador reached a peak in the late 1980s. It sent the message that toughness and female masculinity could be expressed through a militarized effort to create an image of a Chicana dyke who is legitimized through militarization. Still, regardless of the political issues implicated in the militarized Latina/o queer persona, the image of Vasquez, a jota lesbian dyke, was the only image of a Latina dyke on screen ever imagined and no other has registered since Vasquez and her AK47 graced the cinema screen.

La Vida Loca

Puerto Rican singer and performer Ricky Martin became a music sensation at the age of twelve when he joined the pop group Menudo in 1984. Along with music and acting to add to his long list of accomplishments throughout the 1980s and 1990s, Martin released his own self-titled album *Livin' La Vida Loca: Ricky Martin*, which featured his most famous song from the album, "Livin' La Vida Loca," the song that made Ricky Martin the Latin Explosion of the 1990s. After achieving major international success with "Livin' La Vida Loca," Ricky Martin also became a sex symbol who epitomized Latino good looks with Latin flair on the music scene. The irony of "Livin La Vida Loca" is that the song became emblematic of the queer Latina/o experience and was fully appropriated by joteria culture as a coded message of queer life—La Vida Loca. As a different generation of Latina/o performers did not adhere to the rules and precepts of Latina/o culture, Ricky Martin's good looks and bold expression meant that he could stand on his own as a performer without risking damage from the media. After all, this was the age of coming out of the closet for numerous celebrities like Ellen DeGeneres, Melissa Etheridge, and Rosie O'Donnell. Ricky Martin's good looks and sensitive style exuded an acceptable way of expressing Latina/o gay masculinity.

In his autobiography titled simply *Me*, published in 2010, he finally answers his critics. After years of speculation over his sexual orientation, Ricky Martin had publicly come out of the closet in a posting on his website in March 2010. In a thoughtful note to his fans published in Spanish and English, Martin says writing his memoir got him "very close to my truth" and that hiding his sexuality any longer would "indirectly diminish the glow that my kids are born with," referring to his twin sons, who were born in 2008 to a surrogate mother. In the note to his fans he explains, "These years in silence and reflection made me stronger and reminded me that acceptance has to come from within and that this kind of truth gives me the power to conquer emotions I didn't even know existed." Many in the LGBTQ community applauded his decision to come out at the height of his career. He has continued to be an influence as a Latino by lending his support and sponsorship to numerous foundations. In 2012, he delivered a speech at the UN conference on homophobia. ("Ricky Martin to United Nations: 'I Lived In Fear.'" *Huffington Post*, December 12, 2012.)

Translocations

If living "la vida loca" signals a queer affect in the pop culture scene, then it is worth looking into what is meant by a "loca" lifestyle. Within the context of joteria Latina/o popular culture, Larry La Fountain-Stokes examines Latino music to discuss the role of the Bolero transgression of the gender and sexual boundaries. La Fountain-Stokes introduces and elaborates on the concept of the *transloca* that consists of the prefix "trans-" (from the Latin for "across" or "over") and the Spanish word *loca*, meaning "madwoman" and widely used in slang as a synonym for "effeminate homosexual". The term "*transloca*" offers an enabling vernacular critical term that accounts for the intersection of space (geography) and sexuality in the work and lived experience of queer.

The idea of the "transloca" applies famously to the work of Adelina Anthony whose repertoire of performance comedy engages an ethno camp style that achieves and delivers on the madwoman or loca. The Los Angeles-based performance artist's numerous performance pieces and publications capture the efficacy of the transloca whose excess and campy style evokes the lunacy of Latina/o life or better yet, the *locuras* of Latina/o life.

Anthony self-identifies as a "two-spirit Xicana lesbian multi-genre artist, cultural activist, teaching artist, director and producer" where she address themes of "colonization, feminisms, traumas, ancestral memorias, gender, health, race & ethnicity, immigration, sexuality, land & environment & issues generally affecting the two-spirit/ queer/ lesbian/ Gay/ bisexual/ transgender communities." There is nothing covert about her sexuality within the joteria scheme of her plays. She is out, proud, and certifiably *loca*. In one of her main character from her numerous performance plays. In *La Angry Xicana?!*, a full-length comedy that weaves together a critique of Hollywood, the U.S. corporate media, purported lesbian gang epidemics, The L Word, conservative politics, health issues, religious icons, post-welfare life, and the semi-sacred courtship that happens only among queer womyn of color. As in all of her works, the show commits to positioning lesbian Xicana/Latinas as the ideal viewership and operates from queer/ feminist/ indigenous perspectives. Using comedy as a weapon of choice, the show examines possible sources of contemporary and historical anger among womyn. Directed by fellow performance artist D'Lo, she uses the edgy anger-based vernacular of the city to issue a joteria-based critique of social life. Cultural critic Aimee Carrillo Rowe writes about Anthony's ability to draw from the past and future to create indelible characters. Carrillo Rowe writes,

> With her unabashed tongue-in-cheek portrayals of queer lovers, Mexica spirituality, and dysfunctional family life, Anthony's panoply of characters animates marginal subjectivities with subversive and sacred life. Her performances generate what I call an abundant present that binds disparate temporal registers: a pre-Conquest past, when ancestors lived and Mexica spirituality was prevalent, interanimates contemporary queer Xicana life to generate present moments in which prior rhythms and life forms come to life..
>
> (247)

La Fountain-Stokes notes the *transloca* can be many things, but especially "performers, queers, innovators, marginals, exiles, eccentrics, beauties, troublemakers, lovers, loners, and friends … To be a transloca is to dis-identify with dominant social mores in the sense advanced by José Esteban Muñoz (1999): to tread dangerous ground, make and break allegiances, and redefine meanings and sensibilities" (pp 194–195). Is there a place for the angry lesbian who traverses spatial geographies? La Fountain-Stokes specifically identifies and links the concepts of migration and transvestism with the hope of creating a new possibility of identification. In thinking about this heterogeneous group, one might not identify with the neologism of the loca. In its own right, it also suggests a form of hysterical identity (that of individuals lacking sanity, composure, or ascription to dominant norms) that is pathologised at the clinical level, seen as scandalous at the popular one, and celebrated as a site of knowledge and resistance in psychoanalytically inspired cultural critique. *Locas* include effeminate homosexuals, madwomen, and rebels for any cause.

Ella Es Diferente

Riding the wave of the same-sex marriage movement in the United States, Los Tigres del Norte, the acclaimed *norteña* band, recorded a song about a woman who is in love with her best friend—another woman. Here we should extend further the aim of joteria culture to include the support and contributions of family, friends and allies. After all, what would the Latina/o queer community be without the support of their allies? Los Tigres del Norte released their first corrido about lesbian love by lending support to a community that continues to encounter rejection. While many open their eyes with astonishment to hear for the first time at their concerts the leader of the group, Jorge Hernández says that he feels proud of their song (Associated Press interview). The singer and front man for Los Tigres del Norte related in his interview that the group's fan base had asked they also be represented in the corrido band's music. He had waited for the right time to complete something meaningful that would offer something special that would dignify their lives.

What resulted in their efforts to record a song was "Era diferente" from their album *Realidades*. Written by Mexican song writer Manuel Eduardo Toscano, who has collaborated with the best in the *música norteña* scene, the song is about a young, beautiful girl known to all that she was in fact in love with her best friend. The song "Era diferente" goes to great lengths to emphasize the young girl's attractiveness and in a subtle manner suggests that she could have been with any man of her choosing, except for the fact that she is in love with her best friend.

Eras mas linda, mas bella que luna de octubre,
su voz era tan dulce trino de gorrión
Era la chica mas tierna de aquel viejo barrio,
los hombre se peleaban su fiel corazón.
Ellos hacían sus apuestas para conquistarla
pero ningún muchacho se ganó su amor
Ella era tan diferente a las otras muchachas
jamás le interesó el amor de algún varón.

At the completion of recording the song, the group believed they had a song that would allow them to communicate their sentiments about the LGBTQ community. They went ahead with the release of the song and the results, according to Hernández, have been great. For the LGBTQ fans and their supporters, the backing of Los Tigres del Norte has been critical and an invaluable alliance because music is able to reach into communities where there may not be other means of relating their message of acceptance.

Hernández notes that "Still there is much more that needs to be done because sadly there are many people who are queer and transgender in this country (Mexico) and many parts of the Américas whose lives are made very difficult." The song "Era diferente" is probably the first sympathetic gay themed song in the *música norteña* tradition. According to Hernández, "We have never heard another group like ours who has recorded this type of song," with respect to all *norteña* groups. He goes on, "I believe it is really about us as a group where we have dedicated much of our music to communicate important messages about issues in the community, recording the issues in society in which we live," adding "We live together in the world and it is important we share regardless of the situation. That is what makes song great." When responding to the song's reception at concerts, Hernández notes that it has been generally positive.

Girl in a Coma

San Antonio-based indie rock group, Girl in a Coma, from Texas, plays to an eclectic mix of fans that include your typical rock with a culturally dissident style, so unlike Texas or even Tejano music. Lead singer and songwriter Nina Diaz, 23, is the youngest member of the band while her older sister Phanie plays the drums with Jenn Alva on bass guitar. Known for their rebel style when it comes to music, the band is signed to Blackheart Records—a label owned by rocker Joan Jett (National Public Radio, NPR). For Texas, the all-female band follows in the tradition of Dixie Chicks, Cowboy Junkies and Nora Jones, but unlike other better known Texas bands, Girl in a Coma also appeals to gender queer and trans folks because two of its band members are out lesbians. While the members take pride in their Chicana/o heritage, their style is not typical of Tejano music. In an NPR interview, "Diaz says she grew up very much like the slain Tejano singer Selena: an English speaker who listened to English-language radio and didn't pay attention in Spanish classes at school. She says she often regrets not taking the time to learn her elders' language when she was younger. Still, the band's indie reputation has garnered appeal from a collective array of fans who adore Girl in a Coma for its artsy and yet distinctively rock sound. By the time they cut the album *When I'm Gone* in 2007, Jenn Alva was already an out lesbian, which gave the band a queer appeal and following. *The Advocate* interviewed the band members in 2009, when asked by Graham Kolbeing, Mexican culture is not traditionally known for being open and accepting toward homosexuality. Jenn and Phanie, how did your parents deal with your sexuality when they found out? Band member Phanie responds: "Well, for me, it's really not a big deal. My mother is a huge supporter of the band and always supports me in general. To her, as long as I'm happy, that's all that matters." Bass guitar player Jenn Alva recounts:

> Although the Mexican culture is not traditionally known for its acceptance of homosexuality, it is well known that Mexican families are very passionate and try to maintain a strong bond with every member of the household. My family has been very supportive, and although it took my parents a while to come to an understanding about it, they are my number one supporters today. That had nothing to do with our nationality; it was more so the fact of learned behaviors. This is why it is very important to educate every person, young and old, about homosexuality. It has been dubbed an ugly word for too long.
>
> (Graham 2009)

Phanie publicly acknowledges that she is also a lesbian and explains why she was hesitant at the start of Girl in a Coma's career. "My friends and band knew, but not my mother," Phanie said. "I wanted to come out to her first. I wrote her a letter and, as expected, she was wonderful about it—didn't care and nothing has changed in our relationship. Another reason I took a while to come out is because I didn't want the public to focus on that and put us into a gay band box. We are just a band" (NPR).

Joteria in Film

As already mentioned by Cecilia Josephine Aragón and Ben Chappell in this volume, joteria themes play a central role in Peter Bratt's 2009 film, *La Mission*. It is about a reformed ex-convict, Che (played by Benjamin Bratt), a low-rider car aficionado whose relationship with his gay son is the subject of the film. After discovering that the boy has been living a secret gay life, Che has a difficult time accepting him. Still, every day is a struggle as he battles alcoholism and drives a bus in order to support his family. When the work day is done, Che and his friends, the "Mission Boyz," pass the time by restoring junked cars to mint condition. Feared by his peers yet deeply respected as the toughest Chicano on the block, Che is the kind of guy whose entire existence is defined by his macho reputation. There's no one in the world that Che loves more than his adolescent son, Jesse (Jeremy Ray Valdez), but both father and son are about to discover that love isn't exactly unconditional. Upon discovering that Jesse has been living a secret life, Che flies into a violent rage, assaulting the boy and kicking him out onto the street. Meanwhile, Che's attractive and headstrong neighbor Lena (Erika Alexander) challenges the ultra-macho gearhead to step back for a minute and take stock of the life he thought he had. The film received mixed reviews, but it stands as one of the few full-length feature films that deal specifically with the subject matter of gay sexuality. There is no reconciliation at the end of the film, as Che, the father, refuses to accept his son's sexuality and is seen driving south in the direction of Los Angeles.

In 2013, director Aurora Guerrero, created the first lesbian subject matter film entitled *Mosquita y Mari. New York Times* critic writes

> *Mosquita y Mari* is an unassuming indie jewel, resists all of the clichés that its story of the fraught friendship between two 15-year-old girls invites. Yolanda (Fenessa Pineda) and Mari (Venecia Troncoso) are high school classmates and neighbors growing up in Huntington Park, a struggling, predominantly Mexican neighborhood in Los Angeles County.

When Yolanda Olveros meets her new neighbor Mari Rodriguez, all they see in each other are their differences. An only child, sheltered Yolanda's sole concern is fulfilling her parents' dream of a college-bound future. With her father's recent death, street-wise Mari, the elder of two, carries the weight of her sister as their mother works to keep them above water. But despite their contrasting realities, Yolanda and Mari are soon brought together when Mari is threatened with expulsion after saving Yolanda from an incident at school. The girls forge a friendship that soon proves more complex than anticipated when the girls unexpectedly experience a sexually charged moment between them. At a loss for words, the girls ignore their moment and move on to become best friends, unaware they have set in motion an unstoppable journey of self-discovery. As Yolanda and Mari's feelings reach new depths, their inability to put words to their emotions leads to a web of unspoken jealousy, confusion, and a sudden betrayal that ultimately rattles them at their core.

Conclusion

This chapter outlines some of the fundamental aspects of joteria in popular culture. There are certainly more people that warrant mention, but these are the central representative figures and leaders of the early era of joteria popular culture as well as more recent figures who have informed our notion of how joteria. One major current that was followed throughout this chapter outlines the perspectives and issues associated with the coming out process. It would be erroneous to begin in the 1990s when we see a visible and expressive articulation of many queer characters and outlined perspectives on and issues associated with the coming out process. It would be erroneous to begin in the 1990s when we see a visible and articulation of many characters and performers for the first time. Our cultural history is much broader and more complex than beginning with the 1990s or even 2015. In fact, more research on the subject is needed. This chapter, I hope, will lead to more interest on the subject and invites other to look for other ways that joteria are represented, not only those moments and people that have chosen to be out in some way or dimension but for the purpose of informing the public about the contributions of Chicana/os and Latina/os in popular culture.

Bibliography

Aliens. Dir. and Prod. James Cameron. 20th Century Fox, 1986.

Association for Joteria Arts, Activism, and Scholarship [http://www.ajaas.com/services.html] 2015

Bejarano, Yvonne Yabro. "Crossing the Border: A Chicana Femme's Tribute to Chabela Vargas." *Sex and Sexuality in Latin America: An Interdisciplinary Reader*. Eds. D. Balderston and D. J. Guy. New York: New York University Press, 1997. 33–42.

Carillo Rowe, Aimee. 2013. 'Your Ancestors Come…': Tracing an Abundant Present in Adelina Anthony's *La Hocicona Series*. GLQ: *A Journal of Lesbian and Gay Studies* 19, no. 2.

Decena, Carlos Ulises. *Tacit Subjects: Belonging and Same-Sex Desire among Dominican Immigrant Men*. Durham, NC: Duke University Press, 2011.

Halberstam, Judith. *Female Masculinity*. Durham, NC: Duke Press, 1998.

Holden, Stephen. *New York Times* Review "Bravado and Caresses: Girls on the Way to Life" August 2, 2012.

Kolbeins, Graham. "Coming Out of the Coma." *Advocate*, 10 June 2009. Available at: http://www.advocate.com/arts-entertainment/music/2009/06/10/coming-out-coma

La Fountain-Stokes, Larry. "Translocas: Migration, Homosexuality, and Transvestism in Recent Puerto Rican Performance." *Hemispheric Institute E-misférica* 8:1 (2011) http://hemisphericinstitute.org/hemi/en/e-misferica-81/lafountain

Lederer, Edith M. "Ricky Martin to United Nations: 'I lived in Fear'". *Huffington Post*. 12 December 2012.

Martin, Ricky. "Livin' La Vida Loca." *Living La Vida Loca*. Columbia Records. 1999.

Muñoz, Jose Esteban. *Disidentifications: Queers of Color and the Performance of Politics*. Raleigh Durham: Duke University Press, 1999.

National Public Radio. Girl in a Coma Interview. 19 October 2011.

Perez, Daniel Enrique. *Rethinking Chicana/o and Latina/o Popular Culture*. New York, NY: Palgrave Macmillan, 2009.

"Tigres Del Norte Lanzan Corrido Dedicado a Comunidad LGBT." *La Prensa Grafica*. 10 April 2015 http://www.laprensagrafica.com/2015/04/10/tigres-del-norte-lanzan-corrido-dedicado-a-comunidad-lgbt

Vargas, Chavela. *Y Si Quieres Saber de Mi Pasado*. Mexico City: Aguilar, 2002.

26

RAZA ROCKABILLY AND GREASER CULTURA

Nicholas Centino

Sixty years out of vogue, rockabilly music has garnered a tremendous following in the post-industrial urban metropolis of greater Los Angeles. Characterized by rollicking tempos, the staccato "click-clack" of a slapped upright bass, machine gun guitar solos, and an echoing southern-drawled vocal delivery, rockabilly is best remembered as the 1950s genre of music performed by a young Elvis Presley, or Carl Perkins of "Blue Suede Shoes" fame. However, since the turn of the century, young Latinas and Latinos have become a critical mass of the scene's performers, promoters, fans and enthusiasts, effectively transforming the scene's mid-century style, stance, and sound, to meet their own needs and sensibilities: transforming rockabilly into razabilly.

Ask any rockabilly enthusiast to characterize the community of cultural producers and consumers and the sites they frequent, and most will describe it as a *scene*. Coined by John Irwin in *Scenes*, scenes provide participants with an explicit and shared lifestyle that changes and evolves as enthusiasts phase in and out over time. Sites of leisure provide the Los Angeles rockabilly scene space to construct, reinforce, and challenge racialized and gendered notions of scene membership and identity, and have remained an integral element since the genre's rediscovery. While racialized spaces and cultural practices are hardly rare, the extraordinary claiming of the scene by Los Angeles Chicana/os and Latina/os is worthy of distinction given the reactionary and even racist meanings ascribed to rockabilly via its country and western roots. To put it plainly, rockabilly, as a genre of music, a distinct style/ fashion, a type of space such as a bar or shop, or as an attitude or stance, is imagined as a white person's fixation everywhere else but Los Angeles.

Emerging from the American South during the 1950s, rockabilly is a hybrid musical form that combines elements of white country music with black R&B. Decades later in de-industrial Great Britain, young rockabilly revivalists imagined and invented a look, sound, and accompanying activity system based on their own interpretive vision of the United States of the 1950s. Despite its British roots, Los Angeles became the liveliest local scene for rockabilly by the early 2000s, with venues throughout greater LA offering retro and roots music almost any night of the week for a near exclusive clientele of Latinas and Latinos. Leisure sites such as bars, nightclubs, fairgrounds, and social halls allowed for rockabilly enthusiasts to engage in their own adaptation of the cultural practices codified by the European rockabilly revivalists. In an embodied, way, the rockabilly scene provided cultural consumers and producers to communally enact a form of memory that simultaneously spoke to their lived experiences, and also allowed them to re-write themselves into the history of Los Angeles, and the history of rock and roll.

The Los Angeles rockabilly scene engages in a contemporary form of community building and imagining of cultural histories tied to an era its enthusiasts largely did not experience. Yet, to dismiss rockabilly's engagement with the past simplistically as regressive nostalgia would be a mischaracterization. Far from navel gazing, the rockabilly scene's open engagement with the past can provide a broader and more fulfilling understanding of their present. Operating at both a cognitive and affective level, this interpolation of the past, as imagined at that moment, places people, all too objectified and dehumanized, as subjects and actors with a valuable history of their own. Far from regressive nostalgia, this historical placemaking focuses on the present, reinforcing contemporary bonds and senses of belonging.

Examined against the backdrop of W. Bush–Schwarzenegger era politics, the obsessive drive to craft a sense of authenticity speaks to the rendering of the Latina/o body in the United States as inauthentic, unwelcome, and uninvited. Federal legislation aimed at addressing social justice, especially immigrant justice, was thrown asunder after the attacks of September 11. The DREAM act, a congressional bill that sought to provide a pathway to higher education for undocumented youth and that faced bright prospects when it was introduced on August 1, 2001, was ultimately derailed by the subsequent terror attacks. Meanwhile on a statewide level, the anti-immigrant and anti-Latina/o rhetoric crafted during the Wilson administration was joined by new discursive maneuvers to oppose measures to reinstate the ability of non-U.S.citizens to apply for and obtain Californian driver's licenses. Following Arnold Schwarzenegger's 2004 veto of AB 2895, assembly Republican leader Kevin McCarthy equated undocumented laborers with the types of terrorist that attacked the World Trade Center and the White House.

The equation of Latinas/os with terrorism was facilitated, in part, by the media coverage of the apprehension of José Padilla, a former member of the Latin Kings street gang who was detained as an enemy combatant for aiding Al-Qaeda. Within this context, razabilly's drive for authenticity pushes back against an American popular imagination that seeks to render the marker of brown skin as one of inauthenticity and un-American-ness. As Michelle Habell-Pallán argues in Loca Motion, Chicana/os like El Vez who re-inscribe the symbolism of rockabilly and Elvis, the "supreme icon of Americana" (189), for themselves, not only upset Chicano cultural nationalist assumptions, but hegemonic Anglo-American ones as well. If the national imaginary wishes to deny how Chicanas/os and Latinas/os have contributed to twentieth-century American popular culture, then razabilly can serve as a visual and sonic reminder to the contrary.

The Performers

Robert Williams: Born and raised in Southern California, Robert Williams is veritably the ambassador of rockabilly. With featured guest spots on NPR's Fresh Air and All Things Considered, consistent booking on Conan O'Brian's late night talk shows, regular national and international touring schedules, including a performance at Nashville's Grand Ole

Opry, it is little wonder why Williams as Big Sandy is one of the contemporary rockabilly scene's most recognizable faces. Williams is a popular choice for rockabilly festival promoters looking for an MC with the type of charisma and stage experience to command a passionate and often unruly audience. A veteran performer with over 25 years' experience and 12 albums under his belt, Williams as well as his band, Big Sandy and the Fly Rite Boys, are an institution in and of themselves. Beginning as a rockabilly outfit in 1988, Williams and his ever-evolving band delved deeper into history and began performing western swing style tunes from an earlier era by the mid-1990s. While few printed reviews raised the issue, it was not uncommon for observers to remark on the seeming incongruity of Williams's music choice, 1940s and 1950s style country boogie, and his brown skin and Latina/o features.

Yet to dwell on such contradictions serves to trivialize and diminish Williams's own musical roots, and the very cultural memories wrapped therein. Williams's father, Robert James Williams, "a blond-haired, blue-eyed okie" and welder by trade, met his mother, Angelina Avila, a second generation Mexican, at a dance held at the long since demolished amusement park The Pike, in Long Beach, California. As Williams has stressed throughout his career, his home was full of music: old country, rockabilly, and surf records of his father, and jump blues, doo-wop, and R&B records of his mother. Echoing Gaye Johnson's challenge to claims that youth cultures naturally rebel against their parents, in a 1998 interview, Williams stated "some kids rebel against what their parents are into, but I really dug it."

Even Williams's stage name reflects the raced and classed experiences of his family in working class Southern California. Williams had inherited a work jacket once owned and worn by his uncle, Santiago, who labored as a mechanic. Deemed too long a name to fit on a patch by the manager, "Santiago" was shortened to "Santy," and subsequently misspelled as "Sandy" on the finished product. Bassist Wally Hershom suggested the moniker to Williams, who was looking for a stage name. Hershom, referencing the patch on Williams's jacket came up with the name Big Sandy.

Formed in 1988, Big Sandy and the Fly Rite Trio featured Williams on rhythm guitar and vocals, and recorded its first album on Dionysus Records in 1990. The album was entitled "Fly Right With ... ," and was recorded in a studio built by Hershom in his grandmother's tool shed using vintage equipment. After their album was reviewed in an English fanzine, Big Sandy and the Fly Rite Trio were booked in 1991 for Tom Ingram's Hemsby Rock and Roll Weekend, at that time, the premiere rockin' festival in the world.

The band, lauded for their 'authentic' approach to the genre, were embraced by European audiences, leading to consistent bookings year after year. However, the jarring contrast felt by Williams between his rock stardom overseas and his mundane life stateside has certainly been felt by subsequent performers in the Southern California rockabilly scene, especially Latinas and Latinos. Despite the affective sense of empowerment performers may gain while commanding cheering crowds at a rockabilly weekend festival, come Monday they are still due back at work, more often than not, in the service industry. While they may find adoration in Callafel Spain, Heathfield UK, or Munich Germany, at the end of the day, they have to return to a home where Latinas/os and the working poor are rendered to the margins and increasingly penalized.

Williams's solo album, "Dedicated To You" draws upon the musical genealogies inherited from his mother, namely the soulful R&B later dubbed the eastside sound. Released in 1998, Williams's "Dedicated to You" and his forays into R&B and later doo-wop with the group The Lonely Blue Boys helped to establish a musical landscape within the rockabilly scene that was familiar to Los Angeles and Southern California raza. The album is a virtual love letter to predominantly African American Los Angeles-based vocal groups, including appearances by the Calvanes on "Every Where I Go" and Dewey Terry of Don and Dewey on "I'm Leavin' It All Up To You."

As Williams's career progressed, he felt less bound to rigid borders placed upon the genre, recording songs such as the late 1960s Stax-influenced "Slippin' Away" on 2006's Turntable Matinee, or the ska-inspired "Baby Baby Me" and "I Know I've Loved You Before" in 2013's "What A Dream It's Been." In some ways, Williams has been able to have his cake and eat it too. He is still considered a traditionalist and lauded for his and his band's authenticity. Yet his longevity has afforded him the opportunities to perform, record, and draw from the musical genealogies he has inherited.

Vicky Tafoya: Based in the Inland Empire, Vicky Tafoya is the scene's reigning diva of doo-wop and R&B. Performing her first major gig in 1989, Tafoya is more than just a singer: her ability to emote and transmit lyrical content, be it teen angst in "So Young" or sheer joy in "Jump Children" captivates audiences. That ability is combined with the uncanny knack to not only convincingly sound like original artists, especially Frankie Lymon, but to also carry key inflections and subtle changes to place her own unique stamp on the music. Tafoya's performances speak to the cultural memory and legacy of women of color wielding a powerful stage presence. As a multi-faceted text, Tafoya's use of music cues in audiences affectively and cognitively to a sense of historical place as opposed to nostalgia.

Born and raised in Orange County, Tafoya was the youngest of twelve children. Her father, a mechanic who worked on the replica tramp steamers on the jungle cruise ride in Disneyland, passed away when she was very young, leaving her mother, Eleanor, to raise her children on her own. With her brothers caught up in gang life in her neighborhood in Santa Ana, Tafoya recalls her mother striving to divert her away from the pain of street life. Channeled into school and singing, Tafoya recalls her mother providing support, love, and guidance as she grew up.

Attending doo-wop shows around southern California, Tafoya saw and met many of the vocalists familiar to her from records passed down to her from her mother and older sisters. The people she met formed a veritable who's who of African-American and ethnic white vocal artists of the 1950s, including groups like Vito and the Salutations, and Jimmy Merchant and the Teenagers. Although Tafoya was attending the shows, she did not begin performing at them until the 1990s when she was tapped to sing a Frankie Lymon tribute at a Classic New York Doo Wop Show. More than just a lucky break, for Tafoya, the honor was not just in recognition of her singing prowess, but also of her love and knowledge of doo-wop and 1950s R&B by the pioneers of the genre. Through the 1990s, Tafoya continued to perform on the doo-wop circuit as well as small scale local private and public gigs around southern California.

By 2000, Tafoya formed and fronted her own band, Vicky Tafoya and the Big Beat. Crafting the band's look, her backing musicians donned vintage style suits to match Tafoya, who had already adopted a vintage aesthetic for her stage presence. Aided by a duet on Big Sandy's 1998 cover of Oscar McLollie and Jeannette Baker's "Hey Girl, Hey Boy," Tafoya made a name for herself in the rockabilly scene. Vicky Tafoya and the Big Beat became a popular draw in the rockabilly scene given the band was one of few R&B vocal groups in the scene, and quite unique given that Tafoya, as a woman, fronted the group. As argued by Sara Cohen in *Rock Culture in Liverpool*, rock and roll music is neither naturally masculine, nor expresses a predetermined male culture. Rather, rock, and by extension rockabilly, is actively *produced* as male through the everyday practices that make up that activity system. Musical instruction and mentoring is largely a gendered practice among men. While there are dozens of original vintage recordings featuring women musicians in regular rotation in the rockabilly canon, there are hundreds of recordings featuring solely men. Yet, while the promoter and performer networks are made up of almost exclusively men in the rockabilly scene, women are its most fervent and die hard enthusiasts.

Tafoya in her stage persona plays with gender norms and expectations. Countering the de-sexualization of full figured women, Tafoya crafts a hyper feminine pachuca-inspired look, with exaggeratedly ornate hair and make-up, often paired with a fitted eye catching blouse and drape zoot suit slacks. Harkening to the dangerous sexuality of the pachuca, Tafoya dons draped pachuco slacks with thick-soled bluchers. She also often switches gendered voices on stage, easily covering Frankie Lymon's "Why Do Fools Fall in Love" or Rosie and The Originals' "Angel Baby."

Through her music, Tafoya connects not just to her audience, but to their cherished memories as well. The songs she performs serve as cues, reminding and renewing significant bonds and relationships for her predominantly Latina/o audience. It is not uncommon to spot emotional tears when Tafoya performs, or for spectators to call out dedications and requests the same way a caller might phone in a request to Art Laboe. After performing, Tafoya can be found chatting with spectators, many of whom have approached her to share their own intensely personal memories called up by her song choice, memory that is intimately tied to a sense of belonging developed with loved ones.

That affect is fueled in part by Tafoya's performance of memory. Tafoya has more than proven that she is able to express her artistic creativity as a musician who is capable of creating new hybrid sounds with projects like Vicky and The Vengents. Furthermore, she clearly puts her own spin on classic R&B and doo-wop numbers as the frontwoman for the Big Beat. To put it plainly, her live renditions sound and feel more like the original recordings than those performed by surviving original artists on the oldies circuit who are all too often saddled down with overwrought electronic production and cheesy arrangements in hopes of keeping their best loved songs palpable to modern tastes. Tafoya's audience adores her music precisely because it carries a dated sensibility. For the majority of audiences, especially at rockabilly sites of leisure, the memories called up by songs like "So Young" or "ABC's of Love" are not of a 1950s they did not experience, but rather of moments and people they know, love, and cherish, and hold significance for them.

Wild Records: Few bands speak to Latinas/os arrival and mark on the international rockin' scene quite like those signed to Reb Kennedy's Wild Records. Established in 2001, Wild Records has grown into a force to be reckoned with, both locally and abroad. Wild currently is home to a growing stable of over 17 bands, predominantly made up of working class Latina and Latino musicians from the greater Los Angeles area. Organized more like a family than a business, Kennedy serves as the label's patriarch, singularly overseeing the recording, promotion, and bookings of the majority of his bands, as well as the day to day operation of the label, including mundane tasks such as answering emails and even putting records in sleeves for sale. Shows promoted by Kennedy, as well as performances booked by other promoters, are popular draws locally, but immensely successful overseas where Wild has developed an intense following. Yet it all started with a single 45' record featuring Lil' Luis y Los Wild Teens fronted by Pacoima's Luis Arriaga.

While Arriaga was hardly the first Latino to play 1950s style rock and roll long after the genre's midcentury heyday, the global popularity of his band Lil' Luis y Los Wild Teens and his role in building Reb Kennedy's Wild Records helped usher in and cement raza rockabilly as a Los Angeles phenomenon in the early 2000s and beyond. Born in San Fernando and raised in Pacoima, Arriaga grew up in a working class Spanish-speaking home, picking up English as a second language from school and friends. Like many Southern California

Mexican-American teenagers in the 1990s, Arriaga gravitated to the look, sound, and feel of rockabilly. Unlike many of his contemporaries, Arriaga picked up a guitar and started his own band. As Lil' Luis, Arriaga was backed by Los Wild Teens consisting of Angel Hernandez on drums, Richard Coronado on lead guitar, Alex Vargas and Omar Romero on bass, and Alex "Howlin' Al" Cadena and David Acosta on sax.

Arriaga and Kennedy first met after the latter drove from San Francisco to Downey after seeing a xeroxed flyer of the band's gig promising a night of "Mexican Rock and Roll" in 2000. Kennedy, an Irish North Dubliner from a working class family who grew up in London, had worked as a teacher and child care specialist by day, and a DJ and rockin' promoter by night in the United Kingdom. Like many disaffected youth in the 1970s, Kennedy was a punk during the genre's first wave, eventually working at Rough Trade Records, an independent London-based record label established in 1978. A self-professed vinyl junkie, Reb dove into American roots music, finding punk's raw and raucous energy retroactively infused in 1950s rock and roll records like "Jungle Rock" and "Lil Lil." Yet by the end of the 1990s, he relocated to San Francisco, in part because he felt that the spark in London's rockin' scene had since extinguished and was a shadow of its former self.

Despite the relatively diminutive size of the rockabilly scene of San Francisco at the turn of the century, Kennedy found success booking monthly shows featuring original acts. Yet, he sought to promote a sound that was vibrant and fiery. Kennedy began making monthly forays to Los Angeles with his wife Jenny, getting booked for DJ gigs, and checking out bands. While not technically proficient, what Kennedy saw in Lil' Luis Y Los Wild Teens' chaotic performance was a spark of raw talent that could eventually germinate. The band became Wild Records' first signed act.

Under the guidance of Kennedy, Arriaga and his bandmates reverse-engineered familiar Mexican rock and roll numbers into fresher, rawer, and grittier versions of those of the original artists. While Arriaga drew upon the genealogies inherited from Mexican rock and roll, the unique ways in which they interpolated bands like Los Gliders, Los Teen Tops, and others provided raza rockabilly with a soundtrack that was familiar enough to draw upon shared genealogies, but fresh enough to speak to their contemporary moment and mark on history. "La Rebeldona," a song the band had largely dismissed, was released as the band's first recording at the urging of Kennedy. As originally performed and recorded by Los Gliders, "La Rebeldona" is a pop surf rock tune driven by lead singer Carlos Guevara's smooth vocals. As performed by Lil' Luis y Los Wild Teens, the same song is transformed into a gritty stroller featuring Arriaga's growling vocals and Carlos Gomez's lo-fi guitar work.

Released as a 45 record, "La Rebeldona" completely sold out at a time when CDs reigned supreme. The band recorded a full-length album entitled "Rip It Up" in 2003. Black and white photos in the liner notes posed the Latino band members in slick black leather jackets and greased hair stripping a Ford Thunderbird. The cover art featured the band behind a gated fence meant to evoke bars of a jail cell with the subheading "Wild Juvenile Rock n' Roll." Amidst interpolations of English language rock and rollers like Jerry Lee Lewis's "Wild One," and Florian Monday and his Mondos' "Rip it, Rip it Up" are Spanish language covers of Los Teen Tops' "Presumida," Los Beatniks' "Mucho Amor," and Los Boppers' "Porque Soy Rebelde." The majority of tracks on the album consist of original material, including "Delincuente," "Oye Mi Chiquita," and "Solo No Quiero Estar," which are penned in Spanish and performed in the raucous late 1950s style developed by the band. Lil' Luis and his band's look, sound, and attitude spoke to the way Chicana/o and Latina/o young adults, many of them immigrants, sought to shape the music of the Los Angeles rockabilly scene into a soundscape that was appealing and useful to them. Far from being just a band in the right place at the right time, Lil' Luis y Los Wild Teens under the guidance of Kennedy were instrumental architects in shaping the sonic landscape of Los Angeles rockabilly.

This infusion of a band's unique synergy into familiar and not-so familiar vintage guitar-driven rock genres would become one of Wild Records' hallmarks and drive their popularity locally and abroad. Within the greater Los Angeles area of the early 2000s, Lil' Luis y Los Wild Teens' open engagement with material more familiar with transnational immigrant Latina/os than with third and fourth generation Chicanos, speaks to the broader shifts in the make-up of the local Latina/o community as immigration status rose to be as pertinent an identity as race, ethnicity, and gender, given the rise in nativist sentiment and anti-immigrant measures reignited in the 1990s. Described in Eric Zolov's book, *Refried Elvis*, Mexican rock and roll bands of the late 1950s and 1960s re-interpreted popular American rock and roll songs in Spanish for a middle class urban male audience. While Zolov bases this claim on the population buying records and attending concerts, the proliferation and continued rotation of these songs via radio expanded the consumption of Mexican rock and roll beyond the middle class and beyond national borders. Although decades old, songs such as Los Teen Tops' "La Plaga" and "El Rock de la Carcel" can still be heard in radio rotation in Los Angeles, especially on the Univision-owned station KRCD/KRCV "El Recuerdo," a Spanish language "oldies" station.

Yet while the original rendition of these songs reflected the increasingly British influence upon rock music in the early 1960s, Arriaga's band reverse-engineered the songs, suturing the Spanish language lyrics to re-arranged pre-Beatle instrumentation. Arriaga added a gritty snarl to his delivery far removed from the almost pop sounding clarity of the original Spanish language recordings. Complimentarily, Los Angeles-based Latina/o DJs began adding Spanish language music to their rotation, including Roberto Carlos's "Es Prohibido Fumar" from 1964, Los Loud Jets' "Sputnik," and Los Milos' "Pitagoras" among others. For raza rockabilly in Los Angeles, bands like Lil' Luis y Los Wild Teens provided a soundscape that was familiar, but also uniquely their own and created by their peers. Omar and The Stringpoppers and Dusty Chance and All-Nighters, two rockabilly outfits who also infused their own unique sound into traditional genres, followed Arriaga's band.

Wild's stable grew through the 2000s, comprised mostly of Los Angeles-based bands with a majority of Latina/o musicians, including San Fernando's Chuy and the Bobcats, blues rockers The Hi-Strung Ramblers, R&B and soul diva Gizzelle, Salvadoran-American Santos, and the rockin' country sounds of the Vargas Bros. Kennedy, well familiar with the networks of rockin' festival promoters and music dealers secured bookings and CD and record distributions for his bands throughout Europe. Wild artists gained a strong following overseas, consistently selling more records and playing to exponentially larger audiences than in the United States. Wild's bands, consisting of young working class Latinas/os from greater Los Angeles, quickly became the most sought after acts from the United States. Yet, this hardly transformed into commercial success for the bands or label. Nearly all of Wild's musicians work day jobs to support themselves and their families. The money Kennedy makes as the label's head is put back to the label itself as his family's income largely relies on Jenny Lin-Kennedy. In addition to working a day job, Lin-Kennedy also serves as Wild's coordinator of retail sales and is responsible for the label's website.

Many of Wild's musicians from the early years have remained with the label, both out of their love for the music as well as the bonds they developed with each other after nearly a decade of touring and recording. Many of them serve in different capacities in each other's bands as well. In addition to fronting his own band, Alex Vargas also plays bass for Gizzelle (Gizzelle Becerra), Santos and the Hi-Strung Ramblers. Victor Mendez, who plays bass for

Marlene Perez's Rhythm Shakers, also plays bass for Omar and the Stringpoppers and piano for Gizzelle. Many serve as mentors to the label's up and coming artists. Romero, a full time barber, also serves as the label's chief engineer. All of Wild's releases are now recorded in their studio, a one-room shack in Kennedy's backyard in Altadena. Engineered by Omar Romero using a secret rig, the recordings are captured on analog 8-track and then flipped over to16 track. Recording sessions are typically held on Sundays, the only day that most of their young working class musicians consistently have off. Wild is known for recording their artists in a single 14- to 16-hour day. While considerable prep work goes into a recording, Reb, who produces all of the recordings, is hardly aiming for perfection. Mistakes and flubs are often included in a band's final recording.

Of Arriaga's body of work, few speak to the diversity of genealogical roots that raza rockabilly draws from quite like "Dame Una Señal," a song he penned in 2006. Arriaga was contracted to work with Cesar Rosas of Los Lobos on Los Straightjackets' *Rock En Español Vol. I* to compose a Spanish language translation of Brenton Wood's "Gimme a Little Sign," a song that Arriaga had grown up listening to in Pacoima. "Gimme a Little Sign," resignified as "Dame Una Señal," was recorded for the 2007 album with Robert Williams appearing on lead vocals. Taken as just another track on a musically solid album, the recording is not particularly groundbreaking.

Nevertheless, the production of "Dame Una Señal" brings contemporary raza rockabilly in Los Angeles full circle, and speaks to its impact on American popular culture. With Los Lobos, Cesar Rosas laid the groundwork for generations of Chicana/o and Latina/o roots rockers. In some circles, Los Lobos are recognized as the original Chicano rockabilly band playing in Los Angeles alongside contemporary bands and collaborators like the Blasters years prior to the stateside landing of the European-influenced rockabilly revival. While Los Lobos' repertoire draws from a broad swathe, their rockabilly and 1950s rock and roll -inspired music, including 1985's "We're Gonna Rock," 1987's "Shakin' Shakin' Shakes," as well as their work on the soundtrack to Luis Valdez's 1987 film "La Bamba," cemented their relationship to rockabilly both within the Chicana/o and Latina/o community as well as the world of American roots music. The East Los Angeles sensibilities they brought to their performances presaged what raza rockabilly bands would be doing a decade or two later.

The choice of a Brenton Wood song is a callback to a genealogical root little recognized or understood outside of the Chicana/o community of greater Los Angeles. Wood, a former track star from Compton, California, still performs, largely to Chicana/o and Latina/o audiences, singing a small catalog of songs he made famous in the late 1960s including "The Oogum Boogum Song," "Me and You," "Baby You Got It," and the song that Arriaga translated, "Gimme a Little Sign." Considered a part of the canon of lowrider music, or the eastside sound, a Spanish language cover of "Gimme a Little Sign" is seemingly a strange choice for Los Straightjackets, a Nashville-based surf rock band made up of white musicians. Yet given the involvement and collaboration of Rosas and Williams, who as previously detailed, readily pays homage to Southern California's black and brown R&B and soul roots, the song is a fitting tribute. As Big Sandy, Williams tore the roof off when he closed out his set fronting Los Straightjackets by singing Arriaga's composition of "Dame Una Señal" at the sixteenth Viva Las Vegas rockabilly weekender. By the end of the song, the crowd, predominantly Chicana/os and Latina/os well familiar with the original and quick to pick up on the Arriaga's lyrics in Spanish, joined Williams in singing the song's signature refrain.

Now in their thirties, Arriaga and his peers largely remain stable elements at Wild. Romero, now a small business owner, employs a handful of his label mates at "Vinnie's," his Silverlake barbershop. Well aware of the generational shifts and the limits of rockabilly's sites of leisure, Kennedy regularly books performances for Wild bands at seemingly unlikely locations, such as the Santa Fe Swap Meet, targeting new audiences be they already interested in the music of Wild Records or not. The Swap Meet, as well as Wild's own shows held at the Observatory in Santa Ana, are all ages, attracting mostly Chicana/o and Latina/o rockabilly fans too young to get into a rockabilly show, which are almost exclusively hosted at bars and nightclubs for adults only. In many ways, Wild Records has transformed into a lifestyle brand, a rebranding of a Chicana/o or Latina/o re-inscription of the "rockabilly hepkat" with scores of raza, mostly men, looking to take up the rebellious and hard partying attitude portrayed through stage performances, CDs, and YouTube clips.

Bibliography

Cohen, Sara. *Rock Culture in Liverpool: Popular Music in the Making.* Oxford: Clarendon, 1991.

Habell-Pallán, Michelle. *Loca Motion: The Travels of Chicana and Latina Popular Culture.* New York: New York University Press, 2005. 189.

Irwin, John. *Scenes.* Beverly Hills: Sage Publications, 1977.

Johnson, Gaye Theresa. *Spaces of Conflict, Sounds of Solidarity, Music, Race, and Spatial Entitlement in Los Angeles.* Berkeley: University of California, 2013.

Vale, V. *Swing!: The New Retro Renaissance.* San Francisco, CA: V/Search, 1998. 152.

Zolov, Eric. *Refried Elvis the Rise of the Mexican Counterculture.* Berkeley: University of California, 1999.

27

BODIES IN MOTION

Latina/o Popular Culture as Rasquache Resistance

Marivel T. Danielson

Within the realm of discourse on immigration, there is perhaps no image more iconic than that of a silhouetted migrant family running against the bright yellow backdrop of roadside traffic warning signs posted along San Diego freeways in the late 1980s. Created for California Department of Transit by graphic artist John Hood, the now ubiquitous image depicts two adults running alongside a young girl who struggles to keep up with their pace.[1] The extreme angles of the adults' posture, their wide gait, and even the young girl's flying pigtails all bear witness to their urgency. Designed to alert drivers to the potential foot traffic of migrants across busy roadways, the sign's graphic impact and symbolism have far exceeded their original intent.[2] From surfers to graduates, the silhouetted family has been revised and reborn myriad ways in the decades since it first emerged on California roadways.

For some the image represents a gesture to the value of migrant lives, since they advise drivers to "CAUTION" so as to avoid harming anyone crossing on foot. For many others, though, the image inscribes narratives of fear, criminalization, threat, and invasion onto the bodies of migrant communities, locking migrant lives into a limited reality of danger, fear, and flight. Even the caption "CAUTION" floating above the running figures could suggest a multi-layered reading—"be afraid for the migrants crossing" versus "be afraid *of* the migrants crossing."

In his study of Latina/o representation in the public sphere, Otto Santa Ana employs the field of cognitive science to understand how "Metaphor is the mental brick and mortar with which people build their understanding of the social world" (xvi). Beyond addressing a particularly dangerous transit issue, Hood's traffic sign creates a rich space for discourse around migrant identity and inclusion in the United States popular imaginary. Community activist groups, like southern California's Orange County Dream Team (OCDT)—a group of organizers mobilizing around providing support, access, and resources for undocumented students in higher education—identify the problematic nature of the migrant family frozen in fear and flight. The organization's own image builds upon Hood's silhouetted creation, with the addition of caps, gowns, and diplomas to suggest the promise and potential of migrant youth. This reinscription portrays the student figures standing taller, stepping forward from a more relaxed stance, as though walking through a graduation ceremony, not running for their lives. The image also plays on the heteronormative and patriarchal notion of family as depicted in Hood's original design. The original image uses loose fitting pants and shirt to suggest a father figure in a leadership position, a dress to suggest the mother, and a child he specifically chose to designate female because "there is something about a little girl running across with her parents that we are more affected by."[3]

In contrast, OCDT's logo portrays three students of similar build, though interestingly the one figure with short hair that could be coded as masculine maintains his lead position at the front of the line. Like Hood's family, OCDT's trio also holds hands, but rather than the suggestion of a heterosexual couple with a child, the linked group stand as a testament to the power of coalition and collaboration within social justice movements. The students accomplish their goals through their unity and commitment to community. OCDT's image also removes the "CAUTION" label of the original sign, removing the suggestion of danger or threat to either onlookers or the students themselves.

It is this type of movement, the ideological shifts and transformations through images and frames of public and popular culture, which will be my focus in this current chapter on bodies in motion. How does the theme of movement, and in particular corporeal movement, play out in Latina/o popular culture with the aid of technology and social media? Looking at several different types of cultural expression, I will begin by tracing some of the pertinent theoretical frameworks useful in studying these works, and provide a basic introduction to some key innovations taking place at the intersection of moving bodies, social media, and Latina/o popular culture. Subsequently I will move into analyses of work in varying genres of popular cultural expression by Latina/os that exemplify this critical and creative movement within the realms of political protest and related visual art production and blogging/vlogging sites.

In her introduction to the edited volume *From Bananas to Buttocks: The Latina Body in Popular Film and Culture*, Myra Mendible notes a particular challenge when creating scholarship around the genre of popular culture:

> There is a tendency to imagine the popular in terms of oppositions between high and low, vulgar and elite, center and margin, while ignoring the cross-fertilization that is itself a mark of the popular ... [Popular culture productions] create a spectacular 'peep show' where all of us can catch glimpses of our various others *and* form identificatory bonds and affiliations.

(16)

For the current chapter, I ground my definition of the genre of popular culture in Mendible's notion of "cross-fertilizations," which call to mind Fernando Ortiz's transculturation[4] and Gloria Anzaldúa's mestiza consciousness[5], both of which address the multidirectional impact of cultural being and transformation. Each of the works chosen here builds upon existing forms, frameworks, and histories while simultaneously innovating the aesthetics and content of the original models to challenge stereotypes and silences around Latina/o bodies, communities, and experiences.

In thinking about movement as a critical lens, no more fitting conceptualization can be found within Chicana/o and Latina/o studies than that of literary and cultural studies scholar Tomás Ybarra-Frausto. In Alicia Gaspar de Alba's 2003 edited collection *Velvet Barrios: Popular Culture & Chicana/o Sexualities*, Ybarra-Frausto rearticulates his highly applicable critical lens of rasquachismo through which to study the layers of subversion and innovation in popular culture and beyond:

> *Rasquachismo*, the cultural sensibility of the poor and excluded is a core aesthetic category in Chicano/a cultural production. A rasquache world-view is a compendium of all the *movidas* [moves or plays] improvised to cope with adversity. *Rasquachismo* is a sort of voluntary post-modernism, a dynamic sensibility of amalgamation and transculturation that subverts the consumer ethic of mainline culture with strategies of appropriation, reversal, and inversion.
>
> (Gaspar de Alba xvii)

In earlier conceptualization of rasquachismo, Ybarra Frausto explains how movidas factor into daily practices of resistance:

> In an environment always on the edge of coming apart (the car, the job, the toilet) things are held together with spit, grit and *movidas*. *Movidas* are whatever coping strategies you use to gain time, to make options to retain hope. *Rasquachismo* is a compendium of all the *movidas* deployed in immediate, day-to-day living.
>
> (5–6)

Ybarra-Frausto's theorization of improvisational movidas as interventions into discourses of poverty or marginalization lends itself to the study of Latina/o popular culture as exemplified by OCDT's silhouetted graduates image. The art of making something from nothing, and the fashioning of something new from something old epitomize the work and creative aesthetic of the artists, scholars, and community organizers discussed in this chapter. For Ybarra-Frausto, the sensibility of rasquachismo is a uniquely Chicana/o aesthetic. Claiming this body of knowledge, survival, and inspiration represents a powerful act of presence in the context of art history. Alicia Gaspar de Alba performs a similar act of holding space, for a view of Chicana/o popular culture not as marginal or supplementary to U.S. popular culture, but rather as an autochthonous part of "American" cultural production:

> I argue that Chicano/a culture is not a subculture but rather an *alter-Native* culture, an Other American culture indigenous to the landbase now known as the West and the Southwest of the United States. Chicano/a culture, then, is not immigrant but native, not foreign but colonized, not alien but different from the overarching hegemony of white America.
>
> (xxi)

Indeed, for the OCDT, they are not simply migrants, but students, scholars, and graduates. Their popular culture intervention enables them to voice their position as what Gaspar de Alba would term alter-Native cultural practitioners. Both Ybarra-Frausto and Gaspar de Alba's work centralizes Chicana/o and Latina/o cultural production within the frame of analysis, rewriting brown bodies as subjects rather than objects, Latina/o communities as empowered and active agents of inquiry and social transformation.

Demonstrating Bodies

While migration is not a universal trope within Latina/o popular culture, it does provide an extensive body of related narratives and imagery with which many Latina/o artists, performers, and community organizers must contend as they move through the world and seek out spaces to launch their own unique voices and representations. There is perhaps no geographical space more engaged with issues of migration and Latina/o community than that of Phoenix, Arizona. As a result of governmental programs, Operation Gatekeeper and Operation Hold the Line funneled unauthorized migration into the United States away from Texas and California and towards the harsh Arizona/Mexico border during the 1990s. Arizona stands as a key context from which national debates over immigration policy, militarized borders, and human rights emerge (Magaña 152). Within Arizona's court systems and law enforcement agencies, controversial legislative moves like SB 1070[6] (the "show me your papers" bill signed into law by then Governor Jan Brewer in 2010), and HB 2281, a bill purporting to protect school children by removing curriculum focused on the history and culture of ethnic and racial minorities,[7] stand as bastions of the conservative right.

In this chapter on "bodies in motion," the parallel between physical movement of a body or bodies through space, and the social justice movements of activist communities through times of violence and oppression, presents a rich arena from which to look at Latina/o popular cultural production. At the intersection of community organizing, and social media technologies, Puente Movement represents a key voice for migrant rights advocacy in the Phoenix Metro area. Puente Movement is a collective of community organizers who describe themselves as "a grassroots migrant justice organization … We develop, educate, and empower migrant communities to protect and defend our families and ourselves."[8] Since establishing themselves in 2007, Puente Movement has organized numerous campaigns to challenge discriminatory legislation, U.S. Immigration and Customs Enforcement policies on deportation and family separation, and violations of human rights by law enforcement officers in the Phoenix Metro area and beyond.

As an organization, Puente Movement has employed visual arts and popular culture in innovative ways to add strength, vibrancy, and energy to their actions. Frequently creating their own art, members of the silkscreen collective Puente Ink design, produce, and distribute powerful signage that contributes to the visibility and graphic presence of the organization's actions.[9] In addition to silkscreened artwork, the organization regularly collaborates with local photographers to document the actions and transmit the message of the movement to wider audiences through social media. One particular image and its movement through social media channels will be the focus of the current section.

On April 25, 2012, Puente planned and carried out a public protest and action on the public stage of busy Central Avenue in bustling downtown Phoenix in full view of the Immigration and Customs Enforcement (ICE) building. Fighting what Puente Movement's director Carlos García calls "Arizonification"—a violent mix of anti-immigrant legislation, repeated workplace and sidewalk raids, a policy granting local police the right to enforce federal immigration policy, and an overarching discourse of hostility toward Latina/o and immigrant communities[10]—the organization staged the action to bring national and global attention with the sustained hope of social transformation, "Life in Arizona for undocumented immigrants since SB 1070 passed is a combination of basic survival under a climate of hate and inspiring organizing that will one day turn hate to love."[11]

Medical anthropologist Seline Szkupinski Quiroga details the devastating impact of anti-immigration legislation in a study of one South Phoenix community. Pointing out a fallacy in perhaps the most infamous legislation in the State's recent past, Szkupinski Quiroga asserts, "SB 1070 is titled 'The Support Our Law Enforcement and Safe Neighborhoods Act' but ironically, many Latinos no longer feel safe in their homes and neighborhoods" (582). Szkupinski Quiroga traces recurrent themes of vulnerability, panic, and anxiety among Phoenix residents, but in her conclusions also offers a hopeful finding in that, "a resistance and dignified presence in the face of fear and aggression, and further reveals the resiliency found within the Latino community" (584).

Certainly this determination to survive also speaks to Ybarra-Frausto's critical rasquachismo since "Resilience and resourcefulness spring from making do with what's at hand (*hacer rendir las cosas*). This utilization of available resources makes for hybridization, juxtaposition and integration" (5–6). Making do, in this context, will emphasize the creative production related to this particular social justice movement coming out of Puente Movement. How do artists and community organizers use popular culture distributed through social media, to create a movement whose energy and message travel far and wide? Like OCDT's clever redux of John Hood's silhouetted migrant family, Puente Movement activists also utilize visual arts to captivate and move their public into action.

Graphic designer, photographer, and videographer Chandra Narcia—who also designed Puente Movement's logo—documented the March for Justice on April 25, 2012, capturing an image that resonated with individuals and communities around the country. As an Arizona-based indigenous artist and activist, Narcia offers unique insight into border debates:

> The [Tohono O'odham] tribe is constantly under border militarization, which prevents our people from coming across for even ceremonial purposes. The injustice and attacks on human rights through terrible laws being past [sic] have been very upsetting and I feel the need to speak my opinion through my art. I feel a connection to the struggles and will help in any way I can to get across a message of change, inspire action and to call attention to the issues.[12]

In the image Narcia captured during the demonstration, Puente Movement organizer Sandra Castro Solis stands in profile, facing off against a police officer in full riot gear. The photograph is a stunning portrayal of power and resistance, particularly because of the juxtaposition of the two figures at the far left and right of the frame. On the left we see one of many police officers called to the scene that day to arrest demonstrators blocking traffic in front of ICE. The officer, whose chest tag ironically reads "HUNT," also stands in profile, his intense gaze directed at Castro Solis is filtered through a dusty plastic face shield. On the right side of the frame, the young organizer stands perhaps 4 or 5 inches shorter than the officer. In contrast to the officer's downward gaze, Castro Solis's face raises up to meet his, her chin thrusts upward in an expression of both pride and defiance. She is not afraid. The space between the two, marked by a pale, clouded sky and the partial view of additional police nearby, reiterates the ideological distance between them. Yet the police officer's riot gear—in particular his helmet and full face cover—create a sense of insularity, seemingly closed off to the voices and plight of those demonstrating before him that day.

At the close of that day's demonstration, Castro Solis was arrested for civil disobedience. After her release, the image Narcia captured continued to move throughout the country, her powerful work speaking to many working for social justice throughout the nation. One individual moved by Narcia's photograph was San Francisco-based artist and community organizer Julio Salgado, who quickly created a graphic version of the image from his own colorful lens. Salgado's work emphasizes representations of queer people of color from both activist and artistic communities. Through his use of bright colors and sharp lines, Salgado banishes the margins and peripheries of identity, creating portraits that center queer, brown, migrant bodies and experiences as they defiantly declare their survival in a hostile world.[13] Of his own positionalities and creative motivation Salgado explains,

> I use two identities that are supposed to make me weak and empower myself. As an undocumented person, I am seen as a criminal. As a queer person, I am seen as somebody who is going to go to hell. So how do you turn that [around]? For me, through the art ...
>
> (Seif 305–6)

Salgado's take on Narcia's photograph shifts the color palette from overcast greys and blacks to a bright orange background. He simplifies the duo's surroundings, leaving views to focus in on the relationship between Castro Solis and the officer. Salgado maintains the spatial dynamics of the moment, with the police officer bowing his head down in an expression of guilt or impotence, while the young woman again raises her expression to meet his authority.

While Salgado simplifies the detail of the piece, he interjects a layer of complexity with several textual additions. Written on the bodies of each figure, Salgado places the words "Protect who?" on the officer's helmet, questioning his pledge to "serve and protect" in light of the numerous complaints of police brutality, unlawful arrest, detention, and deportation in migrant communities. On Castro Solis's head—as though woven through the strands of her hair—the words STOP SB1070 signify the mission underlying her actions. The work's title "Muxer Fuerte" suggests both the power and strength of this woman organizer, and an alignment with an indigenous identity given the spelling of "muxer" rather than the more Europeanized "mujer."[14]

Beneath the work's title, Salgado includes a final phrase, "Comunidad Unida," calling to mind Castro Solis's fellow organizers as well as all those viewing her image and moved to act based on her example of civil disobedience. This united community to which Salgado's work refers calls to mind Mendible's earlier framing of popular culture texts as sites with the potential to afford audiences "glimpses of our various others *and* form identificatory bonds and affiliations" (16). Within the context of a social justice and civil rights movement, one can see the immediate applicability of an expressive medium defined by its ability to connect and engage artists and audiences. While both Narcia and Salgado's works should rightfully be considered part of conversations of a more formal approach to visual arts production, I believe it is also important here to recognize the role of social media in creating opportunities for communicative exchange for the artists and their audiences. Popular cultural expression, in this case visual art propagated through social media, serves to enhance the ripples of a revolution.

The Big Girls Code

On September 15, 2012, graduate student Leigh-Anna Hidalgo Newton posted the first entry in her blogging site *The Big Girls Code*, a project she describes as a "body positive and fat positive space for women of all sizes."

Flipping the script on the fashion industries' obsession with thin women's bodies as the epitome of beauty, bloggers like Hidalgo Newton use the popular genre of blogging to gain access to a wide audience—anyone with a laptop or smartphone and an internet

Figure 27.1   Leigh-Anna Hidalgo Newton

connection. In this way cultural production disseminated via the internet becomes an intervention into mainstream media representations of women's bodies as impossibly thin, largely white, and cis-gendered. Hidalgo Newton's blog production illustrates both Ybarra-Frausto's critical notion of rasquachismo as well as Gaspar de Alba's alterNative lens. In contrast to the billion dollars spent by top fashion magazines to shoot glamorous photo layouts, Hidalgo Newton's images include shots of her journey from wearing a bathing suit on a public beach[15] to her embracing of traditional practices of "babywearing" as a new mother.[16] Her deployment of the popular culture medium of blogging gives her a platform from which to center her own body within a discourse on fashion, lifestyle, and culture, rather than fighting to be in the margins of mainstream production.

Hidalgo Newton not only challenges mainstream beauty standards, but also relishes in the complication of femininity and Latinidad. Identifying herself as "chapina/guanaca/chicana," she celebrates her mixed heritage as a woman of Guatemalan, Salvadoran, and Chicana culture and/or descent. Even as she incorporates an emphasis on style and fashion, she challenges popular notions of these topics as superficial or inconsequential. Instead she posits "'fatshion' is a form of resistance to mainstream standards of beauty and other forms of subordination, including race, ethnicity, class, sexuality and gender."[17] Yet the potential subversive nature of her joyful approach to body positive self-expression and representation is also guided by a desire to avoid self-exploitation.

In her study of the representation of Latina bodies in popular film and culture, Mendible too acknowledges this risk of a misread or objectified body: "For many women of color in the

United States, even a simple act—dancing—is loaded with gendered, racialized baggage; in a single butt-shaking instant, this Latina body can resurrect a history of stereotypes, preconceptions, and prejudices" (20). Yet Mendible also acknowledges the powerful interventions possible when the transgressive discourses and bodies of Latinas enter into the public sphere. For Hidalgo Newton the risk of sexual objectification is measured against her determination to embrace and embody her sensuality and sexuality in a public forum without shame. She identifies the tensions involved in her own self-representation as a curvy woman of color, "Many full figured women are shamed into covering up every inch of their bodies. At the same time women of color are often over-sexualized in media representations. As a Chicana, my challenge is how to represent myself in ways that are body positive & not self-exploitative."[18] Yet Hidalgo Newton understands the specificity of her body in motion—referring both to the movement of her own vibrant, transformative body moving through her own life, and the way her blogging presence moves as a communicative agent through the lives of her readers and followers.

To fully comprehend the social impact of the cyber medium beyond simple voyeurism or self-objectification, Laura J. Gurak and Smiljana Antonijevic emphasize the need to understand "blogs as communicative events" (64). While one might assume that the primary communicative exchange takes place between blogger and reader(s), Gurak and Antonijevic's analysis suggests that an even more primal communicative pairing is made up of the blogger engaged with her/himself through time since, "Unlike personal Web presentations, structured around 'the essence of me,' blogs are structured around 'the process of me'" (65). Because blogging allows for extended timelines of self-reflection, someone like Hidalgo Newton is able to share not just her day-to-day thoughts and experiences, but her reflective process of growth from one day and experience to the next. As readers we observe these daily personal revolutions, as Hidalgo Newton worries about an upcoming trip to the beach, her intense schedule and struggles as a doctoral student, or the fears and worries of motherhood. We move through the anticipation and fear and into the reality of a beautiful body positive vacation, a successful academic presentation, or a happy thriving child. We bear witness to her journey alongside her.

The code after which the site is named includes a list of style-related pledges such as "not hiding my body behind over-sized clothes," health-related pledges like "to practice self-love by making an effort to pamper myself," as well as a final promise to "practic[e] more of the physical activities I enjoy (i.e. dancing and jiggling my bits, making out, and having SEX)."[19] Here we see the significance of movement, both physical/corporeal and her emotional shift towards embracing her body while engaged in these movements.

Ultimately Hidalgo Newton's presence offers her greatest affront to mainstream media's limited representation of women's bodies:

> As a large woman I am embracing a body that does not fit into the mainstream view of 'beauty'. Representations of large woman are invisible. They are missing in mainstream media. Our voices, our faces, and our bodies, are missing from dominant discourse.[20]

Regarding one particular dominant sphere—the world of fitness broadly and yoga specifically—Hidalgo Newton experienced an almost complete disregard for the unique needs of curvier yoga practitioners. On January 7, 2014, she posted a blog detailing a collaborative project with Phoenix-based yoga instructor Mary Canisales. In her experiences attempting to explore the tradition and practice of yoga, Hidalgo Newton identifies a key contradiction in how larger bodies are both policed and restricted within the public domain:

The contradiction in the absence of visual representations of *mujeres* like me is that dominant society demands that fat people MUST exercise, yet whenever fat people are moving their bodies in public spaces we are called names, shamed, humiliated, seen as a giant eye-sore and a nuisance.[21]

In response to this public shaming and erasure of larger bodies in literal motion, Hidalgo Newton and Canisales created *Rasquache Yoga*, a video featuring both women moving through a routine that includes modified poses for a variety of different body sizes and abilities. Their use of Ybarra-Frausto's rasquache aesthetic underlines his notions both of a "sensibility of the … excluded" and a practice that "subverts the consumer ethic of mainline culture with strategies of appropriation, reversal, and inversion" (*Velvet Barrios* xvii). The women clearly see their visible bodies in motion as a key component in their public intervention, explaining "We want to challenge fitness & health paradigms that shame people with large bodies engaging in physical activity and believe it is empowering to see *mujeres* who are large moving their bodies."[22] Even Hidalgo Newton's invocation of code-switching—seen in her choice of "mujeres" in Spanish, rather than "women" in English—offers insight into the intended frame of reference for *Rasquache Yoga*, not "women" generally, but perhaps Latina women specifically.

Hidalgo Newton's blog production of The Big Girls Code can be seen to employ Ybarra-Frausto's conceptualization of movidas, "[the] coping strategies you use to gain time, to make options to retain hope" (5). While conversations around eating disorders, self-harm, and bullying are present in her postings, Hidalgo Newton is able to transform trauma into hope as she engages community and establishes the "identificatory bonds and affiliations" Mendible associates with popular cultural production and reception (16).

Crafty Chica

Another illustration of Ybarra-Frausto's rasquache aesthetic in Latina/o popular culture can be found in Kathy Cano-Murillo's creative line of products and productions billed under the label "Crafty Chica." Cano-Murillo defines herself as "A crafty version of Selena-meets-the Hallmark Channel-with a dash of Oprah optimism."[23] It is in keeping with a rasquache worldview that she fashions her public persona from the remnants of popular predecessors, icons of the crafting/gifting world, self-improvement world, and the Chicana/o popular culture world. Dividing her time between her Crafty Chica website, her book publications, her craft supply and merchandise lines, and her journalistic endeavors, outwardly Cano-Murillo seems more aligned with a Mexican-American version of Martha Stewart. However the language with which she describes herself suggests a conscious effort to avoid marginalized representations of self. While a Mexican-American version of Martha Stewart would suggest an Anglo original against which all subsequent models are measured, Cano-Murillo's patchwork persona—fashioned from pop music icons, crafty corporations, and an international self-help guru—represents an original creation, as she is not attempting to reproduce the basic template of Selena, Hallmark, or Oprah, but to identify aspects of herself within their pre-existing projects while maintaining her own unique presence.

Cano-Murillo self-identifies on her site as a "third-generation Mexican-American, a native Phoenician, mom of two, wife, with five Chihuahuas!"[24] In Phoenix, Arizona, a city known for the sort of tensions and struggle exemplified above by Puente Movement's community organizing as well as Julio Salgado's visual representations of these actions,

Cano-Murillo's art may serve, for some, as a balm of bright color, sequins, and glitter to soothe weary spirits. Ybarra-Frausto notes of these visual markers of excess, "The *rasquache* inclination piles pattern on pattern filling all available space with bold display. Ornamentation and elaboration prevail, joined to a delight for texture and sensuous surface" (6). Because while Ybarra-Frausto's rasquachismo necessarily comes from a working class background of struggle and oppression, the emphasis of the worldview is on resilience in the face of a challenge:

> To be rasquache is to be down but not out (*fregado pero no jodido*). Responding to a direct relationship with the material level of existence or subsistence is what engenders a *rasquache* attitude of survival and inventiveness ... This constant making do, the grit and obstinacy of survival played out against a relish for surface display and flash creates a florid milieu of admixtures and recombinations.
>
> (5–6)

Cano-Murillo's employment of the term "crafty" in the construction of her brand speaks to this very "inventiveness" about which Ybarra-Frausto theorizes above. Her site includes "Do It Yourself" projects featuring a mix of crafting leftovers and more high-end tools. One example of Cano-Murillo's rasquache form appears in an August 2015 post that detailed her instructions to create "Mexi-fotonovela flowers."[25] The basis for the project, old magazines and surplus Mexican fotonovelas—another popular culture genre made up of literary merging of a romance novel and a comic book—establish a fittingly rasquache start to the project. Ybarra-Frausto identifies reused and recycled materials as a foundation of a rasquache aesthetic, "Limited resources means mending, re-fixing and reusing everything. Things are not thrown away but saved and recycled, often in different context" (6). Although the project could easily be done by hand, cutting flowers of various sizes and shapes from the novela pages to be colored and pinned together, Cano-Murillo's approach integrates her crafting expertise by employing a die-cut machine and flower template. "Grit and obstinacy" ebb and flow as she exchanges them for glitter and determination.

Though not a central focus, Cano-Murillo's Crafty Chica site also has a thread of body positivity from the perspective of a full figured Latina. While Hidalgo Newton's The Big Girls Code's focus on style tends to emphasize the colors, textures, and shapes adorning the canvas of her own body, Cano-Murillo's canvas varies from project to project and frequently does not focus on her own body within the creative process. DIY projects like Day of the Dead pillowcases or repurposed milagro charm jewelry link crafting knowledge with the specificity of Cano-Murillo's Mexican-American cultural identity for audiences. Particular projects where the author integrates a sense of her own racialized and ethnic body within the creative process provide a fuller illustration of an intersectional body in motion.

With two sub-sections on the Crafty Chica site with the titles "Fat Girl Confessions" and "Chubby Girl Delights," readers can immediately identify what seems to be a conscious engagement with body politics alongside crafting, food, and entertainment topics. In one craft project Cano-Murillo details the steps through which she redesigns an ill-fitting Mexican embroidered dress due to her body's seeming excess, "I tried it on and my bootie would not compromise."[26] Rather than leave the beautiful garment unworn, Cano-Murillo simply "makes do" and uses her creative skills to fashion a new wearable garment. In that instance, the garment, and not the body, is seen as the obstacle to looking and feeling good.

The site does, however, reveal some dissonance, as pages shift from delight in decadent dessert recipes to her shame about indulging in a late-night donut run. Yet as her audience we see these shifts as installments in what Gurak and Antonijevic would call Cano-Murillo's "process of me."

In thinking about the presence of the body as a moving, shape-shifting entity in both Hidalgo Newton and Cano-Murillo's blog sites, it is important to understand the way these Latina popular culture producers situate their work at the intersection of gender, ethnicity, and sexuality. Findings in a 2013 study of Latina youth and body image by Schooler and Daniels "indicate that ethnic identity may not fully protect Latina girls from negative feelings about their bodies, but it might lessen the impact of exposure to idealized, White media images" (16). Might we extend this finding, that a strong sense of cultural or ethnic identity might help young girls resist the tendency to measure themselves in painful ways against unattainable models of thin, white, femininity, to Hidalgo Newton and Cano-Murillo's adult engagement with body image, beauty, and identity?

While the examples cited in the current chapter stem from the rich community of Chicana/o and Latina/o community, arts, and activism in Phoenix, Arizona,[27] the theme of "bodies in motion" speaks powerfully to myriad other Latina/o pop culture productions. Of particular significance are those forms of cultural expression, like those of Narcia, Salgado, Hidalgo Newton, and Cano-Murillo, that call on technology and social media to build community and inspire movements of social justice, self-love, and rasquache innovation.

Notes

1 Berestein, Leslie. "Highway safety sign becomes running story on immigration."
2 Berestein, Leslie. "Highway safety sign becomes running story on immigration."
3 Berestein, Leslie. "Highway safety sign becomes running story on immigration."
4 See Ortiz, Fernando. *Cuban Counterpoint: Tobacco and Sugar*. 1995.
5 See Anzaldúa, Gloria. *Borderlands*. 2007.
6 Magaña 157.
7 For an analysis of both 1070 and 2281 in relation to intergroup relations, see: Bean, Meghan G., and Jeff Stone. "Another View from the Ground: How Laws Like SB1070 and HB2281 Erode the Intergroup Fabric of our Community." 2012.
8 Puente Movement. "Puente Arizona | Our History." puenteaz.org. Available at: http://puenteaz.org/about-us/our-history/
9 Puente Ink's founders "Are active in the Civil and Human Rights, Anti-War, Indigenous, Environmental, Migrant and Womyn's movements, [and] envision a full service print shop that would support the movement for political and social change" (facebook.com/PuenteInk)
10 www.huffingtonpost.com/jeff-biggers/arizona-immigration-law_b_1450818.html
11 www.huffingtonpost.com/jeff-biggers/arizona-immigration-law_b_1450818.html
12 www.pcasc.net/2011/09/20/4-artists-who-are-reshaping-america%E2%80%99s-immigration-debate/
13 One of many examples of Salgado's work highlighting the trope of survival can be seen in his #QueerArtistsAlive exhibit that opened at the San Francisco LGBT Community Center September 17, 2015.
14 For additional discussion of the invocation of the 'X' in Raza and Xicana/o Studies, see Mireles 570.
15 www.thebiggirlscode.com/yay-im-at-the-beautiful-beach-in-oaxaca/
16 www.thebiggirlscode.com/rebozo-love/
17 Hidalgo Newton, Leigh-Anna. thebiggirlscode.com. www.thebiggirlscode.com/sample-page/
18 Hidalgo Newton, Leigh-Anna. thebiggirlscode.com. www.thebiggirlscode.com/im-contemplating-belly-tops-becoming-a-summer/

19 Hidalgo Newton, Leigh-Anna. thebiggirlscode.com. www.thebiggirlscode.com/the-code/
20 Hidalgo Newton, Leigh-Anna. thebiggirlscode.com. www.thebiggirlscode.com/the-code/
21 Hidalgo Newton, Leigh-Anna. thebiggirlscode.com. www.thebiggirlscode.com/big-girls-code-rasquache-yoga/
22 Hidalgo Newton, Leigh-Anna. thebiggirlscode.com. www.thebiggirlscode.com/big-girls-code-rasquache-yoga/
23 Cano-Murillo, Kathy. craftychica.com. www.craftychica.com/bio/
24 Cano-Murillo, Kathy. craftychica.com. www.craftychica.com/bio/
25 Cano-Murillo, Kathy. craftychica.com. www.craftychica.com/2015/08/paper-flowers/
26 Cano-Murillo, Kathy. craftychica.com. www.craftychica.com/2011/06/how-to-transform-a-mexican-embroidered-dress-into-a-top/
27 Though based currently in Los Angeles, California, Hidalgo Newton is a former Arizona resident and continues to be active in community organizing and arts communities in the Phoenix Metro area.

Bibliography

Anzaldúa, Gloria. *Borderlands: The New Mestiza*. 3rd ed. San Francisco: Aunt Lute Books, 2007.

Baksh, Stokely. "4 Artists Who Are Reshaping America's Immigration Debate." *colorlines.com*, 20 September 2011. Available at: www.colorlines.com/articles/4-artists-who-are-reshaping-americas-immigration-debate

Bean, Meghan G., and Jeff Stone. "Another View from the Ground: How Laws Like SB1070 and HB2281 Erode the Intergroup Fabric of our Community." *Analyses of Social Issues and Public Policy* 12:1 (2012): 144–50.

Berestein, Leslie. "Highway Safety Sign Becomes Running Story on Immigration." *utsandiego.com*, 10 April 2005. Available at: www.utsandiego.com/uniontrib/20050410/news_1n10signs.html

Biggers, Jeff. "At Supreme Court, Arizona Leaves Affected Voices at Home: Q & A With Carlos Garcia, Puente Human Rights Advocate." *huffingtonpost.com*, 24 April 2012. Available at: www.huffingtonpost.com/jeff-biggers/arizona-immigration-law_b_1450818.html

Cano-Murillo, Kathy. *Crafty Chica*. Blog. Available at: www.craftychica.com

Gaspar de Alba, Alicia, ed. *Velvet Barrios: Popular Culture and Chicana/o Sexualities*. New York: Palgrave Macmillan, 2003.

Gurak, Laura J., and Smiljana Antonijevic. "The Psychology of Blogging: You, Me, and Everyone in Between." *American Behavioral Scientist* 52:1 (2008): 60–8.

Hidalgo Newton, Leigh-Anna. *The Big Girls Code*. Blog. Available at: www.thebiggirlscode.com/

Magaña, Lisa. "SB 1070 and Negative Social Constructions of Latino Immigrants in Arizona." *AZTLÁN – A Journal of Chicano Studies* 38:2 (2013): 151–62.

Mendible, Myra. *From Bananas to Buttocks: The Latina Body in Popular Film and Culture*. Austin: University of Texas Press, 2007.

Mireles, Ernesto Todd. "'We Demand Xicano Studies': War of the Flea at Michigan State University." *Latino Studies* 11: 4 (2013): 570–9.

Moreno, Carolina. "Julio Salgado's 'UndocuQueer Billboard' Explores Intersection Of LGBTQ And Undocumented Communities." *Huffington Post* 21 June 2013. Available at: www.huffingtonpost.com/2013/06/21/julio-salgado-undocuqueer_n_3480327.html

Ortiz, Fernando. *Cuban Counterpoint: Tobacco and Sugar*. Trans. Harriet de Onís. Durham, NC: Duke University Press, 1995.

Santa Ana, Otto. *Brown Tide Rising: Metaphors of Latinos in Contemporary American Public Discourse*. Austin: University of Texas Press, 2002.

Schooler, Deborah, and Elizabeth A. Daniels. "'I Am Not a Skinny Toothpick and Proud of it': Latina Adolescents' Ethnic Identity and Responses to Mainstream Media Images." *Body Image* 11:1 (2014): 11–18.

Seif, Hinda. "'Layers of Humanity': Interview with Undocuqueer Artivist Julio Salgado." *Latino Studies* 12:2 (2014): 300–9.

Szkupinski Quiroga, Seline. "Vamos a Aguantar: Observations on How Arizona's SB 1070 Has Affected One Community." *Latino Studies* 11:4 (2013): 580–6.

Ybarra-Frausto, Tomás. "Rasquachismo: A Chicano Sensibility." *Chicano Aesthetics: Rasquachismo.* Eds Rudy Guglielmo, Tomás Ybarra-Frausto, Lennee Eller, and Rudy Guglielmo. Exhibition catalog. Phoenix, AZ: MARS/Movimiento Artístico del Río Salado, 1989. 5–8.

28

CLAIMING STYLE, CONSUMING CULTURE

The Politics of Latina Self-Styling and Fashion Lines

Stacy I. Macías

From the iconic zoot suits of pachucas and high pomps of rockabilly chicas to the mainstreaming of chola style and ass-enhancing jeans, Latina fashion and self-styling practices are as much transcendent as they are anchored by oppositional formations, shifting popular trends, and transnational politics.[1] Latinas have reached for recognition—a move from mere object to self-determining subject—through their creative deployments and passionate re-workings of aesthetic elements. While Latina style accommodates changing fashion trends, it is also marked by incorporations of historical representations like the sensually stylized flair of señorita femininity, the excessiveness of the hot, fleshy body, or the reinscription of old school, gangsterette wares. Commenting on Latina fashion and style, however, requires more than surveying iconic figures or popular taxonomies. To consider Latina fashion—*what* one wears—and style—*how* one wears 'the what'—requires that we attend to the dialectical relationship among everyday style makers, mainstream fashion producers, and the fraught and fabulous socio-cultural processes through which dominant and subversive aesthetic practices enter into our collective imagination.[2]

In this chapter, I show how Latina self-styling practices and a self-described Latina fashion line emerge messily from socio-cultural forces that include the historical fetishizing of Latina sexuality and the neoliberal marketing of racialized Latina excess. Such contexts also create the conditions for Latinas to manipulate and negotiate their "exotic" racialized gender identities toward re-imagining and thus constructing alternative, expressive, and queerly feminine representations. I name this style *racialized rasquache raunch*, in which rasquache gestures to "a working-class style with vivid colors, vernacular forms, and recycled materials."[3] By racialized, I am indexing how Latinas evoke a non-white racial identity that cannot be congruent with universality, unmarkedness, and social privilege, while raunch, or excess, can be understood as "an acceptable form of embellishment [...] where exaggeration and surplus are signs of abundance" as Ellie Hernández offers (121). Racialized rasquache raunch signifies an explicit Latina aesthetic that is not merely the preserve of individual identity, a performance of racialized gendered clichés, or a simple subversion of the dominant. Style and fashion enable and legitimize expressions and desires of Latina self-identity that potentially queer—or disidentify with and critique the authority of—normative aesthetics, white femininity, and disembodied subjectivity.[4] As a compelling technology of the self, style is also an individual signifying practice woven with threads of shared ethnic-racial conflict, social class barriers, gender limitations, and symbolic cultural meaning. The resulting products and practices are neither whole reflections of interiority or all-unifying community representations of social defiance. Latina self-styling and fashion, instead, reveal how racialized gender identity formation is in part produced through the negotiation of raw materials like clothing, makeup, accessory, hairstyle, and the body. I proceed with a genealogy of my mother's underground styling practices and fashion purchases to illustrate the interaction of myriad social forces that historically situate how self-styling and a Latina fashion line matter to politics—the struggle for and over power—even under the weight of neoliberal capitalism.[5]

Latina Style/Custom-Made, Part I

I recall always being fascinated by the spectacle of my mother: her full-figured, curvaceous body; her ever-changing hairstyles and hues; her flashy taste in clothes, jewelry, and high heels; her infamous bold laugh; and her power. Styling herself in a way that reflected her working-class, Mexican-American ethno-racial historical markings, images and memories of my mother sequentially reveal an Eastside pachuca in the 1950s, a rockabilly chick and mod-esque beatnik in the 1960s, a blonde-bouffant bell-bottom wearer in the 1970s, and a permed-hair, sequined disco queen in the 1980s. The styling choices she made veered far from the images of adoring wife, selfless mother, coy virgin, or dutiful activist that comprised some of the ideal categories of Chicana/Latina womanhood circulating in the 1950s, 60s, 70s, and 80s. While I never personally encountered my mother as a young consumer who worked in and made studied purchases all over the urban centers of Los Angeles, I came to know the tangible manifestations of that young woman embodied in my mother's style: an amalgamation of a discount-driven, ostentatiously imagined, and sensually embodied Latina rasquache style. On *rasquachismo* as a Chicana cultural form, scholar Amalia Mesa-Bains states that it materializes out of "an imposed Anglo-American cultural identity and the defiance of a restrictive gender identity within Chicano culture" (160). A second-generation Mexican-American woman, my mother's rightful place seemed to be alongside the forbidden figures associated with bad behavior, subversive style, and raunchy excess best epitomized, for example, in the figure of the streetwise, publicly scorned chola whose precursor, la pachuca, was considered a national threat to U.S. American patriotism due to her excessive, non-normative femininity.[6]

Alongside my mother, I made discount shopping trips, frequented the local mini-malls, and participated in other mundane consumptive practices of pleasure and survival in South El Monte, a working-class, Latino/a neighborhood within walking distance from the apartment complex where in 1995 one of the most egregious examples of sweatshop labor exploitation involving young, undocumented, Thai women would be uncovered.[7] As a young Catholic school student, my body was assigned daily to a drab-colored, plaid uniform, which offered little occasion to veer from an unadventurous dress routine. Luckily, "free-dress days" allowed my mother the opportunity to hurl my body into an imaginative universe replete with endless color, shape, material, and style options. Our excursions usually landed us in one of the mini-malls owned by non-English speaking Asian immigrant owners and working-class Latina customers. In these stores existed the best low-priced, low-end stylish items. Whether it was at the "5-7-9" or "Susie's Deals," my mother was always able to locate the most expensive-looking clothing item, the latest avant-garde runway copy, or the conversation-inciting accessory. My mother reveled in the process of coordinating colors, matching fabrics and details, and assembling the most fashion forward creation with only a fifteen-dollar budget. The knack that my mother possessed was an under-recognized talent—at least before professional costumers and celebrity stylists were lucrative, legitimate professions.

My mother also shopped for my clothes at "Nena's," a neighbor who regularly hosted invitation-only clothes buying parties. During such events, mothers and daughters opened the door to Nena's house to find piles of girls' sized tops, skirts, dresses, jackets, and pants complete with Broadway, Buffums, Bullocks, and Robinson's department store hangers and price-tags spilling out of dark plastic garbage bags. Nena never displayed the clothes with flourish or removed store tags, but she personally sifted through the trash bags literally dumped on her carpet to find the items that she knew would most attract each mom and daughter duo. With four young daughters of her own, Nena's informal business served less as a means to clothe her children and more to sustain her family economically while the neighborhood's blue-collar kids got a taste of fancy department store threads. Nena's business acumen, like my mother's homegrown style logic, was organically shaped by challenges of economic instability, social access, geographic location, and racialized gender difference.

As I recall, the democratization of fashion started when I entered the first grade and stayed active for the length of Nena's tenancy in my neighborhood. My mother not only shopped at Nena's home willingly and knowingly, but she also communicated the size, colors, and styles in which she preferred to dress me. Although my inquiries about the source of the overflowing disarming garbage bags were never honestly answered, the open secret of Nena's supply was surely known. Eventually my mother would confirm my instinct that the clothes were "hot," and she provided details on how Nena and her employees would lift clothes from major department stores. Because the level of in-store surveillance was minimal, Nena and her co-conspirators would use pillows as pretenses for very pregnant bellies, which in the store's dressing rooms they would empty then refill with clothes.

My mother's styling practices, Nena's entrepreneurial feats, and my budding femme fashionista all form part of a style story that sheds light on the art of underground Latina styling practices. This custom tale, however, cannot be understood outside of its structuring pieces such as the impact of urban economic restructuring, transnational border politics, and outstanding epistemological shifts in consumer identity. Not only over are the days when Nena could manage such stealth activity in a department store due to the high level of surveillance inside and outside a building's parameters; moreover, Nena as the local Robin Hood of fashion has become an irrelevant, obsolete figure. Mega chain stores like Forever 21 litter the consumer landscape while mainstream fashion lines like those sold at K-mart, Sears, and Kohl's provide to young, working-class women of color immediate access to designer knock-offs. At considerably inexpensive prices, department store chains that sell self-designated "Latina"-themed fashion lines offer low-priced items—lower than the prices Nena would have been able to negotiate because her informal business endeavors sustained her entire family. From a reliance on the manufacturing industry to its decline and the domination of the service sector in a post-Fordist economy, it is even more likely that I would bear witness to Nena having to keep her side business afloat while punching in at a store like Forever 21 complete with its lack of access to health care insurance, fair employee wages, and workplace respect.[8] To find my mother's racialized rasquache raunch style streamlined into a corporate fashion line is to encounter the rampant contradictions of Latina style and fashion in which Latinas may partly achieve recognition of their racialized gender subjectivities, yet precisely through a reliance on hegemonic tropes of Latina identity—not to mention the female bodies of color that design, cut, and sew so many different fashion materials in sweat shops locally and transnationally. In the following section, I explore these entanglements by examining the cultural politics of a Latina-themed fashion line and the discourses surrounding it.

Assembling Ensembles: Latina Life™ and the Exceptional Latina Consumer

In October 2005, the global corporation Cotton Incorporated issued, "Latina Fashion: From Vogue to K-Mart," a press release corresponding with national Hispanic Heritage month. In a description of Latina style, the press release states:

> If the retailers are benefiting from the Latina surge, general consumers are also benefiting from the Hispanic woman's special style. Today, colors and embellishments traditionally favored by Latina women, such as reds, lace, and beading are finding a place in the closets of stylish women everywhere.
>
> (*Cottoninc.com*)

The above statement of Latina style is clearly informed by how the racial-ethnic identity of Latinas is co-constructed through dominant gender, class, and sexuality conceptions. The press release's vivid description of the style "traditionally favored by Latina women … " correlates with dominant historic tropes and archetypes of Latina representation. In particular, the stylized costume-y aesthetic of excess captured in the press release through reference to "embellishments" that one may assume more apt for a Vegas club night or special undergarments—reds, lace, and beading—emphasize racialized sexuality and unruly working-class Latina femininity and correspond with how the institution of media has treated Latinas historically. Whether in painting and photography, film and literature, or other popular mediums of representation like television, commercial advertisements, and an assortment of consumer products, the representation of Latinas falls within a set of taxonomies that many media, feminist, and Latina and Chicana studies scholars have analyzed in depth.[9]

In the introduction to her edited collection, *From Bananas to Buttocks*, editor Myra Mendible delineates the Latina archetypes on which mass media and other social institutions have ubiquitously depended (1). Mendible describes how all too predictably Latina representation historically does not deviate from a discursive arc that oscillates among a few popular tropes: the saucy, aberrant, and hypersexual Latina embodied in The Spitfire; a palatable yet still exotically coy and highly feminine Latina epitomized in La Señorita; and finally the maternal, desexualized, working-poor yet criminal immigrant Latina enfigured in La Domestica (3). Thus, the historical tropification of Latinas as alternately illegible (domesticas and garment workers), sexually exotic (screen sirens and industry darlings), criminally-minded (immigrant women regardless of documentation status), and pathological (pachucas, cholas, and other gangsterettes) is what forms the arc of predominating Latina popular representations.

While Cotton Incorporated's dependence on and reproduction of a Latina archetype is clear, I also view the press release's discourse as contradictorily legitimizing racialized rasquache raunch aesthetics. The press release is in direct contrast with the interests of Latina politicians, some ethnic studies scholars, and immigrant rights activists to move Latina femininity away from racialized embodiments and into "appropriate" gendered territory. In this way, the corporate valorization of Latinas' "special style" concomitantly validates racialized rasquache raunch aesthetics and thus self-styling techniques that Latinas consciously and creatively deploy. Latina aesthetic practices that are representative of excessive embellishments, sensual accents, and vibrant colors resist the call to subscribe to historically dominant models of white femininity and also validate the relationship of Latina consumers to a historically racist fashion industry. As the press release indicates, non-Latinas have begun to benefit from the aesthetics that Latinas have long exhibited and prized.

In *Latino Spin*, Latina/o cultural studies scholar Arlene Dávila astutely reveals the contemporary contradictions of market reconfiguration:

> In the contemporary neoliberal context, contests over the 'values' people are given as constituencies are more than ever exacerbated by the spin created by marketers and political pundits. And in these realms, Latinos are more than ever recognized to be the one group that will provide institutions and marketers with the most consumers and constituents.
>
> (164)

Dávila's insights about the role that media and political institutions play in constructing the specialized consumer market worthiness of Latinos in general instructively applies to the ways in which department stores, magazines, corporate research, and Hollywood celebrities form a powerful nexus to mediate racialized, gendered ideologies of Latina femininity. In this sense, I extend Dávila's analysis to consider the value that Latinas have acquired through a product line specifically catered to their marked style sensibilities. In other words, the cultural by-products that neoliberal models contradictorily produce as an effect of their proliferation are significant to consider given that economic globalization is not a homogeneous process with purely predictable outcomes.

Another interesting highlight from the press release compares the remarkable position of Latina consumers to other female consumers to "explain why the Latina consumer spends significantly more time shopping than her Caucasian and African-American counterparts" (*Cottoninc.com*). The press release quotes Kim Kitchings, the director of research and strategic planning for Cotton Incorporated:

> We know from our research that the female Hispanic consumer is highly cognizant of trends and styles and likes to shop for fashion … This customer likes to jump on a trend as it's happening, rather than catching it when it's reached the mainstream.
>
> (*Cottoninc.com*)

Additionally, the press release shows the statistical differences that Cotton Incorporated's "Lifestyle Monitor" tracked:

... Hispanic females spend an average of 135.1 minutes in stores shopping for apparel whereas Caucasian and African-American female respondents recorded an average of 89.4 and 109.27 minutes, respectively. Latina women are also more fastidious about their appearance than women of other ethnicities. A significant 57% of Hispanic females told the Monitor that they preferred clothing that looked better on them, over clothing that was comfortable for an evening of dinner and dancing. This was considerably higher than Caucasians (45%) and African-Americans (46%).

(*Cottoninc.com*)

The above data not only captures that the fashion industry in general is deeply enmeshed in idioms of temporality, but it also reveals the significance of time in relation to racialization strategies. In particular, media represents Latinas (and Latinidad in general) in provincial and backward ways to associate Latinas with the past and old traditions rather than with present contexts or future possibilities. For example, the Suarez family of the ABC dramedy, *Ugly Betty*, may live in the fashion capital, New York, but both Betty and Hilda Suarez represent outdated aesthetic styles in comparison to their on-screen fashion forward, white feminine counterparts. In the press release, however, Latina consumers surpass other consumer groups because of their style perspicacity and forecasting of fashion trends. To further solidify this finding, the press release quantifies the exceptional devotion of Latinas to shopping activities. Through its research and report, Cotton Incorporated constructs the unlikely model consumer—a modern Latina who perpetually shops ahead of the crowd and wears clothing regardless of the cost to her body or bank account.

During the same period of Cotton Incorporated creating media buzz around the female "Hispanic" consumer, Sears, Roebuck, and Co. strategically premiered Latina Life™, its fashion line that catered to the specific style propensities of Latinas. This was not Sears's first attempt, however, to market and design a fashion line to "Hispanic" women. In 2003, Sears chose to collaborate with Lucy Pereda, a Cuban-born television host, anchor, and cookbook author who was popularly dubbed the "Hispanic Martha Stewart," to launch the first ever Latina fashion line in the U.S. (Yerak). After a two-year period of low sales, Sears dropped the Lucy Pereda apparel line and formally cut its ties with Pereda. Sears's executive vice president and general merchandise manager, Gwen Manto, explained the company's decision: "Lucy [Pereda] had a limited appeal. It was barer, more sexy, more clubby-type looks ... [the new apparel line] is very body-conscious with a lot of detail and print but not 'cha-cha-cha'" (Anderson). While Sears attributed the apparel line's lackluster success to its elements of design that seemingly too heavily relied upon youth driven trends and sexual appeal, Manto's use of "cha-cha-cha" revealed that Sears could embrace racialized gender difference but only to a corporate limit. In other words, the Latina aesthetic of Lucy Pereda had moved from acceptable to sullied when the design elements were as identifiably ethnic as the rhythmic hip-centric dance and music beats of the Cuban cha-cha-cha. In place of the Pereda line, Sears pursued *Latina* magazine and debuted Latina Life™ to reignite its appeal to a broader female Hispanic clientele.

The aesthetics of Latina Life™ and the customers shopping at Sears for the apparel line originally caught my attention, as I wondered how someone like my mother, who initially informed me that there was a "really cute Latina fashion line at 'the Sears,'" would manage to wear these clothes. It is plausible to discern that my mother—in her mid-sixties, a former janitorial worker, and by Western medical standards considered overweight—would not be the targeted consumer of Latina Life™. Yet, on my various ethnographic visits to Sears's department stores throughout greater Los Angeles County, I noted that a range of ages from adolescent youth to women older than my mother bought and wore similarly fashioned and styled clothes. Disproportionate, middle-aged, and ample body types encompassed the prevailing Latina customer and her look, which obscured any norms that attempted to prescribe an ideal wearer. It became clear to me that Sears, like Cotton Inc., had likely researched and thus catered to the Latina demographic that would come to patronize its Latina Life™ fashion line.

Sears and *Latina* magazine in their joint fashion line's marketing campaign narrate what they understand as Latina style aesthetics,

> Key Latina Life™ wardrobe separates include animal print faux fur jackets, embellished camis, shrug sets with velvet piping, sheer mesh tops, ruched paisley skirts and fitted pants with contoured yokes, rich colors in lux suede, metallic, faux fur, croc leather and animal print, along with studs, beading and rhinestone embellishment … a little more colorful, always a little spice, a little flavor, and something flirty.
>
> (*WebProNews*.com)

Presumably, Sears in their revamping efforts to appeal to a larger Latina constituency would have forgone design elements like those mentioned above, all of which accentuate rather than deemphasize sexual, racialized allure, or the dominant "cha-cha-cha" look of Pereda's line from which they sought to create distance. While Sears claimed to redirect its Latina-themed fashion line toward a more sedate, professional look, the clothing and accessory products actually *re-inscribed* the racializing tropes of Latina femininity. In other words, Sears's desire to overcome the archetype of a *too* sexy señorita was discursively undermined with "colorful," "spice," and "flirty" in conjunction with the material products that posited it once again as a working-class, sexually titillating style, or what I have termed as a racialized rasquache raunch aesthetic. Latina Life™, touted as the corrective apparel line to its edgier precursor, not so subtly succumbed to the same terms of representation.

Despite that the fashion lines—much like Cotton Incorporated's research and press release—may consciously uphold and reproduce historical tropes of Latina racialized representations of femininity, they also unwittingly and ironically provide Latinas the means to display their racialized rasquache raunch style. Visual art historian Laura E. Pérez provides a productive point of entry for apprehending alternative meanings of self-styling and fashion. Pérez proposes that the body, dress, and body ornamentation can be viewed as social garments or "writings on and about the body." In Pérez's view, such social texts have the ability to mark and produce gender and racial identities, "whether these be normative or historically newer forms of constructing and representing femaleness, femininity, or the undecidability of gender" (51).

For all of Sears's desire to overhaul and thus upgrade Latina Life™ in the direction of a normative, digestible, yet still explicitly racialized Latina articulation of femininity, Sears also provides the means to legitimize Latinas who shop for fashion and style their clothes in ways that exceed normativizing systems of feminine gender. Latina Life™ can be read as harkening back to tropes of hyperbolic sexuality, unabashed embodiment, and excessive pleasures, yet it also reorients feminine aesthetics away from disembodied, modern, and assimilating versions. The social texts of Latina Life™ nestle power within its Latina fashion lines and style options. I find it useful here to consider a Foucauldian notion of power to highlight the complex, un-inducted, horizontal, and proleptic forms of power that subjects negotiate between individual agency and social structures.[10] Rather than relying on a model that only legitimizes a hierarchically ordered system of power between oppressors and the oppressed—in this case, between neoliberal capitalism/corporations like Sears and Latina consumer subjects—I draw upon Foucault to emphasize how power circulates contextually and contingently through a variety of networks. Within this frame, I view Latina femininities as sites of non-centralized power that through self-styling and consumption of fashion come to mean something other than what is historically invoked as frivolous and meaningless consumption. The range of bodies and sizes engaged in the artful acts of wearing and consuming Latina Life™ symbolize the contradictions of consumer capital that proliferate through Sears's commodification of Latina femininity, yet not without Latinas inventing, negotiating, and subjectivizing their styles and selves to their own desires and effects. The racialized rasquache raunch aesthetic of Latina Life™ invests Latina style and femininity with a sense of power that is opaque in both the mainstream fashion world and the universe of respectable Latina style.

Perhaps in its desire to distance itself from figures of bodily excess, unruly sexuality, and racialized rasquache raunch that during the so-called era of the "Latin Boom" in the mid-1990s through the early 2000s had circulated more widely (the onscreen portrayals of Salma Hayek in films like *From Dusk Till Dawn* (1996) and *Fools Rush In* (1997); the off-screen tabloid talk of Jennifer Lopez, her infamous revealing green Versace dress, and her relationship with the gun-toting, hip hop mogul, Sean "Puffy" Combs; the cinematic scenes of Mexican-American gang members depicted in *Mi Vida Loca* (1993); and the cross-over successes of Tejana singer, Selena, and Latin American songstresses like Thalía Sodi, Alejandra Guzmán, and Gloria Trevi, Sears and *Latina* magazine could not imagine an alternative to the "timeless" trends of representing Latina femininity. However, Latinas' apparel purchases from fashion lines like Latina Life™ also result in a self-styling pattern that do not conform to the cultural edicts of what and how to wear clothes. The visual schism between the clothing item and its consumer is a cultural indicator of how regimes of normativity like neoliberalism through technologies like self-styling may fracture under the pressure of targeted, ethnic consumption.

The Latina consumers patronizing Sears—a department store historically serving hardworking, average-earning, all-American citizens—are more than simple signs that Sears, like other large retail corporations, knows how to remain culturally relevant and profitable. Néstor García Canclini theorizes that minoritized subjects' participation in the exchange of goods and services indexes a process that may also mark oppositional rationalities and creative tactics. I identify these oppositional rationalities and creative tactics as alternative practices that constitute cultural sites in which style and fashion matter politically. Like other types of non-remunerative labor, I understand Latina consumers to be queerly exhibiting their racialized, working-class femininity, and subsequently engaging in a real kind of labor required "to work" such a stylized outfit. Wearing clothing items such as fitted mini-skirts, leopard print faux fur shrugs, and glittery accessories does not necessarily amount to a critically resistant practice of femininity; however, contextualizing that the subjects of such a practice are diversely bodily shaped, Spanish-speaking immigrant and non-immigrant Latinas who don clothing during the day to participate in a mundane activity like shopping within the confines of a department store setting that is located in a working-class barrio signifies a different relationship to racialized gender identity formation, consumptive behavior, and self-styling practices.

Some may interpret this relationship as a catastrophic symbol of how neoliberalism through transnational capital has managed to, as Angela Davis states, "create new structures of feeling and insinuate itself into our intimacies and intimate lives" (2010). In this frame, shopping is no more than another normativizing technique for aspiring populations like

Latinas who clumsily attempt to mimic their white feminine counterparts by spending their time and (likely scarcer) expendable income on trivial commodity-buying. On the other hand, one can view such Latina self-styling measures as purely resistant practices of marginalized groups proactively opposing hegemonic structures that dictate normative ideologies of femininity and consumer identity. Yet another way to view this relationship is to search beyond the design of the garment, the identity of its wearer, and the place of its purchase, and instead look behind the garment's label and its politics of production. It is nearly impossible in our contemporary transnational moment to consider fashion products and purchases without concomitantly conjuring up images of sweatshop fabrication and racialized women's labor. In this real-life scenario, often the labor of women of color in the U.S. and the global South working under sweatshop-like conditions is rampant, which enables companies like Sears to mass produce semi-quality goods at lower price rates and to pass on these "savings" so that working-class, racialized, and immigrant Latinas increase their store brand purchasing power.

The operations of capital in the U.S. that invent, manage, and discipline Latinas are worth re-contextualizing given how neoliberalism tethers Latina femininity to concepts of labor, sexuality, and nation. However, to draw attention only to Marx's "murderous, meaningless caprices of fashion" is to participate directly in a form of misogyny with charges of frivolous consumption, auto-commodification, and near complete capitulation to neoliberal global capitalism (525). In all of these understandings, assimilation/capitulation and resistance/counter-hegemony are set up in an unproductive binary that releases from this relationship its rhizomatic features of contradiction, negotiation, and heterogeneity. And because nothing can completely escape commodification, it is essential to acknowledge, to explore, and to continue to ask what popular Latina styling practices and Latina-themed fashion lines have to offer to an analysis of Latina identity formation in the contemporary moment of neoliberalism.

Latina Style/Custom-Made, Part II

A few years ago, my mom tried on a black and white leopard printed stretchy fabric blouse and asked me to help her adjust its unflattering neckline. She assumed that the blouse was marked down to $4.99 because the elongated keyhole crossing her chest had been sewn incorrectly, as there was too much loose fabric that covered up rather than showcased her décolletage. Rather than toss out the inexpensive top, she turned to her neighbor to reconstruct the neckline so that her vision of it could be brought to life. With a deeper plunge and tauter fit, my mother achieved the aesthetic outcome that she had hoped for when she originally made the purchase. As my mom and her neighbor spent several minutes discussing the fit and design options, finally settling on attaching a dome-shaped sparkly button to hold together the neckline's structure, I realized how that moment animated the politics of style and fashion among Latinas. The blouse and its redesign not only capture my mother's racialized rasquache raunch aesthetic, but her decision to deploy her neighbor to rework the blouse crystallizes that self-styling desires, existing fashion designs, and consumption practices are collaborative endeavors as much as they are about constructing individual subjectivities. The moment also encapsulated an alternative temporality—talking, considering, and reconstructing a clothing article that some may believe is not worth its cost. When that blouse recently reappeared—only this time worn by my mom's older sister, my Aunt Alice, on the occasion of her seventy-fourth birthday brunch—I further realized the value of racialized rasquache raunch not only as a technique of self-styling and fashion designer ideals but also as a negotiated process of underground commodity exchanges.

To consider that Latinas like my mother and aunt can claim unique racialized gendered subject positions in the U.S. through innovative reworkings of clothing and bodily texts urges us to see how styling practices are politically infused strategies of self-formation, community identity, and creative consumption. Furthermore, racialized rasquache raunch aesthetics function to denaturalize overdetermined notions of femininity as white, middle-class, and normative. My mother's choices of how to spend her time and money make legible the racialized gender identities of Latinas that are often construed as too festive, too brash, too materialist, and too excessive. In this way, methods of self-styling and Latina-themed fashion lines form critical sites of Latina cultural politics that legitimate Latina-style aesthetics while serving to counter hegemonic norms of feminine propriety and taste.

Notes

1 A version of this essay was originally written for and will appear in the anthology *meXicana Fashions: Self-Adornment, Identity Constructions, and Political Self-Presentations*, co-edited by Norma Elia Cantú and Aída Hurtado. I thank Drs. Hurtado and Cantú profusely for their astute critical feedback. I would also like to thank my mother, Sally Najar, and my aunt, Alice Melendez, for always sharing their inspired and inspiring stylish selves.

2 Through social media sites like Instagram, YouTube, and Facebook, Latina fashion and style have democratized rapidly, enabling the rise of new and multiple style icons, non-commercial D.I.Y. Latina fashion lines, community-organized runway shows, and other subterranean cultural producers and products.

3 CARA Exhibition. n.p. n.d. Web. 30 April 2010.

4 For further elaboration on Jose Muñoz's theory of disidentification, see his *Disidentifications: Queers of Color and the Performance of Politics*. Minneapolis and London: University of Minnesota Press, 1999.

5 Under late capitalism, neoliberalism, or market globalization, is a political philosophy and economic policy that has established a new regime of order, power, and politics. David Harvey argues that under neoliberalism, capital is the primary motor that fuels all political, structural, and cultural shifts. Within this purview, there is little space for individuals and communities to resist meaningfully the omnipotent regime that is neoliberal global market capitalism. See David Harvey, "Neoliberalism as Creative Destruction." *Annals of the American Academy of Political and Social Science*. 610 (March 2007): 22–44.

6 For more on pachuca style, see Catherine S. Ramírez, *The Woman in the Zoot Suit*. Durham, NC: Duke University Press, 2009. For more on chola style, see Norma Mendoza-Denton, *Homegirls: Language and Cultural Practice among Latina Youth Gangs*. Malden: Blackwell Publishing Co., 2008; and more recently, Barbara Calderón-Douglass, "The Folk Feminist Struggle Behind the Chola Fashion Trend." *VICE.com*. 13 April 2015. Available at: www.vice.com/read/the-history-of-the-chola-456

7 For further details on the experience of the over 70 workers who endured months of slave-like conditions sewing garments for nearly no compensation and what happened in its aftermath, see Penda D. Hair, "Client-Centered Lawyering: Garment Worker Advocacy in Los Angeles." *Louder Than Words: Lawyers, Communities, and the Struggle for Justice: A report to the Rockefeller Foundation*. New York: The Rockefeller Foundation, 2001.

8 Since 2001, there have been several active girlcott/boycott campaigns against the corporate chain store, Forever 21 (http://la.indymedia.org/news/2004/05/111521.php). One campaign resulted in a successful lawsuit brought by three former employees, who sued and were awarded an undisclosed sum. The three-year court battle and counter suit was the subject of the documentary, *Made in LA/Hecho en Los Angeles*.

9 For scholarship on popular Latina stereotypes, see Frances R. Aparicio and Susana Chávez-Silverman, eds. *Tropicalizations: Transcultural Representations of Latinidad*. Hanover, NH: University Press of New England, 1997; Mary Beltran, *Latina/o Stars in U.S. Eyes: The Making*

and Meanings of Film & TV Stardom. Chicago: University of Illinois Press, 2009; Suzanne Bost, *Mulattas and Mestizas: Representing Mixed Identities in the Americas, 1850–2000*. Athens, GA: University of Georgia Press, 2003; Rosa Linda Fregoso, *MeXicana Encounters: The Making of Social Identities on the Borderlands*. Berkeley: University of California Press, 2003; Myra Mendible, ed., *From Bananas to Buttocks: The Latina Body in Popular Film and Culture*. Austin: University of Texas Press, 2007; Isabel Molina-Gúzman, *Dangerous Curves: Latina Bodies in the Media*. New York: New York University Press, 2010; Clara E. Rodríguez, ed., *Latin Looks: Images of Latinas and Latinos in the U.S. Media*. Boulder, CO: Westview Press, 1997.

10 Specifically, I draw upon Michel Foucault's *Discipline and Punish* (1977) and *Abnormal* (2004).

Bibliography

Anderson, George. "Sears Looks for Broader Appeal With Latinas." *Retail Wire.com*. 20 April 2005.

Canclini, Néstor García. *Consumers and Citizens: Globalization and Multicultural Conflict*. Minneapolis: University of Minnesota Press, 2001.

Dávila, Arlene. *Latino Spin: Public Image and the Whitewashing of a Race*. New York: New York University Press, 2008.

Davis, Angela Y. *Abolition Democracy: Beyond Empire, Prisons, and Torture*. New York, NY: Seven Stories Press, 2005.

Hernández, Ellie D. *Postnationalism in Chicana/o Literature and Culture*. Austin: University of Texas Press, 2009.

"Latina Fashion: From Vogue to K-MART." *The Lifestyle Monitor*. Cottoninc.com. Cotton Incorporated Press Release, 5 October 2005.

Marx, Karl. *Capital: A Critique of Political Economy Vol. 1—Part I, The Process of Capitalist Production*. New York: Cosimo, 2007.

Mendible, Myra, ed. *From Bananas to Buttocks: The Latina Body in Popular Film and Culture*, Austin: University of Texas Press, 2007.

Mesa-Bains, Amalia. "Domesticana: The Sensibility of Chicana Rasquache." *Distant Relations: Cercancías Distantes/Clann I Gcéin. Chicano, Irish, Mexican Art and Critical Writing*. Ed. Trisha Ziff, Santa Monica, CA: Smart Art Press, 1995.

Pérez, Laura E. "Writing on the Social Body: Dresses and Body Ornamentation in Contemporary Chicana Art." *Decolonial Voices: Chicana and Chicano Cultural Studies in the 21st Century*. Eds Arturo J. Aldama and Naomi H. Quiñonez. Bloomington, IN: Indiana University Press, 2002. 30–63.

"Sears And Latina Team Up On Apparel Line." *WebProNews.com* Ientry Inc. 20 April 2005.

Yerak, Becky. "Sears drops Lucy Pereda, adds line of Latina Life." *Chicago Tribune* 20 April 2005.

29

LATINA/OS AND THE AMERICAN SPORTS LANDSCAPE

Christopher González

The sports industry in the United States is a multi-billion dollar enterprise that impacts and influences American life and popular culture in numerous and consequential ways. From the merchandising of sports drinks such as Gatorade and Powerade, to basketball shoes made by Nike and Adidas, to the imitation of pro football players' touchdown celebrations by children not even in their teenage years, sports in the U.S. holds vast sway in a nation of over 300 million and also across the globe. In a culture where athletes are revered for the number of championships they have garnered, their mantles weighted with Most Valuable Player trophies, where head football coaches of collegiate power football conferences like the Southeastern Conference (SEC), Big Ten, and Pac 12 are paid millions of dollars per year, where sports legends like O.J. Simpson, Ray Rice, Tom Brady, Aaron Hernandez, and Adrian Peterson can fall from grace and into public disfavor, sports is at least one metric by which we might measure the prosperity, progress, and collective ethics of the United States.

Because of its privileged status, sports is a critical space of visibility and representation for Latina/os in the U.S. Moreover, the history of organized sports in America begins as a monolithic representation of whiteness that in its beginning actively sought to exclude minority groups from entering these arenas of competition and athleticism. Since the defining feature of high-level competition is equality on the field of play—call it sportsmanship—granting players from marginalized groups the opportunity to play against white players on an equal site was anathema. It is only through the efforts of athletes such as Jim Thorpe, Jackie Robinson, Roberto Clemente, Babe Didrikson Zaharias, among others, that barriers of entrance into sports are overcome. On the other hand, institutionalized and systemic racism, sexism, and classism are never completely eradicated with the advent of a singular, pathbreaking player. It has taken many generations of athletes to truly level the playing field, and we have only seen significant diversity in sports writ large as we moved into the early part of the twenty-first century.

In this chapter, I take stock of the progress Latina/os have made to change and shape the American sports landscape. In particular, I want to acknowledge those pioneering Latina/

os who helped cross the Brown Color Line in a wide range of American sports, while also discussing the changes in society that have helped make these athletes possible in the first place. I also want to place emphasis on the importance of visibility and media coverage on Latina/os in sports, and why the recognition of Latina/os—the idea of representation—is so crucial to a viable Latina/o sports demographic.

Before Clemente

Organized sports are, by definition, exclusive. For a team to be successful, it must cull only the best players from all those available. This assertion is both logical and reasonable to anyone who has winning in mind. However, the early- to mid-twentieth century was a time in which social stigmas and segregationist ideals dominated the country, and so too did it dominate collegiate and professional sports. The all-white football clubs of the Ivy League and the all-white basketball teams, perhaps best embodied by coach Adolf Rupp's unshakable belief that the best Kentucky Wildcats basketball team was one that would be composed only of all-white players. Rupp's notions of athletic superiority came crashing down in one devastating defeat. As Todd Boyd writes of the 1966 National Collegiate Athletic Association (NCAA) basketball finals,

> The all-Black, Don Haskins-coached Texas Western team had won the NCAA championship in 1966 against legendary coach Adolph Rupp and his consciously all-White Kentucky team. From that moment onward, college basketball became an integrated affair for the most part. Eventually, Black players would come to dominate most rosters as time passed. Adolph Rupp, nicknamed The Baron, had once taken his team off the floor because his opponents featured Black players, and this went against his Southern code of conduct. Texas Western, which would later be called the University of Texas at El Paso (UTEP), not only beat Kentucky that night, but also made a statement to the world about the limits of segregation and the ridiculous posture that Rupp had assumed.
>
> (75)

Rupp was far from the only coach who excluded athletes not on the basis of athletic ability but rather because of melanin levels, phenotype, and hair. Some marginalized groups such as Native Americans and African Americans were forced to create their own baseball leagues. And, because Latinos easily complicate strict understandings of race in the U.S., their entry into professional baseball was not a simple matter of whether or not they were black or white. As Adrian Burgos observes,

> Latinos did not enter the U.S. playing field as simply black or white. Rather, most occupied a position between the poles of white (inclusion) and black (exclusion). […] Just as significant, the process of incorporating Latinos [in professional baseball] illustrates the participation of league and team officials in the production of racial categories to accommodate the limited inclusion of nonwhite Others.
>
> (4)

As professional baseball is one of the oldest sports organizations in the U.S., its handling of Latinos in the sport would influence how other sports industries and organizations would engage with the so-called nonwhite Others. To make matters worse, because collegiate sports has historically been used as a training ground for professional sports, access to higher education became inextricably linked to a career in sports.

For marginalized groups, and Latina/o athletes in particular, difficulties in being admitted to the university, over time, impacted their ability to train and compete at a high level. Socioeconomic status often proved to be insuperable,

> Poverty was the central factor that kept Latinos off the playing field. The majority of young Latinos did not enter high school due to the economic limitations of most families. This lack of opportunity made it problematic to even consider athletic participation. Strong young men had no time for sports when they were needed to help the family as they worked in the sugarcane, cotton, or vegetable field.
>
> (Hawkins 205)

One concrete example is Jim Plunkett, who quarterbacked for Stanford University in the late 1960s and the Oakland Raiders in the 1970s and early 1980s. Plunkett, who suffered from Osgood-Schlatter disease at a young age, also had to take care of his parents, both of whom were blind. He "picked fruit in the summers" and "worked at a gas station cleaning up for two hours before they closed," only to get home late and study for school (Aldama and González 102). Though he worked hard enough to earn a scholarship at Stanford, Plunkett did not have it easy: "It was tough for me. I had no money. My parents didn't have some of the basics that other kids had like a car, for instance. I felt a little embarrassed and out of place" (Aldama and González 102). It is easy to see just how close Plunkett was to allowing the hardships he faced prevent him from pursuing football. Instead, not only did he win the highest individual award in collegiate sports, the Heisman trophy, he went on to lead his Raiders to two Super Bowl championships, including the Super Bowl XV Most Valuable Player (MVP) in 1981.

Though work often takes precedence over athletics in many Latina/o families, it would be a mistake to say Latina/o communities do not appreciate or enjoy sports. The key here is that sports are often seen as recreation. With Latina/os often employed in physically demanding work, and at a young age, participation in sports could easily be seen as mere fun and thus a waste of time and money. Sports and income-earning work were not seen as being one and the same. Here the necessities of home, of providing for the family, took precedence over the promise of being a successful athlete for many Latina/os in the early twentieth century. It was almost natural to have such dreams deferred, as the possibility of having a career as an athlete was still a rarity as the postwar mid-twentieth century approached.

According to Michael Lomax, the postwar moment helped usher in a proliferation of Latina/os in American sports:

> The height of the civil rights movement coincided with the massive expansion of profession team sports, as teams relocated and leagues added new franchises in response to declining markets, the development of new markets, and challenges from rival leagues. Expansion not only created new opportunities for black and Latino players but also meant that southern cities seeking to lure sports franchises had to come to grips with Jim Crow segregation.
>
> (xxxi)

Yet despite progressive legislation such as the G.I. Bill, the Civil Rights Act of 1964, and the landmark Supreme Court decision in 1954 *Brown v. School Board of Topeka, Kansas,* such a long absence of Latina/os in sports hindered their chances, even if there were increasing opportunities. For instance, Richard Santillan points to the "hiring of Mexican American [baseball] umpires and league officials" as a "major breakthrough" (156), and it certainly was. However, Latina/os were hindered because, outside of baseball where they would become increasingly overrepresented, they were essentially invisible in other sports. Pervasive stereotypes of Latina/os—that they were short, meek, and lazy—continued to inform the decisions of coaches and scouts across the nation.

While many Latina/o athletes in the early- to mid-twentieth century helped lay the foundation for future Latino/a athletes to come, it is important to note that the breakthrough of these athletes into their respective sports did not suddenly create hospitable spaces for all Latina/o athletes. Quite often they were harassed, bullied, belittled, and ridiculed, often by their own teammates. As Hank Olguin, who made Latina/o history in 1959 when he and Joe Kapp took Cal to the Rose Bowl, remarks in an interview, this was a period when

> it was not exactly cool or fashionable to be Mexican … we weren't down at Sather Gate waving Mexican flags and yelling "Viva Zapata." This racial consciousness came a few years later, in the 60s when we would more publically embrace and celebrate our ethnic background.
>
> (Aldama 67)

Sports, as a reflection of society, continued to hold minorities with little regard except for what they were able to contribute to the greater good, in this case on the field of play. Similar attitudes continue to prosper into the twenty-first century when critics of undocumented Latina/os are not similarly outraged that large industries such as agribusiness, restaurants, and hotels often employ these very same individuals. It is a position that wants the benefits a group of marginalized peoples provides without having to recognize them or their rights. Of course, such a position is both unethical and untenable. Nevertheless, it persists.

Perhaps the most significant and influential Latino sports figure in this early group was Roberto Clemente. The Puerto Rican baseballer is an athlete akin to Jackie Robinson in that he was seen as a "colored player" in a time of severe racial strife in the U.S. Because he was not born in the U.S. nor inculcated in the ways of Jim Crow south, his stresses off the field threatened to topple his on-field achievements. Samuel O. Regalado outlines Clemente's struggle in this way:

> Puerto Rican blacks, like Clemente, were not ignorant of racism in the states. Stories of racial discrimination were in abundance from those that had spent considerable time in the states and had returned to the island. However, the degree of resistance to integration raised, by the 1950s, a new level of intensity in the struggle to bring about civil rights.
>
> (168)

Clemente also had the added struggle of speaking Spanish in an English-only time in U.S. history. Despite the many challenges Clemente faced, he became a revered figure not only in Pittsburgh Pirates history or Major League Baseball (MLB) history, but in the history of American sports. Clemente became the first Latino player in the major leagues to achieve 3,000 hits—a significant statistic that almost always ensures hall of fame status, as it did for Clemente. As the first Latino inductee into the MLB Hall of Fame, Clemente did not live to see this honor bestowed upon him. On a humanitarian mission to bring aid to the victims of a massive earthquake in Nicaragua, his plane crashed shortly after takeoff killing everyone on board.

For many baseball and sports aficionados, Clemente's tragic and sudden death effectively raised him to the status of martyr and saint. Not only was he one of the greatest players the MLB had ever seen, an assertion made all the more significant because of the sport's long history and position of prominence in the American psyche, he died while trying to help people whom he had never met. Clemente helped dislodge held stereotypes and prejudices by the manner in which he played and lived. His death on December 31, 1972, serves as an important historical marker for Latina/os in American sports. There are the Latina/os who, along with Clemente, gained entrance into the upper echelons of competitive sport—what I call the Pre-Clemente group of Latina/o athletes. And there are those Latina/os who came Post-Clemente, athletes who understood that superstardom was a possibility in their sport. Clemente proved to be the paragon of what Latina/o athletes might achieve.

After Clemente

The early 1970s was a tumultuous time for the U.S., and the counterculture movement was in high gear. The women's liberation movement, now emerging as what would come to be known as second-wave feminism, continued to decry sexism in all arenas, including sports. American football was now on its way to displacing baseball as the nation's sport spectacle of choice, thanks in large measure to the emergence of the National Football League's (NFL) merger and championship game. The Super Bowl, as the game has come to be known, helped solidify the television sports medium. The game perennially ranks as the most watched television event in the U.S. In terms of visibility, the NFL deserves credit for helping sports become a viable and, indeed, desirable choice for programming. Thanks to this increased visibility, Latina/os would soon take an important place in sports. Casual fans could now turn on the television and see Latina/os participating in high-level competition shoulder to shoulder with their white teammates. The power of sports television can never be overestimated.

The NFL soon came to be emblematic of sports in the U.S., and it is the most dominant sports league in terms of revenues generated, visibility, and publicity. Additionally, football ended up being a sport that was perfectly suited for television. Because of the time between plays, producers devised a process by which footage already captured was played again while the players prepared for another play. The instant replay, as it came to be known, bombards viewers with close ups, alternate angles, and other techniques that heighten player visibility. If a Latina/o athlete wanted to be noticed, he could do worse than the NFL.

With the Super Bowl just on the horizon, right before the modern era of the NFL (i.e., since the official merger of the AFL and the NFL in 1970), a Latino quarterback emerged in California. Tom Flores, who had excelled at University of the Pacific, was finally picked up by the Oakland Raiders after stints in the Canadian Football League and the Washington Redskins. His first Super Bowl championship came as a player for the Kansas City Chiefs, when he served as Len Dawson's backup in the 1969–70 season. In time, Flores would go on to coach another Latino, quarterback Jim Plunkett, to two Super Bowl victories. Never before had a pair of Latinos made such an impact on professional sports in the U.S. It is so significant an achievement, it has never been duplicated. Flores, mentored by John Madden and supported by owner Al Davis, flourished in a professional sport where he was the only Latino head coach at the time. He was just the second Latino head coach after Tom Fears, and would be the only one for decades until Ron Rivera became the head coach of the

Carolina Panthers in 2011. These three men, Fears, Flores, and Rivera, comprise the history of Latino head coaches in the NFL.

Joe Kapp, whom *Sports Illustrated* once called "The Toughest Chicano" (Aldama and González 93), let the Minnesota Vikings to the Super Bowl championship game in 1970, where they lost to the Kansas City Chiefs. This Super Bowl featured two Latino quarterbacks on either team (Kapp and Flores), another first for the game. Kapp was a confident leader on the field and off. Rather than play down his ethnic heritage, Kapp reveled in his Chicano identity, often speaking in Spanish on the field and the sidelines. However, because of his non-Hispanic surname, Kapp is often forgotten today when discussions of Latino athletes take place.

Other Latinos would follow, achieving even greater levels of success. Plunkett, a two-time Super Bowl champion and also a Super Bowl MVP, came after Flores and Kapp. As one of the few Latino quarterbacks of his time, Plunkett is generally considered the most successful. In Cincinnati, Anthony Muñoz was redefining the position of offensive tackle for the Bengals. Because of his sheer domination during his career, Muñoz was enshrined in the NFL Hall of Fame. Max Montoya, a teammate of Muñoz's, helped the Bengals reach two Super Bowls in the 1980s. These men also helped dispel the notion that Latinos could only play football at the highest levels if they were punters and placekickers.

Outside of the NFL, other Latinos were making their marks in sport. Latino, and specifically Latin American born, baseball players followed in the wake of Clemente—far too many to list here, but players such as Fernando Valenzuela, Jose Reyes, Pedro Martinez, Alex Rodriguez, Ivan Rodriguez, Mariano Rivera, Moises Alou give an indication. These players and others have made the MLB the sport with the greatest number of Latinos on their roster. They are often the norm on an MLB team rather than the exception.

Latina/os have left their mark in other sports as well. Tennis and golf are two sports that tend to bear the connotation of being elitist or upper class. Latina/os have proven to be among the best in these sports as well, though fame and success in these sports have come at a high price. Richard Alonso "Pancho" González fought through prejudices of others to become the top ranked tennis player for nearly a decade. His Latino heritage was easy fodder for the sports media of the 1950, and they continued to use the nickname "Pancho," which his former high school coach, Chuck Pate, had given him despite the fact González detested it (Alamillo 125). The media consistently played up his "bad boy" image, which always seemed to undermine the remarkable feats he accomplished on the tennis court. Once, the image of his body was manipulated to downplay his ethnicity, as José M. Alamillo explains:

> The image of González was "whitened" for the front cover of the 1959 program of Jack Kramer Presents World Championship Tennis. The image featured the body of Richard González but with blond hair, lighter skin, a smaller nose, and smaller lips. There is no mention of the player's identity on the front cover, but compared to another image inside the 1957 program, it closely resembles González.
>
> (139)

González's whitening is another instance of a long tradition of objectification and commodification of the Latina/o athlete's body. Often the Latina/o athlete is whitened or exoticized.[1] Despite his sustained success in a sport where he felt like an outsider, González's final years facing stomach cancer, living in poverty, and being effectively fogotten by erstwhile friends are a sad commentary on the seemingly disposable nature of sports athletes in general.

Golf, like tennis, has the air of the affluence that permeates it. That did not stop Latina/
os such as Juan "Chi Chi" Rodriguez, Lee Trevino, and Nancy Lopez from becoming among
the best golfers in the world during their careers. They were a part of the initial wave of
diversity to crash upon a sport that historically excluded men of color, as well as all women.
A player like Nancy Lopez, without many Latinas to help pave the way for her, benefitted
from the efforts of Babe Didrikson Zaharias, who regularly beat men on the golf circuit and
other sports endeavors. And men such as Rodriguez and Trevino would help usher in players
such as Vijay Singh and Tiger Woods. Today professional golf is truly a global sport, which
allows it to claim a kind of diversity not shared by other sports such as American football.
However, the economic point of entry into the world of golf is far too high for many young
athletes in the U.S., making it a paradoxically diverse and elitist sport.

The ESPN Era

Though the Super Bowl generated great interest in the NFL that had never been seen
before, it was arguably the establishment of a twenty-four-hour sports channel named ESPN
that would ultimately help increase the visibility of athletes across a host of sports. While
there is no denying that heightened opportunities for Latina/os to participate and excel in
sports was paramount in an ever-increased engagement of Latina/os in careers in athletics,
another crucial component was the presentation of sports programming to an audience. It
may be easy to forget that sports fans did not always have such easy access to multimedia
information concerning their favorite sports. Before ESPN debuted, the major networks had
weekly programs such as ABC's "Wide World of Sports" that highlighted sports. Audiences
might rely on sports articles and essays in their local newspapers or in magazines such as
Sports Illustrated or *The Sporting News*. This is to say, sports news was constrained in what it
reported because of the limitations of the medium. That is, until ESPN.

I mention the advent of ESPN as a high water mark for sports industries across the
nation. What is more, ESPN would have a large role in creating sports as an entertainment
commodity. With twenty-four hours of programming to fill per day, ESPN found itself
interested in athletes not just for their statistical significance but also for the kinds of
narratives they could bring to audiences. In the late 1980s, for example, ESPN broadcast
many of the now iconic mini-documentaries produced by NFL Films and its mastermind
Steve Sabol. NFL Films cameras could go where network cameras could not and capture
moments as they happened on the field and sidelines. These documentaries, shot on film
rather that video, brought a theatrical quality to the NFL that enthralled audiences and
made players and coaches into legends. By making sports into a commodity, ESPN, NFL
Films, and later entities such as Fox Sports and internet sites such as Bleacher Report have
been able to grant fans the kind of access to athletes and coaches that few in the early days
of sports could have envisioned.

It is not difficult to surmise the effect such coverage had on young athletes who
aspired to be a pro. Consider the influence Tiger Woods had on children of color and low
socioeconomic status when he burst on the pro golf scene in the late 1990s. The Nike
television commercials suddenly made golf, a game seemingly from another planet for many
inner city children, a worthwhile pursuit. Or consider Venus and Serena Williams, sisters
who grew up in Compton, California, and have come to dominate the tennis world for
most of their career. Their childhood neighborhood now boasts a tennis center for the
development of youth talent. The visibility of minority athletes on television, in magazines,
on award shows, on sports drinks, and so on generates an unquantifiable interest within the

hearts and minds of young children born and raised in similar cultures and circumstances as those athletes from which they draw inspiration.

We might do a simple thought experiment and wonder how much of a greater impact on Latina/o athletes players such as Jim Plunkett, Tom Flores, Joe Kapp, and Roberto Clemente might have had if they had lived and played in the ESPN era. Would it have resulted in more Latinos in the NFL like Jeff Garcia, Mark Sanchez, Antonio Ramiro "Tony" Romo, or Tony Gonzalez? We can't know, but we might watch what effect these recent players that do play in this all-access sports environment will have on Latinos in the next few generations of players in the NFL.

What we do know is that when Latina/os do break into areas of sport where they have not been before, there is the potential for backlash. Another contributor to this volume, Jorge Iber, has written elsewhere about the success and controversy of Mark Sanchez's tenure as quarterback of the prestigious University of Southern California (USC) Trojans. As a Mexican American, Sanchez's significant achievements were, for many, erased when he had a special mouthguard made that looked like the Mexican flag. Sanchez was the subject of the ire of many USC fans:

> While many teammates similarly personalized this equipment, the fact that an individual of Mexican descent had openly demonstrated pride in his family's history helped spark a controversy. Instead of commenting on Sanchez's on-field accomplishments, one fan grumbled that the young man needed to discard the specialty mouthpiece because many "will think that he is a Mexican citizen, and it is an insult to this country, where he was born and raised. Mexico is not giving Sanchez the opportunity that he is getting right now, so why is he showing his love for Mexico?"
>
> (Iber 7)

Interestingly, Iber goes on to note how Sanchez's mouthguard was the subject of pride for Latina/os in Los Angeles and across the U.S. (8). Sanchez's decision reveals the tension that exists when Latina/os achieve high levels of success in American sports. There are many fans who would prefer that Latina/os not acknowledge their family history and heritage. On the other hand, Latina/os, who have been shut out from many of the major sports organizations for much of their history, cannot help but celebrate and acknowledge a fellow Latina/o's success. The athletes remain caught in the middle, and their actions are destined to slight one group or another, regardless of the level of engagement with their Latinidad.

But something else has resulted in the proliferation of sports media coverage. Though there is no doubt that the NFL, NBA, and the MLB get the greatest amount of media exposure by far, there has been a growing interest in sporting events that at one time would scarcely have received attention by ESPN or Fox Sports. We might think of boxing, which at one time boasted large audiences but has recently been gutted by the rise of Mixed Martial Arts, or MMA. Boxing once had terrific Latino fighters such as Roberto Durán and Julio César Chávez, and even in the twenty-first century, Manny Pacquiao has been a key figure in keeping audience interest in the sport high. As ratings for MMA fights continue to increase, Latino fighters such as Tito Ortiz, Cain Velasquez, and Ricardo Lamas are helping ensure a strong Latino presence in the sport. In addition, there is no question that promoters of MMA understand audience and fan affiliation with these fighters. One of the key reasons for the surge in interest and revenue in MMA is the marketing to Latina/o audiences, both in the United States and in Latin America.

The marketing of sports in America, in effect the programming that is available for an ever-widening audience, continues to preview what the future holds for Latina/os in sports in the U.S. This targeted sports marketing to Latina/os is a direct reflection of both the increasing numbers of Latina/os and, perhaps just as importantly, the purchasing power of Latina/os in the twenty-first century. Like virtually all television programming, sports programming is driven by advertisement revenues. By 2003, major networks had already come to the realization that a market for Latina/os and sports had achieved a tipping point. This push was intended to heighten interest by Spanish-speaking Latina/os in traditionally American sports such as football and basketball, specifically with the advent of ESPN Deportes ("Latinos"). While this trend of offering Spanish-language broadcasts has continued, sports programming directors also recognize that many Latina/os in the U.S. speak English as their primary language. By the end of the first decade of the twenty-first century, even the NFL wanted to boost viewership of the Super Bowl by Latina/os. In 2010, Peter O'Reilly, NFL vice president of fan strategy and marketing, stated, "We are thrilled with the way this season has been going from a Hispanic fan perspective. But the growth is not limited to TV. We are seeing growing engagement across all platforms, including online, radio and print." (Martinez 24). If the NFL, which already enjoys the largest viewership for its championship game, recognizes the swell in the Latina/o demographic, other sports will continue to take notice.

Still, Latina/os have helped shape larger American interests in sports such as *fútbol* (soccer). More networks have signed on to broadcast soccer, historically a marginalized sport in the U.S., though among the most popular sports on the global stage, mostly because there is a growing audience that craves soccer and is willing to purchase network packages, team merchandise, and tickets. Without the increase in spending power, it may be that sports such as MMA and soccer would be largely ignored in the U.S. Alternatively, because these two sports have deep connections to Latina/os, savvy sports network executives and marketing strategists recognize that not only is the U.S. coming closer every census to becoming a majority-minority nation, Latina/os as an ever expanding demographic will continue to enjoy an increasing amount of influence.

Conclusion

Like other forms of popular culture, sports in the U.S. exert a tremendous amount of influence on trends and perceptions. Professional athletes are often trendsetters when things go well, and object lessons when they don't. For some fortunate athletes, salaries are stratospheric. As a result of our media saturated society, certain sports figures can hold as much influence as Hollywood movie stars or politicians. Such is the power of sports in the twenty-first century. Despite the exclusionary history of sports in the U.S., and for all of the shortcomings that remain, we can take stock and recognize that American sports are more diverse than they have ever been before. The NBA inches toward becoming more of a global league with each passing season, and the MLB also recruits and drafts players from Latin America, Japan, and South Korea with great regularity. The NFL and NBA acknowledge the influence and importance of the Latina/o demographic during their respective seasons, a sign that Latina/os can no longer be ignored or disregarded.

Where Latina/os were once excluded, they are now invited. Where Latina/os were thought of as not smart enough, they now hold roles of leadership in such powerful leagues as the NFL. Where Latina/os were once invisible, sports network executives actively create programming with Latina/os in mind. All of this is not happenstance or accident.

Courageous and determined individuals such as Roberto Clemente and Tom Flores faced the barriers of racism and prejudice with persistence and aplomb. These sorts of individuals do a different kind of activisim, one that is based on their visibility and presence in the larger American consciousness rather than those comprised of speeches and protests. It is important work, and it continues.

Most important of all, Latina/os are now truly poised to claim their stake in American sports, not as outsiders looking in but as participants, shapers, and consumers of a multi-billion dollar industry. Latina/os have the power to shape part of their own narrative by exploding long-held notions of an inferior body. It makes a tremendous difference to see actual Latina/o bodies among the elites of American athletics. Having Latina/os on such display comes with a cost, of course. Objectification and commodification of the Latina/o body is a downside to the adulation of sports media and fans. But that is a consequence of fame and popularity, and so athletes and fans must be vigilant against such appropriations of the body. For now, Latina/os continue to show and fulfill the promise of their potential, not only by the labor of their bodies in physically demanding jobs, but in the highest reaches of human physical achievement. And that is certainly something worth cheering.

Note

1   One notable example would be the difference in how the media treats two specific quarterbacks: Tony Romo and Mark Sanchez. While Sanchez appeared shirtless on magazine covers and profiles that underscored his Mexican heritage, Tony Romo's Mexican heritage is only rarely mentioned. For a sustained discussion of Sanchez and Romo, as well as the Latino/a athlete and the body, see chapter 4 of Aldama and González's *Latinos in the End Zone: Conversations on the Brown Color Line in the NFL*.

Bibliography

Alamillo, José M. "'Bad Boy' of Tennis: Richard "Pancho" González, Racialized Masculinity, and the Print Media in Postwar America." *More Than Just Peloteros: Sport and U.S. Latino Communities*. Ed. Jorge Iber. Lubbock, TX: Texas Tech University Press, 2014.

Aldama, Frederick Luis. "Aldama: Shaper of Sports History: An Interview with Latino Football Pioneer Hank Olguin." *Journal of the West* 54:4 (Fall 2015): 66–70.

Aldama, Frederick Luis and Christopher González. *Latinos in the End Zone: Conversations on the Brown Color Line in the NFL*. New York: Palgrave Macmillan, 2014.

Boyd, Todd. *Young, Black, Rich, and Famous: The Rise of the NBA, the Hip Hop Invasion, and the Transformation of American Culture*. Lincoln, NE: University of Nebraska Press, 2003.

Burgos, Adrian. *Playing America's Game: Baseball, Latinos, and the Color Line*. Berkeley, CA: University of California Press, 2007.

Hawkins, Billy. "Conclusion: A Contested Terrain: The Sporting Experiences of African American and Latino Athletes in Post-World War II America." *Sports and the Racial Divide: African American and Latino Experience in an Era of Change*. Eds. Michael Lomax and Kenneth L. Shropshire. Jackson, MI: University Press of Mississippi, 2008. 196–208.

Iber, Jorge. "Introduction: The Perils and Possibilities of 'Quarterbacking While Mexican': A Brief Introduction to the Participation of Latino/a Athletes in U.S. Sports History." *More Than Just Peloteros: Sport and U.S. Latino Communities*. Ed. Jorge Iber. Lubbock, TX: Texas Tech University Press, 2014.

"Latinos make mark on U.S. sports; Acculturation extends to games people play, giving marketers chance to tap larger fan base." *Advertising Age* 27 October 2003.

Lomax, Michael E. "Introduction: The African American and Latino Athlete in Post-World War II America: A Historical Review." *Sports and the Racial Divide: African American and Latino Experience in an Era of Change*. Eds. Michael Lomax and Kenneth L. Shropshire. Jackson, MI: University Press of Mississippi, 2008. xiii–xxxix.

Martinez, Laura. "NFL to Blitz Latinos at Super Bowl; League Plans Major Events Surrounding Feb. 7's Big Football Game in Miami." *Multichannel News* 25 January 2010.

Regalado, Samuel O. "Roberto Clemente: Images, Identity, and Legacy." *Sports and the Racial Divide: African American and Latino Experience in an Era of Change*. Eds. Michael Lomax and Kenneth L. Shropshire. Jackson, MI: University Press of Mississippi, 2008. 166–77.

Santillan, Richard. "Mexican Baseball Teams in the Midwest, 1916–1965." *Sports and the Racial Divide: African American and Latino Experience in an Era of Change*. Eds. Michael Lomax and Kenneth L. Shropshire. Jackson, MI: University Press of Mississippi, 2008. 146–65.

30

LATINA/OS IN THE AMERICAN HIGH SCHOOL, COLLEGIATE, AND COMMUNITY SPORTING LANDSCAPE

Jorge Iber

In his chapter in this volume, Christopher González deals with the increased presence and significance of Latina/os in the U.S. sporting landscape. Importantly, he focuses on the role of professional athletes in a wide variety of sports and their impact on the cultural scene of the U.S. González details the role of Latino major stars such as Oakland Raiders' quarterback Jim Plunkett, and his coach, Tom Flores, during two Super Bowl victories. He mentions the careers and impact of other athletes in the highest ranks of football such as the Vikings' Joe Kapp, and the Bengals' Anthony Munoz and Max Montoya, for instance. González then moves on to other accomplished Latina/o athletes such as the great Pancho González in tennis and Lee Trevino and Nancy Lopez in golf. My chapter picks up from González's important contribution by filling in details of the various communal contexts—from high school, community, and collegiate competition networks—that grew such Latina/o athletes. In this chapter I flesh out the stories of other *atletas* who challenged racial stereotypes and brought pride to their *comunidades*. I then give historical depth to how prejudice has miscast Latina/os as athletically inadequate and limited. I follow this with the recounting of various stories of young Latinos and Latinas who, through their participation in high school, community, and collegiate sport directly challenged notions of Latina/o inadequacy, all the while using the power of sport to break down barriers to greater acceptance by the gatekeepers of athletic spaces.

In the late nineteenth and early twentieth centuries prejudice against Mexicanos filled the air at the street level as well as in pages of both academic scholarship and the mainstream press. For instance, nineteenth century Anglos in Texas referred to their Tejano/Mexicano neighbors variously as pagan, depraved, and primitive. (See Arnoldo De Leon's *They Called Them Greasers*.) Within this general atmosphere, Latina/os were considered predisposed to be lazy and mentally inferior, their bodies as preternaturally foul, filthy. (See the work of Natalia Molina.) On a larger scale, the mainstream press constantly linked the internal turmoil of Mexico as a nation with the backwardness and moral decrepitude of Latina/os. (See the work of Mark C. Anderson.)

This racist ideology continued to grow and branch into other areas of material and intellectual life in the twentieth century. In 1922, physical education specialist Elmer D. Mitchell published in *American Physical Education Review* a series of essays entitled "Racial Traits in Athletics." In these articles, Mitchell ranked and detailed the characteristics of "15 different races" then present in the American sporting scene. He considered the Anglo-American, English, Irish, and German "races" the most physically gifted and intellectually able; they were, according to Mitchell, the ones who consistently lead teams to national and international victories. The second tier of athletes included "Latins" and African Americans, among others. Within the category of "Latins" were the French and the Spaniards. At this level of athleticism Mitchell identifies serious limitations and issues, including that they were driven more by emotions than reason, leading to either being lighthearted, indolent, or fiery in temper. He cites Mexican bullfighting as one manifestation of this predisposition. For Mitchell, so-called Latins didn't have the reasoning system for becoming tier one athletes. And, like the Latins, South American athletes (who were in a third tier) were "undisciplined" and lacked the "physique," "environment," and "disposition" to make a "champion" athlete. He writes, "The Indian in him chafes at discipline and sustained effort, while the Spanish side is proud to a fault [his] disposition makes team play difficult."[1]

These are but a few examples of the many that speak to the deep prejudice that Latina/o athletes faced in the early history of sports in the U.S. Yet many did overcome the odds. Many did succeed at the vigorous sports of the American nation.

Baseball

In baseball in the 1920s there were athletes such as Al Lopez (the Tampa area) and Leo Najo (the Rio Grande Valley of Texas). Lopez and Najo distinguished themselves at the high school and community levels. Lopez went on to a legendary career as both a player and manager in the Majors. And Najo, who did have a tryout with the White Sox in 1925, toiled for numerous squads as a player, manager, and promoter on both sides of the southern Texas border until the 1950s. In southern California, as Jose Alamillo notes, Mexican Americans utilized the sport as a tool for community cohesion, labor union recruitment, as well as an opportunity to gain better jobs in corporations such as Sunkist by playing on company teams. In *barrios* from California to Kansas, Mexican American teams played against all comers, including teams from the "old country," during the years through World War II. Among some of the legendary and successful squads involved in such efforts were the clubs representing Carmelita Chorizos and the El Paso Shoe Store. These teams were the center of after-church community activities on most Sundays, and were able representatives that showed the abilities of Latina/os in athletics as well as acumen in business and promotion.[2] In a locale such as Hawaii, for example, similar squads existed among the Puerto Ricans who lived in Honolulu and elsewhere. Teams with names such as San Juan, Ponce, and Arecibo competed against other ethnic groups in the Hawaii League. Further, as noted by author Norma Carr, the Puerto Rican organizations that sponsored clubs prior to World War II were often quite progressive in their willingness to field teams (both baseball and softball) comprising women. Carr remarks on the attrition of female athletes from the 1940s to their disappearance in the 1960s.[3]

Still, there is an extensive history of Latinas participating in baseball and softball. Latinas often participated in baseball and softball. As Jose Alamillo notes, "thanks to public works projects of the New Deal, recreation facilities were constructed and available in many working-class neighborhoods." Teams such as Las Senoritas de Glendale from East Los Angeles took advantage of these parks to play and gain both "a degree of emancipation from their family guidelines [and] exposure to areas outside of their close-knit neighborhoods when they traveled to compete in different communities within the county" (Iber et al. *Latinos in U.S. Sports*, 123–4). The story of Las Senoritas is similar to that of Las Estrellas, a women's baseball team that existed in Lubbock, Texas, in the early 1950s and which worked closely with the men's squad, known as Los Aguilas. (See Christy Martinez-Garcia, "'On an Equal Playing Field.")

Football

Football was also a significant pastime, though the relatively small number of Latina/os attending high school in the years before the 1950s did limit the number of athletes in this endeavor. Still, there are great stories of men who proved themselves worthy of competing in locales such as Edinburg, Texas (Amador Rodriguez), and Kingsville, Texas (E.C. Lerma). The Lerma story is particularly significant because he not only played at the high school level, but was also very successful in the collegiate ranks, starring for the Texas A&I (now Texas A&M University-Kingsville) Javelinas in the later years of the Great Depression. After graduation, Lerma went on to have a legendary career as one of the most successful Mexican American coaches (he also coached track and basketball), athletic directors, and educators in the history of the state of Texas. Shortly before his death in 1998 the first stop in a fabulous coaching career, the community of Benavides in Duval County, named its high school football stadium in Lerma's honor.[4]

Another recent work on Lerma expands upon his significance, and that of his athletes, as counterhegemonic examples of Mexican American athletic pride and achievement. In his article, "Friday Night Rights," Joel Huerta not only lists the long string of accomplishments by the Benavides Eagles teams coached by Lerma, but also goes on to examine how he shaped a generation of young men in south Texas, many of whom went on to success in business, politics, education, and other fields. He accomplished this endeavor by defying many of the prejudices seen in the mainstream press and of supposed scholars like Mitchell. Lerma instilled in his players toughness and pride as well as academic discipline; he was mindful of academics and careful to impose strict curfews. He showed his athletes that they too could overcome prejudice.[5]

Basketball

On the basketball court, similar stories abound. Organizations such as El Club Deportivo Los Angeles staged all-Latino basketball tournaments in southern California. In *When Mexicans Could Play Ball*, Ignacio Garcia considers how Texas head coach, Nemo Herrera, led the all-Mexican American squad of Lanier High School (south San Antonio) to several appearances in the state finals, including claiming titles on two occasions. Further, after Herrera moved to El Paso in the mid-1940s (for his wife's health), he then coached the Bowie High Bears to the first Texas baseball state title in 1949. To this day, Herrera remains the only coach in state history to have ever won titles in two different sports at separate institutions. (See also Jorge Iber, et. al., *Latinos in U.S. Sports*.)

There was also a close connection between basketball and the Catholic Church, which was (at least nominally) the religious institution with which most Latina/os affiliated. After the founding of the Catholic Youth Organization (CYO) in 1930, parishes throughout the nation fielded teams. Not surprisingly, many of the Mexican-dominated institutions did likewise. Again, Alamillo's research has confirmed the widespread existence of such clubs, with his work focusing on teams such as a squad from Our Lady of Guadalupe in Chicago, as well as CYO teams in places such as Los Angeles and San Antonio. After one team called the Mateo Bombers won a tournament in southern California in 1945, their sponsor, Father John Birch, articulated some of the goals for the young men in these clubs/programs: "The basketball program is part of the Catholic Youth Organization's plan to make wide participation in athletics a weapon to combat delinquency and to encourage qualities of leadership" among these Spanish-surnamed individuals.

Alamillo's work has also focused on the existence of similar endeavors for young women. During the 1930s, for example, an entire league, La Liga Femenina Hispano-Americana de Basketball, which was completely composed of Mexican Americans, emerged in the city of San Antonio. This league was clearly a community effort as mutual aid societies, fraternal organizations, civil rights groups (such as League of United Latin American Citizens – LULAC), and other such entities helped raise money, purchase equipment and uniforms, and paid for teams to travel outside of the metropolitan area. One of the most famous "graduates" of this league, who played for a team called the Modern Maids, was legendary labor leader and civil rights activist Emma Tenayuca, who would go on to lead the historically significant pecan shellers' strike in the Alamo City in the late 1930s (Iber, et al., *Latinos in U.S. Sports*, 136).

Boxing

Of course, boxing has always been a major sport among Latina/os, and the first Spanish-surnamed athlete to medal in an Olympics for the United States, Joe Salas, earned a silver medal for pugilism in the 1924 Paris Games. Bert Colima was another boxer of great repute in the 1920s and 1930s, including holding the Pacific Coast titles in three weight categories over his career. Other pugilists who achieved wide acclaim before the 1950s were Cubans such as Kid Chocolate and Kid Gavilan. The squared ring gave Latinos a direct chance to prove themselves against other (as Mitchell would call them) "races." As early as the 1920s, Gary Mormino notes that sell out crowds of whites and other groups would eagerly snap up tickets to watch bouts between "a Latin (meaning Cuban) and a Cracker" in the Ybor City area of Tampa, Florida.[6]

Wrestling

Individual Latinos also excelled in other athletic endeavors. I recently had the opportunity to research the role of Spanish-surnamed athletes in the sport of high school and collegiate wrestling for the National Wrestling Hall of Fame, located on the campus of Oklahoma State University (OSU) in Stillwater. While many today are familiar with the incredibly inspiring story of Henry Cejudo, the participation of Latinos of various backgrounds in this sport goes back to the early 1900s. The research uncovered stories of men such as Cuban-born Fred Narganes, who wrestled for Columbia University and the New York Athletic Club and earned U.S. amateur national titles in 1907, 1909, and 1910. Another individual of note is Joe Puerta, who wrestled for the University of Illinois and finished first in the 123-pound classification in 1931. He defended his championship the next year, but lost in the national finals to a wrestler from OSU. Manuel Gorriaran, a native of Cuba, was also instrumental in the history of the sport, even though he never competed in the U.S. Instead, Gorriaran helped establish the sport in the Pan American Games and was also a long-time supporter and promoter of wrestling at the collegiate and Olympic levels. The grappling equivalent of the Heisman Trophy, given to the athlete with the most pins in the NCAA Championships, is named in his honor. Not only was Gorriaran a successful promoter of the sport, but he was also a well-respected entrepreneur and engineer, owning and operating the Providence-based Hook-Fast Company for many years. Over his career, the Cuban expatriate became world famous for the pins and emblems which he manufactured, and that competitors wore and traded at international and national competitions.

Of all of the pre-World War II grapplers researched, however, the most impressive was an individual named Morey Villareal, who not only won a high school state title in Oklahoma in 1933, but also went on to earn a scholarship at Central Oklahoma and earned All American status in both 1936 and 1937. He then served his country in the Navy during the conflict, and proceeded to have a highly successful career as head coach of Tulsa Rogers High School, capturing the state team title in 1959. He was then president of the state wrestling association for several years and was inducted into the state Oklahoma High School Wrestling Coaches Hall of Fame in 1973. All of this was accomplished during a time when Mexican Americans suffered great amounts of discrimination in this state.[7]

Post World War II Latina/o Atletas

While all of the athletes noted above helped challenge cultural stereotypes of Latina/os' intellectual and athletic abilities, the number of such men and women increased rapidly in the years after World War II. Given the number of Latinos who fought for their country in this conflict, and the benefits accrued justly to these warriors in the areas of housing, health, and education, these Spanish speakers were not about to sit idly by and face discriminatory practices after having helped put down the racial beliefs of the Nazis.

Two prime examples of such athletes/teams won titles in basketball in Arizona in 1951 and in football in Texas in 1961. The story of the Miami Vandals of that season provided a fine example of the athletic ability of Mexican American athletes on the hardwood. This team, with an almost all-Latino starting lineup, earned national attention in publications such as *Spark* magazine for their high scoring ways and for defeating an all-African American team from Phoenix for their state title. In addition, as author Christine Marin noted, participation in sport allowed most of the players a chance to move beyond the blue-collar lives they had known in the mining-based economy of their hometown. "Their rise through sports and education enabled families to realize their American dreams of equality for their children."[8]

Likewise, as this author articulated in his article on the Donna Redskins, the only team from the Rio Grande Valley to win a state title in football-mad Texas produced not only success on the field, but also in education. "For many Valley youths, the Redskins provided an example of what they could accomplish, both in the classroom and on the gridiron.

The success of these players permitted many of the Valley's Mexican American youth to envisage goals that previous generations could not."[9]

In the late 1950s, on the collegiate level, an important individual who contested stereotypical notions such as those held by Mitchell was Puerto Rican Juan "Pachin" Vicens while on the court for Kansas State University (KSU). Born in 1934, he joined an elite team, the Ponce Lions of the National Superior Basketball League in his homeland. He played an excellent point guard, and guided the Lions to two league titles. This success eventually led to his recruitment by Tex Winter, first to play at Marquette, and then with the Wildcats in Manhattan. The highlight of Vicens's time in the U.S. came when he was the team's second leading scorer in 1956, helping KSU achieve a berth in the National Collegiate Athletic Associaton (NCAA) national tournament that season. "Pachin" was recruited to play professionally, but decided to return to Puerto Rico and played again for the Lions and the island's teams in numerous international tournaments, such as the Central American and Caribbean Games, plus the World Championships and two Olympics (1960 and 1964). At the World Championships in Chile in 1959, he was voted the tournament's most valuable player. Vicens retired from the court in 1966 and became a bank manager and commentator for sports radio. In gratitude for his positive portrayal of Puerto Ricans and his success on the court, his hometown of Ciales named its basketball arena in his honor in 1972.[10]

Alexander Mendoza's research on distance runners, primarily in the Laredo area, makes a similar argument. His work details the careers of thin-clads going back all the way to the 1930s, four of whom have represented the U.S. in the Olympic games. Among the men who participated in this sport, and who have done much to challenge the cultural belief of many whites about Latina/o athletic and intellectual inferiority, is the current president of the University of Texas at San Antonio, Dr. Ricardo Romo, one of the most important writers on the Chicano experience in the Lone Star State and a highly decorated runner during a career that featured breaking the four minute barrier while competing for the University of Texas.[11]

Another individual who contested notions of inadequacy was a player known as the "Cuban Comet," Carlos Alvarez of the University of Florida. When his family moved to Miami in the early 1960s, he became very active in academics at North Miami High School, as well as a standout receiver for the Pioneers' football team. His success on the field earned him a scholarship with the Gators and he paid dividends on Florida's investment in his first game, catching a 78-yard touchdown pass from John Reaves on the opening drive of the 1969 season. He earned All-American status that season, and All-Southeastern Conference honors in 1971. A knee injury slowed his progress on the gridiron, but he completed a degree in political science in 1972. Even with his impairment, the Dallas Cowboys took a flyer on this *Cubano* in the fifteenth round of that year's draft. Instead of packing up to work with Roger Staubach and Tom Landry, however, the opportunity to pursue a law degree proved more enticing. Alvarez attended Duke University Law School, graduated in 1975, and has been a practicing attorney in the Tallahassee area ever since.[12]

In more recent times, the presence of Spanish-surnamed athletes has continued to increase at the high school and collegiate levels, and in "newer" areas of concentration: in smaller communities located in states such as Iowa, Nebraska, and Kansas. As noted in a 2006 ESPN article by Wayne Drehs entitled "Cultures are Teammates at Iowa High School," athletic competition and camaraderie are helping to bridge gaps between the sons and daughters of long-time residents and the newly arriving Latina/os. In the community of West Liberty, Drehs noted the relationship forged by two players, Joe Yoder and his teammate Manny Gamon, the son of two Mexican-born parents. The two youths, players on the Comets' football team and classmates since second grade, argued that "athletics has provided a level of acceptance and entry into the broader American society for the young Gamon." Indeed, Manny has become so much a part of the community, that his mother is concerned he is losing his *Mexicanidad*. As Wayne Drehs sums up: "Hispanic parents are growing increasingly frustrated that their teenage children are becoming too Americanized. They're playing American sports, they're eating American food and they're speaking Spanish with an accent."[13]

In Lexington, Nebraska, where there has been an influx of Latina/os just like in West Liberty, Iowa, school administrators have worked diligently to break down cultural barriers on both sides of the communal fence in hopes of attracting participation by the newest Latinas in school athletics, especially in basketball, soccer, and track (see Elizabeth Merrill article, "Changing the Game for Hispanic Girls"). This has not been easy to accomplish, as many Central American parents are hesitant to have their daughters play as well as needing them at home to take care of younger siblings while toiling in the nearby meat and poultry processing plants. Still, there has been substantial progress and the make-up of the hoops and other squads now reflects the community's composition more accurately. Further, some of the Latina athletes who have been in the local schools for a few years are now reaping both the sporting and academic rewards for their efforts. Kyle Hoehner, the Lexington High School Athletic Director, noted to Merrill that,

> One of Lexington's biggest success stories is depicted in a giant frame in Hoehner's office. It's a former cross-country star who was headed for the Tyson plant after graduation. Her family wanted her to quit running, to stay at home and help. After an emotional tug-of-war, she accepted a scholarship at a community college in another state. She's now studying to be a nurse and has been an inspiration to other Hispanic athletes.
>
> [Another competitor named] Anely Laguna ... knows she is one of the lucky ones. She's been in Lexington since fifth grade ... and her parents encouraged her to play. Soccer has made huge strides in Lexington ... Nearly half of the girls' squad is Hispanic. [Days later] Laguna walks back to campus, and tells Hoehner some news: She's just accepted a soccer scholarship at Concordia, a NAIA school in Seward, Nebraska. "It's a great college," he tells her. In most towns, it's not huge news. In Lexington, it's another small victory.[14]

In my own research on Latino wrestling, I came across similar stories in two other communities: Garden City, Kansas, and Randall County, Texas. At both schools, Mexican American former athletes, Martin Segovia at GCHS and David Quirino at Randall, have risen to important institutional positions after earning scholarships to participate in the collegiate wrestling program of the University of Nebraska-Kearney. Both men now are passing along what they learned to a new generation of Spanish-surnamed athletes. Further, they are Latinos in positions of influence in local communities (Athletic Director and Head Coach of wrestling teams), helping to reshape the perception of our population's capabilities not just on the mat, but also in the classroom and administrative offices.[15]

The stories noted above are just a few of the examples of the research that has been produced in regard to both academic and popular literature on the role of Latina/os in sport at the non-professional level over the past few years. While the Anely Lagunas and Martin Segovias of the world many not be as well known as personages such as Tony Romo of the Dallas Cowboys and Art Moreno (owner of the Los Angeles Angels of Anaheim), they are, I would argue, making an even more significant contribution to our culture and the demographic transformation of the U.S.

Latina/os who are winning in the classroom, the field, and the bureaucracies of local communities are changing the way that the majority population perceives Latina/os in the U.S. We are seen less as a threat—as the outsiders taking over. Rather, we are seen more as a part of the communities in which we live. Our young men and women—some of whom will make it to the pros, no doubt—are transforming the civic and daily life of the U.S. Latina/o youths are increasingly bearing the names of their towns on jerseys, and their successes and failures capture the emotions and acceptance of all. While the people in Lexington might still root for the Minutemen and Minutemaids, the players' names that run the back of athletic jerseys are now: Sanchez, Rodriguez, and Perez. Standing on the shoulders of those who struggled before, today's Latina/o players at all levels of the athletic space are changing the way of life of sports in our the U.S.

Notes

1 See Elmer D. Mitchell, "Racial Traits in Athletics," *American Physical Education Review* 3 (March, 1922): 93–9; *American Physical Education Review* 4 (April 1922): 147–52; and *American Physical Education Review* 5 (May 1922): 197–206.
2 See Jose Alamillo, "Peloteros in Paradise: Mexican American Baseball and Oppositional Politics in Southern California, 1930–1950; Samuel O. Regalado, "Baseball in the Barrios: The Scene in East Los Angeles Since World War II"; and Douglas Monroy, *Rebirth: Mexican Los Angeles from the Great Migration to the Great Depression.*
3 Norma Carr, "The Puerto Ricans in Hawaii," Doctoral Dissertation, University of Hawaii, 1989, 265–81.
4 Todd Marveles, "Bobcat Pride Spans More than 80 Years"; and Jorge Iber, "Mexican Americans of South Texas Football: The Athletic and Coaching Careers of E.C. Lerma and Bobby Cavazos, 1932–1955." *Southwestern Historical Quarterly* 55:4 (April 2002): 617–33.
5 See Joel Huerta, "Friday Night Rights: South Texas High School Football and the Struggle for Equality, 1930s–1960s."
6 William Estrada, "The Triumph of Joe Salas: The First Latino Olympian"; and Jorge Iber, et al., *Latinos in U.S. Sports*, 117.
7 All of this information is gleaned from Jorge Iber and Lee Maril, *Latino American Wrestling Experience: Over 100 Years of Wrestling Heritage in the United States.*
8 See Christine Marin, "Courting Success and Realizing the American Dream: Arizona's Mighty Miami High School Championship Basketball Team, 1951."
9 See Jorge Iber, "On-Field Foes and Racial Misperceptions: The 1961 Donna Redskins and Their Drive to the Texas State Football Championship."
10 Quoted in Jorge Iber, et al., *Latinos in U.S. Sports*, 177.
11 See Alexander Mendoza, "Beating the Odds: Mexican American Distance Runners in Texas, 1950–1995."
12 Quoted in Jorge Iber, et al., *Latinos in U.S. Sports*, 204.
13 Wayne Drehs, "Cultures Are Teammates at Iowa High School."
14 Elizabeth Merrill, "Changing the Game for Hispanic Girls."
15 All of this information is gleaned from Jorge Iber and Lee Maril, *Latino American Wrestling Experience: Over 100 Years of Wrestling Heritage in the United States.*

Bibliography

Alamillo, Jose. "Peloteros in Paradise: Mexican American Baseball and Oppositional Politics in Southern California, 1930–1950." *Mexican Americans and Sports: A Reader in Athletics and Barrio Life*. Eds. Jorge Iber and Samuel O. Regalado. College Station, TX: Texas A&M University Press, 2007. 50–72.

Anderson, Mark C. "'What's to be Done with 'Em': Images of Mexican Cultural Backwardness, Racial Limitations and Moral Decrepitude in the United States Press, 1913–1915." *Mexican Studies/Estudios Mexicanos* 14:1 (Winter, 1998): 23–70.

Carr, Norma. "The Puerto Ricans in Hawaii." Doctoral Dissertation, University of Hawaii, 1989.

Drehs, Wayne. "Cultures Are Teammates at Iowa High School." 11 October 2006. Available at: http://sports.espngo.com/espn/print?id=2618295&type=story

Estrada, William. "The Triumph of Joe Salas: The First Latino Olympian." *The Latino Olympiads: A History of Latin American Participation in the Olympic Games, 1896–1984*. Eds. Antonio Rios-Bustamante and William Estrada. Los Angeles Olympic Organizing Committee, 1984. 29–43.

Garcia, Ignacio. *When Mexicans Could Play Ball: Basketball, Race and Identity in San Antonio, 1928–1945*. Austin: University of Texas Press, 2014.

Huerta, Joel. "Friday Night Rights: South Texas High School Football and the Struggle for Equality, 1930s–1960s". *More Than Just Peloteros: Sport and US Latino Communities*. Ed. Jorge Iber. Lubbock, TX: Texas Tech University Press, 2014. 206–31.

Iber, Jorge. "Mexican Americans of South Texas Football: The Athletic and Coaching Careers of E.C. Lerma and Bobby Cavazos, 1932–1955." *Southwestern Historical Quarterly* 55:4 (April 2002): 617–33.

Iber, Jorge. "On-Field Foes and Racial Misperceptions: The 1961 Donna Redskins and Their Drive to the Texas State Football Championship." *Mexican Americans and Sports: A Reader in Athletics and Barrio Life*. Eds. Jorge Iber and Samuel O. Regalado. College Station, TX: Texas A&M University Press, 2007. 121–44.

Iber, Jorge and Lee Maril, *Latino American Wrestling Experience: Over 100 Years of Wrestling Heritage in the United States*. Stillwater, OK: National Wrestling Hall of Fame, 2014.

Iber, Jorge, Samuel O. Regalado, Jose M. Alamillo, and Arnoldo De Leon, *Latinos in U.S. Sports: A History of Isolation, Cultural Identity, and Acceptance*. Champaign, IL: Human Kinetics, 2011.

Leon, Arnoldo de. *They Called Them Greasers: Anglo Attitudes Toward Mexicans in Texas, 1836–1900*. Austin: University of Texas Press, 1983.

Marin, Christine. "Courting Success and Realizing the American Dream: Arizona's Mighty Miami High School Championship Basketball Team, 1951." *More Than Just Peloteros: Sport and US Latino Communities*. Ed. Jorge Iber. Lubbock, TX: Texas Tech University Press, 2014. 150–83.

Martinez-Garcia, Christy. "'On an Equal Playing Field: Las Estrellas-The Stars, Lubbock's First All-Latina Baseball Team. *Latino Lubbock* (March 2009).

Marveles, Todd. "Bobcat Pride Spans More than 80 Years." *McAllen Monitor*, 30 July. www.accessmylibrary.com/coms2/summary_0286-16149227_ITM

Mendoza, Alexander. "Beating the Odds: Mexican American Distance Runners in Texas, 1950–1995." *Mexican Americans and Sports: A Reader in Athletics and Barrio Life*. Eds. Jorge Iber and Samuel O. Regalado. College Station, TX: Texas A&M University Press, 2007. 188–212.

Merrill, Elizabeth. "Changing the Game for Hispanic Girls." 24 March 2009. Available at: http://sports.espn.go.com/espn/print?id=4012596&type=story

Mitchell, Elmer D. "Racial Traits in Athletics," *American Physical Education Review* 3 (March, 1922): 93–9.

Molina, Natalia. *Fit to Be Citizens?: Public Health and Race in Los Angeles, 1879–1939*. Berkeley: University of California Press, 2006.

Monroy, Douglas. *Rebirth: Mexican Los Angeles from the Great Migration to the Great Depression*. Berkeley: University of California Press, 1999.

Regalado, Samuel O. "Baseball in the Barrios: The Scene in East Los Angeles Since World War II." *Baseball History* 1:2 (1986).

Part V

POP RITUALS OF LIFE IN DEATH

31

SAINTS AND THE SECULAR

La Santísma Muerte

Desirée Martin

Sandra Cisneros's short story, "Little Miracles, Kept Promises," demonstrates the hope and desperation, the affection, and especially the intimacy that devotees in the U.S.-Mexico borderlands feel towards their favorite saints. The men and women who leave notes, gifts, and offerings for the saints at public shrines or at their own home altars address them like friends, confidants, relatives, lovers, and sometimes even antagonists. One couple, Sidronio Tijerina and Brenda A. Camacho de Tijerina of San Angelo, Texas, hints at a litany of enduring pain and suffering as they give thanks to the Blessed Santo Niño de Atocha for helping them "when Chapa's truck got stolen," stating matter-of-factly that "he's been on probation since we got him to quit drinking," and "Raquel and the kids are hardly ever afraid of him anymore, and we are proud parents" (116). The couple does not expect a complete reversal of fortune or a perfect solution for their troubles, instead focusing on their debt of gratitude to the saint: "We will light a candle to you every Sunday and never forget you," indicating the degree to which their relationship with the saint is integrated into their everyday lives. Another devotee, Ms. Barbara Ybañez of San Antonio, Texas, behaves even more familiarly with her chosen patron, defiantly threatening San Antonio de Padua, "I'll turn your statue upside down until you send [me a man who isn't a pain in the *nalgas* (ass)]" (117–18). Ms. Ybañez's plea demonstrates that she feels comfortable enough with San Antonio de Padua to playfully scold him as she would a friend, relative, or lover, rather than simply appease him. At the same time, Ms. Ybañez's threat indicates that she retains the power of negotiation with the saint, for she is free to switch patrons if necessary.

In the same way, devotees of Santa Muerte (Saint Death), folk saint and guardian of the dispossessed (Figure 31.1), pray novenas to her that suggest more than a simple request or a promise to worship the saint from a passive believer.

The refrain of the best-known novena to Santa Muerte reads: "Beloved Death of my heart, do not abandon me, protect me, and do not allow [name] a single moment of peace, bother him constantly, torment him, worry him, worry him, so that he will think of me always. Amen" (Gil Olmos 183). The novena begs not just for the lover's return, but for

Figure 31.1 Santa Muerte (Saint Death)

total domination over him, imploring: "I want him to fall before me prostrate, surrendered at my feet, to fulfill all of his promises," and "I want you to make him beg me to forgive him, as docile as a lamb, faithful to his promises, that he may be loving and submissive for the rest of his life" (Gil Olmos 184, 186). In a sense, the female supplicant asks Santa Muerte to transfer some of her formidable power onto her. The enduring control over the lover requested by the devotee reflects the power she exercises as a result of her relationship of devotion and exchange with Santa Muerte. Ultimately, the novena reflects a circuit of intimacy between the saint, the devotee, and the lover. Santa Muerte touches both the devotee and the lover through the novena, transforming their relationship by entering their lives to bother, torment, or worry them (in the case of the lover) or protect them (in the case of the devotee).

More importantly, the novena portrays a mutually constructed relationship between the devotee and the saint. Addressing Santa Muerte like a lover ("Beloved Death of my heart"), the supplicant pledges an intimate relationship of devotion with the saint that resembles the one she seeks with her earthly lover. Like a bride or groom, the devotee pledges lifelong devotion to the saint in exchange for the favors received. However, in this relationship, the devotee is not totally powerless and subservient, nor is the saint infallibly powerful. Although the connection between saint and believer may be inherently unequal, both parties engage in a give-and-take relationship with each other. While supplicants may pledge total allegiance to Santa Muerte, for example, such loyalty is possible only if the saint fulfills the request: "make me believe in only you by granting me this miracle" (Gil Olmos 185). Through this relationship of exchange, the devotee enters into the "consciousness" of Santa Muerte as much as the saint enters into that of the devotee. Many believers threaten saints with the withholding of their belief and favors, and it is common for devotees to shift allegiances between different saints. Some saints, like Santa Muerte, have a reputation for being more loyal than others, but this constancy frequently comes at a price. Devotees accept that if they neglect the death saint or dare to stray from her fold, they will face her sacred retribution.

While the advantage in the relationship between devotee and saint may shift over time, popular devotional practices in the borderlands and among Latinos/as in general fundamentally emphasize the personal, intimate relationship between them. Popular rituals like the exchange of relics or sacred images, the placement of altars, street processions like the Via Crucis (Way of the Cross), faith healing and *curanderismo*, spirit possession and the recitation of rosaries, novenas, and other prayers all shape relationships of exchange and identification. The supplicants who recite novenas to Santa Muerte frequently also appeal to Jesus Christ and recite the Lord's Prayer as part of their petition, reflecting their willingness to blend popular and orthodox spirituality. The ecclesiastical status of these sacred figures—whether they are canonized saints, folk saints, manifestations of Christ or the Virgin Mary, mystics, faith healers, or are not even routinely considered saints at all—has little impact on the masses' desire to worship on their own terms. Meanwhile, devotees incorporate a wide variety of cultural and spiritual traditions in their rituals, drawing upon Catholic, Protestant, Evangelical, indigenous, and African beliefs.

In this chapter I will explore the ways in which Latino/a borderland spirituality is a flexible and diverse practice. Latino/a spiritual practices, including the veneration of saints, reorder and transcend ecclesiastical authority. In the process, they blur the boundaries and highlight the intersection between orthodox and popular belief, between private and public worship, and especially, between the human and the divine.

Saints and the Secular

Scholars agree that "the saint is a familiar figure in all world religions," while many political leaders, celebrities, performers, artists, royals, and other cultural heroes are "candidates for 'sainthood' treatment," thus blurring the lines between sanctity, iconicity, and celebrity (Woodward 16; Hopgood xi). Reinforcing this multiplicity, James F. Hopgood argues that it is difficult to distinguish the "truly sacred" from "folk saints, near-saints, or saintlike personages" in any context. He concludes that it is unnecessary to hold "firm conceptual divides" between the saint, folk saint, icon, and others (xii, xvii). Hopgood asserts, "it is best to use concepts with few constraints" in an exploration of "human behavior in the area of the sacred and in religion" (xvii). He associates the icon with the "secular saint," suggesting that any cultural figure that undergoes a process of "popular canonization" can be considered a secular saint, for he or she highlights the juxtaposition of sacred and profane (xvii).

While such spiritual and conceptual variability is certainly the norm in the borderlands and for U.S. Latinos/as in general, it frequently contradicts Roman Catholic doctrine. The Catholic Church is the only one to feature "a formal, continuous, and highly rationalized process for 'making' saints," a process that requires copious research to determine and prove the presence of holiness and miracles (Woodward 16). Yet even within official Catholic doctrine, sanctity is an inherently contradictory concept for it juxtaposes the human and the divine, the holy and the profane, the secular and the sacred. Jacques Douillet indicates that the Bible refers repeatedly to the simultaneous presence of elements both holy and profane, suggesting that one cannot exist without the other (10–11). In a sense, it follows that all sanctity is fundamentally secular, because it is always both holy and profane. Nevertheless, Douillet's analysis of the duality between the holy and the profane is decidedly orthodox, for he insists that the two poles cannot be equal. He asserts that "things are holy because they are set apart from the profane world; just so, God is holy because he is not a part of the world. [Although] the world is separate from him ... he is not a being among other beings. He surpasses them infinitely" (13). Catholic doctrine generally supports Douillet's assessment of the transcendence of the divine, but devotional practices in the borderlands produce much more ambivalent and flexible understandings of the duality of human and divine.

Saints are clearly extraordinary figures, for within Catholic cosmology they are holy, frequently miraculous men and women who, rendered sacred, have ascended into heaven. As men and women, they are like the rest of us, inherently secular. Since they are both human and divine, saints are at once different from and similar to ordinary, flawed people on earth. Saints are not gods but rather mediators, benefactors, and protectors. From the perspective of the faithful, the status of saints as intermediaries between heaven and earth renders them preferable to gods who, by definition, are too distant and too unlike humans, so that most devotees find it difficult to form meaningful relationships with them. It is this human aspect of saints that renders them fallible and accessible, and points toward the possibility of reciprocal relationships of devotion and exchange. By straddling the divide between divine and mundane, saints both underscore the gulf between the two realms and paradoxically blur the line that separates them. The counterpoint between accentuating and erasing the boundary between human and divine reflects the ambivalent essence of secular sanctity. The contradiction goes beyond a simple juxtaposition of two seemingly opposed poles. In Theresa Delgadillo's analysis of "spiritual mestizaje," which she defines as "the transformative renewal of one's relationship to the sacred through a radical and sustained multimodal and self-reflexive critique of oppression in all its manifestations and a creative and engaged participation in shaping life that honors the sacred," secular sanctity reveals that the divine and the mundane are deeply intertwined in everyday life (1). In secular sanctity, as in spiritual mestizaje, life "honors the sacred," while the sacred becomes a means through which to engage with secular society, signaling a "way of being in the world" (Delgadillo 4).

Woodward contends that while saints were "venerated for their holiness, [they] were invoked for their powers" (64). These miraculous powers are what attract humans and (perhaps paradoxically) permit the closeness between saint and human. This closeness is present not necessarily because humans wish to assume the miraculous powers of saints—though there are some examples of popular ritual, like spirit possession or faith healing, that do purport to transmit divine powers, at least from the perspective of believers. Rather, devotees identify with saints because of their human qualities. While the hierarchical process of saint-making in the Catholic Church effectively severs the link between saint and devotee by distancing the saint from ordinary humanity, devotees everywhere seek to reinforce their connection with favored saints by focusing on the union of human and divine.

Borderlands and Latino/a Spiritual Practices

Popular and official notions of sanctity are deeply intertwined in the borderlands. Although the official markers and celebrations of sanctity have declined steadily since the mid-twentieth century as a result of shifting cultural norms and the liturgical changes instituted in 1969 after the Second Vatican Council, the worship of popular or folk saints has flourished in the borderlands, throughout Mexico, and in Latino/a communities in the

United States.[1] Andrew Chesnut indicates that devotion to Santa Muerte, for example, has been transformed in less than a decade "from an occult practice, unknown to most Mexicans, to a burgeoning public cult that counts millions of devotees in Mexico and the United States among its followers" (4). Nevertheless, theorists and critics vary in their assessment of the intersection between popular and official spirituality and sanctity in the borderlands and among Latinos/as in general. In her discussion of "la facultad," the spiritual sixth sense that she describes as "the capacity to see in surface phenomena the meaning of deeper realities … an instant 'sensing,' a quick perception arrived without conscious reasoning," Gloria Anzaldúa suggests that institutionalized religion rejects the possibility of any intersection between the human and divine (60). Anzaldúa argues, "Institutionalized religion fears trafficking with the spirit world and stigmatizes it as witchcraft … It fears what Jung calls the Shadow, the unsavory aspects of ourselves. But even more it fears the supra-human, the god in ourselves" (59). Following Anzaldúa's terms, there is nothing more threatening than an intimate, egalitarian relationship of exchange between human and saint, especially because it implies that divinity can reside within the human.

Meanwhile, Timothy Matovina and Gary Riebe-Estrella argue that some celebrations like the *Día de los Muertos* (Day of the Dead) "make more visible or even accentuate the separation and tensions between church officials and Catholic liturgy, on the one hand, and Chicano/a community leaders and ritual traditions" on the other (6–7). At the same time, however, they contend that some "pastoral ministers" (representing orthodox Catholicism) readily "incorporate devotions like those to Our Lady of Guadalupe into parish life and even into sacramental celebrations," or "engage traditions like the Via Crucis as a means to call Mexicans and Mexican Americans (and others) to live gospel and church teachings on social justice" (6). Drawing upon the work of Virgilio Elizondo, Matovina and Riebe-Estrella cite the "*segundo* [second] *mestizaje*" inherent to Mexican American spirituality and saint worship—denoting "the mixture of two elements (cultures, religious systems, races) in such a way that a new element (a new culture, a new religious system, a new race) is created" (8). This second mestizaje is unique because it illustrates both "the Spanish conquest of the indigenous peoples in the territories that became New Spain (and later Mexico) and the U.S. conquest of what is now the Southwest" (8). It is precisely through this second mestizaje, or the blending that Gastón Espinosa identifies as the "rearticulation of Mexican and American traditions, customs, practices, symbols, and beliefs," that the intersections between human corporeality and the sacred in borderlands and Latino/a saint devotion are possible (4).

Matovina and Riebe-Estrella argue that for Mexican-American devotees, ritual practices like the Via Crucis or Guadalupan devotion "are not mere pious reenactments but corporeal encounters with sacred times, places, persons and events that shape their everyday world and its meaning" (15). In other words, such rituals enact bodily incorporation with and into the sacred. For these believers, the sacred is a "constant presence" in daily life, not something that they merely access from afar or through mediators (15). Luis D. León reinforces the agency that borderlands and Latino/a devotees exercise through popular spirituality and practices of exchange and identification with their favored saints. He argues: "religious belief and practice are continuously redefined by devotees of various traditions that started in and were transformed by, brought to and found, throughout the borderlands as a creative and often effective means to manage the crisis of everyday life" (5). León is quick to acknowledge that religion still "serv[es] power as an ideological mechanism of social control, exploitation, and domination" for many, if not most Latino/a devotees (5). Nevertheless, he posits that those "who have access to only the bare resources that constitute conventional power," actively deploy spiritual practices—such as saint worship—to "destabilize those very same forces" of power and control (5). There is tremendous appeal in creating one's own narratives of faith without the influence of institutions or authority figures, especially for marginalized peoples who may have no other recourse to challenge the primacy of church and state.

For the Latino/a faithful, particularly for Chicanos/as or Mexican-Americans, the destabilization of the "forces of power and control" through religious ritual frequently coalesces through the articulation of community and self in intimate communion with the divine. Roberto S. Goizueta argues that ritual performances such as the celebration of Día de los Muertos, the construction of and worship at home altars, "the carrying of the cross, the physical reenactment of Jesus's crucifixion, the recital of the *Pésames* or condolences to Jesus's grieving mother on Good Friday" reveal "the very identity … the very existence of the Mexican-American people as a people," which fundamentally "depends upon the people's ability to maintain an intimate connection with one another, their ancestors, and the divine" (123, 122). Goizueta further emphasizes that the connection between the Latino/a faithful, their dead ancestors, and the divine is one of equals. Like the believers who worship Santa Muerte alongside orthodox figures like La Virgen de Guadalupe and San Judas Tadeo, Goizueta indicates that Latino/a saint worship does not place the saints in competition with Jesus Christ "for primacy in the religious pantheon" (134). Instead, the church consists of a "communion of saints," as the "primary locus in which the church takes root" (134). That is, the egalitarian relationship between saint and believer is the very basis of religious belief for Latino/a Catholics. Rather than promoting an "individualistic theological anthropology, in which the atomic individual exists over against other individuals," for Latino/a Catholics, "the primacy of Christ implies and demands a communion of the saints," while the reverence and love demonstrated to deceased relatives and ancestors reflects a "representation of divine nearness [that] is lived out every day of the year, but especially in celebrations such as the Day of the Dead and the Way of the Cross" (134–5).

Such "divine nearness" is particularly enacted through the relationship of exchange between saint and devotee in the borderlands. Many of the attributes and practices associated with popular sanctity reflect the bond between saint and believer, for they emphasize interaction, communication, exchange, and even identification with the saint. However, such practices of exchange and identification are not direct or straightforward; instead, they reflect a process of disidentification with the awareness that, although the devotee can never fully approximate the saint, saints must approximate humans in order for the faithful to access them. Nevertheless, the "disidentificatory subject," as José Esteban Muñoz puts it, retains a measure of power, for he or she "tactically and simultaneously works on, with, and against a cultural form" (12). Reflecting such agency, Latino/a and borderlands devotees are not passive supplicants. They circumvent authority, for they do not primarily interact with saints through priests or in the context of the Catholic mass. They modify devotional practices as they see fit and reserve the right to seek more acquiescent patrons as needed (though they may do so at their own risk). Devotees build home altars to their favored saints; wear them on their bodies in the form of amulets, jewelry, or tattoos; dress statues of their saints in elaborate handmade clothing; and communicate with diverse saints through prayers and petitions that range from traditional votive offerings like candles, *retablos* (votive oil paintings on tin or metal), or *milagritos* (tiny charm-like metal renderings of body parts) to more secular gifts like liquor or cigars. León stresses the importance of gifting and the *promesa* (promise) or *manda* (obligation or errand) within the devotee–saint relationship (67). In fact, most devotional practices in the borderlands are predicated upon exchange, especially the giving and receiving of tangible and intangible favors. The saints might grant the return of a wayward lover or a sense of spiritual well-being, while their devotees exchange and transfer relics or images of saints, embark on pilgrimages, present votive offerings, recite prayers and novenas, construct home altars, and wear amulets, jewelry, or tattoos.

All of these devotional practices involve some sort of transfer (as in the offering of gifts to the saint in return for good health or a job), but the exchange between saint and devotee is necessarily unequal. The gift of a healthy childbirth or a son released from prison before his sentence is completed, for example, is not directly equivalent to an offering of lit candles or homemade tamales, or even to an act of sacrifice like walking to a saint's temple on one's knees. Devotees accept this disparity because they know that the saints are innately different in their divinity, even though they were once human and reflect the essential human condition. The faithful simultaneously disidentify with their favored saints by revering them for their extraordinary qualities and access them because of their ordinary human characteristics. Many devotees emphasize points of physical, emotional, or spiritual identification between themselves and their favored saints or virgins. Various authors cite the link between the Virgin of Guadalupe's bronze-colored skin and that of many of her mestizo followers.[2] Meanwhile, other devotees accentuate their temperamental similarities with certain saints. For example, many people venerate Santa Muerte precisely because they identify with her transgressiveness or her lawlessness, and they feel that she can understand them better than other divine figures because of it. In fact, it is because Santa Muerte is so contradictory and transgressive that she is so appealing to many marginalized borderlands and Latino/a believers in the first place.

La Santa Muerte

"Santa Muerte hears prayers from dark places. She was sent to rescue the lost, society's rejects. 'She understands us, because she is a cabrona like us ... We are hard people and we live hard lives. But she accepts us all, when we do good and bad," claims Haydé Solís Cárdenas, a resident of Mexico City's infamous barrio Tepito and devotee of Santa Muerte (Thompson n.p.). Solís Cárdenas, a street vendor who sells smuggled tennis shoes for a living, feels an affinity with Santa Muerte not as a righteous, holy inspiration but as a tarnished outsider much like herself. Saints like Santa Muerte, who is the unofficial patron of the poor, the criminals, and the sinners, are outsiders who straddle the line between secular and sacred. Devotees from all walks of life worship Santa Muerte, but she is especially important to those who live on the margins of society, such as undocumented migrants, taxi drivers, prostitutes, drug addicts, and criminals in Mexico, the United States, and beyond. Perhaps because of her link to marginalization and illegality, she has exponentially risen in popularity on both sides of the border in terms of media attention, cultural production, and academic studies. Many scholars attribute the death saint's increase in popularity in Mexico to the economic crisis of 1994, also known as the *efecto tequila* (tequila effect), during which the Mexican peso sharply decreased in value and the middle class lost most of its buying power (Gil Olmos 91–2). The crisis intensified Mexican migration to the United States, as many sought to escape ever more precarious economic conditions. In the past fifteen years or so, Santa Muerte has found a home in cities and regions of the United States with large populations of Mexican and Central American migrants, while in Mexico today only Jesus and the Virgin of Guadalupe have more devotees.[3] Whether Santa Muerte is viewed as a solution in times of crisis or as just another manifestation of crisis, she is popular precisely because of her controversial and contradictory nature. Devotees and critics alike are simultaneously fascinated and frightened by her.

Santa Muerte is the most contradictory figure within the contemporary culture of secular, seemingly sinful or lawless, and explicitly cross-border sanctity. While the death saint is famous for being very miraculous and loyal, she is also known for being a jealous, vengeful patron who requires the utmost devotion and respect. Santa Muerte prefers offerings of fruit, candy, liquor, and cigars. She is known by a variety of nicknames, such as "La Niña Blanca" (White Girl) or "La Flaca" (Skinny Girl), and many of her followers refer to her with loving, familiar endearments such as "Mi Reina" (My Queen), "Mi Niña Bonita" (My Beautiful Girl), "Madrina" (Godmother), or "Holy Mother," even as they may be very fearful of her. She is represented as a skeleton, dressed in hooded robes, as a bride, or in other elaborate, hand-made clothing, wigs, and jewelry that change depending on the calendar or on the moods of her devotees.[4] She often carries a sickle, a globe of the world, an hourglass, and the scales of justice. Like her followers, and indeed, like any human, she is potentially good and bad at once. A true secular saint, Santa Muerte is not venerated for her purity or holiness but for her accessibility to the masses on both sides of the border and her resistance to the powerful forces of the state, the Catholic Church, and wealthy elites.

As a symbol of death—both the only certainty of life and its polar opposite—Santa Muerte fully embodies the duality between accessibility and inaccessibility that all saints represent. Since all humans must face death, both that of others and their own, Santa Muerte is the great equalizer across class and social distinctions and racial, gender, or sexual hierarchies. Judith Butler reiterates the unifying power of death, suggesting that it is the only thing that might collectively unify diverse people, however reluctantly: "Despite our differences in location and history, my guess is that it is possible to appeal to a 'we,' for all of us have some notion of what it is to have lost somebody. Loss has made a tenuous 'we' of us all" (20). Santa Muerte's devotees certainly embrace her role as an equalizer and unifier of the human race. At the same time, they are acutely aware that she is illegible, for she represents life's greatest mystery. While devotees might request protection from violence, pray for help finding work, love, or happiness in their personal lives, or ask Santa Muerte to bring harm to their enemies, they can never expect her to protect them from death forever. As Enriqueta Romero (known as Doña Queta), the caretaker of the best-known shrine to the death saint, says: "You are born with a destiny, from the day you are born ... your destiny is marked" (Hernández 156). The first order of this destiny is the inevitability of death.

Nevertheless, devotees like Doña Queta take great comfort in putting their lives in Santa Muerte's hands. In the film La Santa Muerte by Eva Aridjis, Doña Queta affirms, "Oh Skinny Girl, I know you're the one who's going to take me away. But while I'm still in this world, take care of me, help me, keep me company." (All quotes from the film La Santa Muerte are taken from Eva Aridjis's English subtitles.) In this sense, the death saint walks with her devotees in life as well as in death. Yet despite the intimacy and solace that Santa Muerte's followers find in her cult, they do not presume to understand her, identify with her, or possess her. Death remains impenetrable to humans; as such, in relation to Santa Muerte, a practice such as spirit possession—that is, the possibility of assuming her image, whether literally or figuratively—is frowned upon by most of her followers. At the same time, Santa Muerte represents the universality of death and its proximity for the faithful. Reflecting the contradiction between accessibility and inaccessibility, Santa Muerte's devotees understand that, rather than their possessing death, death must possess them.

Rather than serving as an obstacle, the ambivalent, contradictory character of Santa Muerte allows devotees to articulate their own narratives of transcendence and equality. By asserting equality and modes of belonging through the death saint, marginalized devotees may embrace their own ambiguous status in society. Overall, worship of Santa Muerte allows for contradictory modes of belief and belonging. For example, some devotees flout the primacy of Christ or the Virgen de Guadalupe—and even of Catholicism in general—through their worship of the death saint, like Haydé Solís Cárdenas, who declares that "the Virgin of Guadalupe, Mexico's patron saint, would not sympathize with a life like hers, tending rather to well-off people with college degrees and nice clothes" (Thompson n.p.). Still others, like Doña Queta, reject hierarchies by emphasizing their roles as good Catholics, as when she insists that Santa Muerte is on an equal plane with orthodox divinities: "Unless I am ignorant, there is only one Death and one God. And the Death that is going to take me is going to take everyone. And the God that people believe in … is the same God that I pray to. So I pray to the same God as the Church … " (Aridjis, *La Santa Muerte*). Similarly, during one of his masses in honor of Santa Muerte, Jesse Ortiz Peña encourages the first-time congregants, saying, "As you can see, [the cult] is not diabolic, it is not Satanic. I am glad you decide to break the barrier … of ignorance." Significantly, both of these examples reverse the terms of ignorance in a society that usually accuses Santa Muerte's devotees of ignorance. Here, Doña Queta and Ortiz claim ownership over God, saints, altars, prayer, and the ritual of the mass, emphasizing that the truly ignorant are those who do not believe in Santa Muerte's power.

Needless to say, Santa Muerte's ambivalent nature remains a serious threat to her critics, such as the Catholic Church, the Mexican state, and many middle- and upper-middle class Mexicans and Chicanos/as. While such criticism is usually attributed to Santa Muerte's status as a pagan or satanic icon, in reality she and her devotees are most threatening because they disrupt the status quo of class-based, racial, gender, and sexual hierarchies on either side of the U.S.-Mexico border. The ambiguity, mobility, and transgressivity symbolized by Santa Muerte is so menacing to the dominant powers of state, church, and social elites that its true significance is frequently elided or denied. Ultimately, Santa Muerte frightens her critics because she fills a void against the failure of civil society and the state for those on the margins, especially migrants, impoverished barrio dwellers, and most contentiously, for criminals, to establish alternative forms of spatial and temporal communities, commerce or trade, and social services through secular sanctity.

La Santa Muerte by Eva Aridjis

Civil society and the state have failed many of the death saint's devotees in the borderlands, Mexico, and the U.S., and religious institutions and groups also often exclude them. Nevertheless, Santa Muerte's followers articulate alternate forms of identity, community, or social and civil services in a world that frequently considers them disposable and denies them basic human rights. In her documentary film *La Santa Muerte*, Eva Aridjis focuses on the nuances of Santa Muerte's criminal devotees, a group that is almost always painted in broad strokes, and their use of the death saint to challenge social and economic hardships, even as they may depend upon violence or delinquency to achieve them. In fact, the majority of the people Aridjis interviews in the film, including those who live on the margins of society like prison inmates and transvestite prostitutes, focus on ordinary concerns, such as the desire for lost lovers, for a reunion with a beloved mother, or for money and employment. Several of the criminals that Aridjis interviews are artists—both tattoo artists and visual artists—and poets who are inspired by and dedicate their work to the death saint. As always, these artists' uses of Santa Muerte are contradictory. One artist shows Aridjis an unfinished sketch titled "With her tears I pay for my sins." The poem that accompanies the sketch cites indigenous gods like Tonatiuh (the Aztec sun god) alongside the death saint, demonstrating the syncretic religious beliefs that many historians emphasize in their discussions of the cult of Santa Muerte. The poet affirms: "The penitentiary is my university, it's the place where I received my education, and learned how to survive within the demented." This powerful statement situates Santa Muerte not only as a protector or guide to navigate the treacherous world of the penitentiary but also as a teacher for those (like most of the inmates portrayed) who do not have the opportunity to receive a traditional education.

At the same time, many inmates and Tepito residents portrayed in the film subtly reveal unpleasant or potentially threatening emotions or actions that relate to different forms of illegality. Aridjis meets with Tepito resident Ernestina Ramírez Hernández's daughter, an inmate at the Women's Social Readaptation Center, who nervously equivocates when the filmmaker asks her how she landed in jail: "For pickpocketing. Well, for robbery. Of a ... they say I stole a wallet ... 1,700 pesos. But I didn't do it. On Tuesday when I had my hearing, the guy kept on contradicting himself ... him and the police. My lawyer said I'll probably beat them." When Aridjis asks about her devotion to Santa Muerte, the woman animatedly describes her daily prayers and her desire for her freedom. Whether or not the woman is guilty of committing the petty theft, what is certain is that both her criminal activity and her devotion to the death saint are transgressive.

While Ernestina Ramírez's daughter vacillates about her likely criminal past, another woman in the film is more upfront about her transgressive life. This woman, who paints murals and other images of Santa Muerte for other inmates, openly situates the death saint as both an economic succor and a guardian for her drug habit. She asserts, "a lot of people have asked me to paint her for them. And from that I get some money for food ... and to buy myself whatever I want ... And it's like she's my friend, because ... when I get high, she holds my hand. She's right by my side. Because what if I overdose and die? She's there with me." It is fascinating that this woman seems to expect neither judgment for nor deliverance from her drug habit. Instead, she considers Santa Muerte a friend who will not only protect her from overdosing but will stay with her as she gets high, perhaps implicitly participating in her illicit journey. Such a friend is certainly threatening to mainstream society and reflects the illegality that is so appealing to many of the death saint's marginalized devotees.

One of the few detailed descriptions of the use of Santa Muerte to harm others is the testimony of Ernestina Ramírez Hernández, who describes her son's violent death on the streets of Tepito and her pleas to the death saint for retribution. Ramírez, who claims that her son never did drugs and was killed because he refused to join a gang or to "be like the other guys from here," prays to Santa Muerte in a reversal of Jesus's proverb "turn the other cheek": "You know that a tooth for a tooth and an eye for an eye ... and those who do bad things receive bad things. So I place them in your hands. And that's what happened to them." Of one gangbanger in particular, Ramírez asks, "O Saint Death, I know that guy was involved. Mark him. How are you going to punish him? Don't let him die, but leave him so he's useless." The bereaved mother proudly asserts that her prayers have been answered. Whether her narrative of an innocent, upstanding son is accurate or not, it avoids the threatening possibility that the gangbangers who killed her son might have been followers of Santa Muerte as well, or that he might have been involved with them somehow. In an inversion of the negative perspective typically held by many cosmopolitan Mexicans and the Catholic Church, Aridjis's film presents an optimistic, perhaps occasionally one-sided portrayal of Santa Muerte and her followers.

Ernestina Ramírez's example of the use of Santa Muerte for "bad things" is fundamentally ambiguous, for her prayers seek retribution and justice in an area where most residents completely lack legal, economic, or social justice. In a sense, Santa Muerte might be their only hope for justice. The marginalized people featured in Aridjis's film allude to their social status in oblique, matter-of-fact terms, as when Ernestina Ramírez affirms that her son refused to join a gang or do drugs like all of the other guys from Tepito simply because he lived there, or when Doña Queta's son (Omar Romero, named only in the film credits) casually discusses his multiple brushes with death. Looking like a typical gangbanger with a shaved head, muscular, heavily tattooed arms, and a wife-beater t-shirt, Romero asserts that Santa Muerte has saved his life at least three times. He claims, "Well at times when I've been unwell. About to ... die. It's only been a few times, like two or three times ... The police beat me up and ... I was dying. My mother was already going to bring a priest. The liquid was going into my brain. My skull was split open. And ... that's when I pray to her. Because ... I'm not going to ask her for things all the time." The matter-of-fact attitude he adopts toward his near death experiences is both chilling and logical given his dangerous environment and his possible involvement in the criminal underworld. Omar Romero's reluctance to call upon Santa Muerte arbitrarily, instead only appealing to her in truly life or death situations, reflects a code of justice and retribution that rewards those who know when and how to best summon the death saint. Since death surrounds so many of the residents of Tepito, they must be judicious in calling upon Santa Muerte.

Doña Queta herself alludes to the economic privation most Tepito residents contend with when she intimates that her public altar to Santa Muerte is something of an extension of her home. When describing her decision to bring her large Santa Muerte statue out to build a street altar, Doña Queta tells Aridjis, "And since I live in a very small room, you've seen the room where I live ... My bed is there, but there's really not much space." For Doña Queta, the public shrine extends her private space not only because of her dedication to the death saint or her position of leadership in the community of the faithful, but because her living quarters consist of just one tiny room. Rather than inhabit a subordinate role, the devotees featured in *La Santa Muerte* proudly articulate their own narratives of equality and resourcefulness through Santa Muerte, even as they sometimes give lip service to established hierarchies such as those decreed by the Catholic Church. Much of this narrative of equality celebrates the democratic nature of the death saint, for many of those interviewed in the film reiterate that Santa Muerte does not discriminate: she will eventually take everyone, no matter how much money they have or how dark or light their skin is, or whether they are citizens or migrants, straight or gay, good or bad, young or old.

Thus, the cult of Santa Muerte articulates equality for marginalized groups of people and spaces that fundamentally lack it. Several of the devotees in the film invoke the power of the death saint through street or home altars, amulets, jewelry, or tattoos as a kind of neighborhood watch to protect them in Tepito, where the police often refuse to tread. Many of the devotees that Aridjis interviews, including Doña Queta and Jesse Ortiz Peña, claim that Santa Muerte has protected them from danger in the neighborhood. Doña Queta asserts that the death saint protected her when she was on her way to see her critically injured son Omar late at night with a group of women friends, by covering them "with her holy shroud" so that a group of muggers would not see them. Meanwhile, Ortiz discusses an encounter with thieves and kidnappers that was defused when he informed them that he gives masses to Santa Muerte. The film also demonstrates that worship of the death saint produces much more routine, permanent benefits, such as the establishment of public social space for the inhabitants of Tepito. Doña Queta's street altar expands the available safe space in which to live, pray, work, and socialize for all of Santa Muerte's devotees. The death cult in prisons or around shrines like the one on Alfarería Street—with its attendant preachers, dressmakers, caretakers, and especially, the congregation that attends the monthly masses—serves as confessor, social worker, therapist, friend, and family for the faithful.

Doña Queta suggests that what is most empowering about Santa Muerte is her universality, as she asserts, "She is inside of you just as she is inside of me ... Once you peel this [your skin] ... you are the Muerte. You already have her ... in you" (Hernández 156). Doña Queta's powerful, simple image conjures the idea of a saint that believers do not necessarily have to invoke, because she is always with them. In other words, everyone already possesses her inside; or more accurately, Santa Muerte possesses us. This accessibility is surely what makes the death saint so threatening to her critics and popular with her devotees, for it suggests that all of her contradictions are universal. Santa Muerte's fundamental ambivalence—as a secular saint who is simultaneously sacred and profane, good and evil, and fair and arbitrary—permits her often marginalized devotees to embrace their own contradictions as the essence of the human condition. While Santa Muerte's secular sanctity exceeds the grasp of church and state, it also transforms the abject condition of marginalized groups into a double-edged sword of empowerment and menace. As novelist Homero Aridjis argues, while most of the saint's followers "seek protection from the evil that lurks in their lives, others ... seek darker blessings no other saint would approve" (Thompson n.p.). Santa Muerte is undeniably a refuge for criminals as well as for their victims, as some devotees "ask [her] for protection from harm even as they harm others" (Thompson n.p.). But all too often, the hyperbolic association of the death saint with criminals and narcos obscures the fact that her followers are well aware of her potential for harm, and the possibility that she could turn on them if they do not treat her with care. Ultimately, the understanding that Santa Muerte represents both empowerment and menace reflects her accessibility and ambivalence for her devotees. Whether they use her for good or ill, Santa Muerte's followers respect and embrace her because she signifies the choices that are frequently denied them as marginalized subjects in the borderlands and beyond.

Notes

1 Richard Kieckhefer argues, "Through the 1960s most days of the year were special feast days of saints ... Liturgical changes in 1969 included the deletion from the calendar of 52 saints whose very existence was questioned ... Although some recent saints were added, the net effect was to diminish attention given to the saints" (Kieckhefer and Bond 9).

2 One of the Virgin of Guadalupe's monikers is La Virgen Morena (the dark-skinned virgin). See Sandra Cisneros, "Guadalupe the Sex Goddess," and León, who cites an East Los Angeles woman named Señora de la Cruz who feels an affinity with Guadalupe because "she looks like me" (León 115).

3 Journalist José Gil Olmos cites Katia Perdigón, a Mexican anthropologist whom he interviews in his book La Santa Muerte, on this point. According to Perdigón: "today the devotion to Santa Muerte is only below that of Jesus and the Virgin of Guadalupe, and equal to that of San Judas Tadeo" (92). Gil Olmos also cites an interview with Manuel Valadez, a seller at the Mercado de Sonora (Sonora market), a traditional public market in Mexico City famous for its collection of merchandise dedicated to medicinal plants, spirituality, and the occult. Valadez claims, "of all the figures available at the market, the most sold is that of Santa Muerte" (82).

4 Many devotees, like those featured in Eva Aridjis' documentary La Santa Muerte, make or order new dresses and outfits for their Santa Muerte figures to correspond to religious or national holidays or simply to reflect the change in season. Gil Olmos notes that devotees dress their Santa Muerte figures in special outfits and costumes such as those of a china poblana, Aztec dancer, mariachi, or football (soccer) player. Gil Olmos argues that the wide variety of outfits and accessories manifest the agency that stems from the connection between saint and devotee "since the figures belong to them" (103).

Bibliography

Anzaldúa, Gloria. *Borderlands/La Frontera*. 2nd ed. San Francisco: Aunt Lute Books, 1999.

Aridjis, Eva (dir). *La Santa Muerte*. Dark Knight Pictures, 2007.

Butler, Judith. *Precarious Life*. London and New York: Verso, 2004.

Chesnut, R. Andrew. *Devoted to Death: Santa Muerte, the Skeleton Saint*. New York: Oxford University Press, 2012.

Cisneros, Sandra. *Woman Hollering Creek*. New York: Vintage Books, 1991.

Cisneros, Sandra. "Guadalupe the Sex Goddess." *Goddess of the Americas*. Ed. Ana Castillo. New York: Riverhead Trade, 1996. 46–51.

Delgadillo, Theresa. *Spiritual Mestizaje*. Durham, NC: Duke University Press, 2011.

Douillet, Jacques. *What Is a Saint?* New York: Hawthorn Books, 1958.

Espinosa, Gastón and Mario T. García, eds. *Mexican American Religions: Spirituality, Activism, and Culture*. Durham, NC: Duke University Press, 2008.

Gil Olmos, José. *La Santa Muerte: La Virgen de los Olvidados*. Mexico City: Debolsillo, 2010.

Goizueta, Roberto S. "The Symbolic World of Mexican American Religion." *Horizons of the Sacred: Mexican Traditions in U.S. Catholicism*. Eds. Timothy Matovina and Gary Riebe-Estrella. Ithaca, NY: Cornell University Press, 2002.

Hernández, Daniel. *Down and Delirious in Mexico City: The Aztec Metropolis in the Twenty-First Century*. New York: Scribner, 2011.

Hopgood, James F. *The Making of Saints: Contesting Sacred Ground*. Tuscaloosa, AL: University of Alabama Press, 2005.

Kieckhefer, Richard and George D. Bond, eds. *Sainthood: Its Manifestations in World Religions*. Berkeley, CA: University of California Press, 1988.

León, Luis D. *La Llorona's Children: Religion, Life, and Death in the US-Mexican Borderlands*. Berkeley and Los Angeles: University of California Press, 2004.

Matovina, Timothy and Gary Riebe-Estrella. *Horizons of the Sacred: Mexican Traditions in U.S. Catholicism*. Ithaca, NY: Cornell University Press, 2002.

Muñoz, José Esteban. *Disidenfitications: Queers of Color and the Performance of Politics*. Minneapolis: University of Minnesota Press, 1999.

Perdigón Castañeda, J. Katia. *La Santa Muerte: Protectora de los hombres*. Mexico City: INAH, 2008.

Thompson, Ginger. "Mexico City Journal; On Mexico's Mean Streets, the Sinners Have a Saint." *New York Times* 26 March 2004.

Woodward, Kenneth. *The Making of Saints*. New York: Simon and Schuster, 1990.

32

DAY OF THE DEAD

Decolonial Expressions in Pop de los Muertos

Cruz Medina

Sweet smells of pan de los muertos and sugar candy skulls, vibrant pastel paper cutouts lining the streets for processions in skeleton face paint, with oversized papier-mâché figures and altars decorated with pictures of family members lead the way to the cemetery with offerings of bottles and plates of food at tombs and headstones, with golden bouquets of marigolds adorning burial plots.[1] These familiar sights, smells, and tastes of Día de los Muertos pop cultural memory possess distinct layers of indigenous, colonial, and decolonial expression. The indigenous Mexican practices associated with Pre-Columbian Nahua and Mayan civilizations surviving the Conquest would be adopted by mainstream Mexican artists and intellectuals following the Revolution, translating into more current U.S. representations that gained popularity via the Chicana/o art movement. That struggle and resistance can be identified with each of these time periods when Día de los Muertos re-emerges "suggest[s] an almost irreverent, macabre confrontation with mortality" (Brandes, "Day of the Dead, Halloween" 360). Día de los Muertos expressions derive much of their rhetorical power from Pre-Columbian roots and the anti-colonial ethos of the Mexican Revolution that express not only a distinct visual aesthetic, but more importantly, symbolize the decolonial belief system that resists Western traditions. That the popularity of Día de los Muertos continues to grow demonstrates an exigency for conceptualizing death in a manner that diverges from a Western ideology of imperialism through consumption and fear of the afterlife.

Contemporary productions of Día de los Muertos reflect the traditional skeleton art popularized by José Guadalupe Posada and his image of "La Calavera Catrina," which was meant as social criticism of the elites in Porfirio Díaz's pre-Revolution Mexico. The anti-colonial ethos of this aesthetic levied towards Spain further emphasized the importance of Día de los Muertos as a cultural practice that was indigenous to Mexico. Building on this tradition, Regina Marchi notes that "[m]any Chicano artists were inspired by José Guadalupe Posada's satirical calavera caricatures, and began to create stylistically similar drawings that critically commented on California's politicians, urban youth, and other political topics" (40). The self-determination embodied by the art created before and after the Mexican

Revolution provided a clear inspiration for the Chicana/o art movement that paralleled the civil rights movement and the spirit of anti-colonial resistance.

The incorporation of anti-colonial messages into popular cultural productions such as theater can, in fact, be traced to the project of the conquest of the Americas. While some argue that there is a lack of explicit connection between Día de los Muertos and its Pre-Columbian roots, this argument remains indicative of the colonial project that sought to erase the history, literacy, and knowledge of Pre-Columbian populations through the burning of codices. Pre-Columbian culture served to differentiate Mexico from Spanish colonialism, and Día de los Muertos highlights the difference in how death is represented in Western pop culture amidst the current popularity of zombies in TV, comic books, and movies, providing an alternative—even liberatory—worldview that values family, communing with the dead, and cultural memory.

Framework of the Dead

In the pop culture imaginary, death is often associated with Halloween and the fantastic and fear-eliciting zombies populating a "hell on earth" that fits within a Western colonial religious belief system. Día de los Muertos serves as a cultural practice that not only differentiates how death is represented in film, movies, and comics, but the celebration of the dead signifies a cultural break from Halloween, which in Mexico "has become a symbol of the United States and its cultural imperialistic designs" (Brandes, "The Day of the Dead, Halloween" 371). Although Stanley Brandes also speculates about the connection between Dia de los Muertos and Pre-Columbian traditions ("Day of the Dead, Halloween" 366), it is important to keep in mind that decolonialism is not just a study of history, culture, and artifacts. Decolonialism offers a framework for interpretive projects and the creation of knowledge: "A delinking that leads to de-colonial epistemic shift and brings to the foreground other epistemologies, other principles of knowledge and understanding and, consequently, other economy, other politics, other ethics" (Mignolo 453). Decolonial epistemologies can develop when we authorize Pre-Columbian fragments remaining from the codices and archives of knowledge burned in the project of the Conquest. In both authorized and unauthorized epistemologies, fragments of texts provide sources of background knowledge and evidence that generate arguments with decolonial methodologies that recognize the hermeneutic potential of indigenous culture and practices.

To study how pop culture expresses particular rhetoric related to death, it is important to recognize how a decolonial methodology offers alternatives for how death is conceptualized. In his discussion of sacred rhetoric, Morgan Marietta examines the psychology behind "sacred" topics in political arguments often associated with religious beliefs. Marietta concludes that sacred rhetoric possesses absolutist reasoning that influences "public discourse rather than public opinion" (777). Although the dominant epistemologies in the U.S. purport to rely upon logic as a guiding principal, the ideological underpinnings of U.S. politics demonstrate that even logic fails to effectively persuade audiences with entrenched beliefs. In keeping with the psychology undergirding rhetoric of the dead, Joshua Gunn's "Refitting Fantasy: Psychoanalysis, Subjectivity, and Talking to the Dead" conceptualizes communication with the dead as "a conspicuous and exaggerated elaboration of the underlying fantasy that is central to the ways we think about rhetoric: the mediation or reconciliation of self and other across a terrible, yawning gap" (2). Gunn's main site of analysis is the television psychic John Edward who channels the dead for the members of his studio audience. That Edward remains something of a punch line shows how communicating with the dead is viewed pejoratively; in addition, the ability to speak to the dead is defined by Gunn as a fantasy, and death "a terrible, yawning gap" as opposed to an inevitable stage of life.

Día de los Muertos pop culture express layers of semiotics associated with these representations beyond the yawning gap of zombies. By following decolonial scholar Walter Mignolo's advocacy to examine parallel "loci of enunciation," sites of analysis related to Día de los Muertos stem from the distinct epistemologies associated with the history and people of that geographical space, rather than the thoughts from imperial outposts of power. After contact, the Franciscans recognized Aztec rhetoric that connects with the Día de los Muertos practice of speaking the words of the ancients and elders:

> What the Franciscans recognized as rhetoric the Aztecs themselves called *huehuetlahtolli*. This Nahuatl word is formed by compounding *huehue*, "old man" or "men of old" and *tlahtolli*, "word," "oration" or "language." Thus *huehuetlahtolli* is variously translated as "the ancient word," "the speeches of the ancients" or "the speeches of the elders."
>
> (Abbott 252)

Pre-Columbian *huehuetlahtolli*, or speech of the ancients, can be traced to the tradition of pláticas in Día de los Muertos celebrations. The holiday serves as a time for children

> to listen to these pláticas (talks) because they are expected to embrace these stories [of the deceased] and retell them in other venues. It is understood, and often explained by the family's leader to the child, that he or she will eventually lead these discussions in the future.
>
> (Pimentel 264)

These pláticas perform an important role in the remembrance of the deceased. Like Día de los Muertos, huehuetlahtolli performs an epideictic role that "consists of orations relative to the life cycle. These speeches were delivered by elders or parents at crucial junctures in human experience: birth, infancy, marriage, death" (Abbott 255). Día de los Muertos ritualizes the remembrance of the deceased, so it possesses elements of epideictic rhetoric.

By speaking the speeches of the ancients, celebrators are also reminded to think about death as more than fantasy, or acting as willing colonial subjects to earn passage into the afterlife. Día de los Muertos supports a decolonial ideology because the holiday "helps to create an interpretation of the world in which Mexico is unique, culturally discrete, and above all different from the two powers that have dominated the country throughout its long existence: Spain and the United States" (Brandes, "Day of the Dead, Halloween" 359). Rather than fearing zombies who hunt the living to feed, or praying to saints who mediate prayers for the dead, Día de los Muertos symbolizes a liberating worldview that draws on ancient indigenous practices that continue to resonate.

Day of the Dead Expressions

When it comes to Latina/o representations of the dead in the pop culture collective unconscious, Cuban filmmaker George Romero occupies a sacred space due to his iconic, cult cinematic representations of the dead. In the U.S. tradition of Halloween zombies, Romero's *Dead* series established a blueprint of cinematic tropes and rules about what the dead can do when they come back to life in an unthinking form in search of living humans for consumption. Because Romero's 1978 *Dawn of the Dead* takes place against the backdrop of a shopping mall, the critique of consumerism rings through because in an unthinking, zombie state, the dead return to the mall as they were trained to in life (Bishop; Harper; Walker). The horror genre remains popular in the U.S. because it is inexpensive, and much like the artisans of Día de los Muertos crafts, "they [traditional Mexican artisans] do not object to the introduction of Halloween symbols, so long as their handiwork sells" (Brandes, "Day of the Dead, Halloween" 377). Still, the critique of western imperialism through the metonymy of consumerism reflects the decolonial ethos that expressions of the dead facilitate.

The characters in Romero's films remain in the colonial paradigm that focuses on the catharsis of fear through *schadenfreude* for characters finding themselves in post-rapture storyworlds. In *Gospel of the Living Dead: George Romero's Visions of Hell on Earth*, colonial morality plays "a part of Romero's symbolism that the characters who do reject the sinful perversions of reason and violence are once again people who ... stand outside the power structure of the 'normal,' pre-zombie, prejudgement America" (Paffenroth 89). The western religious paradigm represented in Romero's films that include the judgment and rapture exhibits the enduring tradition of evangelical passion plays that the Franciscans employed in the conversion during the Conquest of the Americas. However, even the Nahua (Aztecs) infused the evangelical theater with messages of resistance: "This [evangelical] theater gave the Nahuas the opportunity of managing public space again, of showing their unrivaled ability to incorporate new meanings ... and possibility of encoding 'hidden transcripts of resistance' for the consumption of the indigenous audience only" (Balsera 63). Similar to the Nahua during the Conquest, Romero composes within the expectations of the horror genre, although he manipulates the conventions to communicate social critique.

Without explicitly drawing on Día de los Muertos beliefs, practices, or ritual, George Romero's 1985 film with the title *Day of the Dead*—the third film following Romero's *Night of the Living Dead* (1968) and *Dawn of the Dead* (1978)—demonstrates a subversive translation of the deceased occupying the same space as the living. Taking place in an underground Florida missile silo, *Day of the Dead* (1985) centers on a tyrannical military leader who takes over a scientific mission to reverse the zombie outbreak. Romero's social critique is evidenced by the location of Florida, where many Cubans sought refuge following Fidel Castro's *paredón* firing squads, as well as the resemblance of the soldier named Rickles, portrayed by actor Ralph Marrero, to Cuban revolutionary soldiers, wearing a thick black beard and up-turned army cap. Though Romero does not widely discuss his Latino heritage, his father was born in Cuba; and in an interview with the *Daily News*, Romero said that he traveled with his family to Cuba during his youth before Castro came to power (Monell).

The military tyrant's isolation from the world of the living in *Day of the Dead* is analogous to the disconnection of Romero's cultural homeland of Cuba. In Joe Kane's book *Night of the Living Dead: Behind the Scenes of the Most Terrifying Zombie Movie Ever*, Romero explains that the *Day of the Dead* depicts a world where structure and communication are suddenly removed. He says,

> [W]hen that structure is gone, they don't quite know how to behave or they cling to old behaviors and no one talks to each other and no one communicates. So there's this sort of tragedy about how a lack of human communication causes chaos and collapse even in this small little pie slice of society.
>
> (Kane 140)

On the surface, the scientist character's experiments in *Day of the Dead*, attempting to reverse the zombie process, portray Gunn's explanation of the death fantasy as communicating across the "terrible, yawning gap" (2). Still, many Cubans in the U.S. like Romero literally experienced "a lack of human communication" once Castro seized power and the U.S. placed an embargo on Cuba (Kane 140). When Russia experienced economic hardships during the Cold War and it could no longer financially assist Cuba as the Communist outpost in close proximity to the U.S., the small island nation also experienced the structural "collapse" that Romero's films portray.

The political commentary of Romero's zombies functions as critique within the horror genre, although Romero's influence in popular culture extends outside of the U.S. film industry. The influence of Romero's *Dead* series can be seen, as both parody and homage, in the Spanish-Cuban zombie comedic satire *Juan of the Dead/Juan de los Muertos* (2011). *The New York Times* film review calls attention to how *Juan of the Dead* follows in the tradition of Romero's social commentary in the political context of Castro's Cuba: "As the zombies turn Havana into a gory circus of flying limbs and severed heads, the nightly news anchors continue to calmly assert the government line, that the attacks are not the work of the undead but dissidents in the pay of the United States" (Burnett). Independent from the state-financed Cuban film industry, *Juan of the Dead* has a title character that connects with Día de los Muertos pop culture with Spanish influence from pre-Revolution Mexico: "In the year 1847, a play by the Spanish playwright Jose Zorilla arrived in Mexico. The play, 'Don Juan Tenorio,' ... takes place in a cemetery where statues and spirits come to life. It became a popular play, often performed during the Days of the Dead" (Moss 5).

Even if *Juan of the Dead* does not follow the belief system represented by Día de los Muertos, the social criticism follows the traditional use of death in Latina/o pop culture. Sarah Misemer explains,

> death invokes the ongoing syncretic nature of the fight to integrate all segments of the Mexican population—a goal of the Revolution. Artistic figures such as Diego Rivera, José Clemente Orozco, and Guadalupe Posada among others used the trope of death to make social and political commentary through their art.
>
> (763)

The zombie plague metaphorically standing in for Cuban unemployment and crumbled infrastructure in *Juan of the Dead* hardly mirrors Día de los Muertos philosophy about death, yet the powerful critique of government embodies the same decolonial ethos of resistance to an oppressive authority.

Pop de los Muertos

In the genre of documentary, Lourdes Portilla's *La Ofrenda: The Days of the Dead* captures the preparation, the cleaning of cemetery headstones, the offering of traditional food dishes, and the construction of altars in Oaxaca, Mexico. Often overlooked, Juan Velasco (40) explains that "La Ofrenda *rescata dos elementos memorables de la tradición Mexicana del día de los muertos: el altar y el acto de ofrecer* [La Ofrenda rescues two memorable elements of the Day of the Dead tradition: the altar and the act of offering]" (author's translation). Marta Turok explains that in Mexico "[t]he *ofrenda* has also taken on new values ... it becomes a medium for reaffirming Mexican cultural values in schools, countering the Anglo-Saxon tradition of Halloween" (79). Portilla's focus on the *ofrenda* in both Mexico and in San Francisco, California, shows how the traditional cultural practice provides a decolonial space where altars and offerings draw attention to the impact of AIDS in the LGBTQ community.

Portilla channels the rhetorical power of "remembering loved ones through ofrendas [that] could also serve as a way to publically commemorate individual and collective experiences of the Mexican American community" (Marchi 39). The Día de los Muertos expressions engage in critique of what mainstream society has ignored.

In music, Día de los Muertos is represented in multiple genres ranging from traditional son jarocho from Veracruz, Mexico, to Latin American electronic dance pop, as well as the fusion of hip hop and cumbia by musicians in the U.S. (Raygoza). A salient example of the conflation of Día de los Muertos pop culture and western ideology is the traditional son jarocho song called "La Bruja" about a drunken man who is held hostage by a witch. The song has become associated with Día de los Muertos because of the influence of traditional western Halloween symbolism, and it additionally reveals "insight into Catholic-Latin sexuality; the enticing fear of the woman who 'consumes' men in the wee hours of the night and is promiscuous even in her cannibalism" (Garsd). Though a traditional folklore song, colonial ideology permeates the negative portrayal of female sexuality.

The mestizaje of Día de los Muertos culture with Halloween can also be seen with Gilbert Hernandez's, of *Love and Rockets* notoriety, contribution of a variant cover of *The Walking Dead* for the Las Vegas Wizard World Comic Convention. Still, Día de los Muertos iconography is fundamental to the aesthetic and storyline in the film *The Dead One* (2007) from the comic by the name *El Muerto: The Aztec Zombie* by Javier Hernández. In *El Muerto*, the main character Diego is killed by "Mictlantecuhtli, the Aztec God of Death, also known as Mictlan" before Diego is reborn as *El Muerto* with a Chicana/o consciousness of Pre-Columbian history (Foster 235). Unfortunately, the attention to Día de los Muertos in the U.S. also attracted the colonizing efforts of the Disney Corporation that attempted to copyright the holiday in May 2013, leading to Lalo Alcaraz's "Muerto Mouse" image that circulated through social media (Medina 2015).

With the original working title *Day of the Dead*,[2] the animated film *The Book of Life*[3] (2014) exemplifies Día de los Muertos imagery expressed in mainstream pop culture with notable Mexican actors Diego Luna and Kate del Castillo, as well as Zoe Saldana, Channing Tatum, Ron Perlman, Christina Applegate, Ice Cube, Cheech Marin, Danny Trejo and Gabriel Iglesias lending their voices. Told in a frame narrative, Christina Applegate portrays La Muerte in human form, working as a museum tour guide for children, exposing them to the "wonder of Mexico." In a decolonial gesture, Applegate as the museum guide tells the children that "Mexico is the center of the universe" as an image of Mexico appears with a comically large mustache across the center of the country. While non-Mexican audiences may resist the assertion that Mexico is the center of the universe, the caricatured mustache softens the remark and positions the belief system of the film within a non-U.S.-centric worldview. *The Book of Life* appeals to audiences with "the humor and gaiety that pervade the holiday," along with visually lush and arresting colors and imagery from the traditional celebrations (Brandes, "Day of the Dead, Halloween" 363).

Guillermo Del Toro's role as producer accounts for the level of detail and aesthetic feat that *Book of Life* achieves, given the arresting visuals in *Pan's Labyrinth* (2006); however, Del Toro's first feature film *Cronos* (1993) reveals the Mexican director's long fascination with the themes of death and resurrection. Discussing *The Book of Life* in an interview with *The Telegraph*, Del Toro espouses the Día de los Muertos belief that the dead co-exist with the living:

> Ultimately you walk life side-by-side with death … and the Day of the Dead, curiously enough, is about life … Because I'm not a guy that hides the monster: I show it to you

with the absolute conviction that it exists. And that's the way I think we view death. We don't view it as the end ...

(Harrod)

In addition to a non-western view of death, Del Toro also acknowledges his rejection of western culture's emphasis on materialism. He explains, "I think we live in a culture that is actually hedging all of it towards comfort and immediacy, things that scare me. All the things that they sell us as a way of life scare me" (Harrod). Del Toro's perspectives illuminates a decolonial stance in opposition to both western beliefs about death and consumerism, which manifest in the rejection of military power and fame in favor of love and artistic endeavors in *The Book of Life*.

In the film, the first Day of the Dead celebration occurs when the main characters Manolo Sánchez, Joaquín Mondragon, and María Posada are children playing in a cemetery while their families honor the dead who appear as ghost-like figures alongside the living who decorated the headstones with marigolds, altars with offerings of *pan de muerto* and pictures of the deceased. The central narrative of *The Book of Life* takes place against the backdrop of multiple Days of the Dead in the town of San Angel. The town name San Angel relates to the intended audience of children and underscores the Mexican belief system, in which "*angelito*, literally 'little angel,' the word used to describe a child who dies in sexual innocence and therefore is destined to go directly to heaven, without having to pass through purgatory" (Brandes, *Skulls to the Living* 4). The storyworld of the film operates outside of the belief system of purgatory, further undercutting the existential burden imposed by colonial religious paradigms.

Above the cemetery, La Muerte, the goddess of the Land of the Remembered, and Xibalba (from the Mayan *Popol Vuh*), the god of the Land of the Forgotten, place a bet. La Muerte wagers that Manolo will win María's heart while Xibalba bets in favor of Joaquín. In the Spanish audio of the film, La Muerte is called La Catrina, which refers specifically to the popular Día de los Muertos figure. In addition, the characters Maria and her father General Posada also pay homage: "[Dia de los Muertos] decorations often center on images of La Calavera Catrina, a skeleton of an upper-class woman whose image was made popular by the late-Mexican printmaker Jose Guadalupe Posada" (Contreras). Following the bet, Xibalba bestows upon Joaquín a magical medal that gives him indestructible power to help the young man win Maria's heart through military glory. Even though Xibalba's name comes from the Mayan *Popol Vuh*, his intervention supports the belief that Pre-Columbian "Nahua gods were tricksters ... [Tezcatlipoca for example] sowed discord and trouble both among and within opposite parties" (Balsera 29). Xibalba further reveals himself as unscrupulous in his desire to win his wager with La Muerte when he sends his snakes to strike, killing Manolo, and thereby winning the bet by default.

Even though the god and goddess of the underworld place bets on and trick the living, death is portrayed as a celebratory stage of life connected to the living and to ancestors. When Manolo arrives at the Land of the Remembered, it is a colorful place where skeleton figurines celebrate the Day of the Dead while an upbeat anthem called "El Aparato/Land of the Remembering" by Gustavo Santaolalla and Café Tacvba plays. The song is a lush arrangement with a familiar indigenous chant in accompaniment. Manolo crosses realms of the underworld from the Land of the Remembered to the Land of the Forgotten, where he finds La Muerte and notifies her of Xibalba's meddling. In another bet with Xibalba to return to the world of the living, Manolo faces an enormous bull that Manolo has the chance to defeat, although, instead of finishing off the bull, he sings a song of apology. The bull stops charging and disintegrates into dust, rising into the air as marigold petals. The dust from the dead alludes to a deeper level of Aztec mythology in which Quetzalcoatl was said to have gathered bone fragments in the land of the dead to carry them back to other gods in order to give new life:

> Quetzalcoatl was the god appointed to go down to Mictlan to collect bones and ashes of the previous, deceased generation of men ... The bones were ground into fragments by a goddess, at which point the rest of the assembled gods proceeded to bleed themselves or to perform self-sacrifice so that life could spring forth from the bone mass.
>
> (Nicholson, quoted in Balsera 32)

This mythology provides an additional layer of understanding to the Land of the Forgotten in *The Book of Life* where relatives who no longer have families to remember them go and fade into dust.

The historical context of *The Book of Life* is particularly indicative of the moment after Mexico had earned its independence from Spain. Mexico continued to face civil war in the form of bandits such as the character in *The Book of Life* named Chakal who threatens the safety of San Angel. Cristina Ramírez explains, "The Revolution, which had started out as a movement through which she hoped to bring justice for the campesinos and fair wages for industrial workers, turned into a movement of power grabbing among the elites" (149). The threat of Chakal and his bandits motivates María Posada's father to pressure her into marrying Joaquín, so that he will stay to protect the city from Chakal and his men.

María's elite class position and education abroad support her articulation of opposition to the gendered expectations of her father Joaquín and Manolo, although she remains strategic in her stance for the safety of the town. Even though María embodies strong feminist qualities such as superior sword-fighting skills and education, she acquiesces to her father's patriarchy because "feminism is not only an active stance against oppressive systems but a strategic critical position emerging from a newly acquired literacy" (Ramírez 17). Comparatively, Manolo's dead female cousins Scardelita and Adelita make visible the role of Mexican women in the Revolution through their appearance by wearing ammunition belts, long skirts, and large sombreros.

The Book of Life concludes with Manolo and María teaming up to defeat Chakal with self-sacrifice on the parts of both Manolo and Joaquín. Neither act on motivations for power or glory, but rather in service of friendship and concern for the town. The message communicated to the younger audience is an anti-colonial argument for family, true love, and artistic passions, rather than the destructive imposition of desire for meaningless glory. At the very least, the representation of death in *The Book of Life* undermines the western religious paradigm that provides a blueprint of the living co-existing with the dead "as zombies, who are walking damned, robbed of intellect and emotion, or as surviving humans, barricaded and trapped in some place from which there is no escape ... a shadowy, trapped, borderline existence that resembles hell" (Paffenroth 22). As a Día de los Muertos pop culture expression, *The Book of Life* and other pop culture offer an alternative history, perspective, and culture for conceptualizing relationships with the dead.

Conclusion

The decolonial ethos of Día de los Muertos transmits distinctly Latina/o messages about indigenous cultural memory, political critique, and the stages of life. The holiday and its pop culture productions persist through conquest, genocide, revolution, civil war, and cultural imperialism because they are "a product of changing political agendas and economic circumstances ... the symbolic value of this holiday for those who might draw upon it to define personal and collective identity" (Brandes, *Skulls to the Living* 11). The differing genres and manifestations of Día de los Muertos portray the history and cultural identity that the projects of imperialism and colonialism actively sought to erase.

The proliferation of Día de los Muertos is related to the spread of culture through the Mexican and Latin American diasporas, yet the Pre-Columbian belief about death as a stage of life persists because it is rhetorically effective. Without Día de los Muertos, death falls into the colonial Halloween paradigm where it threatens purgatory through pop culture manifestations of dystopian *Walking Dead* realities. Although George Romero's *Dead* series defines the contemporary tropes of the zombie horror genre by personifying colonial Catholic beliefs about death (Paffenroth 2006), Romero's Cuban heritage informs the film series's rhetorical commonplace of losing communication. Día de los Muertos emphasizes cultural memory as it celebrates communicating with the dead.

Death dances among the bodies of the living as long as they are remembered and their stories passed down through the discursive power of plática. If history endures through cultural expressions, then the presence of death is merely a stage in the cyclical movement of bone and blood to dust and spirit. Decoloniality opens the free flow of knowledge and history from parallel sites of cultural creation—burrowing further deeper through the mouth of Xibalba's cave into lands and histories that extend beyond the reaches of colonial outposts in the collective unconscious, warning of damnation, yawning gap embargos, and limitations on how the deceased may be remembered. Día de los Muertos pop expressions give cultural communion to those who choose to celebrate belief systems that reinforce family rather than occupy the superego with threats for defying the corrupt power structures of the living.

Notes

1 Thanks to the generous feedback from Juan Velasco and Enrique Reynoso during the writing of this chapter.
2 "Guillermo Del Toro Joins with Reel FX to Produce Epic Animated Adventure Day of the Dead." Reel FX. 21 February 2012.
3 The title *The Book of Life* appeals to Judeo-Christian ideology, although the title was no doubt influenced by the subtitle applied to the *Popol Vuh* of *The Mayan Book of the Dawn of Life and the Glories of Gods and Kings*.

Bibliography

Abbott, Don P. "The Ancient Word: Rhetoric in Aztec Culture." *Rhetorica* 5:3 (1987): 251–64.
Balsera, Viviana Díaz. *The Pyramid Under the Cross: Franciscan Discourses of Evangelization and the Nahua Christian Subject in Sixteenth-Century Mexico*. Tucson, AZ: University of Arizona Press, 2005.
Bishop, Kyle W. "The Idle Proletariat: Dawn of the Dead, Consumer Ideology, and the Loss of Productive Labor." *The Journal of Popular Culture* 43:2 (2010): 234–48.
Brandes, Stanley. "The Day of the Dead, Halloween, and the Quest for Mexican National Identity." *The Journal of American Folklore* 111:442 (1998): 359–80.
Brandes, Stanley. *Skulls to the Living, Bread to the Dead: Day of the Dead in Mexico and Beyond*. Malden, MA: Blackwell Publishing, 2006.
Brugués, Alejandro (dir). *Juan of the Dead (Juan de los Muertos)*. La Zanfoña Producciones, 2011.
Burnett, Victoria. "Socialism's Sacred Cows Suffer Zombie Attack in Popular Cuban Film." *The New York Times* 10 December 2011.

Contreras, Russell. "'Day of the Dead' Expanding in U.S." *Huffington Post Latino Voices* 19 October 2011.

Del Toro, Guillermo (dir). *Cronos*. CNCAIMC, 1993.

Del Toro, Guillermo (dir). *Pan's Labyrinth*. Estudios Picasso, 2006.

Foster, David W. "Latino Comics: Javier Hernandez's *El Muerto* as an Allegory of Chicano Identity." *Latinos and Narrative Media: Participation and Portrayal*. Ed. Frederick Luis Aldama. New York: Palgrave Macmillan, 2013.

García, Peter J. "Día de los Muertos." *Encyclopedia of Latino Popular Culture*. Vol. 1. Eds. Cordelia Candelaria, Peter J. García, and Arturo J. Aldama. Greenwood Publishing Group, 2004.

Garsd, Jasmine. "Latin Roots: Son Jarocho." *National Public Radio*. 16 May 2013.

Gunn, Joshua. "Refitting Fantasy: Psychoanalysis, Subjectivity, and Talking to the Dead." *Quarterly Journal of Speech* 90:1 (2014): 1–23.

Gutierrez, Jorge R. dir. *The Book of Life*. Reel FX Creative Studios, 2014.

Harper, Stephen. "Zombies, Malls, and the Consumerism Debate: George Romero's *Dawn of the Dead*." *Americana: The Journal of American Popular Culture* 1:2 (2002): n.p.

Harrod, Horatia. "Guillermo Del Toro Interview for *The Book of Life*: What is it with Mexicans and Death?" *The Telegraph* 25 Oct 2014.

Hernández, Javier. *The Dead One/El Muerto*. Peninsula Films, 2007.

Kane, Joe. *Night of the Living Dead: Behind the Scenes of the Most Terrifying Zombie Movie Ever*. New York: Citadel Press, 2010.

Marchi, Regina. *Day of the Dead in the USA: The Migration and Transformation of a Cultural Phenomenon*. Piscataway, NJ: Rutgers University Press, 2009.

Marietta, Morgan. "From My Cold, Dead Hands: Democratic Consequences of Sacred Rhetoric." *The Journal of Politics* 70:3 (2008): 767–79.

Medina, Cruz. *Reclaiming Poch@ Pop: Examining Rhetoric of Cultural Deficiency*. Latin Pop Culture Series. New York: Palgrave MacMillan, 2015.

Mignolo, Walter D. "Delinking." *Cultural Studies* 21:2 (2007): 449–514.

Misemer, Sarah M. "Pedagogía de la Participación: Entering Elena Garro's Un Hogar Sólido through the Body, Enacting Death and Politics in Mexico." *Hispania* 92:4 (2009): 762–73.

Monell, Raymundo. "George Romero: Our Zombie in Havana." *New York Daily News* 14 February 2008.

Moss, Jean. *The Day of the Dead: A Pictorial Archive of Dia de Los Muertos*. Dover Pictorial Archive. Mineola, NY: Courier Corporation, 2010.

Nicholson, Henry B. "Religion in pre-Hispanic Central Mexico." *Handbook of Middle American Indians* 10:1 (1971): 395–446.

Paffenroth, Kim. *Gospel of the Living Dead: George Romero's Visions of Hell on Earth*. Waco, TX: Baylor University Press, 2006.

Pimentel, Octavio. "El Dia De Los Muertos." *Encyclopedia of Latino Culture: From Calaveras to Quinceañeras*. Ed. Charles M. Tatum. Santa Barbara, CA: Greenwood, 2013.

Portillo, Lourdes (dir). *La Ofrenda: The Days of the Dead*. Xochitl Films, 1988.

Ramírez, Cristina Devereaux. *Occupying Our Space: The Mestiza Rhetorics of Mexican Women Journalists and Activists, 1875–1942*. Tucson, AZ: University of Arizona Press, 2015.

Raygoza, Isabella. "Days of the Dead: 10 Songs for Remembering Your Ancestors." *MTV Iggy.com*. 12 January 2015.

Romero, George A. (writer/dir). *Night of the Living Dead*. Laurel Group, 1968.

Romero, George A. (writer/dir). *Dawn of the Dead*. Laurel Group, 1978.

Romero, George A. (writer/dir). *Day of the Dead*. Laurel Entertainment Inc., 1985.

Santaollalo, Gustavo and Café Tacvba. "El Aparato/Land of the Remembering." *The Book of Life (Original Motion Picture Soundtrack)*. Sony Classical, 2014.

Tedlock, Dennis, ed. *Popol Vuh: The Definitive Edition of The Mayan Book of The Dawn of Life And The Glories of Gods and Kings*. New York: Simon and Schuster, 1996.

Tlen Huicani. "La Bruja." *Trovadores de Veras*. 2007.

Turok, Marta. "The Altar: a Creative Horn of Plenty." *Artes de Mexico* 62:1 (2002): 77–9.

Velasco, Juan. "Performing Multiple Identities: Guillermo G.mez-Pe.a and His 'Dangerous Border Crossings.'" *Latino/a Popular Culture*. Eds. Michelle Habell-Pallán and Mary Romero. New York: New York University Press, 2002.

Walker, Matthew. "'When There's No More Room in Hell, the Dead Will Shop the Earth': Romero and Aristotle on Zombies, Happiness, and Consumption." *The Undead and Philosophy*. Eds. Richard Greene and K. Silem Mohammad. Chicago: Open Court, 2006. 81–9.

33

LIBERANOS DE TODO MAL/BUT DELIVER US FROM EVIL

Latina/o Monsters Theory and the Outlining of our Phantasmagoric Landscapes

William A. Calvo-Quirós

At first, they made me think
that I was a monster,
then they "made" me a monster,
and at the end... I saved them,
but I remain a monster.

Monsters are unique historic and epistemic cultural products. According to Stephen T. Asma, the word "monster derives from the Latin word *monstrum*, which in turn derives from the root *monere* (to warn). To be a monster is to be an omen" (13), a portent. However, according to David Wardle the term comes from Cicero's verb *monstra*, to show or to demonstrate (75). In this sense, monsters work both as omens and signs. They are never culturally silent, as they "speak" aloud about the conditions and communities from which they emerged and lived. For the most part, monsters terrorize, repulse, scare, and haunt our existence, but they also fascinate and attract us. They can bring out the best and the worst of human beings.

Monsters and phantasmagoric creatures populate our Latina/o culture(s), our landscapes (physical and imaginary), and our histories. They exist everywhere, both in the tangible and intangible parts of our worlds. Monsters have accompanied our existence as faithful reminders of our fragile realities. In many ways, monsters are central to our consciousness as Latina/os, not just because we have grown up with their terrifying stories told to us by our families and friends, but also as racialized subjects. Latina/os in the United States have been construed as monsters, as subjects of terror, as the Other. Being a Latina/o in the United States carries the burdens of the legacies of racism (and orientalism) that permeate all aspects of our social lives in regard to the access to resources for health care, housing, education, job security, etc., to the point of "premature death" (Gilmore 28).

I argue that the duality of studying/analyzing monsters while simultaneously being construed as social monsters is what differentiates Latina/o Monsters Theory (LMT) from mainstream traditional monster theory, as it allows for a unique standpoint in which to approach the imaginary. In this chapter, I explore both of these realities. In the first part, Monsters, and the Exorcising of Knowledge, I present the basics of monster theory, and the work done by Latina/os in expanding the analysis of these complex entities. I am particularly interested in exploring the nuanced approaches and interventions created by Latina/o feminist, queer, and race scholars in this field. This section will explore the epistemic knowledge value of monsters in the Latina/o community. The second section in this chapter, Monstrous Encounters and Crisis Monsters, will outline the trajectory of U.S. Latina/o monsters; in particular how they have been defined by what I call *monstrous colonial encounters*, or moments of crisis created by political and socio-economical transformations. I call these encounters monstrous because they are characterized by violence, cruelty, and the creation or perpetuation of vulnerability. I define these encounters as "colonial," because they preserve the legacies of European colonial disparity of power and distribution of resources and knowledge. In this section, I discuss five main monstrous encounters. The main objective of this chapter is to present monsters as important entities to understand the Latina/o experience of oppression, and the possibilities the imaginary provides to envision alternative worlds outside racial and colonial models of subjugation.

Monsters, and the Exorcising of Knowledge

The process of colonial subjugation of a community happens at the physical, emotional, aesthetical, intellectual, spiritual, and imaginary levels. The control of the transit and the processes of validation of knowledge about a community and its histories are central parts of the process of colonization. As Michael Foucault has observed, our society works within a system of knowledge hierarchy where some types of knowledge are "subjugated" (7), disqualified, or defined as inadequate and naïve (7), while others are reproduced and utilized to define progress, civility, and the sense of what it means to be human. Being a minority or a subjugated community, as Latina/os in the United States, means to develop a unique relationship to this hierarchy of knowledge. Many of our community knowledge[s] have been defined as invalid, backward, or useless for the "development" of the nation. Therefore, the process of assimilation has implied the "suppression" of those knowledge[s]. This occurred, for example, through the control of school curriculum, language, history narratives, and more recently, by the banning of books dealing with the Latina/o experience in the American Southwest. Simultaneously, false and/or misleading knowledge about the Latina/o community is created and disseminated. Latina/os have been portrayed as lazy, noisy, welfare "vampires," hypersexual, and violent. In other words, knowledge has been created to construe Latina/os as social monsters that must be controlled, reeducated, segregated, or "deported" into invisibility. It is in this epistemic context that imagination can provide an invaluable source for the transfer and dissemination of in-situ knowledge about these communities, to envision a "different" world and to propose social and economic changes that recognize their experiences. The world of the imagination allows for the opening of possibilities beyond the "norms" of what is possible, and the assumptions about what it means to be a Latina/o. Furthermore, the imaginary provides a venue to create new knowledge about the world and the self.

In this sense, the Latina/o monsters are materializations of what Rossana Reguillo calls "critical social knowledge" (40), which in these cases have been inscribed strategically within the flexible spaces of the vernacular. I say strategically, precisely because vernacular productions that have been disqualified as valuable or "serious" knowledge can travel, for the most part, outside the "interest" of the mainstream. Labeled as "superstitions" or "folk myths," these monsters and popular legends can navigate undetected outside the gaze that polices and maintains the social hierarchy of knowledge. In a high level of refinement the Latina/o community maneuvers the process of knowledge "subjugation" (Foucault 7), that has been imposed on them in order to construct a venue, the imaginary, to transport knowledge useful for their survival. Using Walter Mignolo's arguments in *Local Histories/ Global Designs: Coloniality, Subaltern Knowledges, and Border Thinking*, we can call these subversive epistemic maneuvers as truly "subaltern modernities" (13), or sophisticated productions generated by oppressed communities in order to deal with the effects of their subjugated status. Furthermore, these monsters are not alone as they form part of a larger network of other epistemic oral productions such as corridos, jokes, and legends that exemplify what Américo Paredes studied and referred to as "sabidurías populares" (Saldívar 56) or popular/vernacular knowledge (Paredes I).

For Stephen T. Asma, a "monster is more that an odious creature of the imagination; it is a kind of *cultural category*" (13), as important and crucial as many of the other categories we have constructed in our societies, such as aesthetics, religion, literature, and politics. For Asma, monsters have been used to construct, control, and regulate many of these domains (13). He writes, a

[m]onster ... is a product of and a regular inhabitant of the imagination, but the imagination is a driving force behind our entire perception of the world. If we find monsters in our world, it is sometimes because they are really there and sometimes because we have brought them with us.

(14)

This argument highlights the intimate connection between the real and the imaginary, a connection that mutually feeds each other and cannot always be differentiated. This is why Jacques Lacan rejects the argument that the imaginary, the real, and the symbolic are separate (Gallop 162), as he understands how interconnected they actually are. This is precisely the argument behind underpinning Emile Durkheim's explanation that "to be able to call certain facts supernatural, one must already have an awareness that there is a natural order of things" (24). In other words, our imagination responds to the real, as the real is affected by our imagination. Monsters, as outrageous and out of this world as they may appear, are intimated and defined by the real, as well as the context from which they were created.

Monstrous Encounters and Crisis Monsters

In his essay "Seven Theses," Jeffrey Jerome Cohen reminds us how a "monster is born only ... as an embodiment of a certain cultural moment of a time, a feeling, and a place ... The monstrous body is pure culture" (4). Monsters are cultural products that, much like legends and myths, hold cultural knowledge. They are records of collective memory encrypted within a cultural and socio-political context. A monster is foremost history turned into uncanny flesh that is mobile. They remind us, as Cohen describes, of "times of crisis" (6), or as Marina Levina and Diem-My T. Bui explain, monster narratives "offer a space where society can safely represent and address anxieties of its time" (1). In other words, we can reveal the history of a community by the different monsters that have inhabited and haunted their cultural territories over time. In this sense, monsters are quite valuable for the study of a community, and in the case of Latina/os, they can help us to understand the effects of systematic oppression and discrimination, as well as the many coping and resilience mechanisms developed by this community over time.

Monsters are never naïve; on the contrary, they are very sophisticated productions that not only materialize social anxieties and fears, but also call attention to the effects of subjugation upon a community. For Avery Gordon, phantasmagoric entities such as ghosts are symbols of something that is missing or of something that remains to be resolved (139). They have the ability to expand our expectations of the future, precisely because they remind us about our haunted past. For Gordon, "to be haunted is to be tied to historical and social effects" (190), deeply interconnected to the past, in the case of the Latina/o community a past defined by violence and subjugation. Ghosts and monsters tie us to a past, to the social conditions that allowed for their emergence, and their existence in the first place. They certainty are both evidence and an omen at the same time.

By weaving these concepts of being "haunted" by our past, and the emergence of monsters during "times of crisis" proposed by Gordon and Cohen, I argue that the Latina/o monster experience in the United States, especially for those in the American Southwest, has been defined by five main monstrous encounters: (1) the Spanish conquest experience; (2) nineteenth century U.S. expansionism; (3) the twentieth century's interwar period; (4) the World Trade Organisation (WTO) era; and more recently, (5) the millennium neo anti-immigrant nativist movements. I argue that each one of these "crisis" periods is characterized by unique transformations on the landscape of the imaginary, precisely because they demarked monstrous transformations in the socio-economic everyday life of Latina/o communities with new layers of out-of-this-world cruelty and violence. Each one of these periods has it own monsters. These monsters are multilateral, as they work as projections (monsterizations) of the Latina/o community, and simultaneously as a materialization of the monstrous conditions experienced by Latina/os. In many ways these monsters are an uncanny ideology that "haunts" the imaginaries of our history. Because of limitations of space, and the introductory scope of this chapter, I will not expansively describe each of these periods. However, I will try to give the readers sufficient information to understand the monstrous forms that characterize and differentiate each one of these periods, as well as the pantheon of monsters that they fostered. I argue inspired by Cathryn J. Merla Watson's words that our Latina/o history is "haunted by an invisible net of histor[ies] and embodied memor[ies], specters of colonialism and misogynist transnational imaginaries" (236). What follows is a brief description of some of these monsters.

The Spanish Conquest Experience: Keeping the Cry for Our People

The Spanish Conquest is a period in the Latina/o history defined by out-of-this-world apocalyptic transformations, the genesis of our "modern" mestizo Latina/o monstrous history. This period of extreme crisis was built on the premise of the cultural supremacy of European settlers in the Americas. The horrors of forced acculturation, sexual policing and rape, biological warfare, and the imposition of foreign religious, social, and economical norms called for the emergence of unique monsters that haunt us until today, as 'reminders' of the horror of cultural genocide and colonial violence. La Llorona or Weeping Woman with its pre-Columbian conquest and postcolonial imperial connections, expansions, and evolutions, signifies an entity that represents this period. It is because of its great geographic dissemination within the Americas, its vast variations but simultaneous consistency at the core of the legend, that we can conclude the emergence of La Llorona during the conquest/colonial era (Perez 17) as a mix of indigenous and Spanish elements, as a mestizo product. The earliest account related to La Llorona in Mexico, and the American Southwest has been linked with the Aztec goddesses Cihuacoalt, an ancient Mexica-Aztec mother goddess. In particular, La Llorona has been connected to one of the eight omens believed to occur in Tenochtitlan (Mexico City today), before the arrival of the Spanish conquistadors in 1519, and presented by Fray Bernardino de Sahagún in his *Historia genera de las cosas de la Nueva España*.[1] In his account, a woman was heard weeping and crying throughout the city and by Lake Tetzcoco, "O my children, we are about to go forever. Oh my children, where am I to take you?" (Perez 17).

One of the tales about La Llorona depict an indigenous woman in a relationship with a Spanish man, who killed their children by drowning them in water (in a river, lake, or the ocean) after betrayal. She will become La Llorona. In many cases La Llorona has been connected to La Malinche, the indigenous Nahua slave given to Hernán Cortés. For centuries, La Malinche has been represented negatively and erroneously as a traitor, and in part responsible for the defeat of the Aztecs. Chicanas and third world feminists of color in the U.S. have challenged this reading, and have re-signified La Malinche as the "mother" of a mestizo race, as a symbol of resilience of women to their mistreatment and abuse by patriarchy. Foremost, her desperate weeping has been interpreted as crying for the "ongoing colonial project" (Perez 19) that connects the Americas, the South and the North, their past and present. It is in this context that La Llorona is called the "eternal mother who refuses to give up on her children" (Perez 36), always weeping and looking for them. For Mark Glazer, La Llorona cries for her "children [that] are lost because of their assimilation into the dominant culture or because of violence and prejudice" (77). La Llorona calls for a community emancipated from the haunting effects of our oppressive condition. As Alicia Gaspar de Alba explains, La Llorona through her cry gives a community "voice lessons" (292) to express its despair and cry for justice.

Nineteenth Century U.S. Expansionism: The Dangerous Bandido

The ideology of exceptionalism, as exhibited by Manifest Destiny and its continental expansions, defined in particular the second half of the nineteenth century in the United States. This ideology (and the tensions about race) framed the Mexican/United States war and the implementation of the Treaty of Guadalupe Hidalgo. This period is particularly important for those studying monsters in the Latina/o-U.S. context because it is deeply defined by the "construction" of Others, in this case Mexicans and Mexican Americans, as monsters, despite their categorization as "whites." Framing these communities as violent uncivilized savages, as dangerous subjects, was one of the crucial technologies used to justify exclusion and segregation. One example of these social "freak" monsters can be illustrated by the case of Joaquin Murrieta, a bandit famous in California during the California Gold Rush that followed the Mexican/American war. I chose the legend around Murrieta purposely to demonstrate how the construction of a Mexican bandit worked as a tool to present them as monstrous outlaws. Despite the controversy over whether he was a real historical figure, his legend follows many of the characteristics associated with monsters. First, he is presented as a dangerous figure to society, one that threatens social order and attacks "good citizens." In addition, the state not only sponsored the hunting of Murrieta, but it institutionalized the California State Rangers led by a former Texas Ranger, Captain Harry Love. Furthermore, after Murrieta's alleged capture and execution, a monster-freak spectacle was created around this severed head, and people in the state of California were able to pay $1 in order to see his head in a jar at traveling fairs. His dual monsterization and mythification help us to navigate the double representation of Mexicans in the United States, in particular in the Southwest during this period. For example, it is believed that the legend of Murrieta contributed to the creation of the fictional character of El Zorro by Johnston McCulley. The ties between the legend of Murrieta and his Mexican immigrant status, the previous conflict between the United States and Mexico, and the turbulent racial and class relationship between Anglos and Mexicans are evident not only in the narration of the legend, but in the politics of his existence, and the spectacle of monstrosity created around him and the people he represented. Murrieta exemplifies a valuable cultural tool to study a period demarked by the transformation of Mexicans into Americans, from landholders and state runners into farmhands, wage-dependent poor workers, and barrio-segregated second tier citizens. Murrieta as a monster materialized the ideologies of subjugation of the period.

The Twentieth Century Interwar Period and World War II: Monsters Within

In the context of Monster Latina/o Theory, the period after World War I and during World War II in the United States is important because it witnessed the emergence of a different type of social monster. In this case, Latina/os are presented, not only as foreign invaders (as in the case of Joaquin Murrieta) but rather as in-house monsters, blood suckers of social services, incapable of being educated, unwilling (by their nature) to assimilate into the American melting pot and consequently, "harmful" to the progress of the nation and democratic civilization. The notion of Latina/os as social failures, unclean, and violent achieved new proportions during this period. It is precisely during this era that in 1924 the U.S. Border Patrol was established.

The Stock Market Crash of 1929 marked the beginning of the Great Depression, and the subsequent forced relocation of 500,000 to 2 million Mexicans and Mexican Americans to Mexico (Balderrama and Rodriguez 265). The fictitious argument used to justify the forced removal of these communities during the Great Depression, as Francisco Balderrama and Raymond Rodríguez explain, was that they "were on [welfare] relief or were public charges" (99) which was not true. This argument was not the only one used to control, demonize, and monsterize this community in the Southwest during this period. In other areas, like San Antonio, Texas, the rhetoric of poor sanitation and cleanliness, used previously against Chinese immigrants, was used against Mexican Americans, in particular by using the typology of the Chili Queens, or tamale and chili female street vendors that were famous landmarks of the city. As Jeffrey M. Pilcher describes, in 1937, the San Antonio city health officials started an official campaign against these vendors (Pilcher 173) by presenting them as unsanitary examples of the dirty Mexicans, who needed to be controlled, reformed, and contained (Castañeda 223). This monsterization followed a long tradition that began several decades before these food vendors were reconstructed through exotification, over-sexualization, and the xenophobic statements. Nevertheless there was something new:

as Pilcher writes, "the chili queens thus helped create a stereotype of dusky, sharp-witted women, waiting to be tamed by Anglo men." Here, race and class are used to construct undesirable "fictional" subjects for containment, where gender and sexuality are controlled and intersected.

However, it is the pachuco/zoot suiter that, in my opinion, exemplified the social monsters of this era. Despite the fact that the famous Sleepy Lagoon (1944) and Zoot Suit Riots of Los Angeles (1943) happened during World War II, the construction of these monsters was a process that started several years before. Consequently, I do not frame the pachuco/zoot suiters simply as war monsters, but rather as monsters whose genesis happened in the years leading up to the war. Certainly, it is during the Sleepy Lagoon murder case that the pachuco is presented "publically" by state authorities as a bloodthirsty violent monster, with the previous help of the newspapers and the media. For example, Deputy Sheriff Edward Duran Ayres, head of the Foreign Relation Bureau of Los Angeles County Sheriff's Department testifying to the court about the pachuco monster, argued that "all he knows and feels is a desire to use a knife or some lethal weapon ... his desire is to kill, or at least let blood" (Obregón Pagán 162). It is in this context, that Mauricio Mazón in his book *The Zoot-Suit Riots: The Psychology of Symbolic Annihilation* explained the process of monsterization that took place during the Sleepy Lagoon trial. For Mazón, the refusal of the judge to allow the incriminated Mexican American youths to shave, shower, or change clothes during the trial was no different from "carnival freak shows and the display of deformities, aberrations, and the paraphernalia of criminals" (Mazón 28). This was possible, as Mazón explains, because during those turbulent war years "the boundaries between the real enemy and imaginary enemies were fluid" (Mazón 28). As in the case of Murietta, the spectacle of the pachuco was necessary to assert their monstrosity in the collective imagination.

Here, the process of epistemic subjugation enacted by the re-signification of social monsters as manifested in the murder trial is particularly important. Mazón writes,

> The most immediate impact of the [Sleepy Lagoon] case was that it introduced a new way of thinking about zoot-suiters. They were bizarre creatures, somewhat fantastic, subterranean, clearly identifiable by their garb and argot, yet elusive and of uncertain origins. They represented a social anomaly; still they provoked anomalous behavior from the law-abiding citizen ... [They] saw them as a sinister group capable of inflicting great moral and physical harm on society.

> (Mazón 29)

As he presents it, the monsterization of pachuco/zoot suiters was a fictional/imaginary project within the real context of xenophobia and racism, meant to consolidate and perpetuate social inequalities. Here the monster becomes a tangible space of intersection between social fear, racial anxieties, and economic subjugation. The demonization of the pachuco/zoot suiter as a social monster combines both ideology and aesthetics within a judicial system purposely created to contain and domesticate subjects. The core of this particular type of Latina/o monster has remained almost immutable during the rest of the twentieth century and the first decade of the twenty-first; despite the changes experienced in its social form and body, the ideological core has remained consistent.

The Twentieth Century Free Trade-WTO Era: Blood Sucking Vulnerability

Karl Marx described capitalism as a "vampire thirst for the living blood of labour" (Marx 367), a particular entity that "lives only by sucking living labour, and lives the more, the more labour it sucks" (Marx 342). At the same time, Fredric Jameson called our attention to how during the last decades of the twentieth century the world experienced an "original space of some new 'world system' of multinational or late capitalism" (Jameson 50), with unprecedented global spread and strength (Hardt and Weeks 164). These two realities defined the monsters that emerged during this period.

Certainly, one of the characteristics of late capitalism is the creation of transnational market blocs through the signing of multilateral "free" trade agreements between nations. Centralized and organized following colonial paths of exploitation, these free trade blocs regulate the transit of goods, services, labor, taxation, intellectual property rights, and access to markets. As of 2015, most nations in the world are members of the World Trade Organisation,[2] the governing entity for international trade. Latina/os in the United States have been deeply affected by the changes generated by late capitalism; in particular, changes that came in the form of the North America Free Trade Agreement (NAFTA) between Canada, Mexico, and the United States, which came into effect on January 1, 1994—not, coincidentally, the same day that the insurgent Zapatista Army went public in Southern Mexico.

The last decade of the twentieth century saw the emergence of a new type of blood-sucking creature, one that exemplified the characteristics of late capitalism, El Chupacabras, the goatsucker. This creature manifested the atrocities of this period, and the effects of a system based on sucking vulnerability (Calvo-Quirós "Chupacabras" 98). This is a Latina/o monster that materialized the horrendous transformations experienced by these communities, as well as the anxieties and fears projected upon them in the post cold war years. Like the decentralization and outsourcing practices of late capitalism that make it almost impossible to locate, equally the Goatsucker cannot be captured or domesticated. The Chupacabras is the monster of forced migration, proletarization of rural areas, wage dependency, land privatization, unemployment, and the destruction of welfare safeguards for the poor in what Jean Comaroff and John Comaroff call "Millennium Capitalism" (779). In this sense, the Chupacabras is a millennial child. Let us review the context of this blood-sucking creature.

The tryouts of late capitalism were first implemented within the borderlands and the colonies of today's empires. In the case of North America, these experiments first affected, in particular, Puerto Rico and Mexico, as a process of mass decentralization and privatization that defined the 1990s. This monstrous process happened on two levels. First by the reinforcement and re-signification of old colonial laws, such as the Jonas Act (1917), that forced Puerto Rico to only purchase goods from American-made ships with an "American" crew. These colonial laws exponentially continued to increase the prices and restrictions on local business growth.

Secondly, this late capitalism process happened through the implementation of new neoliberal regulations and privatizations. This included, as in the case of Puerto Rico, the sale of telecommunications (1992/1998) and the government shipping company (1995), as well as the implementation of the Executive Reorganization Act of 1993 that restructured key components of local government including public finances, industry, agricultural activities, and social services. The dismantling of several fiscal protections for corporations investing in Puerto Rico was also manifested in this process. The end of fiscal breaks, such as section 936 of the U.S. Internal Revenue Code during this period, proved particularly devastating as it promoted the exodus of pharmaceutical companies, one of the most important sources of revenue and jobs for the island.

It is precisely in this context that the Chupacabras emerged in Puerto Rico, as they witnessed a slow but consistent bleeding-out of their resources and revenues. During the following decades, Puerto Rico as a colonial territory of the U.S., experienced as a consequence of these policies, an overwhelmingly high rate of unemployment and poverty as well as a mass exodus, especially of youth, to the continental United States. By 2015, the "vampire" effects of this slow and chronic colonial death have left the island in a virtual zombie-like state with a deficit of almost $72 billion.

On the other hand for Mexico, the decade leading to the 1990s was defined by similar changes meant to facilitate the implementation of the North American Trade Agreement (NAFTA). These changes included the privatization of *ejidos* or communal landholdings by indigenous communities; the deregulation of import restrictions on grains, particularly of U.S. subsidized corn; and the mass privatization of the government's own infrastructure and services (Calvo-Quirós "Sucking Vulnerability" 97). As in the case of Puerto Rico, the effects of these massive changes did not translate to equal advances for its inhabitants. On the contrary, between 1993 and 2000 "Mexico lost 1.3 million agricultural jobs [...] as little farmers and peasants struggle to complete with large-scale U.S. Producers" (Anderson 94), leaving the poor more dependent upon wage income (World Bank 172). As I explained before,

> Clearly, for those on the losing end, the experience of land dispossession, forced migration, and the loss of their sources for maintaining their families and preserving their culture, could have been perceived as the effects of a monster that was attacking them, one that little by little, was sucking their lives away. In those days, just as today, there were more than just livestock animals dying and succumbing, there were also communal histories, and traditions at stake.
>
> (Calvo-Quirós "Sucking Vulnerability" 215)

The Chupacabras exemplifies the effect of neoliberalism in Latina/o communities as well as the anxieties generated by a post-cold war United States. This monster's form and its characteristics are not random: for those experiencing the effects of mass socio-economic transformations, the realm of the imaginary, provides a useful venue to materialize the hyper-real devastations of exploitation and the implementation of a "new 'world system'" (Jameson 50). As the free trade market territories expanded simultaneously, the habitat and dominion of the Chupacabras increased. Today the Chupacabras can be found as far away as Asia and Russia.

The Neo Anti-Immigrant Nationalist Movements: Slow Dead and La Santa Muerte in the New Millennium

New increased levels of xenophobic violence, the reiteration of anti-immigrant and nativist sentiments have characterized the first decade of the twenty-first century, in particular against Latina/os, Arabs, and Muslims in the United States. As the U.S. (primarily the middle and upper middle classes) started to experience the negative effects of neoliberal policies in their lives, including the erosion of many of their safety-nets such as job security, house ownership, and the questioning of many of their racially based privileges, they turned their anxieties and fears toward more vulnerable communities, part of what I call the terrorizing technologies of distraction of capitalism.

The out-of-this-world violence experienced by marginalized communities did not happen in a vacuum. On the contrary, this was the result of the long-standing legacies of colonialism, the effects of neoliberal policies (e.g. the end of the welfare state, employment outsourcing, the privatization of education, massive incarceration, police brutality, etc.) and the constraints amplified by the "Great Recession." For example, the conjunction of these factors and long-lasting War On Drugs had devastating effects for those communities located along the U.S.-Mexico border, as they experienced the increased slaughter of civilians, state-sponsored trafficking of guns from the U.S. to Mexico and Central America (e.g. Operation Wide Receiver, and Operation Fast and Furious), and the impunity of police corruption. Death, whether coming fast and furiously by violence or long and slowly from the low-intensity war experienced by marginalized communities, has become an everyday experience along the border and the intercities. It is in this context that the devotions to La Santa Muerte (as discussed by Desirée Martin in another chapter in this volume), Jesús Malverde, and Saint Toribio Romo have increased in recent decades. For example, Toribio Romo, an official Catholic saint, has been appearing and assisting migrants as they cross the deadly Sonora Dessert from Mexico to the U.S., especially as immigration policies (e.g. Operation Gate Keeper) have forced displaced workers to leave the usual San Diego and Texas paths of transit for the more deadly routes of Arizona (see Figure 33.1).

The inter-city has become a zombie-like entity, a nightmare-city that is simultaneously dead and alive, depleted of services and investments for its survival, where gentrification has created unconnected hipster-oases within the urban desert. Even before the sub-

Figure 33.1 Deadly Vulnerability: A child playing innocently with a mural of the Santa Muerte in the background, San Antonio Tultitlán, Mexico City (photo by Daniel Hernandez)

prime mortgage crisis, Latino and black barrios experienced the effects of racial steering, poor urban planning, inflated loan rates, pollution, and police surveillance. In this context, La Santa Muerte's increased veneration in Mexico and the United States has been exemplified by the deadly effects of social violence on Latina/os as a predominantly working class urban phenomenon. If the veneration of the Santa Muerte is an example today of a "crisis cult," it is because the values of life, and of life as a human right are in crisis, as are the lives of marginalized poor communities which are "valuated" only through a vampire's notions of labor, and the normalization of race categorizations. Indeed, as Achille Mbembe asserts, we are living in times where we are experiencing the "subjugation of life to the power of death (necropolitics)" (39) to the point that "vast populations are subjected to conditions of life conferring upon them the status of living dead" (40). Certainly, as the nation debates the political correctness of "Black lives matter," Mbembe's assertion that "the function of racism is to regulate the distribution of death and to make possible the murderous functions of the state" (17) is as real as ever. The proliferation of La Santa Muerte among the disposed and the working class is not coincidental, as the experience of death by violence has become the norm of the new millennium. La Santa Muerte is the saint of a millennium where death reigns.

Conclusion

Certainly, monsters have been faithful companions of the Latina/o existence, as well as our consciousness and history of violence. They have scared us, tortured our psyche, and haunted our lives. But foremost they have consistently reminded us about our vulnerabilities and trajectories of oppression. We ourselves have been turned into monsters and freak shows through the social normalization of race, prejudice, and ignorance. Furthermore, each monster's genesis, modus operandi, habitat, preferences, and characteristics have showed us the intrinsic interrelations that exist between the real and the imaginary. Monsters have provided a method to unpack the effects of violence and a forced early death upon our communities. Their study has shown how marginalized communities truly understand their oppressed conditions, and utilize the imagination and the fantastic as tools for emancipation, liberation, and to envision a different world, one outside the constraints of a vampire-like system that feeds on their vulnerability. For communities of color the imaginary is about the real, as the real transforms how they envision their futures. Monsters denounce violence, but they are also tools to defeat the oppressor and ultimately to combat or negotiate violence. Fortunately, because many of these monsters are unnatural racialized fictions, they cannot live forever. The more we know about them, the easier it is to eradicate them. Until then, we keep fighting and exorcising our society.

Notes

1 Based on the written accounts of Fray Bernardino de Shagún, who wrote between 1540–1585, Historia general de las cosas de la Nueva España, known today as the Florentine Codex.
2 The WTO officially started on January 1, 1995, a year after the signing of the Marrakech Agreement (1994).

Bibliography

Anderson, Sarah., et al. *Field Guide to The Global Economy*. New York, NY: The New Press, 2005.

Asma, Stephen T. Introduction. *On Monsters: An Unnatural History of our Worst Fears*. New York, NY: Oxford University Press, 2009. 1–15.

Balderrama, Francisco and Raymond Rodríguez. *Decade of Betrayal: Mexican Repatriation in the 1930s*. Albuquerque: University of New Mexico Press, 1995.

Calvo-Quirós, William A. "Chupacabras: The Strange Case of Carlos Salinas de Gortari and his Transformation into the Chupatodo." *Crossing the Borders of the Imagination*. Ed. María del Mar Ramón Torrijos. Madrid: Instituto Franklin de Estudios Norteamericanos, Universidad de Alcalá, 2014. 95–108.

Calvo-Quirós, William A. "Sucking Vulnerability: Neo Liberalism, The Chupacabras, and the Post Cold-War Years." *The Un/Making of Latina/o Citizenship: Culture, Politics & Aesthetics*. Eds. Ellie D. Hernandez and Eliza Rodriguez Gibson. University of Indiana Press, 2014. 211–34.

Castañeda, Antonia I. "'Que se pudiera defender (So You Could Defend Yourselves)': Chicanas, Regional History, and National Discourses." *Frontiers* 22:3 (2001): 116–42.

Cohen, Jeffrey Jerome. "Seven Theses." *Monster Theory: Reading Culture*. Minneapolis: University of Minnesota Press, 1996. 3–5.

Comaroff, Jean and John Comaroff. "Alien-Nation: Zombies, Immigrant, and Millennial Capitalism." *The South Atlantic Quarterly* 101:4 (2002): 779–805.

de León, Arnoldo. *They Called Them Greasers: Anglo Attitudes Toward Mexicans in Texas, 1821–1900*. Austin: University of Texas Press, 1983.

Durkheim, Emile. *The Elementary Forms of Religious Life*. New York: The Free Press, 1995.

Foucault, Michel. *Society Must be Defended: Lectures at the Collège De France 1975–1976*. New York: Picador, 1997.

Gallop, Jane. *Reading Lacan*. New York: Cornell University Press, 1987.

Gaspar de Alba, Alicia. *'Bad Woman': Sor Juana, Malinche, Coyolxauhqui, and Other Rebels with a Cause*. Austin, TX: University of Texas Press, 2014.

Gilmore, Ruth Wilson. *Golden Gulag: Prisons, Surplus, Crisis, and Opposition in Globalizing*. Berkeley, CA: University of California Press, 2007.

Glazer, Mark. "La Llorona, Magic Realism, and the Frontier." *Beyond Bounds: Cross-Cultural Essays on Anglo, American Indian, and Chicana Literature*. Alburquerque: University of New Mexico Press, 1996. 110–27.

Gonzalez Obregón, Luis. "La Llorona." *Las Calles de México: Leyendas y Sucedidos, Vida y Costumbres de Otros Tiempos*. Mexico City: Editorial Porrúa, [1922] 1988. 9–10.

Gordon, Avery. *Ghostly Matters: Haunting and the Sociological Imagination*. Minneapolis, MN: University of Minnesota Press, 2008.

Hardt, Michael and Kathi Weeks. *The Jameson Reader*. Malden, MA: Blackwell Publishers, 2000.

Hoffman, Abraham. *Unwanted Mexican Americans in the Great Depression: Repatriation Pressures, 1929–1939*. Tucson: University of Arizona Press, 1974.

Jameson, Fredic. *Postmodernism or, The Cultural Logic of Late Capitalism*. Durham: Duke University Press, 2003.

Levina, Marina and Diem-My T. Bui, "Introduction: Toward a Comprehensive Monster Theory in the 21st Century." *Monster Culture in the 21st Century: A Reader*. New York: Bloomsbury, 2013.

Marx, Karl. *Capital Volume 1: A Critique of Political Economy*. Trans. Ernest Mandel. New York: Penguin Books, [1867] 1976.

Mazón, Mauricio. *The Zoot-Suit Riots: The Psychology of Symbolic Annihilation*. Austin, TX: University of Texas Press, 1984.

Mbembe, Achille. "Necropolis." *Public Culture* 15:1: (2003): 11–40.

Merla-Watson, Cathryn J. "Hauted by Voices: Historical Im/materialism and Gloria Anzaldúa's Mestiza Consciousness." *El Mundo Zurdo 3: Selected Words from the 2012 Meeting of the Society for* the Study of Gloria Anzaldúa. Eds. Larissa M. Mercado-Lopez, Sonia Sladívar-Hull, and Antonia Castañeda. San Francisco: Aunt Lute, 2013. 225–41.

Mignolo, Walter. Local Histories/Global Designs: Coloniality, Subaltern Knowledges, and Border Thinking. Princeton, NJ: Princeton University Press, 2000.

Obregón Pagán, Eduardo. Murder at the Sleepy Lagoon: Zoot Suits, Race, and Riot in Wartime L.A. Chapel Hill, NC: University of North Carolina Press, 2003.

Paredes, Américo. "Folklore, lo Mexicano, and Proverbs." Aztlán, The Journal of Chicano Studies, 13:1–2 (1982): 1–11.

Perez, Domino Renee. There Was a Woman: La Llorona from Folklore to Popular Culture. Austin, TX: University of Texas Press, 2008.

Pilcher, Jeffrey M. "Who Chased Out the 'Chili Queens'? Gender, Race, and Urban Reform in San Antonio, Texas, 1880–1943." Food and Foodways: Explorations in the History and Culture of Human Nourishment. 16:3 (2008): 173–200.

Reguillo, Rossana. "The Oracle in the City: Beliefs, Practices and Symbolic Geographies." Social Text 22:4 (2004): 35–46.

Saldívar, Ramón. The Borderlands of Culture: Américo Paredes and the Transnational Imaginary. Durham: Duke University Press, 2006.

Wardle, David. Cicero on Divination, Book 1. Oxford: Oxford University Press, 2007.

World Bank Report, A Study of Rural Poverty in Mexico. Washington, D.C. 2004, http://siteresources. worldbank.org/INTMEXICO/Resources/A_Study_of_Rural_Poverty_in_Mexico.pdf

34

NARCO CULTURA

Ryan Rashotte

On an August morning last July, two fathoms above the delusive white bass of Lake Ontario, my father gave me a piece of advice that I've been turning over with some soreness ever since. "Whenever you feel like friending a member of the Sinaloa Cartel on Facebook," he told me, "… *don't do that.*"

He never said anything about the other major Mexican drug cartels with social-media presence; or about the street gangs and politicians who double their friend requests (so to speak); or about the underworld networks who transport their contraband across Asia, Africa, Europe, and the Americas; or about the Citibank and Wachovia and HSBC Cartels who've laundered their money with what might as well be called judicial impunity;[1] but I understood by the look of disgust on his face that my father meant a great deal more than this, Sinaloa being symbolic of that pernicious shebang, and, moreover, that his concern about my recent academic proclivities was sincere, if a touch melodramatic for 6 a.m. on a family vacation.[2]

What is it about the cartels' use of social media that people find so distressing? Is it the virtual proximity? The surprising e-aptitude? Maybe. Does the brazenness with which *sicarios* forgo privacy and security to look cool to millions of strangers on-line illuminate the dire self-obsession at the heart of social media today? Yes, it's probably some of that, too. For my part, however, what it comes down to is a matter of depth.

When the speed of intercultural dissemination is broadband, and its scope is what Herodotus called "what has come to be," there's a kind of autotelic tendency to skim the surface for whatever is most reflective. Often these days it's four or five pages into a Google search for "narco media," below the WhatsApp ransom notes,[3] the selfies with pet tigers,[4] deep down into the dense and rich abscesses of the Latina zeitgeist, that the old media—the films, the clothes, the songs, even the religious icons—tend to get buried. And this is a real shame. Damn skippy it is.

With the hope of raising these traditional, more durable forms of narco culture back to the critical forefront, where they belong, I've prepared below a little primer in which each of those forms is addressed, their existent scholarship (where applicable) vetted, and brief, largely implicit cases made as to why they should matter, what fungible strain of humanity lies in their profound inhumanity that's worth our attention, our pathos, and, at the very least, a higher Google ranking.

I don't really have a thesis per se, or even at all. And, to be completely honest, this study will probably digress in ways that are at best scholastically irresponsible. But in trying to make sense of a culture developed around a billion-dollar industry that annually destroys thousands of lives while it mellows, wilts, inspires, and unhinges millions more, a culture whose relevance has managed to supersede that ginormous industry by drawing fans from a whole spectrum of Latino pop and beyond, I promise: it may be old-school, it may be deficient in hashtags and continental theory, it may have several more than the zero references to testicles I'd allotted in mind, but the last thing this study will be is disinterested.

So, caveat lector, let's get right to it.

Narco Santo

Across the tracks from the country club in the west end of Sinaloa's modern capital Culiacán stands an 18-foot chapel made of frosted glass and cinder block where the faithful come to split their whiskey with the genius loci.[5] Several chambers lead in to the chapel, each gleaming with the refracted city and packed with oblatory clutter: cola bottles, votive candles, flowers, figurines, knickknacks, artificial limbs, even—what is that? Is that live ammunition? Where the walls aren't covered with plaques and fading photographs they are plastered with American dollar bills and cursive requests for mercy. A three-piece *tambora* band waits at the archway to the inner sanctum, fielding requests for narcocorridos, and one wonders if on a quiet afternoon the accordion's frazzled rumpus could reach the doors of the National Migration Institute, 100 meters west on Indepedencia.

This is the chapel of Jesús Malverde, folk saint of the narcosphere, and though it seems a natural place to begin, I don't want to mislead you. Like the raw material that engenders it, narco culture is vigorously diffuse—its power is in motion, not stasis. At the same time, by its own nostalgia, there can be a deep reverence for origins, which is why we take our hats off as we approach the altar of the handsome saint. Most of the major capos have knelt here, blessed themselves, regarded the plaster bust, argent in the votive light. Its hand-painted visage is said to have been inspired by pictures of Pedro Infante and Jorge Negrete, two of Mexico's golden-age cinema idols,[6] and the resemblance comes across most dapperly in the soft matinée eyes and thick black mustache. Such a handsome mustache, the common *selleckus mexicanus*. Such a prodigal center for a centerless world.

There are other centers, too, of course. Outside the chapel, in the mountains looming beyond the souvenir stands, lies the town of Mocorito, where legend says the saint was born in 1870. And 50-odd kilometers east of Mocorito are the scattered villages of Badiraguato, an agricultural hinterland practically teeming with origins. This is where, in the nineteenth century, Chinese immigrants began cultivating plots of marijuana and poppies, and where, in the late 1920s, Mexican farmers called in the law to help muscle out the Chinese.[7] It's where generations of dirt-poor laborers learned to diversify crops, foster political ties, and accumulate the prestige to turn their households into dynasties.[8] Finally, it was here, in the 1970s, that these nouveau riche barons shrugged off their rustic trappings and ventured forth into the city, bringing to Culiacán, along with their money and grudges, the seeds of a unique narco culture: songs, stories, even a saint, enshrined in 1979 by the railroad tracks where his bones were said to lie (the original stone sepulcher was razed to make room for the state capitol, so sort of an apt center there, as well).[9]

Whether a flesh-and-blood Malverde ever existed is unlikely— his legend draws heavily on the biographies of Heraclio Bernal and Felipe Bachomo, two earlier bandit heroes— but the faithful insist: he was a poor railroad hand, or construction worker, who found his métier stealing from local landowners after his parents died of starvation.[10] Much of his loot was divvied up among the peasants, a point that has inspired some scholars to take him

Figure 34.1   Jesús Malverde (Artwork: Ayumi Shimizu)

primarily as a symbol of class struggle.[11] After his execution, in 1909, his earliest adherents included beggars and prostitutes, and today, migrants are just as likely as drug smugglers to petition him for *un buen camino* to the U.S.[12] Only a fraction of the prayers he's ever received have been illicit in nature.

But Malverde also had a randy side. A heavy and braggy drinker whose idea of wealth redistribution often meant rounds at the cantina,[13] it's fair to say his Robin Hood had some Friar Tuck in him. In fact, you might also say that what makes him such an attractive saint to drug dealers is the fluency with which the two personas conform to one mask, one face, one legend. To the heavyweights who admire him, this synthetic appeal is obvious. How manly your indulgences must look when they append your heroics; and how forgivable your crimes must seem when you accept them as acts of social conscience.

Despite what Rome or the Drug Enforcement Agency (DEA) has to say on the matter, thousands will testify to Malverde's sanctity. And be they criminal or civilian, rich or poor, these adherents will continue making the pilgrimage beyond the tracks to share their whiskey, continue dividing their petitions between the preacher on the cross, the virgin on the hill, and the bandit hanging from the mesquite bough. A dark and taciturn bandit whose mustache has become its own form of ideology in this macho world.

It is an excellent 'tache. Please take a moment in the inner sanctum to admire it yourself. And know that any donations you leave behind will cover the medical expenses of the local poor, and pay for their funerals when all else fails.[14]

Do ut des, motero.

Narco Corrido

Alright, that was "El Bandido Generoso," by Chalino Sánchez, one of Sinaloa's favorite sons, here on WNCO: Narco Radio.

How many traumatic polkas you can croon along with on the flatbed from greater Tucson to the watermelon fields will demonstrate an affinity with narco culture that may be held against you in a court of law. How many of those polkas are Chalino's, how many of his three-minute ballads, comic and tragic, knightly and orcish: here's the measure of a true crimin—connoisseur. For though not the first troubadour of drug trafficking (narcocorridos date back to the 1930s, and are themselves modern versions of nineteenth-century folk songs about bandit heroes battling oppressive *federales*[15]), experts nevertheless agree that Chalino was the original bad ass. Straight outta Sinaloa, a migrant, hustler, smuggler, killer, and, from the day he began charging local traffickers to hear their crimes sung in major keys, a folksinger, and a thoroughly grisly one at that. His clothes were plain, but tidy. His eyes were slits. His lyrics could be tea-spittingly graphic in their depiction of execution and torture.[16] The searching quiver of his high A is the pitch that led the genre from its spiffy 1970s revival (associated with groups like Los Tigres del Norte) toward the violent street-smart *valiente* style still favored by superstars today.[17] And so before we move on, let's give it up one more time for Chalino Sánchez (b. 1960, Sinaloa—d. 1992, Sinaloa).

Commercially speaking, narcocorridos are commissioned by both traffickers and professional studios. Generically, they're composed in first- or third-person, and classified as *bandas* (performed by brass bands, a style associated with north-western Mexico) or *norteños* (accordion-led, associated with the north).[18] Sonically, despite these differences, it's all real zesty stuff. Part Guthrie, part Dre, part Shmenge. Songs of marrow and brass. Sponsored testimonials of gonadal amplitude.[19] Octosyllables, monomyth, perfect fourths. Accordion that flits and probes around the bass's *oom-pah-pah* like a hummingbird at the lip of a whiskey jug. And the trumpet blasts. And the tuba poots. And the pre-recorded gunspray, which rang out at a hundred decibels on a dark dance floor in L.A. will instantly mark all underpants in the house belonging to newbies.

And then of course, there's the academic *grito*—"counter-hegemonic"[20] —, which has played high in the mix since scholars discovered this music and made it the centerpiece of narco-cultural studies. Luís Astorga calls the corridist the "true creator of the constitutive myths of the trafficker's world vision ... of [his] transmutation from stigma into emblem;"[21] Mark Cameron Edberg identifies the genre as "both contemporary narrative and homage to a transcendent myth;"[22] and John H. McDowell argues that this music offers Latinos "a zone of commemorative practice where disruptive historical events can be processed through artistic conventions."[23]

Objections have been raised against the genre's brazen consumerism and misogyny;[24] and full-scale attacks levied against its self-purported "authenticity" (deconstruction remaining a strong moral imperative in today's humanities departments, the corridists' claim to speak *la pura verdad* to power has occasioned more thoughtful antagonism,[25] by and large, than lyrics like, "Their intestines were hanging out and a dog was eating them,"[26] or, "We're bloodthirsty madmen, we like to kill,"[27] or, "I got plastered ... and then fucked [her] 'til I was retarded").[28]

But even the most disparaging scholars are downright cordial compared to the genre's true enemies. For decades, the Mexican government has been passing legislation to prohibit the retail and performance of narcocorridos under auspices of public morality.[29] Currently, the national Army and Air Force Studies Center offers a module on the genre, in which "officers deconstruct [!] the songs to learn more about the enemy."[30] And for every Luís Astorga insisting the corridist is the "organic intellectual" of drug trafficking,[31] there's probably a group of interns at News Corp scanning the linear notes for just the right couplet to evince the horror of a roving Mexicanidad. Reading highlights of Donald Trump's presidential bid (recent at the time of writing), some of the mogul's views on migrants couldn't help cue a track by Sinaloan quartet Calibre 50 in my subcortical playlist. See if you can guess whose bombast is whose:

> When Mexico sends its people … They're sending people that have lots of problems and they're bringing those problems with us [sic].
> The guys come around, chugging Johnnie Walker and Buchanan's … Enjoying the best because life is short.
> They're bringing drugs. They're bringing crime.
> They're packing bazookas and grenades.
> They're rapists.
> [They're] disturbed.[32]

I'm not suggesting the song's hyperbole gives credence to Trump's own (at this point it's hard to take anything the Donald says as more than just smoke from a noxiously fading GOP); rather I'm evoking the scholarly argument that by reclaiming stereotypes so exaggeratedly, sometimes to the point of cynicism,[33] but always with an auxiliary accordion lick to corral hard feelings back to the fiesta, the narcocorrido allows fans to reimagine what it means to be "criminal," even what it means to be Mexican, in a country where discrimination against Latina/os is a national tradition, and people like Trump loudly exist.[34]

As for the violence—the hyper-violence—well, sure, some of it can be pretty unsettling. And citing lyrics about decapitation isn't likely to win you any post-docs (trust me). But that doesn't mean the fantasy-reality barrier is somehow more breachable here than in other pop cultural avenues, and it's to their credit that academics who study the corrido tend to accept this as a given. Shaylih Muehlmann argues that "rather than naturalize violence or desensitize the public to its horrors, corridos are locally understood to heighten awareness of the violence," telegraphing info that the government *and the narcos* would otherwise suppress.[35]

As for the misogyny: nope, not going to defend that on any grounds.

As for the conspicuous consumption—sure, for some listeners, this makes a fair strike three. But the kind of greed these songs extol is hardly exclusive to borderlands folklore. Zadie Smith once defended charges of hip hop's materialism by reminding us that "boasting is a formal condition of the epic form. And those taught that they deserve nothing rightly enjoy it when they succeed in terms the culture understands."[36] It would be hypocritical of me to criticize Gerardo Ortíz's paean to Prada sunglasses and Hugo Boss,[37] all cavalier and Marxist-like, when the truth is, if that was my wardrobe, I'd sing songs to people about it, as well.

Finally, as for the notion that a minor academic's ambivalence should have any import whatsoever on the evolution of a hugely successful populist Latino music, it's like songwriter Mario Quintero says, "The people want to hear narcocorridos. We are not going to give meat to an audience of vegetarians."[38]

Narco Gastronomy

Hold on. Can we go back to the corridos for a second?

I don't know if it was the full moon, or the soft tacos (about which, *yikes!*, more in a moment); it could have been the fact that I cited Calibre 50 to support a thesis on counter-hegemony—Calibre 50, whose major hit, "El Tierno Se Fue" (Tender No More) is sung from the rapist's point of view—but I was up all night rethinking my conclusions on the narcocorrido. Some of the issues just can't be resolved in the space I've allowed them.

The issue of censorship, for example. Not exactly a controversial one in the current discourse. Many scholars avoid it, or treat it as anecdotal, and the ones who deal with it substantially seem to be in resounding agreement: no. Banning the corridos to stop the violence is just the sort of patronizing, head-in-the-sand legislation you'd expect from a government hoping to divert publicity from its ineptitude (not to mention its collusion) in dealing with the cartels.[39] Hector Amaya calls it an "antiquated" solution, "blind to the increasing centrality of transnationalism and new media technologies;"[40] and journalist Elijah Wald, the genre's Alan Lomax, argues that prohibition is an attack on the subaltern class as much as on the narcos.[41]

Such criticism is valid, and on brighter days, it would be unimpeachable. What I'm wondering is, in the midst of an ongoing drug war, which in addition to being a war that takes thousands of lives each year, is very much a battle of representation—a battle being won in Nuevo Laredo and Ciudad Juárez by the cartels who now control the presses,[42] a battle that's taken the lives of over a hundred journalists and bloggers, and threatened thousands more[43] for reporting basic details such as these[44]—might we instead see censorship as a progressive measure intended to tip the representational scale toward realism and objectivity, to encourage journalistic solidarity by demanding nothing but the truth?[45]

> Okay, that makes … some sense (says my inner contrarian, whom let's call here Deconstructive Steve). But if you allow the government to censor music they consider propaganda, what's to stop them from restricting any sort of cultural production that makes them look bad? Remember, historically, the federal government has shown a tendency to reserve statistics that are particularly grisly.[46] And if the Sinaloan state legislature had its way in 2014, crime scenes would be off limits to the media altogether,[47] giving presses little to report other than handed-down pieces of an official narrative about waning violence and victory to come.[48] The horizon is being crayoned pastel by a government that we know has ordered troublesome journalists beaten and killed, sometimes in collaboration with the cartels,[49] and you're taking their side against the poets?

Well, but consider, too, that—I'll get to food in a moment—by lauding the corridos, you're encouraging musicians to take assignments that are potentially fatal. This isn't hyperbole: writing a corrido for the wrong man can get you killed.[50] Agreeing to perform at the wrong party can get you killed.[51] And as the assassinations of Valentín Elizalde, Sergio Gómez, and Chalino Sánchez, and the recent attack on Gerardo Ortíz have proven, even the superstars aren't safe from retaliation. This is about public safety.

> Whoa, slow down there, *Footloose*. It takes a "public" to make a case for "public safety." Who, besides government detractors, would support such oppressive policy in this day and age?

Figure 34.2 El Gallo (Artwork: Ayumi Shimizu)

Um, how about 64 percent of people living in Mexico?[52] That includes politicians from the left, right, and center,[53] public intellectuals like Javier Sicilia,[54] ex-corridists and film-makers who've seen the body counts rise and chosen to stop making art "that encourage[s] admiration for the narcos."[55] If scholars insist on condemning the censorship pro forma, they should know that by doing so, the burden of that less fashionable pro-censorship argument falls harder on those who deal with narco violence on a daily basis.

> I see what's going on here. You don't actually endorse censorship. You know there are talented musicians and songwriters in the narcosphere, that it's not all eve-teasing and blood for blood's sake. And yet the opportunity to call out a bunch of scholars for arguing the subaltern's perspective in a voice only grad students could love—this strikes you as irresistible, doesn't it? Probably because it implies your own street smarts by comparison. The thing you don't seem to realize, though, jerk, is that by siding with that 60 percent—

64 percent

> —64 percent, you're also using the narcocorrido to signal your radical cred, just in a different key. I bet this whole thing ends with some punch line about how obtuse academic jargon sounds when it's applied to real-life problems. As if you've got a better handle on those problems than scholars from Sinaloa. You ever think shenanigans like this have something to do with why you're still an "independent scholar"?

Look, I don't have a good answer. What I have is a word count, a strict one, so let's leave this for now. As for the narco gastronomy stuff, I'm afraid we'll have to let that go, too. By way of summary, I'll mention that in 2015 it was widely reported that one of the main syndicates in Michoacán was forcing recruits to eat human hearts to demonstrate their loyalty.[56] To the government who officially condemns the violence, and to those corridists who trade on it, at least here's some propaganda to benefit both sides. And to scholars who'll go on praising the corrido's subaltern "counterdiscursive" narrative while overlooking its power to encourage the violence by eliciting public support for the cartels (*oh boy, here it comes*), for realism's sake, could we maybe just get a moratorium on "simulacra,"[57] and "zone of the imaginary,"[58] at least until the heart-eating stops?

Alright. You and me? We're done here. Finish this thing on your own.

Moving on.

Narco Husbandry

A brief lesson in narco slang: *gallo* (rooster) = marijuana, *chiva* (goat) = heroin, and *perico* (parakeet) = cocaine.[59] Which, verbum pro verbo, must make for some pretty Mad Libbish obituaries.

Narco Couture

The balaclava's garnered something of a harsh rap this season. What was once the mask of Mexican-rebel chic[60] is now widely panned by police, both fashion and *federale*, as the crude disguise of goons like al-Qaeda and ISIS ... or like Horacio, strutting down the runway in this field ensemble from *Chacaloso Homme*. The black Kevlar body suit and scuffed camo boots might not be dashing in the Pedro Infante sense, but what they take away from agility they redouble in hit points—not to mention *fit* points. Whether cruising the streets of Nuevo Laredo in a steel-plated tank or beheading rivals on YouTube, our model's not afraid to go ballistic in this tactical outfit that howls and pleads, "fashion!" Thank you, Horacio.

Since 37-year-old capo Edgar Valdez Villarreal was photographed wearing one at his arrest in 2010, no fewer than seven major traffickers have been hauled before the cameras sporting the relaxed-fit "Big Pony" jersey from Ralph Lauren, a trend that has sent admirers flocking to flea markets all over Mexico for $13.50 knock-offs.[61] Says one vendor, "The guys who buy them want people to think they're tough. It's about putting on a look."[62] And what a look! Cotton mesh with vented hem, it turns out, offers the perfect backdrop for the ten pounds of jewelry our next model is dangling below his sneering handlebar. Gold crosses, encrusted pendants,[63] enough gilded swag to illuminate, Damascus style, that narcos are among the most fashion-conscious of culture villains. Some cartels have even begun manufacturing uniforms with their own logos.[64] For us civilians, indie houses like Antrax and El Cartel Clothing offer everything from t-shirts with fake bullet holes to custom bullet-proof vests interwoven with Burberry appliqué.[65] But it's an open market, yet. According to the DEA, Hollister, Abercrombie, and Ed Hardy are the hottest brands for today's *narco juniors*[66] (which proves a pet theory of mine that anyone in this hemisphere wearing an Ed Hardy t-shirt is probably a career criminal, if only in the *Scarface*-postered walls of his imagination).

Next on the catwalk is ... oh my. Hello, "dark eyes." Hello, "round, swelling breasts." And hello to you, "curves of overwhelming sensuality."[67] Could it be? Why it must! No narca could turn our lupine friends in the press box more sheepish than Sandra Ávila

Beltrán, *la Reina del Pacifico*, herself; and no-one else so yowserfully fleshes out the stereotype of the sensuous narca, which Elaine Carey argues is frequently pushed to the point of caricature (read: nymphomania) by the U.S. and Mexican media.[68] As those curves pop left, pop right, wheel around, and flounce away from my defibrillating heart, it would be useful to remind everyone that this "skintight-jeans-clad stunner" (in the words of *Marie Claire*)[69] is an exception to the rule. None of the other 46 female cartel leaders arrested in recent years have sat down with Anderson Cooper on CNN, or inspired literary biographies replete with silly quotable descriptions of eyes and curves.[70] In fact, most women in the drug trade tend not to see their work as heroic escapade, but rather as family sacrifice, one which can shame them deeply if discovered—and one much more lucrative when undertaken anonymously.[71]

Our final model, on the other hand, here's a stereotype more than happy to shake that ass all over the narcosphere. Fernando's sporting the classic *chero* look: cowboy hat, pavonine silk shirt, blue jeans prêt-à-monter, belt buckle with marijuana-leaf inlay. And, of course, what accessory better says *bona fide traficante* than boots of distressed alligator (it's a fact that alligator is wildly expensive, and tenderer feet must contend with lesser lizard).[72] According to corridists, filmmakers, and pretty much the entire narco-culture industry, this is what a trafficker looks like: browbeating and gimcrack, shirts of a faded brightness, cocked smile, big gut, eyes full of rustic mettle. Ready at the crack of life's thunder to draw his pistol and strike ... a pose, that is. Chicness, thy name is Fernando Bustamante Perez de Tres Iglesias.

Narco Cinema

One of the great scholastic rewards of narco cinema is its ability to combine the other forms of narco culture—the songs, the saints, the snazz—into a 90-minute narrative full of explosions and moral lessons about staying true to your roots.[73] I'm not talking about *Miss Bala* or *Traffic*, no no no. These b-films are some of the b-est productions in world cinema, sparing almost every expense to deliver us their formulaic and *à clef* versions of narco lore. Weeks after a kingpin is brought to justice, you can count on a studio like La Raza Mex or JS Films to dump his legend, prepackaged, into the discount DVD bin at Wal-Mart. Give it a week for that same legend to begin amassing view counts on YouTube.

As far as indie cinema goes, there is a lot to be desired. No, that's not good enough. In many cases, there are still entire films to be desired. With maximum budgets of $50,000, even the best movies at times seem intolerant of basic cinematographic principles.[74] Expository in dialogue, melodramatic in plot, ketchupy in violence, they offer a ruthless affront to connoisseurs who might appreciate the folkways quality of the corridos but would squirm at the sight of an unshorn Mario Almada stabbing men in the blood packs, or laying down with women four decades his junior. In short, narco cinema draws out to make inescapable the underlying violence and kitsch and machismo of narco culture in the most banal of ways, and by doing so, it becomes that culture's epitomic form. I'm not ashamed to say that it tickles me right under the chin. Scholars can keep their vinyl *Corridos Prohibidos*; I'd rather hear Los Tigres del Norte harmonize over the psychedelic title sequence to *Contrabando y traición* (*Smuggling and Betrayal*), or watch them serenade a Brownsville pool hall in *La banda del carro rojo* (*The Red Car Gang*), knowing that beyond the next chorus looms a cheesy shoot-out and one to grow on.

Contrabando and *Carro rojo* both premiered in 1976, and are the two defining films of the genre.[75] Over the next fifteen years, and sometimes with cartel funding, narco cinema would develop a robust catalog, and habitually win the approval of working-class audiences in Mexico and the U.S. borderlands. If quality took a fatal stumble behind quantity in the 1990s, when production budgets declined and most films went straight to VHS (as many as 200 of them a year),[76] things have lately turned around. Digital video is the medium of choice for today's directors, and the explosions look brighter, the screams cut through cleaner than ever. As long as the drug war continues, narco cinema will endure as a unique borderlands art form sure to delight its core audience, and alienate the holy hell out of most everyone else.

I'm not being coy. Even academics and journalists have tended to keep a wide distance.[77] Until recently, the most thorough study of the genre was a 20-minute *Vice* doc (which predictably was a bit solecistic and brocephean for scholarly taste). And this is just one reason why it was a tremendous boon to academe and the wider world beyond when Ryan Rashotte's *Narco Cinema: Sex, Drugs and Banda Music in Mexico's B-Filmography* appeared in 2015 to bung that scholarly void. What a handsomely composed survey this is. Its analyses of key films are by turns lean and sinewy, its study of aesthetic criteria firm and lustrous as marble, marble buttocks. This is scholarship with just tremendous hair. (I'm really sorry about this, but imagine what poor verisimilitude I'd be responsible for without some obnoxious self-promotion. If it helps, please know that like most braggadocio, these claims come courtesy of some very broken places.)

Anyway, seductive as that tome may appear, one of the thousands of films it doesn't consider is *La Fuga del Chapo* (*Chapo's Escape*), a fictional account of Sinaloan godfather Joaquín "El Chapo" Guzmán's escape from jail in 2001. After serving almost eight years for drug trafficking and sundry kingpin behavior, Chapo was able to bribe his way out of the federal penitentiary and, for the next thirteen years, confound authorities by constantly changing locations while turning his Sinaloa Cartel into one of the world's most formidable criminal organizations. When he was finally captured, in 2014, his mug shot signaled that the era of impunity had passed, and that the government had finally taken the upper hand in its war with the narcos.

Then, on July 11, 2015, the actual no-fooling day I sat down to write this subsection, the unthinkable happened: El Chapo escaped from prison again, enraging the DEA, and sending Mexico into a metaphysical freak-out over the scale of its political corruption and ineptitude. Since there's no more appropriate way for me to honor that synchronicity, or to pass the time until a sequel appears, let's take a brief look at this film, directed by Arturo Martínez, Jr. and released, on video, just months after the original flight.[78]

We begin in Guatemala, rainy season, 2001. Over the opening credits, a dour manacled Chapo (Everardo Licea) is led in slow motion toward a holding cell by Lt. Rodriguez (Rogelio Guerra), a grizzled federal narcotics officer so disgusted by El Chapo and his criminal antics he must be restrained from drawing his pistol, delivering the capo instead a swift knee to the groin, an act of vigilantism which, unfortunately for Chapo, initiates a series of copycat assaults. By the time Chapo's been processed, and the warden's gone over the prison rules in a deep voice, his poor avocados will have been kneed and butted so many times I can taste that bilious guacamole myself.

While Chapo recovers in a holding cell, over in Mexico a kindly, slow-witted journalist named Francisco (Alberto Estrella) is researching an editorial on drug trafficking. Knowing nothing about the subject by his own goofy admission, he seeks out Lt. Rodriguez and, over several meetings, manages to pester the *federale* to the point of endearment with trenchant journalistic questions along the lines of, so who is this Guzmán character, anyway? And what exactly *is* a maximum-security prison? Is it possible anyone might escape one?

We interrupt this exposition to bring you a car chase! Spinning out over the Texcoco desert, two mini-cyclones of white sand, Capcom Rock at full blast, chrome erumpent and lapping at the day's good light—apropos of nothing at all. Or almost nothing: this is one of several action sequences meant to show how ruthlessly the cartel deals with snitches and deadbeats—i.e., by outracing and outarming them, and then making them beg in vain for their lives. The problem is there are so many of these scenes, and they're all basically the same, that if you can't muster the adrenaline to get on board, you're stuck checking your watch until *bang! Bang! Bang!* Down they go. *Bang!*

Meanwhile, since his transfer to Mexican prison, El Chapo, too, has become restless. With the pressure of his 20-year sentence mounting, the walls of his cell close in. "I need air!" he yells out, and instructs his lawyer to bargain with the corrupt warden for a few afternoons of prison leave. Fortuitously, when Francisco gets lost on his way to interview the warden, he happens to spot El Chapo gallivanting in a nearby park. Francisco proceeds to show photos of said gallivanting to Lt. Rodriguez, and the two storm back to the prison in search of answers. So furious are they in their righteousness, however, that when a garbage truck passes them at the prison gates, they barely notice. With Chapo nowhere to be found, Rodriguez and Francisco must satisfy their justice lust by arresting the warden. End scene. Score one for the good guys, kind of.

In case you nodded off at some point, denouement is a highlight reel of the previous 80 minutes—Chapo pacing his cell, blasting suckers—while a corridist, hunkered over his guitar, sings surely of arms and the man. This is the seventh corrido to be played at full length. That's a lot of music. In fact, if we break down the film's running time, we see that 11:56 minutes (13 percent of the film) have been allotted to non-essential fight and chase scenes; 1:06 minutes (1 percent) to a cock fight, an actual real-life animals-were-harmed-in-the-making-of-this-film cock fight; and 22:17 minutes (a whopping 25 percent) to narcocorrido interludes, which take the form of montages like this one, or ersatz music videos, like the one featuring Los Zainos del Norte, which stands out as a cinematographic WTF in this film of heavy boom mics (as if nursing a grudge, the lead singer keeps turning a sharp 90 degrees away from the cameraman, who eventually retaliates by snaking backward from the singer in wide decentering pans, at one point blocking him entirely behind a tree, the effect of which mutual repulsion is like being in an intermittent staring contest with a stranger).

What this means is that 39 percent of the film isn't concerned with advancing the plot at all. It's a testosterone drip. It's accordion solos and offings. His delivery of this excess, by word or buckshot, is what makes Chapo the film's hero, the patron with the best fireworks. We shouldn't underestimate the catharsis in this. When Chapo is booked into Guatemalan prison, in midst of all that testicular violence, the warden informs him, "your constitutional rights are now suspended … from now on you are no longer a person." Things improve steadily in Mexico, where his commissary pushes ten figures, but under cellblock lights the luxuries seem so basic: a platter of finger foods, a couple bottles of good booze, a mini TV, some private time with his lawyer and girlfriend. What Chapo really wants is mobility, a little air, a little music, a chance to see the horses gallop freely now and then so as to make his 20-year sentence endurable. Viewers who can appreciate the monotony of his routine and the stigma of his criminality (a stigma earned for providing Americans a basic agricultural service, you see where I'm going with this)—not to mention his genuine pride in rural roots—may naturally cheer when he's able to confound his oppressors.

The problem, as far as character development is concerned, is that this is where Chapo's ends. Licea's stubborn Napoleonic features may give his capo the façade of a strategist, but his actions are more impulsive than tactical. When it's time to flee the prison, all he has to do is pay his bills and then creep real cat-like toward the garbage truck waiting to take him home; there's no final test of wits, the wooden gate slides open, and this viewer is left imagining how much more exciting Chapo's real escape must have been. In the end, it's Francisco the simple journalist who grows under the tutelage of the good cop, and therein lies the audience's sympathetic dilemma: if we want maturity from our hero, we identify with the journalist learning to make sense of this corrupt world; if we wouldn't mind getting a little corrupted ourselves, high-stepping to those *norteño* grooves, Chapo's our guy. Ultimately, it's the latter identification that proves most realistic. Everyone knows that making sense of the narcosphere is a fool's errand; and that the capo with the most money always goes free.

Narco Morbo

Two klicks east of the Malverde Chapel in the west end of Culiacán are the Jardines de Humaya, a 50-year-old funerary grounds named for the river that joins the city to the mighty Pacific. Many of Sinaloa's heroes are interred here, some beneath slabs of unchiseled cement, others in two-story mausoleums with bullet-proof cupolas and security cameras.[79] The higher-end crypts, which can retail for just under half a million USD,[80] come equipped with solar panels to power their central-air units and entertainment centers. Around one of the slabs, a group of coeds who've been drinking all night in memoriam, declares proudly, "We have narco culture running in our veins."[81]

Malverde statues appear from time to time,[82] but in these disparate and ostentatious pastures it's the other folk saint who holds sway. *La Flaquita*, the Skinny Girl, as she's known, or *la Madrina*, the Godmother, though you might recognize her formal title: *Nuestra Señora de la Santa Muerte*, Our Lady of Holy Death. Often depicted as a scythe-wielding skeleton in a bridal gown, she is said to be particularly merciful to devotees.[83]

Santa Muerte is the most-recent avatar of death in over five centuries of Mexican syncretism. The affinity with criminals that marked the early stages of her cult, in the 1980s, has grown to include as many as 12 million followers today, regular folk who visit her shrines throughout the borderlands to pray for good health, and better luck.[84] Even police and military now count themselves by the regiment among her adherents,[85] a fact that didn't stop President Calderón from singling her out as the symbol of narco culture most offensive to his iconoclastic vision of a post-war Mexico. In an act that has proved just as futile as banning the corridos, the Mexican army demolished 40 Santa Muerte shrines in 2009.[86] Predictably, statues of the Godmother continue to turn up at drug raids. And with violence increasing, and no end to the drug war in sight, the capos who commissioned her original public shrines have more reason than ever to rebuild them.[87] What better protectorate could one ask for in a perpetual war that's already killed over a hundred thousand?[88] Does the government really expect to win the battle against Death herself?

In his analysis of the narcocorrido, Mark Cameron Edberg argues that "the narco trafficker persona is not complete unless he or she has been betrayed or is dead ... death is an ontological stage in the completion of this character."[89] I would take this further. What narcocorridist Paulino Vargas calls the *morbo*—and what Elijah Wald translates as "a sickness unto death," "a weird attraction," and "a particular style of speaking, a twist one gives to language"[90]—this may be the animating force behind the forms of narco culture we've studied today. It's the fake bullet holes in the t-shirts. It's the gore onscreen and the ironic remove salutary to our receiving it. It's the hegemony scholars don't mean when they

Figure 34.3   Santa Muerte (Artwork: Ayumi Shimizu)

talk about "counter-hegemonic" folk songs. It's the saint sipping whiskey with his everlasting stare, and the saint sewing bones into the earth's shallows at sundown. No matter how cartoonishly rendered, no matter how analogously received, the intrinsic morbidity of narco culture is what habitués of that culture know all too well, and what future scholars might keep in mind. Drugs may be the matter, death is the art.

On that note, it's time for us to part ways. The urge in the graveyard is to continue philosophizing over the silence, but what more could I say? When the solutions to the drug war are so simple and yet so utterly impossible, restating them by way of conclusion might make that nihilism a bit more palatable, but it would be rude of me to hog the catharsis, which I hope to have shown is already abundant in narco culture itself.

The gate's to the left. Follow the echo of accordion down Godfather's row. Stop by to watch a DVD in the *Jefe de Jefe's* mausoleum.

Or try another route. Wherever you wish to seek your communion, the paths in this narcosphere are short and twisted, glitzy and dim, and at last they pull back to the same place.

Notes

1 Rafa Fernandez De Castro, "A Drug Cartel Guide to Laundering Millions." *Fusion* (2014).
2 This intro is a conceit—I do not use the Facebook. The cartels, however, they've been all over social media since the MySpace era. See Katie Collins, "Guns, Gore and Girls: The Rise of the Cyber Cartels." *Wired* (2014); Priscila Mosqueda, "Mexican Drug Cartels Are Using Social Media Apps to Commit Virtual Kidnappings." *Vice* (2014); S. Womer and R.J. Bunker, "Sureños Gangs and Mexican Cartel Use of Social Networking Sites." *Small Wars & Insurgencies.* 21:1 (2010): 87; Karla Zabludovsky, "Public Relations, Narco Style." *Newsweek* (January 15, 2014).
3 Mosqueda.

4 Joseph Cox, "Mexico's Drug Cartels Love Social Media." *Vice* (2013).

5 Heh, heh—never been there, myself. The description in these opening paragraphs has been assembled from details in: James H. Creechan and Jorge de la Herrán Garcia, "Without God or Law: Narcoculture and Belief in Jesús Malverde." *Religious Studies and Theology*. 24:2 (2005): 8–13; Sam Quinones, *True Tales from Another Mexico: The Lynch Mob, the Popsicle Kings, Chalino, and the Bronx* (Albuquerque: University of New Mexico Press, 2001), 225–29; Ida Rodríguez, "El Culto a Jesús Malverde." Instituto de Investigaciones Estéticas, Universidad Nacional Autónoma de México, 11; Elijah Wald, *Narcocorrido* (New York: HarperCollins, 2001), 61–2.

6 Wald, *Narcocorrido*, 67.

7 Jorge Alan Sánchez Godoy, "Procesos de institucionalización de la narcocultura en Sinaloa." *Frontera Norte* 21:41 (2009): 87–8.

8 Luís Astorga, "Drug Trafficking in Mexico: A First General Assessment." *UNESCO*.

9 Creechan and de la Herrán Garcia, 8; Wald, *Narcocorrido*, 62.

10 Quinones, 227; Rodríguez, 7.

11 Creechan and de la Herrán Garcia, 16.

12 Creechan and de la Herrán Garcia, 12; Rodríguez, 8; Wald, *Narcocorrido*, 64.

13 Wald, *Narcocorrido*, 66.

14 Quinones, 232.

15 Helena Simonett, *Banda: Mexican Musical Life Across Borders* (Middletown, CT: Wesleyan University Press, 2001), 203; Wald, *Narcocorrido*, 13.

16 Cathy Ragland, *Música Norteña: Mexican Migrants Creating a Nation Between Nations* (Philadelphia: Temple University Press, 2009), 10; Wald, *Narcocorrido*, 73.

17 Wald, *Narcocorrido*, 71–2.

18 Helena Simonett, "Narcocorridos: An Emerging Micromusic of Nuevo L.A." *Ethnomusicology* 45:2 (2001): 316.

19 Not just male gonads; see Jenni Rivera's "Ovarios."

20 Hector Amaya, "The Dark Side of Transnational Latinidad: Narcocorridos and the Branding of Authenticity." *Contemporary Latina/o Media: Production, Circulation, Politics* (New York: New York University Press, 2014): 226; Chris Muniz, "*Narcocorridos* and the Nostalgia of Violence: Postmodern Resistance *en la Frontera*." *Western American Literature* 48:1 (2013): 56. Mark Cameron Edberg also uses the term, but hedges, "the picture is more complex than that." See *El Narcotraficante: Narcocorridos and the Construction of a Cultural Persona on the U.S.-Mexico Border* (Austin: University of Texas Press, 2004), 104–5, 127.

21 " … verdadero creador de mitos constitutivos de su visión de mundo … de la transmutación del estigma en emblem." Luís. A. Astorga, *Mitología del "Narcotraficante" en México* (Mexico City: Universidad Nacional Autónoma de México, Plaza y Valdés Editores, 1995), 38. Translation mine.

22 Edberg, 112.

23 John H. McDowell, "The Ballad of Narcomexico." *Journal of Folklore Research* 49:3 (2012): 268.

24 Amaya, "Dark Side," 235–39; Amanda Maria Morrison, "Musical Trafficking: Urban Youth and the Narcocorrido-Hardcore Rap Nexus." *Western Folklore* 67:4 (2008): 390–91; José Manuel Valenzuela, *Jefe de Jefes: corridos y narcocultura en México* (Havana: Fondo Editorial Casa de las Américas, 2003), 156–60.

25 See Amaya, "Dark Side," and José Pablo Villalobos and Juan Carlos Ramírez-Pimienta, "*Corridos* and *la pura verdad*: Myths and Realities of the Mexican Ballad." *South Central Review* 21:3 (2004): 129–49.

26 From "El Crimen de Culiacán," by Nacho Hernández. Quoted in Wald, *Narcocorrido*, 73.

27 From "Sanguinarios del M1," by Movimiento Alterado. Quoted in Kai Flanders, "The Deadly World of Mexican Narco-Ballads." *Vice* (2013).

28 "me alcoholice … también foquie hasta quedar mongolo." From "El Trokero Lokochon," by Gerardo Ortíz. Translation mine.

29 Hector Amaya, "Authorship and the State: Narcocorridos in Mexico and the New Aesthetics of Nation." *A Companion to Media Authorship* (West Sussex: John Wiley, 2013), 509–10; Wald, "Drug Ballads and Censorship in Mexico," *ElijahWald.com* (2002).

30 Anabel Hernández, *Narcoland: The Mexican Drug Lords and Their Godfathers* (London: Verso, 2013), 200.

31 Astorga, *Mitología*, 38.

32 Trump, Calibre, Trump, Calibre, Trump, Calibre. Trump quoted in Alexander Burns, "Choice Words from Donald Trump, Presidential Candidate." *New York Times* (2015). Lyrics from "Plebada Alterado": "La plebada anda pisteando Johnny Walker y Buchanan's ... Disfrutando de lo bueno/ Porque la vida se acaba"; "Trae besucas y granadas"; "La plebada anda alterada." Translation mine.

33 A former foreign secretary of Mexico explains, "The songs are born out of a traditional Mexican cynicism: This is our reality, we've gotten used to it." Quoted in Josh Kun, "Minstrels in the Court of the Kingpin." *New York Times* (2010). See also, Edberg, 112.

34 Shaylih Muehlmann, *When I Wear My Alligator Boots: Narco-Culture in the U.S.-Mexico Borderlands* (Berkeley: U of California P, 2013), 93–4; see also Ryan Rashotte, *Narco Cinema: Sex, Drugs and Banda Music in Mexico's B-Filmography* (New York: Palgrave, 2015), 17–18.

35 Muehlmann, 86–7, 102–4. See also, Villalobos and Ramírez-Pimienta, 143–44.

36 Zadie Smith, "The House That Hova Built." *New York Times* (2012).

37 The song is "A La Moda."

38 Quoted in Kun.

39 Muehlmann, 99; Wald, "Drug Ballads."

40 Amaya, "Authorship," 516.

41 Wald, "Drug Ballads."

42 Randal C. Archibald, "Mexico Paper, a Drug War Victim, Calls for a Voice." *New York Times* (2010); Mike O'Connor, "The Press Silenced, Nuevo Laredo Tries to Find Voice." *Committee to Protect Journalists* (2011); Ed Vulliamy, *Amexica: War Along the Borderline* (New York: Farrar, Straus and Giroux, 2010), 233, 283.

43 225 journalists were attacked between January and September 2013. See Gloria Leticia Díaz, "Con 225 agresiones, este año el más violento contra periodistas: Artículo 19." *Proceso* (2013).

44 Rafa Fernandez De Castro, "Mexican Journalist Beheaded for 'Poking the Hornet's Nest.'" *Fusion* (2015); Mosqueda.

45 I raise this argument elsewhere with regard to narco cinema. See Rashotte, 8–11.

46 John P. Sullivan, "Measuring mayhem: The challenge of assessing violence and insecurity in Mexico." *Baker Institute Blog, Huston Chronicle* (2013).

47 Martin Duran, "Mexican Law 'Worthy of an Authoritarian State' Will Be Repealed." *Vice* (2014).

48 Sullivan.

49 Fernandez De Castro, "Mexican Journalist."

50 Scholars have acknowledged this occupational hazard. See, for example, Muehlmann, 97.

51 Leila Cobo, "'It's Like a Horror Movie': The Grisly Details Behind Mexico's Narcocorrido Murder Epidemic." *Billboard* (2015).

52 According to a phone survey conducted by the national paper *Excélsior*. Quoted in Lizbeth Diaz, "Ban on Mexico drug ballads no match for YouTube." *Reuters* (2011).

53 Amaya, "Authorship," 509–10; Wald, "Drug Ballads."

54 In Sicilia's own words: "because the narcos have exalted this way of life, of criminal power, I think it's fair to prohibit this type of thing. But it must be accompanied by a U.S. policy ... to silence celebrities like Charlie Sheen or Paris Hilton who exalt drugs." "Estoy de acuerdo porque los narcocorridos han exaltado como un camino de vida y de poder a los delincuentes, creo que es justo que se prohíba este tipo de cosas. Pero debe de ir acompañada por una política de los estados unidos de prohibir también a gente del espectáculo, elogian la droga, la exaltan como Charlie Sheen o Paris Hilton, habría que silenciarlos también." "Palabras a los Graduados de la Escuela de Periodismo Auténtico 2011. Ciudad de México, 21 de mayo." *Narco News* (2011). Translation mine.

55 Filmmaker Mario Hernández, quoted in Valeria Perasso, "Reality Took Over from the Imagination of the Film Maker," *BBC Radio World Service*.

56 Gabriel Stargardter, "Cartel cannibalism: Mexico says drug gang members ate human hearts." *Reuters* (2015).

57 Edberg, 126–7; Muniz, 57.

58 Edberg, 106.

59 Wald, *Narcocorrido*, 28.

60 You may recall that Benetton once solicited Subcommandante Marcos for a fashion campaign. See Guillermo Gómez-Peña, *Dangerous Border Crossers* (New York: Routledge, 2000), 84.

61 Muehlmann, 171; Mark Stevenson, "Mexico's Latest Fashion Craze: 'Narco Polo.'" *NBCNews.com* (2011).

62 Stevenson.

63 For descriptions of some of the jewelry for sale at a recent auction, see Jo Tuckman, "Mexico Sells Off Narco-Bling Seized from Traffickers." *The Guardian* (2010).

64 Elyssa Pachico, "Narco-Uniforms Mark Authority in Mexico." *InSightCrime.com* (2011).

65 "Songs of the Drug Lord: 'Narcocorridos' Impose Their Own Fashion Trends." *Hispanically Speaking News* (2011).

66 El Paso Intelligence Center, "Language of the Cartels: Narco Terminology, Identifiers and Clothing Style," in Dane Schiller, "Uncle Sams's Guide on How to Speak Narco, Language of Mexico's Drug Cartel." *Houston Chronicle* (2012); Muehlmann 170.

67 Víctor Ronquillo, *La Reina del Pacífico y otras mujeres del narco* (Mexico City: Editorial Planeta Mexicana, 2008), 27. Translation mine.

68 Elaine Carey, *Women Drug Traffickers: Mules, Bosses, and Organized Crime* (Albuquerque: University of New Mexico Press, 2014), 195–6.

69 Monica Campbell, "Mexico's Female Drug Lords." *Marie Claire* (2011).

70 Pablo Perez, "Women on the rise in Mexican drug cartels." *Agence France-Presse* (2012).

71 Carey, 196; Muehlmann, 43, 47, 54–5.

72 Muehlmann, 69–70.

73 Rashotte, 3–4.

74 Bernardo Loyola, "Narcotic Films for Illegal Fans." *Vice* (2009).

75 Rashotte, 50–1.

76 Iván Cadín, "Narcos metieron dinero al cine." *El Universal* (2011); Rashotte, 71.

77 Routledge's collection *Latsploitation* contains a few tangential essays, and O. Hugo Benavides' *Drugs, Thugs and Divas* theorizes at length on the politics of the "narco-drama" (though it never discusses any actual narco films).

78 His father directed *Contrabando y traición*, among other classics.

79 "Descansan capos entre lujo y opulencia en narcopanteón de Culiacán." *Proceso* (2014); "Lujo post mórtem: la dorada paz de los narcos." *Excélsior* (2011); Jasmine Garsd, "This Narco Cemetery has Graves with Air Conditioning and Cable TV." *Fusion* (2104).

80 Javier Angulo, "Here Lies a Bunch of Mexican Drug Dealers." *Vice* (2011); Jo Tuckman, *Mexico: Democracy Interrupted* (New Haven, CT: Yale University Press, 2012), 39.

81 Garsd.

82 "Lujo post mortem."

83 Andrew R. Cheshnut, *Devoted to Death: Santa Muerte, the Skeleton Saint* (Oxford: Oxford University Press, 2012), 103; Claudio Lomnitz, *Death and the Idea of Mexico* (New York: Zone Books, 2005), 490.

84 Lomnitz, 491–2; Rick Paulas, "Our Lady of the Holy Death Is the World's Fastest Growing Religious Movement." *Vice* (2014).

85 Chesnut, 102, 107.

86 Chesnut, 113.

87 Chesnut, 103; Lomnitz, 492.

88 Mark Karlin, "Fueled by War on Drugs, Mexican Death Toll Could Exceed 120,000 as Calderon Ends Six-Year Reign." *TruthOut* (2012).

89 Edberg, 113.

90 Wald, *Narcocorrido*, 35.

Bibliography

Amaya, Hector. "Authorship and the State: Narcocorridos in Mexico and the New Aesthetics of Nation." *A Companion to Media Authorship*. Eds. Jonathan Gray and Derek Johnson. West Sussex: John Wiley, 2013.

Amaya, Hector. "The Dark Side of Transnational Latinidad: Narcocorridos and the Branding of Authenticity." *Contemporary Latina/o Media: Production, Circulation, Politics*. Eds. Arlene Dávila and Yeidy M. Rivero. New York: New York University Press, 2014.

Angulo, Javier. "Here Lies a Bunch of Mexican Drug Dealers." *Vice* 1 April 2011.

Archibald, Randal C. "Mexico Paper, a Drug War Victim, Calls for a Voice." *New York Times* 20 September 2010.

Benavides, O. Hugo. *Drugs, Thugs and Divas: Telenovelas and Narco-Dramas in Latin America*. Austin: University of Texas Press, 2008.

Astorga, Luís A. "Drug Trafficking in Mexico: A First General Assessment." UNESCO Management of Social Transformations—MOST, United Nations Educational, Scientific, and Cultural Organization. Discussion Paper 36. 1999. Available at: http://www.unesco.org/most/astorga.htm

Astorga, Luís A. *Mitología del "narcotraficante" en México*. México, D.F.: Universidad Nacional Autónoma de México: Plaza y Valdés Editores, 1995.

Burns, Alexander. "Choice Words from Donald Trump, Presidential Candidate." *New York Times* 16 June 2015.

Cadín, Iván. "Narcos metieron dinero al cine." *El Universal* 25 April 2011.

Calibre 50. "Plebada Alterada." *Renovar O Morir*. Disa, 2010.

Campbell, Monica. "Mexico's Female Drug Lords." *Marie Claire* 20 July 2011.

Carey, Elaine. *Women Drug Traffickers: Mules, Bosses, and Organized Crime*. Albuquerque: University of New Mexico Press, 2014.

Cheshnut, Andrew W. *Devoted to Death: Santa Muerte, the Skeleton Saint*. Oxford: Oxford University Press, 2012.

Cobo, Leila. "'It's Like a Horror Movie': The Grisly Details Behind Mexico's Narcocorrido Murder Epidemic." *Billboard* 10 April 2015.

Collins, Katie. "Guns, Gore and Girls: The Rise of the Cyber Cartels." *Wired* 5 November 2014.

Cox, Joseph. "Mexico's Drug Cartels Love Social Media." *Vice* 13 November 2013.

Creechan, James H. and Jorge de la Herrán Garcia. "Without God or Law: Narcoculture and Belief in Jesús Malverde." *Religious Studies and Theology*. 24:2 (2005): 5–57.

"Descansan capos entre lujo y opulencia en narcopanteón de Culiacán." *Proceso* 18 August 2014.

Díaz, Gloria Leticia. "Con 225 agresiones, este año el más violento contra periodistas: Artículo 19." *Proceso* 11 October 2013.

Diaz, Lizbeth. "Ban on Mexico drug ballads no match for YouTube." *Reuters* 27 June 2011.

Duran, Martin. "Mexican Law 'Worthy of an Authoritarian State' Will Be Repealed." *Vice* 19 August 2014.

Edberg, Mark Cameron. *El Narcotraficante: Narcocorridos and the Construction of a Cultural Persona on the U.S.-Mexico Border*. Austin: University of Texas Press, 2004.

El Paso Intelligence Center. "Language of the Cartels: Narco Terminology, Identifiers and Clothing Style." In Dane Schiller, "Uncle Sams's Guide on How to Speak Narco, Language of Mexico's Drug Cartels." *Houston Chronicle* 3 May 2012.

Fernandez De Castro, Rafa. "A Drug Cartel Guide to Laundering Millions." *Fusion* 20 September 2014.

Fernandez De Castro, Rafa. "Mexican Journalist Beheaded for 'Poking the Hornet's Nest.'" *Fusion* 27 January 2015.

Flanders, Kai. "The Deadly World of Mexican Narco-Ballads." *Vice* 28 May 2013.

Garsd, Jasmine. "This Narco Cemetery has Graves with Air Conditioning and Cable TV." *Fusion* 19 May 2014.

Gómez-Peña, Guillermo. *Dangerous Border Crossers*. New York: Routledge, 2000.

Hernández, Anabel. *Narcoland: The Mexican Drug Lords and Their Godfathers*. London: Verso, 2013.

Karlin, Mark. "Fueled by War on Drugs, Mexican Death Toll Could Exceed 120,000 As Calderon Ends Six-Year Reign." *Truth Out* 28 November 2012.

Kun, Josh. "Minstrels in the Court of the Kingpin." *New York Times* 5 March 2010.

Latsploitation: Exploitation Cinemas and Latin America. Eds. Victoria Ruétalo and Dolores Mary Tierney. New York: Routledge, 2009.

Lomnitz, Claudio. *Death and the Idea of Mexico*. New York: Zone Books, 2005.

Loyola, Bernando. "Narcotic Films for Illegal Fans." *Vice* 1 September 2009.

"Lujo post mórtem: la dorada paz de los narcos" *Excélsior* 7 August 2011.

McDowell, John H. "The Ballad of Narcomexico." *Journal of Folklore Research* 49:3 (2012): 249–74.

Morrison, Amanda Maria. "Musical Trafficking: Urban Youth and the Narcocorrido-Hardcore Rap Nexus." *Western Folklore* 67:4 (2008): 379–96.

Mosqueda, Priscila. "Mexican Drug Cartels Are Using Social Media Apps to Commit Virtual Kidnappings." *Vice* 27 September 2014.

Muehlmann, Shaylih. *When I Wear My Alligator Boots: Narco-Culture in the U.S.-Mexico Borderlands.* Berkeley: University of California Press, 2013.

Muniz, Chris. "*Narcocorridos* and the Nostalgia of Violence: Postmodern Resistance *en la Frontera.*" *Western American Literature* 48:1 (2013): 56–69.

O'Connor, Mike. "The Press Silenced, Nuevo Laredo Tries to Find Voice." *Committee to Protect Journalists* 22 December 2011.

Ortíz, Gerardo. "A La Moda." *Ni Hoy Ni Mañana.* DEL Records, 2010.

Ortíz, Gerardo. "El Trokero Lokochon." *Ni Hoy Ni Mañana.* DEL Records, 2010.

Quinones, Sam. *True Tales from Another Mexico: The Lynch Mob, the Popsicle Kings, Chalino, and the Bronx.* Albuquerque: University of New Mexico Press, 2001.

Pachico, Elyssa. "Narco-Uniforms Mark Authority in Mexico." *InSightCrime.com* 20 April 2011.

Paulas, Rick. "Our Lady of the Holy Death Is the World's Fastest Growing Religious Movement." *Vice* 13 November 2014.

Perasso, Valeria. "Reality Took Over from the Imagination of the Film Maker." *BBC Radio World Service.* n.d.

Perez, Pablo. "Women on the Rise in Mexican Drug Cartels." *Agence France-Presse* 27 May 2012.

Ragland, Cathy. *Música Norteña: Mexican Migrants Creating a Nation Between Nations.* Philadelphia: Temple University Press, 2009.

Rashotte, Ryan. *Narco Cinema: Sex, Drugs and Banda Music in Mexico's B-Filmography.* New York: Palgrave, 2015.

Rivera, Jenni. "Ovarios." *Jenni: Super Deluxe.* Fonovisa, 2009.

Rodríguez, Ida. "El Culto a Jesús Malverde." Instituto de Investigaciones Estéticas, Universidad Nacional Autónoma de México. n.d.: 1–28. Available at: http://www.esteticas.unam.mx/edartedal/PDF/Bahia/complets/RodriguezMalverde.pdf Web. 10 Aug. 2015.

Ronquillo, Víctor. *La Reina del Pacífico y otras mujeres del narco.* Mexico City: Editorial Planeta Mexicana, 2008.

Sánchez Godoy, Jorge Alan. "Procesos de institucionalización de la narcocultura en Sinaloa." *Frontera Norte* 21:41 (2009): 77–103.

Sicilia, Javier. "Palabras a los Graduados de la Escuela de Periodismo Auténtico 2011. Ciudad de México, 21 de mayo." *Narco News* 1 June 2011.

Simonett, Helena. *Banda: Mexican Musical Life Across Borders.* Middletown, CT: Wesleyan University Press, 2001.

Simonett, Helena. "Narcocorridos: An Emerging Micromusic of Nuevo L.A." *Ethnomusicology* 45:2 (2001): 315–37.

Smith, Zadie. "The House That Hova Built." *New York Times* 6 September 2012.

"Songs of the Drug Lord: 'Narcocorridos' Impose Their Own Fashion Trends." *Hispanically Speaking News* 19 December 2011.

Stargardter, Gabriel. "Cartel Cannibalism: Mexico Says Drug Gang Members Ate Human Hearts." *Reuters* 6 January 2015.

Stevenson, Mark. "Mexico's Latest Fashion Craze: 'Narco Polo.'" *NBCNews.com* 10 June 2011.

Sullivan, John P. "Measuring mayhem: The challenge of assessing violence and insecurity in Mexico." *Baker Institute Blog, Huston Chronicle* 23 October 2013.

Tuckman, Jo. "Mexico Sells Off Narco-Bling Seized from Traffickers." *The Guardian* 19 November 2010.

Tuckman, Jo. *Mexico: Democracy Interrupted.* New Haven, CT: Yale University Press, 2012.

Valenzuela, José Manuel. *Jefe de Jefes: corridos y narcocultura en México.* Havana: Fondo Editorial Casa de las Américas, 2003.

Villalobos, José Pablo and Juan Carlos Ramírez-Pimienta. "*Corridos* and *la pura verdad*: Myths and Realities of the Mexican Ballad." *South Central Review* 21:3 (2004): 129–49.

Vulliamy, Ed. *Amexica: War Along the Borderline*. New York: Farrar, Straus and Giroux, 2010.

Wald, Elijah. *Narcocorrido: A Journey into the Music of Guns, Drugs, and Guerillas*. New York: HarperCollins, 2001.

Wald, Elijah. "Drug Ballads and Censorship in Mexico." *Elijahwald.com* 2002.

Womer, S. and R.J. Bunker. "Sureños Gangs and Mexican Cartel Use of Social Networking Sites." *Small Wars & Insurgencies*. 21:1 (2010): 81–94.

35

SMUGGLING AS A SPECTACLE

Irregular Migration and Coyotes in Contemporary U.S. Latino Popular Culture

Gabriella Sanchez

On the morning of May 14, 2003, sheriff deputies from Victoria County, Texas, made a macabre discovery. The remains of 17 irregular migrants from Mexico, El Salvador, Guatemala and Dominican Republic—including those of a 5-year-old boy—lay inside and next to a trailer that had been abandoned by its driver, along with 46 other survivors, in the parking lot of a gas station in a desolate stretch of Interstate highway 77. Those who had perished died of suffocation and hypothermia after having spent close to four hours riding in the back of a locked trailer with no ventilation as they attempted to reach Houston, Texas, undetected by U.S. immigration authorities.

The magnitude of the case—eventually defined by the U.S. Department of Justice as the single largest loss of life in a human smuggling operation in U.S. history (2010)—immediately generated widespread outrage and condemnation, and strong demands for the arrest of those responsible. In the days that followed 13 people—including the driver of the truck, Tyrone Williams, a Jamaican immigrant, and Karla Perez, a woman of Honduran origin who coordinated some of the migrants' journeys—were arrested. The case's extreme visibility relied on the mobilization of graphic, sensationalistic images of migrant suffering and death, and detailed descriptions of their agony. Latina/o media hunted the survivors for their testimony, and even made a documentary where four of the survivors retraced their journey for the voyeuristic pleasure of the masses. The depictions of suffering depended upon the characterizations of those behind their journeys—known in the lingo of irregular migration as *coyotes* or *polleros*—as heinous merchants of life, blinded and driven by greed, exploiting their own kin. Yet once the appeal of the case subsided in the days and weeks that followed, the tragedy of the 77 migrants from Victoria was forgotten by the media—and the public.

Human smuggling-related tragedies of the kind that occurred in Victoria are most often traced to *coyotes*: the men or women who for a fee or in-kind payment facilitate the extralegal journey of migrants into a country or countries different than their own. Coyotes have historically been central actors of U.S.-bound migration processes, facilitating the cross-border transits of thousands of irregular migrants into the country avoiding government controls, and are therefore an ever-present element of irregular border crossing narratives.

The experiences of irregular migrants with coyotes as agents of human mobility vary widely. Empirical work on border crossings indicates some migrants describe coyotes as benefactors and supporters of migration goals and hopes (Hagan, 2008) while others see them as a necessary, if at times unpleasant, evil (Andreas 2015, 306), next to the testimonies of those who having endured dramatic cases of abuse, violence, and death, define coyotes as abominable predators (Ochoa O'Leary 2009).

For decades, this last characterization is the one that has dominated the narrative of the coyote in Latino popular culture. Corridos and films on *indocumentados* have historically been prolific grounds for references to the violent, greedy, two-timing coyote who preys upon the naïve, poor, and hopeless migrant, whose journey is defined by pain, suffering, and often tragedy (Herrera-Sobek, 1999). While more recent representations of irregular migration (namely the onslaught of films of a fictional nature, inspired by what are marketed as "true stories" of migration, or documentaries that focus on the experiences of Central American migrants and children traversing along Mexico atop of cargo trains) tend to reflect changing trends in irregular U.S. bound migration, the coyote continues to appear as an inescapable, pervasive character that preys on the weak and poor.

While Latino popular culture has found in the most dramatic characterization of the coyote and the irregular border crossing an important mechanism to narrate many of the injustices migrants face in the context of their irregular journeys, mainstream media has not resisted the opportunity to cash in on the anxieties of an entire population marked by migration by appropriating the character. The coyote—as the inherently predatory and violent, greed-driven, hypersexual *Mexican* male, who exploits the naïve, defenseless, and ignorant "illegal" migrant (another favorite character in both the Anglo and the Latino *imaginaria*)—has now been vastly incorporated into the narratives of irregular migration. By saturating the voyeuristic instincts of an audience not vested in deconstructing the real reasons behind irregular migration and its tragedies—the increase of immigration enforcement mechanisms on the part of the nation state as the means to deter those in transit at all costs being one—media have relied on the character of the coyote or human smuggler to communicate the collective, xenophobic fears over the presence of irregular migrants. Personified as a *male* of color of the global South, who preys upon the misery of his own people, the coyote has become a metaphor for death: the quintessential predator of late modernity (the migrant preying upon him/herself).

Simultaneously, while embedded in a dominant media system that has historically supported and perpetuated Latina/os' invisibility and negative representations (Escalante 134), the fixation of Latino popular culture with the portrayal of the coyote as a victimizer stands as a clear reflection of Latina/os' own tensions and anxieties over irregular migration.

Inspired by Nicholas de Geneva's notions of migrant "illegality" and *border spectacle*, this chapter surveys the transformation of the coyote in contemporary popular culture's representations of irregular migration. It argues that the treatment and the embracing of the coyote as foreign and abject reflects collective, widespread, and long-lived tensions and anxieties of Latina/os' own experiences on irregular migration by virtue of being "inserted in a comprehensively racialized social structure" (Omi and Winant 60).

The chapter begins by introducing some of the linguistic and anthropological dimensions of the concept of coyote, followed by a summary of the engagements of U.S. Latina/o popular culture and migration scholarship with the coyote as an actor. A second section relies on current representations of the coyote in popular media that reinscribe notions of coyotes as threatening, greedy, and cruel, while simultaneously allowing for the reification of Latina/o migrants as criminal and abject. In closing, a third section raises questions over the transformation of the coyote from an element of popular culture to its current positioning in state discourses of border protection and immigration control as a global merchant of death, all part of the border spectacle where the suffering and death of the migrant body become justified/justifiable, constitutive elements of immigration enforcement and control practices.

Coyote: a Definition

The term coyote has historically been used in the colloquial language of border crossings to designate a person who facilitates the transit of those seeking to enter the United States without official authorization. Yet the coyote has had a long trajectory in Latin American native, colonial, and post-colonial narratives. Its presence in native traditions antecedes the arrival of the Spanish conquerors—where gendered as a male the coyote stands as the trickster-culture hero of multiple Mesoamerican traditions (Melendez 296). In the Nahua pantheon, the Old Coyote God, Huehuecoyotl, "represented the fundamental concepts of pleasure and lust … [and as a coyote] Huehuecoyotl gave testimony of one of the world's realities: eroticism." (Lopez Austin, 1996:163 in Rodriguez Valle 80).

Melendez and Rodriguez Valle suggest that native views of animals and deities shifted with the arrival of Catholicism. Both authors make reference to the texts of Fr. Bernardino de Sahagun, who after careful observation of the coyote's behavior in the wild establishes that the coyote's supernatural characteristics can only emanate from its relationship with the devil (Rodriguez Valle 81–5).[1]

While the religious perceptions of the coyote as evil form part of the term's current iteration, it is also during colonial times that the word started to be used as a proxy for *mestizo*. In the intricate chart of New Spain's caste system, coyote was a quasi-pejorative designation that conveyed mixed ancestry (a quality that would eventually be shared by most Mexicans) and which turned those of mixed origin into what Melendez refers to as "perpetual outsiders": coyotes were indeed the eternal outcasts (Melendez 298–9). In this context, and by virtue of their marginal and ambiguous condition, coyotes emerge as those who "bridge opposing forces or cross boundaries" (Melendez 299), those who navigate the boundaries between the admissible and the unacceptable.

It is in these engagements with notions of difference and ethnicity where the first notions of the coyote as a reflection of a self arising from the Conquista and the tensions over identity become patent. There is a shift towards the development of informal social mechanisms that, while embedded in the larger, official, colonial system of classification, justify and allow distinctions among groups that ironically are so closely related to exist and be enforced.

It is also in the context of the colonial system of labor that the fights between "both Spanish and colonial governments … over the supply of labor and its production" gave room to the emergence of a series of agents or brokers who could accommodate the needs of both entities. Coyotes become "an army of the disinherited" (Wolf in Melendez 298), "the ones who carried out … society's illicit but indispensable transactions" (Spener 87). Still used in this fashion throughout Latin America, the word coyote refers to this underground facilitator or expeditor of bureaucratic or government transactions. Despised by many, but desperately needed by many more, coyotes are what Gomez de Silva refers to as "illegitimate intermediaries" (Spener 86), whose contacts and knowledge can reduce the frustrations associated with red tape—for a price.

Coyotes as Facilitators of Irregular Migration Processes

The designation of coyotes as able to navigate marginal or marginalized spaces, as abject yet necessary members of complex social structures, and as capable of performing the acts that others would consider immoral or illicit, seems to fuse in some of the earliest references to their work on the U.S. Mexico border, where they first appear as illicit employment brokers by the late 1800s. Coyotes identified and recruited Mexican nationals seeking employment for American companies and contractors, charging them a fee for each recruit (Gamio, 1931; Spener, 2014). Minding the costs and the bureaucratic delays involved in hiring workers through legal channels, some American contractors turned to coyotes to fulfill their labor needs.

Gamio provides a detailed description of the role of coyotes in the mid and late 1920s on the U.S. Mexico Border. Coyotes provided would-be migrants (who were many times members of rural or indigenous communities unfamiliar with bureaucratic processes) with the documents they needed for their employment authorization interviews with U.S. officials. Yet coyotes also worked on facilitating the border crossings of those whose interviews had been unsuccessful. In the testimonies of Gamio's respondents, the facilitation of this form of irregular migration constitutes a multi-faceted enterprise, involving both individuals and gangs, working together but haphazardly at transferring Mexican nationals into the United States. Coyotes lend—rent—passports, visas, cars, and hiding places to each other, guide people through the river, land, or by vehicle, while all along seeking to fulfill the needs of American contractors or *enganchistas* looking for workers. Gamio seems troubled by the practices of American companies and the way they violate labor practices, which often lead to the exploitative conditions many irregular workers face. The coyote in Gamio's work appears to be a by-product of the unwillingness of American companies to comply with government regulations, a quasi-problematic agent whose actions allow for the migration of the Mexican workers, but also their mistreatment.

Contemporary scholarship on the facilitation of irregular migration, although scant, suggests that while state measures to criminalize migrants have now become rather formal and punitive in nature, the overall organization of the activity has in some instances not changed much from Gamio's time.

The role coyotes take as facilitators of irregular migration constitutes what in legal terms is referred to as human smuggling. Specifically, the practice refers to the consensual, negotiated process that, for a fee or in-kind payment, facilitates the transit of an individual into a country or countries other than his or her own. This process is facilitated by a broker or series thereof while avoiding government controls. Smuggling has a variable nature. It can be altruistic (organized to guide or accompany friends and families on their journeys), while in many other cases it involves the payment of fees to groups of varying sizes which may charge for facilitating only specific legs of a journey, or coordinate an entire trans-continental journey (Sanchez, 2015).

There is no specific profile of a smuggler facilitator, other than that it often involves people living along the migrant trail who face similar levels of marginalization themselves, and with the ability to perform a conventional, socially situated, often unremarkable task. Entering and participating in smuggling requires minimal or no initial investment, as it relies on resources already at the facilitator's disposal (a vehicle or a house; a valid driver license and/or the ability to drive; access to a specific road or route; friends or family members at a specific location, etc.). While men tend to be more often represented and identified as smuggling facilitators, women do perform important roles. In fact, tasks in smuggling are highly gendered (for example, women are more often involved in activities like cooking, providing room and board, or child or elder care than men, who usually work as guides or drivers) (Zhang, Chin and Miller, 2007; Sanchez, 2015). Most smuggling facilitators are employed either in the mainstream economy or in less formal occupations. Few can afford to live off smuggling alone—the practice's irregular, infrequent nature means it only generates and can only be relied upon as supplementary income (Zhang, 2008). Furthermore, and contrary to widely held perceptions, smuggling earnings are often small and also vary significantly by gender, with male facilitators earning more than their female counterparts, whose participation is often perceived as peripheral, unimportant, or not worthy of compensation.

Most facilitators have a tendency to work within their immediate social circles, as a means to protect those who travel with them, themselves, and their reputation. Smuggling facilitation is primordially a referral-based occupation, which relies on perceptions of trust and reliability built over time. In other words, customers seeking to travel will be more likely to travel with a facilitator with a good delivery "track record" and references. Facilitators build a reputation through the provision of successful, uneventful, effective journeys, considering migration of the kind they enable involves a high level of uncertainty and inherent precariousness. Facilitating the transit of people known by virtue of kinship or friendship may also ensure that in the event of detection, those in transit will be less likely to report the facilitator to the authorities. Traveling with a known facilitator is also perceived by those who travel with them as a way to reduce the potential for violence, abuse or accidents that could be experienced at the hands of an unknown or less experienced facilitator. Friendship and family ties may also ensure a quicker response in the event a situation of danger arises, the facilitator feeling more inclined to protect his own friends or relatives from risk (Khosravi, 2007).

Smuggling transits are not necessarily linear—that is, they do not have a specific trajectory and do not always follow the same steps or routes. Facilitators must adapt to the changing conditions that surround them. Weather, surveillance, the activities of other groups in the region, and even holidays play a role in facilitators' decisions to move an individual or group in transit or to stay put in a specific location (Icazara-Palacios, 2015). For this reason, the duration of a smuggling transit cannot always be determined in advance, being intricately tied to conditions along the route.

Another important characteristic of the facilitation of irregular migration by smuggling is the highly specialized nature of its tasks. By specialization I do not suggest tasks are complex (one of the advantages of smuggling is precisely the fact that it does not require specialized training), but rather that they are specific to a facilitator, each task constituting an element of the larger chain that will eventually—with luck—allow for a successful crossing (Zhang, 2007; Sanchez, 2015). Examples of tasks include recruiting customers; guiding a group along a specific route; driving a vehicle; providing room and board; maintaining a safe house or resting point stocked with food and water; serving as a messenger; providing childcare; ensuring the payment of fees from those in transit or the distribution of compensation to all participants; mediating between parties in the event of misunderstandings, etc. While on occasion, a facilitator may opt to perform a different task in the event of need, substitutions are rare. Some groups prefer cancelling entire trips if someone is unavailable in order to avoid mistakes or detection by law enforcement. It is also preferable among many to attempt a crossing multiple times with the resources they have available rather than altering plans drastically. Altering tasks may be the difference between a successful crossing and a mistake that may cost lives.

Coyotes and Contemporary Latino Popular Culture

Given the impact of U.S.-bound migration upon entire generations of U.S. Latina/os, the ubiquitousness of the migratory experience in popular culture representations should not come as a surprise. Yet Mexican cultural production on migration has been the one most often examined by scholars, and its products the ones with the most diffusion, due in part to the overrepresentation of Mexican migrants in the U.S. The thematic of the heroic, martyrized, irregular migrant who crosses the border looking for the elusive dream of *El Norte* despite *la migra* and *los coyotes* dominated the narratives of corridos (folk ballads) and *peliculas de indocumentados* for the majority of the twentieth century. Herrera-Sobek in her study of corridos as hypertext remarks how "ideological configurations directly connected either to nationalistic processes or to the structuring of social protest expressions" (282) are present in the lyrics and dialogues of folk ballads and films narrating the experiences of irregular migrants in transit. Until the 1980s, corridos were always present in the films describing the fictionalized, and almost always tragic, border crossings of migrants, whose inherent naiveté, nobleness, and passiveness made them easy prey of the cruel, inhumane Border Patrol agent or coyote.

The advent of the internet and the proliferation of cable TV options, however, changed not only the ways in which media messages were distributed and consumed. It also allowed for the circulation of newer, more cluttered narratives of migration reflecting the deep changes to U.S. immigration law of the 1990s on the one hand, and the post 9/11 hysteria over national security on the other. The alleged failure of the 1986 Immigration Reform and Control Act (IRCA) in addressing U.S. irregular immigration led to the imposition of stricter rules and sanctions pertaining to the presence of irregular migrants in the country through the 1996 Illegal Immigration Reform and Immigrant Responsibility Act (IRIRA). The implementation of this newer set of laws—which established severe penalties for those caught crossing the border irregularly, including provisions for permanent removal and the inability to regularize immigration status in the event of arrest, as well as a significant growth of border enforcement—has been linked to the interruption of the migration patterns that for decades had allowed irregular migrants to return to their places of origin seasonally. Facing increased surveillance and criminalization mechanisms, many migrants opted not to risk a journey back "home" that could not only land them in immigration detention, but which would ultimately curtail their very ability to return to and remain in the U.S. and legalize their presence. The magnitude of the events of 9/11 also gave rise to a new series of propositions that situated the borderlands as the frontline of the domestic war against terror, a claim that transformed irregular migration and its facilitation into a threat to the security of the nation, the migrant into an invader that had to be contained at all costs.

The changes to federal immigration and border enforcement resulted by the first half of the 2000s in a humanitarian crisis of unprecedented magnitude. The intentional funneling of the flow of irregular migrants into the Arizona desert as part of enforcement measures aimed at controlling undocumented immigration resulted in the deaths of thousands of irregular migrants, but had little impact in reducing the number of irregular border crossing attempts. Stepped up enforcement forced border crossers to seek alternative routes in their journeys that often placed them in places or situations where help was not only unavailable, but improbable. And in this context, new technologies allowed the live broadcasting of highly dramatic scenes—the arrests of groups of irregular migrants during their treks through the desert; the detection of and raids on safe houses in urban areas; the rescue of men and women too weak or injured to continue with their journey or even to survive. The images not only consolidated the role of irregular migration as a public spectacle. They were a central component of the construction of migrants' very "illegality." Transformed into public evidence, the images served to explain and justify the conditions and the treatment that migrants faced during their transit. The display of images of fear, overcrowding, physical pain, suffering, and death has become a required element of the state's discourse and processes of discipline for migrants. By doing this, the state has also established the migrant body as inherently damaged, weak, and disposable. Death, when present, is nothing but a mere natural consequence of migrants' own legal transgressions.

It was in the context of the panic over the presence of irregular migrants in the country when the figure of the coyote re-emerged, aggrandized through the xenophobic and anti-immigrant rhetoric that would accompany the language of a nation's borders in siege. Multiple movies and documentaries, instantly available through internet streaming, piracy, cheap DVD sales, and mail order delivery have facilitated the diffusion of images of migrants, coyotes, and the border to audiences who base their knowledge of the border on images of lawlessness, sexual violence, death, and drugs (Staudt 2014). Rather than framing violence against migrants in the context of failed immigration control policy, these media position coyotes once again as the ideal perpetrators: they are blamed of abandoning their clients in the desert to their fate; of raping women as part of depraved rituals, of loading children with drugs and even of beheading those who failed to abide by their rules. These images reproduce dominant hegemonic narratives of the borderlands as wild, chaotic, sexualized and violent (Staudt, 2014). Furthermore, and while focused on the actions of the coyote, the images assist in the racialization process that furthers dominant narratives of the people of the border and Latina/os in general as criminal and deviant.

The Victoria Tragedy

One of the most covered narratives of smuggling was the Victoria tragedy in 2003 which involved the death by suffocation and hyperthermia of 19 out of 75 irregular migrants riding in the back of a sealed truck. The group had boarded the vehicle in the hope of being transported to Houston, Texas, undetected (ICE, 2009). The trailer had a refrigeration device but it was not turned on. As soon as the doors of the trailer were locked, the temperature inside it began to escalate, making it hard if not impossible for those inside to breath.

The driver, Tyrone Williams, had been aware of the nature of his cargo all along. A few days earlier he had been offered U.S. $3,500 by two young Mexican men to transport irregular migrants. He had initially declined but reconsidered as one of his trailers needed expensive repairs. In court records, two other men who were accused testified that they usually transported the migrants in vans, but on that occasion the number of people who had recruited their services was such that they believed using a truck would make things easier (U.S. vs Rodriguez, 2008).

Williams covered the entire distance to Victoria from Harlingen, Texas (the place where the migrants entered the vehicle, an estimated three and a half hours away), without making a single stop, driving under the speed limit so as not to attract the authorities' attention. He stopped at the gas station in Victoria that night most likely at the behest of other drivers who pointed out that something was wrong with his taillights.

The scene inside the truck must have made Williams realize something had gone terribly wrong. The Dantesque display of collapsed bodies and arms reaching out for help must have been overwhelming. An old security video shows him walking twice into the gas station to buy a few bottles of water, which he allegedly distributed among the survivors waiting outside. It was perhaps at that moment that Williams began to grasp the magnitude of the event. He disconnected the trailer from his truck and fled the scene, leaving all the victims behind. A few hours later he checked himself into a hospital in Houston, claiming overwhelming stress. By then 19 people—all male—were dead. A 5-year-old boy had died in his father's arms. The other 44 survivors had been treated for borderline critical heat exhaustion, and the state-wide manhunt for those responsible was well on its way.

Karla Lopez, a 25-year-old single mother of three, was following the news coverage of the event in disbelief. She had coordinated the journeys of several of the people in the truck. Lopez had just recently started participating in the facilitation of extralegal journeys, following the arrest of her children's father, who was a coyote. The Victoria trip was the fifth she organized and would be her largest. Until then she had relied on friends and acquaintances to secure clients, transportation, and locations to house migrants, earning a few hundred dollars each time. This time things had become cumbersome. Multiple recruiters had been calling her requesting seat assignments in the vans that she would load with border crossers trying to reach Houston. She had lost track of how many people she was expecting to transport that time, but she was not very concerned. This time, the man in charge of securing the vans believed switching to a larger vehicle would reduce costs and expedite the transit, and she did not oppose the change. She was particularly strapped for cash after covering the legal expenses of her former partner. She estimated that once all costs were covered, the trip would leave her an estimated U.S. $500 in profits, which was not much given the number of travelers and the time she had invested, but would help her provide for her children. Shortly after the news of the accident broke, she fled the country and moved back to Honduras with her family. Fearing repercussions from the families of the deceased, Lopez left her three children in the custody of her mother and fled to Guatemala, where she was arrested and extradited to the United States to face her process, and was eventually sentenced to 17 years in prison (U.S. Department of Justice, 2010).

The Victoria tragedy was indeed an event of massive proportions. Yet its scope was magnified by the sensationalist coverage that surrounded it, and which was in great measure the responsibility of Latina/o broadcasting companies. While the international media descended on the small community (the naked feet of one of the victims inside the truck becoming a symbol of the tragedy), a local Univision station (the top U.S. Latino broadcasting company) became the source of coverage on the tragedy and had unlimited access to the site and the victims. Jorge Ramos, Univision's main correspondent, located the survivors and interviewed them as part of an hour long special recreating the tragedy. For *Viaje a la Muerte*,[2] Ramos traveled to Victoria with four male survivors and filmed them as they walked around the parking lot where Williams had abandoned them. A mix of recreated scenes, media clips, and interview footage (which includes scenes of Williams and Chavez in custody), the documentary is a visual narrative comprising dead migrants' bodies, images of "Mexican" poverty, and the survivors' suffering.

Viaje, as in many other more recent productions showcasing the U.S.-bound irregular migrant journey, seeks to insert narratives of "humanitarianism" (attempting to "give a human face" to the "drama" of undocumented migration) yet does little other than fetishize the survivors' physical suffering, often reducing the experiences of migrants to tragedy.[3] *Viaje*, for example, closes by blaming the events in Victoria on the very poverty afflicting the migrants, and their almost irrational search for the "American dream," rather than considering the much larger and stronger structural mechanisms that as forms of institutional violence deliberately target the migrant body and its survivability. In this sense, smuggling and the work of the coyote become further reinscribed, rather than as attempts of those unable to secure the protection of visas or passports to develop their own forms of human security (what we can effectively describe as a form of 'protection from below') as the natural consequence of opting for traveling with smugglers (in other words, it makes the migrant responsible for his or her own victimization, or even death).

Conclusion: Coyotes, Migrants, and the Border Spectacle

While Latina/o media could provide a platform to contest the way dominant media has constructed Latina/o migrant identities, it has most often supported, legitimized, and reproduced narrow and negative characterizations of Latina/os, particularly in the discourses pertaining to migration. Two fundamental characters in this process have been the irregular migrant and the human smuggler or coyote. While for decades corridos and *películas de indocumentados* were effective at communicating the experiences of irregular migration to a specific population, changes in the distribution of media in the streaming era, alongside the rhetoric of national security and the demand for racialized, gendered identities that can embody global threats of late modernity, have changed some of those culturally-specific, community-centered mechanisms. Within current global anxieties over human mobility that have framed irregular migration as a phenomenon of unprecedented proportions, the human smuggler stands as a quintessential predator, so it should not come as a surprise that contemporary iterations of irregular migration on popular Latino media most often include a greedy, violent, and often hypersexual coyote as part of their narratives.

Globally, narratives of tragic irregular migrations and despicable smugglers have become necessary elements of what Nicholas De Genova refers to as *border spectacle*, "the enactment of exclusion through the enforcement of the border, which produces illegalized migration as a category and literally and figuratively renders it visible" (2013). He further argues that "the representation of illegality is imprinted on selected migration streams and bodies," suggesting that the coverage of tragedies like the one documented by Univision in Victoria, and fictional or "factual" representations of irregular migration, "serve to enact the spectacle of the border and deepen the architecture and practices of the border regime" (Kasparek, De Genova, and Hess, 2013: 67).

Yet the presence of the coyote, and the cultural fixation with the most violent of their actions, also reveal historically specific tensions with identity formation. As the term coyote transitions from native traditions into the caste system of Colonial Mexico, it becomes marked by people's collective anxieties over the presence of those who are forced to be on the margins by virtue of their mixed ancestry, by those who perform the tasks that no other person would do. Coyotes could then be perceived as simply another product of mestizaje, yet they are a reflection, a constant reminder of our own identities as colonial subjects—a reminder of our own selves.

The rejection expressed against the acts of coyotes allows them to be swept to the margins, yet they remain as part of our collective consciousness and identity. Furthermore, the illicit nature of coyotes' actions make it easier for those who have relied on their services to distance themselves from the life of precarity and risk of their own migrant experiences, and facilitates the embracing of mainstream discourses that may condemn the violence that irregular migrants face, yet see it as an inherent element of their journeys. In that sense, the spectacle of migrant illegality becomes, as De Genova states, "a scene of exclusion, and the obscene of inclusion."

Notes

1 "A mi ver, ni es lobo ni zorro, sino animal propio de esta tierra … . Es diabólico este animal." (In my perception, it is neither wolf nor fox, but an animal of this land. This animal is diabolic.)
2 "Journey to Death." Ramos also authored a best seller based on the case.
3 A few examples stand out: Luis Mandoki's *La Vida Precoz y Breve de Sabina Rivas*; Pedro Ultreras' *Siete Soles* and La *Bestia*; Mark Silver's *Who is Dayani Crystal?*; Cary Fukunaga's *Sin Nombre*; Diego Quemada-Diez *La Jaula de Oro*, etc.

Bibliography

Andreas, Peter. *Smuggler Nation: How Illicit Trade Made America*. New York: Oxford University Press, 2014.

De Genova, Nicholas. "Spectacles of Migrant Illegality: The Scene of Exclusion, the Obscene of Inclusion." *Ethnic and Racial Studies* 36:7 (2013): 1180–98.

Escalante, Virginia. "The Politics of Chicano Representation in the Media." *Chicano Renaissance: Contemporary Cultural Trends*. Eds. David Maciel, Isidro D. Ortiz and Maria Herrera-Sobek. Tucson: The University of Arizona Press, 2000. 131–68.

Gamio, Manuel. *Mexican Immigration to the United States: A Study of Human Migration and Adjustment*. New York: Dover Publications, 1971.

Hagan, Jacqueline. *Migration Miracle: Faith, Hope and Meaning on the Undocumented Journey*. Boston: Harvard University Press, 2012.

Herrera-Sobek, Maria. "El Corrido como Hypertexto, las Peliculas de Indocumentados y la Balada Chicano/Mexicana." *Cultura al Otro Lado de la Frontera*. Eds. David R. Maciel and Maria Herrera-Sobek. Mexico City: Siglo XXI Editores, 1999.

ICE. "12th Individual Sentenced in 2003 Texas Human Smuggling Tragedy." ICE Newsroom Press Release. 9 November 2009.

Izcara-Palacios, Simón P. "Coyotaje y Grupos Delictivos en Tamaulipas." *Latin American Research Review* 47:3 (2012): 41–61.

Kasparek, Bernd, Nicholas De Genova and Sabine Hess. "(4) Border Spectacle." In Nicholas De Genova, Sandro Mezzadra and John Pickles (eds.). New Keywords: Migration and Borders. *Cultural Studies* 29:1 (2015): 55–87.

Khosravi, Shahram. *Illegal Traveler: An Auto-Ethnography of Borders*. London: Palgrave, 2010.

López-Austin Alfredo. *Augurios y Abusiones. Fuentes Indígenas de la Cultura Náhuatl. Textos de los Informantes de Sahagún*. 4. Mexico City: UNAM, Instituto de Investigaciones Históricas.

López-Castro, Gustavo. "Coyotes and Alien Smuggling." *Binational Study of Migration between Mexico and the United States, Vol. 2. Research Reports and Background Materials*. Washington: U.S. Commission on Immigration Reform, 1998. 965–74.

Meléndez, Theresa. "Coyote: Towards a Definition of a Concept." *Aztlan* 13 (1982): 295–307.

Ochoa O'Leary, Anna M. "The ABCs of Migration Costs: Assembling, Bajadores and Coyotes." *Migration Letters* 6:1(2009): 27–35.

Omi, Michael and Howard Winant. *Racial Formation in the United States*. New York: Routledge, 2015.

Ramos, Jorge. *Morir en el Intento: La Peor Tragedia de Inmigrantes en la Historia de los Estados Unidos*. New York: Harper Collins, 2005.

Rodríguez Valle, Nieves. "El Coyote en la Literature de Tradición Oral." *Revista de Literaturas Populares* 5:1 (2005): 79–112.

Sanchez, Gabriella. *Human Smuggling and Border Crossings*. London: Routledge, 2015.

Spener, David. "The Lexicon of Clandestine Migration on the Mexico-US Border." *Aztlan* 39:1 (2014):71–103.

Staudt, Kathleen. "The Border, Performed in Films: Produced in Both Mexico and the U.S. to 'Bring Out the Worst in a Country.'" *Journal of Borderland Studies* 29:4 (2014): 465–79.

U.S. v. Rodriguez. United States Court of Appeals Decision No 06-20774. December 15, 2008.

U.S.Department of Justice. "Last Defendant in Deadliest Smuggling Operation Sentenced." Press Release,. The United States Attorney's Office, Southern District of Texas. 7 June, 2010.

Wolf, Eric. *Sons of the Shaking Earth*. Chicago: University of Chicago Press, 1959.

Zhang, Sheldon X. *Smuggling and Trafficking in Human Beings: All Roads Lead to America*. Westport CT: Praeger, 2007.

Zhang, Sheldon X. *Chinese Human Smuggling Organizations: Families, Social Networks and Cultural Imperatives*. Palo Alto: Stanford University Press, 2008.

Zhang, Sheldon, Ko-lin Chin and Jody Miller. "Women's Participation in Chinese Transnational Human Smuggling. A Gendered Market Perspective." *Criminology* 45:3 (2007): 699–733.

AFTERWORD

A Latino Pop Quartet for the Ontologically Complex Smartphone Age

William Anthony Nericcio

It was the best of times, it was the worst of times, it was the age of wisdom, it was the age of foolishness, it was the epoch of belief, it was the epoch of incredulity, it was the season of Light, it was the season of Darkness, it was the spring of hope, it was the winter of despair, we had everything before us, we had nothing before us, we were all going direct to Heaven, we were all going direct the other way.

Charles Dickens, *A Tale of Two Cities*[1]

Anxiety is not only anxiety about ... , but is at the same time, an attunement, anxiety for ... In anxiety, the things at hand in the surrounding world sink away, and so do innerworldly beings in general. The "world" can offer nothing more, nor can the Dasein-with of others. Thus anxiety takes away from Dasein the possibility of understanding itself, falling prey, in terms of the "world" and the public way of being interpreted.

Martin Heidegger, *Being and Time*[2]

I: Smörgåsbord with a Trumped-up Dressing

When all is said and done ...

"When all is said and done ... "—*the* very definition of an *Afterword*.

We close this magnificent show, this down and brown album of intellectual firepower and savvy artistry with Charles "El Carlos" Dickens' well-known dictum, adapted somewhat for our present circumstances: "it [is] the best of times, it [is] the worst of times" for (among other things) Latina/o Pop culture.

And we close it as well with some anxiety—Heideggerian anxiety, to be sure, (and to seem smart) but regular run-of-the-mill anxiety as well. "Being-in-the-world" is tough enough when one is trafficking in existential philosophy, but *being-in-the-world*, what Heidegger tagged with the catchy moniker *Dasein*, is damn well next to impossible when it comes to the conundrum of Latinas/os in American mass culture, where Hamlet's ontological birthright (to query whether "to be, or not to be") is not always our choice, has not always been our possibility.

But we must move on—*kinesis* always at least guarantees the appearance of progress.

Back to Carlitos Dickens.

It is the best of times because never before have there been so many avatars of Latina/o deliciousness splashing across the televisions, movie screens, and smartphones of the American population: from Robert Rodriguez (can you say *Machete III*?) to *Jane the Virgin* with its Golden Globe award-winning actress Gina Rodriguez, from Mexican cinematic gurus Alfonso Cuarón, Alejandro González Iñárritu, and Guillermo del Toro (along with three-in-row best cinematographer Oscar winner Emmanuel Lubezki—for *Birdman*, *Gravity*, and *The Revenant*) to Emmy award-winning phenoms Sophia Vergara and America Ferrara, you can't flip a channel (or load a web page) without washing your eyes in the rich semiotic tapestry that is the Latina/o body politic writ large in pulsing photons bouncing off your retinas with the regularity of the sunrise—our aural world gets a workout too with the musical mesmerism of Shakira and groovy street rock/bebop of Chicano Batman providing the background score for our twenty-first century travails. Gustavo Arellano, scabrous scribe of *Ask-A-Mexican* and contributing producer for Fox TV's new animated series *Bordertown* (premiering January 2016) keeps calling for #televisionreconquista on all his social media channels—it might just be here!

Or not …

And so, *it is the worst of times* because never before has racist hate against (primarily, but racists are not picky) Mexican bodies (legal and "illegal", documented and undocumented) and Latina/o *gente* been so in vogue in our peculiar nation of once-immigrants/now

Figure 36.1   Lalo Alcaraz's "Liberty's On the Run," 2010

425

xenophobes (the irony of this too rich to ignore, the Statue of Liberty now reduced from a symbol of freedom to mocking idol) (Figure 36.1).

This de-evolution did not begin with talk radio—did not commence with the seductive neo-fascist dulcet tones of Fox News—but ever since fat, cigar-chomping speed-freak Rush Limbaugh, germophobe hypocrite Lou Dobbs, sorority-girl-channeling Ayn Rand, neo-Nazi Ann Coulter, and now, tele-celebrity, billionaire fascist Donald Trump started filling American ears and souls with wave after wave, sound bite after sound bite, hate-smeared speech act after hate-smeared speech act of anti-Mexican, anti-Latina/o aural and visual vitriole, it suddenly became OK to loathe ethnic bodies in public. In conversation, I have called this trend our twenty-first century Latina/o *Kristallnacht*.[4]

Random and planned acts of violence have accompanied Trump's smashing rise in the polls (and when you read this, we will perhaps finally know the electoral fate of that plump 'short-fingered vulgarian,' *Spy Magazine's* telling take on *the Donald*) with undocumented workers beat–up in Boston, and anti-Trump protestors attacked in Florida—Latina/o telecelebrities are not immune from this treatment with even Jorge Ramos, our Latino Walter Cronkite, rudely manhandled out of a Trump press conference.[5]

In my own scribblings on the *Tex[t]-Mex Galleryblog*, I have documented Trump's rise in the wake of Dobbs's, Coulter's, and Limbaugh's (at least) decade-long monologue of hate-speech on right wing talk radio outlets and the Fox News channels. But you don't need the reincarnated body of Marshall McLuhan to remind you that talk radio itself did not come out of some vacuum—the seething, writhing hate was more of a spoor in an already robust and fecund Petri dish; anti-Latina/o racism, a virally adaptive organism, given new hosts via radio. Seeding an American soil already ripe for racist hate, the biracial body of President Barack Obama had already served as a spur to the rise of hate groups from California to Maine.[6] With anguished cries of "I want my country back," these mobs (think *The Walking Dead* but driving, with Trump bumper stickers) of haters now span the country, entertaining themselves with reruns of *Duck Dynasty* and *Honey Boo Boo* as they burn images of Obama or harass undocumented immigrants along the U.S./Mexican border with flashlights (or worse).

II: Gus Arriola's *Gordo* and the Semiotics of Mexicanicity in America

Writers of Afterwords are a lucky lot. Before *you* ever got your eyes on these pages, dear reader of *The Routledge Companion to Latina/o Popular Culture*, I have already encountered all its resplendent voices and scholarship. I've delved deep into Camilla Fojas's mad-smart findings with regard to Latino film, reveled in Osvaldo Cleger's musings on videogames, danced with Pancho McFarland's hip hop findings, broken bread (or tortillas) with Paloma Martínez-Cruz's culinary ruminations, cruised in Ben Chappell's lowrider, jumped offside with Christopher Gonzalez's sporting contemplations, and channeled Frederick Aldama's calculated, orchestrated curation of all of the above.

Said exercise gets you through *the worst of times*.

What we find here gathered is a constellation of smart people, intellectuals whose collective imaginations work as a salve, an existential balm, calming our worst of fears from worst of times scenarios where the hate does not go away—this anxiety must be kept at bay in order for the Latina/o *Dasein* to emerge, in order for complex subjectivities to evolve with Darwinian cunning.

These chapters, these interventions inspire a force of action, a matrix of engaged contestations and discoveries that force readers to re-align their views of our Latina/o *Dasein*. Or to see it for the first time: Touch it. Feel it. Want it.

And the anxiety, for the moment, abates—retreats to the dark shadows and hopefully into hibernation; it won't really die. The anxiety of ontology, of being, of being-in-the-world itself, is unimaginably difficult for Americans of Latina/o descent.

Heidegger never ran with *carnales* in the ivory tower, with *vatos locos* and *cholas chingonas* in the barrio.

He missed out.

Myself? I am pleased to get this chance to return to writing after spending the better part of two years trying to get away from it.

Let me explain (and please forgive this self-indulgent slide into autobiography).

One of the consequences of having written *Tex[t]-Mex: Seductive Hallucinations of the "Mexican" in America,* my magnum opus on Latina/o stereotypes, is that I got to become a curator. Better put, I got to channel my hoarding tendencies into something I would like to think of as Museum Studies, but is actually closer to me being a pack-rat.

Born from the assembled artifacts, newspaper clippings, advertisements, and whatnots I had collected over the years since graduate school, my ridiculous graphic art experiments, and my own collection of Mexican American/Latina/o art and photography, *Mextasy: Seductive Hallucinations of Latina/o Mannequins in the American Unconscious* is a pop-up gallery exhibition that evolved out of my book with the University of Texas Press.

I have thought of this traveling exhibition as a way to reach out to throngs of Latina/o culture vultures who don't have the time to read heady treatises written by professor-types (present company in this book excepted) only available in college bookstores (sometimes, when the logo-ridden sweatshirts sell out) and in musty university libraries.

The move to gallerize my academic work revealed something to myself I had not really understood: that I yearned to do more than *study pop culture*—in a sense, in some weird Dorian Gray meets the Twilight Zone sort of way, I wanted to *become* one of the many artifacts I accumulated along the way. Not to become a pop artist (*estilo* Andy Warhol, Selena-style), but to engage with pop aesthetics in simulcast, to develop a work that functioned in parallel with an emerging Latina/o pop critical aesthetic.

To have my *pan dulce* and eat it too, *por supuesto.*

In order to do that, I had to change the way I write—instead of pursuing publications in scholarly tomes, I had to start writing for a more general reader—less professorial, more street; less academic, more intimate.

For three years or so now I have been writing for the wonderfully titled *hilobrow.com*—an online magazine edited by Joshua Glenn of *Hermenaut* fame back in the day.

Glenn, trained as a newspaper editor in Boston, is a monster with the editing knife—a blue editor's pen is too sweet for his Jack the Ripper expurgations, his manic exercises in rhetorical pruning that always left your baroque wordsmith gasping for air.

But it was through these exercises—simultaneously mounting a traveling museum show and learning to write for a broader audience (unlearning the ghastly jargon-laden writing academe had rewarded me for), that the ground was set for my next adventure/experiment in television.

But I am getting ahead of myself.

Here, unexpurgated, is my riff on Mexican American cartoonist Gus Arriola, a singular and powerful twentieth-century presence in the history of Latina/o pop:

> GUS ARRIOLA: Long toward the end of a long timeline that begins with the Lascaux cave paintings, there, just after the turn of the last century between Winsor McCay and genius-of-the-present-moment Chris Ware, rests the redoubtable master of sequential art, Gus Arriola.

A Mexican-American artist from Arizona who ended up spending the rest of his life in California, Arriola's comic strip *Gordo* delighted, bemused, and confused readers from November 24, 1941 to March 2, 1985. "Confused" because Arriola's ambition, particularly in his Sunday splash-page cartoons, were the stuff of comic book legend, marrying the semiotic ambition and range of McCay's earlier work, with a baroque, jazzy color palette (and a sublime disregard for the precision of the square panel—a precision, I might add, that has led to the banal cacophony of boring, shrunk, stiff compositions that fill the daily fishwrap today: yes, Mary Worth and Beetle Bailey, I am talking about you).

Arriola's *Gordo* is best remembered for being one of the few daily, mainstream, narrative artifacts that was focused on Mexico, Mexicans, Mexican-Americans and Mexican culture—also one of the few that was positive and evocative (though, irony of ironies, Gordo begins as a strip focused on a fat, lazy, "Mexican"—scare-quotes necessary, *por favor*).

In an American popular culture sea of stereotypes featuring raping bandit Mexicans (in case you're wondering where idiot Donald Trump gets his ideas), dirty, pre-civilization Latinas/os, and the rest, Gordo evolves as *a brimming visual cauldron of subterranean semiotic insurrection*, surreptitiously introducing readers to Mexicans and Spanish-language culture with a light touch, and a rigorous and disruptive compositional eye.

Old school hands in the comics trade like Mort Walker and Charles Schulz envied Arriola's eye and pen, with Charlie Brown's father touting Arriola's strip as the "the most beautifully drawn strip in the history of the business." Like the aforementioned Chris Ware, Arriola's genius rested with what used to be called postmodern aesthetics— as much as Arriola loved to tell a story he also (and simultaneously) told a story about stories—meta-narrative from a Chicano *meta-mensch*.

For me, a little Mexican-American kid growing up in the 1960s, Arriola's warped and warping lines did a number on my imagination—though I was born on and in the U.S./ Mexico border in Laredo, Texas, and was, as a result, submerged in Tex-Mex/Mexicano *cultura*, the English-language/ 'Merican side of my psyche was utterly bereft of Mexican influences—in this regard, both Speedy Gonzales and Gordo are like bizarre twin devils perched upon my shoulder, speaking in English (but with a decidedly "Mexican" accent) and seducing my psyche with parsed and unparsable utterances that moved and delighted me on the surface and had deeper, unknowable impacts elsewhere, marking my career in cultural studies.[7]

III: Severo Sarduy, Translation, Transubstantation, and Transvestismo

It was natural for someone who serves at the foot of Latina/o pop culture to write about comics—in this regard my piece on Arriola joined other things I wrote on www.hilobrow.com on Bill Elder, Chris Ware, and Charles Burns. But in order to do Latina/o Pop right, to give the credit where credit was due, I also had to stay true to my roots—as a PhD child of the Postmodern 1980s, high theory had to have a home in my popular culture spelunkings but it had to do so in a way that would not alienate the masses. Here again, unexpurgated, but deriving from my dabbling in online writing is my homage to Severo Sarduy!

SEVERO SARDUY: He is the toast of Paris, by way of Havana—a Cuban scribe with a lithe mind (and a body subject to metamorphosis). Poised between the at-times bitter taste of full-on Euro Structuralism (note the capital "S") and, just-on-the-horizon, Post-structuralism (and Postmodernity, aka *Pomo*, for that matter), his evolving fragmented literary and theoretical escapades will bridge the gap between Latin American and European intellectual history.[8]

"He" is the one and only Severo Sarduy: Roland Barthes's student, fixture of *Tel Quel* intellectual covens, lover/partner of François Wahl (editor at Éditions du Seuil), and matchmaker for French readers with the likes of Gabriel García Márquez and Jose Lezama Lima.

Novelist (*Gestos*, 1963; *Cobra*, 1972; *Maitreya*, 1978), Essayist (*Written on a Body*, 1969), Poet (*Big Bang*, 1974), and more (I am told his radio plays are legendary, shades of Orson Welles, or, better, a Welles rolled in with a Nabokov, with Gore Vidal tossed in for good measure), Sarduy weaves a literary tapestry noted for its grandiloquence and sassy wit.

His wordplay is serious and his essays formidable. For English readers, the most accessible entry into Sarduy's wicked mind is *Written on a Body*, from 1989, translated by Carol Meier (which combines Sarduy's *Escrito sobre un cuerpo* from 1969 with the first half of *La simulación* from 1982). In these essays, musings, and fragments, one runs into a Cuban Jean Baudrillard (of course you can look at it backwards: Baudrillard was merely a straight, Frenchy Severo Sarduy—no doubt they cribbed notes from each other at *Tel Quel* cocktail parties).

In these pages, Sarduy anticipates much of what passes for queer theory and gender and post-gender studies these days with riveting biology-inspired passages that wow the reader with their audacity.

Did you know that transvestites are like butterflies and other insects that use camouflage and metamorphosis in a headlong pursuit of pleasure? (or is it erasure? Sarduy: "[N]othing insures that the chemical—or surgical—conversion of men into women does not have as its hidden goal a kind of disappearance, invisibility, effacement" (*Written on a Body*, 94).

Like Octavio Paz on LSD, or maybe ecstasy, Sarduy's hedonistic theorization of transvestism reveals the domain of the human through entomology-smeared lenses resulting in some of the best critical theory since Deleuze and Guattari went gardener on our asses with their *rhizome*-laced theoretical soliloquies.[9]

IV: Mextasy—Seductive Hallucinations on Latina/os in the American Unconscious

In a sense I am forged or formed as a writer, and now an artist, by my transmogrified synapses—neurons *de-ranged* by chance encounters with, among others, a Mexican-American experimental cartoonist, Arriola, and a genius Cuban shapeshifter, Sarduy.

I see both of their influences in the aforementioned *Mextasy*, a traveling pop-up art exhibition that has changed my life and just might lead to a career in/on television (don't hold your breath!).

More on that in a minute.

As these words go to press, I have just closed my twentieth *Mextasy* exhibition/ presentation, this one at the Gallery@SWC, on the Southwestern College campus in Chula Vista, California.[10] There, under the curatorial guidance of Italian-American artist/director, Vallo Riberto, *Mextasy* has emerged as a full-blown museum installation replete with didactics, openings, and more. *Mextasy* appeared as part of a show entitled *1+1*, featuring a veritable who's who of Baja California-based Mexican artists affiliated with the CECUT, the

Centro Cultural Tijuana, including Hugo Crosthwaite, Alejandra Phelts, Marcos Ramirez, Roberto Gandarilla, Manuel Luis Escutia, and Mely Barragán.

I want to share two new pieces here I did for the show—these pieces debuted at Gallery@ SWC but they will stay in the show as it moves to Tucson (University of Arizona), Ithaca (Cornell University), and Lawrence (University of Kansas) in the Spring of 2016. Both works conjoin my ongoing attack on Mexican stereotypes that was born in the pages of *Tex[t]-Mex*, but both also move forward, attempting to engage with audiences fed up with the mainstreaming of anti-Mexican, anti-Latina/o hate.

What this means is that I am no longer really writing about Latina/o Pop; it means that I am trying to engage with the mass cultural visual effluvia on its own terms, in its own medium—only time will tell if this attempt to speak the language of the boob tube, to surf the televisual waves that constitute and shape us, will have any impact at all.

The centerpiece of the Southwestern College Art Gallery show is a towering composite sculpture entitled "The {New} Statue of Liberty," a work that combines a Donald Trump piñata my sister picked up for me off of San Bernardo Avenue in Laredo, Texas, this past summer, and a tire-besmirched road sign gifted to me by my dear friend Dee Reed, an avocado-grower (and cultural studies graduate student), from East County near San Diego (see Figure 36.2):

Figure 36.2   Trump Statue of Liberty

Figure 36.3 As part of rewriting the history of Latinas/os in the Americas, we felt we had to go to the Hollywood sign near Griffith's Park in LA to symbolize our planned reinscription, our semiotic Reconquista.

I am the grandson of a Sicilian immigrant who came through Ellis Island in 1906—the other three abuelos/as were Mexican and Mexican-American. So, as you might imagine, the symbolic reverberations of the giantess sculpture France gifted to the United States, Lady Liberty, looms large in my psyche—Trump's latest statements on Mexican immigrants triggered a rage I could not root out with pleasant, logical arguments, with patient, wisdom-laced footnotes.[11]

So I turned to sculpture.

To art.

And to television. The last thing I have up my sleeve is to try to enter into the maelstrom of American cable television via a travel show also called *Mextasy*.[12]

The show itself is an experiment—whether in televised entertainment or in intellectual pedagogy I have yet to determine. You can mark this undecidability in the supporting verbiage we've grafted onto our written pitches for network executives:

> *Mextasy* surfs the waves of a Latina/o tomorrow! Imagine a Latino-focused travel show where your tour guide is an ex-bartending, pool-playing, rock-guitar strumming, mad doodling, Latino English Professor. Mextasy is a show about a man that is driven by a quest to travel, discover, and celebrate Latina and Latino communities and their vibrant artists throughout the U.S. and beyond.
>
> Mextasy breaks the stereotypical mold. No roundup of domestic maids, no casting call for devious narco traffickers. Instead, Mextasy samples the delicious smörgåsbord of Latina/o humanity—each episode focused on what's going down now in a major planetary metropole: Mextasy San Antonio, Texas? Check! Mextasy New York City? Of course! But Mextasy Paris, Mextasy London, Mextasy at the Oscars, as well.
>
> Mextasy's host, Dr. William "Memo" Nericcio, a popular Ivy League-trained, California-based cultural studies maniac/English Professor, thinks of the University

as an asylum, a crazy house he has to escape in search of Latina/o innovation and artistry—join him on his quest in search of Mextasy!

That's entertainment!

The one-page pitch for the show reveals the show is financed for three quarters of a million dollars by Blindspot Productions based out of Mexico City, DF, and Madrid, Spain.

Where did this come from? What does it all mean?

Mextasy derives from a frustration and an itch—a frustration with an American mass culture addicted to the broadcast and dissemination of idiots, malcontents, and fools; a frustration, too, with an American telespace of entertainment content with repeating stereotypes ad infitum and ad nauseum.

Now, the "itch": Mextasy seeks to immerse its watchers in the unknowable exquisiteness that is the world of Latina and Latino women and men in the United States and beyond. As this chapter comes to press I have been trying to sell the show across the U.S. and Mexico—in the process, I have become an expert of the "elevator pitch," a bizarre performance wherein you condense 20 years of work into a 2 to 5 minute sound bite. I have pitched to studio heads at Lionsgate (*Mad Men, Orange is the New Black*), rubbed shoulders with Norman Lear, interrogated Eva Longoria, eavesdropped on Vince Gilligan's (*Breaking Bad*) conversations—all of that, and I still don't have a show, still don't have a distribution deal.

The moral of the story, dear Professor friends? Don't quit your day job.

The future of Latinas/os in American pop culture is bright—as Timbuk 3 had it back in the day, "The Future's So Bright/Gotta Wear Shades," but the opportunity to create intelligent television across platforms (broadcast, streaming, cable) is difficult for all Americans, perhaps especially those who would swim against the stream of a cascading wave that might just abate, or might, as with a tsunami, return with a violent force that ultimately we must be prepared for.

Notes

1 Charles Dickens, *A Tale of Two Cities* (London: James Nisbet & Co., Limited, 1902), 3.
2 Martin Heidegger, *Being and Time* Joan Stambaugh, translator, Dennis J. Schmidt, editor. Albany: SUNY Press, 2010, 185.
3 Lalo Alcaraz, "Liberty's On the Run," 2010, *Migration Now* (website: http://migrationnow.com/post/26916960183/lalo-alcaraz-lalo-alcaraz-is-a-political). From the *Migration Now* site: "Lalo Alcaraz is a political cartoonist, visual artist, designer, poster-maker, satirist, and writer. He draws the nationally syndicated comic strip "La Cucaracha" and is an award-winning editorial cartoonist. Alcaraz is also the Jefe In Chief of the satirical website *Pocho.com*, and host of KPFK Radio's weekly *Pocho Hour of Power* program. "Liberty's On The Run" was visually inspired by the ubiquitous immigrant crossing sign and thematically, it was inspired by the continuing efforts of Arizona's right wing politicians to harass undocumented immigrants. The image suggests [among other things] a violation of brown people's human rights.
4 *Kristallnacht* as described on the U.S. Holocaust Memorial Museum website: "literally, 'Night of Crystal,' is often referred to as the 'Night of Broken Glass.' The name refers to the wave of violent anti-Jewish pogroms that took place on November 9–10, 1938. This wave of violence took place throughout Germany, annexed Austria, and in areas of the Sudetenland in Czechoslovakia recently occupied by German troops … *Kristallnacht* owes its name to the shards of shattered glass that lined German streets in the wake of the pogrom—broken glass from the windows of synagogues, homes, and Jewish-owned businesses plundered and destroyed during the violence." U.S. Holocaust Memorial Museum website (www.ushmm.org/wlc/en/article.php?ModuleId=10005201)
5 See Russell Berman's "A Trump-Inspired Hate Crime in Boston," *The Atlantic* (August 20, 2015), www.theatlantic.com/politics/archive/2015/08/a-trump-inspired-hate-crime-in-boston/401906/;

Kim Bellware's "Pro-Immigration Protester Violently Dragged Out Of Trump Rally" *Huffpost Latino Voices* (October 25, 2015), www.huffingtonpost.com/entry/donald-trump-florida-rally_562ce403e4b0ec0a3894ba2d; and Theodore Schleifer's "Univision anchor ejected from Trump news conference," www.cnn.com/2015/08/25/politics/donald-trump-megyn-kelly-iowa-rally/

6   The go-to group for information on hate groups in the United States is the Southern Poverty Law Center, www.splcenter.org/issues/hate-and-extremism

7   A version of this sequence first appeared as "Gus Arriola" (July 17, 2015). http://hilobrow.com/2015/07/17/gus-arriola/

8   With the United States, sadly, lagging behind—sorry Jonathan Culler!

9   The best web-based reverie on Sarduy is from *The Independent*, by the late English writer James Kirkup, "Obituary: Severo Sarduy" (October 22, 2011). www.independent.co.uk/news/people/obituary-severo-sarduy-1491791.html

10 Take a virtual tour of the installation here: https://vimeo.com/145141793

11 Trump's actual words? Mexico is "sending people [to the U.S.] that have lots of problems. They are bringing drugs, and bringing crime, and their rapists." See Rupert Neate's "Donald Trump doubles down on Mexico 'rapists' comments despite outrage" in *The Guardian* (July 2, 2015) .www.theguardian.com/us-news/2015/jul/02/donald-trump-racist-claims-mexico-rapes

12 https://vimeo.com/117076126

INDEX

Bold page numbers indicate figures

Abarca, Meredith E. 246, 252; *Rethinking Chicana/o/Literature through Food* 257
ABC 29; *a.k.a. Pablo* 28; *Common Law* 28; *Cristela* 30; *I Married Dora* 28; *Kukla, Fran and Ollie* 45; *Modern Family* 7; *Ugly Betty* 6, 7, 9, 24, 25, 30, 328; "Wide World of Sports" 340
"ABC's of Love" 305
Acevedo, Elizabeth: "Invocation" 158; "Spear" 159; "Volver, Volver" 18; "Wolfchild" 158
Acción Chicano 27
Acosta, David 306
Acosta, Oscar Zeta 156, 306; *Autobiography of a Brown Buffalo* 110; *The Revolt of the Cockroach People* 103
Activision: *Call of Duty: Black Ops* 87; *Call of Duty: Black Ops II* 89; *Call of Duty: Modern Warfare II* 87
The Adventures of Jonny Quest 46
The Advocate 298
AFNs. *See* Alternative Food Networks
Afrofuturism 112, 115
Aguilar, Laura: *Fuerzas Naturales* 231
Aguilar, Mario 134
Ahora! 27
AJAAS. *See* Association of Joteria Arts and Activism Scholarship
Al-Qaeda 302, 401
Alambrista 35
Alba, Jessica: *Machete* 40
Alberto, Lourdes 137
Albertson, Jack: *Chico and the Man* 27–8
Alcalá, Rita Cano 230–1
Alcaraz, Lalo: *Coco* 54; "La cucaracha" 432n3; "Liberty On The Run" **425**, 432n3; "Muerto Mouse" 375; *Pocho Hour of Power* 432n3; *Pocho.com* 432n3
Aldama, Arturo 132, 137

Aldama, Frederick Luis 337, 426; "Confessions from a Latino Sojourner in *SciFilandia*" 110; "Getting Your Mind/Body On" 92; *Latino Comic Book Storytelling* 102, 104, 107; *¡Muy Pop!* 216
Alejandro, Kevin: *True Blood* 9
Alex, Stacey 14
Alexander, Erika: *La Mission* 299
Alexander, Michelle 164, 170
Alfaro, Luis: *Deep in the Crotch of My Latino Psyche* 206
Algarín, Miguel 152, 154, 155, 157; *Nuyorican Poetry* 153, 156
Almada, Mario 402
Alonzo, Cristela: *Cristela* 31
Alternative Food Networks (AFNs) 243, 245, 246, **246**
Alurista 165; "El Plan Espiritual de Aztlán" 152, 246
Alva, Jenn 298. *See also* Girl in a Coma
The Alvin Show 46
American Culinary Federation 243
American Entertainment Marketing 5
American Family 30
American Girl Dolls 4
American Idol **62**
American Me 3, 35
Amundson, Daniel 24, 25
Anders, Allison: *Mi Vida Loca* 3
Andersen, Lemon 157
Annual Festival of Nations 134
Anthony, Adelina 296
Anthony, Marc 3, **62**, 176, 177
Anzaldúa, Gloria 73, 76, 112, 115, 137, 139, 194, 197, 199–200, 256–7, 263, 311, 361; *Borderlands/La Frontera* 133, 265n1; *La Danza Azteca* 134, 136; "Now Let Us Shift" 133, 263; "Speaking Across the Divide" 133, 134; *This Bridge We Call Home* 133

Applegate, Christina: *Book of Life* 375
Aquaman 46
Aquí y Ahora 176
Aragón, Cecilia Josephine 12–13, 298
Archie 46
Arellano, Gustavo 240, 246; *Ask-A-Mexican* 425
Ariaza, Albert Antonio: *Deep in the Crotch of My Latino Psyche* 206
Aristotle 2, 127n3
Arnaz, Desi: *I Love Lucy* 25; *Too Many Girls* 143
Arriola, Gus: *Gordo* 104, 426–8, 429
Arteaga, A. 171
Asimov, Isaac 112; *I, Robot* 120, 126; "Runaround" 126
Asma, Stephen T. 381, 383
Assassin's Creed 12, 90; *III* 92; *IV: Black Flag* 90, 92, 94; *Freedom Cry* 93
Association of Joteria Arts and Activism Scholarship (AJAAS) 291–2
Astorga, Luís 397, 398
Avant-Mier, Roberto 182–3
Avila-Saavedra, Guillermo 24
Ayres, Edward Duran 387

Baby Zoot 145
Baca, Jimmy Santiago 13, 168
Baca, Judy 199
Bachomo, Felipe 395
Báez, Jillian 24
Baker, Jeannette: "Hey Girl, Hey Boy" 304
Balderrama, Francisco 386
Ball, J. 162–3
Ball, Lucy: *I Love Lucy* 25
Banda Blanca 186
Banderas, Antonio: "Puss in Boots" 70
Banet-Weiser, Sarah 46
Baraka, Amiri: *Black Magic* 152
Barber, Dan: *The Third Plate* 243
Barks, Carl: "Lost in the Andes" 103
Barnes, Clive 147
Barney and Friends 50
Barrera, Aida: *Carrascolendas* 47; *Looking for Carrascolendas* 47, **48**
Barrera, María Canals: *Camp Rock* 6
Barry, Jack: *Juvenile Jury* 45
Bartes, Roland 112, 429
Batman 46, 106
Battlestar Galactica 32, 111, 115–17, **116**
Bayless Deann Groen 248
Bayless, Rick: *Authentic Mexican* 248; Frontera Grill 248; Topolobampo 248
Bejarano, Yvonne Yabro: "In Crossing the Border" 292
Beland, Tom: *Chicacabra* 107; *True Story* 107
Belmore, Rebecca: *Indian Factory* 136
Beltrán, Mary 10, 25; *Chico and the Man* 24

Beltrán, Sandra Ávila: *la Reina del Pacifico* 402; *Latina/o Stars in U.S. Eyes*, *Chico and the Man* 28
Belz, Adam 181, 183
Bendis, Brian Michael 105, 106
Bennett, Tony 176, 177
Bennett-Weiser, Sarah: *Authentic* 60–1
Bergad, Laird 192
Bernal, Gael García: *César Chávez* 34
Bernal, Heraclio 395
The Big Girls Code 315–18, 319
BIP. *See* Border Industrialization Program
Birmingham School 1
Black Arts Movement 152
Black Arts Repertoire Theatre School 152
Blackheart Records 298
Blades, Rubén 177
Blomkamp, Neill: *Elysium* 5
Blue Beetle 106
bodies in motion 310–22; The Big Girls Code 315–18 (*see also* The Big Girls Code); Crafty Chica 318–20; demonstrating 313–15; racialized rasquache raunch 16, 323–4, 326, 327, 329, 330, 331, 332
Bogdanovich 37
The Book of Life 11, 54, 68–72, 74, 375–7, 378n3; casting 72–3; *Day of the Dead* working title 375
Border Industrialization Program (BIP) 35, 38
Boston Tea Party 37
Bourdieu, Pierre 181
branding 8, 287, 309; "Latinohood" 59–67; mobilizing identities to create personal brands 78–80
Brando, Marlon: *Viva Zapata!* 3
Brandon, Jorge 160n3
Brant, Beth: *Bay of Quinte Mohawk* 131, 139; "The Good Red Road" 131, 136–7
Bratt, Benjamin: *La Mission* 9, 137–8, 273–4, 298–9
Bratt, Peter: *La Mission* 9, 13, 138, 273–4, 298–9
Breaking Bad 30, 176, 432
Breakthrough: *I Can End Deportation* 12, 91, 92; *ICED!* 12, 91
Breinig, Jeane T' áawxíaa 132
Breitbart News Network 184
Brilliant, Richard 234
Broadway 143–50, 157, 177, 325
The Brothers Garcia 30
Brown, Arian 13, 158
Brown, Ed: *Chico and the Man* 27
Brown, Jeffrey: *Black Superheroes*, *Milestone comics and their Fans* 106
Brown Berets 227
Brown Color Line 335
Brown v. School Board of Topeka, Kansas 336
brownface 3, 8

"Browning of America" 3
Broyles-Gonzales, Yolanda 146, 150n1; *El Teatro Campesino* 144
Buck-Morss, Susan 34
The Bugs Bunny 46
Bui, Diem-My T. 384
The Bullwinkle Show 46
Burciaga, José Antonio: "After Aztlán" 240
Bureau of Prisons 164
Burns, Charles 428
Burton, LeVar 50
Burton, Tim 73

Café Tacuba 13, 176
Calibre 50 398; "El Tierno Se Fue" 399
California Association of Bilingual Education 51
California Association of Latins in Broadcasting 49
Call of Duty 12, 90; *Black Ops* 87, 90; *Black Ops II* 87–88, 90; *Modern Warfare II* 87
Calvo, Luz 205, 246, 258–60; *Decolonize Your Diet!* 252
Calvo-Quirós, William A. 17–18
Camayd-Freixas, Erik: *US Immigration and Its Global Impact* 182
Cameron, James: *Alien* 294
Canclini, Néstor García 330
Candelaria, Cordelia 132
Candy, Dulce Candy 11, 78, 79–80; *Maquillaje Estilo a JLo en los Oscars* 80; *The Sweet Life* 79
Cano-Murillo, Kathy *Crafty Chica* 318–20
capcom Rock 403
Čapek, Karel: R.U.R. 124, 126
Captain Kangaroo 45
Cardenas, Rene 48, 49
Cárdenas, Solís 363, 365
Cardenas, Steve 50
The Care Bears 49, 55n3
Carey, Elaine 402
Carnegie Corporation 46
Carrascolendas 11, 27, 47–8, **48**, 50
Carrillo, Leo 25
Carrillo Rowe, Aimee 296
Carson, Rachel: *Silent Spring* 244
Casanova, Erynn Masi de 8, 24, 68
Casillas, Dolores Inés 179
Castañeda, Mari 24, 32n1, 179, 183, 184
Castillo, Ana 10, 230
Castillo-Garsow, Melissa 14
Castro, Fidel 90, 373, 374
Castro Solis, Sandra 314–15
Catholic Youth Organization 348
Catholicism 233, 364–5, 366, 367, 415; allegory 228; basketball 348; dance 133; death 378; heroism 101–2; identity 209; liturgy 361; mass 362; ritual 281–2, 283; saints 390;

sanctity 359–60; sex 284, 375; uniforms 324–5
CECUT 429
Center on Media and Human Development 88
Center Theatre Group 144
Centino, Nicholas 16
Centro Cultural Tijuana 429
César Chávez 11, 34–7, **36**, 38, 39, 40, 41
Chan, Sucheng 217
Chappell, Ben 15, 298, 426
Chavez, Cesar 11, 34–7, 38, 39, 40, 41, 127, 245, 246
Chavez, Julio Cesar 341
Chavira, Antonio: *Desperate Housewives* 6
Chee, Fabio 12, 120, 121
chica lit 4, 9
Chicanafuturism 12, 111, 112, 115
Chicano Art Movement 152
Chicano Environmental Justice Movement 246
Chicano hip hop 13, 162–72; colonialism, capitalism, and the War on Drugs 163–5; identity 171; *maiz* narratives 165–8; place and identity in Xicana/o culture 165–8; place in new pinto poetics 168–71
Chicano Hip Hop Nation (ChHHN) 167
Chicano pinto 13
Chico and the Man 24, 25, 27, **27**, 28
Children Now 31
children's animation 68–75; Latinidad 69–70; problematic children 71–2
children's television 44–58; *Dora the Explorer* reinvents bilingual children's television 50–2 (*see also* Dora the Explorer); early years 45–7; (live)action 47–9; 1980s and 1990s 49–50; post-Dora inspired contemporaries and mishaps 52–5
Children's Television Act 50
Children's Television Workshop 46
Chilpancingo Collective for Environmental Justice 37, 41
Chinese-Chicano installation art and transnationalism 214–25
"Cholo Adventures" 82, 83
Chomsky, Aviva 184
Chupacabras 18, 388, 389
"Cielito Lindo" 73
Cienfuegos, Lucky 152
The Cisco Kid 25
Cisneros, Sandra 10, 157; "Little Miracles, Kept Promises" 357
CivCity 93
Civilization 93
Clark, Larry: *Marfa Girl* 8, 9; *Wassup Rockers* 8
Cleger, Osvaldo 12, 426
Clune, Michael 160n6
Coalition of Immokalee Workers (CIW) 245

Cohen, Jeffrey Jerome: "Monster Culture (Seven Theses)" 383–4
Cohen, Sara: *Rock Culture* 304
Colima, Bert 348
Colombian RCN Television 4
Colón, David 13
Colonche 259
Comaroff, Jean 388
Comaroff, John 388
comic books 101–9; digital media 107–8; ethnic authorship and parody 101–5; Latina/o subjects and non-Latina/o author 105–7
Comics Code Authority 102–3
Comixology 12, 104, 107
commodification 9, 17, 59–66, 135, 232, 330, 331, 339, 343
Common Law 28
content and form 4–10
Contreras, S. 171
Cooper, Anderson 402
The Corpse Bride 73
Correa, Teresa 78
Cortés, Hernán 207, 385
Cortez, Constance 229, 234
Cortez, Nike 268
Cortez, Raul 183
Coulter, Ann 426
counter-hegemony 331, 397, 405
The Couple in the Cage 136–7
coyotes 18, 114; contemporary Latino popular culture 418–19; definition 415–16; facilitators of irregular migration processes 416–18
Crafty Chica 318–20
Craig, Daniel: *Spectre* 5
Crespo, Jaime 104
Cristal, Linda: *The High Chaparral* 26
Cristela 6, 30, 31
Crosser and La Migra 98
Crosthwaite, Hugo 429
Crumb, Robert 104
Cruz, Celia 177
Cruz, Nilo: *Anna in the Tropics* 147
Cruz, Penelope: *G-Force* 8
Cruz, Terri "Lil Loca" Lynn 231–2
Cruz, Victor Hernández 152
Cruz, Wilson: *My So-Called Life* 291
CSI Miami 30
Cuarón, Alfonso 34, 425; *Children of Men* 111; *Gravity* 111
Cuban island culture 2
Cuban Revolution 128n2, 373
Cyber Arte 231

Daddy Yankee: "Limbo" 177
Dalleo, Raphael 148

Dana, Bill: *The Bill Dana Show* 26; *The Danny Thomas Show* 26
Danielson, Marivel T. 16, 205
The Danny Thomas Show 26
Dark Horse Digital 107
Dasein 424, 425, 426
Davidson, Gordon 144
Dávila, Arlene 24, 29, 84n1, 196, 327; *Latino Spin* 55n17
Davis, Al 338
Davis, Angela 330
Davis, R. G. 147
Day of the Dead 72, 73, **135**, 361, 362, 370–80; DIY projects 319; elements 374; expressions 372–4; framework of the dead 371–2; pop 374–7
DC Comics 2–3, 102, 104, 10: *Batman* 106; *Young Justice* 106
de Casanova, Erynn Masi 8, 24, 68
de Genova, Nicholas 421, 422
de la Torre, Sergio: *Maquilapolis* 10, 11, 35, 37–9, **38**, 41, 80
De Niro, Robert: *Machete* 40
de Silva, Gomez 416
DEA. *See* Drugs Enforcement Agency
Deal, Gregg: *The Last American Indian on Earth* 136 •
Decena, Carlos 293–4
Deer, Thomas 92
DeGeneres, Ellen 291, 295
del Castillo, Kate: *Book of Life* 375
del Toro, Guillermo, 34, 425; *Book of Life* 375; *Cronos* 111, 375; *Día de los Muertos* 375–6; *Mimic* 111; *Pacific Rim* 111; *Pan's Labyrinth* 375
Delgado Bernal, Dolores 180, 181
Dell: Disney comics 102
Desperate Housewives 6, 30
Development, Relief, and Education for Alien Minors (DREAM) Act 182, 302
Devious Maids 6, 32
Día de los Muertos (Day of the Dead) 3, 5, 17, 73, 74, **135**, 207, 361, 362; Disney copyright controversy 54, 375. *See also* Day of the Dead
Diamond, Betty 147
diaspora 134, 137, 139, 156, 160, 181, 184, 207, 278
Díaz, Junot 4, 105; *The Brief Wondrous Life of Oscar Wao* 110; "Monstro" 110
Diaz, Nina 298
Díaz, Porfirio 370
Díaz-Wionczek, Maríana 51
Dickens, Charles: *A Tale of Two Cities* 424, 425
digital divide 77, 83, 84
digital media 76–86; contexts and approaches 77–8; digital pop economy 80–1; mobilizing identities to create personal brands 78–80; online Latinidad 82–4

Dinsdale, Shirley: *Judy Splinters* 45
disidentification 324, 332n4, 362, 363
Disney 7, 8, 26; *Camp Rock* 6; *Coco* 54;
    copyright controversy for Día de los Muertos
    54, 375; *Good Luck Charlie* 53; *Handy Manny*
    53; *Junior* 54; *The Mickey Mouse Club* 45;
    Marvel Studio 5; *Saludos Amigos* 70; *Shake It
    Up* 53; *Sofia the First* 53, 55n18; *Special Agent
    Oso* 53; *The Three Caballeros* 70; *Wizards of
    Waverly Place* 6, 31, 53
Dobbs, Lou 426
Dobson, Kit 214
Dominguez, Ricardo: *El gato negro* 102; *Turista
    fronterizo* 12, 91
Dora the Explorer 8, 11, 30, 44, 50–2, 53,
    54, 55n6, 68, 69, 176; branding and
    commodification 59–62, **60**, **63**, 66, **66**, 67
Downs, Lila 14, 177
Dragon Tales 50
DREAM Act. *See* Development, Relief, and
    Education for Alien Minors (DREAM) Act
Drugs Enforcement Agency (DEA) 396, 403
Duck Dynasty 426
Dulché, Yolanda Vargas: *Lagrimas y risas/Posesión
    diabólica* 101
DuPuis, E. Melanie 243
Durán, Carmen 39
Duran, Roberto 341
Durcal, Rocío 294

East Los High 6, 10, 24, 31, 32
East WillyB 10, 24, 31
Edberg, Mark Cameron 397, 405, 407n20
Eddy, Terry: *Learning Construction Spanglish,* 177
Edward, John 371
Egan, Hannah Palmer 243
Eisenberg, Jesse: *Rio* 70
El Gallo **400**
El Rey Network 31, 81: *From Dusk Till Dawn* 5;
    Lucha Underground 5
Elder, Bill 428
The Electric Company 49
Eleveld, Mark: *The Spoken Word Revolution* 153
Elizalde, Valentín 399
Ellis, Edward: *The Steam Man of the Prairies* 124
Eppert, Claudia 222
Erickson, Leif: *The High Chaparral* 26
Erlmann, Veit 186
Esparza, Moctesuma: *Villa Alegre* 49
Espinosa, Frank 110
Espinosa, Gastón 361
Espinosa, Paul: *… and the earth did not swallow
    him* 3
Estefan, Gloria 3, 176, 177
Esteves, Sandra María 152, 156, 160n7
Estrella, Alberto: *La Fuga del Chapo* 403
Etheridge Melissa 295

Europa Universalis I–IV 93
European Frankfurt School 1
Eva Luna 4
Executive Reorganization Act of 1993 388

Faber, Daniel 243
Faison, Donald: *Scrubs* 7
Fajardo, Rafael: *Crosser and La Migra* 98
The Fantastic 4 46
Farm Security Administration 227
fashion. *See* self-styling and fashion lines
Federal Communications Commission (FCC)
    49, 183
Feniger, Susan: Border Grill 249
Fernandes, Leela 222
Fernández, Laura 11
Fernández, María Teresa (Mariposa) 157
Ferrera, America: *Ugly Betty* 6
Fiddler on the Roof 148
FIFA series 12, 90
film in the end times 34–43
Fisher, Bryan: "Bringing Home the Bacon" 283
Fitting, Elizabeth: "Cultures of Corn and Anti-
    GMO Activism in Mexico and Columbia"
    242
Flamin' Hot Cheetos 82
The Flintstones 46
Flores, Juan 142, 143, 191, 194, 268, 269; *The
    Diaspora Strikes Back* 158
Flores, Nelson: "Has Bilingual Education Been
    Columbused?" 180
Flores, Paul 159
Flores, Tom 338–9, 341, 343, 345
Fojas, Camilla 10–1, 426
folklore-popular culture borderlands 279–90;
    overview 280–1; quince as retroacculturative
    practice 288–9; quince motif 282;
    quinceañeras and cultural identity 285–6;
    quinceañeras as consumer rite 287–8;
    quinceañeras as family ritual 283–5; secular
    re-vision 281–2
Fonseca, Vanessa 246
food 239–55; decolonizing haute cuisine
    247–52; food as medicine 258–60
Foucault, Michel 181, 330, 382; *Abnormal*
    333n10; *Discipline and Punish* 333n10
"The Four Horsemen of the [Neo-Fascist]
    Apocalypse" 430
Fox 29, 30, 429; *Knock Knock Live* 279;
    MundoFox 4; News 239, 426; Sports 340,
    341
Francisco, Don 175–6
Frank, Kathryn M. 11–2
Fraser, Nancy 148, 269
Fregoso, Linda: "Born in East L.A. and the
    'Politics of Representation'" 120
The Friendly House 134

From Dusk Till Dawn 5, 330
From the West: Chicano Narrative Photography
  226
Funari, Vicky: *Maquilapolis* 10, 11, 35, 37–8, **38**,
  41
Furman, Jill 148
Fusco, Coco 13; *The Couple in the Cage* 136–7;
  Two Amerindians 136; *Turista fronterizo* 12, 91
Futurama 50
Futurestates 123, 125

G. I. Joe 49
Gabriel, Juan 16, 293–4
Gaines, Reg E. 157
Gallery@SWC 429
Gamio, Manuel 416
Ganz, Marshall 35–6
Garcia, Carlos E. 288–9, 313
García, Enrique 10, 12
Garcia, Ignacio: *When Mexicans Could Play Ball*
  347–8
Garcia, Jeff 341
García, Lilly 107
García, Peter J. 132, 137, 139
Gaspar de Alba, Alicia 231, 312, 316, 385;
  Velvet Barrios 311
Gates, Henry Louis 65, 112
Gay and Lesbian Alliance Against Defamation
  291
Gears of War 4
Geneva, Nicholas de 414
George of the Jungle 46
Get Me High Lounge 153
Gifford, Chris: *Dora the Explorer* 51
Gilligan, Vince: *Breaking Bad* 432
Gioia, Dana 151, 154, 159
Giovanni, Nikki 152
Giraldo, Greg: *Common Law* 28
Girl in a Coma 16; *When I'm Gone* 298. *See also*
  Alva, Jenn; Diaz, Nina; Diaz, Phanie
Glass, Bryan 94
Glazer, Mark 385
GLBTQ. *See* LGBTQ
Glenn, Joshua 427
Global Conflicts 97–8
Go Diego, Go! 30, 53
Goldman, Shifra M. 194
Goldstein, Jenette: *Aliens* 294
Gomez, Selena 6; *Barney and Friends* 50; *Wizards
  of Waverly Place* 53
Gómez, Sergio 399
Gómez-Peña, Guillermo 13, 211–2; *The Couple
  in the Cage* 136–7; "Naftaztec" 211; *Two
  Amerindians* 136
Gonzales, Patrisia: *Red Medicine* 260, 261
Gonzáles, Rudolfo "Corky": *I am Joaquín* 152

González, Christopher 17, 110, 114, 121, 345,
  426; "Latino Sci-Fi" 111
González, Jennifer A. 226
Gonzalez, Ricardo 274
González, Richard Alonso "Pancho" 339, 345
González-Martin, Rachel V. 15–16
Good Neighbor Policy 70
Goodman, David 243
Goodman, Michael 243
Goodwin, Mathew David 12–13, 110
Gordon, Avery 384
graffiti 1, 14, 165, 170, 192, 193–8, 201n7, 212,
  228, 229, 232
Graham, Laura 132
Grand Theft Auto 12, 90; V 88
Grangel, Carloa: "Corpse Bride" 73
Graue, Jennifer 249
Great Depression 347, 386
Great White Way 143, 145, 146, 150
Green, Rashaad Ernesto: *Gun Hill Road* 9
Greenaway, Twilight 245
Grupo Factor X 37, 41
Guars, Estar: *Star Wars* 207
Guerra, Juan Luis: *Ojalá que llueva ca* 176;
  "Woman del Callao" 176–7
Guerra, Rogelio: *La Fuga del Chapo* 403
Guerrero, Aurora: *Mosquita y Mari* 299
Guevara, Carlos 306
Guevara, Che 167
Guevarra, Rudy 215
Guidotti-Hernandez, Nicole 24
Gunckel, Colin 226
Gunn, Joshua: "Refitting Fantasy" 371–2, 373–4
Guthman, Julie 245
Gutierrez, Fernando "Pisket HAR INK" 197
Gutiérrez, Jorge: *The Book of Life* 11, 54, 68–73,
  74–5, 375–7, 378n3; *The Corpse Bride* 73–4;
  El Tigre 8, 11, 68, 69, 73
Gutierrez, Patricia 275
Guzman, Alejandra 330
Guzmán, Joaquín "El Chapo" 403–5

Habell-Pallán: *Loca Motion* 302
Halberstam, Judith 294
Halo 2 87
Hamann, Edmund T. 181
Handy Manny 8, 30, 53
HAR 193, 197
Har, Sarck 191, 193, 194, 195, **195**, 197–9
Har NYC 197–8, 199, 200
Haraway, Donna: 111–2, 115
Har'd Life Ink (Hermandad, Arte y Rebeldía)
  194–5, 197–200; Arts Collective 14, 192,
  198
Hastrup, Kirsten: "Siting Culture" 180
Hatfield, Charles: *Alternative Comics* 103
Hathaway, Anne: *Rio* 70

haute cuisine, decolonizing 247–52
Havana Cathedral 94, **95**, 95–6
Hayek, Salma 34; *Fools Rush In* 330; *From Dusk Till Dawn* 330; *Ugly Betty* 30
He-Man and the Masters of the Universe 49
healing 256–66; food as medicine 258–60; time as a ritual in healing 260–5
Hearts of Iron 93
Hedrick, Tace 9
Hendershot, Heather 46
Hernandez, Aaron 334
Hernandez, Angel 306
Hernandez, Ellie D. 16, 324
Hernández, Ernestina Ramírez 366
Hernandez, Ester 209; *Sun Mad* 208, 246, 252
Hernandez, Gilbert 4, 103, 104–5; *Chance in Hell* 105; *Love and Rockets* 375; *María M* 105; *Palomar* 104, 105; *Speak of the Devil* 105; *The Troublemakers* 105. See also Los Bros Hernandez
Hernandez, Jaime 103; *Locas* 104, 105, 296. See also Los Bros Hernandez
Hernández, Javier 3, 102, 106; *El Muerto* 375
Hernández, Jorge 297. See also Los Tigres del Norte
Hernández, Leticia 160n7
Hernandez, Robb: "Drawing Offensive/Offensive Drawing" 210
Herrera, Alberto: *Learning Construction Spanglish*, 177
Herrera, Nemo 348
Herrera-Sobek, Maria 418
Herrmann, Rachel 96
Hey, Hey, It's Fat Albert 46
Heyn, Pieter 94
High Chaparral **26**, 26–7
Hilton, Perez 78, 79, 80
hip hop 8, 13, 147, 148, 154, 160n6. See also Chicano hip hop
Hispanic Heritage Month 326
Holden, Stephen 41
Holman, Bob 159; *Aloud!* 152–3; *Burning Down the House* 151
Holmes, Seth 244
Homeland Guantanamos 98
Horta, Silvio: *Ugly Betty* 30
"Hot Cheetos and Takis" 82, 84
Hot Wheels 46, 49
Hoult-Saros, Stacy 8
House of Buggin' 28
Howdy Doody 45
Hudes, Quiara Alegría: *Eliot, A Soldier's Fugue* 147; *In the Heights* 13, 143–4, 147–48, 150, 177; *Water by the Spoonful* 147
Hudson Street 28
Huerta, Dolores 246; *César Chávez* 41
Huerta, Joel: "Friday Night Rights" 347

human smuggling 413–23; coyote definition 415–16; coyotes and contemporary Latino popular culture 418–19; coyotes as facilitators of irregular migration processes 416–18; Victoria County, Texas tragedy 419–21
Hyde, Lester 64, 65

I Can End Deportation 12, 91, 92, 98
I Love Lucy 3, 25, 102
I Married Dora 28
Iber, Jorge 17, 41
Ice Cube: *Book of Life* 375
identity and culture 84n1, 133, 163
Iglesias, Enrique 176
Iglesias, Gabriel: *Book of Life* 375
Iglesias, Julio, 176
Illegal Immigration Reform and Immigrant Responsibility Act 418
immigration 98, 113, 147, 181, 192, 194, 198, 208, 239, 307, 310, 413, 415; activism 77; enforcement 182; films 137; interventions 187; laws 418; phobia 39; policy 40, 179, 313, 390, 419; reform 114, 182. See also human smuggling; U.S. Immigration and Customs Enforcement
Immigration Reform and Control Act 192, 418
In the Heights 13, 143–4, 147–48, 150, 177
Iñárritu, Alejandro González 34, 425
Indelicato, Mark: *Ugly Betty* 7
Independent Television Service 37, 123. See also *Futurestates*
indigenismo 137, 139
indigenous epistemologies 132
Ingle, Zachary: "The Border Crossed Us" 40–1
Inside the Haiti Earthquake 98
International Game Developers Association 88
International Worker's Day 54
Ivy Queen: "Somos raperos pero no delincuentes" 177

Jameson, Fredric 388; *Archeologies of the Future* 112–13
Jane the Virgin 6, 23, 24, 30, 425
Jenner, Brody 83
Jeong, Sun Ho 78
The Jetsons 46
Jett, Joan 298
Johnson, Don: *Machete* 40
Johnson, Gaye 303
Jonas Act 388
Jones, Alex 41
Jones, Meta DuEwa 154; *The Muse is Music* 151
Jones, Nora 298
Joseph, Michael 65–6
joteria 16, 291–300; in film 298–9; Latina lesbians 294–5; "lo que se ve, no se pregunta"

293–4; *música norteña* 297; translocations 295–6. *See also* Gabriel, Juan; Girl in a Coma; Los Tigres del Norte: "Era diferente"; Martin, Ricky; Vargas, Chavela
JS Films 402
Juan Bobo 11, 59, 60, 62–7; *Juan Bobo Busca Trabajo* **64**
Juan of the Dead 374
Juarez, Benito 166
Juarez, Raquel 184
Judy Splinters 45
Junior Jamboree 45
Jurado, Katy 25
Juvenile Jury 45

Kahlo, Frida 157, 194, 232, 292, 293
Kalem, T. E. 146
Kant, Nancy 53, 186
Keating, AnaLouise: "'I'm a Citizen of the Universe'" 134
Kinky: "Más" 73
Kinto Sol 13, 165–6, 167, 168; *Hijos del Maiz* 165
Kline, Kevin: *The Road to El Dorado* 70
Knight, Etheridge 157
Kolbeing, Graham 298
Kortezua 195, 198
Kristallnacht 426, 432n3
Kukla, Fran and Ollie 45
Kun, Josh 185, 186; "Aural Border" 182
Kurtzman, Harvey: *Mad* 103
Kusama, Karyn: *Girlfight* 8
Kustritz, Anne 115

La Angry Xicana?! 296
La Bamba 3, 35, 308
La Danza Azteca 9, 13, 132, 134–6, 138–9
La Estrellas 347
La Fountain Stokes, Larry 295, 296
La Fuga del Chapo 403
La Llorona 18, 232–3, 280, 385
La Mission 9, 137–8, 273–4, 298–9
La Raza Mex 402
La Santa Muerte 357–9, **358**, 360, 362, 363–5, 368n3, 390, **390**, 391, 405, **406**
labor, migration, and protest 120–8; migrants without migration 123–5. *See also A Robot Walks into a Bar*
Lacan, Jacques 383
Lastra, Sarai 62, 63
LatCrit. *See* Latino Critical Race Theory
Latina Life 328–30
Latino Critical Race Theory (LatCrit) 181
Latino Cuban culture 2
Latino pop art 205–13; artists re-define the past to create present 206–7; future 211–2; politics role 207–11

Latino population 24, 82, 183; Iowa 181, 182
Latorre, Guisela 15, 222
Lavandeira, Mario 78
Laviera, Tato 152
Law and Order 28
Le Espiritu, Yen 217
Leguizamo, John: *Freak* 13, 144, 149; *House of Buggin'* 28
Leonard, Elisabeth Anne 112
lesbians 9, 209, 292–3, 294–5
Levina, Marina 384
Lewthwaite, Stephanie 15
Leyvas, Henry 145
LGBTQ 16, 79, 105, 162, 291, 295, 296, 297, 298; AIDS 374
Licea, Everardo: *La Fuga del Chapo* 403, 404
Lichter, S. Robert 24, 25
Lima, Frank 160n3
Lima, Jose Lezama 429
Limbaugh, Rush 426
Lionsgate 34, 432
Lippi-Green, Rosina 220
Lipsitz, George 179
"Little Loca" 82, 83, 84
Loggia, Robert 26
Lohan, Lindsay: *Machete* 40
The Lone Ranger 46
Longoria, Eva 432; *Desperate Housewives* 30; *Low Riders* 273
Looney Tunes and Merrie Melodies 45
Lopez, Al 346
Lopez, Alma 206, 212; "Our Lady" 209, 210, 230, 231
Lopez, George: "Bringing Home the Bacon" 283; *The George Lopez Show* 7, 16, 23, 24, 25, 30, 283
López, Gustavo 82
Lopez, Jennifer (JLo) 3, 50, 68, 176, 330; *American Idol* **62**; "I Luv U Papi" 9; *Maid in Manhattan* 9
Lopez, Jessica Helen: *Always Messing With Them Boys* 156; *Cunt Bomb* 156
Lopez, Karla 420
Lopez, Nancy 340, 345
Lopez, Luis: *GTA* 92
Lopez, Priscilla: *A Chorus Line* 149; *In the Heights* 148
Lopez, Yolanda: "Grandma's Story" 223; *Guadalupe Series* 223, 230; "Who's the Illegal Alien, Pilgrim?" 208
Lorde, Audre 112, 115
Los Americans 10, 31
Los Angeles County Museum of Art (LACMA) 205, 208
Los Bros Hernandez 106, 110. *See also* Hernandez, Gilbert; Hernandez, Jaime
Los Gliders: "La Rebeldona" 306

Los Loud Jets: "Sputnik" 307
Los Milos: "Pitagoras" 307
Los Tigres del Norte 16, 18, 177, 183, 397;
    Contrabando y traición 402; "Era diferente" 297;
    La banda del carro rojo 402; Realidades 297
Los Zainos del Norte 404
Lost 4, 30
Lou, Gloria: "Grandma's Story" 223; Stories on
    My Back 214, 219, 220, 221–3; "A Love
    Letter to my Mother" 221, 222
Lou, Magda: Stories on My Back 214, 219, 220,
    221
Lou, Maricela: Stories on My Back 214, 218, 219,
    220, 221
Lou, Ming: Stories on My Back 214, 219, 220,
    221
Lou, Richard 214; "A Love Letter to my
    Mother" 221, 222, 223; "On the Shore of the
    East China Sea" 218–24; Stories on My Back
    15, 214–18, **215**
Louder Arts 159
Lovato, Demi: Barney and Friends 50; Camp Rock
    6
lowriders 267–78; barrio publics 272–3; family
    276; space in publics 274–6; studios 270–1.
    See also La Mission
Lubezki, Emmanuel: Birdman 425; Gravity 425
Lucas, Ashley 146
Luche Libre 91
Lucha Underground 5
Luján, Lourdes 39
Luna, Diego: Book of Life 72, 375; César Chávez
    10, 34–7, **36**, 38, 39, 40, 41
Lunda, James: Take a Picture With a Real Indian
    136
Lymon, Frankie 304; "Why Do Fools Fall in
    Love" 305

McFarland, Pancho 13, 426; The Chican@ Hip
    Hop Nation 199; Chicano Rap 199
Machete 10, 11, 35, 39, **40**, 40–1, 176, 267, 268
Machete Kills 39
Machete Kills in Space 39
Machida, Margo 215, 217, 219
Machinima 81
Macías, Stacy I. 16–17
Maciel, David 34
McNally, Terrence: The Ritz 143
maiz narratives 13, 163, 164, 165–8
Malcom X 152
Maldonado, Sheila 159
Malverde, Jesús 390, 395–6, **396**, 405
The Man and the City 26, 27
Mann, Denise 80, 81
Mansfield, Pancho 30
Maquilapolis 10, 11, 35, 37–9, **38**, 41, 80
Marchi, Regina M. 207, 370

Maya and Miguel 8, 53, 66, 69
Maker Studios 81
maquiladoras 34, 35, 38, 39, 97
Marchetti, Gina 217
Marie, Constance: The George Lopez Show 7, 283;
    Union Square 28
Marie Claire 402
Marietta, Morgan 371
Marin, Cheech 40; The Book of Life 375; Born in
    East LA 3, 120; Dora the Explorer 62
Marin, Christine 349
Mark Taper Forum 144–5
Markie, Biz: "Just a Friend" 73
Márquez, Gabriel García 51
Martin, Akwiratékha 92
Martin, Darnell: I Like it Like That 3
Martin, Desirée 17
Martin, Ricky 3, 16; "Livin' La Vida Loca" 14, 16,
    176, 295; Livin La Vida Loca 295; Me 295
Martínez, Arturo, Jr. 403
Martínez, Elizabeth Coonrod 246
Martínez, Félix 229, 231
Martinez, Pedro 339
Martinez, Zarela 251, 252
Martínez-Cruz, Paloma 15, 132, 257, 426
Martinez Pompa, Paul: "The Abuelita Poem" 241
Marvel Comics 5, 102, 103, 107; Avengers 105;
    Blatino Spider-Man Miles Morales 106;
    Ultimate Spider-Man 4
Marvel Live Action films 106
Marvel Studios 5
Marx, Karl 331, 388
Marxism 61, 103, 135, 162, 163, 398
Massey, Douglas S. 200n2
Matcek, Trevin: As You Were 125
Maya & Miguel online game 52
Maya and Miguel 8, 53, 66, 69
Mayer, Vicki 24
Mazón, Mauricio: The Zoot-Suit Riots 387
Mbembe, Achille 391
McCall, Jeremiah: Gaming the Past 93
McCourt, Tom 183
McDowell, John H. 397
McGlynn, Áine 214–15
McLollie, Oscar: "Hey Girl, Hey Boy" 304
Mcnamara, Sean: Bratz 6
Medina, Cruz 17
Melendez, Alice 332n1
Melendez, Theresa 415
Mendoza, Alexander 246, 350
Mendoza, Ruben 271
mestizaje 131–41; body, space, and place 133–6; body
    as theory 133; Indian identity and performance
    art 136–7; indigenismo 139; indigenous
    representation in Latina/o film and TV 137–8;
    La Danza Azteca 9, 13, 132, 134–6, 138–9; (re)
    creating indigenous performances 133–6

mestizo 132, 137, 175, 194, 239, 363, 384, 385, 415; definition 139

Mexican-Cuban culture 7

Mexican food 239–42, 247, 248, 252, 260

Mexican popular art in New York City 191–204; background 193–7; "Hermandad, Arte y Rebeldía 197–9

Mexican population in New York City 192–3

Mextasy 427, 429, 431–2

Miami Sound Machine 3

Micheline, Jack 156

The Mickey Mouse Club 45

Microsoft 81, 87

Middleton, Peter 151

Mighty Morphin Power Rangers 50

Mignolo, Walter 240, 372; *Local Histories/Global Designs* 383

migration 121, 123, 158, 162, 168, 192–3, 197, 200n2, 215, 217, 218, 219, 223, 313, 363, 413–15; forced 388, 389; irregular processes 416–18, 419, 421; labor 34, 125; transvestism 296; undocumented 421. *See also* coyotes; human smuggling

Migration Now 432n3

Milestone 105–6

Millán, Isabel 11

Milliken, Mary Sue: Border Grill 249

Minnesota YMCA 82

Miranda, Keta 270

Miranda, Lin-Manuel: *Hamilton* 148, 177; *In the Heights* 13, 143–4, 147–8, 150, 177

Mister Roger's Neighborhood 46, 47

MiTú multichannel network 81

Modern Family 6, 7, 30, 32

Molina-Guzmán, Isabel 3–4, 24

Molina-Guzman, Laura 9

monster theory and the outlining phantasmagoric landscapes 381–93; encounters and crisis monsters 383–91; exorcising of knowledge 382–3; new anti-immigrant nationalist movements 389–91; nineteenth century U.S. expansionism 385–6; Spanish Conquest experience 384–5; twentieth century interwar period and World War II 386–7

Montalban, Ricardo 25; *Star Trek II* 110

Montes, Amelia M. L. 15, 258–9

Montes, Brian 106

Montoya, Delilah 226–36; *Chicano Art* 227; *Contemporary Casta Portraiture* 228, **228**, 231; *El Sagrado Corazón/The Sacred Heart* 227–8, 229, 231; "La Familia" 231; "La Genízara" 227–8, 229; *La Guadalupana* 229–30; *Las Lloronas* 232–3; "Los Jovenes" 228, 231; *Our America* 227; *San Sebastiana: Angel de la Muerte* 233; *San Sebastiana:*

Lengua Negrá 234; "Terri 'Lil Loca' Lynn Cruz" 231, **232**; Women Boxers 231–2

Morales, Alejandro: *The Rag Doll Plagues* 110

Morales, Diana: *A Chorus Line* 149

Morales, Esai: *Caprica* 111, 117; *Los Americans* 10, 31

Morales, Evo 97

Morales, Gil: *Dupie* 104

Morales, Sylvia: *Sesame Street* 49

Morales, Taina: *Taina* 53

Moreno, Art 352

Moreno, Belita: "Bringing Home the Bacon" 284

Moreno, Rita: *Dora the Explorer* 54; *The Electric Company* 49; *The Ritz* 143; *West Side Story* 149; *Where on Earth is Carmen Sandiego?* 50

Morin, Jose Luis 164

Mucha Lucha! 8, 53, 69

Muehlmann, Shaylih 398

Muir, E. Roger: *Howdy Doody* 45

Multi-Ethnic Coalition 29

MundoFox 4–5

Muñoz, Anthony 339, 345

Munoz, Jose Esteban 296, 332n4, 362

Mun2 30

Murguía, Alejandro: "Nineteen Men" 156

Murillo, Enrique 181

Murray, Zachiah: *Mindfulness in the Garden* 244

Murrieta, Joaquin 18, 385–6

música norteña 297

Mutaner, Frances Negrón 24

My Little Pony 'n Friends 50

My So-Called Life 291

Myspace 84

NAFTA. *See* North American Free Trade Agreement

Nakamura, Lisa 76, 84

narco cultura 394–412; cinema 402–3; corrido 397–8; couture 401–2; gastronomy 399–401; husbandry 401; Jesús Malverde 390, 395–6, **396**; morbo 405–6; santo 395–6

Natalicio, Diana S. 47

National Chicano Youth Liberation Conference 152, 208

National Council of La Raza 5, 24

National Endowment for Children's Educational Television 50

National Hispanic Foundation for the Arts 29

National Hispanic Media Coalition 5, 54

National Hispanic Media Council 29

National Public Radio. *See* NPR

National Restaurant Association 243

Nava, Gregory: *American Family* 30; *El Norte* 3, 137; *Mi Familia* 3

NBC 29; *Chico and the Man* 27; *Howdy Doody* 45; *Kukla, Fran and Ollie* 45; *NBC News* 44;

The Office 9; *Today* 44; *Union Square* 28; Universo 30
Negrete, Jorge 395
Nericcio, William Anthony: *Tex[t]-Mex Galleryblog* 426; *Tex[t]-: Seductive Hallucinations of the "Mexican" in America* 427, 430; Trump Statue of Liberty **430**, 431
"The [New] Statue of Liberty" 430
New York Undercover 28
Ni Hao, Kai-Lan 53, 55n15, 66
Nickelodeon: *Dora and Friends* **60**; *Dora the Explorer* 8, 11, 30, 44, 50–2, 53, 54, 55n6, 59–62, 66, 67, 68, 69, 176
The Nine Lives of Elfego Baca 25
Nitz, Jai: *Blue Beetle* 106
Noel, Urayoán 154, 155, 160n3; "The Body's Territories" 158; *In Visible Movement* 152
Noriega, Chon 24, 226; *Shot in America* 27
Norse, Harold 156
North American Free Trade Agreement (NAFTA) 38, 208, 260, 265n6, 388, 389; post- 12, 211
Noticiero Univisión 176
NPR, 298; *All Things Considered* 302; *Fresh Air* 302; "Move Over, Dora" 54; "From Ricky Ricardo to Dora" 44
Nuesta Señora de la Santa Muerte (La Flaquita, the Skinny Girl, la Madrina, the Godmother, Our Lady of Holy Death) 405
NuvoTV 31
Nuyorican Poets Café 152
Nyberg, Amy 103
Nyong'o, Lupita: *Star Wars* 111

O'Donnell, Rosie 295
O'Neill, Ed: *Modern Family* 7
Obama, Barack 117, 184, 239, 426
Ochoa, Eric G: "Cholo Adventures" 82, 83
Ochoa, Enrique C. 246
Olguín, Ben 169, 171, 172n1
Olguin, Hank 337
Olivas, Alex: *East Metropolis* 104, 107
Olmec 241–2
Olmos, Edward James: *American Me* 3, 35; *The Ballad of Gregorio Cortez* 176; *Battlestar Galactica* 111, **116**, 116–17; *Blade Runner* 110; *Miami Vice* 28; *Zoot Suit* 145, 150
Olmos, José Gil 368n4; *La Santa Muerte* 368n3
Olvera, Enrique: Cosme 247, 249
Olveros, Yolanda 299
Olwig, Karen Fog: "Siting Culture" 180
"On the Shore of the East China Sea" 217–19
105.5 FM La Ley 14, 180, 183
One the Rocks 28
1 + 1 429
Orchard, William 1, 13
Ordonez, Juan 182

Orozco, José Clemente 193
Ortiz, Ana: *Ugly Betty* 6
Ortiz, Fernando 311
Ortíz, Gerardo 308, 309
Ortiz, Michelle 89
Ortiz, Tito 341

Paffenworth, Kim: *Gospel of the Living Dead* 373
PageSixSixSix.com 78
Pak, Greg: *Happy Fun Room* 125
Palacios, Monica: *Deep in the Crotch of My Latino Psyche* 206
Papo y Yo 4
Paradas, Daniel: *Serpent and the Shield* 102
Pardue, Derek: "Putting Mano to Music" 185
Paredes, Americo: 383; *With a Pistol in His Hand* 216
Parra, Sonia 184
Patinkin, Mandy: *Dora the Explorer* 54
Payback Gardia 165
Paxman, Andrew 49
PBS: *The Electric Company* 49; Kids network 46; KLRN 47; *Maya and Miguel* 8, 53, 66, 69; *Mister Roger's Neighborhood* 46, 47; *Point of View* 41; *Reading Rainbow* 49, 50; *Sesame Street* 11, 46, 47, 49, 50; *The Sixth Sense* 200n1; *Villa Alegre* 11, 47, 48, 49; *Where in the World is Carmen Sandiego?* 50; *Zarela!* 251
Peña, Devon 246; *Mexican Americans and the Environment* 243–4
Peña, Elizabeth: *I Married Dora* 28
Peña, Jesse Ortiz 365, 367
Peña, Luis Fernando: *Sleep Dealer* **114**
Peña, Michael: *Ant-Man* 5
Penix-Tadsen, Phillip 90, 93; *Latin American Ludology* 92
Penny, H. Glenn 132
Perdomo, Willie 159; "How Beautiful We Really Are" 157; "Nigger Reecan Blues" 157
Perez, Daniel Enrique: *Rethinking Chican/o Popular Culture* 292
Pérez, Domino R.: *There Was a Woman* 280
Pérez, George 106; *Avengers Omnibus* 105
Perez, Karla 413
Pérez, Laura 230, 329
Perez, Marlene: Rhythm Shakers 308
Pérez, Rosie 44; *The Road to El Dorado* 7
Pérez-Firmat, Gustavo 24, 25
performing indigeneity 131, 132, 136, 137
Perlman, Ron: *Book of Life* 375
Phelts, Alejandra 429
Pietri, Pedro: "Puerto Rican Obituary" 152
Pilcher, Jeffrey 240, 246, 386–7
Piña, Michael: *César Chávez* 36
Piñero, Miguel 152; *Nuyorican Poetry* 153; *Short Eyes* 147
pinto poetics 13, 163, 164, 168–71

Pita, Beatrice: *Lunar Braceros* 110
Pitbull 4, 68
Plana, Tony: *Ugly Betty* 7
Plascencia, Luís F. B. 271
Plascencia, Salvador: *People of Paper* 1
Points of Entry 98
Popi, 28
Popples 50
Portilla, Lourdes: *La Ofrenda* 374
Posada, Jose Guadalupe 207; "La Calavera
    Catrina" 370
Posada, María 74, 376, 377
Pound Puppies 50
Povod, Reinaldo: *Cuba and His Teddy Bear* 147
Prado, Rocío Isabel 14–15
Pregones Theater 142, 156
Presley, Elvis: "Blue Suede Shoes" 301; "Can't
    Help Falling in Love"
Pretty Little Liars 32
Prinze, Freddie: *Chico and the Man* 27–8
Psycho Realm 13, 169; "Palace of Exile" 170; *A
    War Story* 170
Puente, Tito 177
Puente Ink 313
Puente Movement 313, 314, 318
Pulido, Albert 271–2, 274
Pulido, Jose 207
Pulido, Laura 245
punk Spanglish 14, 173–8
Puss in Boots 70

Qué Pasa 27
Quesada, Joe 105, 107; *Daredevil* 102
Quiero Mis Quinces 15, 16, 287
Quijano, Aníbal 240
Quinn, Anthony 25; *American Idol* **62**; *The Man
    and the City* 27
Quiñonez, Naomi: "La Diosa in Every Woman"
    230
Quintero, Mario 398
Quinto Sol 118

racialized rasquache raunch 323–4, 326, 327,
    329, 330, 331, 332
radio and counter epistemologies 179–88
Rae, Issa: "The Misadventures of Awkward
    Black Girl" 83
Raíces de Sangre 34, 35, 38, 39
Ramírez, Catherine S. 113; "Chicanafuturism"
    111, 112, 115
Ramírez, Cristina 377
Ramírez, Ernestina 366
Ramirez, Marcos 429
Ramirez, Sara: *Grey's Anatomy* 9
Ramírez Berg, Charles 111, 115
Ramírez Hernández, Ernestina 366–7

Ramos, Jorge 426; *The Other Face of America* 176;
    Viaje a la Muerte 420–1
Ramos, Manuela Nathalia: *Bratz* 6
Rashotte, Ryan 18; *Narco Cinema* 403
rasquache raunch 323–4, 326, 327, 329, 330, 331,
    332
razabilly 16, 302. *See also* rockabilly
Reading Rainbow 49, 50
Realidades 27, 297
Red Dead Redemption 12, 90
Reed, Peyton: *Ant-Man* 5
Resurrection Blvd. 25, 30
Reyes, Jorge: *Lost* 30
Reyes, Jose 339
Reyes, Judy: *Scrubs* 7
Reyes, Rigo 272
Rice-Cisneros, Dominica 251–2
Riebe-Estrella, Gary 361
Rio 70; *2* 70
Rios, Diana 24
Risomena, Fernando 200n2
Rivera, Alex: *A Robot Walks into a Bar,* 12, 120,
    121–23, 125, 127, 127n1; *Sleep Dealer,* 12,
    111, 113–14, **114**, 120, 121, 122, 123, 127;
    The Sixth Section 200n1; *Why Cybraceros?* 122
Rivera Chita: *Kiss of the Spiderwoman* 149; *West
    Side Story* 143, 149
Rivera, Christina 11
Rivera, Diego 193, 292, 374
Rivera, Lysa 110, 113
Rivera, Mariano 339
Rivera, Naya: *Glee,* 3, 9
Rivera, Ron 338–39
Rivero, Yeidy 24
The Road to El Dorado 7, 70
A Robot Walks into a Bar, 12, 120–8
rockabilly 16, 301–9, 324; performers 302–5;
    Wild Records 305–9
Rockband 3 90
Rockstar: *Grand Theft Auto V* 8
Rodriguez, Adam: *CSI Miami* 30
Rodriguez, Alex 339
Rodriguez, Amador 347
Rodriguez, Chris: Decolonial Food for Thought" 258
Rodriguez, Eric 198
Rodríguez, Fernando: *Aztec of the City* 102
Rodríguez, Freddy: *Chico and the Man,* 3
Rodríguez, Gina 425; *Jane the Virgin* 31–2
Rodríguez, Isis 230
Rodriguez, Ivan 339
Rodriguez, Juan "Chi Chi" 340
Rodriguez, Luis 153
Rodriguez, Michelle: *Avatar* 111; *Girlfight* 8;
    Machete 40
Rodriguez, Paul: *a.k.a. Pablo* 28
Rodriguez, Phillip: *Brown is the New Green* 26
Rodríguez, Raymond 386

Rodriguez, Rico: *Modern Family* 7

Rodríguez, Robert 76, 425; *El Mariachi* 3, 176; El Rey Network 5, 31, 81; *From Dusk Till Dawn* 5; *Machete* 10, 39, **40**, 176, 267; *Machete Kills* 39; *Machete Kills in Space* 39; *Spy Kids* 176

Rodriguez, Roberto Cintli 165; *Our Sacred Maíz Is Our Mother* 241

Rodríguez, Spain: *Trashman* 103

Rodriguez, Vittoria 32

Rojas, Viviana: "Language and Cultural Identity in the New Configuration of the Latino TV Industry" 32n1

Román, David 149

Román, Estela 257, 260–1, 265n2

Rome 93

Romero, Enriqueta 364

Romero, George: *Dawn of the Dead* 372–3; *Day of the Dead* 373; *Dead* series 372, 374, 378; *Night of the Living Dead* 373

Romero, Omar 306, 308, 309, 367

Romero, Romero 367

Romo, Antonio Ramiro "Tony" 341, 343n1, 351

Romo, Ricardo 350

Romo, Saint Toribio

Roosevelt, Franklin D. 70

Rothenbuhler, Eric 183

Rudd, Paul: *Ant-Man* 5

Ruiz, Dulce "Dulce Candy" 11, 78, 79–80

Russell Simmons Def Poetry Jam 157

Ryan, Erin L. 61

Ryan, Stevie: *Stevie TV* 83

Sábado Gigante 175

Sáez, Elena Machado 148

Sahagún, Bernardino de 385, 415

saints 357–69; borderlands and Latino/a spiritual practices 360–3; *La Santa Muerte* 365–8, 368n4; Santa Muerte 357–9, **358**, 360, 362, 363–5, 368n3, 390, **390**, 391, 405, **406**; and the secular 359–60

Saldaña, Carlos: *Burrito* 3

Saldaña, Kenia 246

Saldaña, Zoe: *Avatar* 111; *The Book of Life* 375; *Star Trek* 111; *Star Trek: Into Darkness* 111

Saldívar, Ramón 224

Saldívar, Samuel, III 116

Salinas, Raul 13, 168

Sánchez, Chalino. *See* Sánchez, Rosalino

Sanchez, Gabriella 18

Sánchez, George: *Becoming Mexican American* 194

Sanchez, Gody 209

Sanchez, Mark 341, 343n1

Sanchez, Ricardo 13, 168; "Tiers/Tears" 169

Sánchez, Rosalino "Chalino" 18, 177, 399; "El Bandido Generoso" 397

Sánchez, Rosaura: *Lunar Braceros* 110

Sanchez, Sonia: *Sister Son/ji* 152

Sánchez, Stephanie M. 246

Sandoval, Chela 111–2, 115, 132, 137, 139

Sandoval, Denise: *Velvet Barrios* 274–5

Sandoval-Sánchez, Alberto 143

Santaolalla, Gustavo: "El Aparato/land of the Remembering" 376

Santiago, Wilfred 103; *In My Darkest Hour* 3

Sara Solves It 66

Sarduy, Severo 428, 429, 433n9

Schirrmeister, Fabiola 185

Scholz, Trebor 80

Schwarzenegger, Arnold 302; *The Running Man* 111

science fiction 12, 91, 110–19, 120, 121, 123, 124, 126

Scolieri, Paul: *Dancing the New World* 132

Scooby-Doo 46

Scott-Heron, Gil: "The Revolution Will Not Be Televised" 152; *Small Talk at 125th and Lenox* 152

Scrubs 7

Segall, Steven: *Machete* 40

Segovia, Martin 351

Self-Help Graphics 207

self-styling and fashion lines 16–17, 80, 228, 231, 233, 234, 316, 318, 320, 323–33; Latina consumers 326–31; Latina style/custom-made 324–6, 331–2; narco couture 401–2. *See also* Latina Life

Semana Primavera 135

Senarens, Luis 12; *The Electric Man* 124; *Frank Reade Jr., And His New Steam Man* 124; *The Frank Reade Library* 121, 124–5, 127

Serious Games Interactive: *Global Conflicts* 97–8

Serrato, Claudia 258

Serrato, Philip 68

Sesame Street 11, 46, 47, 49, 50

Sesame Workshop 46

Sex Pistols 174

Shake It Up 53

Shakira 52, 68, 425

Shanke, Ntozake 152

She-Ra 50

Showtime: *Weeds* 30

Shubert Organization 145–6

Sí TV 30

Sicario, Thief: "Tearz of Rage" 169

sickside 169

Sicilia, Javier 400, 408n54

Sierra, Gregory: *Hudson Street*

Silva, Gomez de 416

silva, ire'ne lara 261, 263

Simon, Roger I. 222

The Simpsons 50, 231

Sinaloa Cartel 394, 403

Siqueiros, David Alfaro 193

The Sixth Sense 200n1
Skribe 165, 167
Sleepy Lagoon Riots 145, 387
Small Fry Club 45
Smith, Linda Tuhiwai 248–9, 250
Smith, Marc 153
Smith, Patti 174
Smith, Robert: *Mexican New York* 192
Smith, Zadie 398
Smits, Jimmy: *L. A. Law* 28; *Star Wars* 111
smuggling, human. *See* human smuggling
Sofia the First 53, 55n18
Soldatenko, Michael 240
Soler, Nieves Pascual: 252; *Rethinking Chicana/o/*
    Literature through Food 257
Solís Cárdenas, Haydé 363, 364
Solorzano, Daniel 181
South Park 50
Spang, Bently: *Tekcno Powwow III* 136
Spanglish 8, 13–14, 174, 175–8. *See also* punk
    Spanglish
Spanish-American War of 1898 175
Spanish Conquest 70, 138, 361, 384
Spectre 5
Speedy Gonzalez 45, 51, 91, 428
Spiderman 46
Spike TV 30
spoken word 13, 151–61, 211; concepts 153–6;
    poets 156–9
sports 17, 176, 275, 334–53; baseball 346–7;
    basketball 347–8; boxing 348; after
    Clemente 338–40; before Clemente 335–8;
    ESPN era 340–2; football 347; post-World
    War II athletes 349–52; wrestling 348–9
Spray Paint LACMA 205
Springsteen, Bruce: "Born in the USA" 120
Sprout 54
Spy Magazine 426
Stavans, Ilan 14, 242; *Latin Music* 174; *Learning*
    Construction Spanglish 177; *¡Muy Pop!* 216;
    Norton Anthology of Latino Literature 156;
    Spanglish 174; "Who Owns the English
    Language" 174
Stevie TV 83
Stop Disasters 93
street hop 13, 168–9, 171
Suarez, Justin: *Ugly Betty* 6–7, 9
Sundance Institute Documentary Fund 37
Superman 46
Sutton, Ryan 249–50
Suvin, Darko 113
Swilky, Jody 181–2

Tafoya, Vicky 16, 304–5; "Angel Baby" 305;
    "Hey Girl, Hey Boy" 304; "Jump Children"
    304; "So Young" 304, 305; Vicky and The
    Vengents 305; Vicky Tafoya and the Big Beat
    304; "Why Do Fools Fall in Love" 305
Taínos 61
TAKI 183
Tassler, Nina 30
Tatum, Channing: *The Book of Life* 68, 72, 375
Teatro VIVA! 142
Telemundo 5, 30, 175; *Una Maid en Manhattan* 176
Televisa 34
television 23–33; early decades 25–7; 1970s
    activism 27–8; 1980s and 1990s 28–9; 2000s+
    29–31; ongoing questions and debates 31–2.
    See also children's television
Tex-Avery 8
Texeira, Erin: "Latino Characters Commonplace
    in Kids' TV" 44; "TV for Kids Courts Spanish
    Speakers" 44
theater, pop culture, and Broadway 142–50; case
    of *Zoot Suit* 144–7 (*see also* Zoot Suite); *In the
    Heights* 147–50 (*see also* In the Heights)
theatrical visibility 155
Third World Farmer 93
This is Oakland 251
Thomas, Roy 103
ThunderCats 49
Tillstrom, Burr: *Junior Jamboree* 45; *Kukla, Fran
    and Ollie* 45
Tolteka: "Map of Disturnell" 168; *Reflexiones en
    Yangna, Califaztlan* 167
Tom and Jerry 46
Torres, Ortiz 209
Torres y Ayala, Laureano de 90, 96
The Transformers 49
translocations 14, 216, 295–6
Trashman 103
Treaty of Guadalupe Hidalgo 168, 175, 385
Trejo, Danny: *The Book of Life* 375; *Machete* 39–41, **40**
Treviño, Jesús Salvador 34
Trevino, Lee 340, 345
Tropical America 98
Trujillo, Ester 82
Trump, Donald 239, 398, 426, 433n11
Turino, Thomas: *Music as Social Life* 185
Turista fronterizo 98
Two Amerindians 136
2001: A Space Odyssey 120

Ubben, M. Lynn 182
UFW. *See* United Farm Workers
Ugly Betty 6, 7, 9, 24, 25, 30, 328
Umbra Workshop 152
U.S. Census 3, 29, 342
U.S. Immigration and Customs Enforcement 182,
    313
U.S. Internal Revenue Code 388–9
Una Maid en Manhattan 176
Union Square 28

United Farm Workers 35–6, 37, 144, 209, 247; Organizing Committee 245–6
University of California 245–6; Levine 118
University of Wyoming 134–5
USA? 27

Vagabundo 98
Valadez, Manuel 368n3
Valadez, Paul: "Bojangles/Gringo" 430; "Spick" 430
Valdes, Alisa 4
Valdez, Alisa: Dirty Girls Social Club 1, 9–10
Valdez, Inés 182
Valdez, Jeremy Ray: La Mission, 299
Valdez, Luis 271; Actos, 110; "La Bamba" 308; Los Vendidos 12, 121, 126; Zoot Suit 3, 13, 143, 144–7
Valdivia, Angharad 24
Valle, Rodriguez 415
van Alphen, Ernst 228
Vargas, Alex 268, 276, 306, 308
Vargas, Chavela 16, 292–3; "Macorina" 293; Y Si Quieres Saber de mi Pasado/If You Want to Know About My Past 293
Vargas, Paulino 405
Vargas Bros. 307
Velez, Ivan, Jr.: Blood Syndicate 106
Vergara, Sofía 68, 425; Modern Family 7, 30
Vicky Tafoya and the Big Beat 304. See also Tafoya, Vicky
videogames 87–100; Latin American history 93–6; ludology 91–3; representation of Latinos 89–91; serious games, serious issues 97–8
Villa, R. H. 163
Villa Alegre 11, 47, 48, 49
Villarreal, Edgar Valdez 401
Vine 77, 84n2
Viva Valdez 28

Wald, Elijah 399, 405
Walker, Alice 115
Walker, Mort 428
The Walking Dead 17, 375, 378, 426
Walsh, Valerie: Dora the Explorer 51
Walt Disney Presents The Nine Lives of Elfego Baca 25
War on Drugs 162, 163, 164, 169, 170, 390
Warde, Alan 247
Wardle, David 381
Ware, Chris 427, 428
Warner Brothers: Looney Tunes and Merrie Melodies 45
Waters, Alice: Chez Panisse 251, 252
Watson, Cathryn J. Merla 384
Wax, Sandy 54
Weeds 30
Weeping Woman 233, 385
Weiner, Eric: Dora the Explorer 51

Welles, Orson 429
Wheeler, Lesley 151
Where in the U.S.A. is Carmen Sandiego? 50
Where on the World is Carmen Sandiego? 50
"whitewashing" 31
Wiggins, Kyle A. 113
Wild Records 305–9
Will & Grace 9
Williams, Frederick 47
Williams, Nathaniel 128n2
Williams, Robert "Big Sandy" 16, 302–4; "Baby Baby Me" 304; "Dame Una Señal" 308; "Dedicated To You" 303; Fly Rite Trio 303; "I Know I've Loved You Before" 304; The Lonely Blue Boys 303; "Slippin' Away" 304; "What A Dream It's Been" 304
Williams, Robin: Happy Feet 3, 8
Williams, Serena 340
Williams, Tyrone 413, 419–21
Williams, Venus 340
Winter Garden 145, 146, 147
Wizard World Comic Convention 375
Wizards of Waverly Place 6, 31, 53
Women's Rights Advocates 37, 41
Wood, Brenton: "Baby You Got It" 308; "Dame Una Señal" 308; "Gimme a Little Sign" 308; "Me and You" 308; "The Oogum Boogum Song" 308
Wood, Natalie: West Side Story 3
Woodall, Joanna 231
Woods, Tiger 340
Woodward, Kenneth 360
World Trade Organization 384, 388
World War I: post 386
World War II 45, 70, 101, 146, 147, 164, 183, 218, 219, 346, 347, 349, 386, 387
Wortham, Stanton E. F. 181
Wu-Tang Clan 82

Xicana/o culture 163, 165–8, 170, 171, 296

Ybarra-Frausto, Tomás 194, 311–2, 314, 316, 318, 319; "A Panorama of Latino Arts" 193
Y.N. Rich Kids 82, 83
Yogi Bear 46

Zamora, Pedro 183
Zamora Entertainment 183
Zapata, Emiliano 246–7
Zarate, Juan: "Santuario" 169
Zarela! 251
Zona Rosa 249
zoot suit 195, 201n6, 305, 323, 387
Zoot Suit 3, 13, 143, 144–7, 148, 150
Zoot Suit Riots 145, 387
Zorilla, Jose 374
Zorro 25